Informatik aktuell

Herausgeber: W. Brauer
im Auftrag der Gesellschaft für Informatik (GI)

Georg Lausen (Hrsg.)

Datenbanksysteme in Büro, Technik und Wissenschaft

GI-Fachtagung
Dresden, 22.–24. März 1995

Springer

Herausgeber

Georg Lausen
Institut für Informatik
Albert-Ludwigs-Universität Freiburg
Am Flughafen 17
D-79110 Freiburg

CR Subject Classification (1995): C.4, D.1.5, D.3.2, H.2, H.5.1, I.2.3, I.3.5

ISBN-13:978-3-540-59095-8   e-ISBN-13:978-3-642-79646-3
DOI: 10.1007/978-3-642-79646-3

CIP-Eintrag beantragt

Satz: Reproduktionsfertige Vorlage vom Autor/Herausgeber

SPIN: 10484638   33/3142-543210 – Gedruckt auf säurefreiem Papier

Vorwort

Angestoßen durch den Einsatz von Datenbanken in der Praxis sind in den vergangenen Jahren zahlreiche Forschungsprobleme und herausfordernde Entwicklungsaufgaben erkannt worden, für deren Lösung sich die derzeit auf dem Markt befindlichen Datenbanksysteme nur bedingt geeignet zeigen. Datenbanken werden seit vielen Jahren erfolgreich in Anwendungen eingesetzt, die durch große Bestände einfach strukturierter Daten gekennzeichnet sind. Im Gegensatz dazu finden beispielsweise Hypertext-Anwendungen im Bürobereich, die Verwaltung von Entwurfsdaten in ingenieurwissenschaftlichen Anwendungen oder auch die Entwicklung von datenbankbasierten Expertensystemen durch Datenbanken keine befriedigende Unterstützung. Es werden deshalb zunehmend Konzepte diskutiert und prototypmäßig implementiert, mittels denen sogenannte Nicht-Standard-Datenbanken realisiert werden können, die den Einsatzbereich bisheriger Datenbanken in die neuen Anwendungsgebiete ausdehnen.

Die 1985 in Karlsruhe begonnene im zweijährigen Turnus veranstaltete Tagungsreihe "BTW" hat es sich zum Anliegen gemacht, vor einem Forum von Datenbank-Forschern und -Praktikern den Enwicklungsstand und die Perspektiven neuer Datenbank-Technolgie in aktuellen Einsatzgebieten zu diskutieren. Über 70 Kurz- und Langbeiträge wurden zur Begutachtung eingereicht. Diese hohe Zahl zeigt, daß auch nach nunmehr zehn Jahren die "BTW" nichts von ihrer Attraktivität verloren hat und nach wie vor als die wichtigste Datenbanktagung im deutschsprachigen Raum gesehen wird. Das Programmkomitee war in der erfreulichen Lage, ein interessantes und qualitativ hochwertiges Tagungsprogramm, bestehend aus 18 Lang- und 8 Kurzbeiträgen, zusammenstellen zu können. Die Beiträge sind in Sitzungen gruppiert zu den folgenden Themen:

- Vorgangssteuerung und Dokumentenverwaltung

- Schemaentwurf

- Speicherungssysteme und Zugriffspfade

- Anfragen

- Modellierung und Konsistenz

- Anwendungen

- Wissensbanken

Drei renommierte Referenten runden mit ihren eingeladenen Beiträgen das Programm ab. Prof. Dr. Erich Neuhold, Institut für Integrierte Publikations- und Informationssysteme der GMD, Darmstadt, mit dem Thema "Multimedia Database Systems – The Notions and the Issues", Dr. Jim Gray, San Francisco, mit dem Thema "Super Servers: Commodity Computer Clusters Pose a Software Challenge" und Prof. Dr. Albrecht Blaser, Universität Heidelberg, mit dem Thema "Die BTW im Wandel der Datenbank-Zeiten".

An dieser Stelle möchte ich allen Autoren danken, die sich die viele Mühe gemacht haben, einen Beitrag einzureichen, und so die Tagung ermöglichten. Danken möchte ich auch den Mitgliedern des Programmkomitees und den zusätzlichen Gutachtern für die sorgfältige Beurteilung der Beiträge. Mein besonderer Dank gilt Herrn Professor Meyer-Wegener von der Technischen Universität Dresden, der als Tagungs- und Organisationskomiteeleiter mit seinem Team mit viel Engagement die Tagung vorbereit und durchgeführt hat. Ebenso bin ich dankbar für die Unterstützung durch meinen Mitarbeiter Jürgen Frohn, die mir die Vorbereitung des Programms und der Proceedings sehr erleichtert hat.

Freiburg, im Januar 1995

Georg Lausen

Veranstalter

Fachausschuß 2.5 der Gesellschaft für Informatik

Tagungsleitung

K. Meyer-Wegener, TU Dresden

Programmkomitee

G. Lausen, Uni Freiburg (Vorsitz)
H.-J. Appelrath, Uni Oldenburg
H. Biller, Siemens-Nixdorf, München
J. Biskup, Uni Hildesheim
A. Buchmann, TH Darmstadt
P. Dadam, Uni Ulm
K. Dittrich, Uni Zürich
H.-D. Ehrich, TU Braunschweig
N. Fuhr, Uni Dortmund
O. Günther, Humb.Uni Berlin
D. Haban, Daimler-Benz, Ulm
T. Härder, Uni Kaiserslautern
R. Haux, Uni Heidelberg
A. Heuer, Uni Rostock
A. Kemper, Uni Passau
H.-P. Kriegel, Uni München
K. Küspert, Uni Jena
H.-C. Mayr, Uni Klagenfurt
K. Meyer-Wegener, TU Dresden
H.-J. Schek, ETH Zürich
G. Schlageter, FernUni Hagen
M. Schrefl, Uni Linz
W. Stucky, Uni Karlsruhe
R. Studer, Uni Karlsruhe
H. Thoma, Ciba Geigy AG, Basel
G. Vossen, Uni Münster

Organisationskomitee

K. Meyer-Wegener, TU Dresden (Vorsitz)

M. Böhm, K. Bruns, R. Bürger, E. Eiselt, T. Hegel, A. Hemm, B. Keller, B. Kochinka,
C. Pietsch, W. Schulze, E. Spudulyte, U. Wloka

Inhaltsverzeichnis

Speicherungssysteme und Zugriffspfade

Anfragen

Modellierung und Konsistenz

Anwendungen

Wissensbanken

Multimedia Database Systems
-
The Notions and the Issues

Thomas C. Rakow[1], Erich J. Neuhold[1,2], and Michael Löhr[2]

[1] GMD - Integrated Publication and Information Systems Institute (IPSI)
[2] Technical University of Darmstadt, Department of Computer Science
Address: Dolivostr. 15, D-64293 Darmstadt, Germany
E-Mail: {rakow, neuhold, loehr}@darmstadt.gmd.de

Abstract. In this article, we give an overview of the usage of database systems in the emerging field of multimedia computing systems. We motivate that management of multimedia information requires support of temporal relationships, interactive operations, high data volume, and transport of multimedia data. The solutions achieved so far vary to which extend multimedia applications are supported. We suggest to use the notions of hybrid, structural, behavioral, and distributed multimedia systems to classify them. We emphasize the current issues in the area of multimedia database research. Multimedia data modeling, content-based retrieval, continuous storage management, and a distributed architecture are the constituents of multimedia database management systems. The developments achieved so far with the AMOS prototype currently under development at our institutes serve as an illustrating example of current efforts. Specifically, the design of a datatype for audio information, the modeling of meta information and of interactive multimedia presentations, the development of an object manager for continuous objects, and the integration of an information retrieval system in our system are described.

1   Introduction

Most multimedia applications involve a diversity of conventional data types like numbers, text, and tables combined with media data like images (bitmaps), graphics, audio, video and animations. Early research results in the area of multimedia systems have shown that object-oriented programming is very promising to provide for the multitude of datatypes and their manipulation features. In multimedia system development a database management system can provide several useful services: transparency from physical aspects of storage, associative access through indexing, data consistency through defined access methods, query facility with descriptive access, multi-user access through concurrency control and reliability through recovery mechanisms. In order to preserve these advantages, it is necessary to integrate multimedia data into database management systems. However, besides the concepts of object-orientation several other concepts need to be employed by a multimedia database management system.

Differently to ordinary data the presentation of multimedia data is not canonical. The types of conventional data usually comprise the types known from programming languages (e.g. character, integer, real or records of these types) and their representation is inherent to a computer system. Multimedia data are not directly supported by programming languages and their presentation depends on special devices as well as additional information such as image format, compression techniques and layout description. The benefits of database systems are especially found in areas were groups of information producers cooperatively create complexly structured multimedia information. This information must be stored and manipulated/updated over long periods of time and is accessed by a multitude of information consumers looking for "individualized" information that satisfies the consumer's information needs of the moment.

A multimedia database management system (MM-DBMS) should have the capability of storing, managing and retrieving information on individual media, managing interrelationships between the information represented by different media, and should be able to exploit these media for presentation purposes. Concepts for modeling time-dependency and synchronized presentation of multimedia data must be added and integrated into the data description and the query language. Furthermore, presentations and control of presentations at the user's workstation requires a client/server architecture, buffering concepts, and networks that support continuous or isochronous transport protocols. The necessary access to existing multimedia data stores (e.g. CD-ROM systems) requires flexible integration techniques.

One of the key obstacles for many multimedia applications is the vast amount of data involved. The use of digital images often is not viable due to high storage or transmission costs, even if image capture and presentation devices are affordable. Modern image compression technology can compress typical images from 1/10 to 1/50 of their uncompressed size without visibly affecting image quality. But the storage requirements for one object still exceed the size of an average object handled by conventional database systems. For example, objects may not fit into main memory in their entirety.

Traditional database applications use data of fixed size, but the size of multimedia data can vary dynamically. A frame in a video can be regarded as a single object and treated accordingly in the database, but this way continuous presentation is not feasible. So far all unformatted data (mainly text and images) has been handled in database systems through long fields or BLOB's (binary large object), but they usually support only a few generic operations such as reading or writing parts of long fields. Moreover, they are excluded from queries. It is necessary to impose some structure to accommodate for example a frame structure in a video sequence.

Within audio, video, and voice the information itself is expressed as a function of time. Synchronization assures a temporal order of events. Examples of synchronization of multimedia data are the playback of a movie with its soundtrack and the alignment of two stereo channels. Conventional databases provide neither mechanisms for expressing these synchronization conditions nor for controlling them.

In contrast to conventional data the production, manipulation, and presentation of multimedia data is performed with special devices or tools. To provide the flexibility needed, generic interfaces must be provided to integrate new devices. The access to these devices by concurrent capturing and presentation processes must be controlled and the interaction with them must be handled (i.e. interrupting the presentation of a continuous multimedia object). The integration of these devices is very appealing from another point of view. They enhance the possibility for user interaction with the database, for example interaction-supported queries (e.g. based on a pointing device) become possible. This can be achieved only partially in case these devices are directly accessed by the application.

1.1 Related Work

Research in the field of storing time-dependent data addressed new solutions for buffering, layout of files, and strategies for accepting requests in parallel of ongoing services. The proposed solutions can be classified into deterministic and statistical approaches regarding the performance guarantees. Deterministic approaches guarantee reliability of services, statistical approaches only provide service reliability with some probability. In the statistical case, unpredictable delays may occur because of resource contention. Another inherent problem is the acuracy of the statistical model. Deterministic approaches usually rely on worst-case scenarious and, hence, involve the risk of underutilized systems, because they often do not take into account variations in e.g., the compression rate of audio and video. For examples the reader is referred to [A+92, GC92, LS93] on continuous media file and storage systems, [YSB+89, WYY91] on efficient storage of audio data on optical discs, [RVR92, RV93] on support for on-demand multimedia services and techniques for interleaving multiple read requests.

Multimedia database systems are a relatively new field due to the fact that the necessary hardware became available only recently and is still developing [AK92, Gro94, MW94]. The first approaches were database systems for specialized data such as spatial databases [OM88], [SR86] and pictorial databases [TY84]. But in some cases a DBMS was only used as a somewhat complex file system. Spatial databases are attractive because the semantics of the objects and operations are clearly defined and their properties can be derived from geometry.

One of the first efforts in managing multimedia data was MINOS, the multimedia object presentation manager developed at the University of Crete [CHT86]. Another early project was the Multimedia Information Manager of the ORION object-oriented DBMS, developed at MCC [WKL87, WK87] and now available as the product ITASCA. The integration of the new datatypes is accomplished through a set of definitions of class hierarchies and a message-passing protocol not only for the multimedia capture, storage, and presentation devices, but also for the captured and stored multimedia objects. This way a high degree of flexibility is achieved since new storage or presentation devices are included easily by providing the corresponding types as subtypes of the existing types. This approach is very promising, but it remains more or less a collection of classes. Specific database issues such as query processing, user interaction and architectural implications are not considered. Furthermore, it can be questioned whether the modeling of devices down to the level of methods such as `get-next-block` lead to efficient realizations.

Sometimes, multimedia systems are designed as *federated* systems because heterogeneous information sources shall be integrated [B+90, Mas91] or conventional and multimedia information are stored in different systems [KMMW94]. The latter system called MOSS aims at the integration of a multimedia set-oriented data server with a relational DBMS. Cooperation of federated systems is a problem not only specific to multimedia systems. Hence, specific requirements for multimedia systems cannot be drawn from these systems. In [Loc88], at least different systems for discrete and time-dependent data were assumed.

At GMD-IPSI, research in the area of MM-DBMS takes place in the AMOS (Active Media Object Stores) department. The objective is the development of the concepts needed for a "true" MM-DBMS and their integration within the existing object-oriented database management system VODAK. Main topics of research are modeling of multimedia information [AK94, BA94, BR94, KNS90] and support for time-dependent data [RM93, RLM+93]. Prototypes were developed and used in applications in telecommunication environments [R+94, TR94]. The AMOS developments serve as an illustrating example of the features and the architecture of a MM-DBMS in this article.

1.2   Overview

In *section 2* of this paper we give a detailed motivation for specific requirements of multimedia data. *Section 3* describes current solutions and introduces the notions of multimedia systems. We emphasize multimedia data modeling, content-based retrieval, continuous storage management, and the architecture of MM-DBMS's. In *section 4*, the developments achieved so far for the AMOS prototype are observed. In *section 5*, we show how our system can be used within a sample application. This application supports the engineering process such that dependencies between different multimedia specification and report documents can be managed automatically and global consistency is ensured. *Section 6* concludes the paper with an outlook.

2   Multimedia Information

The characterizing property of multimedia information in general is the incorporation of continuous media like video, audio, animation together with conventional types of data. This section gives an introduction to multimedia systems as far as it is needed in following sections. Introductions to the basics of multimedia systems and their technical demands in general are given in [EF94, Fur94, Gro94, Ste93].

2.1 Datatypes and Formats

The notion *multimedia data* covers alphanumeric data as known from conventional computer systems, new types of data like *audio, video, graphics, images (pictures), speech, music, animation*, and any arbitrary composition of these data types. The new types of data add new dimensions to the properties of conventional data types and their handling by a computer system. First, data types like *audio* and *video*, often called *continuous data*, are *time-dependent*. Second, these new data types reflect an increased complexity and are no longer just symbolic data, i.e., they usually have associated compression techniques and need complex operations for their interpretation and manipulation. In the following we characterize some of the media data types in more detail in order to derive some important requirements for multimedia database management systems.

Image: In the past images were stored and distributed as drawings, paintings, photographs or prints. A multimedia system has to provide the functionality to import and manipulate digital equivalents of these media. Basic manipulation operations are clipping, scaling, chromatic correction and the composition of several picture sources. To handle image data a database management system has to manage large amounts of simply structured data efficiently. The internal representation of the images should be hidden to end users and applications by an adequate abstraction.

Graphics: The notion of computer graphics includes all concepts that allow to generate drawings and other images based on formal descriptions, programs or data structures. Typical elements of computer graphics are lines, regions and text elements. Several standards [ISO84] have been established and serve as the basis for industrial and scientific applications. The proper integration of graphics with other media types and existing systems as well as the ability to handle the complex-structured data representing graphical objects are the central requirements for a multimedia database management system in this context.

Text: For a multimedia system it is often not enough to process and represent text as simple strings of characters. A useful representation of textual information should include structural information like title, authors, authors' affiliation, abstract, sections, subsections, and paragraphs. An example of a standard which allows to express the logical structure of documents is SGML [ISO86]. In addition to the representation of the logical structure of text a comprehensive representation of textual information has to represent layout information as well. The complexity of all these structures, which arises from concepts like nesting and repetition, requires powerful modeling capabilities from an underlying database management system [BAH94].

Audio: A common property of all the media previously mentioned is their independence from time. In contrast to these time-independent data an implementation of audio has to consider its time-continuous characteristics. Audio data has only a meaningful interpretation with respect to a constantly progressing time scale. Manipulation operations like cut, copy, and paste can still be handled statically, but playback and recording operations will always be associated to a time scale. Time-dependency, the necessity to express temporal relationships, and the support for compression techniques need to be reflected by an implementation of an audio datatype and its associated operations in a multimedia database management system. This allows the database system to provide a basic understanding of the semantics of audio data.

Speech: The media type speech often is not recognized prominently in the context of multimedia systems. At a first glance it seems not necessary to handle speech as something different than audio, because speech is usually stored as audio data, but recent improvements in speech recognition allow to search for characteristic keywords [RJ93] and to identify specific speakers [WB92]. With advanced progress in the field of spoken natural language processing it will become more important with respect to the interaction features of multimedia systems. For example, speech data can serve as input for the retrieval of stored audio and speech data, or speech data can be generated as a result of queries. Advanced retrieval operations like a best-match word retrieval operator for speech documents [SG94] may be defined on audio data. These algorithms need additional abstractions which play a role that is comparable to traditional indexing techniques in information retrieval. Therefore, even if speech shares the characteristics of audio it shows some unique properties of spoken natural language in addition.

Video: Video combines the properties of the media types audio and picture. Like audio data, video data is time-dependent. The manipulation operations like cut, copy, paste, playback, and recording are similar to those defined for audio data. The atomic constituents of video data are video frames which are closely related to picture data. Advanced retrieval operators may be defined on the content of a video, e.g., retrieving particular portions of a video which start with specific scene cuts which are close to a given picture. These properties of video data have a significant impact on the implementation of video data types and the handling of the data by a database management system.

Generated Media: Examples for this category are computer-generated animation and music. If these media are computed in advance and stored as video or audio data there is no difference to other video or audio material. If they are generated in real time during presentation, both can be seen as a special kind of continuous media types. The approach to generate animations and music on the fly during presentation clearly increases the possibilities of interaction. Examples are changes in the visual angle on the scene presented or the manipulation of simulation parameters, if an animation sequence represents a simulation result.

Presentation speed may be changed with less problems than it is for audio or video. The generation process can easily produce sounds of arbitrary length or generate additional pictures to present an animation in slow motion.

2.2 Temporal Relationships

Conventional documents are statically structured compositions of, e.g., text, graphics and pictures. Multimedia documents become dynamic as soon as they incorporate time-dependent media. The dynamics is based on the temporal relationships between the continuous media components that are part of a presentation. Examples for such relationships are playing back a video and an audio *simultaneously*, playing back two videos *in succession* or *after a predefined temporal interval*. While object-oriented database systems provide useful concepts to handle complex static structures, they are lacking the ability to handle the dynamics inherent to temporal relationships. The modeling and presentation of multimedia information, however, strongly depends on the ability to reflect temporal relationships. Static information is usually presented as a whole piece of data or, triggered by subsequent user interactions, piece after piece. The operations on time-independent data do not consume time and their execution can be modeled as a sequence of steps. In contrast to this, the presentation of dynamic media is expected to last for some time. User interaction at any time can change the presentation.

In order to cope with temporal relationships a multimedia database system must provide some notion for *parallelism*, e.g., for executing a playback operation on videos and audios simultaneously or to control user interaction in parallel to media presentation. The system should also provide for the representation of temporal relationships and their composition (see also section 4.4).

Synchronization: As soon as several time-dependent media are to be presented, it is no longer sufficient to merely express the temporal relationships between the continuous media and to lean on the concept of parallelism. Temporal coordination of several media and therefore concepts for *synchronization* become necessary. As the presentation of information to the end user belongs to the tasks of a database management system (at least in some default mode which is already needed if queries against multimedia data are allowed), a multimedia database system must support synchronous delivery of media data all over the way from the storage system to the user interface. Hence, it is necessary to model and store temporal relationships between the media data in addition to the data itself. Based on this information a synchronization mechanism is needed to handle various related continuous data streams during presentation according to temporal relationships defined between the streams.

Processing: A mechanism for the correct processing of temporal relationships should provide certain "concessions" with respect to the actual specification of temporal relationships. To describe the requirements of a multimedia application on one side and the performance of multimedia system components on the other side the notion of *quality of service (QoS)* has been introduced [LG90]. A complete QoS definition consists of the following parameters:

- *Average Delay* describes the time between the triggering event (e.g. user interaction) and the observable reaction of the system by means of executing an operation. For example, the average delay between submitting a query to a database system and receiving the (multimedia) result is a critical parameter for user acceptance.
- *Speed Ratio* is defined as the ratio between the originally intended and the actually achieved presentation rate. This parameter relates the actual presentation speed to real time and therefore allows the specification of increased or decreased playback speed.
- *Utilization* describes the ratio between the amount of media data used for the actual presentation rate and the total amount of data available for this presentation. For example, using only 8bit out of 16bit audio information corresponds to a utilization of 1/2.
- *Jitter* is a measure for the temporal deviation of two simultaneous presentations at a certain point in time.
- *Skew* is a measure for the accumulated temporal deviation of two simultaneous presentations during a certain interval of time [SE93].
- *Reliability* describes the average frequency of errors during a given time interval of media presentation or recording. Reliability may be measured at multiple levels such as bits, packets, or whole frames.

The parameter settings vary depending on the concrete applications. The parameters themselves are subject to complex interactions depending on the QoS requirements of a multimedia application.

2.3 User Interaction

User interaction becomes much more complex if multimedia data is involved in a presentation for a user or dialog with a user. The state-of-the-art concepts like buttons, text entry, scrollable areas for constructing user interfaces do not support the interaction with continuous media. New devices like cameras, microphones may be taken into account in addition to keyboard, mouse, and external equipment like VCRs for input recognition (speech and gestures). Presentations may be directed to various devices like windows, monitors, loudspeakers. To handle multimedia data additional presentation-related services and concepts are needed [RLM⁺93]:

- *Simultaneous control of different devices*, i.e., support for temporal composition and synchronization so that timing constraints between different presentation steps can be handled. The control of these devices may be based on high level abstractions in order to decouple the database system and application from device-specific and low-level synchronization issue.

- *Efficient handling of user interrupts* is crucial for multimedia applications as the interaction with the user is based on a visual (video) and acoustic perception due to the usage of time-dependent data which is much more sensitive to timing than other interaction styles.
- *Standardized interaction paradigms* for multimedia-related interaction like controlling a VCR, continuous media streams and image presentation should provide for a universal interaction paradigm with a universal look and feel.
- *Support for pen and voice input* would allow to make use of advanced technology and extend the range of interaction styles.

2.4   High Data Volume

One common characteristic of all the media types discussed before is the requirement to support the storage and management of huge amounts of data. Figure 1 shows the memory consumption for several common media types and Figure 2 the bottleneck of storage and transfer rates in a workstation-based environment. In the case of time-independent data (text, images, graphics) at least no serious problems in terms of processing speed are imposed on storage devices and networks. As soon as a system has to deal with time-dependent data the problem of very high data volume becomes critical because of the additional timing constraints imposed on the processing of time-dependent data. This may influence the design of operating systems, networks, and hardware. When dealing with such high data volume it may be more efficient to operate on abstractions of the data instead of the data itself. But the final presentation of the media will always rely on the original data. In such a case a form of dynamic data management is needed in order to bridge the gap between resources available and resources needed. Techniques employed in this context are pipelining data, prefetching data, splitting the presentation operation into several processes etc.

Media Type	Format	Volume	Transfer Rate
text	ASCII	1 MB/500 pages	2 KB/page
b/w image	G3/4-FAX	32 MB/500 images	64 KB/page
color image	GIF, TIFF; JPEG [1]	1.6 GB/500 images 0.2 GB/500 images	3.2 MB/image 0.4 MB/image
speech	μ-law, linear; ADPCM, MPEG audio [1]	2.4 MB/5 min.	8 KB/sec.
CD-music	CD	52.8 MB/5 min.	176 KB/sec.
consumer video	PAL	6.6 GB/5 min.	22 MB/sec.
high quality video	HDTV	33 GB/5 min.	110 MB/sec.

Fig. 1. Media types, formats and resource consumption

---

[1] compression formats

Source	Volume	Transfer Rate (BYTE/sec.)
main memory	64 MB	ca. 100 MB
floppy disc	1.5 MB	
MO-disc	300 MB/side	620 KB
CD-ROM	644 MB	150/600 KB
magnetical disc	1/2 GB	5/10 MB
RAID system	30 GB	
MO disc jukebox	50 GB	
tape change system	600 GB	
telephon		ca. 2.5 KB
S-ISDN		2 * 8 KB
Ethernet (typ./1:1)		0.12/1.2 MB
FDDI		2.4/12 MB
ATM		4/20 MB

Fig. 2. storage and channel transfer rates

2.5 Transport of Multimedia Data

Multimedia applications usually require the storage of multimedia data at a server site and the consumption of the data (playback, presentation, or general manipulation) at a client site. Traditional networking environments like LAN do not meet the requirements with respect to high data rate, stream-oriented highly bursty traffic patterns, less rigorous reliability, latency, or synchronized transmission. Specific solutions are needed, e.g. with respect to traffic channels (e.g. separating multimedia traffic from regular network traffic according to priority schemes) [Cri93] and quality of service [LG90].

2.6 Integrated Multimedia System

To justify the notion *Integrated Multimedia System* a system should meet the following demands [HS91, MW91, RSSS90]:

- *Combination of Media:* The system should offer the free combination of different media to one multimedia object. This applies both to the temporal and spatial dimension of multimedia presentations.
- *Integration of Media:* The composition of the media leads to one single object. Manipulation operations on an object should be available in such a way that the work on and presentation of it seems as if it was one new medium.
- *Independent Access to Media and their Parts:* At the same time it must be possible to manipulate single media independently from the whole composition. This applies as well for the parts of a single medium.
- *Translation of Media:* Translation in this context stands for the conversion from one medium into another. Representatives are the conversion of text

into audio by means of speech generation, and the conversion of pictures into text with optical character recognition.

3   Multimedia Database Systems

In this chapter, we emphasize the current issues in the development of multimedia database systems and some solutions achieved so far. We describe four basic mechanisms which can be used in current DBMSs to manage multimedia information. Nevertheless, adequate DBMS support for multimedia systems requires more than just writing a database schema. We introduce four notions to classify multimedia systems: hybrid, structural, behavioral, and distributed multimedia system. A "true" MM-DBMS should support all notions to some degree. We describe in more detail the constituents of a MM-DBMS: multimedia modeling, content-based retrieval, continuous storage management, and a distributed architecture.

3.1   Storing Multimedia Information in Database Systems

Multimedia information can be stored in database systems by different mechanisms [KMMW93, RLM+93]. We describe four basic types which may appear in current DBMSs alternatively or jointly.

- *External References:* Using this mechanism, a database contains references to the original multimedia data. The references may be file names or other identifiers to locate the data in an open environment [ISO91]. In addition to the references the database contains descriptive data modeled as additional attributes or relationships. For example, attributes of a video stream may be its length, the applicable output device, its compression format, and a textual description of the content. Obviously, the database system cannot provide support for the original multimedia data.
- *Long Fields:* A long field or *BLOB* (binary large object) usually can store up to several GBytes of data and can be used as a domain for attributes. Essentially, a long field can be accessed partially. The DBMS provides full support for data stored in long fields. Nevertheless, contents is still uninterpreted, structuring takes place at the (low) level of bytes, and the functions offered to operate on the data are generic only.
- *Using External Functions:* Some database systems allow to call external functions for processing data stored in the database. The limitations on the data manipulation language such as SQL which are not universal programming languages are the reason for introducing this mechanism. Multi-user support and authorization can be applied for the *access* to external functions but their execution cannot be controlled by the DBMS. For example, if an audio is delivered to an audio device using an external function exclusive access cannot be guaranteed by the DBMS. However, external functions are often very useful to reuse existing algorithms and tools in the context of multimedia presentation and capture.

– *Extensible or Object-Oriented System:* Extensible systems allow the programmer to define (at least) abstract data types and to refer to them in applications. Especially, the object-oriented approach supports advanced modeling by building up datatype hierarchies and defining relationships between instances of classes [KAN93]. In some systems, specific indexing mechanisms can be established for user-defined datatypes [SK91] thereby allowing extensibility *within* the system. Object-oriented systems offer the most suitable support for multimedia information but still lack some features such as supporting time-dependent data, user interaction, and content-based query and retrieval techniques.

Most DBMSs support client access to a database which reside at a remote server. Thus, distribution is supported if multimedia information is stored in long fields or an extensible/object-oriented system is used. However, specific transport protocols for streams are not available. Figure 3 summarizes our discussion [RLM$^+$93]).

DBMS Property	External References	Long Fields	External Functions	Extensible/ Object-Orient.
Persistency	No	Yes	No	Yes
Data Independence	No	No	No	Yes
Indexing	No	No	No	Yes, limited
Object Buffering	No	Yes	Yes [2]	Yes
Multi-user Support	No	Yes	Yes [2]	Yes
Recovery	No	Yes	Yes [2]	Yes
Authorization	No	Yes	Yes [2]	Yes
MM Data Types	No	No	No	Yes
Time Dependency	No	No	No	No
Interactivity (i) Presentation	No	No	Yes	Yes
(ii) Control	No	No	No	No
High Data Volume	No	Yes	No	Yes
Distribution	No	Mostly Yes	No	Mostly Yes
Streams	No	No	No	No

Fig. 3. Support for multimedia information by current DBMS mechanisms

3.2 The Notions for Multimedia Database Management Systems

A DBMS can be classified as a multimedia DBMS if - roughly speaking - all entries in Figure 3 contain a "Yes". However, several levels of multimedia support can be distinguished with respect to usage of analog devices, structuring

---

[2] limited for database objects only

features, handling of time-dependencies, and the degree of distribution. Our classification follows the historical developments of multimedia database systems. In our opinion, a current multimedia DBMS should support all levels to some degree. The need to use analog components (hybrid systems) will decrease with the availability of efficient digital components.

- *Hybrid Multimedia System:* A system is called hybrid if analog components as well as digital can be used together [HS91]. Typical hybrid multimedia systems use analog storage devices like VCR and optical disks which are controlled via the digital components and/ or audio and video data are transmitted via analog cables. Because analog components guarantee required data transfer rates, high quality systems can be build. However, specific hardware must be installed and tape technology may result in long start-up delays. Expensive conversion between analog and digital formats is necessary if operations manipulate data or if analog data is stored on a digital storage device.

- *Structural Multimedia System:* As introduced in [Dit86] a system is called structural if composite objects are supported. This includes datatype constructors (e.g. array, set, list) and generic operators to access composite objects in their entirety as well as parts (elements) of structured attributes. Operations offered are generic reads and writes on datatypes, combined with object creation and deletion operations. In [Loc88], a structural multimedia DBMS is preferred because it should not "preempt the semantics of the served systems". Multimedia information like graphics and text require adequate modeling of structural properties. Audio and video can be seen as an array of samples or frames, respectively. A synchronized data stream can be modeled as a list of the single media data objects combined with a description of its timing requirements.

- *Behavioral Multimedia System:* New specific behavior for multimedia data results from the need to present them to the user under particular timing requirements. The same holds for capture of multimedia information but for practical reasons this situation may be handled differently. If data of an video conference, for example, has to be recorded data must not be lost. In the case of a presentation, degradation of QoS parameters may be tolerated temporarily. Thus, a multimedia system is called behavioral if at least time-dependent and synchronized presentation of multimedia data is supported. Note, a behavioral object-oriented system [Dit86] models the behavior of conventional datatypes but not necessarily the behavior of time-dependent data. However, behavior of multimedia data cannot be modeled without a notion for the behavior of conventional data.

  In behavioral systems, we can differentiate levels of assistance for synchronization (see 4.4). *Fine-grained* synchronization is required at the user's workstation for presentation purpose. *Coarse-grained* synchronization is appropriate if less restrictive timing requirements are allowed. A usual technique is buffering of data.

- *Distributed Multimedia System:* It follows from the nature of multimedia data that they have to be viewed or heard by the user at his workstation. Thus, distribution of multimedia data must be enabled by multimedia systems if multi-user access is supported. Transport of multimedia data between the nodes of a distributed system must be supported by the notion of a data stream. We can differentiate between several architectures with respect to object availability. In a *client/server* system objects are transparently transferred from the server to the client. Implementations may or may not support buffering (caching) at the client. Clients can access objects only via the server. In a (fully) distributed system (unrestricted) *object migration* over all participating nodes is supported, allowing access from every node in the system. This mechanism supports applications where users cooperate or data sources at different sites have to be accessed. The advantage of a client/server architecture for DBMSs is its easier implementation and mangement overhead through centralized concurrency control, recovery, and authorization.

An example of a structural multimedia DBMS is the ORION DBMS [WK87]. Multimedia data, their presentation and storage can be modeled, but none of the other characteristics of multimedia systems are supported by the DBMS. The MOSS DBMS is a structural system, too, which includes a comfortable set datatype constructor [KMMW94]. The V^3 Video-Server is a multimedia application based on the VODAK DBMS [RM93]. The object-orientation supports the structural aspects of multimedia data. The transparent access of analog video clips stored on an optical disk classifies the video server as hybrid. Additionally, the video clips are transparently distributed to clients. Because coarse-grained synchronization was not supported by the VODAK DBMS, fine-grained synchronization at the client was realized by prefetching all frames of a requested video clip.

3.3 Multimedia Data Modeling

The relevant quality of service (QoS) parameters from the perspective of the database are the average delay at the beginning of a presentation, the speed ratio between desired and actual speed, and the utilization of stored and presented data. The parameters themselves are not independent of each other, e.g. when presenting a video it might be appropriate to fix the speed ratio and to change the utilization in order to overcome overload situations.

Representation of alphanumeric data is not a problem at all. Formatting problems are mostly settled and supported by default by operating systems and programming languages. The basic datatypes are not adequate to reflect the structure of multimedia data. New built-in datatypes like *bitmap* and *audio* and a notion of *stream* for presentation and capture purposes are needed. These built-in datatypes need to have media-specific operations. Spatial data should be accessible by coordinates (e.g. point, area, volume), time-dependent by their time axis (e.g. in 1/10.000 seconds). Manipulation operations may be available for different media but need different implementations. For example, attack and decay are needed for audio and video datatype(s) but have to be implemented differently. The object-oriented concept of overloading and of overriding of operations can be applied here.

In addition to the datatypes, type constructors which allow to deal with the temporal relationships are very useful. For example, a type constructor which models the synchronized combination of a video (e.g. sequence of bitmaps) and an audio (represented as an audio stream) can be used to create the representation of a video clip including its sound-track.

The introduction of appropriate datatypes and type constructors is complicated by the use of compression techniques. There is not just a single compression technique applicable for all multimedia data and all types of applications. Hence, supporting different compression techniques results in different representation formats which underly the datatypes and type constructors for continuous data. The system must provide for a modular and efficient representation of these standards and should make them transparent to the user.

3.4 Content-Based Retrieval

Retrieval in multimedia databases must include the type of queries known from the field of traditional databases as well as retrieval functionality (such as full text search) known from the field of information retrieval. In the case of videos e.g. content based search means to be able to search for a specific fragment of a video which starts with a given scene, or includes given objects. In the case of audio, one might want to be able to retrieve all those audios which are associated to some given topic. Such a retrieval operator may include interactive input needed to process the query. For example, the user's sketch of the shape of cars he is interested in may be used as parameter of a query. Retrieval/query operators should allow for the composition of new media as the result of a request. An example is the retrieval of a particular video and a particular audio (in a specific language) which returns to the user a synchronized multimedia object which can be played lip-synchronously.

Content-based retrieval may depend on the availability of rich metadata or metaknowledge about the original multimedia data. The metadata can be based on additional knowledge incorporating the semantics of the data and its intended usage in a particular application. Or it might be (semi-)automatically derived from the original data by employing specific analization techniques.

3.5 Continuous Storage Mangement

In order to provide timely delivery continuous data streams may be directed from the storage components (see 1.1) to the consuming component (viewer, application) bypassing other layers of the multimedia database system. This avoids additional overhead but does not allow any further processing (selection of portions, scaling, etc.) of the data by the database system. In this case the storage component must offer some high level delivery protocol for the consuming

components. The protocol itself can be based on network transport protocols
which meet the requirements of transmitting data over networks in terms of
quality of service parameters.

3.6 Architecture

Every system that provides special support for continuous media must deal with
the central aspects of media storage, transport, manipulation, and presentation.
Due to the high expense these aspects should be efficiently managed by one integrated system. An OO-DBMS already allows the modeling of large amounts
of complex structured data for several concurrent users and applications. The
ability to store data together with the appropriate manipulation and presentation methods is of special interest for multimedia because media data are a lot
more dependent from these methods than conventional data.

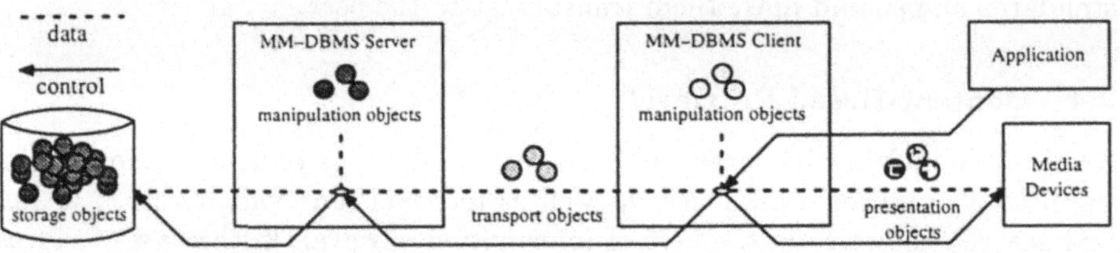

Fig. 4. General architecture of a multimedia DBMS

Figure 4 shows a multimedia application that uses the services of the DBMS
to retrieve multimedia objects from the database, to manipulate them, to transport them over the network and finally to present them at the user's workstation.
The representation of the objects may depend on the task to be executed on the
objects. Objects may be converted between specific representations for storage,
transport, manipulation, and presentation.

A transport protocol that implements the continuous flow of data along with
a mechanism for continuous control is of central importance for an efficient management of presentation and capture functionalities throughout the whole system. Usual applications never get in touch with the data stream itself. They
access their local client of the MM-DBMS to initiate a presentation of data from
a central database at the local workstation. The MM-DBMS then retrieves the
media data in the database of the server and sets up a continuous data connection from the the server through the network to the client. By means of this
connection the data are transferred to the local presentation device(s). The data
connection and a corresponding control connection are working in parallel to the
other components of the distributed DBMS and the application. One data connection can consist of several channels to support the presentation and capture
of a set of media.

4 The Multimedia Database Management System AMOS

So far the properties of an OO-DBMS like **VODAK** are useful for a multimedia system. Our implementation of a video-server [RM93] as a standard **VODAK** application, however, has shown that they are not sufficient. Current OO-DBMSs do not offer support for timing and continuous data transport. To capture the continuous and time-based character of media such as audio and video special solutions for the problems of continuous transport, presentation and control are needed.

Schemas are modeled in the **VODAK** modeling language (**VML**) [KAN93]. Application programs are written **VML**or in C++ using the **VODAK** C++ programming interface. Within a **VML**schema metaclasses, application classes and object types are specified. The inheritance hierarchy of types together with the transformation of types to classes and metaclasses are defined here, too. Every VML application program can use the navigating access facilities of VODAK, which consists of methods to access all instances of a class and the dereferencing of object identifiers. The query and update language of the **VODAK**DBMS is based on a declarative query approach. It differs from SQL mainly by allowing method calls within a query statement.

In this section, the developments achieved so far for the AMOS prototype are observed. The design of the datatype **AUDIO**, the modeling of meta information, multimedia presentations, the development of an object manager for continuous objects, and the integration of the information retrieval system INQUERY in our system are described.

4.1 The AMOS Architecture

In a client/server environment data objects can be partitioned between server and client. In the general architecture of a multimedia DBMS (Fig. 4), full modeling capabilities on both sides are presumed. We decided, however, for ease of implementation and for re-implementation on other platforms to assume an environment with built-in data types. Hence, persistent objects are created only at the server. This restriction is necessary to prevent conflicts and inconsistencies produced by uncoordinated changes on local replicas of the media object. In addition, it may be impossible to copy complete audio objects to the clients due to their limited storage capacity. As a consequence of this partition calls to manipulation methods are always sent to the server for execution. Changes applied to the audio data become visible to concurrent users of the database immediately after the completion of the transaction.

4.2 The Datatype **AUDIO**

The structure of audio data together with methods for their manipulation could be implemented on the level of objecttypes where it could use the available modeling techniques of the **VODAK** modeling language VML. This approach would result in the fact that the underlying system would have no information about the special characteristics of audio as a multimedia type. Especially the need for parallel, continuous I/O and transport as well as the necessity of interactive control could not be expressed by means of the standard modeling capabilities. In addition, the usage of audio should be elementary and simple for the user. Therefore we decided to implement a prototypical audio datatype as the first step towards a complete multimedia DBMS [LR94].

The decision upon the storage format for audio data was based on both our experience with compression techniques and the typical applications we expected:

- *Data Compression vs. Raw Data:* With regard to the storage format of the audio data we had to decide whether any of the currently available compression methods are suitable for our purposes. Compression raises a general problem because manipulation methods usually need access to uncompressed data. Manipulation of compressed audio always means to decode the compressed data, apply the changes and encode it again. For applications like the production of multimedia documents for which editing is one of the main tasks, this procedure causes more than performance problems. Even with the most advanced compression techniques repeated decompression, manipulation, and compression cycles introduce an audible loss of quality due to the effect that minor deteriorations are accumulated. As a consequence of our experiences with the exemplary compression methods and because of the performance and deterioration problems we decided not to use compression for the time being.
- *High Quality Format vs. Parameterized Format:* For all operations manipulating audio data one common high quality format would be a convenient basis. Converting low resolution digital audio to a high definition format, however, would increase space consumption by a factor of at least 20. Further, format conversion may generate false information resulting from the algorithms that generate samples by means of interpolation that were not present in the original. Without careful signal processing this effect may be audible as noise. In addition, frequent format changes are unlikely to happen with typical applications as they are expected to choose a format suitable to their demands in advance. The considerations on available space, computing power, and expected usage lead to the concept supporting a parametrized format. In this context parametrization means to allow any sampling rate and sample sizes of 8, 16 or 32 bits. Linear encoding is supported for all sample sizes. 8 bit samples may be μ-law encoded alternatively. To preserve compatibility between different parametrizations adequate conversions are available on demand.

According to the considerations on data formats and bearing our area of application in mind, we implemented the datatype AUDIO including a set of built-in operations. These operations can be divided into the following groups:

- *Import/Export from/to Files:* We support several common file formats including uncompressed 8- and 16-bit mono and stereo audio data.

- *Recording and Playback:* In contrast to normal operations or method-calls in the **VODAK** environment calls of these operations are executed asynchronously. This allows calls to return before playing or recording is completed. The interface of these operations hides an interrupt-controlled mechanism that switches between two buffers and enables continuous operation. An inquiry operation can be called to detect whether one of the two buffers is free. In this case play or record return immediately. Otherwise these operations have to wait. This dual buffer mechanism allows to call **play** asynchronously once again while the audio from the previous call is still being played [LR94].
- *Inquiry of Attributes:* By means of the operations of this group information about sampling rates and sample resolutions can be obtained. Furthermore the operations allow access to status and current position of ongoing play and record operations. Status and position information are important for the continuous transport mechanism and the synchronization with other media.
- *Audio Manipulation:* Supported manipulations are cut and paste operations, operations to change the volume persistently, to mix several sources into one destination, and to convert between different sample rates and resolutions. The implementation of a low-pass filter operation was necessary to improve the quality of the sampling rate conversion. An attack/decay mechanism and a method for dynamic compression have been implemented as two more complex operations based on volume manipulation. The attack/decay mechanism allows to produce effects such as fade-in and fade-out. Dynamic compression provides selective amplification of passages with low volume and therefore reduces the dynamic range of the audio signal.

4.3   Modeling Meta Information

The rich semantics carried by multimedia data can be utilized be content search, which is a very difficult problem as can be seen from the information (text) retrieval systems. The problems of content-based search lie outside the scope of database research and are difficult to solve. The task of a MM-DBMS is to provide the framework for doing content search. The organization of the data must allow for operations to be added easily. A clear subdivision into different categories of data is necessary: some data are useful for content queries, other data are only needed for internal use such as presentation [TR93]. This implies the need for a meta organization of the data. The following classification of metadata for multimedia objects can be made [BR94]:

- *Metadata for the Representation of Media Types:* This includes format, coding and the compression techniques that have been applied. Either a current name for format, coding etc. may be given, or it may be explicitly described. For example, the datatype **AUDIO** is described by the number of samples per second, number of channels, and the coding in which it has been recorded. From our point of view, certain attributes of textual document components not reflecting the content also fall into this category. An example is an attribute `language` bearing the language a textual component is written in.

- *Content-Descriptive Metadata:* These metadata are determined intellectually or by means of semi-automatic or automatic methods. In the last two cases, these methods are media-type-specific. Examples of content-descriptive metadata are a list of persons or institutions having some relation to a particular multimedia document's content.

- *Metadata for Content Classification:* The distinction between content-descriptive and technical metadata for simple digital media types is well-known (cf. [MW91]). Furthermore, however, while content-descriptive metadata reflect an object's or an object component's content, metadata for content classification are additional information that can be derived from the object's content. For instance, metainformation such as the level of expertise in the field required by the reader of a text falls into this category. To our knowledge, coming up with algorithms how that kind of metainformation can be derived from the document content automatically or at least semi-automatically is an open research issue.

- *Metadata for Composition and Relationships:* The relationships between objects have certain characteristics. Composition-specific metadata are knowledge about these characteristics. As opposed to some other kinds of metadata, this one makes sense only for structured multimedia objects and not for simple media types. For instance, the direct content elements of a document component may be ordered, as with SGML documents [ISO86], or not, as with diverse hypertext models. Using data modeling terminology, the different semantics of these instances of the partOf-relationship is reflected in the operations that would be provided by the corresponding modeling primitives. In the first case a method `getNextComposite` returning the composite that follows the target object makes sense. This method, however, would not have a counterpart in case of unordered composites.

- *Metadata for Location:* Multimedia objects are not inclined to be duplicated and distributed, as compared to conventional ones. Rather they are accessed by the consumer on demand. This facilitates continuous modification of documents' content without that the object actually becomes another one. It is a prerequisite, however, that the multimedia documents can always be localized unambiguously [ISO91].

The kinds of metadata that have been mentioned so far relate to individual multimedia objects. Additionally, there are metadata for collections of multimedia objects. Here, we give an example of such metadata which will be referred to as *statistical metadata*. Consider the case that multimedia documents are stored within a database. Metainformation that may be relevant in this context is the frequency of documents with certain characteristics.

4.4 Modeling Multimedia Presentations

An application on the MM-DBMS-Server can compose a presentation on a high definition level, e.g. HyTime [AK94, ISO92]. We map this high-level description to a simple representation that contains all information that concerns the media and their occurrence in the course of the presentation and use it at the client's site for the actual presentation.

Our system allows the free composition of different media to a new multimedia product, a multimedia presentation. Any combination of both *continouus* media such as audio, video, and text as well as *non-continuous* such as picture can be arranged in one multimedia presentation. This calls for a modeling of a presentation that includes defined temporal time dependencies between the media, defined time intervals in which media are presented to the user as well as media specific characteristics such as the initial playback volume of an audio.

Modeling: The modeling of multimedia presentations has to take the differents aspects important for the presentation into account and has to meet the demands of the users of a multimedia presentation. The essential reflections of the modeling and our solutions can be summarized as follows:

- *Spatial and Temporal Composition:* Our way to describe a presentation is suitable for the definition, storage, and playback of a complex multimedia presentation at the client. The description reflects both all possible temporal relationships between the media, e.g. played in parallel, and necessary media specific information. Besides the description of time in a multimedia presentation a possible spatial position of two-dimensional media on the screen and the overlapping of two-dimensional media are modeled.
- *Time Line:* The selected representation mirrors the entire temporal course of the multimedia presentation. Our solution to keep track of a presentation is to store information only about changes during a presentation. Changes take place in a presentation at certain moments (*events*) on a time line: for each medium in a presentation the start, the end, and every alteration event are stored in a script-like fashion. For each event the time of occurrence is stored by means of (*relative time intervals*) between the events on the time line. The sequence of serial and parallel events during a multimedia presentation including each the necessary presentation parameters is kept in the flat structure of a list, implemented in VML. An interesting difference between our solution and the conventional time line is that media without predefined end can be represented in our system. An example of the necessity of the latter is a help window in the presentation. The end of its presentation is determined interactively.
- *Interaction Capabilities:* One of the main features of a presentation on the client's site is the user interaction in the course of a presentation. As indicated above interactions are treated and modeled as normal media. The standard interaction resemble the typical interactions on the control panel of a video recorder. Over and above that complex interactions such as *selection* are currently under construction.
- *Coarse and Fine Synchronization:* The modeling of multimedia presentations raises the question of how to represent its synchronization features. Timing requirements are subdivided in fine and coarse synchronization. The

coarse synchronization ensures that the time line representation of the presentation is put into action. Coarse synchronization relies on the mere schedule of the presentation stored in the description. The fine synchronization, however, obeys the maximum permissible deviation from refence media. For each single event on the time line one or more reference media to synchronize with are specified in the script-like representation as well as the corresponding deviation limit.

– *Presentation Parameters:* Initial settings such as playback volume for an audio, the playback speed of a video and the like are modeled. The exploitation of the knowledge about the presentation environment at the client's site flows into the script-like representation at the server when it is generated. This improves the quality of the actual presentation at the client.

Presentation: The script-like description of the presentation is transferred from the MM-DBMS-Server to the client, is interpreted there, and the presentation is showed to the user as desired. The interpreting component at the client manages the preparation, startup and termination of the single media presentations that belong to a complex multimedia presentation. The implementation of the interpreter of the script-like representation of a multimedia presentation is currently under construction.

4.5 The Continuous Object Manager

The continuous object manager frees the applications from considering time-dependency during media capture and presentation. Continuous object management functionality is categorized into object handling, direct access, and buffer resource management. Additionally, it has been found that traditional communication protocols, e.g. TCP/IP or OSI-like protocols are not sufficient for real-time requirements of multimedia applications [LG90, Nic90]. Therefore, the integration of a multimedia transport protocol is planned.

The client/server distribution of the AMOS system is constructed in such a way that a distributed database buffer is maintained by the continuous object managers on the server and the client. The support of interactions for continuous data leads to a new understanding of buffer management strategies. The well-known statical buffer preloading and replacement strategies (e.g. most recently used etc.) are substituted by more elaborate algorithms which consider the actual structure and behavior of continuous data streams as discussed in [R+94]. The primary idea is described by an example of the presentation of an M-JPEG (Motion JPEG) video clip (Figure 5).

At the beginning of the presentation the method call `play()` is sent to the respective object `Object`. The continuous object manager initializes its buffer by preloading continuously the JPEG-frames which are needed to best support the presentation state `play`. In our example in figure 5, frame 4 is being presented, 1 to 3 were already displayed and frames 5 to 8 are preloaded. While consuming frame 4, the user changes the presentation status from `play` to `fastplay(doublespeed)`. The operation may be implemented so that every

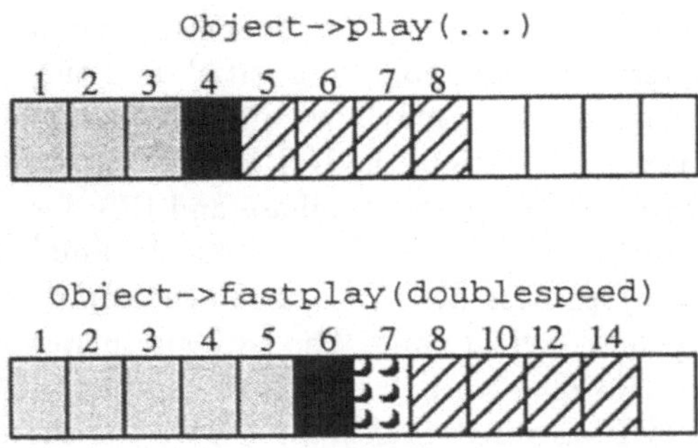

Fig. 5. Continuous Object Management

second frame is dropped. Hence, the new preloaded frames are 10, 12 and 14. Frame 7 is no longer needed. When the presentation direction is changed, the continuous object manager can use the same strategies by preloading "on the left". A state transition from **fastplay** to **play** is realized by frame stuffing of eventual missing frames.

A simple and sufficient replacement strategy is as follows: replace frames which are farthest away from the actual presentation point.

Other relevant questions of continuous object management are the intra-media synchronization of different media streams, how the buffer resource is distributed over several multimedia presentations and how and which scaling [D+93] or adaptation strategies on the client and the server side can be considered.

4.6 Content-Based Text Retrieval

Whereas DBMSs are particularly suited to handle structured information in multi-user environments, complement information-retrieval systems (IRSs) provide content-oriented retrieval capabilities [SM83]. Result of an IRS query are a set of documents and their (probabilistic) *relevance* for the query. We have integrated the IR system INQUERY with the object-oriented DBMS VODAK [VAB95]. Combining structural queries with IRS queries leads to non-trivial questions with regard to retrieval semantics and query processing. Further, the VODAK DBMS supports the management of user-definable typed document structures according to SGML and the hypertext features of HyTime [ABH94, BA94, ISO86, ISO92]. In the sequel, we give some examples of possible queries in this system:

- *"Select the authors of all chapters whose introduction is about multimedia databases"*
- *"Select the titles of all sections on the information highway"*

Naturally, such queries require that the document-type definition contains element types 'chapter', 'introduction', and 'title', and that chapters have an attribute 'author', and that they may have an introduction.

We have coupled the DBMS to the IRS *loosely*. The DBMS facilitates a mapping between logical entities in the database and IRS-documents. The database schema reflects which are the logical units from the application's point of view. We want to remain open for arbitrary document components, not only entire documents, being these logical units. The IRS administer flat text only. Besides that, the result of IRS queries shall always be complete IRS documents. Applications access the DBMS which makes the DBMS the control component of the IRS. Thus, modifying any of the existing systems is not necessary. Queries issued by the application are expressed in the database query language making use of query-processing mechanisms, i.e. analyzing, evaluating and optimizing queries. Formulating complex queries is easy using the database query language. Other database features are "for free". The most important result is that query results can be given which contain the relevance of specifically selected document parts.

5   A Sample Application

In this section, we show how our system can be used within a sample application. Other current applications are a multimedia calendar of events (CoE) [R+94, TR94] and an interactive audiotool for an audio/image database (AAT) [LR94].

This application supports the engineering process such that dependencies between different multimedia specification and report documents can be managed automatically and global consistency is ensured. The $\mathcal{M}uSE$ project [3] aims at the integrated system support of the systems engineering process such that dependencies between different specification and documentation documents can be managed automatically and global consistency can be ensured [DGJ+94] . $\mathcal{M}uSE$ covers various phases of the systems engineering process including design, verification, animation, and simulation, and follows the concurrent engineering paradigm.

In the $\mathcal{M}uSE$-environment the information resulting from the design process, verification of specifications, system simulation and animation, and testing is stored in the underlying object-oriented and multimedia database management system. This includes alphanumeric data as well as graphics, images, audio and video annotations which may originate from simulation and animation results. The system allows for the storage, retrieval and manipulation of highly structured information like 3D-data, part structures, and multimedia and hypertext documents in a multiuser environment which need to be supported by the underlying database management system.

---

[3] $\mathcal{M}uSE$ is the acronym for a project entitled *Multimedia Systems Engineering*. The project is a joint effort of groups at the Technical University of Darmstadt, GMD-IPSI and FhG-IGD, Darmstadt. The project is sponsored by the *Deutsche Forschungsgesellschaft* DFG, grant numbers He 1170/5-1 and He 1170/5-2.

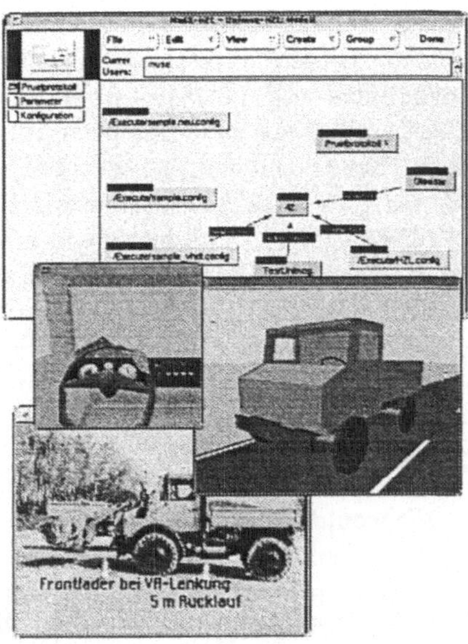

Fig. 6. Screendump of the $\mathcal{M}uSE$ environment

The $\mathcal{M}uSE$ prototype uses hypermedia concepts to organize the documents of the system development process. The complete system model is represented as a hypernetwork containing the different specifications. The hyperstructure is visualized via a hypermedia authoring environment which provides the desktop for the whole $\mathcal{M}uSE$ environment. Figure 6 shows a screendump of the $\mathcal{M}uSE$ environment.

6   Conclusions

In this paper we have investigated the functionality needed to support advanced multimedia applications. We have illustrated how OO-DBMS technology can be applied and what need to be modified and/or extended internally to support such applications. We have compared our approach to other related work and have pointed out differences and advantages of the various systems. However, we do not claim to have found a complete solution for the many features and properties required in such a MM-DBMS. An important open issue remains what the adequate level of application support is.

We also feel that more work has to go into effective storage models and models on how to store but especially retrieve multimedia information. Traditional query based retrieval does not seem feasible as it is nearly impossible to precisely describe, via attributes, the content of a video or image. Imprecise queries as they have been handled in the field of information retrieval will have to be embedded into the database management system. Again how much is integrated and how much is built on top is to be investigated further.

In contrast to the prominent rôle of object-oriented DBMS in this article results of other DBMS research areas have not been applied. Nevertheless, we are sure that the research that is and will be executed in *active DBMS*, *real-time DBMS*, and *distributed* as well as *heterogeneous DBMS* will contribute to solving the problems of MM-DBMS's. The history of scientific research shows that some problems are re-solved by different areas. For example, scheduling of processes takes place in operating systems as well as in DBMS's. We strongly hope that developments in the area of multimedia DBMSs, *multimedia operating systems* (including file systems), and *multimedia network protocols* will benefit from each other. Maybe, that—by the fascinating domain of handling multimedia information—these areas will be tied together.

Acknowledgements: We would like to acknowledge the work of our colleagues *Wolfgang Klas, Karl Aberer, Klemens Böhm, Frank Moser, Heiko Thimm*, and *Marc Volz* contributing to the work on the AMOS system. We also thank the *MuSE* team for providing material, and our many students working with us on the development of the system components. Especially, the participation of *Susanne Boll* in preparing this paper was very helpful.

References

[A+92]   D. P. Anderson et al. A file system for continuous media. *ACM Transactions on Computer Systems*, 10(4):311–337, November 1992.

[ABH94]   K. Aberer, K. Böhm, and C. Hüser. The prospects of publishing using advanced database concepts. In *Proc. of the International Conference on Electronic Publishing, Document Manipulation, and Typography, EP94, Darmstadt, Germany*, pages 469–480. John Wiley & Sons, Ltd., 1994.

[AK92]   K. Aberer and W. Klas. *The Impact of Multimedia Data on Database Management Systems*. Technical Report TR-92-065. International Computer Science Institute (ICSI), Berkeley, CA, USA, 1992.

[AK94]   K. Aberer and W. Klas. Supporting temporal multimedia operations in object-oriented database systems. In *Proceedings of the IEEE International Conference on Multimedia Computing and Systems, Boston, USA*, May 1994.

[B+90]   P. B. Berra et al. Architecture for distributed multimedia databasesystems. *Computer Communications*, 13(4):217–231, May 1990.

[BA94]   K. Böhm and K. Aberer. An object-oriented database application for hytime document storage. In *Proceedings of the Conference on Information and Knowledge Management (CIKM94)*. Gaithersburg, MD, December 1994.

[BAH94]   K. Böhm, K. Aberer, and C. Hüser. Introducing D-STREAT - The Impact of Advanced Database Technology on SGML Document Storage. ⟨*TAG*⟩, 7(2):1–4, February 1994.

[BR94]   K. Böhm and T.C. Rakow. Metadata for multimedia documents. In *SIGMOD Record (Special Issue on Meta-data for Digital Media)*, number 4 in SIGMOD Record. ACM, December 1994.

[CHT86]   S. Christodoulakis, F. Ho, and M. Theodoridou. The multimedia object presentation manager of minos: A symmetric approach. In *Proc. Int. Conf. on Management of Data, Washington*, pages 295–310, 1986.

[Cri93]   S. M. Crimmins. Analysis of video conferencing on a token ring local area network. In *Proceedings of the ACM Conference on Multimedia 93*, pages 301–310, 1993.

[D⁺93]   L. Delgrossi et al. Media Scaling for Audiovisual Communication for the Heidelberg Transport System. In *Proc. ACM Multimedia Conf.*, 1993.

[DGJ⁺94]   M. Deegener, G. Große, W. John, B. Kühnapfel, M. Löhr, and H. Wirth. Rapid Prototyping with MuSE. *International Symposium on Automotive Technology and Automation, Dedicated Conference on Mechatronics*, 1994.

[Dit86]   K. R. Dittrich. Object-oriented database systems: The notion and the issues (extended abstract). In *K. Dittrich and U. Dayal (Eds.): Proc. Int. Workshop on Object-Oriented Database Systems*, pages 2–4. IEEE CS Press, 1986.

[EF94]   J. L. Encarnação and J. D. Foley, editors. *Multimedia*. Springer Berlin, 1994.

[Fur94]   B. Furht. Multimedia Systems: An Overview. *IEEE MultiMedia*, 1(1):47–59, 1994.

[GC92]   J. Gemmell and C. Christodoulakis. Principles of Delay-Sensitive Multimedia Data Storage and Retrieval. *ACM Transactions on Information Systems*, 10(1), January 1992.

[Gro94]   W.I. Grosky. Multimedia Information Systems. *IEEE MultiMedia*, 1(1):47–59, 1994.

[HS91]   R.G. Herrtwich and R. Steinmetz. *Towards Integrated Multimedia Systems: Why and How*. Technical Report 43.9101. IBM, march 1991.

[ISO84]   ISO. *PHIGS - Programmers Hierarchical Interface to Graphics Systems*, 1984. ISO/TC97/SC5/WG2/N305.

[ISO86]   ISO. *Information processing - Text and Office Systems - Standard Generalized Markup Language (SGML)*, 1986. ISO-IS 8879.

[ISO91]   ISO/IEC. *Information Technologie - Text and office systems - Distributed Office Applications Model (DOAM), Part 2: Distinguished-object-reference and associated procedures*, 1991. ISO/IEC 10031.

[ISO92]   ISO. *Information Technology - Hypermedia/Time-based Structuring Language (HyTime)*, 1992. ISO/IEC IS 10744.

[KAN93]   W. Klas, K. Aberer, and E. Neuhold. Object-Oriented Modeling for Hypermedia Systems using the VODAK Modelling Language (VML). In *Object-Oriented Database Management Systems, NATO ASI Series*. Springer Verlag Berlin/Heidelberg, August 1993.

[KMMW93]   R. Käckenhoff, D. Merten, and K. Meyer-Wegener. Eine vergleichende Untersuchung der Speicherungsformen für multimediale Datenobjekte. In *W. Stucky and A. Oberweis (Hrsg.): Datenbanksysteme in Büro, Technik und Wissenschaft*, pages 164–180. Springer Verlag Berlin, 1993.

[KMMW94]   R. Käckenhoff, D. Merten, and K. Meyer-Wegener. MOSS as a Multimedia Object Server. In *Proceedings of the 2nd International Workshop on Advanced Teleservices and high Speed Communication Architectures, LNCS*, pages 413–425. Springer Verlag, 1994.

[KNS90]   W. Klas, E. J. Neuhold, and M. Schrefl. Using an Object-Oriented Approach to Model Multimedia Data. *Computer Communications, Special Issue on Multimedia Systems*, 13(4):204–216, May 1990.

[LG90]   T. D. C. Little and A. Ghafoor. Network Considerations for Distributed Multimedia Object Composition and Communication. *IEEE Network*, 4(6):32–49, November 1990.

[Loc88]   P. C. Lockemann. *Multimedia Databases: Pradigm, Architecture, Survey and Issues*. Technical Report 15. Univ. of Karlsruhe, Dept. of Computer Science, Dec. 1988.

[LR94]   M. Löhr and T. C. Rakow. *Audio Support for an Object-Oriented Database Management System*. Technical Report (Arbeitspapiere der GMD) 890. GMD St. Augustin, Dec. 1994.

[LS93]   P. Lougher and D. Shepherd. The Design of a Storage Server for Continous Media. *The Computer Journal*, 36(1):32–42, 1993.

[Mas91]   Y. Masunaga. Design issues of omega: an object-oriented multimedia database management systems. *J. of Information Processing*, 14(1):60–74, 1991.

[MW91]   K. Meyer-Wegener. *Multimedia Datenbanken*. Leitfäden der angewandten Informatik. Teubner Stuttgart, 1991.

[MW94]   K. Meyer-Wegener. Database management for multimedia applications. In *J. L. Encarnação and J. D. Foley (Eds.): Multimedia*. Springer Berlin, 1994.

[Nic90]   C. Nicolaou. An Architecture for Real-Time Multimedia Communication Systems. *IEEE J. Select. Areas Commun.*, 8(3):391–400, 1990.

[OM88]   J. Orenstein and F. Manola. PROBE Spatial Data Modeling and Queryprocessing in an Image Database Application. *IEEE Trans. Software Eng.*, 14(5), 1988.

[R+94]   T. Rakow et al. Development of a Multimedia Archiving Teleservice using the DFR Standard. In *Proceedings of the 2nd International Workshop on Advanced Teleservices and high Speed Communication Architectures, LNCS*, pages 401–412. Springer Verlag, 1994.

[RJ93]   L. Rabiner and B. H. Juang. *Fundamentals of Speech Recognition*. Prentice-Hall, 1993.

[RLM+93] T. C. Rakow, M. Löhr, F. Moser, E. J. Neuhold, and K. Süllow. Einsatz von objektorientierten Datenbanksystemen für Multimedia-Anwendungen (in German). *it+ti 3/93*, 1993.

[RM93]   T. Rakow and P. Muth. The V3 Video Server - Managing Analog and Digital Video Clips. In *Proc. SIGMOD '93*, pages 556–557, May 1993.

[RSSS90] J. Rückert, H. Schmutz, B. Schöner, and R. Steinmetz. A Distributed Multimedia Environment for Advanced CSCW Applications. In *Proc. IEEE Multimedia*, 1990.

[RV93]   P. Venkat Rangan and Harrick M. Vin. Efficient Storage Techniques for Digital Continuous Media. *IEEE Transactions on Knowledge and Data Engineering*, 5(4):564–573, 1993.

[RVR92]   P. Venkat Rangan, Harrick M. Vin, and S. Ramanathan. Designing an On-Demand Multimedia Service. In *IEEE Communications Magazine*, July 1992.

[SE93]   R. Steinmetz and C. Engler. *Human Perception of Media Synchronization*. IBM European Networking Center, 1993.

[SG94]   P. Schäuble and U. Glavitsch. Assessing the retrieval effectiveness of a speech retrieval system by simulating recognition errors. In *Proceedings of the ARPA Workshop on Human Language Technology (HLT'94)*, 1994.

[SK91]   M. Stonebraker and G. Kemnitz. The postgres next-generation database management system. *CACM*, 34(10):78–92, October 1991.

[SM83]   G. Salton and M.J. McGill. *Introduction to Modern Information Retrieval*. McGraw-Hill, 1983.

[SR86]   M. Stonebreaker and L. Rowe. The Design of POSTGRES. In *Proc. ACM SIGMOD*, 1986.

[Ste93]   R. Steinmetz. *Multimedia-Technologie: Einführung und Grundlagen*. Springer Berlin, 1993.

[TR93]   V. Turau and T. C. Rakow. *A Schema Partition for Multimedia Database Management Systems*. Technical Report (Arbeitspapiere der GMD) 729. GMD St. Augustin, Feb. 1993.

[TR94]   H. Thimm and T.C. Rakow. A dbms-based multimedia archiving teleservice incorporating mail. In W.Litwin and T.Risch, editors, *Proceedings of the First International Conference on Applications of Databases (ADB)*, pages 281–298, Vadstena, Sweden, 1994. Lecture Notes in Computer Science 819, Springer.

[TY84]   H. Tamura and N. Yokoya. Image Database Systems: A Survey. *Pattern Recognition*, 17(1), 1984.

[VAB95]   M. Volz, K. Aberer, and K. Böhm. *A Flexible Approach to Combine IR Semantics and Database Technology and Its Application to Structured Document Handling*. Technical Report (Arbeitspapiere der GMD). GMD St. Augustin, Jan. 1995.

[WB92]   Lynn D. Wilcox and Marcia A. Bush. Training and search algorithms for an interactive wordspotting system. In *Proceedings of the International Conference on Acoustics, Speech and Signal Processing*, March 1992.

[WK87]   D. Woelk and W. Kim. Multimedia information management in an object-oriented database system. In *Proceedings of the 13th VLDB Conference*, Brighton, 1987.

[WKL87]   D. Woelk, W. Kim, and W. Luther. Multimedia applications and database requirements. In *Proc. IEEE Computer Society Symposium on Office Automation*, April 1987.

[WYY91]   J. Wells, Q. Yang, and C. Yu. Placement of audio data on optical disks. In *Int. Conference on Multimedia Information Systems '91*, pages 123–134. McGraw-Hill, 1991.

[YSB+89] C. Yu, W. Sun, D. Bitton, et al. Efficient placement of audio data on optical disks for real-time applications. *Communications of the ACM*, 32(7):862–871, July 1989.

Super-Servers:
Commodity Computer Clusters Pose a Software Challenge

Jim Gray
310 Filbert Street, San Francisco, CA. 94133-3206
Gray @ crl.com

Abstract: Technology is pushing the fastest processors onto single mass-produced chips. Standards are defining a new level of integration: the Pizza Box – a one board computer with memory, disk, baseware, and middleware. These developments fundamentally change the way we will build computers. Future designs must leverage commodity products. Clusters of computers are the natural way to build future mainframes. A simple analysis suggests that such machines will have thousands of processors giving a tera-op processing rate, terabytes of RAM storage, many terabytes of disc storage, and terabits-per-second of communications bandwidth. This presages 4T clusters. To an iron monger or software house: the T stands for Terror! To customers it stands for Tremendous! These computers will be ideally suited to be super-servers in future networks. Software that extracts parallelism from applications is the key to making clusters useful. Client-server computing has natural parallelism: many clients submit many independent requests that can be processed in parallel. Database, visualization, and scientific computing applications have also made great strides in extracting and exploiting parallelism within a single application. These promising first steps bode well for cluster architectures. The challenge remains to extend these techniques to general purpose systems.

Outline:

Introduction

Standards Are Coming!

Business Strategy In An Era Of Commodity Software.

System Integration And Service In A Commodity World

4B Machines: Smoking-Hairy Golfballs.

Future Mainframes: 4T Machines.

Who needs a 4T super-server?

What Are The Key Properties Of Super-Servers?

Clusters and Cluster Software- the key to 4T machines.

Cluster Software – Is It a Commodity Business?

Standards: Tell Me It Isn't SO (Snake Oil).

Clusters versus Distributed Systems, What's The Difference?

Summary.

Introduction

Computers are a key force in the evolution of human civilization. They change the way we communicate, the way we act, the way we play, the way we do science, the way we learn, and even the way we think. I believe that the revolution has just begun -- there is much more coming. As such they are key to the fabric of each society.

Some view the computer is the hardware embodiment -- the box. This paper argues that the boxes will be a commodity by the end of the decade. In the next century, the computer industry will be dominated by the software that animates these boxes with new applications.

The most exciting software will be the new clients: the super-phone, the intelligent-TV, the intelligent-car, the intelligent house, and most exciting of all, the intelligent assistant. These artifacts will all be part the intelligent universe predicted by Herb Simon. In that world, all our artifacts will have behavior and will be programmed to adapt to and assist people.

These billions of clients will need millions of servers. The servers will store, process, and communicate information for the smaller and mobile clients. This paper focuses on the construction of such servers. They will come in many sizes, most will be small. Some servers will need to be very powerful super-servers. This paper argues that these servers must be constructed from commodity hardware. Economics form the basis of these arguments, so the paper touches on the new structure of the computer industry.

This paper was invited by the Deutsche Gesellschaft für Informatik's National Conference. It is good news for Germany and for the EU. Clearly, Europe does not dominate the current hardware or software industries. But, the new software industry is wide open. It is quite reasonable for Europe, with its recognized talent for innovation and design excellence to lead the application-oriented software industry. This paper focuses on the need to design software for super-servers. There is a corresponding need to design software for information appliances (super-clients).

These ideas have been evolving for many years. Gordon Bell is their main and most articulate proponent. This paper grew out of an 1990 taskforce at Digital Equipment chaired by Barry Rubinson. Participants included Bob Bean, Andrew Birell, Verell Boaen, Barry Goldstein, Bill Laing, Richie Lary, Alan Nemeth, Ron Obermarck, Tom Rarich, Dave Tiel, and Cathy van Igen. A confidential version spread widely in the Internet, so in 1992 a public version as Digital SFSC Technical Report 92.1. This is the 1994 revision of that never-published paper.

The 1992 version had two major changes over the 1990 version. (1) High-speed networks were mentioned (gigabit LANs and megabits WANs). This was recognized as the BIG change in computer architecture. Other parts of the computer were getting only ten to one hundred times cheaper and faster in the next decade. Networking was getting thousands or millions of times faster and cheaper in the next decade. (2) Clusters were contrasted with distributed systems. Clusters are simple distributed systems (homogeneous, single site, single administration).

The 1994 version showed four years progress: (early 1991 to late 1994). NT replaces POSIX as the darling operating system. Generic, *Middleware*, replaces the failed POSIX (=UNIX), SAA, and NAS initiatives. Networking promises are more real. Disks and tapes exceeded my technology forecasts. Cpus are on schedule; but RAM is evolving more slowly, more in step with the pessimistic predictions of 4x every 4 years rather than 4x every 3 years. Tape technology and tape robots had been ignored, but are now included in the discussion.

Standards Are Coming!

By the end of the decade, boatloads of NT or POSIX systems, complete with software and hardware, will be arriving in ports throughout the world. They will likely be ten times more powerful than today's Pentium workstation, and will cost less than 10,000$ each, including a complete Microsoft software base (front and back office). No doubt they will come in a variety of shapes and sizes, but typically these new super-computers will have the form factor of a PC or VCR. These products will be inexpensive because they will exploit the same software and hardware technologies used by mass-market consumer products like, HDTV, telephones, desktop teleconferencing, voice and music processors, super-FAX, and personal computers.

How can traditional computer companies add a hundred billion dollars of value to these boxes each year? Such added value is needed to keep computer industry giants like AT&T, Bull, Digital, HP, Hatachi, Fujitsu, IBM, ICL, NEC, Olivetti, SNI, and Unisys alive.

I believe that the 100B$/year will come from three main sources:

Manufacture: Provide the hardware and software components in these boxes.

Distribute: Sell, service, and support these platforms for corporations. Although the boxes will be standard, corporations will want to out-source the expertise to install, configure and operate them and the networks that connect them. Much as they outsource car rentals.

Integrate: Build corporate electronics, by analogy to consumer electronics, prepackaged or turnkey application systems that directly solve the problems of large corporations or provide mass-market services to consumers. The proliferation of computers into all aspects of business and society will create a corresponding demand for super-servers that store, analyze, and transmit data. Super-servers will be built from hundreds of such boxes working on common problems. These super-servers will need specialized application software to exploit their cluster architecture. Database search and scientific visualization are two examples of such specialize application software.

As in the past, most revenue will come from manufacturing and distribution – the traditional computer business. The high profit margins will be in integrated systems that provide unique high-value products. For example, in 1993 Compaq made 7B$ of revenue and .5B$ of profit on Microsoft-based systems. Microsoft made only 4B$ of revenue on those sales but more than 1B$ in profit – 7% profit versus 28% profit. Similarly, Microsoft made as much profit on the average Apple system as Apple Computer did. Adobe's margins are higher than HP's on HP postscript printers.

Integration is not a new business for traditional computer companies, but the business structure will be different. There will be more emphasis on using commodity (outside) products. The development cost of standard products will have to be amortized across the maximum number of units. These units will be marketed to both competitors and to customers. Development of non-standard products will only be justified for items that make a unique contribution with order-of-magnitude payoffs. The cost of me-too products on proprietary platforms will be prohibitive.

This phenomenon is already visible in the PC-marketplace. In that market, standardized hardware with provides the bulk of the revenue, but has low profit margins. A few vendors dominate the high-margin software business (notably Microsoft, Novell, and Lotus).

I conclude from this that the application software business will be the most innovative and most financially attractive sector of the computer industry in the year 2000.

Business Strategy In An Era Of Commodity Components

Profit margins on manufacturing commodity hardware and software products will be modest, but the volumes will be enormous. So, it will be a good business for a few large producers, but a very competitive one. There will continue to be a brisk business for peripherals such as displays, scanners, mass storage devices, and the like. But again, this will be a commodity business with narrow profit margins – much like the commodity PC industry of today.

Why even bother with such a low-margin business? The reasons are simple, jobs and technology. For many nations and companies it is essential to be in the high-volume business. The revenues and technology from this high-volume business fund the next generation and cross-fertilize new products and innovations. This can already be seen in the integrated circuit business where DRAM manufacturing refines the techniques needed for many other advanced devices.

There is a software analogy to this phenomenon visible within IBM, Lotus, Novell, Microsoft, and Oracle. There are economies-of-scale in advertising, distributing, and supporting software. Microsoft's Windows products demonstrate the importance of an installed base and of a distribution network. In addition, the pool of software expertise in developing one product is a real asset in developing the next.

On the other hand, observe that IBM could not afford to do all of SAA and that Digital could not afford to do all of NAS. These projects are so huge that they were stretched-out over the next decade. In fact, they are so huge, that alliances were formed to spread the risk and the workload. This is a root cause of the many consortia (e.g., OSF, COSE, OMG, ...). For IBM and Digital to recover the development costs for SAA and NAS, their software efforts will have to become ubiquitous. NAS and SAA must run on millions of non-Digital and non-IBM hardware platforms. This outcome seems increasingly implausible.

There is no longer room for dozens of companies building me-too products. For example, each operating system now comes with a SQL engine (DB2 on AIX, OS/2, and MVS, Rdb on VMS, SQLserver on NT, NonStop SQL on Guardian,...). It will be hard to make a profit on a unique SQL engine – SQL is now commodity software. A company or consortium must either build an orders-of-magnitude-better unique-but-portable SQL product, or form an alliance with one of the portable commodity SQL vendors. Put glibly: each company has a choice, either (1) build a database system and database tools that will blow away Oracle, Sybase, Informix, and the other portable database vendors, or (2) form an alliance with one of these commodity vendors.

Networks show a similar convergence. The need for computers from many vendors killed IBM's SNA and Digital's DECnet. Customers are moving away from these proprietary protocols to use the TCP/IP protocol instead. The need for interoperability, and especially the need to support desktop and client-server computing has driven this trend more quickly than predicted.

There is confusion about standards. There are committee standards and there are industry standards. For example, the ISO-OSI standards have had almost no impact -- rather it has been a de facto standard (TCP/IP) driven by the PC, UNIX, and Internet that became pervasive. We return to this issue in a later section.

In general, each computer company will both build and buy. This probably represents the way things will be in the future; no company can afford to do everything. No single company can produce the best implementation of all standards. Even Microsoft has its limits: it has 85% of the desktops but Novell has 70% of the servers. Lotus dominates the Mail and Workflow components of the Microsoft desktop.

There will be a good business to migrate legacy systems to commodity platforms -- but that will be a small part of the business of using these new platforms.

System Integration And Service In A Commodity World

The costs of designing, implementing, deploying, and managing applications has always dominated hardware costs. Traditionally, data centers spent 40% of their budget on capital, and 60% on staff and facilities. As hardware and software prices plummet, there is increasing incentive to further automate design, implementation, and management tasks.

Cost-of-ownership studies for client-server computer systems show that most of the money goes to system management and operations. A full-time support person is needed for every 25 workstations. Just that cost exceeds the workstation cost after a year or two.

This is reminiscent of the 1920 situation when a human operator was needed to complete each telephone call. It was observed then that by 1950 everyone would be a telephone operator. Ironically the prediction was correct, direct dialing made us all telephone operators.

If computers are to become ubiquitous, we are all going to become system designers, administrators, and operators. Computer software designers are going to have to automate and elevate the programming process by presenting visual (object-oriented) metaphors for task parameters and sequencing. This should allow "ordinary" people to program, manage, and use information appliances.

Automating the programming, operation, and use of servers and super-servers is equally important. As shown below, the super-server will have thousands of components. Software must manage and exploit these components automatically.

Where will this automated software come from? The computer industry is rapidly moving to a horizontally structured industry as diagrammed in Figure 1. In this model, rather than having one company provide all the services, the customer contracts with a systems integrator who combines products from many vendors into a solution tailored the customer. The customer may operate the resulting system, or may contract with someone to operate it.

Function	Example
Operation	AT&T
Integration	EDS
Applications	Computer Associates
Middleware	Oracle
Baseware	Microsoft
Systems	Compaq
Silicon & Oxide	Intel & Segate

Figure 1: The horizontal structure of the new information industry. In a vertically integrated industry one company provides the complete solution. In a horizontal industry, providers at each level select the best components from the lower levels to provide a product at their level. Few companies are competitive at more than one level.

The super-server will primarily be an applications and integration business. It will not be a shrink-wrapped, mass-market business. It will be more like the business of building bridges, airports, hospitals, or oil refineries. Each is a separate industry.

Systems integrators and applications designers need deep application-knowledge to implement application-specific super-servers. Each problem domain has different needs. There are big differences between a document super-server, a consumer shopping super-server, a stock and commodities trading super-server, and a scientific data storage and analysis super-server. They need some common middleware, but mostly they need domain specific knowledge to build applications and middleware on top of commodity products. It is likely that companies will be built around one or another problem domain -- one specializing in documents, another specialized on geographic data, another specialized on financial systems, and so on. These companies will add considerable value, and so should be profitable. They will write software to adapt commodity middleware, baseware, and systems to the particular problem domain.

4B Machines: Smoking Hairy Golf Balls

Today, the fundamental computer hardware building blocks are cpus, memory chips, discs, tapes, print engines, keyboards, displays, modems, and Ethernet. Each is a commodity item. Computer vendors add value by integrating these building blocks and by adding software to form workstations, mid-range computers, and to some extent mainframes. Apple, AT&T, Compaq, Digital, HP, IBM, Sequent, SGI, SNI, Sun, and Tandem, all follow this model. They use commodity components. Proprietary product lines are shrinking.

The unit of integration has gone from vacuum tube to chip. The next step in integration will be a minimal hardware/software package. By the end of this decade, the basic processor building blocks will be commodity boards running commodity software. The boards will likely have one or more 1 bips cpus (billion instructions per second), 1 GB (Giga byte) of memory, and will include a fairly complete software system. This is based on a technology forecast shown in Table 1.

Table 1: Hardware component technology forecast.						
Year	1 Chip CPU Speed	1 Chip[1] DRAM	1GB Disc	Tape	LAN	WAN
1990	10 mips	4 Mb	8"	.3 GB	10 mbps Ethernet	64kbps ISDN
1995	100 mips	16+ Mb	3"	10. GB	150 mbps ATM	1mb/s T3
2000	1000 mips	64+ Mb	1"	100. GB	850 mbps ATM	1 gbps fiber

This forecast is fairly conservative. It also estimates the following costs for the various 2000 components (see Table 2.)

Table 2: Cost forecast for year 2000 hardware components.						
	CPU	DRAM	1GB Disc	tape robot	LAN	WAN
unit cost	500$	15$	200$	1,000$	200$	200$
1,000$ buys	2 cpus	.5 GB	5x10 GB disk =50 GB array	1TB tape robot	5 x LAN	5 x WAN

These costs must be inflated by about 2x to package the components into a mass-market product. Given these costs, one could build a processor, .5GB of RAM, several high-speed communications chips, and ten discs, package and power them for a few thousand dollars.

Such computers are called **4B machines** (Billion instructions per second, Billion bytes of DRAM storage, and a Billion bytes per second of IO bandwidth, and a Billion bits per second of communications bandwidth). A **5B machine** will support a Billion bit display, that is 4000x4000 pixels and each pixel 32 bits of shading and color[2]. These machines are the natural evolution of the 5M machines that drove the PC revolution of the 1980's (mip, megabyte of ram, megapixel display, 10 megabit per second LAN, and a mouse).

To minimize memory latency these 4B machines will likely be **smoking-hairy-golf-balls**[3]. The processor will be one large chip wrapped in a memory package about the size of a golf ball. The surface of the golf ball will be hot and hairy: hot because of the heat dissipation, and hairy because the machine will need many wires to connect it to the outside world.

Dramatic changes are also expected for storage and networks.

---

1 There is good evidence that DRAMs are evolving more slowly than they have in the past. This slower evolution comes from reduced demand and increased capital costs. If recent trends continue, in 1999 DRAMS chips will be at 64Mb and will cost about 15$ each. Thanks to Steve Culled of Digital for this observation.

2 Some prefer to call these 4G and 5G machines using Giga instead of Billion.

3 Frank Worrell used this metaphor in 1985. Frank is now working at LSI Logic.

Disc farms will be built from mass-produced 1" discs placed on a board; much as DRAMs are placed on memory boards today. A ten-by-ten array of such discs will store about 100 GBytes. Disc array technology will give these disc-boards very high performance and very high reliability[4].

Tape farms will be built from arrays of inexpensive tape robots. Each robot will have about a hundred tapes. Each tape will store 100GB of data. This will give an inexpensive way to store 10 TB nearline. The use of many such robots exploits commodity components, and minimizes queuing delays for tape transports. Multiple transports also increases bandwidth with parallel transfers.

Networks: Networks will be much faster. Fiber based communications will be able to deliver gigabit data rates, but at a high price. Commodity fiber-optic interfaces will run at gigabit speeds. Local communication (LANs) will be able to use this bandwidth, but long haul bandwidth will still be expensive. So, although gigabit-WANs will be possible, and may form the backbones of the Internet, it seems likely that megabit-WANs will be more typical. The transition from the low speed WANs of today running at 64kbps, to the higher-speed commodity ATM WANs of 1999 running at 155 mbps (OC3) will be a major architectural shift for data communications. These changes in network performance and network economics will be key enablers for super-servers. Such networks will allow almost instant access to data and images distributed all over the world.

Baseware: The base software for 4B machines will contain all the elements of X/Open, POSIX, DCE, SAA, and NAS. In particular it will include some standard descendants of Motif, C++, SQL, OSI, DCE-UNIX, X/Open, and so on. The NT operating system along with its GUI, integral database engine, and system management tools is emerging as the commodity baseware of choice.

Perhaps more significant, I believe that Microsoft's OLE standard will become ubiquitous. OLE will be present hundreds of millions of desktops. It's class libraries will be the standard representation for data capture and data display. This will drive all other systems to support OLE. The result is that the OLE class libraries define the standard format for documents, sounds, images, videos, spreadsheets, and other common datatypes. OLE also sets the template for creating new datatypes and representations. It is already the standard way to capture, store, and display data. It will be the mechanism we use to extend databases, operating systems, and viewers.

These basic building blocks will be commodities. That is, the hardware will be mass produced and so will have very low unit price. Standard operating systems, window systems, compilers, class libraries, database systems, and transaction monitors will have high volumes and so will also have low unit prices. This can already be seen in the workstation world. There, NT, OS/2 and NetWare provide complete software systems (database, network, and tools) for less than a thousand dollars.

Today, most applications are not portable from one family to another (e.g., from Intel to Alpha). NT makes applications portable among hardware platforms and provides limited portability from UNIX to NT. The stable interfaces will be software interfaces: windows interfaces, programming languages, file systems, class libraries, databases, and network protocols.

---

4 Patterson, D. A., G. Gibson and R. Katz. (1988). *A Case for Redundant Arrays of Inexpensive Disks (RAID).* Proc .ACM SIGMOD. 109-116. or Schulze, M., G. Gibson, R. Katz and D. A. Patterson. (1989). *How Reliable is a RAID.* 34th IEEE Compcon 89. 118-123.

Future Mainframes: 4T Machines

In a classic paper Gordon Bell and Dave Nelson defined the basic laws of computing[5]. One of their key observations is that there are seven tiers to the computer business. These tiers are roughly categorized by the dollar value of the computers:

        10$: wrist watch computers
        100$: pocket/ palm computers
        1,000$: portable computers
        10,000$: personal computers (desktop)
        100,000$: departmental computers (closet)
        1,000,000$: site computers (glass house)
        10,000,000$: regional computers (glass castle)

Bell and Nelson observed that each decade, computers from one tier move down a notch or two. For example, current portables have the power and capacity approximating that of a 1970 glass-house machine. Machines with the power of 1980 workstations are now appearing as palmtop computers.

Bell and Nelson observed that service workers can be capitalized at about 10,000$ of computer equipment per person on average. That more or less defines the price of the typical workstation.

The costs of departmental, site, and regional servers can be amortize over many more people, so they can cost a lot more.

What will the price structure look like in the year 2000? Will there be some super-expensive super-fast neural-net computer that costs ten million dollars? If future processors and discs are very fast and very cheap, how can one expect to build an expensive computer? What will a main-frame look like?

One theory is that the mainframe of the future will be 10,000$ of hardware and 990,000$ worth of software. Being a software guy, I like that model. Fighter planes work this way. Each new fighter is smaller and lighter – yet costs much more because it is filled with fabulously expensive software and design. It's unlikely that similar mechanisms will operate for commodity super-servers.

OK, so the 99% software theory is blown. What else? Perhaps the customer will pay for 990,0000$ worth of maintenance or service on his 10,000$ box? Probably not. He will probably just buy two, and if one breaks, discard it and use the other one.

I conclude that the mainframe itself will cost about a million dollars in hardware. What will a million dollars buy? It will buy (packaged and powered) about:

~	1,000	processors	= 1 TOP	(tera-op: trillion instructions per second) or
~100,000	DRAMs (@64Mb+)		= 5 TB	(half a terabyte RAM) or
~	10,000	discs (@1GB)	= 10 TB	(ten terabytes disc) or
~	10,000	net interfaces (@1Gbps)	= 10 Tb	(10 terabits of networking)

So, the mainframe of the future is a 4T machine!

---

5 See C.G. Bell and J.E. MacNamera, *High Tech Ventures*, Addison Wesley, 1991, pp. 164-167

Who Needs a 4T Super-Server?

What would anyone do with a 4T machine? Perhaps the mainframe of the future is just a personal computer on each desk. A thousand 4B PCs would add up to a 4T "site" computer. The system is the network! This is in focus of the NOW (Network Of Workstations) project at Berkeley[6]

Each worker will probably have one or more dedicated 4B computers, but there will be some jobs that require more storage or more processing than a single processor, even one of these super-powerful 4B ones.

Consider the problem of searching the 25 terabyte Library of Congress database looking for a for all documents similar to a specified one. A single 4B processor using current software (e.g., Rdb) would take about a month to do this search. By using a thousand 4B processors in parallel, the search would take about a half hour and would cost about 20$. Such searches on a 2 TB database are common today in marketing applications.

Similar observations apply to applications that analyze or process very large bodies of data. Database search is prosaic compared to data visualization algorithms mapping vast quantities of data to a color image. These search and visualization problems lend themselves to parallel algorithms. By doubling the number of processors and memories, one can **scaleup** the problem (solve twice as big a problem), or **speedup** the solution (solve the problem twice as fast).

Some believe that the 4B machines spell the end of machines costing much more than 10,000$. I have a different model. **I believe that the proliferation of inexpensive computers will increase the need for super-servers. Billions of clients mean millions of servers.**

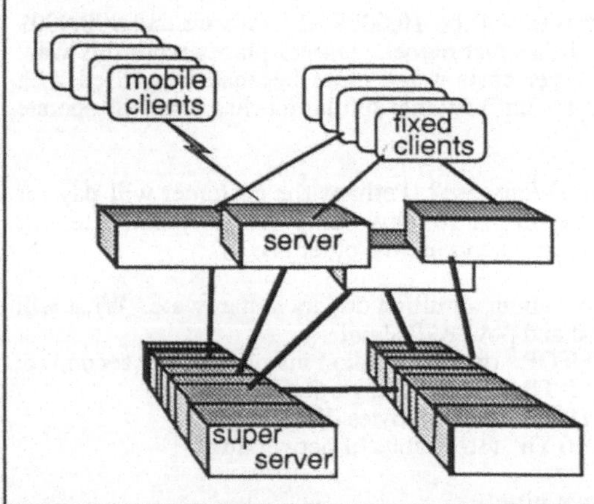

Figure 2: The structure of computer systems. Mobile clients will have low-bandwidth access to the network. All others will have high-speed and low-cost access to local servers and to remote super-servers. Local servers and remote servers will be built from the same hardware and software components. The super-servers will simply be large arrays of processors, disks and tapes. Each server will be functionally specialized to some task like document search and dissemination, video service, intelligent agent shopping, and so on.

---

[6] *Proceeedings of NOW Workshop*, Hennesy, J., & Patterson, D. (ed.), ACM, ASPLOS Conference, San Jose, CA, Sept. 1994.

A fraction, say 25%, of future computer expenditures will go for super-servers. The typical strategy today is to spend half the budget on workstations, and half on print, storage, and network servers. In the end, the split may be more like 90-10, but servers will not disappear. The main arguments in favor of centralized servers are:

Power: The bandwidth and data storage demands of servers supporting hundreds or thousands of 4B machines will be enormous. The servers will have to be more powerful than the clients. Fast clients want faster servers.

Control: The proliferation of machines and bandwidth will make it possible, even easy, to access centralized services and resources. No longer will you go to the video store to get a videotape, you will download it. No longer will you search paper libraries for information, you will have a server do it for you. These resources (movies, libraries,...) will contain valuable information. Central utilities (or at least regional utilities) will want to control access to them. They will set up super-servers that offer an client-server interface to them.

Manageability: People do not want to manage their own data centers. Yet, the trends above suggest that we will all own a personal data center in 1999. Each PC and perhaps each mobile telephone will be a 4B machine. There will be a real demand for automatic data archiving and automatic system management. This will likely be a centralized service. A simple example of this is visible today with the tendency to use X-terminals to move management issues from the desktop to the closet.

What Are The Key Properties Of Super-Servers?

Servers must have the following properties:

Programmable: It is easy to write client and server applications for the server.

Manageable: It is easy to manage the server.

Secure: The server can not be corrupted or penetrated by hackers.

Highly available: The server does not lose data and is always "up".

Scaleable: The server's power can grow arbitrarily by adding hardware.

Distributed: The server can interoperate with other super-servers.

Economic: The server must be built from commodity components to be inexpensive.

Clusters – The Key To 4T Machines

Servers need to be as powerful or more powerful than their clients. They must serve hundreds or millions of clients. How can powerful servers with all these properties be built from commodity components? How can a collection of hundreds of 4B machines be connected to act as a single server? What kind of architecture is needed? What kind of software is needed?

I believe the answer is clusters: Tandem, Teradata, and Digital currently offer clusters that scale to hundreds of processors. Their clusters have excellent programming tools, are a single management entity, and are secure. Clients access servers on the cluster not knowing where the servers are running or where the data resides. So the cluster is scaleable. Processors, storage, and communications bandwidth can be added to the cluster while it is operating. These clusters are fault-tolerant; they mask faults with failover of discs and communications lines. Teradata's TOS, Tandem's Guardian, and Digital's VMS have the transaction concept integrated into the operating system. These clusters are built from commodity processors (Intel x86, MIPS 4000, Alpha), commodity disks and memories, and are among the most economic servers available today as measured by the TPC A, and C benchmarks. In addition they hold the performance records on all those benchmarks because they scale so well.

Well, that is the official marketing story; and there is a grain of truth to it. But, the details of the Teradata, Tandem, and Digital clusters do not deliver on most of these promises. Digital and Tandem clusters do not currently scale much beyond a hundred processors (Teradata scales to about 500.) The programming and management tools of the Digital and Tandem clusters not offer much transparency; each component is managed individually. Few of the tools use more than one-processor-at-a time in running an application; this dramatically limits the ability to scaleup or speedup applications by adding hardware. The cluster price is not especially economic when compared to PC-based servers -- it only compares well to UNIX and mainframe prices. Lastly there are single points of failure in the software and operations aspects of these cluster systems: e.g., software upgrades are not hot-pluggable.

But, these clusters are certainly a step in the right direction. Clusters are the direction that most vendors have adopted. Notable examples are:

AT&T Teradata builds clusters out of the Intel x86 family and proprietary software. These clusters act as back-end SQL servers to mainframes and LANs. Teradata systems feature economy, scaleability, and fault-tolerance. The largest clusters have over four hundred processors and two thousand discs. AT&T hopes to build systems that scale from the palm to the super-computer by building clusters of Intel x86 processors[7].

Digital has long offered the VMScluster and is not evolving it to the AlphaCluster. They have ported the VMS cluster technology to UNIX-OSF and to NT.

IBM Sysplex is a cluster of up to forty eight 390 processors. At present there is very little software to support this cluster hardware. In addition, the IBM AIX system (their UNIX clone) running on the PowerPC-SP2 hardware has a software cluster concept. It supports an array of scientific parallel programming packages and IBM has a large efforts to add parallelism to its DB2/2 products on AIX-SP2 and DB2 MVS.

Intel is building a hyper-cubes of a thousand processors. Unlike the other machines mentioned so far, software, fault tolerance, and input/output seem to be afterthoughts -- rather they are focused on the small high-end scientific computing market. Similar comments apply to Cray's T3D, TMI's CM5, and KSR's machines.

---

7 *NCR's 486 Strategy*, Moad, J., *Datamation*, V36.23, 1 Dec. 1990, pp. 34-38.

Oracle, leveraging its experience on VAX clusters, cloned the VMS distributed lock manager and has ported it to most UNIX systems. Oracle reports excellent scaleup on nCUBE, Sequent, and SP2 clusters. Informix and Sybase report similar scaleups on Sequent and AT&T clusters.

Tandem builds clusters out of a proprietary hardware-software combination running as network servers. Tandem system features match the super-server list above. The systems scale to about 100 processors and to a few hundred discs. Customer complaints center on system manageability. Tandem is working hard on that issue.

Sequent sells a shared memory multiprocessor based on Intel processors. Originally it could scale to about 30 processors, but with the faster Pentium processors, the design peaks at about 9 processors. Next generation processors will require a more partitioned design. Cray T3D, KSR, Encore and SGI all have designs that circumvent these problems.

Silicon Graphics builds shared memory processor arrays based on its MIPS processors. These clusters scale to about 30 processors. SGI hopes to scale to hundreds of processors in the next generation design[8].

Looked at in this light, no one is ready to build a thousand processor 4T machine *and the associated software*. Some are ahead of others. Teradata and Tandem are the leaders today, but IBM's SP2 and Informix or Oracle on SGI are also promising.

---

[8] M. Heinrich, et. al., "The Performance Impact and Flexibility of the Stanford FLASH Multiprocessor, " 6th ASPLOS, Oct. 1994.

Cluster Software – The Key To 4T Clusters

It is important to understand the virtue of clusters. The idea is to add more discs, more processors, more memory, and more communications lines, and get more work out of the system. This speedup and scaleup should go from one processor-memory-disc-communications module to several thousand modules.

Traditionally, multiple processors have been connected by sharing a common memory: Shared Memory Multi-Processors (SMP). The SMP approach does not scale well in a world of smoking-hairy golfballs. The event-horizon of a smoking hairy golfball is on the processor chip; signals from one ball cannot get to the next ball before the processor goes on to the next instruction. A memory shared by two such golfballs looks more like a communications line or a remote processor. SMP designers are aiming for ten-way parallelism. The hundred-fold and thousand-fold speedups available using commodity processors in a cluster have much higher payoff. Most of the machines mentioned above have a cluster architecture. They communicate via messages rather than via shared memory.

Perhaps SMP systems will solve their scaleability problems, but many believe this is not possible. In addition, they must solve the fault-isolation problem. If one part of an SMP fails, it must not contaminate the other parts. In the end, a synthesis of the shared everything and shared-nothing designs will probably prevail[9].

The goal of cluster software is to divide-and-conquer large problems. It must do three things:
1. break the computation into many small jobs,
2. spread the jobs among many processors and memories executing in parallel, and
3. arrange that traffic among the jobs does not swamp the network or create interference.

The challenge has been to extract parallelism from applications. Certain applications like timesharing and transaction processing have natural parallelism. Each client represents a separate and independent request. Each request can go to a separate processor. So, servers with many clients have inherent parallelism. If the number of clients doubles, and if there are no bottlenecks in the hardware or software design, then doubling the number of servers, storage devices, and communications lines will give good scaleup. This is what VMSclusters, Teradatas, and Tandems do today.

The real challenge is recognizing and extracting parallelism *within* applications (big batch jobs). This is an ad hoc field today. SQL servers have discovered how to extract parallelism from large database queries – they search each disc of the database in parallel, they sort in parallel, they join tables in parallel, and so on. These systems display good speedup and scaleup to a hundred processors. Notable commercial examples of this are Teradata and Tandem[10].

Beyond that there have been few successes. Today, recognizing parallelism is an application-specific task. The application programmer must program parallelism into his application by inventing new and innovative algorithms. Automatic extraction of parallelism from applications stands as a major research challenge.

The current situation is (1) 4T machines have a bright future as parallel SQL servers and (2) servers get natural parallelism and scaleup from having many clients. So, no scientific breakthroughs are needed to get the parallelism needed to use 4T machines as data servers. These servers will have lots of opportunities for parallelism.

---

9 Mike Stonebraker, *The Case for Shared Nothing*, IEEE Database Engineering, Vol. 9, No. 1, 1986.
10 David DeWitt and Jim Gray, *Parallel Database Systems: The Future of Database Processing or a Passing Fad?*, CACM, Vol. 35, No. 6, June 1992.

Cluster Software – Is It a Commodity Business?

Once the parallelism problem is "solved" innovation is still needed to make clusters manageable, secure, and highly available. Evolving cluster software to solve any of the major problems (parallel software, manageability, security, fault-tolerance) will be a major software initiative.

There is a fundamental question about whether these initiatives should be based on a proprietary system (NT) or on an Open System (OSF DCE UNIX). I am unclear on the answer to this question. NT is the property of Microsoft and so can only be evolved by them. OSF is in the public domain and so allows much more innovation and experimentation by many different groups. Both are portable to the instruction-set-of-the-month; and both are very large.

The easy way out of this is to base future clusters on UNIX. UNIX is portable and standard. The problem is that UNIX is like stone soup[11]. You have to add a lot to get what you want. If we add 1M lines to UNIX for fault tolerance, 1M lines for distributed databases, and 10M lines for manageability, do we still have UNIX? Have you built a commodity product? Will super-servers be a commodity product – probably not.

Super-Servers will use commodity hardware and proprietary software. Super-servers will have sales volumes measured not in millions of units, but in tens of thousands of units – one super-server per thousands of clients. Super-server operating and management software will have demanding requirements that will not be satisfied by commodity client software. There will be a few server operating systems that offer an open interface (e.g., SAA, NAS, POSIX, X/Open, or the like), run on clusters of commodity devices, but that are proprietary. The software will have many unique performance and management features. It would be best to base this software on NT so that it could run client software at the server. At a minimum, the server will have to support the NT and UNIX application programming interfaces.

This is good news for anyone who wants to make a business of super-servers. If they were easy to build and had huge volumes then there would be a lot of competition for them and margins would be very slim. The key to a successful business is having a product that everybody needs but that few people can build. The software that goes into super-servers may well be such a product.

The next section tries to explain why standard software (e.g., vanilla UNIX-DCE) is unlikely to produce a competitive cluster architecture.

---

[11] The recipe for stone soup calls for a stone to be placed in a large pot of boiling water. Each guest is requested to bring an additional ingredient (e.g., onions, carrots, ...). The quality of the soup depends on the quality of the guests.

Standards: Tell Me It Isn't SO (Snake Oil)

Some believe that all this Open-UNIX-Standards stuff is Snake Oil (SO for short). I do too – well perhaps its not all snake oil, but there is a lot of hype about standards This is an unpopular view – or at least a reactionary one; but it deserves a fair hearing. The SO view proceeds as follows.

Standards are Boring: Customers always want some leading edge feature. They use this as a competitive advantage. Leading edge features have not made it into standards. Parallelism, fault-tolerance, manageability, and high-performance tricks are unlikely to become standards.

Standards are Incomplete: It is standard to see the seven-layer ISO protocol stack. You have seen the 1000-page SQL standard. You have seen the multi-volume X-Windows books. Guess what? They are the tip of the iceberg.
 • The ISO protocol stack has an elevator shaft running down the side called network management. That elevator shaft is not standard. There are implementations that are de facto standards (e.g., NetView-SNMP), but they are not standard. ISO and SNMP ignore issues like security and performance.
 • The SQL standard looks the other way about most errors (they just define a few simple ones), performance (no performance monitor), utilities (no load/dump, import/export,...), and administration (no accounting, space management,...).
The SO reactionaries believe that computing is fractile: there is complexity in every corner of it. Workstations hide this complexity by dealing with a single user and ignoring system management. Consequently, the cost of managing a workstation on a LAN now routinely exceeds the cost of the workstation. SuperServers cannot ignore these problems.

When building a workstation, one aims for simplicity. Microsoft has an *open* standard MS/DOS - a single code body that is its own spec. Apple's Macintosh is a similar story. The UNIX world has a standard *open* application programming interface that allows many simple stand-alone programs to be easily ported from one platform to another. The CICS world has 300,000 programmers who know and love the CICS application programming interface – that is its own spec. These systems are all *open* and standard. Their programming interfaces are published and do not change much, they just grow.

But there is a separate world. There is no real open-standard operations interface for a network of PCs, or for the applications that run them. All the tools to do these operations tasks are proprietary. The CICS operations interface is not well documented, is not open, and it changes from release to release. It is the elevator shaft.

Certainly, the standards organizations have place-holder bodies that are "working" on these elevator shafts, but the SO reactionaries believe such efforts are doomed. These big-systems issues are too specific to become commodity standards or products.

Standards have poor-performance: The standard NFS protocol stack from SUN has poor performance. SUN and other vendors have *deep* ports of this standard code that are much faster. They sell the fact that they have the best NFS. Someone who offers a vanilla NFS server will have a difficult time competing.

Similar comments apply to SQL. Rdb is a deep port of SQL to VMS (actually Rdb was written explicitly for VMS). Other SQL systems do not take advantage of VMS. Rdb consequently displaced other SQL systems on VMS. It was better, less expensive, and came from the hardware vendor. These performance issues are more important for servers than for clients, since servers are resource-poor compared to clients (even in a cluster). I predict a similar scenario for Microsoft's SQLserver on NT -- it will be difficult for "portable" implementations to compete with this native database system.

There is no question that the mass-marketed systems will run standard, mass-marketed software. But, if my model is correct, then a super-server cluster will have commodity hardware and proprietary software extensions. The software may be "open" in the POSIX-Windows sense that applications are portable to it and can interoperate with it. But it will not be the commodity OSF software; it will have LOTS of value added in the areas of scaleability, security, manageability, and availability. In this model, the clients (millions of them) will be running commodity software, but the servers will not.

This reactionary SO view matches the current situation: today the clients are commodity DOS, Windows, or UNIX systems. The small servers are also commodity systems: NetWare. But, past a certain threshold the commodity servers hit a wall. The hardware does not scale up to clusters and neither does the software.

Server vendors have a choice; they can build this super-server cluster software and call it anything they want. They can call it UNIX or NT++. It will be mostly new code. It will surely be X/Open branded, POSIX compliant, and support DCE; so it will be UNIX. But it will have a large body of code that is in neither NT nor UNIX today.

Clusters versus Distributed Systems, What's the Difference?

Why isn't a cluster just a distributed system? Why won't all the wonderful software we have been developing for distributed systems apply directly to clusters? Won't DCE solve the cluster problem? After all, DCE means Distributed Computing Environment.

Well, right! A cluster is a distributed system. Everything, even an isolated PC is a distributed system. That is the virtue of distributed systems, they encompass all and integrate everything.

A cluster a *special* kind of distributed system. It has properties that make it qualitatively different.

Homogeneous hardware and software: A distributed system necessarily involves many types of computers with many different software systems. This heterogeneity comes at a cost. General purpose algorithms are needed to communicate among nodes. Things on one node are slightly different than things on another. It is expensive, if not impossible, to offer transparent access to all data at all nodes.
In a cluster, all the nodes are running the same software and have approximately the same hardware. This simplicity has huge benefits, both for performance and for transparency. It is relatively easy to give the illusion that the entire cluster is a single computer.

Single administrative domain: Distributed systems are designed to cross organizational and geographic boundaries. Each node is considered an independent member of a federation. Since boundaries among nodes of the network are explicit, designers of distributed systems make many design choices that allow fine-grain (node-level) control and authorization.
A cluster is more like a single node of a distributed system. The cluster may consist of thousands of devices, but it is managed as a single authentication domain, a single performance domain, and a single accounting domain. The cluster administrator views it as a single entity with no internal boundaries.

Ideal communication: In a distributed system communication is slow, expensive, and unreliable. The finite speed of light and long distances make it slow - 100 ms round trip is typical. The long distances and huge capital costs of common carriers imply that communications lines are the most expensive part of a distributed computer system. Public networks lose individual connections, and occasionally deny service for extended periods.
By contrast, communication within a cluster is ideal. The distances are short, less than 100 meters; so the speed of light delay is short, less than a microsecond. Bandwidth is plentiful and inexpensive in a cluster. One can just add more ports and fibers. The short distances and low communication complexity within a cluster give highly reliable communication. Since all members of the cluster speak the same language, very efficient communications protocols can be used.

In summary, a cluster is a special kind of distributed system. Distributed systems techniques help build clusters, but the differences make clusters both simpler and faster than distributed systems. In a sense, it is much easier to build a cluster than to build a distributed system.

Of course, a cluster acting as a server will be a key part of a distributed system. It will be a super-server node of the distributed system.

Conclusion

The PC marketplace shows how mass-production and economies-of-scale can mask the engineering costs that dominate minicomputer and mainframe prices today. Technology is pushing the fastest processors onto single mass-produced chips. Standards are defining a new level of integration: the POSIX box. These developments fundamentally change the way we will build computers. Future designs must leverage commodity products.

Clusters of computers are the natural way to build the mainframe of the future. A simple analysis suggests that such machines will have thousands of processors, terabytes of RAM, many terabytes of disc, and terabits-per-second of communications bandwidth. This gives rise to the 4T clusters. These computers will be ideally suited to be super-servers in future networks.

Software that extracts parallelism from applications is the key to making clusters useful. Client-server computing has natural parallelism: many clients submit many independent requests that can be processed in parallel. Database, visualization, and scientific computing applications also have made great strides in extracting and exploiting parallelism. These promising first steps bode well for cluster architectures.

Anyone with software and systems expertise can enter the cluster race. The goal in this race is to build a 2000-processor 4T machine in the year 2000. You have to build the software to make the machine a super-server for data and applications -- this is primarily a software project. The super-server software should offer good application development tools - it should be as easy to program as a single node. The 4T cluster should be as manageable as a single node and should offer good data and application security. Remote clients should be able to access applications running on the server via standard protocols. The server should be built of commodity components and be scaleable to thousands of processors. The software should be fault-tolerant so that the server or its remote clone can offer services with very high availability.

Die BTW im Wandel der Datenbank-Zeiten

Albrecht Blaser
Universität Heidelberg
Interdisziplinäres Zentrum für Wissenschaftliches Rechnen (IWR)
Im Neuenheimer Feld 368
D-69120 Heidelberg
email: blaser@iwr1.iwr.uni-heidelberg.de

Zusammenfassung

Die DB-Szene der 70er Jahre war geprägt von der Anwendung der satzorientierten, navigierenden Datenbanktechnologie, während Forschung und Neuentwicklung vorwiegend die relationale Technologie vorantrieben. Aber noch ehe die ersten relationalen DB-Produkte Anfang der 80er Jahre auf den Markt kamen, begann man besonders in Deutschland über die Grenzen der Anwendbarkeit dieser Technologie für sog. Non-Standard-Anwendungen nachzudenken. Wissenschaftler und Praktiker hatten zwar keinen Zweifel an der prinzipiellen Machbarkeit dieser für die damalige Datenbanktechnologie herausfordernden Anwendungen. Eher bewegten sie Fragen nach Performanz und Aufwand für deren Entwicklung und Nutzung.

Es entstand eine reichhaltige, international einflußreiche theoretische und experimentelle Forschung (etwa komplexe Objekte, NF2/eNF2-Relationenmodell, MAD-Modell), und es wurde schon Anfang der 80er Jahre mit der Entwicklung und Erprobung von Prototypen begonnen (etwa AIM-P, DASDBS, DAMASCUS, PRIMA).

Diese fachliche Aktivität traf sich mit dem Interesse der GI, im deutschsprachigen Raum eine attraktive DB-Konferenzserie zu etablieren. Auf Initiative des Fachausschusses 5.2 „Rechnergestützte Informationssysteme" entstand die GI-Fachtagungsreihe „Datenbanksysteme in Büro, Technik und Wissenschaft", kurz und liebevoll BTW genannt. Die erste Tagung fand 1985 an der Universität Karlsruhe statt. Weitere Tagungen an den Datenbankhochburgen Darmstadt, Zürich, Kaiserslautern, Braunschweig und schließlich Dresden folgten im Zweijahresrhythmus.

Von Anfang an war es das Ziel der BTW, Teilnehmerinnen und Teilnehmer aus Lehre und Forschung einerseits und aus der Entwicklungs- und Anwendungspraxis andererseits zusammenzuführen, um die Praxis zu informieren, was die Forschung über die Evolution der relationalen Datenbanktechnologie und später auch über Alternativen zu ihr dachte, und um durch Berichte aus der Praxis dafür zu sorgen, daß die Forschung nicht „abhob", sondern sich ein realistisches Bild davon bewahren konnte, was die Praxis bewegte (siehe ersten Call for Papers und Vorwort zum ersten BTW-Tagungsband, Springer, Informatik-Fachberichte 94, 1985). Ferner sollte auch ein Bild von den internationalen DB-Entwicklungen vermittelt werden, meist durch eingeladene Vorträge.

Es ist heute wohl unstrittig, daß die BTW ein Erfolg wurde. Sie hat sogar die wirtschaftliche Rezession der letzten Jahre überstanden, zwar mit einigen Blessuren, im großen und ganzen aber doch unbeschadet. Also ist es nach 10 Jahren durchaus angebracht, ein Resümee der BTW zu ziehen und sie daran zu messen, was in diesen Jahren in der Datenbankwelt Realität geworden ist, was sich dort abzeichnet und was sich entwickeln sollte.

Es soll hier also versucht werden, die bisher auf der BTW dominierenden Themen in diesem Licht zu analysieren. Naturgemäß standen am Anfang relationale Weiterentwicklungen verschiedenster Art im Mittelpunkt der Forschungsberichte. Dies wurde in den 80er Jahren begleitet von Praxisberichten über intensive Entwicklung und Nutzung - auch für BTW-Anwendungen - der relationalen Datenbanktechnologie. Im Lauf der Jahre dominierte dann zunehmend das Thema „Objektorientierte Datenbanken" - was immer man darunter verstand - die Welt der Forschung und experimentellen DBS-Entwicklung und damit auch die BTW, und man kann wohl mit Recht vermuten, daß die 90er Jahre als die Jahre der Objektorientierung in die Datenbankgeschichte eingehen werden.

Es läßt sich wohl nicht vermeiden, daß eine Wertung der Tendenzen vom jeweiligen „DB-Glaubensbekenntnis" des Betrachters abhängt. Teil davon ist, daß die alten, ganz fundamentalen Forderungen an Datenbanksysteme immer noch gelten, nämlich:

- Anwendungsentwicklung - aber auch Endbenutzerbetrieb - auf der Basis von Benutzersichten (Subschemata) zu ermöglichen, die auf einer integrierten Gesamtschau (einem globalen, konzeptuellen Schema) der Unternehmensdaten aufsetzen;

- mengenorientierte Datendefinitions- und Datenmanipulationssprachen (mit Anfrageoptimierung) für eine ökonomische Anwendungsentwicklung zu unterstützen;

- Datenunabhängigkeit der Anwendungsprogramme zu gewährleisten, was die Drei-Ebenen-Architektur voraussetzt;

- für Verfügbarkeit, Konsistenz (auch bei Redundanz), Sicherheit/Integrität und Schutz der Daten zu sorgen;

- den Mehrbenutzerbetrieb zu synchronisieren;

- Transaktions-, System- und Media-Fehler beheben zu können.

Diese Funktionalität, gepaart mit vernünftiger Effizienz, ist wohl nach wie vor der Schlüssel für den Markterfolg der Datenbanktechnologie, auch in der Zukunft. Funktionalität ohne Effizienz ist -überspitzt ausgedrückt- mindestens genau so trivial wie Effizienz ohne Funktionalität, eine sich gegenwärtig abzeichnende DBS-Tendenz, die man mit einer gewissen Sorge registrieren muß. Manche Entwicklungen muten oftmals an wie ein Schritt zurück in die satzorientierte Datenbanktechnologie oder gar in die Welt der Dateisysteme und der Datenabhängigkeit. Es mag nostalgisch klingen, soll aber provozieren, wenn dafür plädiert wird, bei der Weiterentwicklung der Datenbanktechnologie -auch für die anspruchsvollen

BTW-Anwendungen- den reichhaltigen Fundus der Ergebnisse der DB-Forschung und -Entwicklung sowie der Anwendungserfahrung aus der Vergangenheit zu nutzen und evolutionär voranzutreiben. Anstatt aus Gründen des vordergründigen Effizienzgewinns auf Funktion zu verzichten, gilt es, das wirkliche Problem kreativ zu lösen, nämlich die auch für BTW-Anwendungen benötigte, obige DBS-Grundfunktionalität gepaart mit Effizienz zu schaffen. Dies sollte die wahre Herausforderung an Forschung und Entwicklung sein, und so sollte man z.B. SQL2 (und noch mehr SQL3) sehen, bei aller Kritik an ihrer überhandnehmenden Komplexität.

Angesichts der auch im internationalen Vergleich hohen Qualität der DB-Forschung und -Nutzung im deutschsprachigen Raum darf man diesbezüglich mit Spannung kommenden BTW-Tagungen entgegensehen.

Supporting Business Transactions
Via Partial Backward Recovery
In Workflow Management Systems

Frank Leymann
IBM Software Solutions Division
German Software Development Lab (GSDL)
Hanns-Klemm-Str. 45
D-71034 Böblingen
Germany
e-mail: frank_ley at vnet.ibm.com

Abstract: *Workflow management systems are used today to realize advanced, distributed application systems, e.g. to support and control real world business processes like office procedures. With the increase of sophistication of these application systems a flexible transaction concept is required to be added to the workflow management system. Business processes exploiting such advanced transaction features are often referred to as "business transactions". We propose to support business transactions by compensation based partial backward recovery of the control flow within an instance of a business process. Work units of a business process which are defined to be potentially subject to such kind of recovery are introduced as "spheres of joint compensation". For the workflow management system IBM FlowMark we show in detail how its metamodel can be extended to support spheres of joint compensation.*

Keywords: Business process management, compensation, recovery, semantic transaction models, workflow management.

1 Introduction

With the introduction of workflow management systems a facility came up that allows for both,

- composing large distributed application systems out of smaller pieces which can be independently developed, and
- supporting real world business processes concurrently performed by many different users exploiting various tools in a network.

While a lot of work has been done over the last decade to broaden the scope of classical transactions (e.g. [7], [13], [16]), the study of transaction models for workflows is much younger (e.g. [2], [17]) and it seems to emphasize on the first bullet (i.e. flow control within applications). In this paper we contribute a semantic transaction model for workflows emphasizing the second bullet (i.e. flow control between tasks of a business process), resulting in the necessity to facilitate even partial backward recovery.

1.1 Advanced Transaction Models And Compensation

It is well-known that the "classical" flat transaction model (although extremely successful) does not sufficiently reflect the processing patterns of complex applications. For that reason a lot of transaction models different from the flat transaction model have been suggested; for example (refer to [6], [18] for more):

- Closed nested transactions [13] allow to structure a transaction in a tree of subtransactions thus striving to enhance intra-transaction parallelism. This should result in improved resource exploitation and response time. But since locks acquired by a subtransaction are inherited by its father the overall concurrency within the system is not improved.

- Open nested transactions [16] strive for enhancing concurrency between (long running) transactions by treating each subtransaction as a separate sphere of control [4]. As a consequence changes of subtransactions become globally visible and the root transaction must be undone by manually scheduling compensation transactions.

- The Saga model [7] structures a (long running) transaction as a sequence of transactions that can be interleaved with other transactions. In case one of the transactions in such a sequence aborts the previous transactions are undone by automatically scheduling compensation transactions removing the burden of manually starting the appropriate compensations.

- The ConTract model [17] allows to view large distributed applications as a collection of steps where a "step" represents an algorithmic part of the application. The control flow between the steps is prescribed via a script. Steps are thus the basic execution units within a ConTract; they can be grouped into flat transactions. Since updates can be externalized at the end of each step a whole ConTract is undone by automatically running the compensation step (which must be defined for each step) of each executed step.

In order to support long-lived computations the proposed models either assume that only forward recovery has to be performed after a crash or that compensating transactions will be performed which semantically undo what previous proper transactions have done [6]. At the first glance it seems to be hard to provide compensation transactions but as a matter of fact "compensation" is a standard technique and is frequently implemented as part of applications already today [17], [18]: For example, the compensation of a credit action is a debit action (and vice versa), the compensation of a reservation is a cancellation (and vice versa). Thus, compensation can be chosen as a base for a transaction model without becoming impractical.

1.2 The Notion Of Business Transactions

We are focussing in the following on the exploitation of workflow management technology to support the automation of *business processes*: A business process is given by an explicit description of the potential flow of control and the flow of data between the different activities. The different activities the business process consists of represent the proper routines making up the functional logic of the associated business process. Business processes may be worked on by different people at the same time. Thus, the activities of a business process must be able to be performed in parallel and by dynamically associated people. The (elementary) activities are in general performed distributed, i.e. at different places in a network. A business process must be explicitly interruptable at any point in time: Since an activity itself may have a long duration it is an important property of the execution behavior of an activity that it must be interruptable. The same is true for the business process as a whole, i.e. a business process must be interruptable whenever control passes from one activity to another.

When an erroneous situation occurs during a workflow representing the execution of a business process features are required to semantically "undo" some work. This turns a business process into a *business transaction*: The effects of some activities within a business transaction are only valid if some other activities are performed successfully. The failing of some activities do not necessarily invalidate the whole business transaction but the results and execution of particular collections of semantically coupled activities. We refer to such a collection as a *sphere of joint compensation*: In case an erroneous situation is signalled for one of the related activities within such a collection all activities of the sphere which have run formerly are compensated.

This notion of backward recovery of business processes captures also the fact from pragmatism that it is not tolerable to undo a whole business process when an failure occurs: Because business processes may last for a long time and may encompass (large amounts of) work performed by many cooperating people, in general, as less work as possible should be undone to recover to a state from where the business process can continue. For the same reason, automatic backout of a business transaction is not tolerable.

1.3 Comparison With Other Work

Beside being compensation based the transaction model we propose in this paper adds the notion of *partial* backward recovery to workflows representing business processes. This feature distinguishes our work from the work performed by others. Proposals which are undoing always complete workflows (e.g. [2], [7], [17]) seem to favor just on one of the major benefits of workflow management systems namely the ability to separate control logic from application algorithms and to provide suitable transaction support for what results. When viewing workflow management systems also as a vehicle for supporting real world business processes (as we do: [11], [12]) one has to deal with the fact that the above does not suffice.

We describe our transaction model in terms of extensions of the metamodel of the workflow management system *IBM FlowMark* [9]. To allow for that we next sketch this metamodel providing an outline of the elements of its syntax and the associated semantics. Then, we define the new elements of the metamodel needed to provide support of business transactions.

2 Modelling And Execution Of Workflows

In [10] we proposed a metamodel based on weighted colored directed graphs for the modelling and execution of business processes. Its applicability has been discussed in [3]. With the enhancements described in [11] it has been implemented in the workflow management system IBM FlowMark [9]. IBM FlowMark can especially be used for business process management [12].

2.1 Control Flow

Figure 1 shows the fundamental elements of our metamodel for describing control flow between activities within business processes (for more details and a complete mathematical description refer to [11]). Note that within IBM FlowMark a workflow can be defined by modelling it via a graphical user interface or by describing it in FlowMark Definition Language (FDL).

The execution steps within a model of a business process are called *activities* (denoted by A1,...,A5). An activity can either be a program, a *subprocess* (activity A3), or a *block* (activity A4). A subprocess is again a complete process model, i.e. our metamodel allows for both, bottom up as well as top down modelling. A block is (nearly: see [11]) a subprocess which is repetitively executed until its exit condition (E4 in figure 1) is fulfilled, i.e. blocks represent "do-until loops". Finally, blocks as well as subprocesses are refined to program activities. Thus programs represent the basic execution steps within a process model; a program can be newly written or can consist of an already existing program which is integrated into the workflow environment. Note, that we do not assume that an activity is a transaction (having ACID properties), i.e. we explicitly support programs e.g. manipulating non-recoverable resources like flat files.

The control flow constructs that we support to bind activities are sequence, loop (via blocks), branch (e.g. A3), fork (e.g. A1), and join (A5). The potential control flow between activities is depicted via a directed edge (*control connector*) from an activity to one of its potential successor activities. Which of the potential successors will become startable in an instance of the process model is determined by the predicates (*transition condition*) associated as weights to the edges: When an activity finishes its execution successfully the predicates of its outgoing edges are evaluated and the endpoints of the edges the predicates of which became "true" will be candidates for follow-on execution. The "successfulness" of the execution of an activity is measured again via a predicate (*exit condition*, e.g. E4) which is evaluated each time the activity terminates. Until its exit condition becomes "true" an activity remains a piece of work which is still to do. Associated to an activity is also an *activation condition* which is a Boolean expression in the transition conditions of the incoming control connectors; the activity finally becomes startable iff its activation condition becomes "true".

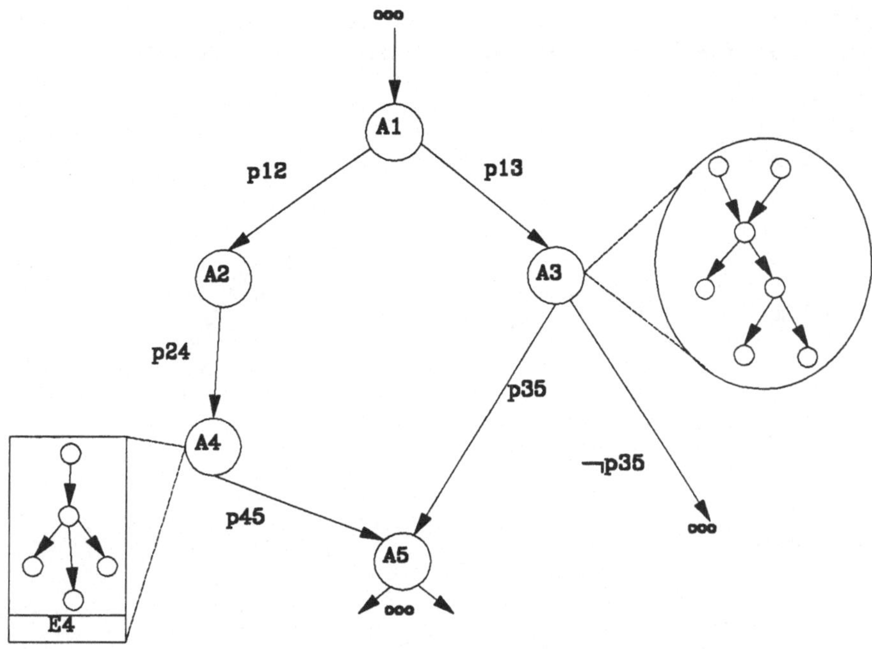

Figure 1. *Control Flow Definition*

2.2 Data Flow

In order to allow for this kind of dynamics predicates are specified as Boolean functions in parameters which are modified by the activities of the business process. Such parameters are bundled into *containers*: Each activity may have an input container and an output container; while an input container represents the input the associated activity expects to be passed to it from the workflow system the output container specifies what will be returned to the workflow system. Since different instances of a given process model may produce different values of the container members and thus different values of the transition conditions different paths through the process model result.

The input and output containers are private to the corresponding activities, i.e. they represent their local context. In order to share container data (e.g. within transition conditions) the construct of a *data connector* is provided: A data connector is a directed edge from an activity to some of its (direct or indirect) successors or a transition condition of an edge contained in a path to a successor indicating that the input container of the target is partially built from the output container of the source. A dedicated container map $\Delta(A, B)$ associated with any pair of activities A and B connected by a data connector specifies which member v_1 of the output container of A is copied to which member v_2 of the input container of B ($\Leftrightarrow (v_1, v_2) \in \Delta(A, B)$). Thus, via data connectors our metamodel allows to define the data flow between activities (and to predicates or conditions, respectively) of a business process.

Figure 2 shows that some members of the input container IC_B of activity B are copies of values of members from the output container OC_A of activity A:

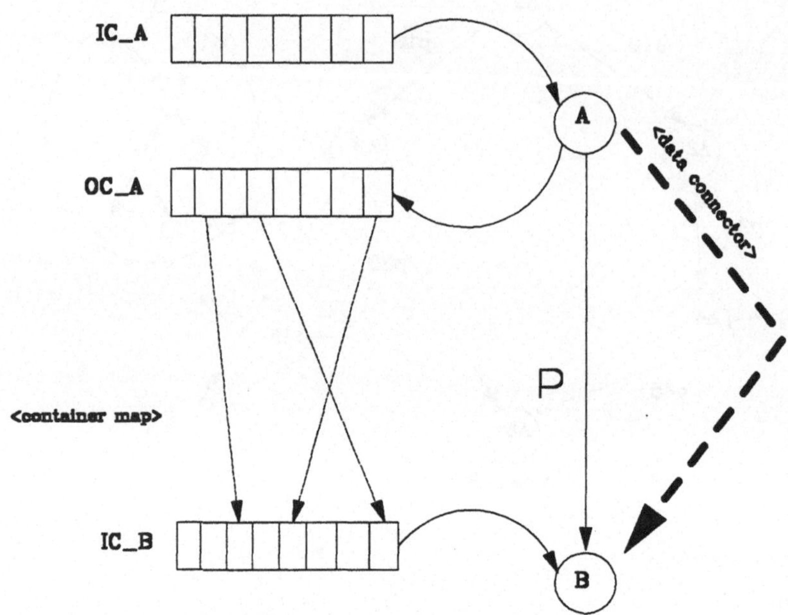

Figure 2. *Container And Data Flow Definition*

With respect to containers activities are isolated: Data connectors are only valid between activities transitively connected via control connectors, so the so-called Bernstein Criterion [1] for parallelizable work is always fulfilled for activities on parallel branches of a process. Moreover, since containers are persistent they provide a persistent context for intermediate results. Also, the state of each process and its contained activities is persistent data. As a consequence, soft-crashes are tolerated: For example, activities which are ended due to a system failure can be restarted. When IBM FlowMark recovers from a system failure the users will have the perception that the active processes are reconstructed until the activities which were worked on at the time the system failed are reached. Similarly, hard-crashes are tolerated. For example, even in case of total losses of work stations a process can be continued correctly based on new a configuration. This is because activities are mapped dynamically to users, nodes, etc. (see 2.3). In this sense IBM FlowMark provides *forward recovery* of processes, i.e. shows behavior which is nicely described as "Phoenix behavior" [6].

2.3 Task Flow

The dynamic mapping of activities to users and nodes is enabled by coupling activities at build time to generic definitions of responsible agents (*staff assignment*). Such a definition can be done in terms of the organization involved in the business process (e.g. "a member of the credit department", "the manager of the person who executed the preceding activity"). The resulting pair consisting of an activity and a staff assignment is called a *task*. Furthermore, activities are attached to definitions of programs and their location in the network. At run time the abstract definition of potential executing agents is resolved into concrete users, the nodes they are logged on etc., finally deriving from a task so-called *work items*. The (elementary) activities are resolved into executable programs. In summary, activities are dynamically mapped to executing resources providing the third "flow dimension" of workflow (beside control flow and data flow) namely the *task flow*, especially capturing the flow of work through the organization.

3 Fundamentals Of Spheres of Joint Compensation

At an abstract level a process model P is perceived as a weighted colored directed graph: The activities build the node set N, the control connectors together with the associated predicates the set of weighted edges E, the exit conditions are the colors of the nodes etc ([10], [11]). For what follows considering the nodes and edges of a process model is sufficient, i.e. $P = (N,E,...)$.

3.1 Metamodel Extensions

Let $P = (N,E,...)$ be a process model. The fundamental concept of "spheres" is defined as follows: Any collection of activities $S \in \wp(N) - \emptyset$ (where $\wp$ denotes the power set) is called *Sphere of Joint Compensation* (or simply *Sphere* for short) iff finally either

- <u>all</u> activities $A \in S$ must have run syntactically successful, or
- <u>all</u> activities $A \in S$ must have compensated.

In this context an activity "run syntactically successful" if it has been activated at some time and terminated meanwhile, or if it will never be able to become activated (e.g. if its activation condition is "false" [11]). An activity that has not run is considered to be compensated via NOP, i.e. in practice only the activities of S which were activated are physically compensated.

We denote by $\mathcal{R}(P) \subseteq \wp(N) - \emptyset$ ("*R*ollback") the set of all spheres of joint compensation defined for the process model P. Considering $\mathcal{R}(P)$ as a new element of our metamodel, i.e. $P = (N, E, ... , \mathcal{R}(P), ...)$, a process model P with $\mathcal{R}(P) \neq \emptyset$ makes an instance of P to become a *business transaction*.

Spheres might intersect, they might especially be contained in each other, etc. Furthermore, a sphere does not necessarily induce a connected subgraph. But we consider each single sphere as a set with the following <u>canonical partial order</u>: Reversing the edges E of P results in the directed graph P^{-1} which induces the assumed partial order on $S \in \mathcal{R}(P)$.

Beside the concept of a sphere we add "compensation" to our metamodel by associating to each activity and to each sphere a *compensating activity*. This is done by including a map κ to the metamodel which associates to each activity $A \in N$ and to each sphere $S \in \mathcal{R}(P)$ a compensating activity $\kappa(A)$ or $\kappa(S)$, respectively ($\kappa : N \cup \mathcal{R}(N) \rightarrow \mathcal{E}$ where $\mathcal{E}$ is the set of all possible activities including NOP). Especially, a compensating activity might be a program, a block, or again a process model. As with spheres before, κ is a new element of our metamodel resulting in process models as tuples $P = (N, E, \dots, \mathscr{R}(P), \dots, \kappa, \dots)$.

3.2 Performing Compensation Of A Sphere

The basic mode of performing the compensation of a sphere is to execute the compensating activities of all activities within the sphere (i.e. $\kappa(A)$ for $A \in S$) in an order which is "reverse" to the order in which the proper activities of the sphere have run (we take the freedom to talk even about a partial order simply as "order"). This order is basically the canonical partial order on S as defined above optionally considering multiple runs of particular activities. The latter is reflected by substituting each of such activity by the linear order induced by the time of termination of the corresponding runs.

Compensating each (semantically not successfully) terminated run of an activity separately is desired if the exit condition of an activity is not only used to measure the semantical successfulness of an execution but in addition as a loop condition: In this situation the exit condition is the conjunct of the "technical" loop condition and the "proper" exit condition. To cope with this one can define via an attribute of the activity (**iterate_compensation** [yes | <u>no</u>]; here and in what follows, the default settings are underscored) whether each terminated run of an activity contributes to a separate compensation instance.

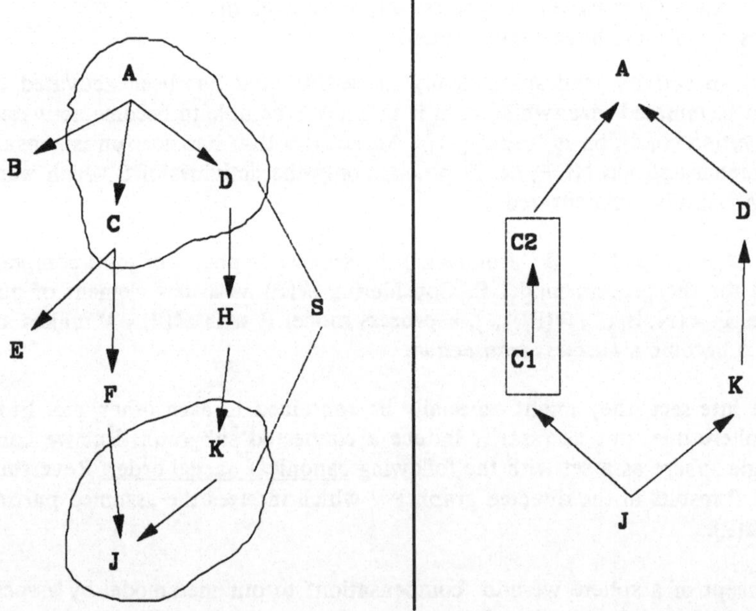

Figure 3. *Compensation Order*

Within the left half of figure 3 S denotes a sphere. Assuming that activity C run twice (instance C1 terminated before C2) the right half of the figure shows the resulting compensation order.

Finally, the proper compensation is performed by executing for each activity <u>instance</u> its compensating activity within this reverse order. Staff resolution does of course also apply to the scheduling of compensation activities. As a default staff assignment the "resource" who executed the original activity is associated with the compensation activity. This can be overwritten when adding a compensation activity to an activity or sphere.

Note, that we do not consider the execution of compensations in an order which is unrelated to the order of the proper activities, e.g. running all compensations in parallel like in [17]. We also ignore cases in which execution of the proper activities can be performed in parallel but compensation can not [14]: If the order of compensation is important a dedicated process must be modelled consisting of the compensating activities in the appropriate order; this process model must then be attached to the sphere as its compensating activity and integral backout (see below) has to be requested.

3.3 Granularity Of Compensation

An activity that is a block or a process is again composed of other activities which also have compensating activities associated to it. In case compensation of such an activity is requested either the original activity's compensation could be performed (called *shallow compensation*) or the compensations of the contained activities could be run (called *deep compensation*). This behavior can be defined with the process model as a property of the activity (**nesting** [deep | <u>shallow</u>]).

Also with the process model it can be specified as a property of each sphere (**integral** [no | <u>yes</u>]) that only the compensating activity associated with the whole sphere of joint compensation is run but none of its encompassed activities (called *integral compensation*). Running the compensation of each encompassed activity is referred to as *discrete compensation*.

Integral compensation might be astonishing but it is desirable in practice: Within the standard "order example" a letter confirming the order is sent to the customer. After passing the order to the production department and then to a carrier it is detected that the ordered item cannot be shipped at the date committed. Compensating what has been done in the "discrete paradigm" will inform the production department about the unavailability of the carrier and will sent out a letter simple notifying the customer about a delay. The "integral paradigm" will sent out a letter with the new ship date and inform the production department accordingly once the usual processing continues.

3.4 Proliferation Of Compensation

The proliferation property of an activity or a sphere, respectively, allows to specify how compensation impacts the neighborhood of the activity or sphere. Proliferation is statically defined with the activity (**proliferation** [local | <u>sphere</u>]) or with the sphere (**proliferation** [sphere | <u>cascading</u>]), or dynamically as parameter of the backout request; dynamic specification overrides the static one. Three degrees of proliferation of compensation are distinguished:

- *Local backout* (of an activity, i.e. activity proliferation = local): Just the particular activity instance is to be compensated. I.e. in case the activity is contained in a sphere of joint compensation the compensations of other activities contained in the sphere are <u>not</u> automatically run).
- *Sphere backout* (of a sphere, i.e. sphere proliferation = sphere): Just the particular sphere is to be compensated. In case other spheres are dependent on this sphere (see below) the other spheres are not compensated (i.e. compensation will not be cascaded).
- *Global backout* (of an activity, i.e. activity proliferation = global): When the activity must be compensated the compensation of the whole sphere is run: Depending on the "integral" property of the affected sphere, either the compensation of each activity within the directly containing sphere or the compensation associated to such a sphere itself will be run. Furthermore, the proliferation property of the sphere determines about cascading or not.
- *Cascading compensation* (of a sphere, i.e. sphere proliferation = cascading): Cascading compensation of a sphere results in the compensation of all dependent spheres of joint compensation.

In case an activity A is contained in more than one sphere and A's global compensation is requested ambiguities w.r.t. cascading compensation might occur. To solve this, the set of all spheres containing A will be determined and via inclusion a finite partially ordered set results. Only the minimal elements of this ordered set are consulted to figure out whether cascading has to take place: The minimal elements having its proliferation scope specified as "cascading" are sources of cascading compensation.

4 Backout Of Spheres

Compensation of a sphere is only one aspect of the general mechanism that is provided to **backout** work: In addition, it has to be determined whether compensation has to be cascaded, and after compensation particular predefined activities have to be determined where work continues.

4.1 Initiating Nodes

Next we define the set of activities $\mathcal{I}(S)$ which potentially initiate the flow of control within a sphere $S \in \mathcal{R}(P)$. Calling $\mathcal{I}(S)$ the set of *formal initiating nodes* of S, it is
$A \in \mathcal{I}(S) :\Leftrightarrow$

1. $A \in S$,
2. A satisfies one of the following conditions:
   - $\{e \in E \mid \pi_2(e) = A\} = \emptyset$
   - $\{e \in E \mid \pi_2(e) = A \wedge \pi_1(e) \notin S\} \neq \emptyset$

Thus, an activity of a sphere S is a formal initiating node of S iff either the activity has no predecessor in the whole process (i.e. it is a start activity), or the activity is target of a control connector which has a source outside of the sphere.

After compensation only those activities are candidates for restart through which the control flow did enter the sphere in the concrete context of the process: The other initiating nodes will not be subject to restart. This set of nodes is called set of *actual* initiating nodes denoted by $\overline{\mathcal{I}}(S)\subseteq\mathcal{I}(S)$. To be more specific, $\overline{\mathcal{I}}(S)$ consists of the following nodes:

1. Each node A corresponding to a start activity (i.e. $\{e \in E \mid \pi_2(e) = A\} = \emptyset$) within $\mathcal{I}(S)$ that has been activated at the time the sphere is requested to be backed out,
2. each node A
   - which is the target of incoming control connectors (i.e. $\{e \in E \mid \pi_2(e) = A \wedge \pi_1(e) \notin S\} \neq \emptyset$) at least one transition condition of which evaluated to 'true',
   - and that has been activated at the time the sphere is requested to be backed out,
   - and that is <u>not</u> reachable from another formal initiating node which has been activated at the time the sphere is requested to be backed out.

Once a sphere has been compensated it is ready to be executed again. By default the execution of a sphere is restarted by scheduling the activities corresponding to the actual initiating nodes of the compensated sphere. After rescheduling the actual initiating nodes the execution of the whole process continues as usual.

4.2 Restart Modes

The major effects of backout as perceived by a user are *compensation* and *rescheduling*. The description of the backout process as described until now represents the default behavior of backout: Both, compensation and rescheduling is performed automatically.

Nevertheless, the two other relevant combinations (i.e. no rescheduling but compensation; no compensation but rescheduling) are desirable in practice too. The resulting behavior of backout is referred to as *restart mode* (a property defined for each sphere). In summary, the following restart modes are relevant:

- *Retry*: After compensation of a sphere all of its actual initiating nodes are by default automatically rescheduled and the execution proceeds as usual.
- *Undo*: In this case compensation takes place but no automatic scheduling of the actual initiating nodes is performed. Thus, 'undo' is like 'retry' but without rescheduling. The sphere is reset for explicit repair actions.
- *Rerun*: No compensation will be run but just the actual initiating nodes are scheduled. This is desirable, for example, in case that instead of sending a countermanding letter a new letter is sent containing both, the countermanding as well as the corrected content.

4.3 Committing Spheres

After having restarted a compensated sphere the control flow will eventually leave the sphere due to the usual execution and navigation behavior. It might be the case that the control flow had already left the sphere before the compensation took place. In this situation some activities outside the sphere might be started again even if they have terminated successfully before.

This seems to be strange at a first glance because an already successfully finished workitem reappears "without any motivation" on a user's worklist. But note that this is inherent to backout of a sphere: If a compensated sphere is automatically restarted the actual initiating nodes (which in general will have been finished successfully!) will reappear on the worklists.

Nevertheless, there might be situations in which reexecution of activities outside the sphere is undesirable. For that purpose spheres can be defined via an associated property (**backout_protected** [yes | <u>no</u>]) to become *backout protected* once the control flow leaves the sphere. To be more precise, the control flow of a backout protected sphere will not leave the affected sphere as long as activities of the sphere are active or may become startable (otherwise the above mentioned side-effect will not be removed!). Furthermore, it has to be ensured that the affected sphere cannot become a victim of cascading backout. Both conditions might result in wait-times: No navigation must take place starting at activities from which the control flow might leave the sphere as long as activities in the sphere are active or could become startable, or as long as cascading backout can occur (caveat: deadlocks!). A backout protected sphere is similar to one that is (implicitly) "committed" (but we do not have an explicit "commit" request).

Neglecting waits induced by potential backout cascades waits in backout protected spheres stem from parallel branches in the sphere inherited by the process model. Since parallel branches of activities within a workflow are desirable in order to speed up the execution of business processes, it has to be decided on a case by case basis whether a sphere has to be defined "commit protected" or not.

5 Cascading

Spheres are in general not independent from each other: If spheres are dependent on each other the backout of one of these spheres will in general result in the backout of the other spheres. In this chapter we describe the various dependencies between spheres which might occur.

5.1 Cascading Backout

If a sphere S is backed out, as a consequence some other spheres $S_1, \ldots, S_n$ might be backed out automatically by the system too. From the process model one can derive already at build time which spheres might interfere at run time:

In case S_i intersects the node set of the sphere S (i.e. $S \cap S_i \neq \emptyset$) both spheres share a common activity and consequently the work represented by the two spheres might interfere at run time. Also, if S_i expects data from the sphere S (i.e. $\exists A \in S \ \exists B \in S_i : \Delta(A, B) \neq \emptyset$) then S_i might depend at run time on results produced by S. In both cases (i.e. *node intersection* and *data expectation*) cascading could be required. In order to determine whether backout has to be cascaded at run time, the actual execution history encompassing activation conditions, activity status, data passing, etc. contribute.

Backout will be cascaded if at ***run time*** the spheres to which backout might be cascaded according to the static conditions above have actually "interfered" with the originating sphere. "Interference" basically means that the spheres of joint compensation had a <u>workitem</u> in common or one sphere <u>consumed</u> data passed by another:

Common Workitem: If S_1 and S_2 intersect in activities none of which have been performed at the time S_1 is backed out, S_2 is not necessarily backed out automatically. Thus, as an additional necessary condition, cascading requires the existence of a shared activity which has been instantiated: $\exists\, A \in S_1 \cap S_2$: A has been active.

Example: In figure 4, if "p1 = FALSE" one cannot infer from "***backout***(S1), S1∩S2 = {A}" that S2 is automatically backed out. ∎

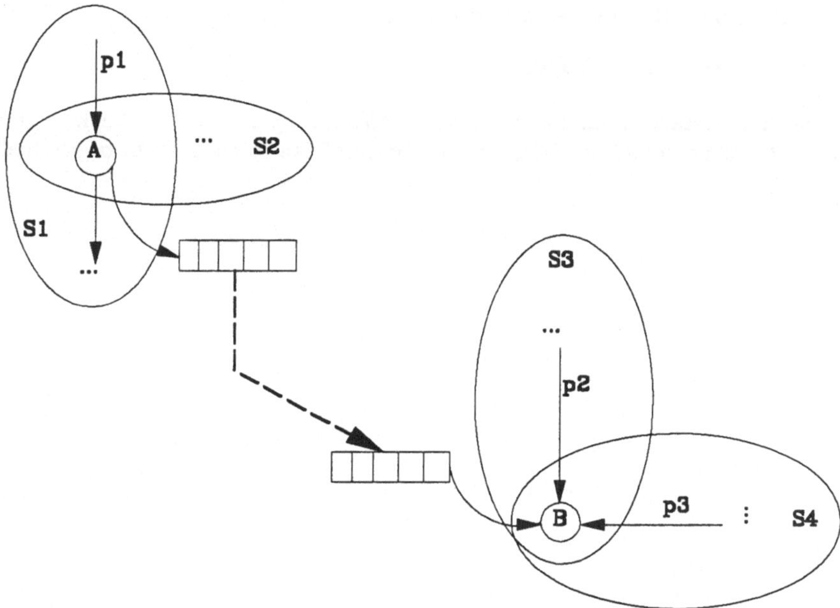

Figure 4. *Backout Cascading*

Furthermore, for conjunctive activation conditions this is also sufficient if cascading applies. In case of a disjunctive cascading conditions the sphere that "did not contribute to the truth" of the disjunction is not automatically backed out.

Example: Assume in figure 4 that the activation condition of B is $p_2 \lor p_3$. If backout(S3) is requested and p_2 = TRUE, p_3 = FALSE, one cannot infer backout(S4). If p_2 = TRUE, p_3 = TRUE and backout(S3) is requested backout(S4) will be automatically performed. ∎

Data consumption: In this case the subject data must have had a chance to be consumed! In order to be allowed to assume that the output produced by $A \in S_1$ has been consumed by $B \in S_3$, A must have terminated successfully and B must have been instantiated: $\Delta(A, B) \neq \emptyset \wedge \varepsilon(A) = \text{TRUE} \wedge B$ has been active, where $\varepsilon(A)$ denotes the exit condition of A.

Example: If in figure 4 A terminated successfully, B has been instantiated and backout(S1) is requested, S3 will be backed out automatically. ∎

Automatic detection of dependencies between spheres and activities can only be based on the definitions of the latter known to the workflow management system. But frequently, dependencies in addition to the ones derivable from these definitions exist: For example, activities in different spheres might exchange data without exploiting the workflow management system's data flow mechanisms for that. We allow to exploit the cascading backout features even in this case via a *join_backout* request: A dependency between S_i and S is established by issuing *join_backout*(...,from = S_i,...,to = S,...) at run time.

5.2 Cascading And Initiating Nodes

In case that a collection of spheres $S_1, \ldots , S_k$ is affected by a cascading backout, the question arises which actual initiating nodes of each of the spheres are to be rescheduled.

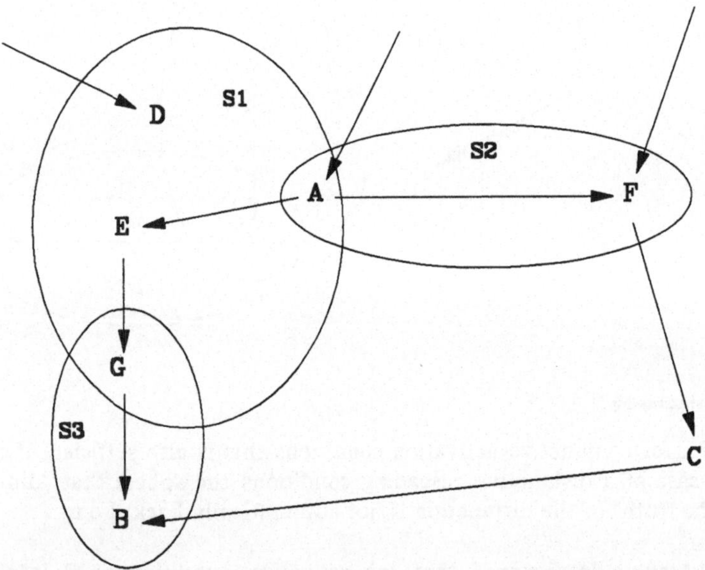

Figure 5. *Rescheduling Nodes For Cascaded Backout*

For example, it might happen that some initiating nodes of an affected sphere are reachable from initiating nodes of other spheres. In case all (actual) initiating nodes of the affected spheres would be scheduled the reachable initiating nodes could be restarted repeatedly. This should be avoided because the backout of the subject collection of spheres will be perceived as a single action. Consequently, only those actual initiating nodes of a sphere will be scheduled which are not reachable from actual initiating nodes from the other spheres.

With $\overline{\mathscr{I}}(M) \subseteq \mathscr{I}(M)$ denoting the actual initiating nodes of a set M, the activities corresponding to the following nodes are scheduled:

$$\overline{\mathscr{I}}\left(\bigcup_i S_i\right)$$

Within figure 5 the formal initiating nodes of the spheres are: $\mathscr{I}(S_1) = \{A, D\}$, $\mathscr{I}(S_2) = \{A, F\}$, and $\mathscr{I}(S_3) = \{G, B\}$; assume all of them have been activated. Then, in case S_1, S_2, S_3 are affected by a cascading backout, only A and D will be rescheduled for restart.

6 Compensation And Data

Compensation requires in general data from the proper activities executed by the business transaction. We describe facilities to provide this data to the compensating activities basically in terms of the process model.

6.1 Rational For Compensation Containers

As with activities themselves compensating activities should be written in such a way that they could be reused in different process models. Thus, a compensating activity should be decoupled from the activity or sphere it is compensating as much as possible. Especially, a compensating activity should not collect its required input data itself (e.g. from the various containers of activities which have run previously, or from some private data stores). Thus, each compensating activity has associated to it a separate input container which is simply called *compensation container*.

6.2 Activity Compensation Container

The compensation container of a compensating activity C_A of a given activity A may be connected by data connectors to various other containers: All of the usual restrictions of our metamodel on data connectors apply (see [11]) with respect to the compensation container of C_A too (e.g. C_A must be reachable from the source of the data connector via a path of control connectors). In addition, data connectors from A's input and output container to the compensation container of C_A are allowed. APIs allow that an activity A puts data into the compensation container of C_A.

6.3 Sphere Compensation Container

Similarly, the compensation container of a compensating activity C_S of a given sphere S may be connected by data connectors to various other containers: To apply the usual restrictions on data connectors, we have to consider the graph $P_{\cdot S}$ which results from the graph P representing the subject process model when S and its edges is "contracted within P into a single node".

I.e. for $P = (N,E)$ and $S \in \mathscr{R}(P)$ we define $P_{\cdot S} = (N_{\cdot S}, E_{\cdot S})$ as follows:

1. It is $N_{*S} = N - S \cup \{S\}$.

2. If $(A, B, ...) \in E$ for $A, B \notin S$ then $(A, B, ...) \in E_{*S}$;

   - if $(A, B, ...) \in E$ for $A \notin S$ and $B \in S$ then $(A, S, ...) \in E_{*S}$;

   - if $(A, B, ...) \in E$ for $B \notin S$ and $A \in S$ then $(S, B, ...) \in E_{*S}$;

   - if $(A, B, ...) \in E$ for $A, B \in S$ then $(A, B, ...) \notin E_{*S}$;

   - this determines E_{*S} completely.

Now, all restrictions on data connectors within P_{*S} apply with respect to the compensation container of C_S. Data connectors from input and output containers of activities contained in S to the compensation container of C_S are allowed. Each activity contained in S may put data into the compensation container of C_S via an API. If C_S is started and data are missing the usual default or prompting behavior, respectively, of IBM FlowMark applies [11].

6.4 Instances Of Compensation Containers

Each instance of an activity must be associated with its own instance of compensation container: This ensures that repeated instantiations of activities are separately compensatable. The compensation container of an activity is instantiated (i.e. filled and made persistent) or manipulated (if it is instantiated already), respectively, at the time

- an instance of the activity terminates (successfully or not: This enables to compensate even activities which have not been finally executed but interrupted only, and it allows for iterated compensation),
- *backout* affecting the activity is requested,
- an API to manipulate the container is issued.

Similarly, the compensation container of a sphere is instantiated or manipulated (if it is instantiated already), respectively, at the time

- an initiating node terminates,
- *backout* affecting the sphere is requested,
- an API to manipulate the container is issued.

Once an activity instance terminated successfully the corresponding compensation container must not be modified. Similarly, when the control flow finally leaves a sphere its associated compensation container must not be modified. All compensation containers are persistent; logically, they belong to the backout log.

7 On Exploiting Spheres

We give some examples where spheres of joint compensation may be used and how this could be done: First, we motivate business transactions from a re-use point of view, next, we sketch how sagas can be modeled via spheres, and finally, we show as an example how mini-batches can be performed based on spheres. It should be obvious how famous examples like "trip reservation" encompassing multiple, independent reservation systems will work.

7.1 Reuse Stimulated Via Workflow

The software community is seeking for technologies allowing to accelerate the software development process. Currently, object oriented techniques and methods are more and more deployed to improve the quality of code and to enhance the productivity of programmers, for example. The crucial aspect here is "reuse". While the basic object technology allows for reuse at a very fine grained level (i.e. objects) *frameworks* (e.g. [15]) allow to provide generic applications which are adapted to particular needs (for example by subclassing). Thus, frameworks strive for reuse at a coarser level hiding much more complexity than plain encapsulation.

Completely independent to this workflow technology allows for reuse at a coarse level by separating the control flow and data flow from the proper business algorithms (i.e. activities). The resulting activities represent business actions which appear in different business processes, in general. Thus, activities are the finest granules of reuse in workflow environments. Applications can be perceived as being build by linking activities together via control flow constructs and data flow constructs which represent the business rules of the how, when and where these activities are exploited.

Now, many activities are usual transactions, i.e. they will commit in case they complete semantically successful. Furthermore, when workflow technology is exploited for business process management activities may be long running, and the time between termination of one activity and the initiation of another one may be long also. As a consequence, binding activities in such an environment into an ACID unit is impractical because concurrency of the overall system will be reduced. But coupling independently developed activities into new semantically correlated entities requires some concepts of "unit of work" for which spheres seems to serve well in many situations occurring in practice.

7.2 Sagas Via Spheres

Our extended metamodel especially allows to basically build and run sagas [7] as well as nested sagas [8]: The root saga is the process model itself and all activities of this process model build a sphere; all control connectors are weighted by "true", and all activities have "true" exit conditions and are started automatically (note the batch-job like behavior resulting from these settings!). A saga within a saga is modelled as a subprocess which is defined as a sphere itself. The restart mode is set to "undo", activity proliferation is set to "global", sphere proliferation is "cascading", compensation is run "discrete" and "deep".

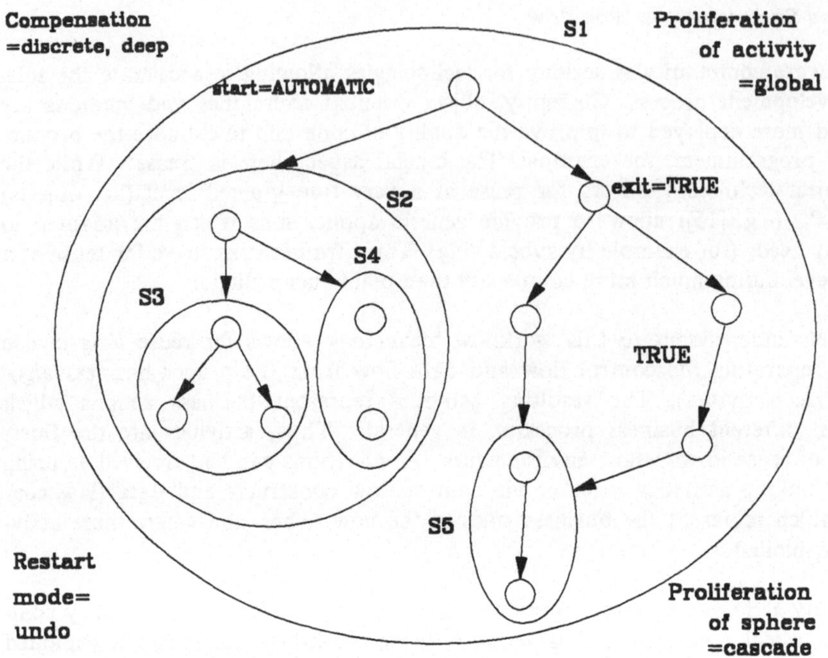

Figure 6. *Nested Sagas Modeled Via Spheres*

7.3 Mini-Batches On Non-Recoverable Resources

Practitioners are using mini-batch techniques in database environments since a long time to split transactions into sequences of smaller ones to reduce the loss of work in case of erroneous situations [6]. The notion of spheres allows to exploit this technique in an easy manner even in cases where non-recoverable resources are affected:

Assume a payroll program P computes the wages of all employees of a company and prints the corresponding wageslips. This is performed by splitting the employees in groups of ten, compute their wages, build the associated slips, and append the slips to an intermediate file from which they could be print. If something happens while writing a stream of ten slips to the file P calls a program Q which removes the new append from the file. Afterwards, the current group of employees is considered again.

This can be modelled as follows: We build a block activity consisting of the activities compute wage, build wage slip, and store. All activities are assumed to be defined as "automatic", i.e. IBM FlowMark will schedule them once they become startable. The activities are connected via control connectors weighted by the constant "true" predicate. The block's input container passes the number of the first employee of a group (first_emp_no) to the block, while its output container contains the number of the next employee of the new group (next_emp_no). A data connector maps next_emp_no onto first_emp_no. The block is a sphere itself having associated to it the compensation activity remove_append the input container of which gets passed a copy of the block's input container member `first_emp_no`. Once the `store` activity detects an error it requests an integral backout with shallow compensation of the block.

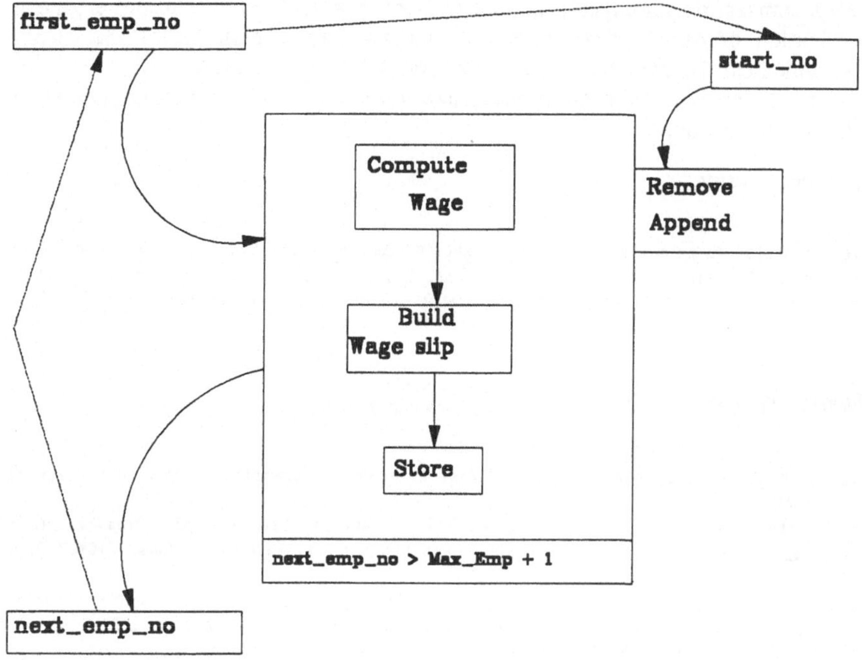

Figure 7. *The Payroll Example*

8 Summary And Future Work

In this paper we introduced the notion of spheres of joint compensation. A sphere defines a work unit within a business process which is backward recovered by automatically running compensation actions when an erroneous situation is signalled. A collection of parameters determines the behavior of a requested backout: The restart mode specifies how to continue after the compensation phase, nesting controls whether subprocesses and blocks are to be "resolved" into their contained activities for compensation, integral compensation performs a compensation action directly attached to the sphere instead of compensating each encompassed activity itself, etc. We identified common workitems and consumed data as basic dependencies between spheres which by default result in cascading backout of spheres.

In principle, our concepts are applicable to all workflow management systems providing for explicit descriptions of control flow and data flow. They enable such systems to support business transactions. For IBM FlowMark we have shown explicitly how the concepts can be added to its metamodel. It has been outlined how nested sagas and mini-batches can be modelled based on spheres indicating the usefulness of our concepts.

Essentially, our future research on business transactions goes into two directions: First, enhancing the sphere concepts towards <u>inter</u>-workflow dependencies, e.g. we will study interleaving workflows striving towards results on concurrent business transactions. Second, providing a design and a prototypical implementation of a "business transaction manager", e.g. we will cover aspects of the kernel engine like the derivation of dependency graphs of spheres from the model of the business process which can be used for efficient determination of cascading paths at run time, or aspects of the build time component like visualizing and animating [12] spheres and their compensation.

Acknowledgements

I am very grateful to my colleagues from IBM who influenced my thinking about this subject over the last months by their critique and discussions, especially Wolfgang Altenhuber, Don Haderle, Robert Junghuber, Susan Malaika, C. Mohan, Dieter Roller, and Dave Shorter. Nevertheless any flaws have to be attributed to me.

9 References

[1] J.L. Baer, *A survey of some theoretical aspects of multiprocessing,* Computing Surveys 5(1) (1973) 31 - 80.
[2] Y. Breitbart, A. Deacon, H.J. Schek, A. Seth, G. Weikum, *Merging application-centric and data-centric approaches to support transaction-oriented multi-system workflows,* SIGMOD RECORD 22(3) 1993.
[3] G. Chroust, F. Leymann, *Interpretable Process Models for Software Development and Adminis-tration,* Proc. 11th European Meeting on Cybernetics and Systems Research EMCR92 (Vienna, Austria, April 21-24, 1992), World Scientific 1992, 271 - 278.
[4] C.T. Davis, *Data processing spheres of control,* IBM Systems Journal 17(2) (1978) 179 - 198.
[5] A.K. Elmagarmid (ed.), *Database Transaction Models for Advanced Applications* (Morgan Kaufmann Publishers, Inc., 1992).
[6] J. Gray, A. Reuter, *Transaction processing: Concepts and techniques* (Morgan Kaufmann Publishers, Inc., 1993).
[7] H. Garcia-Molina, K. Salem, *Sagas,* Proc. ACM SIGMOD (1987).
[8] H. Garcia-Molina, D. Gawlick, J. Klein, K. Kleissner, K. Salem, *Modeling long running activities as nested sagas,* Data Engineering 14(1) 1991.
[9] *IBM FlowMark for OS/2,* Document number GH19-8215-01 (IBM Corporation, March 1994).
[10] F. Leymann, *A meta model to support the modelling and execution of processes,* Proc. 11th European Meeting on Cybernetics and Systems Research EMCR92 (Vienna, Austria, April 21-24, 1992), World Scientific 1992, 287 - 294.
[11] F. Leymann, W. Altenhuber, *Managing business processes as information resources,* IBM Systems Journal 33(2) (1994) 326 - 348.
[12] F. Leymann, D. Roller, *Business process management with FlowMark,* Proc. COMPCON Spring 94 (San Francisco, CA, February 28 - March 4, 1994) IEEE Computer Society Press 1994, 230 - 234.
[13] J.E.B. Moss, *Nested transactions and reliable distributed computing,* Proc. IEEE Symposium on Reliability in Distributed Software and Database Systems 1982.
[14] U. Schmidt, *Transaktionskonzepte in der Fertigung,* Proc. Datenbanksysteme in Büro, Technik und Wissenschaft (Braunschweig, Germany, March 1993).
[15] D. Tkach, R. Puttick, *Object technology in application development* (Benjamin/Cummings, 1994).
[16] I.L. Traiger, *Trends in systems aspects of database management,* Proc. 2nd Intl. Conf. on Databases (ICOD-2), Wiley & Sons 1983.
[17] H. Wächter, A. Reuter, *The ConTract model,* in [5].
[18] G. Weikum, *Transaktionen in Datenbanksystemen* (Addison-Wesley, 1988).

Mentor: Entwurf einer Workflow–Management–Umgebung basierend auf State- und Activitycharts

Dirk Wodtke[1], Angelika Kotz Dittrich[2], Peter Muth[1],
Markus Sinnwell[1], Gerhard Weikum[1]

[1] Universität des Saarlandes
Fachbereich Informatik
Postfach 15 11 50, D–66041 Saarbrücken
E–Mail: {wodtke, muth, sinn, weikum}@cs.uni–sb.de

[2] Schweizerische Bankgesellschaft
UBILAB
Postfach 2336, CH–8033 Zürich
E–Mail: angelika@ubilab.ubs.ch

Zusammenfassung

Der Aspekt der Steuerung von Arbeitsabläufen rückt heute in Unternehmen - gerade auch im Dienstleistungsbereich - immer mehr in den Vordergrund. Eine möglichst optimale Strukturierung und Abwicklung von Unternehmensprozessen spielt, etwa im Rahmen des Business Process Reengineering, für die Wirtschaftlichkeit eine große Rolle. Die aus einzelnen Arbeitsschritten zusammengesetzten Arbeitsabläufe werden auch als "Workflows" bezeichnet. Bei der computerunterstützten Abwicklung von Workflows sollen die einzelnen Arbeitsschritte mittels beliebiger Datenbanksysteme und/oder anderer Systemkomponenten (Dokumentenarchive, Applikationsprogramme etc.) ausgeführt werden; die Workflow–Management–Umgebung soll die Infrastruktur zur koordinierten und fehlertoleranten Ausführung in einer unternehmensweit verteilten und hochgradig heterogenen Informationssystemlandschaft bereitstellen. Dieser Artikel stellt das Projekt *Mentor* vor, in dem eine Workflow–Management–Umgebung entwickelt wird, bei der Workflows mit Hilfe von State- und Activitycharts spezifiziert, ausgeführt, überwacht und gesteuert werden. Die von David Harel entwickelte Spezifikationsmethode der State- und Activitycharts kombiniert die Einfachheit und mathematische Rigorosität von Automatenmodellen mit Möglichkeiten zur Visualisierung von Spezifikationen und hat gleichzeitig eine mit Prädikat–Transitions–Netzen vergleichbare Ausdrucksmächtigkeit. Ausgehend von dem kommerziellen Werkzeug Statemate, mit dem State- und Activitycharts entworfen und simuliert werden können, soll eine komplette Spezifikations- und Laufzeitumgebung für unternehmensweite Workflows entwickelt werden. Diese Umgebung soll verschiedene Middleware-Komponenten wie TP-Monitore und Dienste einer verteilten Programmierumgebung (z.B. OMG CORBA und COSS) integrieren und Workflow–Spezifikationen darauf abbilden.

1 Einführung

Durch den Einsatz von Datenbanksystemen konnten in vielen Dienstleistungsunternehmen in der Vergangenheit große Rationalisierungspotentiale ausgeschöpft werden. Zusätzliche Rationalisierungspotentiale lassen sich erschließen, indem Arbeitsabläufe in einem Unternehmen, die auf die Dienste dieser Datenbanksysteme zugreifen, (teil–)automatisiert werden. Typische Beispiele für solche Arbeitsabläufe sind die Bearbeitung eines Kreditantrages in einem Kreditinstitut, die Bearbeitung eines Schadensfalls in einer Versicherung und die Ablaufplanung und –überwachung eines stationären Krankenhausaufenthalts. Die Bearbeitung eines Kreditantrags beispielsweise beinhaltet u.a. die Prüfung von Firmenkrediten mit entsprechenden Bonitätsprüfungen und Risikoabschätzungen bezüglich des Kreditnehmers sowie seiner finanziellen Verflechtungen mit anderen nationalen und internationalen Unternehmen. Beispielsweise kann es bei der Vergabe eines Kredits an die Firma X von Bedeutung sein, ob bereits an eine Tochtergesellschaft von X ein hoher Kredit vergeben wurde, ob X zu einer Holding-Gesellschaft gehört, für die bereits ein hohes Engagement der Bank existiert, usw. Die zur Entscheidungsvorbereitung notwendigen Arbeitsabläufe erstrecken sich über verschiedene Geschäftsarten (Kredite, Wertpapiere, Devisen, usw.) und verschiedene Niederlassungen, nicht selten sogar auf internationaler Ebene.

Ein *Workflow (Arbeitsablauf)* ist die koordinierte Ausführung einer Menge zusammengehöriger *Arbeitsschritte* in einer verteilten Arbeitsumgebung [Jab93, Rei93, MC94, RS94]. Die einzelnen Arbeitsschritte eines Workflows werden von spezifischen *Ausführungsorganen* bearbeitet; dies können menschliche Sachbearbeiter und Entscheidungsträger wie auch Computersysteme sein oder eine Kombination davon. In der Literatur werden Ausführungsorgane auch als *Ressourcen* bezeichnet. Ausführungsorgane übernehmen bezüglich der Arbeitszuteilung sogenannte *Rollen*; Ausführungsorgane in derselben Rolle sind austauschbar (z.B. verschiedene Sachbearbeiter mit denselben Fähigkeiten und Kompetenzen). Wichtigen Anwendungen in großen Unternehmen liegen häufig hochgradig heterogene Informationssysteme als Ausführungsorgane in einer weitläufig verteilten und damit stark fehleranfälligen Umgebung zugrunde. Die Gesamtheit der organisatorischen und computergestützten Maßnahmen zur Spezifikation, Verifikation, Ausführung, Überwachung und Steuerung von Workflows wird als *Workflow-Management* bezeichnet. Ein *Workflow-Management-System* umfaßt die Gesamtheit aller für das Workflow-Management benötigten Systemkomponenten.

Dieser Artikel stellt das Projekt *Mentor* (Middleware for Enterprise-wide Workflow Management) vor, in dem eine umfassende Workflow-Management-Umgebung entwickelt wird, bei der Workflows mit Hilfe von State- und Activitycharts spezifiziert, ausgeführt, überwacht und gesteuert werden. State- und Activitycharts wurden von David Harel als Spezifikationsmethode für prozeßorientierte, sogenannte reaktive Systeme, entwickelt [Ha87, Ha88, Ha90]. Zur Entwicklung, Visualisierung und Simulation von Spezifikationen wird ein kommerzielles Werkzeug *Statemate* [Ha90, i-Log91] angeboten. State- und Activitycharts wurden primär für die Spezifikation technischer Steuerungssysteme (z.B. in Automobilen oder Flugzeugen) entwickelt und für diesen Anwendungsbereich erfolgreich eingesetzt. Ihre Verwendung für Workflow-Management wird unseres Wissens erstmals in diesem Artikel diskutiert.

1.1 Beispiel einer Workflow-Spezifikation

In Abbildung 1 ist ein Beispiel für einen Workflow wiedergegeben, der mit einem Activitychart und einem Statechart modelliert ist. Das Beispiel zeigt den Workflow "Begutachtung eines Papiers bei einer wissenschaftlichen Zeitschrift".

Der obere Teil der Abbildung enthält das Activitychart *Zeitschrift_AC*, das aus den vier Activities *Einreichung_A*, *Begutachtung_A*, *Entscheidung_A* und *Mitteilung_A*, dem durch die Pfeile dargestellten Datenfluß und einem Verweis auf das Statechart *Zeitschrift_SC* besteht. Das Statechart *Zeitschrift_SC* ist im unteren Teil der Abbildung wiedergegeben und beschreibt das Verhalten des Activitycharts, insbesondere den Kontrollfluß zwischen den Activities. Die Rechtecke mit den abgerundeten Ecken in *Zeitschrift_SC* stellen Zustände dar. Die Pfeile geben den Kontrollfluß an und werden als Transitionen bezeichnet. Sind zwei Zustände durch eine Transition mit der Transitionsbeschriftung $E[C]/A$ verbunden, werden beim Eintreten des Ereignisses E, sofern Bedingung C erfüllt ist, der Ausgangszustand der Transition verlassen, ihr Zielzustand betreten und die Aktion A ausgeführt. Transitionen haben somit dieselbe Mächtigkeit wie ECA-Regeln, wie sie bei aktiven Datenbanken verfolgt werden [WD94], sind aber in übersichtlicher Weise in die Gesamtspezifikation eingebettet und vermeiden damit die Probleme der mangelnden Überschaubarkeit und Beherrschbarkeit umfangreicher unstrukturierter Mengen von ECA-Regeln.

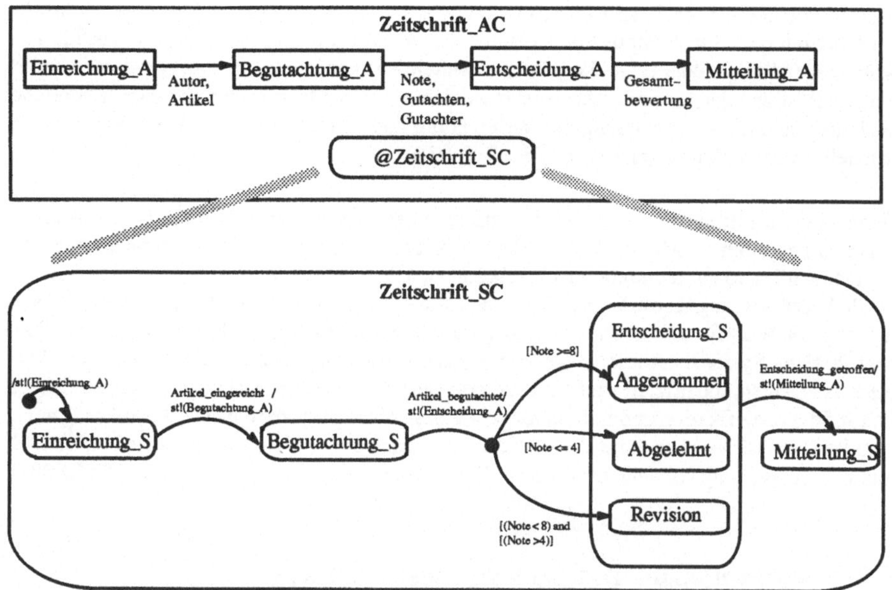

Abbildung 1: Activity- und Statechart zur Modellierung des Begutachtungsprozesses bei einer wissenschaftlichen Zeitschrift

Zu Beginn der Ausführung des Workflows wird die Activity *Einreichung_A* durch die Anweisung *st!(Einreichung_A)* gestartet und der Zustand *Einreichung_S* betreten. Nach der Einreichung eines Papiers (Ereignis *Artikel_eingereicht* wurde generiert) wird die Activity *Begutachtung_A* gestartet und der nächste Zustand *Begutachtung_S* betreten. Liegen die nötigen Gutachten vor, d.h. wurde das Ereignis *Artikel_begutachtet* generiert, wird die Activity *Entscheidung_A* gestartet. In Abhängigkeit von der von den Gutachtern vergebenen *Note* wird einer der Zustände *Angenommen, Abgelehnt* oder *Revision* betreten. Ist die Entscheidung über ein Papier getroffen, wird die Activity *Mitteilung_A* gestartet. Dieser – natürlich etwas übersimplifizierte – Workflow beinhaltet zwei verschiedene Ausführungsorgane, den Editor und den bzw. die Gutachter. (Im Falle elektronischer Einreichungen könnte man die Autoren sogar noch als drittes Ausführungsorgan hinzunehmen.) In Abschnitt 4.1 wird gezeigt, wie der Zustand *Begutachtung_S* verfeinert werden kann.

1.2 Warum State- und Activitycharts?

Die Verwendung von State- und Activitycharts hat sich vor allem in technischen Anwendungen (siehe z.B. [Sta94]) sehr bewährt; ihre Verwendung für Workflow-Management ist dagegen Neuland. Diese Spezifikationsmethode kombiniert die Einfachheit und mathematische Rigorosität von Automatenmodellen [HPSS87] mit weitreichenden Möglichkeiten zur Visualisierung [Ha88, Ha90] und hat gleichzeitig eine mit Prädikat-Transitions-Netzen vergleichbare Ausdrucksmächtigkeit.

Im Gegensatz zu den meisten bisher entwickelten oder vorgeschlagenen Workflow-Management-Umgebungen, die auf Skriptsprachen oder Konzepten aktiver Datenbanksysteme wie ECA-Regeln basieren, ist mit State- und Activitycharts eine theoretisch wohlfundierte Basis gegeben. Von fundamentaler Bedeutung ist außerdem die durch Schachtelung von Zuständen gegebene Möglichkeit, Spezifikationen zu modularisieren – zur schrittweisen Verfeinerung im Entwurfsprozeß oder zur Komposition existierender Workflows zu übergeordneten Worfklows –, wohingegen Skripts oder ECA–Regeln ohne weitere Strukturierung ab einem gewissen Umfang unübersichtlich oder gar undurchschaubar werden. Auch bei Petrinetzen und ihren zahlreichen Varianten sind die Unterstützung der Verfeinerung und Komposition von Spezifikationen tendenziell kritische Punkte (siehe z.B. [Ha87, Fu93]).

Gegenüber Ansätzen, die auf Petrinetz–Varianten basieren, zeichnen sich State– und Activitycharts ferner durch die Möglichkeit aus, beliebige, bereits existierende Subsysteme als Activities in die Spezifikation und Simulation einzubeziehen. Diese "offene Architektur" ist eine entscheidende Voraussetzung für die Verwendung von State– und Activitycharts als Basis der echten Ausführung von Workflows in einer hochgradig verteilten und heterogenen Systemlandschaft. Petrinetz–basierte Systeme erwarten dagegen typischerweise, daß sämtliche Anwendungsteile komplett als Petrinetz spezifiziert sind, und beschränken sich dementsprechend praktisch ausschließlich auf die Spezifikation und Simulation sowie bestenfalls die prototypische Ausführung auf einem Rechner. (Eine Ausnahme, die auch die Anbindung externer Software an eine Petrinetz–Simulationsumgebung vorsieht, ist das in der Entwicklung befindliche INCOME/STAR [OSS94].)

1.3 Forschungsziel und Beitrag dieses Artikels

Dieser Artikel untersucht das Nutzpotential von State– und Activitycharts für Workflow–Management generell und stellt das Mentor–Projekt im besonderen vor. Ziel des Mentor–Projekts ist die Verbindung von State– und Activitycharts als Spezifikationsumgebung mit einer Laufzeitumgebung, die verschiedene sogenannte Middleware–Komponenten integriert und um zusätzliche Infrastruktursoftware zur Ausführung, Überwachung und Steuerung von Workflows erweitert. Mentor sieht als wichtigste Middleware–Komponenten einen TP–Monitor [GR93, Ob94] als Ausgangsbasis zur Erreichung von Fehlertoleranz und eine verteilte Programmierumgebung wie OMG CORBA und COSS [OMG92, OMG94] zur Bewältigung der Heterogenität vor.

Die Ausführung von Workflows soll direkt aus der Spezifikationsumgebung heraus – auf der Basis von State– und Activitycharts – erfolgen. Dazu soll die offene Architektur des Werkzeugs Statemate ausgenutzt werden, bei der Activities beliebigen C–Code und Subsystemaufrufe beinhalten können. Auf diese Weise läßt sich eine Kontrollflußsteuerung auf der Ebene von Statecharts mit Aufrufen beispielsweise eines TP–Monitors koppeln. Während der Workflow–Ausführung sollen umgekehrt die Visualisierungsmöglichkeiten von Statemate auch für die Überwachung von Workflows ausgenutzt werden. Beispielsweise sollen bereits ausgeführte und laufende Arbeitsschritte jederzeit abfragbar und konform zur Spezifikationsumgebung visuell darstellbar sein. Eine derartige Gesamtarchitektur für verteilte, heterogene Workflow–Management–Umgebungen, die alle Ebenen der Spezifikation, Validierung, Ausführung, Überwachung und Steuerung durchgängig überdeckt, ist unseres Wissens neu und hebt sich von bisherigen Arbeiten im Bereich des Workflow–Managements ab.

Im folgenden Abschnitt 2 wird der potentielle Nutzen von Workflow–Management–Systemen diskutiert, und es werden existierende kommerzielle Produkte und Forschungsprojekte im Bereich Workflow–Management kurz charakterisiert. In Abschnitt 3 wird die Architektur unseres Ansatzes für ein Workflow–Management–System vorgestellt. In Abschnitt 4 wird die Spezifikation von Workflows mit State– und Activitycharts anhand eines Anwendungsbeispiels genauer vorgestellt. In Abschnitt 5 folgt eine Diskussion der bei der Ausführung und Überwachung von Workflows zu bewältigenden Probleme.

2 Potential und Stand der Technik von Workflow–Management–Systemen

2.1 Potentieller Nutzen

Der mit der Verbreitung verteilter Systeme einhergehende Einsatz unterschiedlicher Anwendungsprogramme in heterogenen Systemumgebungen zwingt zur Integration der bestehenden Hardware- und Softwarekomponenten. Damit wird es möglich, Arbeitsabläufe in ihrer Gesamtheit stärker zu automatisieren, als dies mit Stand-alone-Ansätzen erzielbar ist. Gelingt es, die Anforderungen, die an solche integrierten Ansätze hinsichtlich Bewältigung der Heterogenität, Fehlertoleranz und Konsistenz gestellt werden, zu erfüllen, läßt sich die Effektivität von Arbeitsabläufen erhöhen, indem zum Beispiel auf die mehrfache Eingabe gleicher Daten in verschiedenen Applikationen verzichtet werden kann. Belegtransporte können eliminiert werden, wenn der Datenfluß automatisiert wird. Als Folge der kürzeren Bearbeitungszeiten der einzelnen Arbeitsschritte und der verkürzten Laufzeiten zwischen den beteiligten Subsystemen ist eine geringere Turnaround-Zeit von Kundenaufträgen zu erwarten.

Positiv für die Unternehmensleitung ist, daß die Überwachung von Geschäftsvorgängen erleichtert und die Transparenz der Arbeitsabläufe für alle Beteiligten erhöht wird. Die Analyse von Arbeitsabläufen (z.B. zur Identifikation von zeitlichen Engpaßstellen) sollte einfacher und besser möglich sein. Die integrierte Sicht auf Arbeitsabläufe erlaubt ferner eine Verbesserung der Informationsmöglichkeit über den Bearbeitungszustand von Arbeitsabläufen. Denkbar ist die Nutzung dieses Informationspotentials auch zum Zweck automatisierter Terminüberwachung. Weisungskonformität kann garantiert werden, wobei das Workflow-Management-System trotz der weitgehenden Standardisierung von Arbeitsschritten und einer Entlastung von Routinetätigkeiten zusätzlich die Möglichkeit kontrollierter, d.h. in der Auswirkung auf den Workflow begrenzter Ausnahmebehandlungen vorsehen sollte. Schließlich sollten Anpassungen von Arbeitsabläufen im Hinblick auf veränderte Marktsituationen oder individuelle Kundenwünsche einfacher und schneller als bisher möglich sein.

Die genannten Anforderungen können als ein Baustein moderner Managementkonzepte im Kontext von Lean Management, Total Quality Management und Kundenorientierung angesehen werden. Dennoch stellt ein Workflow-Management-System kein Allheilmittel für jede Art von Unternehmensproblemen dar, sondern allein ein technisches Infrastrukturmittel, dem eine wichtige Unterstützungsfunktion zukommt.

2.2 Stand der Technik

Das Gebiet des Workflow-Managements ist eng verwandt mit dem Thema CSCW (Computer-Supported Cooperative Work). CSCW zielt jedoch stärker auf ungeplante, spontane Interaktion in einem Arbeitsteam ab, wohingegen Workflow-Management sich primär mit bereits weitgehend strukturierten und vor allem häufig wiederkehrenden Arbeitsabläufen befaßt. Innerhalb der "Routinearbeitsabläufe" sollte Workflow-Management jedoch auch kontrollierte Ausnahmen und manuelle Eingriffsmöglichkeiten zulassen - bis hin zu ausgesprochenen "Ad-hoc"-Workflows. Enge Parallelen gibt es auch mit dem Gebiet des CIM (Computer-Integrated Manufacturing), welches sich allerdings auf Abläufe in Fertigungsunternehmen konzentriert. Workflow-Management wird gelegentlich auch als das "CIM der Dienstleistungsunternehmen" bezeichnet.

Aus Datenbanksicht knüpft Workflow-Management vor allem an die Gebiete der erweiterten Transaktionsmodelle und der aktiven Datenbanksysteme an. In den folgenden Unterabschnitten wird der Stand der Technik auf dem Gebiet des Workflow-Management näher erörtert.

2.2.1 Kommerzielle Produkte

Zur Unterstützung von Workflow–Management werden eine Reihe von Produkten angeboten wie z.B. Lotus Notes, Staffware, FlowMark, ARIS Toolset usw. (siehe z.B. [McC93, LA94, Sch94]). Diese Produkte sind primär für den lokalen Office–Bereich konzipiert und für abteilungsübergreifende, u.U. unternehmensweite Arbeitsabläufe kaum geeignet. Sie sind überwiegend nur in homogenen Umgebungen einsetzbar, bei denen typischerweise alle relevanten Daten auf einem zentralen Server gehalten werden. Heterogenität wird nur auf der Netzwerk– und Betriebssystemebene erlaubt (so daß z.B. eine Koexistenz von DOS–PCs und Unix–Clients möglich ist), nicht jedoch auf der Ebene der Ausführungsorgane (z.B. verschiedene Datenhaltungssysteme). Die Produkte bieten kaum Fehlertoleranzmaßnahmen; sie verwenden z.B. einfache E–Mail und sind weit entfernt von den Fehlertoleranzgarantien, die man etwa vom OLTP–Bereich kennt. Obwohl für einige Einzelprobleme Lösungen in Produkten existieren, gibt es kein Produkt, das alle notwendigen Eigenschaften geeignet kombiniert.

2.2.2 Forschungsprojekte

Workflow–Management wurde in der "Challenges Session" der SIGMOD–Konferenz 1993 zu einem besonders herausfordernden Forschungsgebiet erklärt [Da93] (vgl. auch [De94, Me94]). Dementsprechend gibt es in der Datenbankszene eine stattliche Anzahl von aktuellen Forschungsprojekten zu diesem Thema (siehe u.a. [Bi94, BMR94, Be93, Br93, DHL91, EN93, GGS93 GHKM94, Hsu93, Jab93, KUW94, Ober94, RS94, SK94, ST94, WR92, Wei93]). Eines der ersten und das vermutlich am weitesten fortgeschrittene Projekt ist das ConTracts–Projekt an der Universität Stuttgart [WR92, RSW92, Schw93]. Im Vordergrund dieses Projekts steht die konsequente Erweiterung transaktionsorientierter Mechanismen zur fehlertoleranten Ausführung beliebiger verteilter Abläufe. Insbesondere wurde Wert gelegt auf die saubere Trennung zwischen Ressourcenmanagern und Transaktionsmanagern im Sinne des X/Open–Standards XA und auf die fehlertolerante Verwaltung von Verarbeitungskontexten über Transaktionsgrenzen hinweg. Die Spezifikation von ConTracts beruht auf einer speziellen Skriptsprache, die intern in Prädikat–Transitions–Netze übersetzt wird. Die Tauglichkeit dieser Sprache zur Spezifikation komplexer, unternehmensweiter Workflows und zur Anbindung beliebiger Ausführungsorgane ist nicht weitergehend untersucht worden. An dieser Stelle versprechen wir uns von der Verwendung von State– und Activitycharts ganz entscheidenden Fortschritt gegenüber dem – ansonsten sicherlich wegweisenden – ConTract–Projekt.

Verteilte Abläufe generell werden in einer Vielzahl von Projekten untersucht, insbesondere im Umfeld objektorientierter Systeme (z.B. [CBHR93, Mu93, Sch93, OMG92, OMG94]). Dabei werden allerdings Aspekte der fehlertoleranten Ausführung entweder ausgeklammert oder beschränken sich auf relativ primitive Basismechanismen wie z.B. Prozeßgruppen oder (geschlossen) geschachtelte Transaktionen. Die Spezifikation verteilter Abläufe ist ebenfalls ein breites Forschungsgebiet, bei dem insbesondere Petrinetzvarianten zum Einsatz kommen (z.B. [EN93, OSS94]); die Spezifikation sogenannter "object lifecycles" ist eine spezielle Variante dieser Richtung (z.B. [KS91, Saa93]). Diese Forschungslinie behandelt jedoch die Ausführung von Spezifikationen eher am Rande, ganz zu schweigen von verteilten Ausführungsumgebungen.

3 Architektur von Mentor

Dieser Abschnitt beschreibt die Architektur des Workflow–Management–Systems Mentor. State– und Activitycharts spielen in Mentor sowohl während der Spezifikation von Workflows als auch während deren Ausführung und Steuerung eine zentrale Rolle. Sie stellen für jede dieser

Aufgaben die Schnittstelle zum Benutzer dar. Abbildung 2 zeigt die Systemumgebung von Mentor, bestehend aus Workstations, die von Workflow–Designern, Sachbearbeitern und Mitarbeitern mit Überwachungsfunktion bedient werden.

Die Ausführung der einzelnen Arbeitsschritte übernehmen Mentor-Server, die die Verbindung zu den Ausführungsorganen (z.B. Datenbanksysteme) schaffen und den Kontroll- und Datenfluß zwischen den Arbeitsschritten steuern. In der Regel erstreckt sich ein Workflow über mehrere Server und Workstations, d.h. die Arbeitsschritte des Workflows werden von mehreren Mentor-Servern ausgeführt.

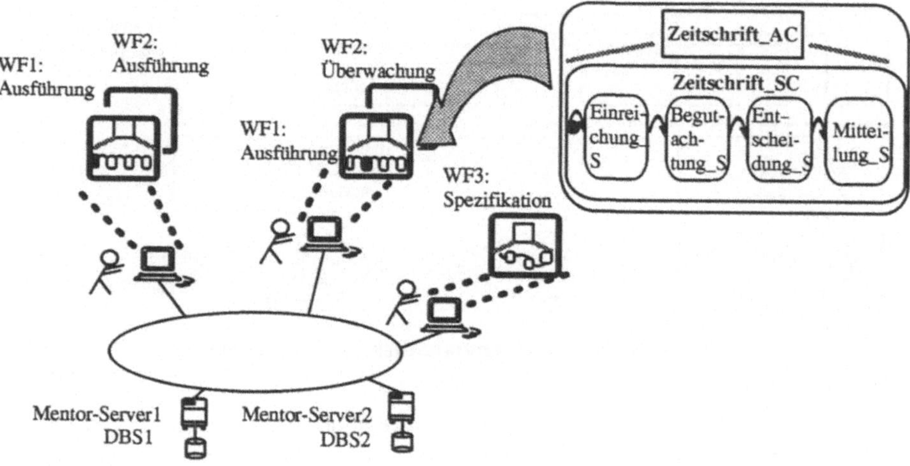

Abbildung 2: Systemumgebung des Workflow–Management–Systems Mentor

Jeder Workstation können zu jedem Zeitpunkt beliebig viele Workflows zugeordnet werden, und ein Workflow kann die Bearbeitung auf beliebig vielen Workstations erfordern. Im Beispiel erfordert die Ausführung des Workflows *WF1* die Bearbeitung durch die ersten beiden Sachbearbeiter. Der Workflow *WF2* kann allein vom ersten Sachbearbeiter bearbeitet werden, Sachbearbeiter zwei übernimmt hier eine Überwachungsfunktion, z.B. um die Effizienz des Ablaufs späterer Ausführungen von *WF2* zu verbessern. Workflow *WF3* wird gerade spezifiziert.

Jeder der drei Mitarbeiter bewegt sich dabei in der selben abstrakten Welt: State- und Activitycharts. Die State- und Activitycharts, die Struktur und Ablauf der Workflows festlegen, sind stilisiert innerhalb der abgerundeten Quadrate wiedergegeben. Innerhalb dieser Quadrate stellt jeweils das große Quadrat ein Activitychart dar, dem das Statechart, das aus den durch Pfeile miteinander verbundenen Quadraten besteht, zugeordnet ist. Ist ein Zustand abgedunkelt, so weist dies auf seine Aktivierung hin. *WF1* wird also zuerst auf der ersten Workstation ausgeführt, nach dem Schalten der Transition zum zweiten Zustand verlagert sich die Ausführung auf die zweite Workstation. Daten- und Kontrollfluß eines Workflows werden mittels Activitycharts und Statecharts vor Ausführung des Workflows spezifiziert, sollen jedoch auch während der Ausführung eines Workflows für kontrollierte Ausnahmen und manuelle Eingriffsmöglichkeiten dynamisch änderbar sein.

Abbildung 3 zeigt die Modularchitektur von Mentor. Das für State- und Activitycharts angebotene Werkzeug Statemate bildet die oberste Schicht und ist auf jeder Workstation lokal verfügbar. Im Sinne der gewünschten durchgängigen Umgebung für Spezifikation, Ausführung und Überwachung von Workflows verwaltet diese Komponente die Daten- und Kontrollflußdefinitionen eines Workflows und visualisiert die Ausführung.

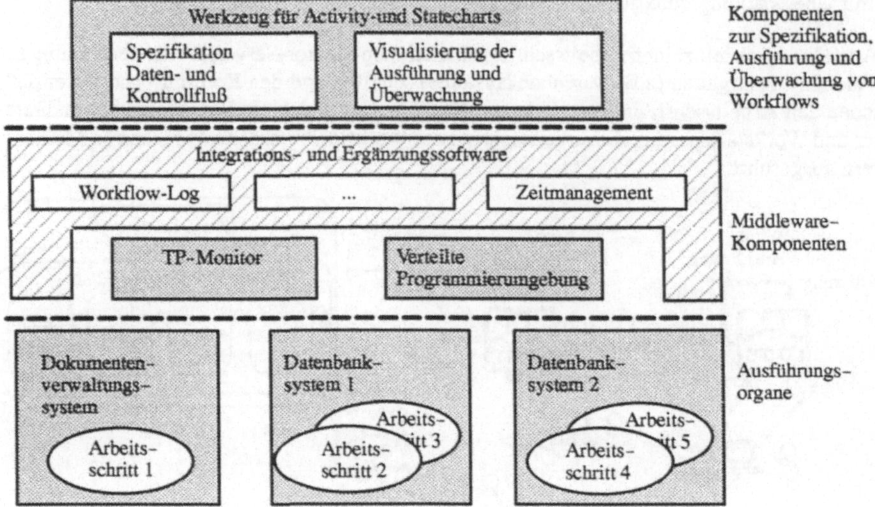

Abbildung 3: Gesamtarchitektur von Mentor

Als Middleware-Komponenten sieht Mentor einen TP–Monitor, eine verteilte Programmierumgebung und einen "Rahmen" von Integrations- und Ergänzungssoftware vor, der die Middleware–Komponenten untereinander verbindet und die Anschlüsse an die State- und Activitycharts nach oben bzw. die Datenverwaltungssysteme nach unten bereitstellt. Die Komponenten der Middleware stehen auf jedem Mentor-Server zur Verfügung. Wir streben eine minimale Menge dieser Komponenten in Mentor an, wobei der notwendige Funktionsumfang noch zu untersuchen ist. Daraus ergeben sich auch die Kriterien für eine mögliche Replikation der Datenstrukturen der Middleware-Komponenten und der Workflow-Spezifikationen auf den Mentor-Servern.

Ein TP–Monitor wird für fehlertolerante Ausführungen benötigt, insbesondere für verteilte Transaktionen und transaktionsgeschützte Nachrichten ("recoverable message queues"). Die verteilte Programmierumgebung (z.B. OMG CORBA und COSS [OMG92, OMG94]) stellt Dienste wie Remote Procedure Call, Naming Service, entfernten Methodenaufruf und Authentifizierungsdienste für heterogene Systeme bereit. Datenbanksysteme und Dokumentenverwaltungssysteme (z.B. Archivierungssysteme für Textdokumente) stellen wichtige Arten von Ausführungsorganen dar.

4 Spezifikation mit State- und Activitycharts

In diesem Abschnitt werden die wesentlichen Konzepte von State- und Activitycharts kurz vorgestellt, die im zweiten Teil des Abschnitts anhand des bereits eingeführten Beispiels erläutert werden.

4.1 Konzepte von Statecharts und Activitycharts

Eine Verhaltensbeschreibung eines Systems muß komplexe Folgen von Ereignissen, Aktionen und Bedingungen berücksichtigen, die häufig in Kombination mit gewissen zeitlichen Restriktionen auftreten. Eine brauchbare Modellierungsmethode muß modular, hierarchisch und gut strukturiert sein und muß Konstrukte enthalten, mit denen parallele Abläufe dargestellt werden können. Diese Anforderungen werden vom Formalismus der State- und Activitycharts erfüllt. Die Grundidee von State- und Activitycharts basiert auf der Darstellung mittels visueller Formalismen. Diese erlauben ein in hohem Maße anschauliches Vorgehen beim Entwurf, wobei durch eine formale Semantik [HPSS87] eine präzise, kompakte und eindeutige Spezifikation möglich wird.

Mit Hilfe von Activitycharts kann ein System aus funktionaler Sicht modelliert werden. Konkret bedeutet dies eine Untergliederung des zu modellierenden Systems in Funktionen (*Activities*) und Datenflüsse zwischen den Activities. Statecharts beschreiben ein System aus Verhaltenssicht. Sie definieren zeitabhängige Vorgänge, die durch Zustandsübergänge modelliert werden. Zusätzlich zu den Darstellungsmitteln der Zustandsübergangs–Diagramme endlicher Automaten bieten Statecharts Konstrukte für die hierarchische Anordnung von Zuständen, für die Darstellung orthogonaler (paralleler) Zustände und für die Kommunikation zwischen Zuständen mittels Ereignissen. In Abbildung 1 sind zum Beispiel die drei Zustände *Angenommen, Abgelehnt* und *Revision* Unterzustände des Zustands *Entscheidung_S*.

Die wesentlichen Eigenschaften von Activitycharts und Statecharts sollen anhand des Beispiels in Abbildung 4 erläutert werden. Das Activitychart *A_AC* besteht aus den beiden Activities *Activity1* und *Activity2* und einem Verweis auf ein Statechart *A_SC*, das den Kontrollfluß zwischen den Activities beschreibt. Außerdem ist der Datenfluß innerhalb des Activitycharts angegeben. Mit Activities kann C–Code assoziiert werden, durch den die Funktionalität der Activity genau ausgedrückt ist. Das Statechart ist im unteren Teil der Abbildung angegeben und besteht aus mehreren hierarchisch aufgebauten Zuständen und den sie verbindenden Transitionen. Beispielsweise besagt die Beschriftung der Transition von *ABB* nach *ABC*: Wenn Zustand *ABB* aktiviert ist, *Activity1* beendet wird und gleichzeitig Bedingung *C1* erfüllt ist, dann schaltet die Transition und die *Activity2* wird gestartet. Im Beispiel ist die Namensgebung der Zustände entsprechend der hierarchischen Einordnung gewählt.

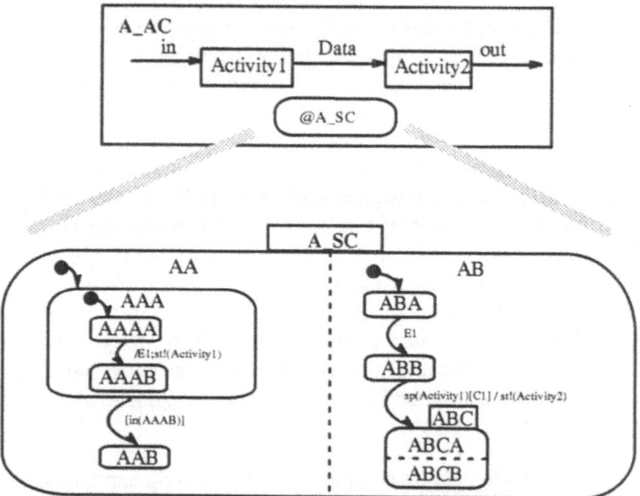

Abbildung 4: Beispiel für ein Activitychart und ein Statechart

Beim Starten des Activitycharts *A_AC* wird automatisch das Statechart *A_SC* aktiviert, d.h. daß mittels der Transitionen ohne Startzustand (die von den kleinen schwarzen Kreisen ausgehenden *Default–Transitionen*) die Zustände *AAA, AAAA* und *ABA* aktiviert werden. Bemerkenswert ist hierbei, daß die Zustände *AAA* und *ABA*, die Unterzustände der orthogonalen Zustände *AA* bzw. *AB* sind, gleichzeitig aktiviert werden.

Im nächsten Schritt schaltet die Transition, die die Zustände *AAAA* und *AAAB* verbindet. Sie löst die Generierung des Ereignisses *E1* aus und startet *Activity1* durch die Aktion *start!(Activity1)* (abgekürzt *st!(Activity1)*). Durch die Generierung des Ereignisses *E1* kann im darauffolgenden Schritt die Transition von *ABA* nach *ABB* schalten. Gleichzeitig schaltet die Transition von *AAA* nach *AAB*, da die Schaltbedingung *in(AAAB)* (d.h. Aktivierung des Zustands *AAAB*) im vorhergehenden Schritt erfüllt war. Das Verlassen des Zustandes *AAA* bewirkt auch eine Deaktivierung aller Unterzustände, in diesem Fall des Zustandes *AAAB*. Terminiert *Activity1* zu einem späteren Zeitpunkt, wird automatisch das Ereignis *stopped(Activity1)* (abgekürzt *sp(Activity1)*) generiert. Als Folge kann die Transition von *ABB* nach *ABC* schalten, wenn die Bedingung *C1* gleichzeitig erfüllt ist. Zeitgleich mit dem Schalten der Transition werden *Activity2* gestartet und der Zustand *ABC* mit seinen orthogonalen Komponenten *ABCA* und *ABCB* aktiviert.

Anhand des Beispiels wird verdeutlicht, wie die Verbindung zwischen Activitycharts und Statecharts die funktionale Sichtweise und die Verhaltenssicht zu einer Gesamtsicht auf ein Modell vereint. Parallelität wird in Statecharts durch orthogonale Zustände dargestellt, Tiefe durch die hierarchische Anordnung von Zuständen und Kommunikation durch Generieren von Ereignissen und Warten auf Ereignisse, auch über die Grenzen von Activities hinweg.

4.2 Anwendungsbeispiel

Ein wesentliches Konzept der Entwurfsmethodik mit State- und Activitycharts besteht in der Unterstützung eines Top–Down–Entwurfsverfahrens, indem bereits entworfene State- und Activitycharts verfeinert werden können. Zum Beispiel lassen sich die Activity *Begutachtung_A* und der Zustand *Begutachtung_S* aus dem Activitychart *Zeitschrift_AC* bzw. dem Statechart *Zeitschrift_SC* aus Abbildung 1 zu dem Activitychart bzw. Statechart in Abbildung 5 verfeinern.

Die Begutachtung eines Papiers geschieht gemäß dem Activitychart durch drei Gutachter, deren Begutachtungstätigkeit in drei Activities *Begutachtung1_A* bis *Begutachtung3_A* modelliert ist. Die zugehörigen Verhaltensbeschreibungen befinden sich in drei orthogonalen Zuständen *Gutachter1* bis *Gutachter3* im Statechart *Begutachtung_SC*. Die darin enthaltenen Zustände *Gutachten_anfertigen* sind dabei Instanzen eines weiteren, gewissermaßen generischen Statecharts. In diesem Statechart wird die Activity *Begutachtung_A* für den jeweiligen Gutachter (*st!(Begutachtung_A)*) gestartet. Ist die Begutachtung beendet, wird das Ereignis *Gutachten_vorgelegt* generiert. Der Begutachtungsprozeß sei hier bereits nach dem Eingang von zwei Gutachten beendet. Da nicht von vornherein bekannt ist, welche beiden Gutachter die Begutachtung als erste beenden werden, wird in einem orthogonalen Zustand die Zahl der angefertigten Gutachten mittels der Zählvariablen *Zahl_Gutachten* protokolliert. Sind zwei Gutachten erstellt worden, ist die Schaltbedingung der Transition von *Start_Begutachtung* nach *Stop_Begutachtung* in einem weiteren orthogonalen Zustand erfüllt und die Transition kann schalten, wobei gleichzeitig die Durchschnittsnote der beiden Gutachten berechnet und das Ereignis *Artikel_begutachtet* generiert werden.

Bei der Modellierung des Verhaltens eines Systems werden häufig explizite Zeitangaben benötigt. Zum Beispiel könnten nach Ablauf einer bestimmten Zeit bestimmte Aktionen oder Zustandsübergänge ausgeführt werden. Der Statechart–Formalismus erlaubt hierfür zum einen die Spezifikation zeitorientierter Ereignisse mittels der Anweisung *timeout (E, n)* (abgekürzt *tm(E, n)*). Diese Anweisung bewirkt das Auslösen eines Ereignisses *n* Zeiteinheiten nach dem Auftreten des Ereignisses *E*. Im Beispiel aus Abbildung 5 wird 100 Zeiteinheiten nach dem Betreten des Zustands *Start* das Ereignis *Frist_naht* generiert, falls die Begutachtung zu diesem Zeitpunkt

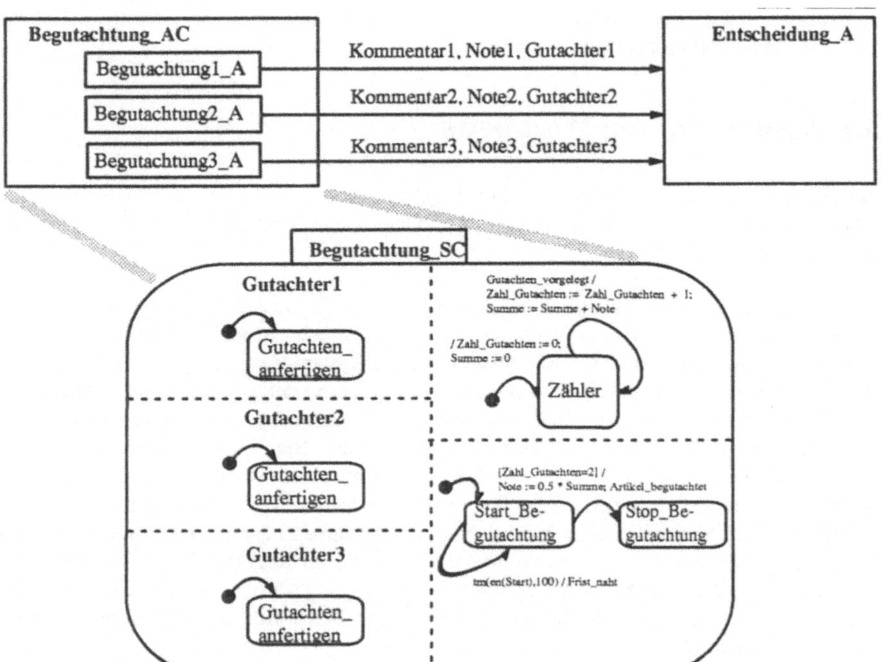

**Abbildung 5: Verfeinerung der Activity *Begutachtung_A* und des
Zustands *Begutachtung_S* aus Abbildung 1**

noch nicht beendet worden ist. Die Generierung dieses Ereignisses könnte zum Beispiel in einer weiteren Verfeinerung des Modells dazu benutzt werden, Aktionen wie eine Beschleunigung der Begutachtung oder eine Begutachtung durch einen weiteren Gutachter auszulösen.

Die zweite Modellierungsmöglichkeit für explizite Zeitangaben sind zeitabhängige Aktionen, die mittels der Aktion *schedule!(E, n)* (abgekürzt *sc!(E, n)*) angegeben werden können. Mit dieser Anweisung wird das Ereignis E n Zeiteinheiten nach der Ausführung dieser Anweisung generiert. Im Beispiel ließe sich mit dem Aufruf dieser Anweisung beim Start von *Zeitschrift_AC* das Ereignis *Frist_erreicht* zu einem festgelegten Zeitpunkt generieren, und zwar unabhängig davon, welcher Zustand zu diesem Zeitpunkt aktiviert ist.

5 Ausführung und Überwachung von Workflows

Dieser Abschnitt diskutiert die bei der Ausführung und Überwachung von Workflows zu lösenden Probleme und zeigt einige Lösungsansätze auf. Wie bereits in den vorangegangenen Abschnitten diskutiert, ist es sinnvoll, für diese beiden Bereiche dasselbe Visualisierungskonzept zu benutzen wie für die Spezifikation von Workflows. State- und Activitycharts leisten dazu in Simulationen, z.B. von Schaltkreisen, gute Dienste. Ein Workflow-Management-System stellt jedoch weit höhere Anforderungen an Ausführung und Überwachung als eine Simulationsumgebung. Es gibt im allgemeinen keine zentrale Instanz, die alle Arbeitsschritte einer Workflow–Spezifikation oder gar alle Workflow–Spezifikationen kennt, und es sollte auch keine zentrale Instanz an der Ausführung oder Überwachung aller Workflows beteiligt sein müssen. Andernfalls ist das System nicht skalierbar. Skalierbarkeit ist aber eine zentrale Anforderung in einer dynamisch wachsenden Workflow-Umgebung. Das resultierende verteilte System muß hohe Anforderungen bezüglich der Fehlertoleranz erfüllen.

5.1 Ausführung von Workflows

Zur Ausführung eines Workflows zählen Aspekte des Kontrollflusses, des Datenflusses zwischen Arbeitsschritten, der Fehlertoleranz von Daten- und Kontrollfluß und der dynamischen Modifikation von Workflows.

Datenbanksysteme bieten mit dem Transaktionskonzept die Basis für eine fehlertolerante Ausführung von Arbeitsschritten. Eine Verbindung mehrerer Arbeitsschritte innerhalb eines Datenbanksystems oder auch zwischen verschiedenen Systemen wird jedoch nicht unterstützt; allenfalls könnte man verschiedene Arbeitsschritte zu einer verteilten Transaktion zusammenfassen. Damit lassen sich jedoch keinesfalls komplexere *Kontrollflußabhängigkeiten* zwischen Arbeitsschritten realisieren, wie beispielsweise die folgende: "Bei Eingang von zwei von drei Gutachten wird die Begutachtung beendet". Einen ersten, aber wesentlichen Schritt zur Lösung dieses Problems stellen TP-Monitore dar. Sie können beispielsweise die Ausführung eines Arbeitsschritts mit dem Versenden einer Nachricht zu einer atomaren Einheit kombinieren, die genau einmal ausgeführt wird. Auf diese Weise kann das Ende der Begutachtung eindeutig bestimmt werden, ohne in der Schicht der Integrations- und Ergänzungssoftware aufwendige Algorithmen implementieren zu müssen. Wir kommen darauf in der Diskussion unseres Beispielszenarios in Abschnitt 5.3 zurück.

Nicht weniger komplex ist die Realisierung des *Datenflusses* zwischen Arbeitsschritten. Zunächst stellt sich das Problem der Heterogenität beim Datenfluß zwischen Arbeitsschritten, die von verschiedenen Datenverwaltungssystemen ausgeführt werden. Um nicht bei n Systemen n^2 Konverter zu benötigen, bedient man sich eines gemeinsamen Standardformates. Standards wie CORBA [OMG92, OMG94] verdecken darüber hinaus die Verwendung unterschiedlicher Implementierungssprachen; eine C++ Methode kann beispielsweise eine COBOL-Routine aufrufen. Zum Austausch komplexer Strukturen wie z.B. Hypertexte oder multimediale Dokumente müssen diese Daten im verwendeten Standardformat darstellbar sein und als Parameter den aufgerufenen Methoden in den Arbeitsschritten übergeben werden können. Dies beinhaltet z.B. die Darstellung und Übergabe von Objektreferenzen als Teil eines Hypertextes.

Nicht jeder Workflow kann im Rahmen seiner Spezifikation zu Ende geführt werden. Äußere Einflüsse können eine Ausnahmebehandlung oder eine dynamische Modifikation nötig machen. Eine Ausnahmebehandlung kann etwa durch außerplanmäßiges Eingreifen eines Vorgesetzten entstehen. Es soll möglich sein, einen Workflow in einem bestimmten Zustand anzuhalten und dann später – zum Beispiel nach dem Treffen intellektueller Entscheidungen – in einem anderen Zustand fortzusetzen. Dynamische Modifikationen werden z.B. bei kurzfristigen Gesetzesänderungen nötig, die Eingriffe in Spezifikationen von laufenden Workflows erfordern. Die Häufigkeit von Ausnahmebehandlungen und dynamischen Änderungen ist anwendungsabhängig. Da in solchen Fällen jedoch Ablaufeigenschaften des Workflows vom System nicht mehr garantiert werden können, sollten Ausnahmebehandlungen und dynamische Änderungen selten bleiben.

Die Verbindung der Middleware-Komponenten mit State- und Activitycharts geschieht durch Programmcode, der den Activities zugeordnet wird. Beim Starten einer Activity wird dieser Code automatisch ausgeführt. Der Programmcode enthält die Anweisungen, die die Dienste der Middleware-Komponenten aufrufen. Konkret bedeutet dies, daß bei der Aktivierung einer Activity A (z.B. mit dem Kommando $st!(A)$) der mit der Activity A assoziierte Programmcode gestartet wird, der wiederum die Dienste der Middleware-Komponenten aufruft.

5.2 Überwachung von Workflows

Die Möglichkeit zur Überwachung von Workflows ist eine wesentliche Anforderung an ein Workflow-Management-System, da sie die Kontrolle über die nun als Workflow implementierten innerbetrieblichen Abläufe ermöglicht. Zur Überwachung der Ausführung von Workflows zählen das Protokollieren der ausgeführten Arbeitsschritte, das Stellen von Anfragen an die entstehende Workflow-Historie, die Berücksichtigung von Zeitaspekten bei der Ausführung sowie Aspekte der Arbeitsverteilung

In Mentor sollen den an einer Workflow–Ausführung beteiligten Sachbearbeitern und sonstigen Personen mit Überwachungsfunktionen dieselben Visualisierungsmöglichkeiten über State- und Activitycharts zur Verfügung gestellt werden, die bei der Spezifikation vorhanden sind. Dazu gehören die graphische Darstellung der verwendeten State- und Activitycharts, die Identifizierung des aktuellen Zustandes, die Trennung in erledigte, gerade bearbeitete und in Zukunft zu bearbeitende Activities, einzuhaltende Fristen und sich evtl. ergebende Wartebeziehungen auf externe Events, z.B. den Abschluß einer für die eigene Arbeit notwendigen Activity eines anderen Sachbearbeiters. Ein überwachender Mitarbeiter muß Zugriff auf die entsprechenden Daten aller von ihm überwachten Mitarbeiter haben. Zusätzlich stehen ihm abgeleitete Informationen zur Verfügung, wie z.B. kritische Pfade für Fristen oder Urlaubsdaten zur Einteilung von Mitarbeitern.

Grundlage für alle Arten der Überwachung sind die bei der Ausführung des Workflows aufgezeichneten Protokolldaten. Dabei werden – auch dynamisch – Anfragen auf historischen Daten durchgeführt. Wir können nicht erwarten, daß die beteiligten Datenverwaltungssysteme die Protokollierung der für uns relevanten Daten der Historie selbst vornehmen. Darüber hinaus wären beispielsweise Einträge aus Logdateien von Datenbanksystemen für unsere Zwecke wertlos, da der Bezug zu den semantisch komplexen Spezifikationen der Workflows nicht hergestellt werden kann. Mentor sieht daher Protokollierungsfunktionen in der Schicht der Integrations- und Ergänzungssoftware vor.

Durch eine laufende Überwachung der Ausführung von Workflows können Informationen über die Lastverteilung gewonnen werden, so daß bei Unbalanciertheit die Ausführungsorgane gleichmäßig mit Arbeit versorgt werden können. Dies kann sowohl für die verwendeten Systemressourcen wie z.B. Workstations als auch für die beteiligten Sachbearbeiter geschehen. Auf der Ebene der Systemressourcen kann die Balancierung weitgehend verdeckt erfolgen. Ergeben sich beispielsweise bei einem Sachbearbeiter zu lange Ausführungszeiten für seine Arbeitsschritte, können diese automatisch zu anderen Rechnern migriert werden. Das Workflow-Management-System entscheidet dies selbständig und für den Sachbearbeiter transparent, oder es gibt dem Systemadministrator zumindest Hilfestellung bezüglich des Verhältnisses von Nutzen durch Verwendung weiterer Rechner und den Kosten der notwendigen Verlagerung von Daten dorthin.

Eine Lastbalancierung auf der Ebene der Sachbearbeiter könnte beispielsweise durch einen allen Sachbearbeitern derselben Rolle gemeinsamen "Eingangspostkorb" unterstützt werden. Darüber hinausgehende Lastverteilungsmaßnahmen können dagegen auf dieser Ebene nur durch explizit erlassene Richtlinien oder durch persönliche Absprachen erfolgen. Ist ein Sachbearbeiter mit der Menge der auszuführenden Arbeitsschritte überfordert, können Arbeitsschritte zu anderen Sachbearbeitern verlagert werden. Das Workflow-Management-System sorgt für die Bereitstellung der erforderlichen State- und Activitycharts und Daten beim übernehmenden Sachbearbeiter.

Durch das Einbeziehen von Zeitaspekten in das Workflow–Management können weitere Verlagerungen von Arbeitsschritten nötig werden. Drohende Terminüberschreitungen können erkannt und vermieden werden, indem vor Überschreitung eines Termins neue Ressourcen alloziert werden oder eine notwendige Lastbalancierung durchgeführt wird. Werden Sachbearbeiter dem in Terminschwierigkeiten befindlichen Workflow neu zugeordnet, muß die Arbeit an anderen

Workflows langsamer ablaufen oder ganz ruhen. Die nun entstehenden neuen Terminverschiebungen müssen vom Workflow-Management-System erkannt und den Vorgesetzten zur Kenntnis gebracht werden.

5.3 Anwendungsbeispiel

In diesem Abschnitt werden die obigen Überlegungen zur Ausführung und Überwachung von Workflows in Mentor anhand eines Beispiels veranschaulicht. Wir legen wieder das Beispiel des Begutachtungsprozesses aus Abschnitt 4.2 zugrunde, konzentrieren uns aber nun auf das Zusammenwirken der Systemkomponenten aus Abbildung 3 zur Laufzeit.

Der Begutachtungsprozeß beginnt mit dem Eintreffen des Papiers. Der Editor registriert das Papier und bestimmt drei Gutachter. Er möchte kompetente Gutachter, die aber nicht gleichzeitig stark überlastet sind. Der Editor stellt also eine Anfrage an seine persönliche Datenbank, die ihm passende Gutachter liefert zusammen mit der Zahl der Papiere, die der jeweilige Gutachter für den Editor schon begutachtet hat. Die Middleware-Komponenten haben die Aufgabe, die Verbindung von den State- und Activitycharts des Editors zu seiner Datenbank herzustellen. Dazu werden C-Funktionen verwendet, die direkt mit Activities assoziiert werden. Im Beispiel aus Abbildung 1 ist dies beispielsweise der Code für die Activity *Einreichung_A*, die beim Schalten der Transition zum Zustand *Einreichung_S* aufgerufen wird. Dieser Code beinhaltet u.a. die Aufrufe an das lokale Datenbanksystem und an das dem Dialog mit dem Editor zugrundeliegende GUI. Die Verbindung zwischen der Activity *Einreichung_A* und der C-Funktion *einreichung* wird folgendermaßen hergestellt; die dabei aufgerufene Funktion `sc_connect_task` gehört zum Laufzeitsystem von Statemate.

> sc_connect_task ("Einreichung_A", einreichung);

Die C-Funktion *einreichung* kann wiederum mit Hilfe von Statemate-Funktionen wie folgt auf die Datenflußelemente des Workflows Bezug nehmen, wobei *autor_name* eine beliebige Variable der C-Funktion sein kann.

> sc_set_string_data_item ("Autor", autor_name);

Für das Aussuchen der Gutachter sind keine speziellen Funktionen der Middleware nötig. Im Fall eines Fehlers bei der Ausführung der beschriebenen Datenbankanfrage sollte sie wiederholt werden, bis ein Ergebnis vorliegt, oder bekannt wird, daß z. B. durch einen Ausfall einer Systemkomponente eine Wiederholung (zu diesem Zeitpunkt) nicht durchführbar ist. Da keine Änderungen in der Datenbank vorgenommen werden, ist dies problemlos möglich; bezüglich Fehlertoleranz liegen keine besonderen Anforderungen vor.

Nach der Auswahl der Gutachter werden mit dem Übergang in den Zustand *Begutachtung_S* die drei Activities *Begutachtung1_A* bis *Begutachtung3_A* gestartet und jeweils der Zustand *Gutachten_anfertigen* betreten (siehe Abb. 5). Diese Activities werden auf dem Rechner des Editors initiiert, müssen aber letztlich auf den Rechnern der jeweiligen Gutachter ablaufen. Wir nehmen an, daß jeder Gutachter für die Erstellung seines Gutachtens eine eigene Workstation benutzt und auf seine persönliche Datenbank wie auch auf öffentliche Datenbanken zugreift, um weitere Informationen zum Wissensgebiet des Papiers zu erhalten. Jetzt kommen wir nicht mehr mit einfachen C-Funktionen zum Ansprechen der Datenverwaltungssysteme aus. Die Papiere müssen an die entfernten Workstations der Gutachter geschickt werden. Dies wird durch den Einsatz des TP-Monitors oder einer verteilten Programmierumgebung in der Middleware realisiert: Die entfernten Systeme werden mittels Remote-Procedure-Call (RPC) angesprochen. RPC-Mechanismen erlauben allerdings meist nicht den Austausch komplexer Datenstrukturen, z.B. strukturierter Dokumente. Soll das eingereichte Papier in einer anderen Form als ASCII oder Postscript an die Gutachter verteilt werden (es könnte sich beispielsweise um einen Hypertext handeln), so sind zusätzliche Komponenten der Integrations- und Ergänzungssoftware nötig, etwa zur Konvertierung des Dokuments in ein geeignetes Datenaustauschformat.

Nach Fertigstellung von mindestens zwei Gutachten soll der Begutachtungsprozeß beendet werden. Die Implementierung dieser Forderung stellt die bisher größten Anforderungen an die Middleware. Die Gutachten liegen verteilt in den Datenbanken der Gutachter vor und werden – wieder mittels RPC und eventueller Konvertierungsfunktionen – an den Editor gesendet. Dort werden die eintreffenden Gutachten gezählt (vgl. Abb. 5). Hier ist eine "Exactly-once"-Semantik des Versendens der Gutachten gefordert. Geht ein Gutachten verloren, wird die nötige Zahl von zwei Gutachten entweder gar nicht oder zumindest erst verspätet erreicht. Wird ein Gutachten mehrfach gesendet, wird es doppelt gezählt und der Begutachtungsprozeß wird fälschlicherweise schon beim Vorliegen eines Gutachtens beendet.

Da die Activities *Begutachtung1_A* bis *Begutachtung3_A* aus Sicht des Editors auf entfernten Rechnern laufen, ihre Beendigung und die (bis zu dreimalige) Generierung des Ereignisses *Gutachten_vorgelegt* aber beim Editor bekannt gemacht werden muß, werden wieder die Kommunikationsdienste des TP-Monitors benötigt. Stellt ein Gutachter sein Gutachten fertig, wird vom TP-Monitor garantiert, daß der Editor genau eine Nachricht über die beendete Begutachtung erhält (in Form des Ereignisses *Gutachten_vorgelegt*). Dies ist die Voraussetzung dafür, daß der *Zähler* des Editors korrekt erhöht wird und sichergestellt ist, daß alle Einzelgutachten berücksichtigt werden. Abbildung 6 verdeutlicht, wie die Information über die Beendigung der Begutachtung unter Zuhilfenahme eines TP-Monitors vom Rechner eines Gutachters zum Rechner des Editors gelangt. Die drei Funktionsaufrufe `Ereignis_generieren`, `Ext_Ereignis_generieren` und `DB_Änderung` werden dabei zu einer atomaren Einheit geklammert.

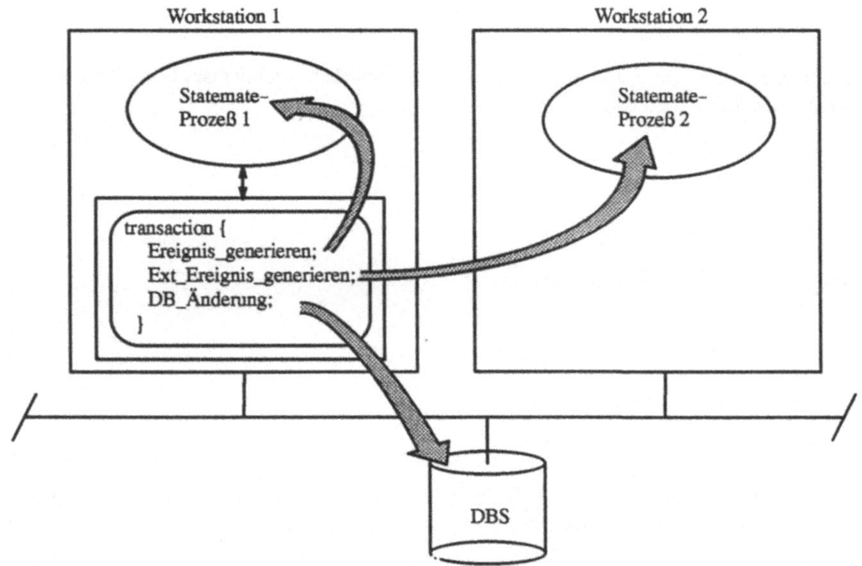

Abbildung 6: Transaktionsgeschützte Prozeßkommunikation mittels TP-Monitor

Der folgende Ausschnitt aus dem C-Code der Activity *Begutachtung1_A* (und analog *Begutachtung2_A* und *Begutachtung3_A*) zeigt exemplarisch eine mögliche Implementierung mit den Sprachmitteln von Encina [Enc93].

```
void Begutachtung1()
{
        ...
        EXEC SQL BEGIN DECLARE SECTION;
                ...
        EXEC SQL END DECLARE SECTION;
        ...
        Gutachten_editieren();
        ...
        sc_set_int_data_item ("Note", meine_note);
        ...
        transaction{
                DB_Änderung();
                Ereignis_generieren("Gutachten_vorgelegt");
                Ext_Ereignis_generieren("Gutachten_vorgelegt");
        }
}
```

In diesem Codestück werden die drei Funktionsaufrufe `DB_Änderung`, `Ereignis_gene-rieren` und `Ext_Ereignis_generieren` zu einer Transaktion zusammengefaßt. Diese Funktionen werden in der Encina-spezifischen "Transaction Interface Definition Language" wie folgt deklariert. Das Schlüsselwort "transactional" bedeutet, daß Aufrufe der deklarierten Funktionen innerhalb einer Transaktion transaktionsgeschützt sein sollen.

```
...
interface ...
{
        [transactional] void DB_Änderung ();
        [transactional] void Ereignis_generieren ([in] char *Ereignisname);
        [transactional] void Ext_Ereignis_generieren ([in] char *Ereignisname);
}
...
```

Die ersten beiden der drei Funktionen werden lokal – auf dem Rechner des Gutachters – ausgeführt; der Code dafür sieht folgendermaßen aus.

```
void DB_Änderung()
{
        EXEC SQL
                UPDATE Meine_Gutachten
                SET Note = :Note
                WHERE ...;
}


void Ereignis_generieren(char *Ereignisname)
{
        sc_do_action(Ereignisname);
}
```

Dabei beinhaltet `DB_Änderung` Aufrufe an das lokale Datenbanksystem, und `Ereig-nis_generieren` ruft die Funktion `sc_do_action` des lokalen Statemate-Prozesses zur Ereignissignalisierung auf.

Die dritte Funktion, `Ext_Ereignis_generieren`, soll auf dem Rechner des Editors entfernt aufgerufen werden und dem dort laufenden Statemate-Prozeß das Ereignis *Gutachten_vorgelegt* signalisieren. Der TP-Monitor setzt den Aufruf dieser Funktion automatisch in einen entsprechenden RPC um, so daß auf dem Rechner des Editors letztlich die folgende Funktion als Teil der verteilten Transaktion ausgeführt wird.

```
void Ext_Ereignis_generieren(char *Ereignisname)
{
        sc_do_action(Ereignisname);
}
```

Auf diese Weise werden also die Zustandsinformationen der beteiligten Statemate-Prozesse beim Gutachter bzw. den Gutachtern und beim Editor synchron aktualisiert, und zwar dank des TP-Monitors auf atomare Art und Weise. Dies ist eine notwendige Voraussetzung für die fehlertolerante Abarbeitung des spezifizierten Workflows, sicher aber noch nicht ausreichend. Im Fehlerfall genügt es nämlich noch nicht, die Effekte einer unvollständigen verteilten Transaktion zurückzusetzen; zusätzlich muß die Transaktion automatisch neu gestartet werden, und zwar so oft, bis sie erstmals erfolgreich beendet wird. Erweiterungen zur Gewährleistung einer solchen "Exactly-once"-Ausführungssemantik sollen in der Ergänzungsschicht von Mentor – aufbauend auf derartigen Diensten eines TP-Monitors – realisiert werden.

Weitere Anforderungen an die Middleware ergeben sich, wenn man zeitliche Beziehungen innerhalb oder zwischen Workflows betrachtet. In unserem Beispiel gibt es eine Frist, nach der alle Einzelgutachten vorliegen müssen. In einem angemessenen Zeitraum vor Erreichen dieser Frist, sollen Erinnerungsschreiben an die verspäteten Gutachter verschickt werden (Ereignis *Frist_naht* in Abb. 5). Dies erfordert eine Schedulingkomponente in der Middleware, die ihre Informationen – wie die anderen Komponenten auch – aus den Definitionen der State- und Activitycharts erhält. Liefert mehr als ein Gutachter gar kein Gutachten, muß mindestens ein weiteres Gutachten von einem zusätzlichen Gutachter eingeholt werden. Die entsprechende Aktivität wird verlagert. Dies zu ermöglichen, ist eine wesentliche Anforderung an ein Workflow-Management-System. In großen Unternehmen müssen ständig Arbeitsschritte von einem Sachbearbeiter an einen anderen delegiert werden, z.B. bei Krankheit. Dabei wird man üblicherweise die vor der Delegation vorliegenden Teilergebnisse mitgeben wollen, um Doppelarbeit zu vermeiden. In der Integrations- und Ergänzungsschicht der Middleware sind entsprechende Mechanismen vorzusehen, die selbst wieder andere Komponenten der Middleware benutzten, um die Delegation durchzuführen. Beispielsweise benötigt man auch dafür eine "Exactly-once"-Semantik, damit nicht später mehrere oder gar kein Sachbearbeiter den betreffenden Arbeitsschritt fortführen.

Die zur Überwachung des Workflows vorgesehene Protokollierungskomponente von Mentor erlaubt Anfragen an die Historie der Workflows. Beispielsweise könnte der Editor in unserem Beispiel wissen wollen, wie oft ein bestimmter Gutachter in früheren Fällen die Frist überschritten hat, oder ein Gutachter könnte in Erfahrung bringen wollen, ob die anderen Gutachter bereits mit ihren Gutachten fertig sind (ohne die Identität der Gutachter preiszugeben). Derartige Möglichkeiten würden hoffentlich zu einem zügigeren Begutachtungsprozeß beitragen.

6 Zusammenfassung und Ausblick

In diesem Artikel haben wir einen neuartigen Ansatz für Workflow-Management vorgestellt, der auf State- und Activitycharts beruht. Diese Spezifikationsmethode hat sich für die Modellierung technischer Steuerungssysteme sehr bewährt; ihre Verwendung für unternehmensweite Workflows wurde unseres Wissens zuvor noch nicht erwogen. Da wir mit dem Mentor-Projekt in diesem Sinne Neuland betreten, liegen natürlicherweise noch keine tiefgehenden Ergebnisse über den gewählten Ansatz vor. Unsere hier vorgestellten Modellierungsüberlegungen weisen jedoch auf ein sehr gutes Potential der verwendeten Spezifikationsmethode hin. Im Vergleich zu anderen Methoden zur Workflow-Spezifikation – Skriptsprachen, ECA-Regeln, Petrinetze oder ähnliches – konnten insbesondere die hervorragenden, intuitiv leicht nachvollziehbaren Möglichkeiten zur Verfeinerung und Komposition von Workflows demonstriert werden. Diese Eigenschaften sind für die Spezifikation komplexer Workflows und die Wiederverwendung existierender Arbeitsabläufe in übergeordneten, unternehmensweiten Workflows von entscheidender Bedeutung.

Über die reine Spezifikation von Workflows hinaus verfolgen wir im Mentor-Projekt das Anliegen, Spezifikationen direkt in der zugrundeliegenden verteilten und heterogenen Systemlandschaft ausführen zu können. Zur Ausführung, Überwachung und Steuerung von Workflows wollen wir die Spezifikationsumgebung Statemate mit geeigneten Middleware-Komponenten koppeln, insbesondere mit einem TP-Monitor. Die grundsätzliche Vorgehensweise für eine solche Kopplung und die damit verbundenen Möglichkeiten haben wir in diesem Artikel demonstriert. Dabei wurde die der State- und Activitychart-Methode innewohnende "offene Architektur" ausgenutzt, indem die spezifizierten Activities um Aufrufe des TP-Monitors und anderer externer Subsysteme erweitert wurden. Zur Realisierung der projektierten vollständigen Workflow-Management-Umgebung ist freilich noch ein gewaltiges Stück Forschungsarbeit zu leisten. Dieses Ziel wird in einem gemeinsamen Projekt der Universität des Saarlandes, des UBILAB der Schweizerischen Bankgesellschaft und der ETH Zürich verfolgt. Im Vordergrund stehen dabei naturgemäß Anwendungen aus dem Bankbereich, beispielsweise die Abwicklung von Kreditanträgen. Das erst vor kurzem begonnene Mentor-Projekt steckt sicher noch in den Kinderschuhen, ist aber nach unserer Überzeugung auf dem richtigen Weg zu ausgereifteren Resultaten.

Literaturverzeichnis

[Bi94] A. Biliris, S. Dar, N. Gehani, H.V. Jagadish, K. Ramamritham, ASSET: A System for Supporting Extended Transactions, ACM SIGMOD Conference, 1994

[BMR94] D. Barbara, S. Mehrotra, M. Rusinkiewicz, INCAS: A Computation Model for Dynamic Workflows in Autonomous Distributed Environments, Technical Report, Matsushita Information Technology Laboratory, Princeton, 1994

[Be93] P.A. Bernstein, Middleware: An Architecture for Distributed System Services, Technical Report, Digital Corporation, Cambridge Research Laboratory, 1993

[Br93] Y. Breitbart, A. Deacon, H.-J. Schek, A. Sheth, G. Weikum, Merging Application-centric and Data-centric Approaches to Support Transaction-oriented Multi-system Workflows, ACM SIGMOD Record Vol.22 No.3, September 1993

[CBHR93] V.J. Cahill, R. Balter, N. Harris, X. Rousset de Pina (Editors), The Comandos Distributed Application Platform, Springer-Verlag, 1993

[DHL91] U. Dayal, M. Hsu, R. Ladin, A Transactional Model for Long-Running Activities, VLDB Conference, 1991

[Da93] U. Dayal, H. Garcia-Molina, M. Hsu, B. Kao, M.-C. Shan, Third Generation TP Monitors: A Database Challenge, ACM SIGMOD Conference, 1993

[De94] P.J. Denning, The Fifteenth Level, Keynote Address, ACM SIGMETRICS Conference, 1994

[Enc93] An Introduction to Programming the Encina Monitor, Transarc Corporation, 1993

[EN93] C.A. Ellis, G.J. Nutt, Modeling and Enactment of Workflow Systems, Invited Paper, 14th International Conference on Application and Theory of Petri Nets, 1993

[Fu93] U. Furbach, Formal Specification Methods for Reactive Systems, Journal of Systems Software Vol. 21, pp. 129–139, 1993

[GHKM94] D. Georgakopoulos, M. Hornick, P. Krychniak, F. Manola, Specification and Management of Extended Transactions in a Programmable Transaction Environment, IEEE Data Engineering Conference, Houston, 1994

[GGS93] M. Gesmann, A. Grasnickel, H. Schoening, A Remote Cooperation System Supporting Interoperability in Heterogeneous Environments, IEEE International Workshop on Research Issues in Data Engineering: Interoperability of Multidatabase Systems, Vienna, 1993

[GR93] J. Gray, A. Reuter, Transaction Processing: Concepts and Techniques, Morgan Kaufmann, 1993

[Ha87] D. Harel, Statecharts: A Visual Formalism for Complex Systems, Science of Computer Programming Vol.8, 1987, pp. 231–274

[Ha88] D. Harel, On Visual Formalisms, Communications of the ACM Vol.31 No.5, 1988

[Ha90] D. Harel et al., STATEMATE: A Working Environment for the Development of Complex Reactive Systems, IEEE Transactions on Software Engineering Vol.16 No.4, April 1990

[HPSS87] D. Harel, A. Pnueli, J.P. Schmidt, R. Sherman, On the Formal Semantics of Statecharts, 2nd IEEE Symposium on Logic in Computer Science, 1987

[Hsu93] M. Hsu (Editor), IEEE Data Engineering Bulletin Vol.16 No.2, June 1993, Special Issue on Workflow and Extended Transaction Systems

[i–Log91] i–Logix Inc., Languages of STATEMATE, in: Documentation for the Statemate System, 1991

[Jab93] S. Jablonski, Aktivitäten–Management–Systeme: Ziele, Grundlagen und Lösungen, Manuskript, 1993

[KS91] G. Kappel, M. Schrefl, Object/Behavior Diagrams, IEEE Data Engineering Conference, 1991

[KUW95] St. Kirn, R. Unland, U. Wanka, MAMBA: Automatic Customization of Computerized Business Processes, Information Systems Vol.19 No.8, 1994

[LA94] F. Leymann, W. Altenhuber, Managing Business Processes as an Information Resource, IBM Systems Journal Vol.33 No.2, 1994

[McC93] T. McCusker, Workflow takes on the enterprise, Datamation, Dec 1, 1993

[MC94] T.W. Malone, K. Crowston, The Interdisciplinary Study of Coordination, ACM Computing Surveys Vol.26 No.1, March 1994

[Me94] W.P. Melling, Enterprise Information Architectures – They're Finally Changing, Invited Industrial Plenary Talk, ACM SIGMOD International Conference on Management of Data, Minneapolis, 1994

[Mu93] S. Mullender (Editor), Distributed Systems, ACM Press, 2nd Edition, 1993

[Ob94] R. Obermarck (Editor), IEEE Data Engineering Bulletin Vol.17 No.1, March 1994, Special Issue on TP Monitors and Distributed Transaction Management

[Ober94] A. Oberweis, Workflow Management in Software Engineering Projects, 2nd International Conference on Concurrent Engineering and Electronic Design Automation, 1994

[OSS94] A. Oberweis, G. Scherrer, W. Stucky, INCOME/STAR: Methodology and Tools for the Development of Distributed Information Systems, Information Systems Vol.19 No.8, 1994

[OMG92] Object Management Group, The Common Object Request Broker: Architecture and Specification, 1992

[OMG94] Object Management Group, The Common Object Services Specification, Volume 1, 1994

[Rei93] B. Reinwald, Workflow–Management in verteilten Systemen, Teubner–Verlag, 1993

[RSW92] A. Reuter, F. Schwenkreis, H. Wächter, Zuverlässige Abwicklung großer verteilter Anwendungen mit ConTracts – Architektur einer Prototypimplementierung, in: R. Bayer, T. Härder, P. Lockemann (Hsrg.), Objektbanken für Experten, Springer–Verlag, 1992

[RS94] M. Rusinkiewicz, A. Sheth, Specification and Execution of Transactional Workflows, in: W. Kim (Editor), Modern Database Systems: The Object Model, Interoperability, and Beyond, ACM Press, 1994

[Saa93] G. Saake, Objektorientierte Spezifikation von Informationssystemen, Teubner–Verlag, 1993

[SK94] A. Sheth, N. Krishnakumar, Specification of Workflows with Heterogeneous Tasks in METEOR, 20th VLDB Conference, Poster Paper Collection, 1994

[Sta94] 2. Deutsches Anwenderforum für STATEMATE/Express V–HDL, Berner & Mattner GmbH, 1994

[ST94] B. Salzberg, D. Tombroff, DSDT: Durable Scripts Containing Database Transactions, Manuscript, submitted for publication, 1994

[Sch94] A.-W. Scheer, ARIS Toolset: a Software Product is Born, Information Systems Vol.19 No.8, 1994

[Schi93] A. Schill (Editor), DCE – The OSF Distributed Computing Environment, Client/Server Model and Beyond, International DCE Workshop, Springer, 1993

[Schw93] F. Schwenkreis, APRICOTS – A Prototype Implementation of a ConTract System – Management of the Control Flow and the Communication System, 12th Symposium on Reliable Distributed Systems, 1993

[WR92] H. Wächter, A. Reuter, The ConTract Model, in: A.K. Elmagarmid (Editor), Database Transaction Models for Advanced Applications, Morgan Kaufmann, 1992

[Wei93] G. Weikum, Extending Transaction Management to Capture More Consistency with Better Performance, Invited Paper, 9th French Database Conference, Toulouse, September 1993

[WD94] J. Widom, U. Dayal (Editors), A Guide To Active Databases, Morgan Kaufmann, 1994

DFR-Dokumentenverwaltung mit verschiedenen Datenhaltungssystemen: Konzepte, Vergleich und Erfahrungen

Uta Störl [1]   Anke Telschow [2]   Bernhard Paul [2]   Norbert Südkamp [3]

[1] Friedrich-Schiller-Universität
Jena
Fakultät für Mathematik und
Informatik
Leutragraben 1
07743 Jena
stoerl@informatik.uni-jena.de

[2] IBM Deutschland
Informationssysteme GmbH
European Networking Center
Vangerowstr. 18
69115 Heidelberg
{telschow, b_paul}@vnet.ibm.com

[3] IBM Deutschland
Informationssysteme GmbH
Wissenschaftliches Zentrum
Vangerowstr. 18
69115 Heidelberg
suedkamp@vnet.ibm.com

Abstract

In Büroanwendungen werden Papierdokumente zunehmend durch elektronisch verarbeitete Dokumente ergänzt und verdrängt. Der Standard 'Document Filing and Retrieval' (DFR) ermöglicht es, diese zwischen verschiedenen Systemen und Netzen auszutauschen. Am IBM European Networking Center (ENC) wurde ein DFR-System entwickelt, das diesen Standard realisiert. Dabei wurden für die Datenhaltungskomponente dieses Systems drei verschiedene Lösungsvarianten geschaffen. Die verschiedenen Implementierungen beruhen auf dem AIX-Dateisystem, dem relationalen Datenbanksystem IBM DB2/6000 bzw. dem objektorientierten Datenbanksystem ObjectStore[1]. Die drei Realisierungen werden in dieser Arbeit vorgestellt. Wesentliche Aspekte der verschiedenen Modellierungen und Implementierungen werden miteinander verglichen.

1. Einleitung

Im Mittelpunkt von Büroanwendungen stehen Dokumente. Dies können z.B Briefe, Bilanzen oder Rechnungen sein. Dabei werden die bisher vorherrschenden Papierdokumente in zunehmendem Maße von elektronisch verarbeiteten Dokumenten ergänzt und verdrängt. Der daraus resultierende Wunsch, diese zwischen verschiedenen Netzen und Systemen herstellerübergreifend austauschen zu können, verlangt ein gemeinsames

---

[1]   ObjectStore ist ein Warenzeichen der Object Design Inc.

Verständnis über die Struktur der Information und die Art der Kommunikation. Dazu wurden entsprechende Standards entwickelt. Der Standard 'Distributed Office Applications Model' (DOAM) [DOAM91] beschreibt eine grundlegende Architektur für verteilte Büroanwendungen. Basierend auf diesem Konzept, setzt sich für den Zugriff und die Speicherung von Dokumenten im offenen, heterogenen Systemverbund immer stärker der internationale Standard 'Document Filing and Retrieval' (DFR) [DFR91] durch.

Am IBM European Networking Center (ENC) wurde deshalb ein DFR-System entwickelt, das diesen Standard realisiert. Die Dokumente werden im DFR-Standard in einer Client-Server-Architektur von einem Server verwaltet. In diesen ist eine Datenhaltungskomponente integriert, welche die eigentliche Dokumentenverwaltung realisiert. Durch die modulare Systemarchitektur des am ENC entwickelten DFR-Systems können ohne Anpassungen der übrigen Komponenten verschiedene Datenhaltungskomponenten in das DFR-System integriert werden. Die Datenhaltungskomponente wurde dabei zunächst mit einem AIX-Dateisystem implementiert. Danach wurden zwei Datenbanksystem-Implementierungen mit dem relationalen Datenbanksystem IBM DB2/6000 und dem objektorientierten Datenbanksystem ObjectStore realisiert. Die dabei gewonnenen Erfahrungen sollen in dieser Arbeit dargestellt werden.

Dazu werden als erstes die wichtigsten Elemente des DFR-Standards kurz vorgestellt. Danach wird das am ENC entwickelte DFR-System mit den verschiedenen Realisierungen der Datenhaltungskomponente erläutert. Es werden Unterschiede in der Modellierung und Implementierung aufgezeigt und bewertet.

Diesem Beitrag liegt in wesentlichen Teilen eine Diplomarbeit zugrunde [Stö94], die in Zusammenarbeit zwischen dem Lehrstuhl für Datenbanken und Informationssysteme der Friedrich-Schiller-Universität (Prof. Dr. A. Blaser) und der IBM in Heidelberg (WZH IDSE, ENC Telekooperation) entstanden ist.

2. Der Standard Document Filing and Retrieval (DFR)

Der ISO/IEC Standard DFR [DFR91] beschreibt drei Aspekte:

- ein **Protokoll**, in welchem der Austausch von Daten und Operationen zwischen DFR-Client und DFR-Server beschrieben wird. Das zugrundeliegende Client-Server-Konzept ist dem allgemeinen Modell für verteilte Büroanwendungen [DOAM91] entnommen.

- ein **Kommunikationssystem**, in dem die Anbindung an die OSI-Kommunikations-schichten festgelegt ist. Dabei benutzt DFR die OSI-Dienste ACSE, ROSE und RTSE.

- ein **Informationsmodell**, in dem die Objekttypen und ihre Beziehungen definiert werden.

Die Objekte werden vom DFR-Server in einem **Dokumentenspeicher** verwaltet. Jedem Server ist dabei genau ein Dokumentenspeicher zugeordnet und umgekehrt.

Das DFR-Informationsmodell unterscheidet vier Objekttypen:

- **Dokument**: der Haupt-Objekttyp mit dem eigentlichen Inhalt des Dokumen-tenspeichers

- **Gruppe**: faßt mehrere Objekte des Speichers zusammen, u.a. auch wieder Gruppen; damit wird eine hierarchische Struktur des Dokumentenspeichers aufgebaut. Eine Gruppe ist mit einer Ablage oder einer Akte vergleichbar. Ein Spezialfall ist hier die Wurzelgruppe, welche die Wurzel des Objektbaumes und damit des ganzen Dokumentenspeichers bildet.

- **Referenz**: damit ein Dokument oder ein anderer Objekttyp auch in mehreren Gruppen oder Dokumentenspeichern gleichzeitig vorkommen kann, wird an dessen Stelle eine Referenz darauf eingerichtet. Eine Referenz kann auch in einen anderen Dokumentenspeicher verweisen.

- **Suchergebnisliste**: bei der (komplexen) Suchoperation können die Ergeb-nismengen als eigenes Objekt angelegt werden; sie können in weiteren Anfragen eingeschränkt oder aktualisiert werden.

Die Objekte werden durch die Gruppenstruktur im Dokumentenspeicher hierarchisch angeordnet. Der mögliche Aufbau eines Dokumentenspeichers soll in der folgenden Abbildung anhand eines Beispiels veranschaulicht werden:

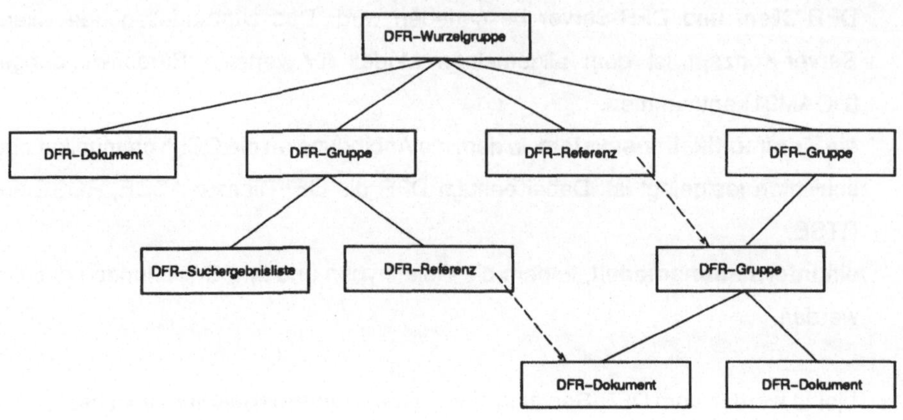

Abbildung 2.1: Beispiel für einen Dokumentenspeicher

Jedes DFR-Objekt besteht aus einem Inhalt und beschreibenden Attributen. Ein Attribut besteht aus einem Attributtyp und einem oder mehreren Attributwerten. Die Struktur des Dokumenteninhalts ist für die Speicherkomponente transparent. Es kann sich deshalb um beliebige Dokumentenarchitekturen handeln, zum Beispiel 'Office Document Architecture' (ODA) [ODA89].

Die DFR-Operationen umfassen das Anlegen (DFR-Create), Löschen (DFR-Delete), Lesen (DFR-Read), Ändern (DFR-Modify), Verschieben (DFR-Move) und Kopieren (DFR-Copy) von Objekten. Es können Zugriffsbeschränkungen für einzelne Objekte vergeben werden (DFR-Reserve). Außerdem können die Mitglieder von Gruppen und Suchergebnislisten mit der DFR-List-Operation aufgelistet werden, und es existiert eine Suchoperation (DFR-Search), die unten detaillierter erläutert wird.

Jedes Objekt besitzt einen Titel, der vom Benutzer festgelegt wird. Zur eindeutigen Identifikation wird vom DFR-Server für jedes Objekt ein Unique Permanent Identifier (UPI) vergeben. Der Zugriff auf DFR-Objekte kann bei den Operationen über den Pfadnamen, d.h. eine Konkatenation der Titel aller Objekte beginnend bei der

Wurzelgruppe, oder direkt über den eindeutigen Identifikator (UPI) erfolgen. Außerdem ist eine Kombination der beiden Verfahren zu einem relativen Pfadnamen möglich, wobei ein UPI einen Einstiegspunkt festlegt, ab dem die Beschreibung durch einen Pfadnamen fortgesetzt wird.

Bei der **Suchoperation** kann im ganzen Dokumentenspeicher gesucht oder aber der Suchraum durch die Angabe einer Suchdomäne eingeschränkt werden. Als Suchdomänen sind sowohl Teilbäume des Dokumentenspeichers, als auch durch vorherige Suchanfragen erhaltene Suchergebnislisten zugelassen. Die Suchoperation erlaubt Anfragen bezüglich der meisten Attribute mit komplexen Filter-Bedingungen, deren Mächtigkeit teilweise über die von SQL-Anfragen hinausgeht. Die Komplexität der Anfrage ergibt sich, neben den Suchdomänen, aus folgenden Eigenschaften:

- Es ist eine beliebige Boole'sche Verknüpfung von Filterausdrücken möglich.
- Für String-Attribute sind auch Partial Match Queries möglich.
- Es sind auch Anfragen für mengenwertige Attribute zugelassen (Teilmengenbedingungen).
- Es gibt viele optionale Attribute, die nicht bei jedem Objekt belegt sein müssen, über die aber auch gesucht werden kann, z.B. auch mit Existenzanfragen.
- Die Anfragen sind unabhängig vom Objekttyp, d. h., in der Suchergebnisliste können Objekte verschiedenen Typs vorkommen.

DFR unterstützt eine **Versionsverwaltung** von Dokumenten. Die verschiedenen Versionen können einen gerichteten Graphen bilden, wobei die Information über Vorgänger- und Nachfolgerversionen bzw. die Ursprungsversion durch spezielle DFR-Attribute verwaltet wird.

3. Das DFR-System TDS

3.1 Überblick und Architektur

Am IBM European Networking Center (ENC) wurde das System **'Telecooperation Document Store' (TDS)** entwickelt, das große Teile des DFR-Standards implementiert.

Das System basiert auf einem modularen Ansatz: Durch die Definition von zwei zueinander äquivalenten DFR-APIs wurden eindeutige Schnittstellen zwischen den Bereichen DFR-Kommunikationssystem und DFR-Anwendungen (Benutzeroberflächen und Datenhaltungskomponenten) geschaffen. Die folgende Abbildung zeigt einen Überblick über die Architektur des Gesamtsystems:

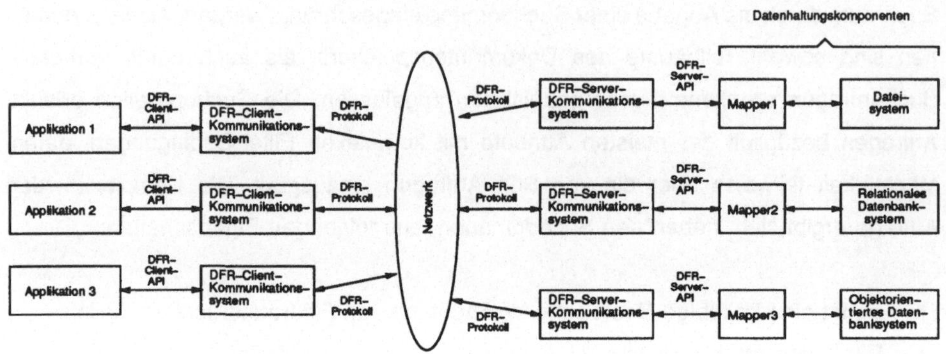

Abbildung 3.1: Architektur des DFR-Systems TDS

Die einzelnen **Komponenten** des Systems haben folgende Aufgaben:

Applikationen/Benutzeroberflächen:

Dies können beliebige Anwendungen sein, z.B. eine einfache zeilenorientierte Testoberfläche oder eine Motif-basierte DFR-Applikation wie z.B. das Bürgerinformationssystem oder ein mutimedialer Veranstaltungskalender. Die DFR-Applikation kann aber auch die Ablagekomponente sein, die in ein Bürokommunikationssystem eingebettet ist. Durch das **DFR-Client-API**, das aus "C"-Datenstrukturen und Funktionen besteht, welche die DFR-Datentypen und DFR-Operationen repräsentieren, wird jeweils die Anbindung an die Client-Kommunikationskomponente realisiert.

Client-Kommunikation:

Diese Komponente realisiert das standardkonforme DFR-Protokoll auf der Client-Seite und benutzt dabei die Dienste und Protokolle der darunterliegenden OSI-Schichten.

Netzwerk:

Hier kann es sich um ein lokales Netz (Token Ring, Ethernet) oder ein Weitverkehrsnetz (z. B. X.25 Datex-P, ISDN) handeln.

Server-Kommunikation:

Diese Komponente realisiert die DFR-Kommunikation auf der Server-Seite, d.h., sie nimmt die Operationen im DFR-Protokoll-Format an und wandelt sie in das DFR-API-Format um.

Datenhaltungskomponenten:

Sie bestehen jeweils aus einem Archiv und einem dazugehörigen Mapper und realisieren die im Standard vorgeschriebenen DFR-Dienste.

Archiv:

Hier werden die DFR-Objekte abgelegt. Es kann sich um ein spezielles Archiv-Produkt, ein Datenbanksystem oder ein einfaches Dateisystem handeln.

Mapper:

Um mit den Strukturen, die das Archiv bietet, einen Dokumentenspeicher nach dem DFR-Informationsmodell zu schaffen, ist eine Abbildung zwischen den beiden Modellen erforderlich. Das **DFR-Server-API** gibt hierbei vor, welche DFR-Funktionen mit welchen Parametern basierend auf dem jeweils gewählten Archivsystem zur Verfügung gestellt werden müssen und gewährleistet so die Anbindung an den Server-Kommunikationsteil und damit an das gesamte TDS-System.

Wegen der modularen Systemarchitektur ist es also möglich, ohne Anpassungen der übrigen Komponenten verschiedene Datenhaltungskomponenten in das TDS-System zu integrieren. Die Alternativen der Implementierung, die in der folgenden Untersuchung betrachtet werden, betreffen genau diesen Bereich.

Es werden in den folgenden Abschnitten Realisierungen basierend auf einem Dateisystem sowie auf einem relationalen und einem objektorientierten Datenbanksystem vorgestellt.

3.2. Realisierung der Datenhaltungskomponente mit dem AIX-Dateisystem

Der Ansatz bei der Implementierung der Datenhaltungskomponente mit einem Dateisystem ist sehr einfach: Attribute und Inhalt eines Objektes werden jeweils in einer Datei abgelegt, die den Namen des UPI trägt, wobei eine Aufteilung auf zwei Verzeichnisse vorgenommen wird. Die Attribut-Dateien bestehen aus einer Menge von Zeilen mit dem Aufbau "Typ=Wert". Für Dokumente enthält die Datei den tatsächlichen Inhalt, für Referenzen ein Ausgabeformat einer Referenz und für Suchergebnislisten den Suchbereich, die Suchbedingung und eine Liste der gefundenen UPIs. Nur die Gruppen bilden eine Ausnahme, da ihr Inhalt (die Liste aller Mitglieder) nicht in einer Datei festgehalten, sondern jeweils dynamisch, aus der unten beschriebenen Baumstruktur, ermittelt wird.

Zur Abbildung der Struktur des Dokumentenspeichers existiert eine spezielle Datei, welche jeweils beim Initialisieren gelesen und nach jeder Änderungsoperation herausgeschrieben wird. Die Datei enthält für jedes Objekt seine UPI, den Titel, den Objekttyp und die Hierarchieebene im Baum. Daraus wird bei zusätzlicher Berücksichtigung der Reihenfolge der Einträge eine Baumstruktur im Hauptspeicher erzeugt, über die navigierend auf die Objekte zugegriffen werden kann. Die einzelnen Knoten des Baumes besitzen dazu folgende Information: UPI, Titel, Objekttyp, Verweis auf das erste Mitglied und Verweis auf den Nachfolger auf der gleichen Ebene.

3.3. Realisierung der Datenhaltungskomponente mit dem relationalen Datenbanksystem IBM DB2/6000

Eine weitere Realisierung der Datenhaltungskomponente erfolgte mit dem relationalen Datenbanksystem DB2/6000. Eine ausführliche Darstellung findet sich in [Jan93]. Es wird für jeden DFR-Objekttyp, außer der Wurzelgruppe, eine Relation definiert. Die Wurzelgruppe wird als spezielle Gruppe betrachtet. Weiter wird eine Relation *DFR-Objekt* eingeführt. Diese enthält den UPI und den Objekttyp jedes DFR-Objektes.

Für zusammengesetzte Attributtypen und mehrwertige Attributausprägungen müssen weitere Relationen definiert werden. Die Attributwerte der DFR-Objekte sind also in verschiedenen Tabellen gespeichert und müssen beim Lesen der Objekte durch JOIN-Operationen wieder zusammengesetzt werden.

Inhalte von Dokumenten werden aufgrund ihrer Größe nicht in einem Feld einer Tabelle verwaltet. Sie sind in einer Datei außerhalb des DBMS abgelegt. In der Datenbank wird für jedes Dokument eine Identifikation der Datei, die den Inhalt enthält, abgelegt.

3.4. Realisierung der Datenhaltungskomponente mit dem objektorientierten Datenbanksystem ObjectStore

Das objektorientierte Datenbanksystem ObjectStore gehört zur Familie der *objektorientierten Datenbank-Programmiersprachen* [Heu92]. Der Strukturteil von ObjectStore stimmt mit dem von C++ überein und beinhaltet zusätzlich generische Klassen zur Verwaltung von Kollektionen, welche Pointer auf Objekte enthalten, sowie Relationships zwischen Instanzen von Klassen. ObjectStore bietet *(1,1)-*, *(1,m)-* und *(n,m)-Relationships* an. Diese unterstützen die Wahrung der referentiellen Integrität der Daten. Der Zugriff auf die Daten erfolgt entweder navigierend, entlang der physisch definierten Beziehungen zwischen Objekten, oder deskriptiv über Queries, die auf Kollektionen von Pointern auf Objekte angewandt werden können. Detailliertere Informationen zu ObjectStore findet man z.B. in [LLOW91].

In der Realisierung der Datenhaltungskomponente mit dem objektorientierten Datenbanksystem ObjectStore [Stö94] werden die im Standard definierten Objekttypen DFR-Dokument, DFR-Gruppe, DFR-Referenz und DFR-Suchergebnisliste direkt als C++-Klassen modelliert. Die DFR-Wurzelgruppe wird nicht als eine eigene Klasse, sondern als eine spezielle Instanz der Klasse DFR-Gruppe abgebildet.

Eine große Anzahl der im DFR-Standard aufgeführten Attribute ist für alle Objekttypen definiert. Außerdem können alle Objekte erzeugt, gelesen, verändert, gelöscht, kopiert, verschoben und reserviert werden. Deshalb wird eine abstrakte Basisklasse *DFR_Object* eingeführt. Die Klassen *DFR_Document, DFR_Group, DFR_Reference* und *DFR_Search_Result_List* werden also von der Klasse *DFR_Object* abgeleitet und erben deren Attribute und Methoden. Die Methoden werden teilweise in den abgeleiteten Klassen redefiniert. Zur Laufzeit wird dann, abhängig vom Typ des aufrufenden Objektes, die richtige Implementierung ausgewählt.

Aus den im Standard definierten Beziehungen zwischen den Objekten ergeben sich mehrere Instanzenbeziehungen zwischen den Klassen. Die Tatsache, daß jedes Objekt, außer der Wurzelgruppe, Mitglied genau einer Gruppe ist, wird durch eine *(1,m)-*

Relationship zwischen den Instanzen der Klasse *DFR_Group* und der abstrakten Basisklasse *DFR_Object* implementiert. Referenzen auf Objekte, die in der Klasse *DFR_Reference* gespeichert werden, werden durch ObjectStore-Referenzen verwaltet. Der Versionierungsmechanismus des DFR-Standards wird durch zwei *(n,m)-Relationships* für die Vor- bzw. Nachfolgerversionen zwischen Objekten der Klasse *DFR_Document* abgebildet. Die folgende Abbildung zeigt die beschriebene grobe Modellierung des Dokumentenspeichers in der Coad/Yourdon - Notation [CY91a und b].

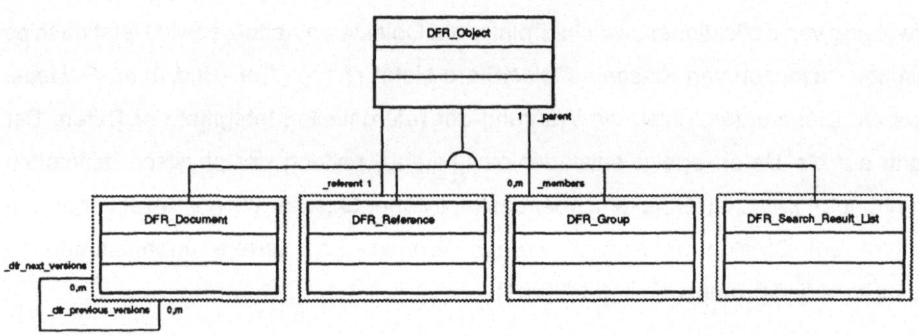

Abbildung 3.2: Objektorientierte Modellierung des Dokumentenspeichers

Wie bereits beschrieben, können die Attributwerte ein- oder mehrwertig sein. Mehrwertige Attributausprägungen werden mit ObjectStore-Kollektionen implementiert. Der Attributtyp ist ein einfacher oder ein zusammengesetzter Datentyp. Für zusammengesetzte Attributtypen werden Komponentenklassen eingeführt. Dadurch werden die oben beschriebenen Klassen weiter verfeinert.

Auf weitere Implementierungsdetails der verschiedenen Realisierungen wird im nächsten Kapitel eingegangen.

4. Vergleich der verschiedenen Realisierungen der Datenhaltungskomponente

In diesem Abschnitt werden einige Aspekte der verschiedenen Modellierungen und Implementierungen miteinander verglichen. Es sollen die verschiedenen Vorgehensweisen, die aus den jeweiligen Systemvoraussetzungen resultieren, aufgezeigt werden.

4.1. Modellierung der DFR-Objekttypen

In diesem Abschnitt soll verglichen werden, wie die Objekttypen des DFR-Informationsmodells in den verschiedenen Realisierungen abgebildet werden.

In der Dateisystem-Implementierung werden alle Attribute eines Objektes in einer Datei und der Inhalt in einer zweiten Datei gespeichert. Die Speicherung erfolgt also typunabhängig. Eine Modellierung der verschiedenen Objekttypen findet dabei nur insoweit statt, als daß für ein Objekt jeweils nur die zum Objekttyp gehörenden Attribute vorhanden sind. Da die DFR-Operationen aber Informationen über den Objekttyp benötigen, wird dieser mit in der beschriebenen Baumstruktur gespeichert.

Beim relationalen Modell werden die Objekttypen als Relationen abgebildet. Allerdings müssen mehrwertige und zusammengesetzte Attribute als einzelne Relationen in der Datenbank gespeichert werden. Die Objekte werden also über mehrere Tabellen verteilt abgelegt. Wird auf ein Objekt zugegriffen, muß dieses erst durch relativ teure JOIN-Operationen wieder zusammengefügt werden. Dies führt zu Performanceproblemen, da die DFR-Operationen, mit Ausnahme der Suchoperation, objektbezogen sind. Es wäre also günstiger, die Attributwerte eines Objektes zu 'clustern'. Dazu wäre aber eine Speicherbeschreibungssprache hilfreich, in welcher die Speicherungsstruktur unabhängig von der Struktur der Objekte beschrieben werden kann. Vorschläge dazu werden z.B. in [KD93], [CSL+90] oder [DPSW92] gegeben.

Im objektorientierten Modell hingegen werden die DFR-Objekte als Ganzes betrachtet und abgebildet. Die physische Speicherung kann damit auch zusammenhängend erfolgen. Für jeden Objekttyp wird eine eigene Klasse definiert. Das Modell des Standards kann in der objektorientierten Modellierung also im wesentlichen 1:1 übertragen werden.

4.2. Speicherung des Inhalts von Dokumenten

Im DFR-Dokumentenspeicher werden Dokumente beliebigen Typs mit beliebiger Größe verwaltet. Bei den Inhalten der Dokumente handelt es sich aus DFR-Sicht um große Mengen unformatierter Daten (Videodaten sind z.B. in der Regel mehrere hundert MB groß). Die für die Speicherung formatierter Daten erkannten Anforderungen (Mehrbenutzerbetrieb, Fehlerbehandlung, Konsistenzerhaltung, Datenunabhängigkeit, Redundanzfreiheit etc.) können auch auf unformatierte Daten übertragen werden [KMM93].

In der Dateisystem-Implementierung werden die Inhalte der Dokumente als Dateien abgelegt. Der Zugriff darauf kann effizient erfolgen. Es bestehen aber weiterhin die generellen Nachteile der Verwaltung von Daten in Dateisystemen (Datenabhängigkeit, eingeschränkte Fehlerbehandlung etc.).

Die Verwaltung beliebig großer Daten in einem Feld einer Tabelle ist in relationalen Datenbanksystemen ein nur teilweise gelöstes Problem. Bei einigen heute auf dem Markt befindlichen Systemen existiert eine Obergrenze für die Größe von Attributwerten [2]. Datenobjekte, die größer als diese Obergrenze sind, können daher nicht in einem Feld einer Tabelle abgelegt werden. Es müßte eine weitere Tabelle definiert werden, in der diese Datenobjekte dann in gesplitteter Form verwaltet würden. Diese Art der Verwaltung ist allerdings sehr aufwendig und erfordert zusätzliche Join- und Sortieroperationen für die Datenobjektfragmente. Deshalb wird der Dokumenteninhalt in dieser konkreten Implementierung außerhalb der Datenbank in einem Dateisystem abgelegt. In der Datenbank wird für jedes Dokument die Identifikation der Datei gespeichert, in welcher der Inhalt gespeichert ist. Die Kopplung zweier Speicherverwaltungssysteme hat Auswirkungen auf die Konsistenzerhaltung der Daten. Datenbanksysteme gewährleisten normalerweise, daß das System nach dem Ausführen von Operationen auf den Daten von einem konsistenten in einen neuen konsistenten Zustand überführt wird. Die Konsistenzerhaltung ist bei der Kopplung mehrerer Speicherverwaltungssysteme problematisch und unter Umständen dem Benutzer überlassen. Für die hier beschriebene Anwendung wird dieses Problem allerdings dadurch entschärft, daß der Benutzer normalerweise auf die Daten nur über den DFR-Server zugreift. Da dieser auf

---

[2] In DB2/6000 Release 1.1 liegt dieser Wert bei 32 kB. Im nächsten Release von DB2/6000 ist ein neuer Datentyp Large Objects (LOBS) verfügbar, der die Speicherung bis zu 2 GB großer Datenobjekte in einem Feld erlaubt.

der Kopplung der beiden Speicherverwaltungssysteme aufsetzt, ist die Verteilung der Daten auf zwei Speicherverwaltungssysteme für den Benutzer transparent.

In objektorientierten Datenbanksystemen ist es prinzipiell möglich, beliebig große Datenobjekte zu verwalten. Der Inhalt der Dokumente wird in der Implementierung mit ObjectStore als ein Attribut der Klasse *DFR_Document* vom Typ *String* abgelegt. Die Verwaltung erfolgt also direkt in der Datenbank. Dadurch wird die Konsistenzerhaltung der Daten vom Datenbanksystem gewährleistet.

Um die Effizienz des Zugriffs auf die Daten zu steigern, wird eine Segmentierung der Datenbank eingeführt. Der ObjectStore-Server ist ein Seiten-Server, d.h., die Daten werden seitenweise vom Server zum Client transportiert. Jede Seite ist genau einem ObjectStore-Segment zugeordnet. ObjectStore bietet die Möglichkeit, beim persistenten Anlegen eines Objektes anzugeben, in welcher Datenbank, welchem Segment oder welchem Cluster das Objekt oder Teile des Objektes gespeichert werden sollen. Abbildung 4.1 zeigt die hier gewählte Datenbankstruktur. Beschreibende Attribute von DFR-Objekten werden im Segment 1 abgelegt, während der eigentliche Inhalt der DFR-Dokumente, der sich jeweils über mehrere Seiten erstrecken kann, in einem zweiten, separaten Segment gespeichert wird. Diese Segmentierung der Datenbank ist insbesondere vorteilhaft für alle Operationen, die nur den Zugriff auf die beschreibenden Attribute benötigen, wie zum Beispiel die DFR-Suchoperation. Diese Art der Clusterung von benötigten Informationen für zeitkritische Operationen ist eine der effektivsten Möglichkeiten zur Verbesserung des Laufzeitverhaltens von ObjectStore Anwendungen. Die vorliegende Segmentierung bietet noch einen weiteren Vorteil gegenüber einer fortlaufenden Speicherung der Objekte in einem Segment: ObjectStore erlaubt für jedes Segment einen eigenen Zugriffsmodus zu definierten. Für den Zugriff auf das Segment mit den beschreibenden Attributen bietet es sich an, jeweils eine Seite an den ObjectStore-Client zu übertragen. Um die Inhalte von DFR-Dokumenten, die sich im Regelfall über mehrere Seiten erstrecken, zu übertragen, ist es sinnvoll, mehrere Seiten mit einem Aufruf zu übertragen

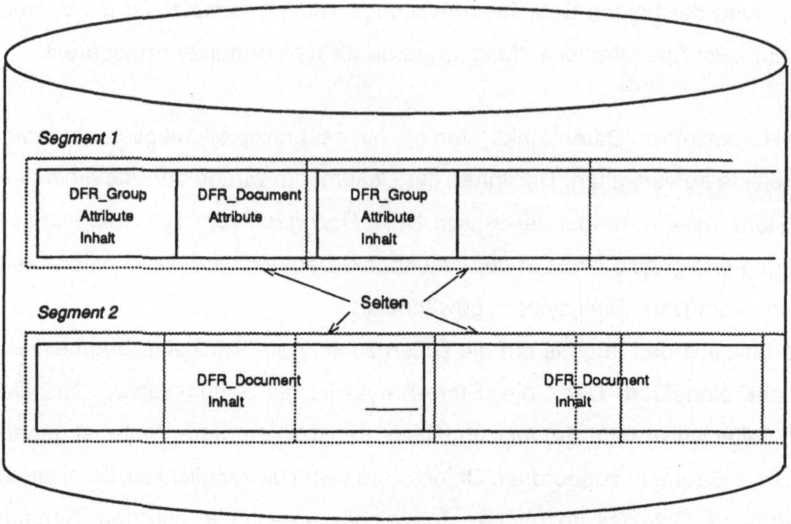

Abbildung 4.1: Segmentierung der Datenbank unter ObjectStore

4.3. Zugriff auf die Objekte im Dokumentenspeicher

Auf die Objekte im Dokumentenspeicher wird mittels der DFR-Operationen im wesentlichen auf zwei verschiedene Arten zugegriffen. Die erste erfolgt bezüglich der hierarchischen Struktur der Objekte im Dokumentenspeicher. Sie wird in diesem Abschnitt beschrieben. Die Erläuterung der zweiten Möglichkeit, der Suche nach Objekten abhängig von einer bestimmten Attributbelegung (DFR-Suchoperation), folgt im nächsten Abschnitt.

Bei allen Operationen zum Erzeugen, Lesen, Auflisten, Ändern, Löschen, Verschieben oder Kopieren der Objekte müssen ein oder mehrere Objekte bzw. deren Eltern-Objekte identifiziert werden. Objekte können, wie bereits beschrieben, über Ihren Unique Permanent Identifier, die Angabe eines absoluten oder eines relativen Pfadnamens identifiziert werden. Daß die Titel der Objekte nicht eindeutig sein müssen, erschwert die Suche nach einem durch einen Pfadnamen identifizierten Objekt. Außerdem ist bei einigen Operationen für eine Gruppe nicht nur die Gruppe selbst, sondern der gesamte von ihr aufgespannte Teilbaum betroffen. Die folgende Abbildung veranschaulicht dies am Verschieben einer Gruppe. Hier müssen die Pfadnamen aller betroffenen Objekte aktualisiert werden.

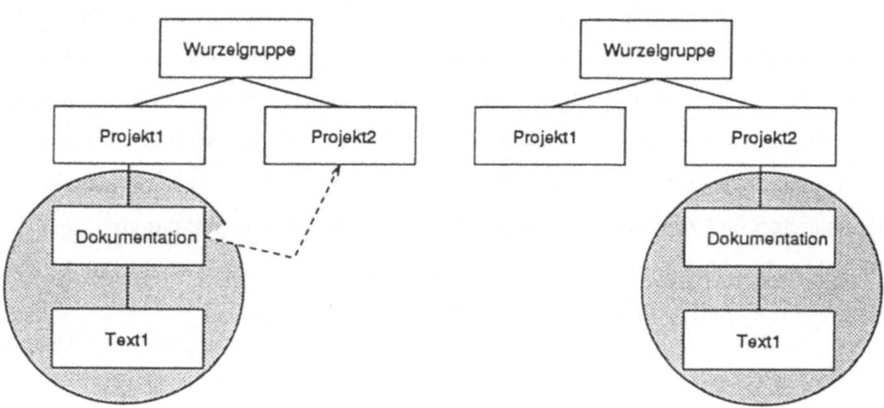

Abbildung 4.2: Verschieben einer Gruppe

Diese Art des Zugriffs erfordert also möglichst effiziente Algorithmen und Zugriffsarten entlang der hierarchischen Struktur der Objekte im Dokumentenspeicher. Sie ist deshalb eng mit der Abbildung dieser Struktur in den einzelnen Realisierungen verbunden.

Die Dateisystem-Implementierung verwaltet die hierarchische Struktur in der bereits beschriebenen Baumstruktur. Der Zugriff auf ein Objekt über seinen UPI ist über eine Tiefensuche im Baum realisiert. Die Implementierung einer effizienteren Variante (Hash-Tabelle) ist geplant. Der Zugriff über den absoluten Pfadnamen wird über eine schrittweise Suche des jeweiligen Titels in der aktuellen Hierarchieebene realisiert. Dabei wird jeweils nur der erste Weg verfolgt, d.h., der Dokumentenspeicher befolgt das Prinzip der "Local Unambiguity", also der Eindeutigkeit des Titels in der Elterngruppe.

Für einen relativen Pfadnamen kann eine Kombination der beiden Verfahren verwendet werden.

Im relationalen Datenbankmodell wird die hierarchische Struktur dadurch abgebildet, daß jede Objektrelation den Unique Permanent Identifier ihrer Eltern-Gruppe als Fremdschlüssel enthält. Außerdem wird der Pfadname jedes Objektes als Attribut mit in der Datenbank gespeichert.

Wird der Identifier des Objektes angegeben, so erfolgt die Suche innerhalb der Relation *DFR-Objekt*. Sie wird durch einen Index auf dem Attribut, das den UPI enthält, unterstützt. Bei der Verwendung eines Pfadnamens hingegen, muß gegen jede Objekttyp-Relation eine SQL-Abfrage mit einem Vergleich des angegebenen Pfadnamens mit dem Pfadnamen des Objektes gestartet werden. Dies führt im ungünstigsten Fall zu einer zeitaufwendigen Suche durch alle Relationen.

Die direkten Nachfolger einer Gruppe können durch eine SELECT-Anweisung innerhalb der Relation *DFR-Objekt* gefunden werden.

In objektorientierten Datenbanksystem ObjectStore können Beziehungen zwischen Objekten mit direkten physischen Verweisen verwaltet werden. Um die hierarchische Struktur des Dokumentenspeichers abzubilden, wird eine *(1,m)- Relationship* zwischen den Instanzen der Klasse *DFR_Group* und allen Instanzen von Subklassen der abstrakten Basisklasse *DFR_Object* verwendet. D.h., von einem Gruppen-Objekt existieren direkte Verweise auf alle Objekte, die Mitglied dieser Gruppe sind. Außerdem existiert für jedes Objekt ein direkter Verweis auf sein Eltern-Objekt.

ObjectStore ermöglicht den Zugriff auf die Daten, wie bereits erwähnt, sowohl navigierend, entlang der physisch definierten Beziehungen, als auch deskriptiv mittels Queries. Bei der Identifizierung eines Objektes durch einen Unique Permanent Identifier wird eine Query über den Extent der Klasse *DFR_Object* gestartet. Diese Query wird durch einen Hash-Index auf dem Attribut, das die Identifier enthält, unterstützt. Bei der Verwendung eines Pfadnamens wird dieser sukzessive abgearbeitet. Es wird entlang der Relationship zwischen Gruppen und Objekten traversiert. Innerhalb der Gruppen wird mit einer Query gearbeitet, die durch einen B-Baum-Index auf den Titeln aller Gruppenmitglieder unterstützt wird. Diese Kombination der Zugriffsmöglichkeiten minimiert die Zahl der 'angefaßten' Objekte und erscheint deshalb sehr effizient.

Auf die Nachfolger einer Gruppe kann sehr schnell entlang der Relationship zwischen Gruppen und Objekten zugegriffen werden.

Für den beschriebenen Zugriff entlang der hierarchischen Struktur des Dokumentenspeichers erweist sich die Möglichkeit des navigierenden Zugriffs innerhalb objektorientierter Datenbanken als sehr vorteilhaft.

4.4. Implementierung der DFR-Suchoperation

Die im Kapitel 2 beschrieben definierte Suchfunktion erlaubt die Angabe komplexer Suchkriterien.

Im folgenden Beispiel soll nach

- allen Dokumenten mit dem Titel "Beschreibung" und

- allen Gruppen, die mehr als 1 Mitglied haben, gesucht werden.

Der Filter lautet also:

((DFR-Object-Class = DFR-Document) AND (DFR-Title = "Beschreibung")) OR

((DFR-Object-Class = DFR-Group) AND (DFR-Number-Of-Group-Members > 1))

Die Suche soll in 2 Suchräumen erfolgen:

- innerhalb der Gruppe *Projekt2* mit der Suchtiefe 3

- innerhalb der Gruppe *TexteMüller* mit der Suchtiefe 2

Außerdem sollen gefundene Referenzen dereferenziert werden.

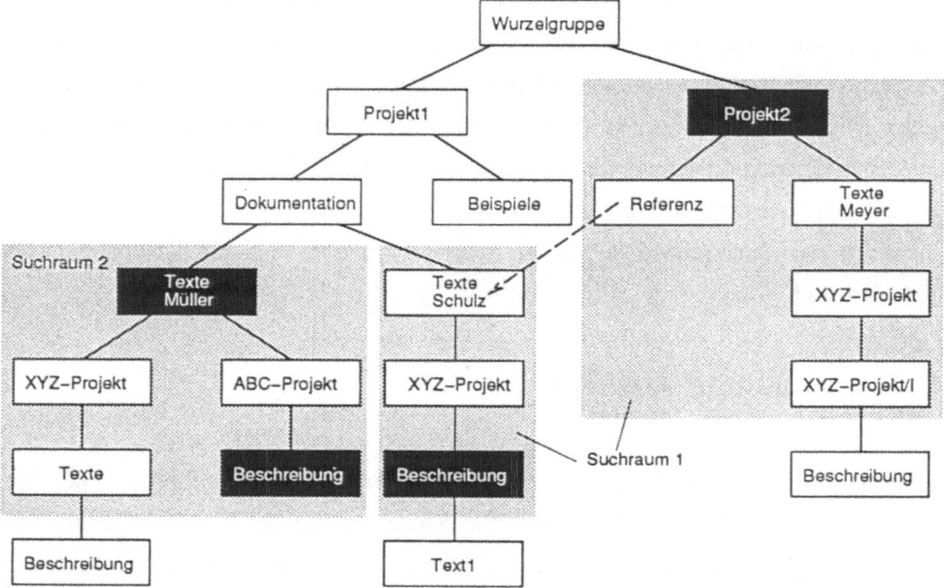

Abbildung 4.3: Beispiel für eine Suche

Die dunkel markierten Objekte bilden die Ergebnismenge dieser Suche.

Um in der Dateisystem-Implementierung zu überprüfen, ob ein Objekt einer Suchbedingung genügt, muß die Attribut-Datei eingelesen und mit dem Filter verglichen werden, und zwar für jedes Objekt des sich durch den Suchbereich ergebenden Teilbaums. Dazu muß jede Attribut-Datei geöffnet, eingelesen und wieder geschlossen werden. Außerdem muß eine Art 'Query-Processor' selbst geschrieben werden. Dies wird bei einer Datenbank-basierten Lösung z.T. vom Datenbanksystem übernommen.

Die relationale Suche wird in zwei Schritten durchgeführt. Zuerst werden alle Gruppen, in denen gesucht werden soll, bestimmt. Dazu müssen für jeden Suchraum alle Nachfolger bis zur angegebenen Tiefe ermittelt werden. Danach wird aus dem Filter ein dynamisches SELECT-Statement aufgebaut. Dieses muß für jede der vier Objekttyp-Relationen ausgeführt werden. Dabei müssen, bedingt durch die Aufsplittung der Objekte in mehrere Relationen, viele JOIN-Operationen ausgeführt werden (entweder im Datenbanksystem oder in der Anwendung 'on top').

In der ObjectStore-Implementierung wird in jedem Suchraum über die Objekte bis zur angegebenen Tiefe traversiert und die Attributbelegung mit dem gesamten Filter verglichen. Eine andere Variante wäre, die Filteratome einzeln abzuarbeiten und für jedes Filteratom eine Query zu stellen. Danach müßten die Ergebnismengen mit den logischen Operatoren verknüpfen werden. Dabei könnte die Suche teilweise mit Indizes beschleunigt werden. Die erste Variante hat aber den Vorteil, daß jedes Objekt innerhalb des Suchraumes nur genau einmal 'angefaßt' wird. Sie ist deshalb hier implementiert.

5. Resümee und Ausblick

Mit allen drei vorgestellten Realisierungsvarianten konnte die volle Funktionalität des DFR-Standards implementiert werden. Die Probleme bei der Implementierung der Datenhaltungskomponente mit einem Dateisystem (fehlende Mechanismen zur Konsistenzkontrolle, für Fehlerbehandlung, Recovery etc.) werden durch die Verwendung von Datenbanksystemen gelöst. Für eine Abbildung des Informations-modells des DFR-Standards erwies sich das Datenmodell des objektorientierter Datenbanksystems ObjectStore als sehr geeignet. Insbesondere die Möglichkeit der

Modellierung komplexer Objekte und die Mechanismen der Vererbung unterstützen und vereinfachen die Implementierung der Datenhaltungskomponente. Die Schwächen von ObjectStore in der Formulierung von Ad-hoc-Queries spielen für diese Anwendung keine Rolle, denn der DFR-Benutzer 'darf' auf die Datenbank nicht direkt, sondern nur über einen DFR-Client mit seinen definierten Operationen zugreifen.

Um die verschiedenen Varianten noch genauer miteinander vergleichen zu können, sollen im nächsten Schritt Performancemessungen durchgeführt werden. Dabei müssen z.B. verschiedene Größen der Dokumentenspeicher, sowie unterschiedliche Zugriffsprofile berücksichtigt werden. So werden auf ein Hauptarchiv hauptsächlich Lese- und Suchoperationen angewendet, während bei einer Gruppenablage Änderungen nach dem Editieren von Dokumenten und das Anlegen neuer Akten im Vordergrund stehen.

Die bisherigen Realisierungen der Datenhaltungskomponente setzen auf einem Dateisystem oder einem Datenbanksystem auf. Die gesamte DFR-Funktionalität der Datenhaltungskomponente wurde selbst implementiert. Eine andere Möglichkeit wäre, auf kommerziell verfügbaren Ablage- und Archivierungsprodukten aufzusetzen. Dann wird die Realisierung der Mapper-Komponente von Abbildung 3.1. entsprechend einfacher, da diese Systeme bereits eine Verwaltung von Attributen und Dokumenteninhalten anbieten. Die DFR-Operationen müssen also nur noch auf die angebotenen Funktionen abgebildet werden. Dies wurde bereits am Beispiel von IBM Image Plus MVS/ESA erfolgreich durchgeführt. Image Plus verwaltet intern die Attribute mit einer Datenbank (DB2) und die Inhalte mit dem 'Object Distribution Manager'. Diese Zweiteilung wird jedoch unter übergreifenden Funktionen verborgen. Allerdings werden von Image Plus nur DFR-Gruppen und DFR-Dokumente, sowie eine kleine vordefinierte Teilmenge der DFR-Attribute unterstützt. Mögliche Einschränkungen des DFR-Modells sind eine genereller Nachteil bei der Abbildung auf vorhandene Produkte. Diese eingeschränkte Funktionalität ist durch verschiedene Anwendungsanforderungen begründet, welche sich in der Standardisierung durch unterschiedliche Profil-Standards widerspiegeln. Für den DFR-Standard ist eine Taxonomie für DFR-Profile entsprechend den Anwendungsklassen entwickelt worden [DFR94].

Andere Erweiterungen des Systems betreffen die Einführung multimedialer Daten mit Audio- und Videoströmen, bei denen die Zeitabhängigkeit der Daten eine zusätzliche Komplexität darstellt. Dies betrifft nicht nur die Kommunikationskomponente [RP93], sondern auch die Datenhaltungskomponente [RDMP94].

Literatur

[CSL+90] M. Carey, E. Shekita, G. Lapis, B. Lindsay, J. McPherson: *An Incremental Join Attachment for Starburst.* In D. McLeod, R. Sacks-Davis, H. Schek (Editors): *16th International Conference on Very Large Data Bases*, 1990

[CY91a] P. Coad, E. Yourdon: *Object-Oriented Analysis*, Prentice-Hall, 1991

[CY91b] P. Coad, E. Yourdon: *Object-Oriented Design*, Prentice-Hall, 1991

[DOAM91] ISO/IEC International Standard 10031: *Information Technology - Text and Office Systems-Distributed Office Applications Model (DOAM)*, 1991

[DFR91] ISO/IEC : International Standard 10166: *Information Technology - Text and Office Systems - Document Filing and Retrieval (DFR)*, 1991

[DFR94] EWOS: DFR ISP Taxonomy: *European Workshop for Open Systems*, July 1994, EWOS/EG SMMI 94/147

[DPSW92] U. Deppisch, B. Paul, H.-J. Schek, G. Weikum, *Managing Complex Objects in the Darmstadt Database Kernel System.* In K. R. Dittrich, U.Dayal, A. P. Buchmann (Eds.): *On Object-Oriented Database Systems*, Springer-Verlag, 1992, Seiten 357-375

[Heu92] A. Heuer: *Objektorientierte Datenbanken. Konzepte, Modelle, Systeme*, Addison-Wesley-Verlag, 1992

[Jan93] H. Jander: *Zugriff auf multimediale Dokumentenablagen in heterogenen Bürosystemen*, Diplomarbeit, Universität Kaiserslautern und IBM European Networking Center, 1993

[KD93] U. Keßler und P. Dadam: *Benutzergesteuerte, flexible Speicherungsstrukturen für komplexe Objekte.* In W. Stucky, A. Oberweis (Herausgeber): *Datenbanksysteme in Büro, Technik und Wissenschaft*, Springer-Verlag, 1993, Seiten 206-225.

[KMM93] R. Käckenhoff, D. Mertens, K. Meyer-Wegener: *Eine vergleichende Untersuchung der Speicherungsformen für multimediale Datenobjekte.* In W. Stucky, A. Oberweis (Herausgeber): *Datenbanksysteme in Büro, Technik und Wissenschaft*, Springer-Verlag, 1993, Seiten 164-180.

[LLOW91] C. Lamb, G. Landis, J. Orenstein, D. Weinreb: *The ObjectStore Database System*, *Communications of the ACM*, 34(10), 1991, Seiten 50-63

[ODA89] ISO/IEC 8613 International Standard: *Information Processing - Text and Office Systems - Office Document Architecture (ODA) and Interchange Format*, 1989

[RP93] J. Rückert, B. Paul, *Integration Multimedia into the Distributed Office Applications Environment.* In W. Stucky, A. Oberweis (Herausgeber): *Datenbanksysteme in Büro, Technik und Wissenschaft*, Springer-Verlag, 1993, Seiten 181-188.

[RDMP94] T. Rakow, P. Dettling, F. Moser, B. Paul: *Development of a Multimedia Archiving Teleservice using the DFR-Standard.* Workshop on Advanced Teleservices and High Speed Communication Architectures, Heidelberg, September 1994

[Stö94] U. Störl: *Dokumentenverwaltung mit einem objektorientierten Datenbanksystem*, Diplomarbeit, Friedrich-Schiller-Universität Jena und IBM Wissenschaftliches Zentrum Heidelberg, 1994

Transformation relationaler Datenbank-Schemas in objekt-orientierte Schemas gemäß ODMG-93*

Christian Fahrner   Gottfried Vossen

Institut für Wirtschaftsinformatik
Universität Münster
Grevenerstr. 91, 48159 Münster
{fahrner, vossen}@uni-muenster.de

Abstract

In vielen Datenbank-Anwendungen stellt sich heute das Problem der Migration von relationalen auf objekt-orientierte Systeme. Zentral hierbei ist eine Schema-Konvertierung, welche bisher in weitgehender Abhängigkeit von dem gegebenen objekt-orientierten System vorgenommen werden muß. Durch den ODMG-93-Vorschlag wurde ein Rahmen geschaffen, in welchem die zentralen Aspekte eines objekt-orientierten Schemas präzisierbar sind, so daß sich eine (system-unabhängige) Konvertierung jetzt auf dieses Modell beziehen kann. In dieser Arbeit wird eine Vorgehensweise beschrieben, relationale Schemas in objekt-orientierte gemäß ODMG-93 zu transformieren. Damit wird es möglich, die Aufgabe des *Reverse Engineering* relationaler Datenbanken rechnerunterstützt durchzuführen und die Lösung von Migrationsaufgaben zu automatisieren.

1   Einführung

In vielen Datenbank-Anwendungen stellt sich heute das Problem der Migration von relationalen auf objekt-orientierte Systeme. Aus der Sicht des Datenbankentwurfs ist hierbei insbesondere eine Schema-Konvertierung vorzunehmen, was bisher in weitgehender Abhängigkeit vom Ziel-System durchgeführt werden muß, da objekt-orientierte Datenbanksysteme (OODBS) keine Einheitlichkeit hinsichtlich des verwendeten Objektmodells zeigen. Durch den ODMG-93-Vorschlag [8] wurde inzwischen ein sprachlicher Rahmen geschaffen, in welchem die zentralen Aspekte eines objekt-orientierten Schemas präzisierbar sind, so daß sich eine (system-unabhängige) Konvertierung jetzt auf dieses Modell beziehen kann. Wir beschreiben in dieser Arbeit eine Vorgehensweise, mit welcher relationale Schemas in objekt-orientierte gemäß ODMG-93 transformiert werden können.

OODBS erlauben im Vergleich zu traditionellen Datenbanksystemen unter anderem eine im Hinblick auf die gegebenen Anwendung angemessenere Modellierung von Objekten, Beziehungen oder komplexen Strukturen; schon aus diesem Grund werden sie für kommerzielle Anwendungen zunehmend interessanter. In dem Fall, daß eine OODB quasi "from

---

*Diese Arbeit wurde von der Deutschen Forschungsgemeinschaft unterstützt (Sachbeihilfe Vo 426/7-1).

scratch" eingerichtet wird, kann man sich beim Entwurf existierender Techniken bedienen, welche z.B. auf dem Entity-Relationship-Modell (ER-Modell) basieren [4, 11, 14, 24, 27] und möglicherweise auch OOA- und OOD-Techniken integrieren, insbesondere aber von den Ausdrucksmöglichkeiten des betreffenden Objektmodells vollen Gebrauch machen. Falls jedoch eine Datenbank bereits existiert, stellt sich die Aufgabe der Konvertierung des Schemas dieser Datenbank in ein Schema des OODBS. (Es stellt sich natürlich auch die Aufgabe der Konvertierung des *Inhalts* dieser Datenbank, was jedoch im Vergleich zu einer Schemakonvertierung einfacher ist und daher hier nicht betrachtet wird.) Die Lösung dieser Aufgabe war bisher system-abhängig, kann jedoch unter Verwendung des Standardisierungsvorschlags ODMG-93 ohne Bezugnahme auf das Objektmodell eines konkreten Systems angegangen werden. Da der ODMG-Standard in gewissem Sinne die kleinste Menge von Modellierungskonzepten beschreibt, welche von einem OODBS unterstützt werden soll, wird es möglich, eine Transformation in diese minimale Menge von Konstrukten zu beschreiben, welche dann "leicht" in die spezifischen Konstrukte eines speziellen OODBS übertragen werden können.

Bereits in vergleichbaren Ansätzen wird deutlich, daß ein zentrales Problem einer relationalen Konvertierung in der "Qualität" des gegebenen relationalen Schemas liegt. Wenngleich dessen Strukturen in Form von Relationenschemas festliegen, ist keineswegs stets sichergestellt, daß der Designer dieses Schemas sämtliche Integritätsbedingungen, welche nicht bereits durch die Strukturen gegeben sind, auch explizit in die Schemadeklaration aufgenommen hat. Zusätzlich können die Elemente eines relationalen Schemas unterschiedliche Interpretationen in bezug auf die zugrundeliegende Anwendung besitzen; es ist z.B. oft schwierig zu unterscheiden, welche Relationenschemas Objekte mit ihren Eigenschaften darstellen und welche Beziehungen (Relationships) zwischen diesen repräsentieren. Daher wird in der Praxis häufig der Umweg über eine ER-Darstellung eines gegebenen relationalen Schemas beschritten, aus welcher dann eine OO-Darstellung gewonnen wird. Als Beispiel für einen solchen Ansatz zum relationalen Reverse Engineering sei hier [25] erwähnt, bei welchem zunächst Primärschlüssel und daraus erkennbare Fremdschlüsselbeziehungen analysiert werden; das Zielmodell ist ein erweitertes ER-Modell mit Generalisierungsstrukturen. Schlüsselkandidaten werden jedoch nicht in vollem Umfang in die Übersetzung einbezogen, und Fremdschlüsselbeziehungen werden lediglich anhand der Namenssemantik erkannt. Ferner werden gegebene Integritätsbedingungen wie z.B. Inklusionsabhängigkeiten bei der Transformation nicht berücksichtigt; der Benutzer muß bei der Erkennung von Generalisierungshierarchien sein Wissen einbringen. Wesentlich erscheint aus unserer Sicht, daß an das relationale Ausgangsschema zwar hohe Anforderungen gestellt werden, wie z.B. die Kenntnis aller Schlüssel, eine eindeutige Attributbenennung und eine 3NF-Normalisierung; andererseits werden jedoch nicht alle diese Informationen ausgewertet, es wird nichts über die Qualität eines relationalen Schema ausgesagt und es wird nicht berücksichtigt, ob Teile des relationalen Schemas einer Optimierung unterzogen wurden (wie z.B. Denormalisierung, horizontale oder vertikale Dekomposition).

In [9, 10] wird eine Instanz des gegebenen Ausgangsschemas betrachtet und versucht, aus dieser die für eine Transformation relevante Information zu extrahieren. Allerdings werden auch hier lediglich schlüsselbasierte Inklusionsbedingungen identifiziert; die Tatsache, daß relationale Strukturen optimiert oder schlecht entworfen sein könnten, wird ebenfalls vernachlässigt. Dies ist anders in [26], deren Ansatz zumindest ansatzweise Optimierungsstrukturen identifiziert. Weitere Ansätze für das Reverse Engineering, die sich rein auf die Auswertung von Inklusionsbedingungen beziehen, sind z.B. [18, 23, 22]; eine Übersicht findet man in [12].

Für die in dieser Arbeit beschriebene Vorgehensweise sind zwei Entwurfsentscheidungen wesentlich: Einerseits wollen wir *direkt* vom relationalen Modell in das ODMG-Modell transformieren, also ohne Rückgriff auf ein Zwischenmodell; andererseits wollen wir an das relationale Ausgangsschema so wenig Anforderungen wie möglich stellen. Wir gehen also grundsätzlich von einem etwa in SQL beschriebenen Schema mit Tabellenstrukturen und eventuell gegebenen Integritätsbedingungen auf diesen aus. Das Zielmodell der Transformation besteht demgegenüber aus Klassen, deren Attribute komplex strukturiert sein und andere Klassen referenzieren können; außerdem können Klassen in einer Vererbungshierarchie angeordnet sein. Das ODMG-93-Modell folgt im wesentlichen dieser allgemeinen Sicht, wobei klassenwertige Attribute als Relationships bezeichnet werden.

Falls der Designer des relationalen Datenbankschemas dessen Semantik so explizit wie möglich gemacht hat, d.h. falls alle für die Transformation nötigen Integritätsbedingungen im Schema deklariert sind und das Schema angemessen annotiert ist (vgl. Abbildung 3), kann eine Transformation nach ODMG-93 in fast kanonischer Weise erfolgen. Allerdings muß der Tatsache Rechnung getragen werden, daß objekt-orientierte Datenmodelle (etwa durch die Orthogonalität von Konstruktoren und Basistypen) reichere Ausdrucksmöglichkeiten besitzen, so daß sowohl auf struktureller als auch semantischer Ebene bei einem Übergang von einem relationalen zu einem objekt-orientierten Schema Information hinzugewonnen werden muß; man muß also darauf gefaßt sein, den Transformationsinput zunächst (strukturell und semantisch) zu vervollständigen. Um dies zu bewerkstelligen, studieren wir zunächst die umgekehrte Transformationsrichtung, d.h. die Darstellung eines objekt-orientierten Schemas durch ein relationales, wie sie z.B. in [16, 17, 28] beschrieben wird. Hieraus ergeben sich wichtige Rückschlüsse auf Eigenschaften des betreffenden relationalen Schemas, welche auch für eine Transformation der hier intendierten Form relevant sind.

Die hier vorgeschlagene Transformationstechnik hat daher einen dreiteiligen Aufbau: In einem ersten Schritt, welcher sich sogar als der wesentliche herausstellen wird, wird ein gegebenes relationales Schema analysiert und für eine Transformation in spezifischer Weise vorbereitet (vervollständigt). Sodann wird in einem zweiten Schritt kanonisch transformiert; insbesondere werden Klassenstrukturen und -zusammenhänge aus dem relationalen Schema abgeleitet. In einem dritten Schritt wird das Ergebnis weiter verfeinert, so daß die spezifischen Möglichkeiten des objekt-orientierten Zielmodells ausgenutzt werden. Das sich am Ende ergebende ODMG-Schema kann sodann leicht in die Modelle konkreter OODBS transformiert werden.

In Abschnitt 2 stellen wir für das weitere Vorgehen relevante Vorüberlegungen an und führen einige Begriffe ein, welche im Kontext der Transformation verwendet werden. In Abschnitt 3 beschreiben wir den ersten Schritt unseres Transformationsverfahren, die Vervollständigung eines gegebenen relationalen Schemas; in Abschnitt 4 werden die beiden nachfolgenden Transformationsschritte beschrieben. Abschnitt 5 enthält eine Zusammenfassung sowie einen Ausblick auf weitere Arbeiten.

2 Vorüberlegungen

2.1 Relationale Darstellung objekt-orientierter Schemas

In einem relationalen Schema kann man strukturell nicht zwischen Objekten und Beziehungen unterscheiden; für ein objekt-orientiertes Schema ist eine solche Unterscheidung jedoch wesentlich. Hinweise darauf, wie eine solche Unterscheidung auf relationaler Ebene herstellbar ist, entnehmen wir einer Analyse der in [17, 28] beschriebenen umgekehrten Transformation. Zur Vereinfachung der Beschreibung nehmen wir im folgenden an, daß alle Literale atomar oder nur durch einmalige Anwendung des Set-Konstruktors gebildet sind (d.h. wir beschränken uns auf die Betrachtung ein- oder mehrwertiger Attribute mit ansonsten atomarem Wertebereich). Dies stellt keine Einschränkung dar, da ein OODB-Schema durch Anwendung einer geeigneten Entnestung und damit verbundener Erzeugung von Klassen und Relationships stets in eine solche Form gebracht werden kann. Ein gegebenes objekt-orientiertes Schema wird dann wie folgt in ein relationales transformiert: Jede Klasse wird durch eine unäre Relation zur Aufnahme der dieser Klasse zugeordneten Objekt-Identifikatoren (OIDs) sowie durch binäre Relationen (je eine pro Attribut) dargestellt. Funktionale Abhängigkeiten bringen Einwertigkeit zum Ausdruck; durch Inklusionsabhängigkeiten wird der Zusammenhang zwischen den Relationen für eine Klasse hergestellt. Weitere Inklusionen zwischen unären Relationen bringen Spezialisierungen (ISA-Beziehungen) zum Ausdruck; Exklusionsabhängigkeiten werden dazu verwendet auszudrücken, daß Subklassen einer Klasse disjunkt oder Klassen bzgl. Vererbung unvergleichbar sind.

Wir erweitern diese Transformation auf die in ODMG-93 vorkommenden Relationships [8] wie folgt: Relationships ohne Inverse werden wie Attribute transformiert, mit der Ausnahme, daß eine zusätzliche Inklusionsbedingung den Zusammenhang zur Wertebereichsklasse herstellt. Falls zu einem Relationship ein inverses existiert, so werden beide zusammen als eine Relation repräsentiert. Da zwischen zwei Klassen mehrere Relationships definiert sein können, muß hierbei auf die Namensgebung geachtet werden, so daß verschiedene Fälle zu unterscheiden sind (Einzelheiten entnehme man [13]).

Ein auf diese Weise gewonnenes Schema besteht lediglich aus unären und binären Relationenschemas und ist daher keineswegs optimal; man kann z.B. unter Verwendung des Synthese-Algorithmus [3, 21, 29, 30] Schemas geeignet zusammensetzen; unter bestimmten Voraussetzungen [13] ist das so gewonnene Ergebnis sogar in 5NF. Durch eine Synthese werden insbesondere elementare Eigenschaften einer Objektklasse sowie einwertige Beziehungen wieder zu einer Relation zusammengefaßt. Jede dieser *Objekt-Relationen* hat ein OID-Attribut als Schlüssel. Mengenwertige Eigenschaften und ein Teil der mengenwertigen Beziehungen einer Klasse sind als eigene Relationen repräsentiert, die im folgenden *Beziehungsrelationen* genannt werden. Die Beziehungen zwischen den einzelnen Relationen sind durch Inklusionen und Exklusionen gegeben, wobei eine Inklusionsbedingung mit Schlüsseln auf der linken und rechten Seite sowohl eine Komponentenbeziehung als auch eine Vererbungsbeziehung darstellen kann. Es sei bemerkt, daß die in einem ODMG-Schema enthaltenen expliziten Schlüsseldefinitionen auch Relationships involvieren können. Im relationalen Schema sind dann unter Umständen interrelationale Abhängigkeiten erforderlich, worauf wir hier nicht näher eingehen.

Über das Ergebnis einer solchen Transformation lassen sich folgende Aussagen machen:

- Es gibt *Objektrelationen*, welche die Eigenschaften genau einer Objektklasse beschreiben, sowie *Beziehungsrelationen*, welche Beziehungen zwischen Objekten oder mengenwertige Attribute beschreiben.

- Alle Beziehungen sind durch schlüsselbasierte Inklusionsbedingungen charakterisiert, und zwar vollständig, d.h. es existiert keine Beziehung, die nicht durch eine Inklusionsbedingung charakterisiert ist.

- Vererbungsbeziehungen sind durch Inklusionsbedingungen mit Schlüsseln auf der linken und rechten Seite und zusätzlich durch Exklusionsbedingungen charakterisiert, aber nicht jede solche Inklusionsbedingung beschreibt eine ISA-Beziehung.

- Objekte im relationalen Schema können durch künstliche Schlüssel repräsentiert sein, die keine beschreibende Eigenschaft haben und im OODB-Schema weggelassen werden können.

Wesentlich ist nun die Beobachtung, daß ein derartig strukturiertes relationales Schema in kanonischer Weise wieder rücktransformiert werden kann: Objektrelationen werden zu Klassen, Beziehungsrelationen zu Relationships oder genesteten Attributstrukturen. Mögliche ISA-Beziehungen sind durch Inklusionsbedingungen mit einem Schlüssel auf der linken und rechten Seite gegeben.

Wir wollen diese Beobachtung für die im weiteren beschriebene Vorgehensweise ausnutzen; die eigentliche Transformation wird also vergleichsweise einfach unter der in Abschnitt 1 bereits erwähnten Voraussetzung, daß das gegebene relationale Schema gewissen Anforderungen genügt. Darüber hinaus wird man das Ergebnis einer kanonischen Transformation im allgemeinen noch einer Restrukturierung unterziehen; dies beinhält z.B. eine Identifikation und Eliminierung von künstlichen Schlüsseln, eine Identifizierung von genesteten Strukturen oder eine Unterscheidung von Objekten und Werten. Die Transformation eines relationalen Schemas in ein objekt-orientiertes Schema wird daher in den Abschnitten 3 und 4 als ein dreistufiger Prozeß beschrieben, der folgende Schritte umfaßt:

1. **Relationale Vervollständigung**: Objekte und Beziehungen zwischen Objekten werden identifiziert und über Inklusions- und Exklusionsbedingungen explizit gemacht.

2. **Kanonische Übersetzung**: Die identifizierten Strukturen werden in Strukturen des OODB-Modells übertragen.

3. **Objekt-orientiertes Redesign**: Das erhaltene Ergebnisschema wird anhand objekt-orientierter Gesichtspunkte restrukturiert.

Zur relationalen Analyse werden dabei Begriffe benötigt, welche wir als nächstes bereitstellen.

2.2   Beziehungsattribute und vollständige Schemas

Zur Beschreibung des relationalen Modells verwenden wir im wesentlichen die Notationen aus [29]. Ein relationales Datenbankschema D ist ein Paar (R, Δ), wobei R eine endliche Menge von Relationenschemas R_i, $1 \le i \le n$, und Δ eine Menge von Inklusions- (*Inclusion Dependencies*, kurz INDs) und Exklusionsabhängigkeiten (*Exclusion Dependencies*, kurz EXDs) ist. Jedes Relationenschema R_i umfaßt eine Attributmenge X_i und eine Menge Σ_i von intrarelationalen Integritätsbedingungen, wobei wir funktionale Abhängigkeiten (*Functional Dependencies*, kurz FDs) und NOT NULL-Bedingungen (NNs) zulassen; U bezeichne die Menge aller Attribute eines Schemas D. Abbildung 1 zeigt ein Beispiel eines

Student (MatNr, Person#, Name, PLZ, Ort, Straße, Betreuer)
Professor (ProfNr, P#, Name, Spezialgebiet)
Institut (I#, Name, Leiter#, seit)
Fach (Fach#, Name)
Ort (Raum#)
Projekt-Antrag (Antragsteller, Projekt#, Version, Datum)
Laufende-Projekte (Pro#, Budget)
Vorlesung (F#, Dozent, Ort, Institut, Datum)
hört (MatNr, Fach#, Dozent, Ort, Institut)

Abbildung 1: Beispielschema für eine relationale Datenbank.

relationalen Schemas für eine Universitätsdatenbank, wobei wir uns zunächst auf die Angabe der Namen der Relationenschemas und deren Attribute beschränken. Wir werden dieses Beispiel im folgenden zur Illustration der einzelnen Schritte unseres Transformationsverfahrens verwenden.

Die grundlegende Idee der relationalen Analyse ist, daß zwei Relationen nur dann miteinander in Beziehung stehen können, wenn sie gemeinsame Attribute mit der gleichen Bedeutung haben. Einer der wichtigsten Schritte der Analyse ist daher die Identifikation von Synonymen und Homonymen. Wir fassen dies formal über den im folgenden eingeführten Begriff des Beziehungsattributs:

Sei $D = (R, \Delta)$ ein relationales Datenbankschema. $A \in U$ heißt *äquivalent* zu $B \in U$, falls A und B Synonyme sind oder die gleiche Bedeutung haben. U ist damit darstellbar als disjunkte Vereinigung der Klassen äquivalenter Attribute; wir bezeichnen diese mit $\kappa_1, \ldots, \kappa_r$. Ein Attribut A heißt dann *Beziehungsattribut* (BZA), falls es eine Klasse κ_i gibt mit $|\kappa_i| \geq 2$ und $A \in \kappa_i$. Im folgenden bezeichne BZA(D) [BZA(R_i)] die Menge aller BZAs eines gegebenen Datenbankschemas D [Relationenschemas R_i]; weiter bezeichne κ_A die Äquivalenzklasse des Attributs A. Ein Attribut A heißt *lokales Attribut* (LKA), falls $A \notin$ BZA(D) gilt. Man beachte, daß durch die Einteilung der Attribute in Äquivalenzklassen eine Umbenennung der Attribute unnötig ist und die Namenssemantik der Attribute erhalten bleibt.

Ein Attribut hat also neben einem Namen und einem Domain jetzt auch eine Äquivalenzklassenzugehörigkeit, welche wir gelegentlich auch als den "Typ" dieses Attributs bezeichnen. Zwei Relationen, die Beziehungsattribute desselben Typs besitzen, stehen direkt oder indirekt miteinander in Beziehung. Beziehungen werden durch Inklusionsbedingungen charakterisiert. Ein Beziehungsattribut heißt dabei *gebunden*, falls es auf der linken oder rechten Seite einer IND vorkommt, und *ungebunden* sonst. Damit läßt sich als nächstes ein Vollständigkeitsbegriff für relationale Schemas festlegen; dieser wird während der Analyse eines relationalen Schemas insbesondere eine Abbruchsbedingung liefern. Der Vollständigkeitsbegriff erstreckt sich dabei auf zwei Teile: die strukturelle und die semantische Vollständigkeit. Ersteren betrachten wir zuerst:

Sei dazu $D = (R, \Delta)$ wie oben mit $R = (R_1, \ldots, R_n)$. Wir definieren einen knoten- und kantenmarkierten gerichteten Graphen $G(D) = (V, E, \gamma, \delta)$, den *Inklusionsgraphen* von D, wie folgt:

(i) $V = R$,

(ii) für $R_i \in V$ sei die Knotenmarkierung definiert durch
$$\gamma(R_i) := \{\kappa_A \mid A \in BZA(R_i)\},$$

(iii) $E = \{(R_i, R_j) \mid (\exists\, X, Y)\, R_i[X] \subseteq R_j[Y] \in \Delta\},$

(iv) ist $(R_i, R_j) \in E$ durch $R_i[X] \subseteq R_j[Y]$ erzeugt, so sei die Kantenmarkierung definiert durch $\delta((R_i, R_j)) := \{\kappa_A \mid A \in X\}$.

Für $Z \in \{\kappa_A \mid A \in U\}$ sei ferner $G_Z = (V_Z, E_Z, \gamma|_{V_Z}, \delta|_{E_Z})$ der Teilgraph von G mit der Knotenmenge $V_Z = \{R_i \in V \mid Z \in \gamma(R_i)\}$ und der Kantenmenge $E_Z = \{(R_i, R_j) \in E \mid Z \in \delta(R_i, R_j)\}$. Ein Schema D heißt Z-*vollständig*, falls G_Z schwach zusammenhängend ist und jedes Attribut A mit $\kappa_A = Z$ gebunden ist; D heißt *strukturell vollständig*, falls D Z-vollständig ist für alle $Z \in \{\kappa_A \mid A \in U\}$.

Strukturelle Vollständigkeit eines Datenbankschemas D verlangt also, daß je zwei Relationen, die ein Attribut der gleichen Äquivalenzklasse κ gemeinsam haben, über einen Weg von Inklusionsbedingungen in dem aus $G(D)$ (durch Ignorieren von Kantenrichtungen) ableitbaren ungerichteten Graphen verbunden sind, wobei jede Inklusionsbedingung bzw. Kante auf diesem Pfad ein Attribut A vom Typ κ beinhaltet. Bemerkt sei an dieser Stelle, daß die Betrachtung des ungerichteten Graphen ausreicht, um bzgl. Δ^+ zu entscheiden, ob ein Schema strukturell vollständig ist. Der gerichtete Graph wird dazu benutzt, sogar Aussagen über die strukturelle Vollständigkeit des Schemas bzgl. $(\Delta \cup \bigcup_{i=1}^{n} F_i)^+$ zu machen, wobei F_i die FD-Menge des Relationenschemas R_i bezeichnet.

Mit Hilfe der strukturellen Vollständigkeit kann man nun entscheiden, wann die Suche nach intra- und interrelationalen Beziehungen abgebrochen werden kann, die über INDs beschrieben werden können: Falls ein Schema nicht strukturell vollständig ist, so existieren noch nicht identifizierte Beziehungen. Allerdings ist diese Information noch nicht ausreichend für eine Transformation, da Strukturen verschiedene *Interpretationen* bzgl. der gegebenen Anwendung haben können. So kann z.B. eine IND mit einem Schlüssel auf der linken und rechten Seite sowohl eine Vererbungsbeziehung zwischen zwei Objektrelationen, eine gewöhnliche 1:1-Beziehung, eine "Link"- Beziehung zwischen einer Objektrelation und einer Beziehungsrelation, aber auch eine einfache Kardinalitätsbedingung beschreiben. Letzteres ist z.B. bei einer totalen 1:1-Beziehung möglich.

Eine rein strukturelle Analyse bzw. Vervollständigung reicht daher im allgemeinen nicht aus, sondern die Struktur muß zusätzlich interpretiert bzw. annotiert werden. Daher definieren wir als nächstes den Begriff der semantischen Vollständigkeit: Ein Schema D heißt *semantisch vollständig*, falls folgende Bedingungen erfüllt sind (vgl. Abbildung 3):

- Die Relationenschemas von D sind in Objektrelationen und Beziehungsrelationen eingeteilt, wobei Objektrelationen auch Aggregationen sein können (*Vorlesung* im laufenden Beispiel).

- Keine Inklusionsbedingung ist redundant bzgl. Δ und Inklusionsbedingungen sind klassifiziert in *ISA-INDs*, die eine ISA-Beziehung beschreiben, *K-INDs*, die eine Kardinalitätsbedingung beschreiben, *B-INDs*, die eine Beziehung beschreiben, die nicht als eigene Relation im Schema abgebildet ist, *L-INDs*, die eine Beziehungsrelation oder eine Aggregation mit einer teilnehmenden Relation verbinden, und *S-INDs*, die für die Strukturabbildung nicht relevante Informationen beschreiben.

- Alle Exklusionsbedingungen zwischen Relationenschemas, welche Subklassen einer Vererbungshierarchie repräsentieren, sind spezifiziert.

- Jede Relation repräsentiert nur eine Objekt- oder Beziehungsmenge mit der Ausnahme, daß in jeder Relation zusätzlich auch Attribute der linken Seite einer B-IND vorkommen dürfen.

Ein relationales Schema heißt dann *vollständig*, falls es strukturell und semantisch vollständig ist.

Es sei bemerkt, daß nur in dem Fall, daß das Ausgangsschema unter Verwendung spezieller Entwurfsmethoden erstellt wurde, aus der strukturellen auf die semantische Vollständigkeit geschlossen werden kann. Viele Ansätze für das Reverse Engineering [23, 9, 25] gehen daher von einer fest vorgegebenen Entwurfsmethode für das relationale Schema aus und sind damit auch automatisierbar. Allerdings liefern die resultierenden Algorithmen nur für Schemata, die genau nach dieser Entwurfsmethode erzeugt wurden, brauchbare Ergebnisse und sind daher für beliebige andere Entwurfsmethoden nicht zweckmäßig. Bei der Vervollständigung im oben beschriebenen Sinne gehen wir demgegenüber von einem relationalen Schema aus, an das keine derartigen Anforderungen gestellt werden; andererseits werden alle verfügbaren Informationen über die Struktur und die Semantik in die Transformation mit einbezogen.

Im nächsten Abschnitt werden noch die folgenden Bezeichnungen benötigt: Für ein Relationenschema R bezeichne Keys(R) die Menge aller Schlüssel von R. Eine IND der Form $R[X] \subseteq S[Y]$ heißt *schlüsselbasiert*, falls $Y \in$ Keys(S) gilt; sie heißt *invers schlüsselbasiert*, falls $X \in$ Keys(R) und $Y \notin$ Keys(S) gilt. Eine invers schlüsselbasierte Inklusionsbedingung $R[X] \subseteq S[Y]$ stellt eine Kardinalitätsbedingung dar, falls die schlüsselbasierte IND $S[Y] \subseteq R[X]$ gilt (andenfalls signalisiert sie eine Optimierungsstruktur). Zwei INDs $i : R[X] \subseteq S[Y]$ und $i' : S[Y] \subseteq R[X]$ heißen zueinander *invers* bzw. i' ist die *Inverse* zu i. Ein Schlüssel $k = \{A_1, ..., A_n\}$ eines Relationenschemas R heißt *Objektschlüssel*, falls kein anderer Schlüssel $k' = \{A'_1, ..., A'_m\}$ eines Relationenschemas S mit $m < n$ und $\{\kappa_{A_i} \mid A_i \in K\} = \{\kappa_{A'_i} \mid A'_i \in K'\}$ existiert. Andernfalls heißt K *Beziehungsschlüssel*.

3   Vervollständigung relationaler Schemas

Wie bereits erwähnt gliedert sich unser Transformationskonzept in drei Schritte; wir beschreiben in diesem Abschnitt den ersten dieser, welcher eine (strukturelle und semantische) Vervollständigung eines gegebenen relationalen Datenbankschemas zum Ziel hat.

Das relationale Ausgangsschema liegt in den wenigsten Fällen in einer Form vor, daß alle Beziehungsstrukturen direkt durch schlüsselbasierte Inklusionsbedingungen beschrieben werden können. In der Praxis sind relationale Schemata oft schlecht entworfen, unvollständig in ihrer Beschreibung oder durch Optimierungstechniken [15] zur Erhöhung der operationalen Performance so verändert, daß die Identifikation von Objekten und deren Beziehungen zueinander nur noch schwer möglich ist. Vererbungshierarchien können nicht direkt dargestellt werden; stattdessen werden sie auf unterschiedliche Weisen simuliert [26]. Dabei kann es z.B. vorkommen, daß Beziehungen zwischen Relationen, welche Spezialisierungen darstellen, nicht mehr explizit über Fremdschlüsselbeziehungen oder Exklusionsbeziehungen, sondern nur noch über Attribute vom gleichen Typ erkannt werden können.

Im folgendem sei ein relationales Datenbankschema D gegeben. Im "worst case" hat dies eine Form, wie sie in Abbildung 1 für ein Beispiel gezeigt ist, d.h. das Schema enthält weder intra- noch interrelationale Bedingungen und auch keine sonstigen Informationen; in einem solchen Fall kann lediglich durch Benutzerinteraktion [1, 6] (wie beim Datenbankentwurf) und gegebenenfalls Analyse der aktuellen Datenbankinstanz [5, 9, 19, 22] versucht werden, Abhängigkeiten, die gelten sollen, zu identifizieren. Wir unterstellen hier, daß anfänglich alle diejenigen Abhängigkeiten bekannt sind, die aus der (etwa in SQL vorliegenden) Schema-Deklaration zu entnehmen sind (wie z.B. schlüsselbasierte INDs aus Foreign-Key Constraints, falls solche existieren). Das Vorliegen einer Datenbankinstanz ermöglicht es, weitere Abhängigkeiten bzw. Kandidaten dafür [19, 5, 22] abzuleiten. Durch SQL-Anwendungsprogramme oder View-Definitionen können ebenfalls Abhängigkeiten abgeleitet werden, z.B. deutet ein Vergleich zweier Attribute in einem SQL-Statement auf eine Synonymbeziehung und gegebenenfalls auf eine Fremdschlüsselbeziehung hin.

Das Ziel einer relationalen Analyse ist die Vervollständigung des Ausgangsschemas unter Berücksichtigung aller gegebenen Informationen. Die strukturelle Vervollständigung konzentriert sich dabei auf schlüsselbasierte INDs, da diese direkt als Strukturen des objekt-orientierten Schemas gedeutet werden können. Die einzelnen Schritte der relationalen Analyse, die zum Erreichen der Vollständkeit nötig sind, werden im folgenden beschrieben.

Schritt 1: Identifikation von Homonymen und Synonymen sowie Einteilung der Attribute in Äquivalenzklassen; Identifikation von Attributgruppen (AGs, "Objekte" im Sinne von [7]).

Schritt 2: Bestimmung von FDs und Schlüsseln, die Objekte beschreiben; Kandidaten hierfür können z.B. über die Namenssemantik der Attribute sowie über die Auswertung der BZAs gewonnen werden: Falls eine Relation ein oder mehrere Beziehungsattribute besitzt, so repräsentieren diese Attribute Schlüssel- oder Fremdschlüsselattribute. Die Auswertung einer Datenbankinstanz im Stile von [5, 19, 22] kann sowohl weitere Kandidaten für Schlüssel und FDs liefern als auch Kandidaten verwerfen. Bei den FDs ist man speziell an solchen interessiert, die von BZAs ausgehen, da diese möglichen Objekten oder Beziehungen ihre Eigenschaften zuordnen. Nicht interessiert ist man hingegen an FDs, die lediglich eine numerische Abhängigkeit [23] zwischen Eigenschaften eines Objektes definieren (Schlüsselabhängigkeiten ausgenommen). Strukturelle FDs [23] werden oft über die Namenssemantik erkannt.

Für jede gegebene Relation muß am Ende dieses Schrittes mindestens ein Schlüssel bestimmt sein. Im Sinne einer "Closed World Assumption" wird im folgenden angenommen, daß weitere als die bisher bestimmten Integritätsbedingungen nicht gelten. Die Integritätsbedingungen für die Beispieldatenbank aus Abbildung 1, welche in den ersten beiden Schritten erkannt wurden, sind in Abbildung 2 gezeigt. In dieser Abbildung verwenden wir bei der Angabe von Elementen einer BZA-Äquivalenzklasse die Notation $R.A$ um anzudeuten, daß Attribut A aus Relationenschema R stammt.

Schritt 3: Normalisierung in dritte Normalform (3NF) [3] unter Berücksichtigung der zuvor bestimmten Attributgruppen (d.h. Synthese im Stile von [7]), struktureller FDs, INDs [22] und EXDs. Durch die Normalisierung wird ein Teil der Optimierungsstrukturen aufgelöst.

Schritt 4: Überprüfung und Auswertung von nicht schlüsselbasierten INDs der Form $i : R[X] \subseteq S[Y]$. Die Überprüfung umfaßt folgende Schritte:

1. Falls i invers schlüsselbasiert ist, so prüfe, ob die zugehörige schlüsselbasierte IND gilt.

2. Falls Y Teilmenge eines Schlüssels von S ist, so prüfe, ob i sich zu einer schlüsselbasierten IND erweitern läßt.

3. Falls X Teilmenge eines Schlüssels von R ist, so prüfe zuerst, ob i sich zu einer invers schlüsselbasierten IND erweitern läßt, und, falls ja, prüfe anschließend 1.

Äquivalenzklassen der BZAs:

$\kappa_{Person\#}$ = {*Student.Person#*, *Professor.P#*, *Projekt-Antrag.Antragsteller*}

κ_{ProfNr} = {*Professor.ProfNr*, *Institut.Leiter#*,
          Student.Betreuer, *Vorlesung.Dozent*, *hört.Dozent*}

$\kappa_{Projekt\#}$ = {*Proj-Antrag.Projekt#*, *Laufende-Projekte.Pro#* }

$\kappa_{F\#}$ = {*Fach.Fach#*, *Vorlesung.F#*, *hört.F#* }

κ_{MatNr} = {*Student.MatNr*, *hört.MatNr*}

κ_{Ort} = {*Ort.Raum#*, *Vorlesung.Ort*, *hört.Ort*}

$\kappa_{I\#}$ = {*Institut.I#*, *Vorlesung.Institut*, *hört.Institut*}

Schlüssel:

Keys(*Student*) = {{*MatNr*}, {*Person#* }}

Keys(*Professor*) = {{*ProfNr*}, {*P#* }}

Keys(*Institut*) = {{*I#*} }

Keys(*Fach*) = {{*Fach#* }}

Keys(*Ort*) = {{*Raum#* }}

Keys(*Projekt-Antrag*) = {{*Antragsteller*, *Projekt#*, *Version*}}

Keys(*Laufende-Projekte*) = {{*Pro#*}}

Keys(*Vorlesung*) = {{*F#*, *Dozent*, *Ort*, *Institut*}}

Keys(*hört*) = {{*MatNr*, *Fach#*, *Dozent*, *Ort*, *Institut*}}

FDs:

Student: PLZ → Ort

Institut: Leiter# → seit

AGs:

Student: PLZ + Ort + Straße

INDs: ∅

NNs: alle Schlüsselattribute

Abbildung 2: Integritätsbedingungen für das Beispielschema aus Abbildung 1.

4. Falls X bzw. Y Superkey ist, so wird i zu einer schlüsselbasierten bzw. invers schlüsselbasierten IND reduziert. Man beachte, daß hierbei redundante Attribute erkannt werden.

Die Auswertung einer nicht schlüsselbasierten IND $i : R[X] \subseteq S[Y]$, die keine schlüsselbasierte Inverse besitzt, erfolgt sodann gemäß [18, 22]: Falls eine schlüsselbasierte IND $S[Y] \subseteq T[Z]$ gilt, so klassifiziere i als S-IND und erzeuge $i' : R[X] \subseteq T[Z]$, andernfalls erzeuge eine neue Relation $T = (Y)$ und ersetze i durch $R[X] \subseteq T[Y]$ und $S[Y] \subseteq T[Y]$. Alle nach diesem Schritt verbleibenden invers schlüsselbasierten INDs werden als K-INDs klassifiziert, alle sonstigen nichtschlüsselbasierten als S-INDs. Die Klassifizierung der schlüsselbasierten INDs bleibt zunächst offen.

Schritt 5: Eliminierung redundanter Relationenschemas und Attribute: Kandidaten für redundante Relationenschemata sind z.B. Relationen, die keine BZAs enthalten (diese repräsentieren eventuell abgeleitete Information) sowie Relationen mit gleicher Attributmenge, z.B. Relationen, die horizontal gesplittet wurden. Redundante Attribute können durch die Überprüfung der Erweiterbarkeit von gegebenen schlüsselbasierten INDs zu solchen aus Schritt 4.4 und durch die Suche nach typgleichen "Attributmustern", die einen Schlüssel beinhalten, gefunden werden.

Schritt 6: Identifikation von Vererbungsstrukturen: Falls mehrere Relationen mit einem Schlüssel vom gleichen "Typ" (d.h. die Attribute der betreffenden Schlüssel sind paarweise äquivalent) existieren, ist dies ein Hinweis auf eine Vererbungsstruktur. Dabei wird unterschieden, ob die typgleichen Schlüssel Objektschlüssel oder Beziehungsschlüssel sind. Im ersten Fall wird überprüft, ob zwischen den betreffenden Relationen eine IS-A- oder eine gewöhnliche Fremdschlüssel-Beziehung besteht, und ob die Relationen eine Beziehungs- oder Objektrelation darstellen. Falls alle durch INDs möglichen Beziehungsstrukturen erkannt sind, können wie in [26] weitere durch eine Auswertung von Attributstrukturen erkannt werden: Eine Vererbungshierarchie kann dadurch repräsentiert sein, daß die Attribute der Superklasse in die Relation der Subklasse eingefügt wurden. Kandidaten für eine solche Beziehungsstruktur sind über typgleiche Attributmuster in Relationen erkennbar. Falls eine derartige Beziehungsstruktur zwischen Relationen $R_1, \ldots, R_l$ gilt, dann wird eine neue Relation H mit den Attributen KX erzeugt, wobei K der gemeinsame Objektschlüssel und X das gemeinsame Attributmuster ist; H wird über entsprechende INDs mit $R_1, \ldots, R_l$ verbunden; die Attribute aus X werden aus den R_i entfernt.

Es kann dann noch verschiedene "Vererbungshierarchien" von Relationen mit Objektschlüsseln vom gleichen Typ geben, die keine gemeinsame Superklasse (Relation) haben. In diesen Fällen kann durch Einführung von *Domain-Relationen* [13] erreicht werden, daß in einem Schema existierende Vererbungshierarchien zusammengefaßt werden. Eine Domain-Relation beschreibt dabei die allgemeinste Klasse von Objekten, die durch den gemeinsamen Objektschlüssel vom gleichen Typ beschrieben werden kann.

Es sei ferner bemerkt, daß Relationen mit gleichen Beziehungsschlüsseln wie Relationen mit gleichen Objektschlüsseln behandelt werden können, mit der Ausnahme, daß keine Domain-Relationen eingeführt werden.

In unserem Beispiel ergeben sich etwa folgende Beobachtungen: Aufgrund der typgleichen Schlüssel sind die Relationen *Student* und *Professor* sowie *Professor* und *Leiter* Kandidaten für eine Fremdschlüssel- oder eine IS-A-Beziehung. Zwischen *Leiter* und *Professor* wird die IND *Leiter[Leiter#] $\subseteq$ Professor[Prof.#]* erkannt und als ISA-IND identifiziert. Zwischen *Professor* und *Student* kann zwar keine IND festgestellt werden, aber aufgrund des typgleichen Attributmusters wird eine Relation *Person(Person#, Name)* erzeugt und über die ISA-INDs *Professor[P#] $\subseteq$ Person[Person#]* und *Student[Person#] $\subseteq$ Person[Person#]* mit *Student* und *Professor* verbunden. Alle betrachteten Relationen werden als Objektrelationen klassifiziert, da alle in einer Vererbungshierarchie angeordnet sind.

Schritt 7: Strukturelle Vervollständigung des Schemas: Die meisten Beziehungsstrukturen können durch Inklusionsbedingungen beschrieben werden, wobei die am häufigsten vorkommende Beziehung die Fremdschlüsselbeziehung ist, die durch schlüsselbasierte Inklusionsbedingungen charakterisiert ist. Nicht schüsselbasierte Inklusionsbedingungen deuten auf eine Optimierungsstruktur hin, über die folgende Aussagen gemacht werden können: Die Attribute auf der rechten Seite der IND beschreiben den Schlüssel eines neuen Objekts, das als eigene Relation repräsentiert werden sollte; aufgrund der angenommenen 3NF kann dieses Objekt aber keine beschreibenden Nichtschlüsselattribute besitzen. Dies wird wie folgt zur Vereinfachung der Suche nach Beziehungsstrukturen und damit zur Vervollständigung des Schemas benutzt:

Schritt 7.1: Falls eine typgleiche Attributgruppe in mehreren Relationen auftaucht, die noch nicht durch Inklusionsbedingungen miteinander in Beziehung stehen, so erzeuge ein Relationenschema, welches die Attributgruppe selbst repräsentiert, und verbinde dieses über Inklusionsbedingungen mit den anderen Attributgruppen.

Schritt 7.2: Identifizierung aller Fremdschlüsselbeziehungen, die in dem Schema gelten. Auf eine Formalisierung der möglichen Fremdschlüsselbeziehungen, die aufgrund der Attributklassifizierung möglich sind, wird hier verzichtet [13].

Nach Schritt 7.2 können noch BZAs im Schema enthalten sein, die nicht gebunden sind. Diese weisen auf eine Optimierungsstruktur oder eine nicht triviale Beziehung hin und werden in den nächsten Schritten behandelt:

Schritt 7.3: Listen- und mengenwertige Eigenschaften werden im relationalen Modell etwa durch Duplizieren von einfachen Attributen innerhalb einer Relation dargestellt; solche Attribute sind in einer Äquivalenzklasse zusammengefaßt. Falls mehrere, noch nicht gebundene Attribute der gleichen Äquivalenzklasse in einem Relationenschema R vorkommen, so wird für diese Attribute ein eigenes Schema erzeugt und an R über eine L-IND angebunden.

Schritt 7.4: Alle Beziehungsattribute, die noch nicht durch eine Inklusionsbedingung gebunden sind, repräsentieren Schlüssel- bzw. Fremdschlüsselattribute von Objekten, die nicht als eigene Relation im Schema repräsentiert sind. Diese können unter Umständen sogar Teilmengenhierarchien bilden, aber neben den Schlüsselattributen, wie bereits erwähnt, keine weiteren beschreibenden Attribute besitzen. Um die exakten Beziehungen und Teilmengenhierarchien zu identifizieren, müßten zuerst alle nicht schlüsselbasierten Inklusionsbedingungen geprüft werden, die aufgrund der Klassifizierung der Attribute in Äquivalenzklassen möglich sind [13], und danach wie in Schritt 4 ausgewertet werden.

Da diese Vorgehensweise aber bestenfalls zu Teilmengen–Hierarchien führen kann, ist in den meisten Fällen eine geeignete Erzeugung der bereits erwähnten Domain-Relationen vorzuziehen. Prinzipiell wird dabei für jede Äquivalenzklasse κ_A, die noch ungebundene BZAs enthält, eine Domain-Relation erzeugt, die mit den ungebundenen Attributen aus κ_A über INDs verbunden werden. Die Domain-Relation wird dann unter Verwendung gegebener Information und von Vererbungshierarchien geeignet in das Relationenschema integriert. In bestimmten Fällen wird auch für mehrere ungebundene BZAs verschiedener Äquivalenzklassen nur eine Domain-Relation erzeugt.

Nach Schritt 7 ist das Ausgangsschema D strukturell, aber noch nicht semantisch vollständig [13].

In unserem Beispiel hat sich nach der Überprüfung der INDs herausgestellt, daß die BZAs *Projekt-Antrag.Projekt#* und *Laufende-Projekte.Pro#* aus der Äquivalenzklasse $\kappa_{Projekt\#}$ noch ungebunden sind. Daher wird eine Domain-Relation *Projekt(Projekt#)* erzeugt, welche mit der Relation *Laufende-Projekte* über die ISA-IND

$$Laufende\text{-}Projekte[Projekt\#] \subseteq Projekt[Projekt\#]$$

und mit der Relation *Projekt-Antrag* über die L-IND

$$Projekt\text{-}Antrag[Projekt\#] \subseteq Projekt[Projekt\#]$$

verbunden wird.

Schritt 8: Eliminierung redundanter Inklusionsbedingungen: Alle aufgrund von Transitivität und Trivialität redundanten Inklusionbedingungen werden in diesem Schritt eliminiert [22]; S-INDs werden dabei nicht betrachtet.

Objektrelationen:

Student (MatNr, Person#, PLZ, Ort, Straße, Betreuer)
Professor (ProfNr, P#, Spezialgebiet)
Institut (I#, Name, Leiter#)
Fach (Fach#, Name)
Ort (Raum#)
Leiter (Leiter#, seit, Person#)
Projekt (Projekt#)
Person (Person#, Name)
Laufende-Projekte (Pro#, Budget)
Vorlesung (F#, Dozent, Ort, Institut, Datum)

Beziehungsrelationen:

Projekt-Antrag (Antragsteller, Projekt#, Version, Datum)
hört (MatNr, Fach#, Dozent, Ort, Institut)

INDs:

$Student[Person\#] \subseteq Person[Person\#]$ *(ISA-IND)*
$Student[Betreuer] \subseteq Professor[ProfNr]$ *(B-IND)*
$Professor[P\#] \subseteq Person[Person\#]$ *(ISA-IND)*
$Projekt\text{-}Antrag[Antragsteller] \subseteq Professor[P\#]$ *(B-IND)*
$Projekt\text{-}Antrag[Projekt\#] \subseteq Projekt[Projekt\#]$
$Institut[Leiter\#] \subseteq Leiter[Leiter\#]$ *(B-IND)*
$Laufende\text{-}Projekte[Pro\#] \subseteq Projekt[Projekt\#]$ *(ISA-IND)*
$Vorlesung[F\#] \subseteq Fach[Fach\#]$ *(L-IND)*
$Vorlesung[Dozent] \subseteq Professor[ProfNr]$ *(L-IND)*
$Vorlesung[Ort] \subseteq Ort[Raum\#]$ *(L-IND)*
$Vorlesung[Institut] \subseteq Institut[I\#]$ *(L-IND)*
$hört[Fach\#, Dozent, Ort, Institut] \subseteq Vorlesung[F\#, Dozent, Ort, Institut]$ *(L-IND)*
$hört[MatNr] \subseteq Student[MatNr]$ *(L-IND)*
$Leiter[Leiter\#] \subseteq Professor[ProfNr]$ *(ISA-IND)*
$Leiter[Person\#] \subseteq Professor[P\#]$ *(ISA-IND)*

EXDs:

$Student[P\#] \cap Professor[P\#] = \emptyset$
$Student[P\#] \cap Leiter[P\#] = \emptyset$

Abbildung 3: Beispielschema nach der relationalen Vervollständigung.

Schritt 9: Jedes Relationenschema kann noch mehrere Objektklassen bzw. Beziehungs-typen repräsentieren. Für diese wird eine vertikale Dekomposition durchgeführt, so daß jede Relation genau eine Objektklasse repräsentiert. Kandidaten für eine solche Dekomposition sind z.B. Relationen mit mehreren Schlüsseln oder Relationen mit einem Beziehungsschlüssel, der sowohl BZAs als auch LKAs beinhaltet. Mehrere Relationen können aufgrund einer vertikalen Dekomposition anhand des Schlüssels auch nur eine Objektmenge beschreiben. Kandidaten hierfür müssen gegenseitig über zwei INDs mit Schlüsseln auf der linken und rechten Seite verbunden sein und werden miteinander verschmolzen.

Schritt 10: Identifikation von Exklusionsbedingungen zwischen Subklassen einer Vererbungshierarchie. Dazu wird ein Schlüssel der Wurzelrelation – im folgenden *Hierarchieschlüssel* genannt – in jede Relation eingefügt, die eine Subklasse repräsentiert. Auf diese Weise werden die Relationen, welche Subklassen repräsentieren, miteinander vergleichbar.

Schritt 11: Klassifikation aller in den Schritten 6 und 7 noch nicht klassifizierten Relationen bzw. Inklusionsbedingungen in Objekt- und Beziehungsrelationen bzw. in ISA-INDs, B-INDs, K-INDs, L-INDs und S-INDs. Eine Relation wird als Objektrelation klassifiziert, falls sie eine Super- oder Subklasse in einer Vererbungshierarchie repräsentiert, einen Objektschlüssel besitzt, der in keiner anderen Relation vorkommt, oder auf der rechten Seite einer schlüsselbasierten Inklusionsbedingung, die keine K-IND ist, steht. Eine Ausnahme, die eine weitere Fallunterscheidung erfordert, ist gegeben, falls zwei INDs (keine ISA-INDs) $R_i[X] \subseteq R_j[Y]$ und $R_j[Y] \subseteq R_i[X]$ mit $X \in$ Keys(R_i), $Y \in$ Keys(R_j) gelten, da hier R_i oder R_j eine Beziehungsrelation darstellen kann [13]. ISA-INDs wurden schon in den Schritten 6 und 7 herausgefunden. Die Klassifizierung der sonstigen INDs ist abhängig von der Klassifikation der Relationen und den NN-Bedingungen. So ist z.B. jede schlüsselbasierte IND,

1. deren linke Seite ein echter Teil eines Schlüssels ist, eine L-IND,

2. deren linke Seite nur Nichtschlüsselattribute enthält, die nicht NN sind, eine B-IND,

3. deren linke Seite nur Nichtschlüsselattribute enthält, die NN sind, eine B-IND oder eine L-IND.

Jede invers schlüsselbasierte IND ist als K-IND klassifiziert. Die genaue Art der Klassifizierung kann in [13] gefunden werden.

Schritt 12: Alle Beziehungen, die durch eine B-IND i dargestellt sind und beschreibende Attribute besitzen, werden in eine eigene Beziehungs-Relation abgebildet und über L-INDs und eventuell K-INDs mit den Relationen der linken und rechten Seite von i verbunden.

Nach Schritt 12 hat das relationale Schema die für die Transformation erwünschte Form. Die Betrachtung weiterer Spezialfälle, wie z.B. die Deutung und Auflösung von Inklusionsbedingungen, deren linke Seiten eine nichtleere Schnittmenge haben, oder die Auflösung von INDs der Form $R_1[k] \subseteq R_2[k]$ bzw. $R_1[k] \subseteq R_2[k] \cup \ldots \cup R_n[k]$, ist in [13] zu finden. Abbildung 3 zeigt das Beispielschema nach der relationalen Analyse.

4 Kanonische Transformation und Redesign

Nach abgeschlossener Vervollständigung des gegebenen relationalen Schemas kann jetzt, wie bereits erwähnt, im wesentlichen kanonisch transformiert werden. Insbesondere werden die Strukturen und die Semantik des Ergebnisschemas der relationalen Analyse in

Relationales Konzept	ODMG-Konzept
Relationenschema R_i	Klasse R_i
LKA A	atomares Attribut A
BZA A	atomares Attribut A, falls A kein Fremdschlüsselattribut ist
Schlüssel k	Key k
ISA-IND $R_i[X] \subseteq R_j[Y]$	Sub/Superklassen-Beziehung $R_i : R_j$
schlüsselbasierte IND (aber nicht S-IND) $R_i[X] \subseteq R_j[Y]$ mit $X \in \mathrm{Keys}(R_i)$ (und eventuelle Inverse)	einwertige Relationships in R_i und R_j, die als invers definiert sind
schlüsselbasierte IND (aber nicht S-IND) $R_i[X] \subseteq R_j[Y]$ mit $X \notin \mathrm{Keys}(R_i)$	einwertiges Relationship in R_i und mengenwertiges Relationship in R_j, die als invers zueinander definiert sind
sonstige FDs, NNs, INDs	(Integritäts-) Operationen

Tabelle 1: Kanonische Transformation in das ODMG-Modell.

Strukturen eines ODMG-Schemas übertragen. Das Ergebnis dieser Transformation ist ein ODMG-Schema, das jedoch noch immer einen "relationalen" Aufbau hat. Die wesentlichen Aspekte der kanonischen Transformation sind in Tabelle 1 zusammengefaßt.

Bei der kanonischen Transformation wird also für jedes Relationenschema eine eigene Klasse erzeugt, wobei alle Attribute des Relationenschemas, die nicht Fremdschlüsselattribute sind, zu Attributen dieser Klasse werden. Schlüsselbasierte INDs bestimmen die Art und die Kardinalität der Beziehungen zwischen den Klassen. Die Relationships werden als invers zueinander definiert, damit die Zugriffspfade des relationalen Schemas im ODMG-Schema erhalten bleiben. Integritätsbedingungen, die nicht direkt über Beziehungsstruktur des ODMG-Schemas ausdrückbar sind, werden in (Integritäts-) Operationen transformiert [13].

Zusätzlich zu den oben erzeugten Strukturen müssen für alle nicht-disjunkten Subklassen einer Vererbungshierarchie, sogenannte "Schnittklassen" definiert werden, da jedes Objekt nur Mitglied einer Klasse sein kann. Falls etwa R_i und R_j zwei Subklassen einer Vererbungshierarchie mit Hierarchieschlüssel k sind, R_s die kleinste gemeinsame Superklasse darstellt, $s \neq i, j$, und die Exklusionsbedingung $R_i[k] \cap R_j[k] \neq \emptyset$ *nicht* gilt, so wird eine für R_i und R_j gemeinsame Subklasse R_i-R_j erzeugt. Für alle auf diese Weise neu erzeugten "Schnittklassen" werden gegebenenfalls weitere Schnittklassen erzeugt.

Abbildung 4 zeigt das Beispielschema nach der kanonischen Transformation. Doppelpfeile kenzeichnen dabei inverse Relationships, dicke Pfeile Vererbungsbeziehungen und Sterne die Mengenwertigkeit von Relationships.

Im letzten Schritt der Transformation — dem objekt-orientierten Redesign — wird das noch relational geprägte Ergebnisschema nach objekt-orientierten Gesichtspunkten restrukturiert:

- Klassen, die binäre Beziehungen darstellen, werden entfernt und durch inverse Relationships ersetzt; dies sind alle Klassen, die eine Beziehungsrelation des relationalen Schemas repräsentieren und genau zwei Relationships, aber keine Attribute enthalten.

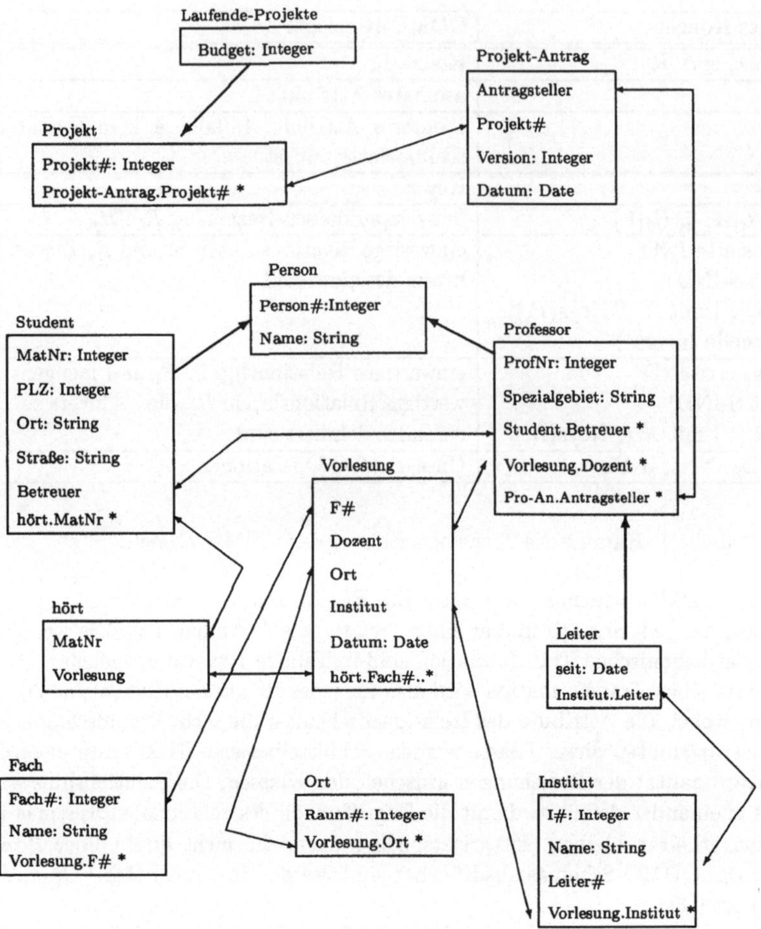

Abbildung 4: Beispielschema nach der kanonischen Transformation.

- Künstliche Schlüssel können aus der Klassenbeschreibung entfernt werden. Künstliche Schlüssel sind alle Schlüssel, die keine "beschreibende Bedeutung" haben und im relationalen Schema nur zur Identifizierung der Objekte verwendet werden. Kandidaten für künstliche Schlüssel sind insbesondere alle Schlüssel, die nur aus einem Attribut bestehen; sie können oft über die Namenssemantik erkannt werden.

- Komplexe Attribut- und Relationship-Strukturen werden erzeugt. Nach der kanonischen Übersetzung haben alle Attribute atomare Wertebereiche. Komplexe Attributstrukturen wie z.B. mengen- oder listenwertige Eigenschaften einer Objektklasse sind durch eigene Klassen im ODMG-Schema oder auch durch ein atomares Attribut [15] repräsentiert. Kandidaten für diese können durch eine Analyse des Schemas und durch die Anwendung von Heuristiken erkannt werden [15, 26]. Zum Beispiel ist jede Klasse, die genau ein Relationship besitzt, welches zusätzlich Teil des Schlüssels ist, ein Kandidat für eine mengenwertige Eigenschaft; Attributgruppen sind Kandidaten für tupelwertige Attribute. Ferner sind im relationalen Schema listen- und mengenwertige Strukturen auch oft durch das Duplizieren von Attributen innerhalb einer Relation dargestellt, so daß im ODMG-Schema mehrere Relationships mit der gleichen Bedeutung zwischen zwei Klassen definiert sein können; diese können zu einem eventuell mengenwertigen Relationship oder einer komplexen Attributstruktur zusammengefaßt werden, wobei letzteres zusätzlich die Umwandlung von Objekt- in Literalstrukturen umfaßt.

- Umwandlung von Objekten zu Literalen: Im Schema können noch Klassen vorkommen, deren Instanzen weniger Objekte als vielmehr Literale darstellen, d.h. die Klassen repräsentieren eher Wertebereiche von Attributen als Objekte mit eigenen Eigenschaften und eigenem Verhalten. Diese werden durch Literalstrukturen ersetzt. Kandidaten dafür sind z.B. alle Klassen, die nur Schlüsselattribute als Attribute besitzen, und Klassen mit nur einem Attribut. Auf die Angabe weiterer semantischer und struktureller Entscheidungskriterien wird hier verzichtet.

In unserem Beispiel ergeben sich für das objekt-orientierte Redesign folgende Beobachtungen: Die Klasse *hört* und die Relationships *hört* in *Student* und *hört* in *Vorlesung* können durch die zwei Relationships *hört.Vorlesung* in *Student* und *hört.Student* in *Vorlesung* ersetzt werden. Kandidaten für künstliche Schlüssel, die entfernt werden können, sind z.B. *Institut.I#* und *Fach.Fach#*. Die Klasse *Ort* ist ein Kandidat für die Darstellung als Literalstruktur in *Vorlesung*. Die Attributgruppe *PLZ + Ort + Straße* wird in ein tupelwertiges Attribut *Adresse* transformiert.

5 Zusammenfassung und Ausblick

In dieser Arbeit haben wir einen Ansatz vorgestellt, Reverse Engineering relationaler Datenbankschemas in Richtung auf objekt-orientierte Schemas zu betreiben, und zwar unter spezieller Berücksichtigung des durch den ODMG-93-Standard vorgegebenen Modellrahmens. Wesentlich an unserer Vorgehensweise ist die Beobachtung, daß eine Transformation relationaler Datenbankschemas in das ODMG-Modell "einfach" wird, falls an das Ausgangsschema gewisse Anforderungen gestellt werden; ein großer Teil unserer Vorgehensweise muß sich daher mit der Frage befassen, wie solche Voraussetzungen in Gegenwart beliebiger Ausgangsschemas erfüllbar sind. Hierzu haben wir eine Reihe von Schritten vorgestellt, deren Ziel die Herstellung eines vollständigen Schemas ist. Ein vollständiges relationales Schema kann dann einer kanonischen Transformation unterzogen werden, deren Ergebnis wiederum nach rein objekt-orientierten Aspekten optimierbar ist. Durch den Begriff der Vollständigkeit ist dem Benutzer insbesondere ein Hilfsmittel an die Hand gegeben, auch verborgene Optimierungs- und Beziehungsstrukturen zu erkennen, die *nicht* direkt über Fremdschlüsselbedingungen bzw. Inklusionsbedingungen beschrieben werden können, sondern zuerst eine Restrukturierung des Schemas erfordern.

Wir haben das ODMG-Modell als Zielmodell gewählt, da es sich hierbei um einen Standardisierungsvorschlag handelt, von dem erwartet wird, daß zahlreiche kommerzielle Systeme ihn in naher Zukunft umsetzen werden, so daß unsere Vorgehensweise allgemein verwendbar wird. Andererseits ist unser Verfahren leicht an die bereits heute verfügbaren Modelle kommerzieller Systeme (etwa O_2 [2] oder ObjectStore [20]) anpaßbar. Wir arbeiten insbesondere an einer Implementierung des Verfahrens, welche als Teil eines Transformationstools in ein rechnergestütztes System zum Datenbankentwurf einfließen soll. Dabei untersuchen wir auch weitere wichtige Aspekte des Reverse Engineering, die hier nicht angesprochen wurden, wie z.B. die Protokollierung der Restrukturierung, um gegebenfalls auch Anwendungsprogramme migrieren zu können, oder formale Eigenschaften der Transformation wie z.B. Informationserhalt. Über Erfahrungen mit diesem Werkzeug wird zu einem späteren Zeitpunkt zu berichten sein.

Danksagung: Wir danken Joachim Biskup sowie zwei anonymen Gutachtern für konstruktive Hinweise zur Verbesserung einer früheren Fassung dieser Arbeit.

Literatur

[1] M. Albrecht: *Ansätze zur Akquisition von Inklusions- und Exklusionsabhängigkeiten in Datenbanken*; Proc. GI-Workshop, Tutzing, Informatik-Bericht Nr. 03/94, Universität Hannover 1994, pp. 162–169.

[2] F. Bancilhon, C. Delobel, P. Kanellakis (Hrsg.): *Building an Object-Oriented Database System: The Story of O_2*; Morgan Kaufmann 1992.

[3] P.A. Bernstein: *Synthesizing third normal form relations from functional dependencies*; ACM TODS 1, 1976, pp. 277–298.

[4] J. Biskup, R. Menzel, T. Polle: *Transforming an Entity-Relationship schema into object-oriented database schemas*; Informatik-Bericht 17-94, Universität Hildesheim 1994.

[5] D. Bitton, J. Millman, S. Torgersen: *A feasibility and performance study of dependency inference*; Proc. 5th ICDE 1990, pp. 635–641.

[6] M. Bouzeghoub, G. Gardain, E. Metais: *Database design tools: an expert system approach*; Proc. 11th VLDB 1985, pp. 82–95.

[7] V. Brosda, G. Vossen: *Update and retrieval in a relational database through a universal schema interface*; ACM TODS 13, 1988, pp. 449–485

[8] R.G.G. Cattell (ed.): *The Object Database Standard: ODMG-93*; Morgan-Kaufmann 1994.

[9] R.H.L. Chiang, T.M. Barron, V.C. Storey: *Performance evaluation of reverse engineering relational databases into extended Entity–Relationship models*; Proc. 12th ERA 1993, pp. 336–352.

[10] R.H.L. Chiang, T.M. Barron, V.C. Storey: *Reverse engineering of relational databases: extraction of an EER model from a relational database*; Data & Knowledge Engineering 12, 1994, pp. 107–142.

[11] R. Elmasri, S. James, V. Kouramajian: *Automatic class and method generation for object-oriented databases*; Proc. 3rd DOOD 1993, Springer LNCS 760, pp. 395–414.

[12] C. Fahrner, G. Vossen: *A Survey of Database Design Transformations Based on the Entity–Relationship Model*; Schriften zur Angewandten Mathematik und Informatik, Universität Münster, Bericht Nr. 14/94-I, August 1994.

[13] C. Fahrner, G. Vossen: *Reverse engineering of relational databases: towards a design tool for ODMG databases*; Technischer Bericht, Universität Münster 1995, in Vorbereitung

[14] M. Gogolla et al.: *Integrating the ER Approach in an OO Environment*; Proc. 12th ERA 1993, pp. 373–384.

[15] J-L. Hainaut, C. Tonneau, M. Joris, M. Chandelon: *Schema transformation techniques for database reverse engineering*; Proc. 12th ERA 1993, pp. 353–372.

[16] A. Heuer: *Equivalent schemas in semantic, nested relational, and relational database models*; Proc. 2nd MFDBS 89, LNCS 364, pp. 237–253.

[17] R. Hull, M. Yoshikawa: *ILOG: declarative creation and manipulation of object identifiers*, Proc. 16th VLDB 1990, pp. 455–468.

[18] P. Johanneson, K. Kalman: *A method for translating relational schemas into conceptual schemas*; Proc. 8th ERA 1989, pp. 271–286.

[19] J. Kivinen, H. Mannila: *Approximate dependency inference from relations*; Proc. 4th ICDT 1992, Springer LNCS 646, pp. 86–98.

[20] C. Lamb, G. Landis, J. Orenstein, D. Weinreb: *The ObjectStore database system*; CACM 34 (10) 1991, pp. 50–63.

[21] D. Maier: *The Theory of Relational Databases*; Computer Science Press, 1983.

[22] H. Mannila, K. Räihä: *The Design of Relational Databases*; Addison Wesley 1992.

[23] V.M. Markowitz , J.A. Makowsky: *Identifying extended Entity–Relationship object structures in relational schemes*; IEEE TSE 16, 1990, pp. 777–790.

[24] B. Narasimhan, S.B. Navathe, S. Jayaraman: *On mapping ER and relational models into OO schemas*; Proc. 12th ERA 1993, pp. 397–408.

[25] S.B. Navathe, A.M. Awong: *Abstracting relational and hierarchical data with a semantic data model*; Proc. 6th ERA 1987, pp. 305–336.

[26] W. Premerlani, M.R. Blaha: *An approach for reverse engineering of relational databases*; Proc. Working Conference on Reverse Engineering, Baltimore 1993, pp. 151–160.

[27] Z. Tari: *On the design of Object-Oriented Databases*; Proc. 11th ERA 1992, pp. 389–405.

[28] J. Van den Bussche, G. Vossen: *An extension of path expressions to simplify navigation in object-oriented queries*; Proc. 3rd DOOD 1993, LNCS 760, pp. 267–281.

[29] G. Vossen: *Datenmodelle, Datenbanksprachen und Datenbank-Management-Systeme*; 2. Auflage, Addison-Wesley 1994.

[30] C.C. Yang, G. Li, P.A.B. Ng: *An improved algorithm based on subset closures for synthesizing a relational database scheme*; IEEE TSE 14, 1988, pp. 1731–1738.

Semantische Anreicherung relationaler Datenbanken

Uwe Hohenstein & Christian Körner

Siemens AG
Zentralabteilung Forschung und Entwicklung
ZFE T SE 44
81730 München
(e-mail: <Vorname>.<Nachname>@zfe.siemens.de)

Kurzfassung

Semantische Anreicherung ist ein Prozeß, der die implizit in existierenden Datenbanken vorliegende Semantik explizit macht. Üblicherweise erfolgt die Anreicherung durch eine Transformation des Datenbankschemas in ein semantisch reichhaltigeres Datenmodell. Dabei werden die höheren Modellierungskonzepte, insbesondere Beziehungen und Subtypen, zur Explizierung der inhärenten Semantik verwendet.

Dieser Beitrag beschäftigt sich mit der semantischen Anreicherung relationaler Datenbestände, indem relationale Datenbankschemata in einem objektorientierten Datenmodell remodelliert werden. Im Gegensatz zu anderen Arbeiten wird eine manuelle Spezifikation vorgeschlagen: Es ist explizit anzugeben, wie relationale Schemata in objektorientierte überführt werden. Somit ist dieser Ansatz in der Lage, jegliche Form von Semantik auszudrücken. Zwei Spezifikationssprachen, eine textuelle Sprache und eine graphische Version, werden vorgestellt.

1 Einleitung

In vielen Unternehmen und Betrieben werden für die Abwicklung der innerbetrieblichen Vorgänge eine Reihe von unterschiedlichen Datenbanksystemen (DBSen) eingesetzt. So koexistieren häufig relationale, hierarchische, Netzwerk- und auch objektorientierte DBSe friedlich nebeneinander. Meist sind es historische Gründe, die zu solchen heterogenen Datenhaltungslandschaften führen. Wenn sich in einem Unternehmen im Lauf der Zeit Organisationsstrukturen, Anforderungen aus dem Anwendungsbereich oder die verfügbare Technologie ändern, werden auch neue DBSe benötigt und eingesetzt; gleichzeitig aber müssen bestehende Systeme und Datenbestände erhalten bleiben. Ebenso können unterschiedliche Rechnersysteme oder kommerzielle Softwareprodukte den Einsatz eines neuen (zusätzlichen) Datenbanksystems zur Folge haben. Aber auch Performanzüberlegungen können dazu führen, spezielle, auf diese Anforderungen zugeschnittene DBSe einzusetzen.

Die Datenbanksysteme bilden innerhalb des Unternehmens Insellösungen, zwischen denen in der Regel keine Verbindung besteht. Steigende Anforderungen an den innerbetrieblichen Informationsfluß und die wachsende Komplexität von Anwendungssystemen erfordern zunehmend einen integrierten Zugriff auf Daten, die innerhalb des Unternehmens an verschiedenen Stellen gespeichert sind. Das Forschungsgebiet der *Integration* von Datenbanksystemen [ShL90, KRS91, HNS92, IMS93] (häufig auch Föderation, Interoperabilität oder 'Multidatabase' genannt) versucht Lösungen dafür schaffen, indem eine einheitliche, systemübergreifende Sicht auf Informationen mit einem transparenten Zugriff unter Wahrung der Autonomie der lokalen Systeme bereitgestellt wird. Alle lokal vorhandenen Datenbestände bleiben weiterhin zugreifbar, und bestehende lokale Applikationen können unverändert weiterlaufen.

[ShL90] geben einen guten Überblick über Ansätze zur Integration von DBSen und definieren eine 5-schichtige Referenzarchitektur. Zwei Schritte dieser Architektur sind grundlegend:

Der erste Schritt, die **Homogenisierung**, widmet sich den unterschiedlichen Darstellungsformen der einzelnen lokalen Datenbankschemata. Die lokalen Datenbanksysteme können eigene Datenmodelle besitzen, die jeweils unterschiedliche Modellierungsmittel und Zugriffsschnittstellen bereitstellen. Diese syntaktische Heterogenität gilt es zu überbrücken. Ein probates Mittel ist eine Transformation in ein einheitliches, sogenanntes *kanonisches* Datenmodell. Jedes lokale Datenbankschema wird im kanonischen Datenmodell remodelliert. Die resultierenden *Komponentenschemata* stellen strukturelle und operationale Aspekte in einheitlicher Form dar.

Anschließend findet die **Integration** der nun homogenisiert vorliegenden Komponentenschemata statt. Die Integration führt zu einem oder mehreren *globalen* (föderierten) Schemata, so daß jedem Anwendungsbereich eine eigene globale Sicht bereitgestellt werden kann. Da jedes lokale Schema unabhängig entworfen wurde, sich andererseits die lokal modellierten Weltausschnitte überlappen, werden in der Regel Diskrepanzen zwischen den jeweiligen Darstellungen der gemeinsamen Teile bestehen. So können gleiche Sachverhalte trotz des kanonischen Datenmodells unterschiedlich dargestellt sein, zum Beispiel einmal als Objekttyp, ein anderes Mal als Attribut oder Beziehung. Derartige semantische Schemakonflikte müssen beseitigt werden, um eine konsistente Sicht auf die globalen Daten bereitzustellen.

Dieser Beitrag befaßt sich mit dem Homogenisierungsschritt im Fall relationaler DBSe. Als kanonisches Datenmodell wird ein objektorientiertes Datenmodell verwendet. Die Objektorientierung bietet bekanntermaßen eine starke Ausdrucksfähigkeit, die die Modellierungskonzepte der gängigen DBSe umfaßt und somit ein breites Spektrum an zu integrierenden Systemen erlaubt [CaS91, Här92]. Prinzipiell kann die Homogenisierung recht einfach gehalten werden, indem jede relationale Tabelle in einen Objekttyp gleicher Struktur überführt wird. Es empfiehlt sich jedoch, eine sogenannte **semantische Anreicherung** [CaS91, Cas93, KPM93, WEZS93] durchzuführen, in der die den Relationen inhärente Semantik unter Nutzung der objektorientierten Konzepte explizit gemacht wird.

In der Literatur gibt es eine Vielzahl an vergleichbaren Datenmodelltransformationen, die sich mit der Remodellierung von relationalen Datenbanken befassen. Ihnen ist gemeinsam, daß sie spezielle formale Information über Relationen wie Namensäquivalenzen und Primärschlüssel [DaA87], Schlüsselkandidaten [NaA87], funktionale Abhängigkeiten und Inklusionsabhängigkeiten [MaM90, YaL92] erwarten, und daraus in einem (semi-)automatischen Prozeß Beziehungen und Subtypen ableiten und in einem Entity-Relationship-basierten oder objektorientierten Datenmodell ausdrücken.

Ein derartiger Automatismus der Remodellierung birgt natürlich Gefahren. Die erforderliche Eingabe ist sehr formal, und die Auswirkungen, insbesondere einer inkorrekten Spezifikation sind nicht unmittelbar erkennbar. Auch sind der Remodellierung Grenzen gesetzt. So werden häufig Subtypen überhaupt nicht erkannt [DaA87, KPM93], oder nur eine Strategie der Subtypbildung remodelliert [MaM90, CaS91, YaL92]. Fehlerhafte Remodellierungen können die Folge sein. Unser Ansatz geht daher von einer weniger formalen, aber dafür direkten und intuitiv verständlichen Spezifikation einer semantischen Anreicherung aus, die andererseits etwas mehr Wissen über die Semantik der Relationen erfordert. Häufig existieren zur Datenbank noch objektorientierte oder Entity-Relationship-Entwürfe, die dann das notwendige Wissen enthalten. Auch eine Wissensakquisition wie in [CaS93, WEZS93], in der diese Semantik anhand des Datenbestands ermittelt wird, kann zu diesem Zweck eingesetzt werden. Unser Schwerpunkt liegt somit auf einer Spezifikation, die jegliche Form von Remodellierungen unterstützt, insbesondere wenn der Entwurf der Tabellen - wie in der Praxis häufig üblich - nicht einheitlichen Strategien folgte und Optimierungen unterlag [PrB94].

Obwohl die Spezifikation der Anreicherung von Hand erfolgt, läuft die eigentliche Homogenisierung aufgrund eines *generativen* Ansatzes automatisch ab. Die Spezifikation ist die Eingabe für einen Generator, der daraus ein objektorientiertes Datenbankschema erzeugt. Im Gegensatz zu anderen Ansätzen, die in der Regel nur eine objektorientierte Struktur erzeugen, beinhaltet das erzeugte Schema auch operationales Verhalten. Im Prinzip besteht das objektorientierte Schema wie in [HoO93] aus C++-Klassen, die generische Methoden einschließlich ihrer Implementierung enthalten. Diese Klassen bilden somit eine vollständige objektorientierte Zugriffsschnittstelle für relationale DBSe. Auf dieser Softwareschicht kann die der Homogenisierung nachfolgende Schemaintegration direkt aufsetzen.

Im folgenden werden zwei Formen der Spezifikation einer semantischen Anreicherung vorgestellt: Eine syntaktische Spezifikationssprache und eine graphische Sprache mit gleich mächtigen Remodellierungsmöglichkeiten. Die folgenden Abschnitte gliedern sich dann wie folgt.

Zunächst wird in Abschnitt 2 das kanonische Datenmodell vorgestellt. Wir verwenden das Objektmodell des zukünftigen Standards ODMG93 [Cat94] für objektorientierte DBSe. Das Objektmodell beinhaltet sowohl strukturelle als auch operationale bzw. Zugriffsaspekte. Anschließend stellen wir allgemeine Konzepte zur semantischen Anreicherung relationaler Datenbestände vor, die die Konzepte des ODMG93-Objektmodells vollständig ausreizen. Die Semantik komplexer Situationen, insbesondere Subtyphierarchien, die durch Anwendung verschiedener Strategien entstanden sind, läßt sich explizit spezifizieren. Wir stellen eine entsprechende Syntax zur Spezifikation einer semantischen Anreicherung anhand eines Beispiels vor. Um unsinnige Spezifikationen auszuschließen, werden Integritätsbedingungen, die ein relationaler Datenbestand zu erfüllen hat, aus der Spezifikation abgeleitet.

Eine komfortable graphische Benutzerschnittstelle zur Unterstützung der semantischen Anreicherung wird in Abschnitt 3 vorgestellt. Das Werkzeug stellt den gleichen Funktionsumfang bereit und erlaubt auf einfache Art und Weise ein inkrementelles Erstellen von Spezifikationen ohne jegliche Syntaxkenntnisse. Aus der graphischen Spezifikation läßt sich automatisch die korrespondierende explizite syntaktische Spezifikation erzeugen.

Die hier vorgestellte Arbeit ist Teil eines Projekts zur flexiblen Integration heterogener Datenhaltungssysteme (FIHD). Abschnitt 4 zeigt weitere Aspekte des FIHD-Projekts auf.

2 Semantische Anreicherung relationaler Datenbanken

Die semantische Anreicherung im Falle relationaler DBSe besteht aus einer Remodellierung der relationalen Schemata in einem kanonischen Datenmodell. Zu diesem Zweck verwenden wir das Objektmodell der **Object Database Management Group** (ODMG). Die ODMG ist von den führenden Herstellern objektorientierter DBSe gegründet worden, die zum Ziel hatten, einen gemeinsamen DBS-Standard zu definieren. Der ODMG93-Standard ist im Herbst 1993 als Buch veröffentlicht und inzwischen in einer revidierten Form [Cat94] erschienen. Wir werden zunächst das ODMG-Objektmodell näher erläutern, bevor unser Ansatz zur semantischen Anreicherung im Objektmodell beschrieben wird.

2.1 ODMG-Objektmodell

Das ODMG-Objektmodell beinhaltet Objekttypen mit Attributen, einfache und multiple Vererbung in Form einer Subtypbildung sowie Möglichkeiten, Beziehungen zwischen Objekttypen auszudrücken. Das folgende Beispiel stellt ein einfaches ODMG-Schema einer Firmendatenbank dar, hier in graphischer OMT-Notation [RBP+91] figuriert:

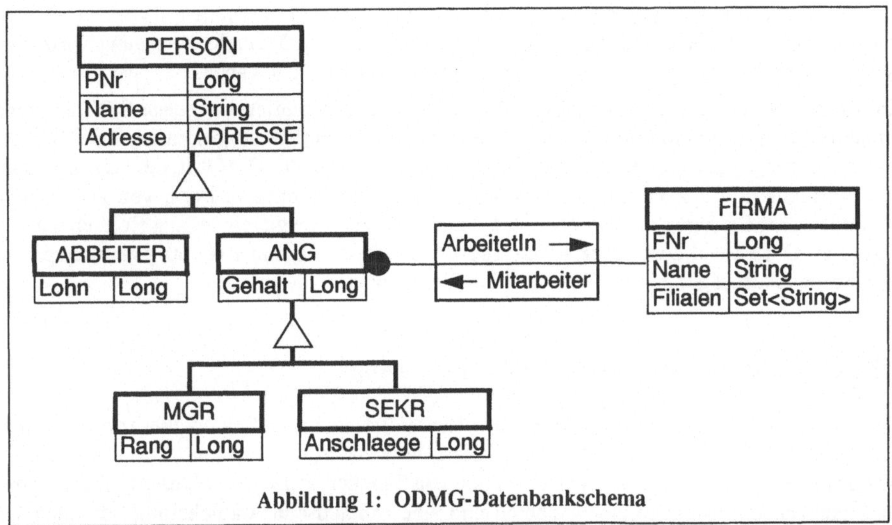

Abbildung 1: ODMG-Datenbankschema

Objekttypen wie PERSON und FIRMA sind als Rechtecke dargestellt. Objekte besitzen wie üblich eine Objektidentität, die ein Objekt zu jedem Zeitpunkt eindeutig identifiziert. Eigenschaften von Objekten werden als *Attribute* spezifiziert. Jede Person (des Typs PERSON) besitzt eine Nummer (PNr), einen Namen und eine Adresse. Attribute sind einer Domäne zugeordnet. Es existieren verschiedene vordefinierte Domänen, im wesentlichen die Grunddatentypen wie Long, Float oder Char, aber auch komplexere Datentypen wie Date, Time und String. Auch Objekttypen sind zulässige Domänen. So soll im Beispiel das Attribut Adresse Werte eines Typs ADRESSE annehmen, der aus Postleitzahl, Ort und Straße besteht. Hierdurch wird jedoch *keine* Beziehung zwischen PERSON und ADRESSE ausgedrückt. Die Adresse einer Person ist kein eigenständiges Objekt, d.h. sie besitzt keine Objektidentität; die Adresse ist lediglich in PERSON quasi als Wert eingebettet und kann nicht als unabhängiges Objekt angesprochen werden. Darüber hinaus gibt es parametrisierbare Datentypen im Sinne von C++-Templates. Mittels Set, Bag, List und Varray lassen sich Mengen, Multimengen, Listen bzw. Arrays über beliebige Domänen bilden, wie z.B. Set<String>. Multimengen sind Mengen mit Duplikaterhaltung. Listen besitzen gegenüber Mengen eine Ordnung, die es erlaubt, auf eine beliebige Position direkt zuzugreifen. Arrays sind den Listen ähnlich, können aber unbelegte Felder aufweisen.

Beziehungen werden über *Referenzen* ausgedrückt. Im Beispiel ist ArbeitetIn eine *einwertige* Referenz: Jeder Angestellte arbeitet in (höchstens) einer Firma. Hingegen ist Mitarbeiter *kollektionswertig* (markiert durch einen Punkt '●'), eine Firma hat eine Menge von Angestellten. Mögliche Formen von Kollektionen sind hier nur Mengen (Set) und Listen (List). Beide Referenzen Mitarbeiter/ArbeitetIn stellen ein und dieselbe Beziehung aus jedoch unterschiedlichen Richtungen dar, modellieren also eine *bidirektionale* Beziehung. Referentielle Integrität wird gewährleistet, d.h. wird ein Angestellter gelöscht, so verschwindet er automatisch aus der Menge der Mitarbeiter seiner Firma. Referenzen können auch *unidirektional*, gerichtet von einem Objekttyp zu einem anderen, sein. Die referentielle Integrität ist dann nicht gegeben, sie muß manuell sichergestellt werden, um 'dangling pointers' zu vermeiden, zum Beispiel indem beim Löschen von Objekten auch die auf das Objekt zeigenden Referenzen gelöscht werden. Mit der Richtung der Referenz ist automatisch die Zugriffsrichtung festgelegt.

Objekttypen können Subtypen haben. So besitzt der Typ PERSON die Subtypen ARBEITER und ANGestellter, und ANG hat selbst wieder zwei Subtypen SEKRetärin und Manager (MGR), jeweils durch Dreiecke dargestellt. Subtypen sind im Objektmodell immer disjunkt.

Mit der Subtypbildung ist eine *Vererbung* von Eigenschaften verbunden; Typen erben von ihrem Obertyp Attribute und die Teilnahme an Beziehungen. Multiple Vererbung wird vom Objektmodell bereitgestellt, ein Typ kann also mehrere Obertypen haben.

Korrespondierend zum Objektmodell gibt es eine Object Definition Language ODL, die eine syntaktische Spezifikation von ODMG-Schemata erlaubt, eine Anfragesprache OQL (Object Query Language) und eine Object Manipulation Language OML. Die OML definiert zu jedem Typ die Signaturen der entsprechenden Manipulationsoperationen in Form von generischen Methoden zum Einfügen und Löschen von Objekten, zum Navigieren entlang Referenzen von Objekt zu Objekt und zum assoziativen Zugriff. Die OML liegt in zwei programmiersprach-spezifischen Ausprägungen für C++- und Smalltalk vor.

2.2 Konzepte zur semantischen Anreicherung

Die Homogenisierung von relationalen Datenbanken erfolgt durch Remodellierung der relationalen Schemata im ODMG-Objektmodell. Die Verwendung eines semantisch reichhaltigen Modells legt nahe, auf eine simple Umsetzung von Tabellen in gleichstrukturierte Objekttypen ohne jegliche Beziehungen zu verzichten und eine semantische Anreicherung vorzunehmen [Cas93]. Ziel sollte es sein, jegliche den Tabellen inhärente Semantik unter Ausnutzung der objektorientierten Konzepte im Sinne eines "Reverse Engineering" [PrB94] zu explizieren.

Um die objektorientierten Konzepte weitestgehend bei der Remodellierung auszureizen, ist es *nicht* ausreichend, nur Beziehungen zu ermitteln, auch eingebettete Objekte oder Vererbung sind zu betrachten. Gedanklich ist hierfür zunächst der umgekehrte Weg zu untersuchen: Wie läßt sich das Objektmodell auf Relationen abbilden, und welche Strategien stehen hierfür zur Verfügung? Erst dann lassen sich die Probleme einer Remodellierung nunmehr in der anderen, Homogenisierungsrichtung erkennen und unterstützen.

Betrachten wir also die möglichen Abbildungen eines objektorientierten Schemas auf relationale Tabellen, um daraus die wichtigsten Regeln abzuleiten, die diesen Vorgang umkehren. Grundlage der Diskussion bildet das objektorientierte Schema aus Abbildung 1. Das Grundprinzip besteht in der Regel darin, zu jedem Objekttyp eine *Basistabelle* einzurichten, welche die Attribute, deren Datentypen im relationalen DBS vorhanden sind, übernimmt. Zum Beispiel ist zum Objekttyp PERSON {...} eine Tabelle T_PERSON (...) einzurichten, die die elementaren Attribute PNr und Name direkt erhält. Für die Anreicherung ergibt sich dann:

Regel 1: Objekttyp aus Tabelle ableiten :

> Relation T_PERSON (PNr, PName, ...) → Objekttyp PERSON { PNr, Name, ... }

Es sollte möglich sein, aus Tabellen wieder Objekttypen und aus relationalen Attributen entsprechende objektbezogene Attribute zu generieren. Umbenennungen sind dabei sinnvoll, sei es, um sprechendere Namen zu wählen (häufig werden in Attributnamen die Fremdschlüsselbeziehungen z.B. als Namenspräfix "hineinkodiert", was bei Objektattributen nicht mehr notwendig ist), oder um späteren Namenskonflikten von vornherein aus dem Weg zu gehen. Der Schritt von einer Tabelle zu einem Objekttyp erfordert demnach entsprechende Namenszuordnungen zwischen Relationennamen und Typnamen (T_PERSON → PERSON) sowie zwischen Attributnamen (T_PERSON.PName → PERSON.Name).

Das ODMG-Objektmodell bietet eine Vielzahl an vordefinierten Datentypen wie String, Time und Date an. Sind diese auch im relationalen System verfügbar, so kann eine direkte Übertragung erfolgen. Ist das jedoch nicht der Fall, so müssen diese entsprechend auf relationale Attribute umgesetzt werden. Angenommen, PERSON besäße ein Attribut GebDat vom Typ Date. Dieses ließe sich dann durch drei integer-wertige Attribute Tag, Monat und Jahr "implementieren". Umgekehrt gilt:

Regel 2: Vordefinierte Datentypen nutzen :

      T_PERSON (..., Tag, Monat, Jahr, ...)   →   PERSON { ..., GebDat:Date, ... }

Entsprechende Zuordnungen müssen spezifiziert werden, um die Umsetzungen rückgängig zu machen: (T_PERSON.Jahr, T_PERSON.Monat, T_PERSON.Tag) → PERSON.GebDat.

Analog lassen sich typwertige Attribute wie Adresse von PERSON dadurch behandeln, daß sie auf mehrere relationale Attribute (teilweise unter Zuhilfenahme weiterer Tabellen) aufgespalten werden: T_PERSON (PNr, PName, PLZ:integer, Ort:String, Strasse:String).

Regel 3: Attribute strukturieren :

      (T_PERSON.PLZ, T_PERSON.Ort, T_PERSON.Strasse)   →   PERSON.Adresse

Kollektionswertige Attribute wie Set<String> müssen ebenfalls bei der Transformation eines Objektschemas auf Tabellen behandelt werden, da sie im relationalen DBS nicht verfügbar sind. Die übliche Vorgehensweise verwendet eine eigene Tabelle für die Kollektion der Attributwerte, die über einen Fremdschlüssel den Bezug zur Basistabelle herstellt. Zum Beispiel läßt sich das Attribut Filialen zu FIRMA durch eine Tabelle T_ORT (FNr, Filiale) realisieren, die zu gegebener Firma FNr die Menge der Filialen als Werte der Spalte Filiale aufnimmt. Im Falle eines listenwertigen Attributs würde T_ORT noch ein Numerierungsattribut Nr beinhalten, um die Listennumerierung explizit zu realisieren. In der anderen Richtung sollte es demzufolge möglich sein, mehrere Relationen zu einem Objekttyp ('Cluster' in [YaL92]) zusammenzufassen, insbesondere kollektionswertige Attribute explizit zu machen. Auch eine Normalisierung im relationalen Datenbankentwurf kann dazu geführt haben, daß Tabellen (die Typen repräsentieren) weiter in mehrere Tabellen zerlegt worden sind.

Regel 4: Bildung von 'Cluster' :

      T_FIRMA (FNr, Name) ;   →   FIRMA { FNr, Name, Filialen:Set<String> }
      T_ORT (FNr, Filiale:String)

Eine entsprechende Regel muß der Tabelle T_ORT das Attribut Filialen zuordnen und den Zusammenhang zwischen T_FIRMA und T_ORT über FNr spezifizieren. Wie immer lassen sich auch hier zusammengesetzte Attribute verwenden. Bei listenwertigen Attributen, realisiert als T_ORT(FNr, Nr, Filiale), ist zusätzlich das Numerierungsattribut Nr erforderlich.

Alternativ kann ein kollektionswertiges Attribut auch durch eine feste Anzahl Attribute abgebildet worden sein, was bei kleineren Kollektionen fester (Maximal-)Größe sinnvoll ist: T_FIRMA (..., Filiale1, Filiale2, Filiale3).

Regel 5: Attributaufzählungen als Array-wertige Attribute explizieren :

      T_FIRMA (..., Filiale1, Filiale2, Filiale3)   →   FIRMA { ..., Filialen:String[3] }

In diesem Fall muß die Zuordnung der Attributfolge zum Attribut Filialen getroffen werden.

Beziehungen zwischen Objekttypen lassen sich relational entweder über Fremdschlüsselattribute oder über eine eigene Tabelle umsetzen. Die Beziehung Mitarbeiter/ArbeitetIn kann beispielsweise als ein Attribut Firma der Tabelle T_ANG ausgedrückt werden: T_FIRMA (FNr, Name) und T_ANG (PNr, Gehalt, Firma) [1]. Das Attribut Firma beinhaltet den Schlüssel der Firma, in der der Angestellte arbeitet.

Beliebige n:m-Beziehungen können aber auf diese Weise nicht auf Relationen abgebildet werden. Hier ist eine eigene *Beziehungstabelle* zur Aufnahme der beteiligten Schlüssel notwendig. Diese Strategie kann natürlich auch für 1:n-Beziehungen wie Mitarbeiter/ArbeitetIn angewendet werden, indem eine eigene Tabelle T_MITARBEITER die Beziehung über PNr und FNr ausdrückt: T_ANG (PNr, Gehalt) ; T_FIRMA (FNr, Name) ; T_MITARBEITER (PNr, FNr). Viele existierende Ansätze sind nicht in der Lage, solche Beziehungstabellen in eine Beziehung rückzuübersetzen. Natürlich sollten beide Fälle invertierbar sein:

---

1. PNr ist das von PERSON ererbte Schlüsselattribut. Näheres zur Umsetzung der Vererbung folgt später.

Regel 6: ***Beziehungen (über Fremdschlüssel oder Beziehungstabelle) explizit machen :***

a) T_ANG (PNr, Gehalt, Firma) ;   →   ANG { PNr, Gehalt, ArbeitetIn:FIRMA } ;
T_FIRMA (FNr, Name)   FIRMA { FNr, Name, Mitarbeiter:Set(ANG) }

Die Umsetzung wird durch eine entsprechende Zuordnung des Referenzpaares ArbeitetIn/Mitarbeiter zu den Attributen T_ANG.Firma und T_FIRMA.FNr charakterisiert.

b) T_ANG (PNr, Gehalt) ;   →   ANG { PNr, Gehalt, ArbeitetIn:FIRMA } ;
T_FIRMA (FNr, Name) ;   FIRMA { FNr, Name, Mitarbeiter:Set(ANG) }
T_MITARBEITER (PNr, FNr)

Dem Referenzpaar sind hier hier zwei Attributpaare (T_MITARBEITER.PNr, T_ANG.PNr) und (T_MITARBEITER.PNr, T_FIRMA.FNr) zuzuordnen.

Die Beziehung kann in beiden Fällen natürlich auch über zusammengesetzte Attribute erfolgen, so daß entsprechend Tupel von Attributen anzugeben sind. Zu beachten ist, daß weder n-äre Relationships noch attributierte Relationships im Sinne des klassischen Entity-Relationship-Modells hier behandelt werden, da das ODMG-Objektmodell diese nicht anbietet. Folglich müssen derartige Relationships als Objekttypen (re-)modelliert werden.

Einige Ansätze [MaM90, YaL92, Cas93, WEZS93] zur semantischen Anreicherung sind in der Lage, Subtyp-Beziehungen explizit zu machen, können jedoch keine mehrstufigen Subtyp-Hierarchien erkennen oder nur die vertikale Strategie der Subtypbildung (siehe unten) umkehren. Gerade die "Implementierung" von Subtypen auf Relationen bietet ein ganzes Spektrum an möglichen Lösungen, die somit bei der Remodellierung unerkannt bleiben:

a) Bei der *vertikalen* Strategie wird für jeden Objekttyp der Hierarchie eine eigene Tabelle mit den typspezifischen Attributen (gemäß oben) eingerichtet. Im Beispiel sind das die Tabellen T_PERSON (PNr, PName, PLZ, Ort, Strasse), T_ARBEITER (PNr, Lohn), T_ANG (PNr, Gehalt, Firma), T_SEKR (PNr, Anschlaege) und T_MGR (PNr, Rang), die allesamt dasselbe Schlüsselattribut PNr erhalten (welches natürlich in den Tabellen unterschiedlich benannt sein kann). Um auf die von Obertypen ererbten Attribute zuzugreifen (z.B. der PName für Angestellte), muß ein Verbund ('join') über den gemeinsamen Schlüssel ausgeführt werden. Jede Tabelle enthält jeweils die *Elemente*, d.h. die Instanzen des Objekttyps einschließlich der Subtypen. Ein Manager wird folglich in T_MGR, T_ANG und T_PERSON mit jeweils gleicher PNr abgelegt, eine Person hingegen nur in T_PERSON. Bezüglich des Schlüssel-attributs bestehen Inklusionen zwischen Ober- und Untertypen:

    T_PERSON.PNr ⊇ T_ANG.PNr,   T_ANG.PNr ⊇ T_SEKR.PNr,
    T_PERSON.PNr ⊇ T_ARBEITER.PNr , T_ANG.PNr ⊇ T_MGR.PNr

b) Die *horizontale* Strategie verwendet ebenfalls eine Tabelle je Objekttyp. Neben den subtyp-spezifischen Attributen finden sich auch die Attribute der Obertypen bei den Tabellen, die einen Subtyp repräsentieren, wieder: T_PERSON (PNr, PName, PLZ, Ort, Strasse) mit dem Subtyp T_ANG (PNr, PName, PLZ, Ort, Strasse, Gehalt, Firma) und dessen Subtyp T_MGR (PNr, PName, PLZ, Ort, Strasse, Gehalt, Firma, Rang), usw. Jede Tabelle enthält jeweils die *Instanzen* des Objekttyps (ohne Subtypen). Ein Manager wird nur in T_MGR (mit der ANG- und PERSON-Information) abgelegt. Die einzelnen Tabellen sind folglich bezüglich PNr disjunkt: T_PERSON.PNr ∩ T_ANG.PNr = ∅, T_ANG.PNr ∩ T_MGR.PNr = ∅, usw.

c) Die *vollständige Materialisierung* verwendet die Schemata aus b), aber die Ausprägungen aus a): Jede Tabelle enthält die Objekte eines Typs und aller Subtypen; die Attribute der Obertypen sind unmittelbar verfügbar. Ein ANG-Objekt findet sich sowohl in T_ANG (PNr, PName, PLZ, Ort, Strasse, Gehalt, Firma) als auch in T_PERSON (PNr, PName, PLZ, Ort, Strasse) unter derselben PNr wieder. Die Informationen zu PName, PLZ, Ort und Strasse liegen somit redundant vor.

d) Beim *Diskriminanten-Ansatz* gibt es genau eine Tabelle für die gesamte Hierarchie. Diese Tabelle nimmt alle Objekte der Hierarchie auf und steuert ihre jeweiligen Typen über boolwertige Diskriminanten ANG?, ARBEITER?, SEKR? und MGR?:

> T_PERSON (PNr, PName, PLZ, Ort, Strasse, ANG?, Gehalt, Firma,
>   ARBEITER?, Lohn, SEKR?, Anschlaege, MGR?, Rang)

Diskriminanten können zwei Bedeutungen haben, je nachdem ob Instanzen oder Elemente charakterisiert werden: ANG? = true kann genau die Angestellten (ohne Manager und Sekretärinnen) oder alle Angestellten kennzeichnen. Im letzten Fall sind die eigentlichen Angestellten durch ANG?=true $\land$ MGR?=false $\land$ SEKR?=false bestimmt. Die nichtspezifischen Attribute sind jeweils mit NULL belegt, beispielsweise Rang für Arbeiter.

Die Diskriminante kann mitunter wegfallen. Die Kennzeichnung der Arbeiter erfolgt dann zum Beispiel über "Gehalt = NULL". Eine andere Alternative besteht darin, beliebige Bedingungen, z.B. "Gehalt > 2000" zur Kennzeichnung zu verwenden. Anstelle der Diskriminanten kann auch ein Aufzählungstyp (Typ:{ang, arbeiter, sekr, mgr}) benutzt werden.

Die Information über die Vererbungsbeziehungen ist in allen Fällen nur implizit in der Datenbank vorhanden und muß explizit gemacht werden. Je nach Strategie ergibt sich:

Regel 7: Subtyp-Beziehungen explizit machen :

   a) T_PERSON (PNr, PName, PLZ, Ort, ...) ; $\to$ PERSON { PNr, Name, Adresse } ;
       T_ANG (PNr, Gehalt, Firma)   ANG : PERSON { Gehalt, ArbeitetIn }

Zusätzlich zur Zuordnung der Tabellen zu den Typen sind hier für jedes Paar Obertyp-Untertyp die Attribute relevant, die eine vertikale Subtyp-Beziehung zwischen den Tabellen herstellen (und über die ein Verbund der Tabellen durchzuführen ist), also beispielsweise (T_PERSON.PNr, T_ANG.PNr) $\to$ ANG : PERSON.

   b) T_PERSON (PNr, PName, PLZ, ...) ; $\to$ PERSON { PNr, Name, Adresse } ;
       T_ANG (PNr, PName, PLZ, ..., Gehalt, Firma)   ANG : PERSON { Gehalt, ArbeitetIn }

Entsprechend sind hier je Obertyp-Untertyp die Attribute, über die partitioniert wird, von Bedeutung, beispielsweise T_PERSON.PNr und T_ANG.PNr. Aufgrund der Disjunktheit der PNr'n, verteilen sich die Obertyp-Instanzen auf mehrere Tabellen, so daß auch semantisch gleichbedeutende Attribute einander zugeordnet werden müssen. Für das Attribut Name ergibt sich beispielsweise: (T_PERSON.PName, T_ANG.PName, T_ARBEITER.PName, T_MGR.PName, T_SEKR.PName) $\to$ PERSON.Name : Alle diese Tabellen enthalten Namen von Personen, je nach dem speziellen Typ einer Person.

   c) T_PERSON (PNr, PName, PLZ, ...) ; $\to$ PERSON { PNr, Name, Adresse } ;
       T_ANG (PNr, PName, PLZ, ..., Gehalt, Firma)   ANG : PERSON { Gehalt, ArbeitetIn }

Hier sind ebenfalls die Attribute, welche die Subtyp-Beziehung zwischen den Tabellen herstellen (wieder T_PERSON.PNr und T_ANG.PNr), einander zuzuordnen. Darüber hinaus ist die Redundanz zu kennzeichnen: T_PERSON.PName = T_ANG.PName enthalten dieselben Werte für Angestellte, usw.

   d) T_PERSON (PNr, PName, PLZ, Ort, $\to$ PERSON { PNr, Name, Adresse } ;
             Strasse, ANG?, Gehalt,   ANG : PERSON { Gehalt, ArbeitetIn } ;
             Firma, ARBEITER?, Lohn,   ARBEITER : PERSON { Lohn } ;
             SEKR?, Anschlaege,   SEKR : ANG { Anschlaege } ;
             MGR?, Rang)   MGR : ANG { Rang }

In diesem Fall muß zu jedem Subtyp spezifiziert werden, wie sich die Elemente des Typs aus den Diskriminanten bestimmen lassen. Zum Beispiel haben die Elemente von ANG die Diskriminantenbedingung ANG?=true, die ANG als Subtyp zu PERSON bestimmt. Das Prinzip ist dabei unabhängig vom jeweiligen Diskriminantenansatz.

Zu beachten ist, daß diese Strategien auch innerhalb einer Hierarchie miteinander vermischt sein können (siehe später in Abschnitt 2.3).

Obertypen, die keine eigenen Instanzen enthalten (sogenannte *abstrakte* Typen), erlauben eine weitere Art der Abbildung. Der Obertyp selbst benötigt dann keine Tabelle, so daß nur Tabellen für die Untertypen erforderlich sind. Angenommen, ANG sei ein abstrakter Obertyp von MGR und SEKR. Dann würden die Tabellen T_MGR (PNr, Gehalt, Firma, Rang) und T_SEKR (PNr, Gehalt, Firma, Anschlaege) eingeführt werden, die jeweils die (ererbten) Attribute von ANG aufnehmen. Der umgekehrte Vorgang entspricht einer Generalisierung:

Regel 8: Generalisierung von Objekttypen zu einem abstrakten Objekttyp :

T_MGR (PNr, Gehalt, Firma, Rang) ;	→	ANG { PNr, Gehalt, ArbeitetIn } ;
T_SEKR (PNr, Gehalt, Firma, Anschlaege)		MGR : ANG { Rang } ;
		SEKR : ANG { Anschlaege }

Hier gilt es, den Objekttyp ANG als Generalisierung von MGR und SEKR wieder explizit zu machen, d.h. die gemeinsamen Eigenschaften der Subtypen in einem gemeinsamen Obertyp zu konzentrieren. In einer entsprechenden Regel sind die in ANG zusammengefaßten Attribute unter Angabe ihres Bezugs zu den Tabellen zu identifizieren, also T_MGR.PNr und T_SEKR.PNr zu ANG.PNr, T_MGR.Gehalt und T_SEKR.Gehalt zu ANG.Gehalt, usw.

Wie bereits erwähnt, sind die Subtypen innerhalb einer Hierarchie im ODMG-Objektmodell immer disjunkt. Beispielsweise kann eine Sekretärin nicht gleichzeitig Managerin sein. Nicht-disjunkte Subtypen lassen sich mit multipler Vererbung modellieren:

```
ANG { Gehalt, ArbeitetIn } ;
MGR   : ANG { Rang } ;
SEKR : ANG { Anschlaege } ;
ANG_MGR_SEKR : MGR , SEKR { }
```

Der künstliche Subtyp ANG_MGR_SEKR repräsentiert die Schnittmenge von MGR und SEKR. Er ist notwendig, um Objekte einfügen zu können, die sowohl Manager als auch Sekretärin sind. Die über MGR und SEKR ererbten Attribute von ANG sind nur einmal in ANG_MGR_SEKR präsent. Der ANG-Typ ermöglicht den Zugriff auf alle Elemente, ob Manager, Sekretärin oder beides. Die Abbildung auf Tabellen erfolgt wie gehabt, da die Tabellen ohnehin Nicht-Disjunktheit erlauben, also T_ANG (PNr, Gehalt, Firma), T_MGR (PNr, Rang) und T_SEKR (PNr, Anschlaege) im Fall der vertikalen Strategie.

Regel 9: T_ANG (PNr, Gehalt, Firma) ;	→	ANG { Gehalt, ArbeitetIn } ;
T_MGR (PNr, Rang) ;		MGR : ANG { Rang } ;
T_SEKR (PNr, Anschlaege)		SEKR : ANG { Anschlaege } ;
		ANG_MGR_SEKR : MGR , SEKR { }

Eine entsprechende Remodellierung muß wiederum angeben, über welche Attribute die Vererbungsbeziehung aufgebaut ist und wie sich die Attribute von ANG aus den Tabellen berechnen.

Die in dieser Liste aufgeführten Remodellierungsmöglichkeiten sind natürlich beliebig miteinander kombinierbar. Weitere Remodellierungen sind im Rahmen der Homogenisierung denkbar. So schlagen [SCG92] Konzepte vor, wie beispielsweise aus mehreren gleichartigen Tabellen IBM (Datum, Wert), AEG (Datum, Wert), VW (Datum, Wert), usw. ein Objekttyp AKTIE { Datum, Firma, Wert } spezifiziert werden kann, welcher die einzelnen Relationennamen als Werte 'IBM', 'AEG', 'VW', usw. des Attributs Firma sieht. Hier findet somit eine Restrukturierung statt, die Metadaten, hier Relationennamen, zu Daten konvertiert.

Wir verzichten auf solche Umstrukturierungen größeren Ausmaßes, um zum einen Problemen mit Sichtänderungen ('view updates') aus dem Weg zu gehen. Zum anderen sind wir der Meinung, daß nur "lokales" Wissen über das zu homogenisierende relationale Schema in die Homogenisierung einfließen sollte. Solch komplexe Remodellierungen sind aber erst sinnvoll, wenn verschiedene Schemata zu einem Gesamtschema zusammengeführt werden, was Aufgabe der anschließenden Schemaintegration ist.

2.3 Beispiel einer semantischen Anreicherung

Nach dieser Übersicht über potentiell rückgängig zu machende Abbildungen widmen wir uns nun einer syntaktischen Beschreibungssprache, die diese Remodellierungsmöglichkeiten unterstützt. Betrachten wir also das in Abbildung 2 gegebene Beispiel eines relationalen Datenbankschemas als mögliche relationale Realisierung des objektorientierten Schemas aus Abbildung 1:

T_FIRMA	FNr	Name		T_ORT	FNr	Filiale
	10	A Inc			10	U
	20	B Ltd			20	V
					20	W

T_PERSON	PNr	PName	PLZ	Ort	Strasse
	1	A	11111	A_Ort	A_Allee
	2	B	22222	B_Ort	B_Strasse
	3	C	33333	C_Ort	C_Weg
	4	D	44444	D_Ort	Hinterm D

T_ANG	PNr	Gehalt	Firma	MGR?	Rang
	2	2000	10	false	NULL
	3	3000	20	false	NULL
	4	4000	10	true	FGL

T_ARBEITER	PNr	Name	PLZ	Ort	Strasse	Lohn
	5	E	55555	E_Ort	E_Weg	1555
	6	F	66666	F_Ort	F_Gasse	1666

T_SEKR	PNr	Anschlaege
	3	150

Abbildung 2: Relationales Datenbankschema

In diesem relationalen Schema repräsentiert T_ANG einen vertikalen Subtyp zu PERSON (T_ANG.PNr $\subseteq$ T_PERSON.PNr), während T_ARBEITER einen horizontaler Subtyp zu PERSON darstellt. T_ARBEITER enthält somit weitere Personen, die zu denen in T_PERSON disjunkt sind (T_ARBEITER.PNr $\cap$ T_PERSON.PNr = $\emptyset$), und trägt die volle PERSON-Information. T_MGR ist ein über den Diskriminanten-Ansatz gebildeter Subtyp von ANG, die Diskriminante ist MGR?. T_SEKR ist wiederum ein über vertikale Partitionierung realisierter Subtyp zu ANG (T_SEKR.PNr $\subseteq$ T_ANG.PNr). Natürlich impliziert jedes Tupel in T_SEKR aufgrund der Disjunktheit von Subtypen, daß der entsprechende Eintrag in T_ANG den Wert MGR?=false aufweist. Auf Instanzebene (PNr) ist 1 nur eine Person, 2 ein Angestellter, 3 eine Sekretärin, 4 ein Manager und 5 und 6 sind Arbeiter. Innerhalb dieser Vererbungshierarchie kommen somit drei unterschiedliche Strategien zum Einsatz. Des weiteren wurde die Beziehung zwischen ANG und FIRMA über den Fremdschlüssel Firma (in Tabelle T_ANG) ausgedrückt und das mengenwertige Attribut Filialen über eine eigene Tabelle T_ORT realisiert.

Es ist offensichtlich, daß ohne Kenntnis der Semantik der Attribute die objektorientierte Modellierung aus Abbildung 1 nur schwer automatisch ableitbar ist. [PrB94] zeigen aber, daß derartige Situationen, insbesondere die verschiedenen Strategien zur Behandlung von Subtypen, in der Praxis nicht selten vorkommen.

Unser Ansatz erlaubt nun eine explizite Spezifikation, mit der sich die objektorientierte Modellierung aus Abbildung 1 wieder herstellen läßt. Die Syntax einer semantischen Anreicherung ist ergebnisorientiert und zäumt gewissermaßen das Pferd von hinten auf: Es wird nicht spezifiziert, wie Tabellen mit ihren Attributen zu Typen kombiniert werden, sondern welche Objekttypen aus der semantischen Anreicherung resultieren und wie ihr Bezug zu den Tabellen ist. Da die Objekttypen im Vordergrund der Spezifikation stehen, bleibt die Syntax intuitiv verständlich: Die Spezifikation bringt das Ergebnis einer Anreicherung unmittelbar zum Vorschein. Die folgende Spezifikation zeigt die vollständige Remodellierung des Schemas:

```
interface PERSON from relation T_PERSON[PNr] + T_ARBEITER[PNr]
    ( extent personen
      key PNr          )
    { attribute Long   PNr      = T_PERSON.PNr + T_ARBEITER.PNr;
      attribute String Name  = T_PERSON.PName + T_ARBEITER.Name;
      attribute struct ADRESSE { Long PLZ ; String Ort ; String Strasse; } Adresse =
                        (T_PERSON.PLZ, T_PERSON.Ort, T_PERSON.Strasse) +
                        (T_ARBEITER.PLZ, T_ARBEITER.Ort, T_ARBEITER.Strasse);
    }

interface ANG : PERSON from relation T_ANG [PNr = T_PERSON.PNr]
    { attribute Long Gehalt = T_PERSON.Gehalt;
      relationship FIRMA ArbeitetIn inverse FIRMA::Mitarbeiter
                        = ( T_FIRMA | T_FIRMA.FNr = T_ANG.Firma );
    }

interface ARBEITER : PERSON from relation T_ARBEITER [PNr]
    { attribute Long Lohn = T_ARBEITER.Lohn; }

interface SEKR : ANG from relation T_SEKR [PNr]
    { attribute Long Anschlaege = T_SEKR.Anschlaege; }

interface MGR : ANG from relation T_ANG [MGR? = true]
    { attribute String Rang = T_ANG.Rang; }

interface FIRMA from relation T_FIRMA [FNr]
    ( extent firmen
      key FNr          )
    { attribute Long   FNr      = T_FIRMA.FNr;
      attribute String  Name  = T_FIRMA.Name;
      attribute Set<String> Filialen = { T_ORT.Filiale | T_ORT.FNr = T_FIRMA.FNr } ;
      relationship Set<ANG> Mitarbeiter inverse ANG::ArbeitetIn
                        = { T_ANG | T_ANG.Firma = T_FIRMA.FNr } ;
    }
```

Im Prinzip erfolgt die Spezifikation der Objekttypen in der ODL von ODMG93, wobei diverse Erweiterungen den Bezug zum relationalen Schema herstellen. Die Objekttypen, die aus der semantischen Anreicherung resultieren sollen, werden wie in der ODL in interface-Spezifikationen definiert. Im Falle eines Subtyps lassen sich hinter dem Typnamen Obertypen angeben: ANG : PERSON besagt, daß ANG Subtyp von PERSON ist. Die extent-Klausel kann angegeben werden, um einen Einstiegspunkt auf den Objekttyp (bzw. die Tabelle) im Sinne des CODASYL 'owner is system' bereitzustellen. Extents bilden die Voraussetzung für assoziative Anfragen; fehlt die Angabe, so kann die Menge der Objekte dieses Typs nicht direkt traversiert werden. Die optionale key-Angabe spezifiziert eine Attributkombination, die als objektorientierter Schlüssel ausgezeichnet wird und demzufolge Eindeutigkeit der Werte fordert. Ansonsten enthält die Spezifikation attribute- und relationship-Vereinbarungen.

Die ODL wird erweitert durch eine from relation-Klausel, die den Zusammenhang zur zugrundeliegenden Tabelle herstellt, und durch Attribut- und Beziehungsgleichsetzungen ('=').

Die from relation-Klausel besitzt mehrere Grundformen, die unter anderem die verschiedenen Subtypstrategien widerspiegeln. Im einfachsten Fall ist es eine direkte Korrespondenz wie in FIRMA from relation T_FIRMA[FNr] : FIRMA-Objekte finden sich einzig und allein in der Tabelle T_FIRMA. Wir setzen voraus, daß jede Tabelle einen Schlüssel besitzt, dieser muß in eckigen Klammern angegeben werden. Jedes T_FIRMA-Tupel, identifiziert durch FNr, entspricht genau einem Objekt des Typs FIRMA. Insofern trägt der Schlüssel zur Bildung von Objektidentifikatoren bei, die zur Objektmanipulation in der ODMG-Schnittstelle benötigt werden. Zusammengesetzte Schlüssel können als (a,b,c) angegeben werden.

ANG : PERSON from relation T_ANG[PNr = T_PERSON.PNr] spezifiziert eine vertikale Strategie: Der Typ ANG setzt sich in erster Linie aus der Tabelle T_ANG zusammen; Attribute des Obertyps PERSON lassen sich in der Tabelle T_PERSON finden, wobei der Zusammenhang beider Relationen über 'PNr = T_PERSON.PNr' hergestellt wird. Die in Beziehung gesetzten Attribute können dabei unterschiedliche Namen besitzen. Auch hier sind zusammengesetzte Attribute (a,b,c) jeweils angebbar.

Während die vertikale Strategie bei den Subtypen spezifiziert wird, ist die horizontale Strategie Bestandteil des Obertyps: PERSON from relation T_PERSON[PNr] + T_ARBEITER[PNr]. Das ist wie folgt zu interpretieren: Die Objekte des Typs PERSON teilen sich auf Tupel der disjunkten Tabellen T_PERSON und T_ARBEITER auf. Personen, die keine Arbeiter sind, in T_PERSON, und die Arbeiter in T_ARBEITER. Die Identifikation erfolgt über die jeweils in eckigen Klammern angegebenen Attribute. Die '+'-Angaben übertragen sich auf die Attribut- und Relationship-Gleichsetzungen, da sich die Attributwerte ebenso auf beide Tabellen aufteilen.

Beim Diskriminantenansatz ist die Diskriminantenbedingung zur Bildung der Subtypen zu spezifizieren: MGR : ANG from relation T_ANG [MGR?=true] besagt, daß alle Tupel in T_ANG mit MGR?=true als MGR-Objekte aufgefaßt werden sollen. Die anderen Diskriminantenansätze lassen sich entsprechend über die Bedingung steuern.

Ist die Zuordnung eines Objekttyps zu einer Tabelle erst einmal definiert, können die jeweiligen Attribute miteinander in Beziehung gesetzt werden. Für Attribute mit Standarddomänen können die Attribute direkt als FNr=T_FIRMA.FNr gleichgesetzt werden, die FNr von FIRMA findet sich in T_FIRMA als FNr. Komplexe Domänen in der Typdefinition lassen sich durch Tupelbildung Adresse = (T_PERSON.PLZ, T_PERSON.Ort, T_PERSON.Strasse) aus elementaren relationalen Attributen zusammensetzen. Horizontale Partitionierung erfordert, wie oben bereits erwähnt, korrespondierende '+'-Angaben.

Für mengenwertige Attribute, die durch eine eigene Tabelle dargestellt werden, ist die Menge der Werte explizit aus der Tabelle zu berechnen: Set<String> Filialen = { T_ORT.Filiale | T_ORT.FNr = T_FIRMA.FNr } drückt aus, daß sich die Filialen als Filiale-Werte der T_ORT-Tupel finden, wobei die FNr der Tupel mit der FNr der betrachteten Firma übereinstimmen muß.

Die relationale Realisierung von Beziehungen läßt sich in ähnlicher Form konkretisieren. Zwischen den Objekttypen ANG und FIRMA besteht eine über das relationale Attribut Firma ausgedrückte Beziehung, die für ANG entsprechend als ArbeitetIn = (T_FIRMA | T_FIRMA.FNr = T_ANG.Firma) bzw. für FIRMA als Mitarbeiter = { T_ANG | T_ANG.Firma = T_FIRMA.FNr } definiert wird. Runde Klammern spezifizieren ein in Beziehung stehendes Objekt, während geschweifte Klammern eine Menge darstellen. In beiden Fällen wird eine Verbundbedingung angegeben, welche die jeweiligen Tabellen in Beziehung setzt. Im Fall von Beziehungen, die über eine eigene Tabelle relational realisiert sind, ist entsprechend der Bezug der beiden Tabellen, die die beteiligten Objekttypen darstellen, zu der Beziehungsrelation auszudrücken.

In der obigen Spezifikation ist zu beachten, daß ADRESSE im Typ PERSON lokal vereinbart und somit für andere Typen nicht sichtbar ist. Die Ursache dafür liegt darin, daß ADRESSE kein eigenständiger Typ ist, er entwickelt keine eigenen Instanzen. Es gibt keine ADRESSE-Objekte, die unabhängig von PERSON existieren.

Alle in Abschnitt 2.2 erwähnten Aspekte sind in der Spezifikationssprache berücksichtigt, auch wenn hier nur ein Teilausschnitt gezeigt werden konnte. Die Sprache erlaubt eine orthogonale Kombination in jeglicher Hinsicht. Es gibt keinerlei Restriktionen hinsichtlich ihrer kombinierten Anwendbarkeit. Die Spezifikation wird wie in [KPM93] als Metainformation in einem Dictionary abgelegt und zur Implementierung des generierten objektorientierten Schemas (C++-Klassen mit generischen Methoden) genutzt.

2.4 Konsistenzprüfungen

Mit der manuellen Spezifikation einer semantischen Anreicherung ergibt sich unmittelbar das Problem, daß auch *unsinnige* Remodellierungen spezifiziert werden können. Der Begriff "unsinnig" ist in zweierlei Hinsicht zu interpretieren: Zunächst einmal können unsinnige Remodellierungen dadurch entstehen, daß die Grammatik (in ihrer kontextfreien Form) zu viele Freiheiten zuläßt. Das Problem kann auf einfache Weise durch kontextsensitive Regeln behoben werden. Rein grammatikalische Einschränkungen betreffen die unterschiedlichen Formen der Gleichungen und der from relation-Klausel. Zum Beispiel hat eine vertikale Subtyp-Strategie die Form relation[attribute = relation.attribute], wobei attribute entweder ein einzelnes Attribut oder eine geklammerte Attributliste bezeichnet. In jedem Fall müssen die Attributlisten dieselbe Kardinalität besitzen und die korrespondierenden Attribute Typkompatibilität aufweisen. Die reine Syntax übersteigend sind Regeln, die den Zusammenhang zum relationalen Schema herstellen. Generell müssen die Relationen auch im relationalen Schema definiert sein, wie auch die Attribute zu den jeweiligen Relationen gehören müssen. Hierfür ist ein Zugriff auf die relationale Schemainformation erforderlich.

Die Einhaltung der kontextsensitiven Regeln ist allein noch nicht ausreichend, um sinnvolle semantische Anreicherungen zu garantieren. Jede Form einer Anreicherung setzt voraus, daß der relationale Datenbestand die explizit gemachte Semantik beinhaltet, d.h. einen entsprechenden Inhalt aufweist. So lassen sich aus der semantischen Anreicherung Konsistenzbedingungen ableiten. Zum Beispiel fordert jedes Auftreten der Form relation[attribute] in der from relation-Klausel, daß Attribute attribute verwendet werden, die in der Relation relation eindeutig die Tupel identifizieren; sie müssen ein Schlüsselkandidat, aber nicht notwendig Schlüssel der Relation sein. Weitere typische Bedingungen betreffen die Subtypspezifikation. Die vertikale Strategie impliziert Inklusionsbedingungen der Art T_PERSON.PNr $\supseteq$ T_ANG.PNr zwischen Ober- und Untertypen. Hingegen fordern horizontale Subtypen eine Disjunktheit der Werte der spezifizierten Attribute: T_PERSON.PNr $\cap$ T_ARBEITER.PNr = $\emptyset$. Und beim Diskriminantenansatz ist T_ANG.MGR?=false $\Rightarrow$ T_ANG.Rang=NULL zu fordern; Nicht-Manager besitzen keinen Rang. Die aus der semantischen Anreicherung ableitbaren Integritätsbedingungen können auch komplexerer Natur werden, wenn Remodellierungskonzepte, insbesondere Vererbungsstrategien, miteinander kombiniert werden. So muß beispielsweise jede PNr einer Sekretärin als ein Tupel in T_ANG mit MGR?=false auftreten, formal notiert als: $(\sigma_{MGR?=false} (T\_ANG)).PNr \supseteq T\_SEKR.PNr$.

Allgemein gilt es zu beachten, daß diese Konsistenzbedingungen permanent zu prüfen sind, es sei denn, sie lassen sich anhand erweiterter Schemainformation wie Schlüssel- oder Fremdschlüsselangaben ermitteln. Eine einmalige Überprüfung der Bedingungen zum Zeitpunkt der semantischen Anreicherung stellt ansonsten nur sicher, daß nur zu diesem Zeitpunkt die Anreicherung Sinn macht.

3 Graphische Unterstützung der semantischen Anreicherung

Korrespondierend zur expliziten textuellen Spezifikationssprache wird nun eine komfortable interaktive Benutzungsschnittstelle zur Anreicherung vorgestellt. Dieses graphische Remodellierungswerkzeug stellt dieselbe Funktionalität bereit und bietet zusätzlich folgende Vorteile:

- Eine semantische Anreicherung läßt sich aus dem vorliegenden relationalen Schema *inkrementell* erstellen, indem die resultierenden Objekttypen wie auch ihr Zusammenhang zu den Tabellen graphisch entwickelt werden. Die Spezifikation der objektorientierten Schemata und der Zuordnungen zu den Tabellen wird somit für einen großen Benutzerkreis leichter *erfaßbar* und handhabbar als die textuelle Repräsentation.

- Der Benutzer wird von den syntaktischen Zwängen einer textuellen Notation befreit, indem kontextfreie und kontextsensitive Zusammenhänge durch eine *syntaxgestützte* Vorgehensweise weitgehend gewährleistet werden.

- Zudem können auf Wunsch unsinnige Remodellierungen durch Überprüfung der Konsistenzbedingungen aus Abschnitt 2.4 anhand des relationalen Datenbestands jederzeit angezeigt werden.

Das Grundprinzip besteht darin, die relationalen Tabellen, die resultierenden Objekttypen und deren Zusammenhänge durch graphische Objekte ('Widget') [2] zu visualisieren. Das Bedienprinzip für die graphische Unterstützung der semantischen Anreicherung beinhaltet das Einfügen und Löschen dieser Widgets sowie das Ändern ihrer Eigenschaften. Soweit möglich, wird beim Einfügen eines Widgets immer eine semantisch richtige Voreinstellung der Eigenschaften gewählt, die durch Benutzereingaben dann geändert oder detailliert werden kann. Aus der graphischen Darstellung kann im Prinzip zu jedem Zeitpunkt eine äquivalente textuelle Schemabeschreibung (gemäß Abschnitt 2.3) erzeugt werden. Umgekehrt kann diese auch eingelesen und zur Darstellung gebracht werden. Spezielle vom Benutzer festgelegte Layoutinformation muß bei einem solchen Schritt natürlich gesondert behandelt werden.

Die graphische Unterstützung der semantischen Anreicherung läßt sich in drei grundsätzliche Schritte unterteilen, wobei - wie bei der textuellen Spezifikation - die Erstellung der aus der Anreicherung resultierenden Objekttypen im Vordergrund steht.

Zunächst wird zu gegebener relationaler Datenbank das Schema, wie es in den Systemtabellen des DBSs vorliegt, erfaßt und mit *Tabellen-Widgets* dargestellt. Diese Graphikobjekte besitzen eine tabellenartige Struktur. Ihre Einträge sind editierbar, um Strukturinformation wie Fremdschlüssel, die nicht explizit in den Systemtabellen abgespeichert ist, hinzufügen zu können. Der Abstraktionsgrad der Darstellung ist wählbar, so daß beispielsweise das Gesamtschema kompakt im Überblick, aber auch alle Details einzelner Typen dargestellt werden können.

Im zweiten Schritt wird zu jedem Tabellen-Widget automatisch ein gleichstrukturierter Objekttyp als *Typ-Widget* erzeugt. Die Visualisierung des nun (erst rudimentären) objektorientierten Schemas basiert auf der Objekttypnotation der Object Modeling Technique (OMT) [RBP+91]. Jedes Typ-Widget enthält die Strukturinformation des Typs, der dazugehörigen Tabelle wie auch deren Zuordnungen. Wegen der strukturell äquivalenten Darstellung von Typen und Tabellen läßt sich der Zusammenhang auf einen Blick erfassen.

Diese Darstellung ist die Grundlage für den dritten Schritt, der eigentlichen semantischen Anreicherung. Alle in Abschnitt 2.2 erwähnten Aspekte einer Remodellierung lassen sich auf den Widgets ausführen, indem graphisch interaktiv das aus dem vorangegangenen Schritt entstandene ODMG-Schema verfeinert wird. Durch entsprechende graphische Symbole werden in komfortabler Weise die Zuordnungen spezifiziert.

Die einzelnen Schritte werden in den folgenden Unterabschnitten beispielhaft erläutert.

---

2. Obwohl wir dazu neigen, keine englischen Begriffe einzudeutschen, verwenden wir im folgenden den Begriff 'Widget', um eine Mehrfachbenutzung von 'Objekt' zu vermeiden.

Die folgenden graphischen Darstellungen sind unabhängig von speziellen Graphiksystemen, um von den jeweiligen Entwurfsphilosophien und Style Guides zu abstrahieren. So wurde beim Entwurf der graphischen Objekte darauf geachtet, daß im Prinzip auch zeichenorientierte Bildschirme verwendet werden können. Dies ist einer der Gründe, warum sich die Objekttypnotation an OMT orientiert; die OMT-Notation wurde gerade mit dem Ziel entwickelt, keine besonderen Anforderungen an Graphiksysteme zu stellen. Die Objektdiagramme von OMT wurden für unsere Zwecke zur Spezifikation von Anreicherungen erweitert und auch für eine äquivalente Darstellung der Tabellen benutzt. Die Eigenschaften der graphischen Objekte, z.B. Attribute eines Typs, werden in tabellenorientierter Form dargestellt. Alternative Darstellungen wie popup-Menüs, Dialogboxen, List- oder Textboxen sowie Unterfenster können nach den Konventionen der jeweiligen Plattform ausgesucht werden. Selbiges gilt für das Anstoßen von Funktionen. Auch hierfür gibt es die verschiedensten Vorschläge und Konventionen in den Fenstersystemen der verschiedenen Plattformen.

3.1 Erfassung und Anreicherung des relationalen Schemas

Zu einer Datenbank lassen sich die Strukturinformationen der Tabellen aus den Systemtabellen ermitteln und entsprechend visualisieren. Die Struktur einer Tabelle beinhaltet den Tabellennamen und je Spalte den Attributnamen, ihre Domäne, Angaben über die Schlüsseleigenschaften (Primärschlüssel, zusammengesetzter Schlüssel, Fremdschlüssel zu welcher Tabelle/Spalte mit welcher Kardinalität), Nullwertverbot (not null bzw. abgekürzt '!') und der Ordnung der Attribute. Die Schlüsselbeschreibung und die Ordnung sind optional und editierbar. Abbildung 3 zeigt das zugehörige Tabellen-Widget der Tabelle T_PERSON.

T_PERSON			▦ ⁘⁙⁙⁙	
Attribut	*Domäne*	*Schlüssel*	*Nullwert?*	*Ordnung*
Prio:1	*Prio:2*	*Prio:2*	*Prio:3*	*Prio:3*
PNr	Long	primary	not null	1
Name	String		not null	2
PLZ	Long			3
Ort	String			4
Strasse	String			5

Abbildung 3: Tabellen-Widget

Diese Informationen nehmen bei der Darstellung mehr Platz ein, als einer übersichtlichen Darstellung mehrerer Tabellen zuträglich wäre. Daher wird pro Strukturinformation eine Priorität vergeben, die ausdrückt, welche Tabelleneigenschaften bei kompakterer Darstellung weggelassen werden können. Die Priorität ist vom Benutzer nachträglich änderbar. Gemäß der vergebenen Prioritätsstufe lassen sich einzelne Details ausblenden.

Die Tabellen werden nach dem Einlesen der Strukturinformationen entsprechend einer totalen Ordnung (z.B. alphabetisch nach dem Namen) unter Berücksichtigung des voreingestellten Abstraktionsgrades zeilenweise von links nach rechts dargestellt. Falls die Graphikplattform Sinnbilder ('Icons') unterstützt, ist es praktisch, den Tabellen Sinnbilder zuzuordnen, da diese das Wiedererkennen von Widgets innerhalb größerer Ansammlungen erheblich beschleunigen. Des weiteren kann es zur Strukturierung größerer Anzahlen von Tabellen sinnvoll sein, diese mit Hilfe von Teilschemata im Sinne eines Modulkonzepts zu gruppieren, so daß diese zur Abstraktion herangezogen werden können. Teilschemata können ebenfalls benannt und zur besseren Wiedererkennbarkeit mit einem Sinnbild versehen werden.

Die Spezifikation kann nachträglich vom Benutzer vervollständigt werden, beispielsweise um Angaben zu Fremdschlüsselbeziehungen, sofern diese nicht direkt der Schemainformation entnommen werden konnten. In einer späteren Erweiterung können hierzu auch Verfahren wie [CaS91, Cas93] eingesetzt werden, die anhand des Datenbestands automatisch diese implizite Semantik ermitteln. Auf Wunsch lassen sich die durch Fremdschlüssel ausgedrückten Beziehungen im Schemagraph entsprechend der OMT-Notation in verschiedenen Abstraktionsstufen anzeigen (vgl. Abbildung 4). Zu beachten ist, daß T_ANG und T_FIRMA ansonsten noch eine relationale Struktur aufweisen. Entsprechende Algorithmen (analog [TBB88]) werden eingesetzt, um eine übersichtliche, kreuzungsarme Darstellung zu erhalten.

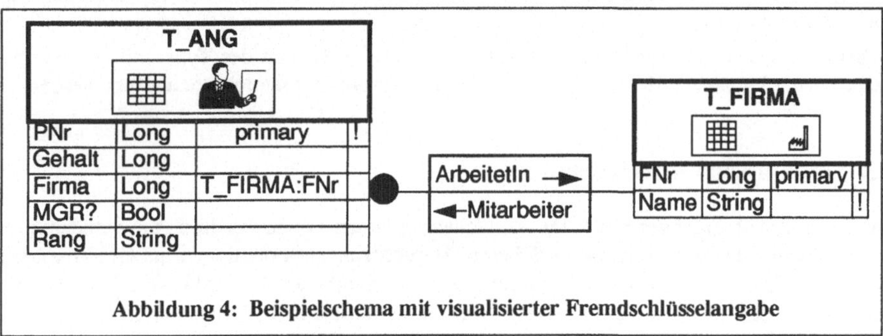

Abbildung 4: Beispielschema mit visualisierter Fremdschlüsselangabe

3.2 Standardschemaabbildung

Die im ersten Schritt entstandenen Tabellenbeschreibungen werden anschließend in äquivalente Typbeschreibungen umgesetzt. Zunächst wird zu jeder Tabelle mit einem Primärschlüssel ein entsprechender Objekttyp als Typ-Widget erzeugt. Die Attribute mit kompatiblen Domänen werden direkt übernommen. Aus den Fremdschlüsselangaben werden explizite Beziehungen abgeleitet.

PERSON						
PERSON			T_PERSON			
Attribut	*Domäne*	*Sichtbarkeit*	*Relationales Attribut*	*Relationale Domäne*	*Schlüssel*	*Nullwert?*
Prio:1	*Prio:2*	*Prio:2*	*Prio:1*	*Prio:2*	*Prio:2*	*Prio:3*
PNr	Long	private	PNr	Long	primary	not null
Name	String	public	PName	String		not null
PLZ	Long	public	PLZ	Long		
Ort	String	public	Ort	String		
Strasse	String	public	Strasse	String		

Abbildung 5: Widget mit integrierter objektorientierter und relationaler Strukturinformation

Jeder Objekttyp muß einen Primärschlüssel besitzen, da ansonsten kein Objektidentifikator abgeleitet werden kann (dieser wird aber für Objektmanipulationen benötigt). Tabellen ohne Primärschlüssel können folglich keinen Objekttyp repräsentieren, sie müssen als Bag<Tupel> remodelliert werden. Existiert jedoch ein Fremdschlüssel zur Tabelle, so kann eine Einbettung in einen Typ erfolgen.

Die graphischen Objekte zur Darstellung dieses nun objektorientierten Schemas sind an die graphische Notation von OMT angelehnt und um zusätzliche Eigenschaften für die Zuordnung zu den entsprechenden Tabellen und deren Spalten erweitert. Abbildung 5 zeigt das anhand von PERSON und T_PERSON.

Diese Darstellung gibt einen sofortigen Überblick über den Zusammenhang der Objekttypen zu den Tabellen einschließlich der Attributzuordnungen, läßt aber andererseits das ursprüngliche relationale Schema verschwinden. Die Tabellenstruktur kann aber jederzeit wieder explizit gemacht werden, indem aus der integrierten Darstellung getrennte Tabellen- und Typ-Widgets erzeugt werden, wobei die Attributzuordnungen durch Verbindungslinien visualisiert werden (siehe Abbildung 6).

In beiden Formen der Typbeschreibung können nun die Namen des Typs und der Attribute geändert werden sowie Sichtbarkeitsbeschränkungen (public, private) hinzugefügt werden.

3.3 Semantische Anreicherung

Zur Spezifikation einer semantischen Anreicherung lassen sich in das durch die Standardabbildung entstandene objektorientierte Schema Anreicherungsinformationen als Graphikobjekte einbringen. Diese ähneln den strukturdefinierenden Symbolen der OMT-Notation, sind aber mit zusätzlicher Information attributiert. Diese Graphikobjekte befinden sich in einem hierarchisch organisierten Werkzeugkasten.

Zum Beispiel ist 'Vererbung' ein Konzept des Kastens, das weiter unterteilt ist in die verschiedenen Einzelstrategien 'vertikal', 'horizontal', 'Diskriminante' und 'Materialisierung'. Je Anreicherungskonzept gibt es ein Sinnbild (siehe Tabelle 1), das aus dem Werkzeugkasten ausgewählt, positioniert und über aktive Enden mit den Typen in Verbindung gebracht werden kann. Die Graphikobjekte sind teilweise attributiert, so daß eine kontextabhängige Anforderung weiterer Information erfolgt: Je nach Anreicherungskonzept sind unterschiedliche Daten zu einer vollständigen Spezifikation erforderlich. Die zusätzlichen Eigenschaften können über drag&drop, durch Hineinkopieren bzw. direkte Eingabe eingefügt werden. Systemvorschläge könnten hier auf der Basis von Namensähnlichkeiten oder Reihenfolgenkonventionen erfolgen. Zufriedenstellende und praktikable Lösungen bedürfen hier aber eines hohen Aufwands.

Strategie	Sinnbild	Attributierung
horizontal	⟷	alle zum Obertyp exportierten Attribute
vertikal	↕	Verbundbedingung, z.B. T_PERSON.PNr = T_ANG.PNr
Diskriminantenansatz	=	Diskriminantenausdruck, z.B. MGR? = true
vollständige Materialisierung	M	gleichzusetzende Attribute
Generalisierung	↑	exportierte Attribute

Tabelle 1: Darstellung der Vererbungsstrategien

Zur Spezifikation von Vererbung lassen sich beispielsweise zwischen den Ober- und Untertypen Vererbungskanten in OMT-Notation einfügen. Da mehrere Strategien zur Remodellierung von Vererbungsbeziehungen unterschieden werden, fordern diese Kanten eine Angabe der jeweiligen Vererbungsstrategie und einer damit verbundenen Eingabe der benötigten Informationen. Deren graphische Umsetzung erfolgt durch Attributierung der Vererbungsbeziehungen. In der OMT-Notation wird entsprechend die untere Kante des Vererbungssymbols mit diesen Angaben versehen. Exemplarisch ist dies in Abbildung 6 für den Fall einer horizontalen Strategie dargestellt: Nach Einrichten der Vererbungskante wird der Benutzer aufgefordert, zu jedem Attribut des Obertyps ein korrespondierendes Attribut des Untertyps anzuwählen. Die horizontale Strategie ist ja dadurch charakterisiert, daß sich die Attribute der Obertyp-Tabelle auch bei der Untertyp-Tabelle wiederfinden. Die Typkompatibilität der Attributpaare wird überprüft. Die einander zugeordneten Attribute werden jeweils bei dem Subtyp ausgeblendet; sie werden von PERSON ererbt. Entsprechende Verbindungen zur relationalen Seite werden hergestellt. Die Vererbungskante wird um die von ARBEITER zu PERSON "exportierten" Attribute versehen.

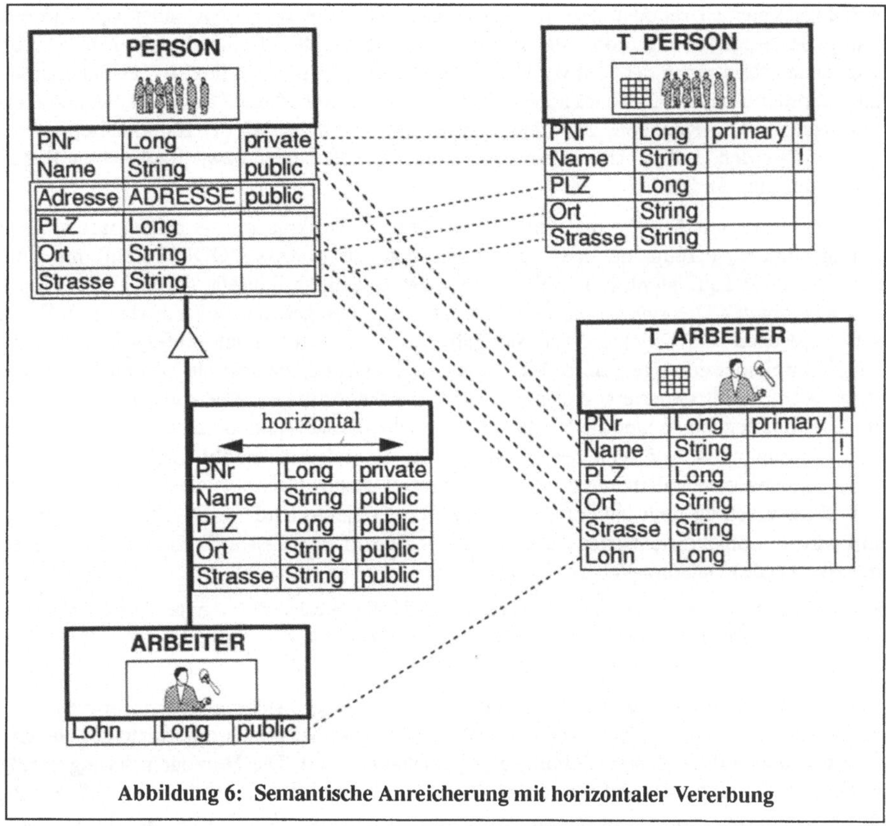

Abbildung 6: Semantische Anreicherung mit horizontaler Vererbung

Für die anderen Vererbungsstrategien sind die Attributierungen in Tabelle 1 zusammengestellt. Der einzugebende Informationsgehalt entspricht der Diskussion in Abschnitt 2.2 bzw. der Syntax in Abschnitt 2.3.

Des weiteren zeigt das Beispiel, wie sich aus den relationalen Attributen PLZ, Ort und Strasse das objektorientierte Attribut Adresse vom Typ ADRESSE restrukturieren läßt. Hierzu ist eine Gruppierung (Doppelumrandung) der drei Attribute im Typ-Widget erforderlich, die anschließend mit der zusätzlichen Angabe des objektorientierten Attributnamens zu versehen ist. Abbildung 6 zeigt die semantische Anreicherung nach Durchführung dieser Aktionen. In ähnlicher Form sind alle anderen in Abschnitt 2.2 diskutierten Remodellierungsregeln graphisch spezifizierbar.

Zu jedem Zeitpunkt läßt sich überprüfen, ob die relationale Datenbank der aktuellen semantischen Anreicherung genügt. Ist eine Konsistenzbedingung verletzt, so wird dem Benutzer automatisch die entsprechende irreguläre Anreicherung angezeigt.

4 Zusammenfassung

Dieser Beitrag hatte zum Ziel, zwei Spezifikationssprachen, eine syntaktische und eine graphische, zur semantischen Anreicherung von relationalen Datenbanken im objektorientierten Objektmodell des ODMG-Standards [Cat94] vorzustellen. Im Gegensatz zu vergleichbaren Remodellierungsansätzen erfolgt die Anreicherung nicht in Form von technischen Regeln wie funktionalen oder Inklusionsabhängigkeiten. Diese Abhängigkeiten sind sehr ungenaue Hinweise für eine Remodellierung, so daß nicht alle beim Entwurf der Tabellen verwendeten Abbildungsstrategien rekonstruiert werden können. Unser Ansatz sieht daher vor, daß eine semantische Anreicherung direkt als ein objektorientiertes ODMG-Schema definiert und der Bezug zu den Relationen herstellt wird. Die Spezifikation ist folglich intuitiv verständlich und erlaubt darüber hinaus, nahezu jegliche in Relationen "hineinkodierte" Semantik wieder explizit zu machen. Alle Konzepte des Objektmodells können dabei bei der Remodellierung voll ausgenutzt werden, indem sie in entsprechenden syntaktischen bzw. graphischen Regeln Berücksichtigung finden.

Während die meisten Ansätze nur eine objektorientierte Struktur aus der semantischen Anreicherung ableiten, erzeugt der hier verwendete generative Ansatz ODMG-konforme C++-Klassen, also ein äquivalentes ODMG-Schema, das sowohl strukturelle als auch operationale Aspekte beinhaltet. Die generierten C++-Klassen beinhalten generische Methoden zum Erzeugen und Löschen von Objekten, zur Navigation und zur assoziativen Anfrageformulierung. Auch die Implementierungen dieser Methoden auf der Grundlage des relationalen Datenbanksystems werden mit generiert, wobei insbesondere die Anfrageübersetzung auf relationales SQL sehr komplex ist, da hier die Vielfalt an unterschiedlichen Remodellierungsmöglichkeiten die zu generierenden Anfragen beeinflußt und die Komplexität erhöht. Insgesamt stellt das ODMG-Schema eine vollständige objektorientierte Datenbankschnittstelle bereit, die in diesem Fall identisch zu dem zukünftigen Standard für objektorientierte Datenbanksysteme ist. Somit wird ein objektorientierter, standardisierter Zugriff von C++ auf relationale (insbesondere existierende) Datenbanken bereitgestellt.

Der präsentierte Ansatz wird zur Zeit noch auf SUN4-Workstations unter Unix und Motif implementiert. Die Implementierung ist flexibel und prinzipiell bezüglich weiterer Regeln zur semantischen Anreicherung erweiterbar.

Weitere Arbeiten beschäftigen sich derzeit mit der Homogenisierung anderer, insbesondere objektorientierter Datenbanksysteme und Dateisysteme, wobei das Grundprinzip der Generierung einer standardkonformen Schnittstelle beibehalten wird. Die Homogenisierung ermöglicht dann auf einfache Art und Weise eine Datenmigration zwischen den jeweiligen Systemen, beispielsweise von Tabellen in ein objektorientiertes Schema. Ein nächster Schritt wird sein, ein Werkzeug zu entwickeln, das automatisch Migrationsprogramme erzeugt.

Die Gesamtheit der homogenisierten Schemata bildet die Basis der Schemaintegration, in der semantische Konflikte zwischen den lokalen Schemata zu eliminieren sind. Analog zur semantischen Anreicherung ist eine *Integrationssprache* in Arbeit, die Konstrukte anbietet, um verschiedene Maßeinheiten (z.B. Dollar / DM, exkl. / inkl. Steuer) aneinander anzupassen, Namenskonflikte wie Homonyme und Synonyme zu beseitigen und Generalisierungen [KDN90] von Typen vorzunehmen, beispielsweise um in unterschiedlichen Systemen abgespeicherte Objekte gleichen Typs zusammenzuführen. Orthogonal dazu lassen sich größere Umstrukturierungen spezifizieren, wie in [SpP91, SCG92] erwähnt, die Typen eine vollkommen neue, aber inhaltlich äquivalente Struktur geben, und neue DBS-übergreifende Beziehungen zwischen den bislang disjunkten Datenbeständen definieren. Im Prinzip ist die Schemaintegration ähnlich handhabbar, generativ mit einer expliziten Beschreibung der Integration, auch wenn die zu behandelnden Probleme im einzelnen andere sind.

5 Literatur

[BLN86]   E. Batini, M. Lenzerini, S. Navathe: *A Comparative Analysis of Methodologies for Database Schema Integration*. ACM Computing Surveys 1986, 18(4) (323 - 364)

[CaS91]   M. Castellanos, F. Saltor: *Semantic Enrichment of Database Schemas: An Object-Oriented Approach*. In [KRS91]

[Cas93]   M. Castellanos: *Semantic Enrichment of Interoperable Databases*. In [IMS93]

[Cat94]   R. Cattell (ed.): *The ODMG-93 Standard for Object Databases*. 2nd edition, Morgan-Kaufmann Publishers, San Mateo (CA) 1994

[DaA87]   K.H. Davis, K. Arora: *Converting a Relational Database Model into an Entity-Relationship Model*. In S. March (ed.): Proc. of 6th Int. Conf. on Entity-Relationship Approach, Chicago 1987

[Här92]   M. Härtig: *An Object-Oriented Integration Framework for Building Heterogeneous Database Systems*. In [HNS92] (33 - 53)

[HNS92]   D.K. Hsia, E.J. Neuhold, R. Sacks-Davis (eds.): Proc. of the IFIP WG 2.6 Database Semantics Conference (DS-5) on Interoperable Database Systems, Lorne (Australia), 1992

[HoO93]   U. Hohenstein, E. Odberg: *A C++ Database Interface Based upon the Entity-Relationship Approach*. In M. Worboys, A. Grundy (eds.): Proc. of 11th British National Conference on Database Systems (BNCOD11), Keele (England) 1993

[IMS93]   Proc. of Conf. on Research Issues in Data Engineering: *Interoperability in Multidatabase Systems* (RIDE-IMS'93). Vienna 1993

[KDN90]   M. Kaul, K. Drosten, E. Neuhold: *ViewSystem: Integrating Heterogeneous Information Bases by Object-Oriented Views*. In: Proc. 6th Int. Conf. on Data Engineering, Los Angeles 1990 (2 - 10)

[KRS91]   Y. Kambayashi, M. Rusinkiewicz, A. Sheth (eds.): Proc. of 1st Int. Workshop on *Interoperability in Multidatabase Systems*. Kyoto (Japan), 1991

[KPM93]   D. Keim, H.-P. Kriegel, A. Mietsham: *Integration of Relational Databases in a Multidatabase System based on Schema Enrichment*. In [IMS93] (96 - 104)

[MaM90]   V. Markowitz, J. Markowsky: *Identifying Extended ER Object Structures in Relational Schemas*. IEEE Transactions on Software Engineering 16(8), 1990

[NaA87]   S. Navathe, A. Awong: *Abstracting Relational and Hierarchical Databases with a Semantic Data Model*. In S. March (ed.): Proc. of 6th Int. Conf. on Entity-Relationship Approach, Chicago 1987

[PrB94]   W. Premerlani, M. Blaha: *An Approach for Reverse Engineering of Relational Databases*. Communications of the ACM 37(5), May 1994

[RBP+91]   J. Rumbaugh, M. Blaha, W. Premerlani, F. Eddy, W. Lorensen: *Object-Oriented Modeling and Design*. Prentice-Hall, Englewood-Cliffs NJ, 1991

[RAD+91]   R. Rafii, R. Ahmed, P. DeSmedt, B. Kent, M. Ketabchi, W. Litwin: *Multidatabase Management in Pegasus*. In [KRS91]

[SCG92]   F. Saltor, M. Castellanos, M. Garcia-Solaco: *Overcoming Schematic Discrepancies in Interoperable Databases*. In [HNS92]

[ShL90]   A. Sheth, J. Larson: *Federated Database Systems for Managing Distributed, Heterogeneous and Autonomous Databases*. ACM Computing Surveys 1990, 22(3)

[SpP91]   S. Spaccapietra, C. Parent: *Conflicts and Correspondence Assertions in Interoperable Databases*. ACM SIGMOD-RECORD 1991, 20(4)

[TBB88]   R. Tamassia, G. DiBattista, C. Batini: *Automatic Graph Drawing and Readability of Diagrams*. In: IEEE Transactions on Systems, Man, and Cybernetics 1988, 18(1) (61 - 79)

[YaL92]   L.-L. Yan, T.-W. Ling: *Translating Relational Schema With Constraints Into OODB Schema*. In [HNS92] (69 - 85)

[WEZS93]   M. Wallrath, H. Esterle, J. Zirbs, E. Steinwand: *Vom relationalen Datenbankschema zum objektorientierten Informationsmodell - Methoden der Informations(rück)gewinnung*. In: 5. Kolloquium der Technischen Akademie Esslingen "Softwareentwicklung - Methoden, Werkzeuge, Erfahrungen 93", September 1993

Unterstützung des korrektheitszentrierten Entwurfs von Informationssystemen

Stefan Conrad

Universität Magdeburg, Institut für Technische Informationssysteme,
Postfach 4120, D-39016 Magdeburg, Germany
E-mail: `conrad@iti.cs.uni-magdeburg.de`

Zusammenfassung Im vorliegenden Beitrag wird ein Ansatz zum Einsatz von Verifikationswerkzeugen in der Entwurfsphase für Informationssysteme vorgestellt. Basierend auf einer einfachen Beschreibungssprache für Struktur und Verhalten von Objekten wird ein geigneter Kalkül präsentiert, mit dem das Beweisen von Objekteigenschaften mittels Herleitung aus der Spezifikation möglich wird. Hiermit ist eine frühe formale Überprüfung des Entwurfes auf wichtige Eigenschaften möglich.

1 Einleitung

Für die Entwicklung von Informationssystemen spielt der konzeptionelle Entwurf eine zentrale Rolle. Fehler, die in dieser Phase gemacht werden, haben weitreichende und damit vor allem kostenintensive Folgen. Kommt zu dem Entwurf der Struktur des betrachteten Weltausschnittes auch noch die Beschreibung des Verhaltens hinzu, erreicht der Entwurf schnell eine Komplexität, die die Entdeckung von Modellierungsfehlern und Beschreibungsfehlern erheblich erschwert. Fehler in der Verhaltensbeschreibung können insbesondere in sicherheitskritischen Systemen hohe Kosten verursachen oder sogar Menschenleben gefährden.

Daher haben wir im Rahmen des BMFT–Verbundprojektes KorSo die korrektheitszentrierte Entwicklung von Informationssystemen untersucht und dabei drei Schwerpunkte gesetzt: die Konzeption einer geeigneten Enwicklungsumgebung, Animation und Verifikation. Als Grundlage unserer Arbeit verwenden wir eine vereinfachte Sprache zur Beschreibung von Objekten (TROLL *light* [CGH92]), die ein Dialekt der Sprache TROLL [JSHS91] ist.

Diese Bemühungen ordnen sich gut in die allgemeinen Bestrebungen ein, formale Methoden schon in den frühen Phasen der Entwicklung einzusetzen. Hiermit kann der immer stärker werdenden Forderung nach Zertifikation von Softwaresystemen Rechnung getragen werden (vgl. [Krü93, Rom93]). Aus unserer Sicht kann sich an die Erstellung einer formalen Spezifikation, ihrer Validierung und Verifikation eine Transformation auf ein bestehendes objektorientiertes Datenbanksystem (siehe [Heu92]) anschließen.

---

[0] Diese Arbeit wurde gefördert durch das BMFT im Projekt KorSo (= KoRrekte Software, Förd. Nr. IT 01 IS 203 D) und durch die ESPRIT Basic Research Working Groups IS-CORE (No. 6071) and ModelAge (No. 8319).

In diesem Beitrag soll der Gesichtspunkt der Verifikation von Objektspezifikationen im Vordergrund stehen, d.h. die Bereitstellung eines geeigneten K'alküls,
der in Form eines Beweisunterstützungssystems als Werkzeug dem Benutzer zur
Verfügung gestellt wird. Der Aspekt der Animation von Objektspezifikationen
ist z.B. in [HFG94, HG94] ausführlicher dargestellt.

Im folgenden werden wir zunächst kurz die Sprache TROLL *light* vorstellen.
Anschließend geben wir eine informelle Einführung in den zugehörigen Basiskalkül, gehen kurz auf Beweisregeln und das Führen von Beweisen ein. Danach
diskutieren wir die Funktionalität des Beweisunterstützungssystems.

2 TROLL *light*

TROLL *light* [CGH92, GCH93, HCG94] ist eine Sprache zur Beschreibung von
strukturellen und dynamischen Eigenschaften von Objekten. Die Beschreibung
von strukturellen Eigenschaften orientiert sich in weiten Teilen an semantischen
Datenmodellen.

- Die in einem Zustand beobachtbaren Eigenschaften eines Objektes werden
  durch Attribute beschrieben. Einfache Attribute sind daten– oder objekt-
  wertig. Darüber hinaus erlauben vordefinierte Sortenkonstruktoren wie *set*
  oder *tuple* auch die Spezifikation komplexer Attributbereiche.
- TROLL *light*–Objekte sind in Objekthierarchien organisiert, die sich aus Unterobjektbeziehungen ergeben. Eine Unterobjektbeziehung ist hierbei als eine exklusive „Teil von "– bzw. Komponentenbeziehung zu verstehen.
- Normalerweise werden Attributwerte direkt durch das Eintreten gewisser Ereignisse bestimmt. Daneben ist es auch möglich, abgeleitete Attribute zu spezifizieren, d.h. Attribute, deren Inhalte sich aus anderer gespeicherter oder
  abgeleiteter Information bestimmen. Zur Formulierung von Ableitungsregeln
  stellt TROLL *light* einen SQL–ähnlichen Anfragekalkül zur Verfügung.
- Der Anfragekalkül von TROLL *light* unterstützt auch die Spezifikation sta-
  tischer Integritätsbedingungen.

Die Beschreibung von dynamischen Eigenschaften basiert auf der Spezifikation
von Ereignissen. Ereignisse sind Abstraktionen von zustandsverändernden Operationen auf Objekten.

- Objektereignisse werden durch eine endliche Menge von Ereignisgeneratoren
  beschrieben. Jeder Ereignisgenerator kann mit einer Liste von Parametern
  versehen sein.
- Die Auswirkung von Ereignissen auf Attribute werden durch Auswertungs-
  regeln beschrieben.
- Ereignisse in verschiedenen Objekten können durch Interaktionsregeln syn-
  chronisiert werden.
- Die möglichen Ereignisfolgen können mit Hilfe CSP-ähnlicher Prozeßbe-
  schreibungen auf zulässige Folgen eingeschränkt werden.

Den Rahmen zur Beschreibung all dieser Objekteigenschaften bilden *Templates*.
Als Beispiel geben wir in Abb. 1 die Beschreibung von Objekten an, die Autoren
in einem Bibliotheksinformationssystem repräsentieren sollen.

```
TEMPLATE Author
   DATA TYPES   String, Date, Nat;
   ATTRIBUTES   Name:string; DateOfBirth:date;
                SoldBooks(Year:nat):nat;
   EVENTS       BIRTH create(Name:string, DateOfBirth:date);
                     changeName(NewName:string);
                     storeSoldBooks(Year:nat, Number:nat);
                DEATH destroy;
   VALUATION    [create(N,D)] Name=N, DateOfBirth=D;
                [changeName(N)] Name=N;
                [storeSoldBooks(Y,NR)] SoldBooks(Y)=NR;
   BEHAVIOR     PROCESS AuthorLife1 =
                   ( storeSoldBooks -> AuthorLife1 |
                     changeName -> AuthorLife2 |
                     destroy );
                PROCESS AuthorLife2 =
                   ( storeSoldBooks -> AuthorLife2 |
                     destroy );
                ( create -> AuthorLife1 );
END TEMPLATE;
```

Abb. 1. Objektbeschreibung für Autoren.

Die so beschriebenen Author-Objekte haben einen Namen, ein Geburtsda-
tum und Anzahlen verkaufter Bücher als Attribute, wobei für jedes Jahr eine Anzahl verkaufter Bücher gespeichert werden kann. Ereignisse, die im Leben eines
Author-Objektes eintreten können, sind sein Geburtsereignis, eine Namensände-
rung, das Abspeichern von Verkaufszahlen und schließlich ein Todesereignis. Im
VALUATION-Abschnitt ist beschrieben, welche Auswirkungen das Eintreten eines
Ereignisses auf Attribute hat. Der Verhaltensteil legt die zulässigen Lebensläufe
von Author-Objekte fest.

```
TEMPLATE AuthorContainer
   DATA TYPES   String, Int;
   TEMPLATES    Author;
   SUBOBJECTS   Authors(No:int):author;
   ATTRIBUTES   DERIVED  NumberOfAuthors:int;
   EVENTS       BIRTH  create;
                     addAuthor(No:int, Name:string, DateOfBirth:string);
                   removeAuthor(No:int);
                DEATH  destroy;
   DERIVATION   NumberOfAuthors=CNT(Authors);
   CONSTRAINTS  NumberOfAuthors<10000;
   INTERACTION  addAuthor(N,S,D) >> Authors(N).create(S,D);
                removeAuthor(N) >> Authors(N).destroy;
END TEMPLATE;
```

Abb. 2. Spezifikation eines zusammengesetzten Objektes.

In TROLL *light* können Objekte hierarchisch zusammengesetzt werden. Der dafür zur Verfügung gestellte Mechanismus sind Unterobjektbeziehungen. In Abb. 2 werden Objekte beschrieben, die Author-Objekte als Unterobjekte haben (im SUBOBJECTS-Abschnitt beschrieben). Im INTERACTION-Teil wird die Kommunikation zwischen dem „Oberobjekt" und seinen „Unterobjekten" festgelegt.

3 Beweisunterstützung

Testverfahren, wie z.B. die Animation einer Spezifikation, können viele Entwurfs- und Beschreibungsfehler entdecken. Allerdings reichen diese Verfahren i.allg. nicht für den Nachweis aus, daß bestimmte Eigenschaften gelten. Insbesondere in Hinblick auf das dynamische Verhalten der beschriebenen Objekte bleibt immer noch eine Unsicherheit darüber übrig, ob die Spezifikation korrekt ist, da immer nur eine endliche Anzahl von Abläufen getestet werden kann.

Daher halten wir ein Beweisunterstützungssystem für notwendig, das uns helfen soll, Eigenschaften einzelner Objekte, aber auch Eigenschaften einer ganzen Objektgesellschaft formal nachzuweisen. Dies erlaubt uns, Eigenschaften zu garantieren, die in allen möglichen Lebensläufen gelten. Allerdings gehen wir davon aus, daß in der Regel nicht jede Eigenschaft formal bewiesen werden sollte, da der Aufwand oft nicht in einem angemessenen Verhältnis zum Nutzen steht. Aber schon der Nachweis wesentlicher Eigenschaften (insbesondere sicherheitskritischer) kann die Zuverlässigkeit des zu entwickelnden Informationssystems wesentlich erhöhen. Eine Reihe von Anwendungsgebieten verlangt in immer größeren Maße verifizierte Software, vor allem wenn fehlerhafte Software große finanzielle Verluste verursachen kann oder sogar menschliches Leben gefährdet.

Auf einer sehr niedrigen Ebene können bereits automatische Werkzeuge eingesetzt werden, die Konsistenzüberprüfungen vornehmen, Mehrdeutigkeiten aufdecken und die Vollständigkeit einer Spezifikation überprüfen können. Auf einer höheren Ebene ist dann das formale Beweisen von Objekteigenschaften möglich. Hier kann das bereits erwähnte Beweisunterstützungssystem eingesetzt werden. Die nachzuweisenden Eigenschaften werden in einem einfachen Kalkül formuliert und können dann interaktiv bewiesen werden, wobei bis zu einem gewissen Grad Beweisabläufe auch automatisierbar sind.

Um eine schnelle Verfügbarkeit für den Einsatz in Fallstudien zu erreichen, haben die Formeln des Kalküls eine sehr einfache Struktur (sogenannte Gentzen-Klauseln). Dadurch läßt sich leicht ein Beweissystem durch Adaption von Inferenzregeln klassischer Sequenzenkalküle erhalten (vgl. [Gen35, Pae88]). Dies erlaubt eine schnelle prototypische Implementierung mit Hilfe eines generischen Theorembeweisers (z.B. ISABELLE [Pau90]).

3.1 Der Basiskalkül

Im folgenden werden anhand von Beispielen Formeln des Kalküls und Inferenzregeln vorstellen. Anschließend zeigen wir mittels eines kleinen Beispiels das Beweisen von Objekteigenschaften. Eine detaillierte Vorstellung und Diskussion des Kalküls ist in [Con94] zu finden.

Formeln des Kalküls sind im wesentlichen Gentzen-Klauseln über einfache Zustandsaussagen, wobei Zustandaussagen folgender Gestalt seien können:

- $t_1 = t_2$ ist eine Zustandaussage über die Gleichheit zweier Terme,
- $p(t_1, \ldots, t_n)$ ist eine Zustandsaussage, wenn p ein Prädikatsymbol ist und $t_1, \ldots, t_n$ Terme geeigneter Sorte sind,
- $\neg P$ ist eine Zustandsaussage, wenn P eine Zustandsaussage ist,
- $[t_o.t_e]P$ ist eine Zustandsaussage, wenn P eine Zustandsaussage ist, t_o ein Term ist, der ein Objekt bezeichnet, und t_e ein Term ist, der ein zu t_o gehöriges Ereignis beschreibt.

$[t_o.t_e]P$ wird gelesen als „wenn als nächstes das Ereignis t_e im Objekt t_o eintritt, dann gilt anschließend P".

Sind also $P_1, \ldots, P_n, Q_1, \ldots, Q_m$ einfache Zustandsaussagen, dann ist

$$P_1, \ldots, P_n \rightarrow Q_1, \ldots, Q_m$$

eine Formel, die wie folgt zu lesen ist: sind P_1 und ... und P_n gleichzeitig erfüllt (in einem beliebigen Zustand der Objektgesellschaft), dann ist gleichzeitig auch Q_1 oder ... oder Q_m erfüllt (in demselben Zustand).

Beispiel:
Betrachten wir die in Abb. 1 gegebene Spezifikation von Author–Objekten, dann beschreiben die folgenden Formeln Eigenschaften solcher Author–Objekte:

(1) $\rightarrow \ [A.changeName(\text{``J.W. Goethe''})]Name(A, \text{``J.W. Goethe''}),$

(2) $\neg \, enable(A.changeName(N)) \rightarrow$
$\qquad [A.storeSoldBooks(Y, C)]\neg \, enable(A.changeName(N)).$

Formel (1) besagt, daß in jedem Zustand (bzw. zu jedem Zeitpunkt) wahr ist, daß nach dem Eintreten eines Ereignisses $changeName(\text{``J.W. Goethe''})$ für ein Author–Objekt A das Attribut $Name$ dieses Objektes den Wert "J.W. Goethe" hat. Dies gilt für jeden Zustand, weil keine einschränkende Vorbedingung auf der linken Seite des $\rightarrow$ gegeben ist. Formel (2) beschreibt, daß, wenn ein Ereignis $changeName(N)$ für ein Author–Objekt A nicht erlaubt ist, es auch nach dem Eintreten eines Ereignisses $storeSoldBooks(Y, C)$ für A nicht erlaubt ist.

Formeln des Kalküls dienen also dazu, Objekteigenschaften zu beschreiben. Damit kann eine ganze Objektgesellschaft durch eine Menge solcher Formeln beschrieben werden. Für die Objektspezifikationssprache TROLL *light* haben wir eine entsprechende Übersetzung entwickelt, die zu einer beliebigen TROLL *light* Spezifikation eine Menge von Kalkülformeln als logische Beschreibung der spezifizierten Objektgesellschaft erzeugt (siehe [Con94]).

Ausgehend von einer Menge solcher Formeln können wir nun unter Anwendung von Inferenzregeln weitere Formeln als logische Konsequenzen herleiten. Eine Zusammenstellung elementarer Inferenzregeln für unseren Kalkül ist in Abb. 3 dargestellt. Diese Regeln konnten im wesentlichen von klassischen Sequenzenkalkülen [Gen35] und einigen neueren Ansätzen für Objektlogiken [FM91] übernommen und auf unseren Kalkül angepaßt werden. Für die hier angegebenen Regeln

$$\frac{}{P \to P} \text{ (axiom)} \qquad \frac{R, P_1, \ldots, P_n \to Q_1, \ldots, Q_m}{P_1, \ldots, P_n \to Q_1, \ldots, Q_m, \neg R} \text{ (negR)}$$

$$\frac{P_1, \ldots, P_n \to Q_1, \ldots, Q_m}{R, P_1, \ldots, P_n \to Q_1, \ldots, Q_m, R'} \text{ (ext)} \qquad \frac{P_1, \ldots, P_n \to Q_1, \ldots, Q_m, R}{\neg R, P_1, \ldots, P_n \to Q_1, \ldots, Q_m} \text{ (negL)}$$

$$\frac{P_1, \ldots, P_n \to Q_1, \ldots, Q_m, R \qquad R, P_1', \ldots, P_k' \to Q_1', \ldots, Q_l'}{P_1', \ldots, P_k', P_1, \ldots, P_n \to Q_1, \ldots, Q_m, Q_1', \ldots, Q_l'} \text{ (cut)}$$

$$\frac{P_1, \ldots, P_n \to Q_1, \ldots, Q_m}{s(P_1), \ldots, s(P_n) \to s(Q_1), \ldots, s(Q_m)} \text{ (sub)} \qquad \frac{occur(E_1) \to occur(E_2)}{[E_2]P \to [E_1]P} \text{ (occ)}$$

$$\frac{P_1, \ldots, P_n \to Q_1, \ldots, Q_m}{[E]P_1, \ldots, [E]P_n \to [E]Q_1, \ldots, [E]Q_m} \text{ (nex)}$$

Abb. 3. Elementare Inferenzregeln.

können wir zeigen, daß sie korrekt sind [Con94]. Vollständigkeit des Beweissystems haben wir nicht angestrebt, weil zu vermuten ist, daß Vollständigkeit aufgrund der Ausdrucksmächtigkeit des Kalküls nicht erreichbar ist.

Eine andere wichtige Eigenschaft unseres Kalküls ist, daß Beweise kompositional sind. Dies bedeutet, daß wir Beweise von Eigenschaften so lokal wie möglich durchführen können (z.B. nur unter Verwendung der sich aus der Spezifikation des betroffenen Objektes ergebenden Eigenschaften). Haben wir beispielsweise eine Eigenschaft von Author–Objekten nur unter Verwendung ihrer Spezifikation bewiesen, bleibt dieser Beweis gültig, wenn wir den Kontext ändern, also wenn wir z.B. die Spezifikation einer Bibliothek betrachten, in der wir die Spezifikation der Author–Objekte verwenden.

Diese Art der Kompositionalität ist unverzichtbar, damit wir nicht dieselben Eigenschaften bei Kontexterweiterungen immer wieder neu beweisen müssen. Die hier angegebenen Inferenzregeln behandeln im wesentlichen den ausagelogischen Teil unseres Kalküls.

Die Eigenschaften, die den TROLL *light* Objekten inhärent sind, werden durch Axiome beschrieben. Zum Beispiel sind die folgenden Formeln Axiome:

$$(1) \quad occur(O.E) \to enable(O.E)$$
$$(2) \quad occur(O.E_1), occur(O.E_2) \to O.E_1 = O.E_2$$
$$(3) \quad Att(O, P_1, \ldots, P_n, V_1), Att(O, P_1, \ldots, P_n, V_2) \to V_1 = V_2$$

Axiom (1) beschreibt, daß ein auftretendes Ereignis auch gleichzeitig erlaubt sein muß. Axiom (2) besagt, daß nicht zwei (oder mehr) verschiedene Ereignisse gleichzeitig in demselben Objekt auftreten können. (3) ist ein Axiomenschema und verlangt, daß für ein beliebiges Attribut *Att* der Attributwert zu jedem Zeitpunkt eindeutig sein muß.

In Fortsetzung des durchgängigen Beispiels werden wir den Beweis einer Objekteigenschaft exemplarisch vorführen. Die zu beweisende Eigenschaft ist dabei:

Nach dem Auftreten eines `addAuthor`–Ereignisses in einem `AuthorContainer`–Objekt hat das Attribut `Name` des neuen `Author`–Objektes den Wert, der als Parameter des `addAuthor`–Ereignisses aufgetreten ist:

$$\rightarrow [AC.addAuthor(Nr, S, S')]Name(Authors(AC, Nr), S)$$

Der Beweis basiert auf den beiden Formeln φ_1 und φ_2, die grundlegende Eigenschaften von `Author`– und `AuthorContainer`–Objekten beschreiben. φ_1 gibt dabei an, daß nach dem Auftreten eines $create$–Ereignisses in einem `Author`–Objekt das Attribut $Name$ dieses Objektes den Wert hat, der als Parameter dem $create$–Ereignis mitgegeben wurde. Die Formel φ_2 besagt, daß das Auftreten eines $addAuthor$–Ereignisses in einem `AuthorContainer`–Objekt das gleichzeitige Auftreten eines $create$–Ereignisses in einem `Author`–Objekt zur Folge hat, das ein Unterobjekt des `AuthorContainer`–Objektes ist. Welches Unterobjekt betroffen ist, wird durch den aktuellen Wert des entsprechenden Parameters des $addAuthor$–Ereignisses festgelegt. Diese Eigenschaften können direkt in den Objektspezifikationen (siehe Abb. 1 und 2) wiedergefunden werden. Der Beweis sieht nun wie folgt aus:

$$\cfrac{\cfrac{\varphi_1}{\varphi_3}\,(\text{sub}) \qquad \cfrac{\varphi_2}{\varphi_4}\,(\text{occ})}{\varphi_5}\,(\text{cut})$$

mit

$$\varphi_1 : \rightarrow [A.create(S, S')]Name(A, S)$$

$$\varphi_2 : occur(AC.addAuthor(Nr, S, S'))$$
$$\rightarrow occur(Authors(AC, Nr).create(S, S'))$$

$$\varphi_3 : \rightarrow [Authors(AC, Nr).create(S, S')]Name(Authors(AC, Nr), S)$$

$$\varphi_4 : [Authors(AC, Nr).create(S, S')]Name(Authors(AC, Nr), S)$$
$$\rightarrow [AC.addAuthor(Nr, S, S')]Name(Authors(AC, Nr), S)$$

$$\varphi_5 : \rightarrow [AC.addAuthor(Nr, S, S')]Name(Authors(AC, Nr), S)$$

Beginnend mit φ_1 liefert die Substitution von A durch $Authors(AC, Nr)$ die Formel φ_3. Formel φ_4 wird durch Anwendung der Regel (occ) auf φ_2 erhalten. Schließlich können wir φ_3 und φ_4 unter Anwendung der Regel (cut) zusammenführen. Das Ergebnis ist φ_5, die Eigenschaft, die wir beweisen wollten.

3.2 Systemfunktionalität

Nach der kurzen Einführung in den Kalkül geben wir nun einen Überblick über die beabsichtigte Funktionalität des Beweisunterstützungssystems. Prinzipiell denken wir dabei an die folgenden Arbeitsschritte (siehe auch Abb. 4):

1. Die (automatische) Übersetzung einer TROLL *light* Spezifikation, die im Template–Dictionary abgespeichert ist, liefert eine zugehörige Template–Signatur zusammen mit einer Menge von Formeln, die die logische Beschreibung der spezifizierten Objekte in unserem Kalkül darstellen. Das Ergebnis dieser Transformation wird wiederum in einer Datenbank gespeichert.

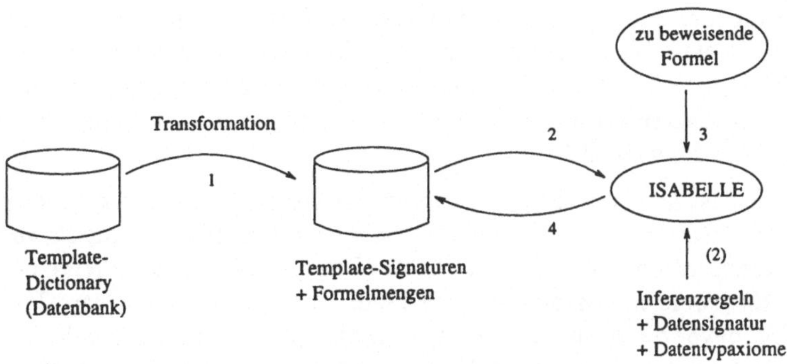

Abb. 4. Das Beweisunterstützungssystem.

2. Wenn die Transformation einer TROLL *light* Spezifikation abgeschlossen ist,
   kann der generische Theorembeweiser ISABELLE [Pau90] aktiviert werden.
   Um diesen Theorembeweiser für unseren Kalkül verwenden zu können, müssen die entsprechenden Syntaxdefinitionen und Inferenzregeln des Kalküls in
   den Beweiser geladen werden. Dann können die Template–Signatur und die
   Formeln aus dem vorherigen Schritt hinzugefügt werden.
3. Nun können wir Eigenschaften als Formeln des Kalküls formulieren, die dann
   bewiesen werden sollen. Auf jede solche Formel können wir dann den Beweiser anwenden. Der Beweis kann interaktiv gesteuert werden, d.h. wir führen
   den Beweis Schritt für Schritt durch Anwenden einzelner Inferenzregeln aus,
   oder wir lassen Teile des Beweises automatisch erzeugen, indem wir eine
   geeignete vordefinierte Beweistaktik auswählen.
4. Wenn der Beweis einer Eigenschaft erfolgreich war, kann die entsprechende
   Formel in die Datenbank eingefügt werden. Dadurch ist es möglich, diese
   Formel für andere Beweise einzusetzen (sozusagen als Lemma).

Natürlich ist dies nur ein erster, sehr grober Ansatz für den Einsatz eines Beweisunterstützungssystems. Jedoch zeigt dies bereits die grundlegenden Funktionalitäten: Transformation in Formeln des Kalküls, interaktive Verwendung eines
(generischen) Theorembeweisers und Abspeichern bewiesener Formeln. Um ein
komfortables Beweisunterstützungssystem zu erhalten, müssen weitere, mächtigere Funktionalitäten integriert werden. Dabei stellen wir uns insbesondere die
folgenden vor:

Protokollieren der Beweisschritte: Damit kann eine Menge Arbeit erspart
werden, wenn nach kleinen Spezifikationsänderungen Eigenschaften nochmal
bewiesen werden müssen, da die meisten Beweisschritte sich erfahrungsge-
mäß nicht ändern.

Entwicklung adäquater Beweistaktiken: Anstelle der schrittweisen Durchführung von Beweisen erlauben es Beweistaktiken, Teile des Beweises automatisch durch den Theorembeweiser finden zu lassen. Hierzu ist es allerdings erforderlich, in größeren Fallstudien typische Beweissequenzen und
–situationen herauszufinden und für diese dann entsprechende Taktiken zu
entwickeln.

Komfortablere Benutzungsschnittstelle: Die aktuell verwendete Version von ISABELLE bietet nur eine sehr „unfreundliche" Benutzungsschnittstelle an. Hier besteht Bedarf an umfangreichen Verbesserungen, um eine höhere Akzeptanz zu erreichen. Insbesondere eine graphische Repräsentation der Beweise wäre sehr hilfreich.

Zunächst ist nur eine erste, prototypische Version des Beweisunterstützungssystems realisiert worden. Sie soll uns helfen, Erfahrungen beim Beweisen von Objekteigenschaften zu sammeln. Erste Beispiele konnten bereits erfolgreich durchgeführt werden. Es sind jedoch mehr und vor allem größere Fallstudien notwendig, bevor die Adäquatheit des Kalküls und die Konzeption des Beweisunterstützungssystems hinreichend beurteilt werden können. Danach könnte dann auf der Basis der erzielten Ergebnisse eine Überarbeitung des Kalküls und des Beweisunterstützungssystems durchgeführt werden.

4 Abschließende Bemerkungen

Das vorgestellte Beweisunterstützungssystem ist im Rahmen des KORSO–Projektes prototypisch realisiert worden und anhand einer Reihe von Beispielen ausgetestet worden. Eine Vervollständigung des Beweisunterstützungssystems, umfangreichere Fallstudien und eine daraus abzuleitende Integration der Verifikation auf Spezifikationsebene in eine geeignete Entwicklungsmethodik (z.B. OMT [RBP$^+$91] oder das V-Modell [BD93]) bieten ausreichende und vielversprechende Ansatzpunkte für weitere Projekte.

Zusammen mit dem hier nicht näher behandelten, aber ebenfalls als Prototyp vorliegendem Animationssystem für TROLL *light*-Spezifikationen sind bereits wichtige Werkzeuge für eine integrierte Entwicklungsumgebung vorhanden.

Die Beschränkung von TROLL *light* in der Anzahl der angebotenen Konzepte war hilfreich, um die prinzipiellen Probleme zu identifizieren und geeignete Lösungen zu entwickeln. Damit bietet sich nun eine Erweiterung auf eine Sprache wie TROLL an, die eine größere Zahl von Konzepten zur Modellierung anbietet und es damit dem Entwerfer ermöglicht, möglichst wirklichkeitstreu modellieren zu können. Je mehr Konzepte eine Spezifikationssprache zur Modellierung anbietet, um so mehr stellt sich die Frage nach einer adäquaten Umsetzung all dieser Konzepte auf mögliche Zieldatenbanksysteme. Gegenwärtig gibt es hier noch eine gewisse Diskrepanz zwischen Spezifikationssprachen und existierenden (objektorientierten) Datenbanksystemen. Diese gilt es in der nächsten Zeit abzubauen, um so einen durchgängigen Einsatz formaler Mothoden bei der Entwicklung von Informationssystemen zu ermöglichen.

Danksagung: Besonderer Dank gilt meinen Kollegen G. Denker, H.-D. Ehrich, M. Gogolla, R. Herzig und N. Vlachantonis, mit denen ich in Braunschweig im KORSO–Projekt zusammengearbeitet habe. Darüber hinaus haben Partner aus dem KORSO–Projekt als auch aus den Esprit BRA Working Groups COMPASS und ISCORE in Diskussionen Beiträge zu unserer Arbeit geleistet.

Literatur

[BD93] A.-P. Bröhl and W. Dröschel. *Das V-Modell: Der Standard für die Softwa-reentwicklung mit Praxisleitfaden.* Oldenbourg-Verlag, München, 1993.

[CGH92] S. Conrad, M. Gogolla, and R. Herzig. TROLL *light*: A Core Language for Specifying Objects. Informatik-Bericht 92–02, TU Braunschweig, 1992.

[Con94] S. Conrad. *Ein Basiskalkül für die Verifikation von Eigenschaften synchron interagierender Objekte.* Fortschritt-Berichte Reihe 10, Nr. 295. VDI-Verlag, Düsseldorf, 1994.

[FM91] J. Fiadeiro and T. Maibaum. Towards Object Calculi. In G. Saake and A. Sernadas, editors, *Information Systems — Correctness and Reusability, Workshop IS-CORE '91, ESPRIT BRA WG 3023, London,* pages 129–178. Informatik-Bericht 91–03, Technische Universität Braunschweig, 1991.

[GCH93] M. Gogolla, S. Conrad, and R. Herzig. Sketching Concepts and Computational Model of TROLL *light*. In A. Miola, editor, *Proc. 3rd Int. Conf. Design and Implementation of Symbolic Computation Systems (DISCO'93),* pages 17–32. Springer, Berlin, LNCS 722, 1993.

[Gen35] G. Gentzen. Untersuchungen über das logische Schließen. *Mathematische Zeitschrift,* 39:176–210, 1935.

[HCG94] R. Herzig, S. Conrad, and M. Gogolla. Compositional Description of Object Communities with TROLL *light*. In C. Chrisment, editor, *Proc. Basque Int. Workshop on Information Technology (BIWIT'94),* pages 183–194. Cépaduès-Éditions, Toulouse, 1994.

[Heu92] A. Heuer. *Objektorientierte Datenbanken — Konzepte, Modelle, Systeme.* Addison Wesley, 1992.

[HFG94] R. Herzig, H. Fischer, and M. Gogolla. Zur Gestaltung der Benutzungs-schnittstelle bei der Animation von Objektspezifikationen. In L. Wegner, editor, *Proc. GI-Workshop "Benutzungsschnittstellen für Datenbanken", Kassel, 17.-18.3.94,* pages 43–45. GI-Datenbankrundbrief 13, Mai 1994.

[HG94] R. Herzig and M. Gogolla. An Animator for the Object Specification Language TROLL *light*. In V.S. Alagar and R. Missaoui, editors, *Proc. Colloquium on Object Orientation in Databases and Software Enginee-ring (COODBSE'94),* pages 4–17. Université du Quebéc à Montréal, 1994.

[JSHS91] R. Jungclaus, G. Saake, T. Hartmann, and C. Sernadas. Object-Oriented Specification of Information Systems: The TROLL Language. Informatik-Bericht 91-04, TU Braunschweig, 1991.

[Krü93] F. Krückeberg. Zertifizierung von Software. *Wirtschaftsinformatik,* 35(2):183–186, 1993.

[Pae88] B. Paech. Gentzen-Systems for Propositional Temporal Logics. In E. Börger, H. Kleine Büning, and M.M. Richter, editors, *2nd Workshop on Computer Science Logic,* pages 240–253. Springer, LNCS 385, 1988.

[Pau90] L.C. Paulson. Isabelle: The Next 700 Theorem Provers. In P. Odifreddi, editor, *Logic and Computer Science,* pages 361–385. Academic Press, 1990.

[RBP+91] J. Rumbaugh, M. Blaha, W. Premerlani, F. Eddy, and W. Lorensen. *Object-Oriented Modeling and Design.* Prentice-Hall, 1991.

[Rom93] H.D. Rombach. Software-Qualität und Qualitätssicherung. *Informatik Spek-trum,* 16(5):267–272, 1993.

Attributierte Grammatiken
als Werkzeug zur Datenmodellierung

Ulrike Stutschka
Siemens AG
ANL A 413

91052 Erlangen

Volker Linnemann
Institut für Informationssysteme
Medizinische Universität zu Lübeck
Wallstraße 40
23560 Lübeck

0. Zusammenfassung

Attributierte Grammatiken sind ein inzwischen weitgehend anerkanntes Verfahren zur Beschreibung der kontextabhängigen Syntax von Programmiersprachen. Sie erweitern kontextfreie Grammatiken um Regeln zur Beschreibung von Kontextabhängigkeiten. Darüberhinaus sind attributierte Grammatiken auch zur Beschreibung von Berechnungsvorschriften für Werte geeignet und stellen daher auch Konzepte zur Semantikbeschreibung zur Verfügung. Die folgenden Überlegungen sollen zeigen, daß attributierte Grammatiken auch in der Lage sind, auf der Datenmodellierungsebene wesentliche objektorientierte Konzepte darzustellen. Sie erlauben die Konstruktion objektorientierter Datenbankschemata unter der Verwendung bekannter Datenstrukturierungsmechanismen wie der Aggregation, der komplexen Typen und der Vererbung in Klassen- (Typ-) Hierarchien. Gleichzeitig wird die Aufnahme expliziter Integritätsbedingungen zur Darstellung sehr komplexer semantischer Bedeutungszusammenhänge in den eigentlichen Datentyp ermöglicht.

1. Einleitung

Mittlerweile existieren eine Reihe von Ansätzen zur Modellierung von Datenstrukturen mittels kontextfreier Grammatiken. Man beschränkt sich dabei nicht länger auf die Darstellung von Dokumenten /Barbic, Rabitti 84/ oder allgemeinen Textstrukturen /Gonnet, Tompa 87/, die in sehr natürlicher Weise Regeln genügen, die einer Grammatik folgen, sondern wendet sich zunehmend auch der Repräsentation allgemeiner hierarchischer Strukturen als einem fundamentalen Repräsentationskonzept von Nichtstandardanwendungen /Gyssens et al 89/ zu.

Für die Beschreibung komplexer Objekte sind hierarchische Strukturierungsmechanismen variabler Tiefe und damit die Verwendung rekursiver Sprachelemente nach /Hoare 75/ oder wie in der Programmiersprache ML /Harper 86/ von grundsätzlicher Bedeutung. Kontextfreie Grammatiken lassen sich nun in sehr natürlicher Weise als rekursives Modellierungskonzept verwenden. Die entsprechenden Strukturen genügen dabei in sehr einfacher Form einer kontextfreien Grammatik, die in generischer Form bereits in /Banerjee 87/ beschrieben wurde.

Die Verwendung grammatikbasierter Datentypen stellt allerdings zunächst eine rein syntaktische Beschreibung dar. Ihre eigentliche Semantik erhalten die entstehenden Objektstrukturen erst durch die Möglichkeit der Definition spezifischer Operatoren /Linnemann 93/.

Bereits der Umgang mit einfachen Textstrukturen, dh. einer sehr typischen Anwendung für kontextfreie Grammatiken, zeigt, daß Abhängigkeiten zwischen Datentypen, die über diese rein kontextfreien syntaktischen Bedingungen hinausgehen, im Rahmen kontextfreier Grammatiken nicht spezifizierbar sind. Als Beispiel würden sich hierbei Textstrukturen anbieten, die aus einer Folge von Kapiteln, Abschnitten, und Unterabschnitten beliebiger Schachtelungstiefe bestehen. Dabei ergeben sich zusätzliche Integritätsbedingungen, die im Zusammenhang mit der Generierung von Kapiteln, Abschnitten, Paragraphen eine konsistente Numerierung gewährleisten. Es sollen nur solche Inhalte von Kapiteln, Abschnitten und Paragraphen erzeugt werden, die eine konsistente Numerierung der gesamten Textstruktur gewährleisten. Konsistente Numerierung heißt in diesem Zusammenhang, daß die Nummern aller auf gleicher Schachtelungstiefe numerierten Abschnitte auch gleich tief geschachtelt, dh. gleich lang sind. Die Problematik einer solchen Repräsentation wurde bereits im Zusammenhang mit rekursiven Datenstrukturen in /Lamersdorf 85/ erkannt.

Aus diesem Grund ist es im Rahmen einer adäquaten Repräsentation von Objektstrukturen notwendig, kontextfreie Grammatiken um Konzepte zur Repräsentation semantischer Strukturen zu erweitern.

Aufgrund der im Bereich von Definition und Übersetzung von Programmiersprachen seit ALGOL 60 geforderten strikten Trennung zwischen Syntax und Semantik und der Konzentration auf kontextfreie Grammatiken im Zusammenhang mit der Syntaxbeschreibung, stellt sich auch im Rahmen der Beschreibung der statischen Semantik von Programmiersprachen (man sollte eigentlich besser von kontextabhängiger Syntax sprechen) ein dem unseren ähnliches Problem. Attributierte Grammatiken haben sich nun in diesem Umfeld als geeignetes Werkzeug einer systematischen semantischen Analyse erwiesen und sind weitgehend anerkannt. Charakteristisch für diesen Ansatz ist die lokale Auflösung der rein hierarchischen Struktur von Datenobjekten, die auf kontextfreien Grammatiken beruhen, und die Verbindung der formalen Definition des Datentyps und der formalen Definition einer semantischen Analyse.

Das Ziel der folgenden Überlegungen soll es nun sein zu zeigen, daß attributierte Grammatiken auch im Rahmen der Datenmodellierung ein geeignetes Werkzeug zur Darstellung sehr komplexer semantischer Bedeutungszusammenhänge sind. Es werden dabei bewußt Beispiele gewählt, die zunächst einmal für eine grammatikbasierte Darstellung "untypisch" sind, um damit den universellen Charakter attributierter Grammatiken zu verdeutlichen.

Die Arbeit gliedert sich wie folgt : In Abschnitt 2.1 wird gezeigt, wie sich Typen und Klassen auf der Grundlage komplexer Objektstrukturen im Rahmen attributierter Grammatiken darstellen lassen. Dabei beschränken wir uns nicht nur auf die Darstellung hierarchischer Objektstrukturen, sondern zeigen in 2.2 die Repräsentierbarkeit von Objekten, deren Struktur allgemeinen azyklischen Graphen genügt. Vererbungsmechanismen werden in Abschnitt 2.3 erläutert. Explizite Konsistenzbedingungen ermöglichen in Abschnitt 2.4 die Integration von Konsistenzbedingungen in den Datentyp. Ihre Aufrechterhaltung ist damit nicht länger allein eine Eigenschaft objektspezifischer Operatoren, sondern wird primär zu einer Eigenschaft der Objektstruktur. Wir werden sehen, daß eine solche Betrachtungsweise gerade im Zusammenhang mit Entwurfsumgebungen wesentliche Vorteile mit sich bringt. In Kapitel 3 wird schließlich eine Anfragesprache auf der Grundlage grammatikbasierter Strukturen umrissen.

2. Repräsentation objektorientierter Konzepte durch attributierte Grammatiken

2.1 Darstellung komplexer Objekte durch attributierte Grammatiken

Datentypen lassen sich durch eine Grammatik in der Weise definieren, daß jedem Nonterminal ein Datentyp zugeordnet wird /Linnemann 80/, dessen Wertebereich aus sämtlichen Syntaxbäumen bezüglich der Grammatik besteht.

Als Beispiel für die Repräsentation hierarchischer Strukturen durch kontextfreie Grammatiken werden wir im folgenden die Modellierung zusammengesetzter, im Rahmen des CSG-Modells dargestellter CAD-Objekte ('Stücklisten - Problem') betrachten. Es handelt sich hierbei um ein Vollkörpermodell, in dem geometrische Körper durch rekursive Anwendung von Mengenoperationen wie Durchschnitt, Vereinigung und Differenz auf einfach zu errechnende Grundkörper z.B. Quader, Zylinder und Kugel dargestellt werden. Somit ist eine Konstruktionsdarstellung in Form binärer Wurzelbäume möglich, in der die Blätter die Grundkörper und die übrigen Knoten die Mengenoperationen darstellen. Als Anwendung ließe sich eine Datenbank denken, die geometrische Körper mit zusätzlichen Informationen speichert.

Die entsprechenden Datentypen lassen sich etwa wie folgt definieren, wobei <REAL> ein vordefiniertes Nonterminalsymbol für alle Gleitpunktzahlen sei. Entsprechendes gilt für die später verwendeten Nonterminalsymbole <INTEGER> und <TEXT>.

```
DECLARE GRAMMARTYPE
    <CSG-Objekt>        ::=  <Grundkörper> |
                             <CSG-Objekt><Mengenoperator><CSG-Objekt>
    <Grundkörper>       ::=  <Kugel> | <Quader> | <Zylinder>
    <Mengenoperator>    ::=  ∩ | ∪ | -
    <Kugel>             ::=  <Radius>
    <Quader>            ::=  <Breite><Höhe><Länge>
    <Zylinder>          ::=  <Radius><Höhe>
    <Radius>            ::=  <REAL>
    <Breite>            ::=  <REAL>
    <Höhe>              ::=  <REAL>
    <Länge>             ::=  <REAL>
END
```

Der Begriff der Klasse läßt sich dabei formal als Menge der Ausprägungen eines Typs im Schema definieren. Ein Objekt ist nichts anderes als eine spezielle Sprachstruktur, die über einem Nonterminal generiert wurde (dh. ein Knoten in einem Syntaxbaum). Klassen und Objekte gehören damit vollständig auf die Datenebene.

Zur Generierung von Objekten lassen sich Generierungsfunktionen definieren, die aus Zeichenketten Syntaxbäume erzeugen. Da die vorliegende Grammatik allerdings mehrdeutig ist, kann sie nicht Grundlage einer direkten Textrepräsentation sein. Grundsätzlich wäre es in unserem Fall jedoch möglich, eine eindeutige Grammatik mit gleicher Mächtigkeit einzuführen und ihre Zuordnung zu unserer Ausgangsgrammatik mittels einer sogenannten Transformationsgrammatik /Salomaa 73/ zu definieren. Da diese Überlegungen nicht Gegenstand unserer Arbeit sind, werden wir uns im folgenden zur eindeutigen Beschreibung von Baumstrukturen einer Präfix-Notation bedienen.

Beispiel:
<CSG-Objekt>(<CSG-Objekt>(x1, ∪, x2), -, x3)

Syntaxbaum:

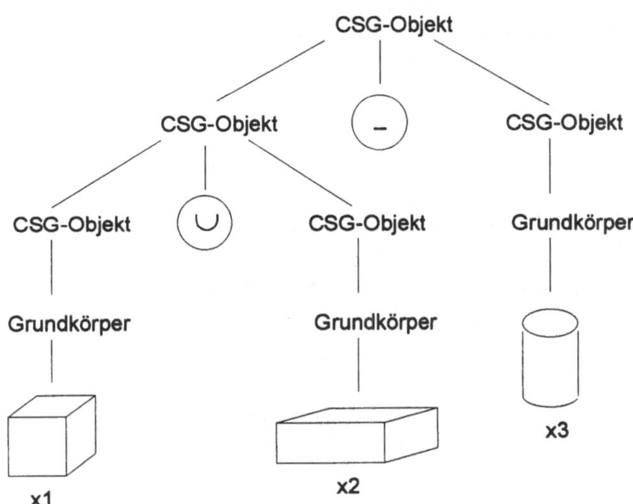

x1, x2, x3 bezeichnen hier vordefinierte Grundkörper.
Dieses Objekt bezeichnen wir im Verlauf der Arbeit mit O.

In objektorientierten Modellen ist das Klassenkonzept mit dem Begriff der Methode verknüpft. Es besteht ein enger Zusammenhang zwischen Methoden und Klassenattributen - so ist die Implementierung einer Methode nichts anderes als ein Klassenattribut. Dies ermöglicht eine Betrachtungsweise, die in attributierten Grammatiken /Knuth 68/ eine Verallgemeinerung des Attributbegriffs auf allgemeine Methoden ermöglicht.

Beispiel:
Es soll neben der Berechnung des Volumens eines Quaders eine Methode definiert werden, die einen Quader mit gleicher Kantenlänge in einen Würfel transformiert. Dazu wird zunächst der

grammatikbasierte Datentyp <Würfel> eingeführt und der Datentyp <Grundkörper> um die Alternative Würfel erweitert.

```
DECLARE GRAMMARTYPE
  <CSG-Objekt>        ::=  <Grundkörper> |
                          <CSG-Objekt><Mengenoperator><CSG-Objekt>
  <Grundkörper>       ::=  <Kugel> | <Quader> | <Zylinder> | <Würfel>
  <Mengenoperator>    ::=  ∩ | ∪ | -
  <Kugel>             ::=  <Radius>
  <Quader>            ::=  <Breite><Höhe><Länge>
  <Zylinder>          ::=  <Radius><Höhe>
  <Würfel>            ::=  <Höhe>
  <Radius>            ::=  <REAL>
  <Breite>            ::=  <REAL>
  <Höhe>              ::=  <REAL>
  <Länge>             ::=  <REAL>
ATTRIBUTES
  <Quader>    [ Volumen:         REAL,
                Transformation:  <Grundkörper>]
  <Radius>    [ Value:           REAL]
  <Breite>    [ Value:           REAL]
  <Höhe>      [ Value:           REAL]
  <Länge>     [ Value:           REAL]
RULES
  <Quader>         ::=  <Breite><Höhe><Länge>:
    [
      <Quader>.Volumen        ←  <Breite>.Value * <Höhe>.Value * <Länge>.Value,
      <Quader>.Transformation ←  IF(<Breite>.Value = <Höhe>.Value
                                    AND <Höhe>.Value = <Länge>.Value)
                                 THEN <Würfel>(<Breite>)
                                 ELSE <Quader>
    ];
  <Radius>         ::=  <REAL>:
    [
      <Radius>.Value ← Value(<REAL>)
    ];
  <Breite>         ::=  <REAL>:
    [
      <Breite>.Value ← Value(<REAL>)
    ];
  <Höhe>           ::=  <REAL>:
    [
      <Höhe>.Value ← Value(<REAL>)
    ];
```

```
<Länge>              ::=  <REAL>:
   [
       <Länge>.Value  ←  Value(<REAL>)
   ]
END;
```

Der Zugriff auf ein Attribut oder der Aufruf einer Methode läßt sich dabei ähnlich der Syntax von Eiffel /Meyer 88/ in der dot-Notation mit dem '.'als Selektor formulieren:

x2.Volumen
x2.Transformation

Die für Quader definierte Methode läßt sich in gleicher Weise auf CSG-Objekte übertragen und ermöglicht, dort in geschlossener Form alle Grundkörper vom Typ <Quader> zu ersetzen. Es ergibt sich damit die folgende Erweiterung der obigen Beschreibung.

```
ATTRIBUTES
   <CSG-Objekt>  [Transformation: <CSG-Objekt>]
   <Grundkörper> [Transformation: <Grundkörper>]
RULES
   <CSG-Objekt>        ::= <Grundkörper>:
      [
          <CSG-Objekt>.Transformation  ←  <CSG-Objekt>(<Grundkörper>.Transformation)
      ];
   <CSG-Objekt>        ::= <CSG-Objekt><Mengenoperator><CSG-Objekt>:
      [
          <CSG-Objekt>[0].Transformation ←
              <CSG-Objekt>( (<CSG-Objekt>[1].Transformation, <Mengenoperator>,
                       <CSG-Objekt>[2].Transformation)¹
      ];
   <Grundkörper>::= <Kugel>:
      [
          <Grundkörper>.Transformation ← <Kugel>
      ];
   <Grundkörper>::= <Quader>:
      [
          <Grundkörper>.Transformation ← <Quader>.Transformation
      ];
   <Grundkörper>::= <Zylinder>:
      [
          <Grundkörper>.Transformation ← <Zylinder>
      ]
END;
```

[1] Die Indices dienen der Unterscheidung der Nonterminalsymbole

Betrachten wir im folgenden ein weiteres Beispiel, das in unseren Überlegungen noch eine wesentliche Rolle spielen wird:

Alternativ zum CSG-Modell wird im CAD-Bereich zur Darstellung von Körpern häufig die sogenannte Begrenzungsflächendarstellung verwendet, die folgende Objektstruktur zugrundelegt.

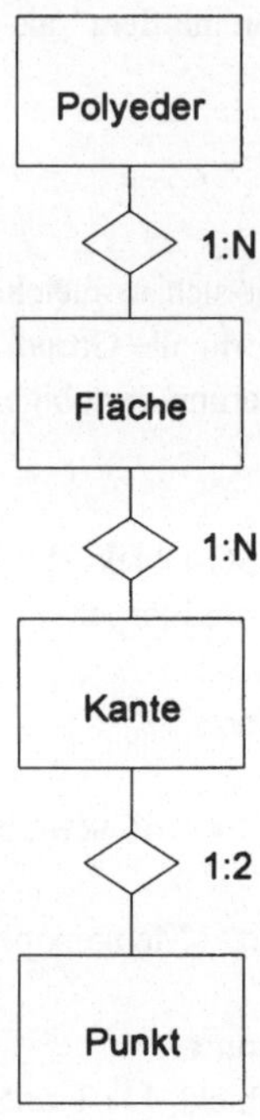

Bei diesem Bild ist die Tatsache, daß eine Kante in der Regel zu mehreren Flächen gehört, nicht berücksichtigt. Entsprechendes gilt für die Beziehung zwischen Kante und Punkt. Wir beschränken also die Kardinalitäten der Objektbeziehungen auf 1:n. Allgemeine n:m-Beziehungen lassen sich durch Kopieren realisieren. (Die Symmetrie dieser Beziehung ist ähnlich zu gemeinsamen Unterobjekten - wie später gezeigt wird - darstellbar.)

```
DECLARE GRAMMARTYPE
  <Polyeder>  ::=  <Fläche>+
  <Fläche>    ::=  <Kante>+
  <Kante>     ::=  <Punkt><Punkt>
  <Punkt>     ::=  <REAL><REAL>
END
```

Das Symbol "+" repräsentiert dabei eine endliche Folge von Objekten des entsprechenden Typs.

Die primär strukturellen Eigenschaften zusammengesetzter Objektstukturen lassen sich in dieser Weise sehr natürlich mit Hilfe kontextfreier Grammatiken darstellen, während die resultierenden Fragen referentieller Integrität, wie in /Ridjanovic, Brodie 82/ gezeigt, vollständig durch attributierte Grammatiken beschrieben werden können.

2.2 Gemeinsame Unterobjekte

Komponentenobjekte sind gemeinsam, wenn sie in mehreren zusammengesetzten Objekten als Komponente auftauchen können. Die Objektstruktur wird damit zu einem allgemeinen, azyklischen Graphen /Kim et al 89/.

Wählen wir eine der Einführung virtueller Records im hierarchischen Datenmodell zur Darstellung von Netzwerkstrukturen ähnliche Vorgehensweise, so läßt sich durch Zerlegung des Objektgraphen in Baumstrukturen und Ergänzung um ein gemeinsames Oberobjekt (vgl. /Ullman 93/) auch diese Bedingung an die Klasse-Komponentenklasse-Beziehung auf Eigenschaften lokaler Baumstrukturen zurückführen und ist ein Spezialfall lokaler referentieller Integrität, deren Einhaltung verlangt, daß referenzierendes und referenziertes Objekt zu dem gleichen zusammengesetzten Objekt gehören.

Beispiel:
Innerhalb einer Bauteilverwaltung sollen im Inhaltsverzeichnis nur solche Referenzen (Nummern) enthalten sein, zu denen auch eine entsprechende Bauteilbeschreibung existiert

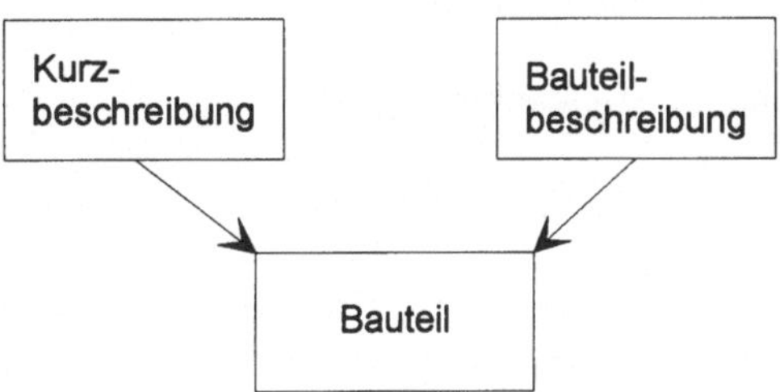


```
DECLARE GRAMMARTYPE
    <Bauteilverwaltung>      ::=   <Inhaltsverzeichnis><Bauteilbeschreibung>+
    <Inhaltsverzeichnis>     ::=   <Kurzbeschreibung>+
    <Kurzbeschreibung>       ::=   <Nummer><TEXT>
    <Bauteilbeschreibung>    ::=   <Bauteil><TEXT>
    <Bauteil>                ::=   <Nummer><CSG-Objekt>
    <Nummer>                 ::=   <INTEGER>
ATTRIBUTES
    <Nummer>                 [ Value:  INTEGER]
    <Kurzbeschreibung>       [ Value:  INTEGER]
    <Inhaltsverzeichnis>     [ Value:  List of INTEGER]
    <Bauteilbeschreibung>    [ Value:  List of INTEGER]
    <Bauteil>                [ Value:  INTEGER]
    <Bauteilverwaltung>      [ OK:     Boolean]
```

```
RULES
  <Kurzbeschreibung>     ::=  <Nummer><TEXT>:
  [
      <Kurzbeschreibung>.Value ← <Nummer>.Value
  ];
  <Inhaltsverzeichnis>   ::=  <Kurzbeschreibung>+:
  [
      <Inhaltsverzeichnis>.Value ← List of (<Kurzbeschreibung>.Value)
  ];
  <Bauteilbeschreibung>  ::=  <Bauteil><TEXT>:
  [
      <Bauteilbeschreibung>.Value ← <Bauteil>.Value
  ];
  <Bauteil>              ::=  <Nummer><CSG-Objekt>:
  [
      <Bauteil>.Value ← <Nummer>.Value
  ];
  <Bauteilverwaltung>    ::=  <Inhaltsverzeichnis><Bauteilbeschreibung>+:
  [
    <Bauteilverwaltung>.OK ←
        <Inhaltsverzeichnis>.Value = List of (<Bauteilbeschreibung>.Value)
  ];
  <Nummer>               ::=  <INTEGER>:
  [
      <Nummer>.Value ← Value(<INTEGER>)
  ]
END;
```

Es bietet sich im folgenden an, die Objektidentität über ein Attribut vom Typ Object_Identifier darzustellen. (Die Attribute vom Typ Integer dienen in unserem Beispiel einem ähnlichen Zweck.)

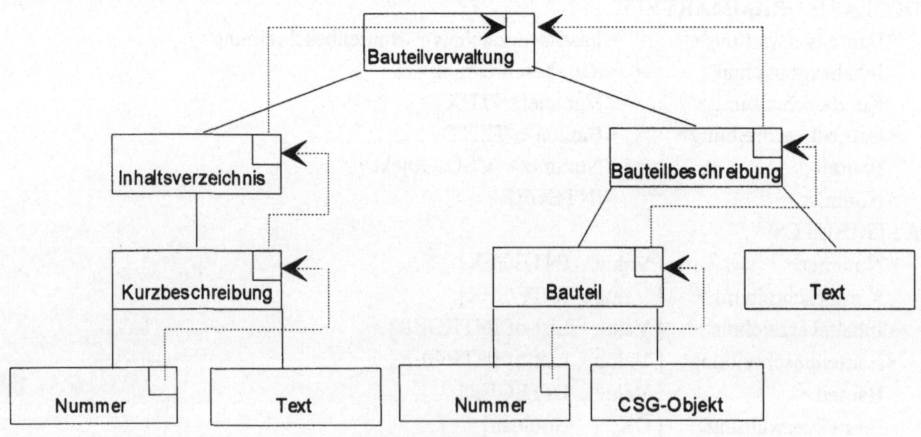

2.3 Vererbung

Innerhalb einer Grammatik lassen sich Superklasse/Subklassenbeziehungen in sehr einfacher Form darstellen. Jede Produktionsregel, deren rechte Seite lediglich aus einem Nonterminalsymbol besteht (<A>::= <B>), repräsentiert eine solche. Werden kontextfreie Grammatiken in dieser Form zur Definition von Beziehungen zwischen Klassen verwendet, so ist es sinnvoll, lediglich Regeln der Form <A>::=<B$_1$> | ... | <B$_n$> und <C>::=γ zuzulassen /Grosch, 90/, wobei γ eine Folge von Terminal- und Nichtterminalzeichen ist, und γ die einzige Alternative für <C> ist. Jede kontextfreie Grammatik läßt sich trivialerweise in diese Form umwandeln.

Die Beschreibung der Superklasse-Subklassen-Beziehung ist natürlich zunächst rein syntaktischer Natur, d.h. lediglich eine Beziehung auf der Ebene der Typbezeichnungen. In der gleichen Weise gelten aber verhaltensmäßige Bedingungen auf der Objektebene. Ist <B> Subklasse von <A> so müssen alle Eigenschaften, die für Objekte der Klasse <A> zutreffen, auch für Objekte der Klasse <B> zutreffen.

Das Konzept der Vererbung von Attributen ist trivialerweise im Konzept attributierter Grammatiken enthalten.

Beispiel:

```
DECLARE GRAMMARTYPE
    <Grundkörper>      ::=   <Kugel> | <Quader> | <Zylinder>
    <Kugel>            ::=   <Radius>
    <Quader>           ::=   <Breite><Höhe><Länge>
    <Zylinder>         ::=   <Radius><Höhe>
    <Radius>           ::=   <REAL>
    <Breite>           ::=   <REAL>
    <Höhe>             ::=   <REAL>
    <Länge>            ::=   <REAL>
ATTRIBUTES
    <Grundkörper>      [ Volumen:   REAL]
    <Kugel>            [ Volumen:   REAL]
    <Quader>           [ Volumen:   REAL]
    <Zylinder>         [ Volumen:   REAL]
    <Radius>           [Value:      REAL]
    <Breite>           [ Value:     REAL]
    <Höhe>             [ Value:     REAL]
    <Länge>            [ Value:     REAL]
RULES
    <Kugel>            ::=   <Radius>:
    [
      <Kugel>.Volumen ←
          4/3π * <Radius>.Value * <Radius>.Value * <Radius>.Value
    ];
```

```
<Grundkörper> ::= <Kugel>:
  [
    <Grundkörper>.Volumen ← <Kugel>.Volumen
  ];
<Quader> ::=  <Breite><Höhe><Länge>:
  [
    <Quader>.Volumen ←
        <Länge>.Value * <Höhe>.Value * <Breite>.Value,<Grundkörper> ::= <Quader>:
  ];
<Grundkörper>   ::= <Quader>:
  [
    <Grundkörper>.Volumen ← <Quader>.Volumen
  ];
  <Zylinder>        ::=  <Radius><Höhe>:
  [
    <Zylinder>.Volumen ←
        π * <.Radius>.Value * <.Radius>.Value *  <Höhe>.Value
  ];
<Grundkörper> ::= <Zylinder>:
  [
    <Grundkörper>.Volumen ←  <Zylinder>.Volumen
  ]
  END;
```

Die trivialen Regeln für <Radius>.Value, <Breite>.Value, <Höhe>.Value und <Länge>.Value
sind weggelassen .

Syntaxbaum:

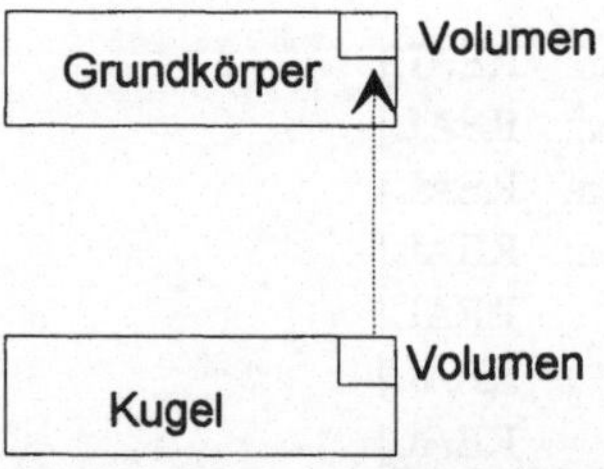

Wie unser Beispiel zeigt, ist es im Rahmen attributierter Grammatiken zur Simulation des
objektorientierten Konzeptes der Vererbung notwendig, gleiche Attribute bzw. Attributwerte
explizit zu definieren.

Erlaubt man Regeln der Art <Grundkörper>.Volumen ← <Zylinder>.Volumen, dh. Regeln, die
lediglich dem Kopieren von Attributen dienen, wegzulassen, erhält man jedoch einen
Mechanismus, der virtuelle Attribute im Sinne von C++ realisiert.

Man kommt dann zu der folgenden Objektdefinition:

```
DECLARE GRAMMARTYPE
   <Grundkörper>      ::=  <Kugel> | <Quader> | <Zylinder>
   <Kugel>            ::=  <Radius>
   <Quader>           ::=  <Breite><Höhe><Länge>
   <Zylinder>         ::=  <Radius><Höhe>
   <Radius>           ::=  <REAL>
   <Breite>           ::=  <REAL>
   <Höhe>             ::=  <REAL>
   <Länge>            ::=  <REAL>
ATTRIBUTES
   <Grundkörper>      [ Volumen:  REAL]
   <Kugel>            [ Volumen:  REAL]
   <Quader>           [ Volumen:  REAL]
   <Zylinder>         [ Volumen:  REAL]
   <Radius>           [Value:     REAL]
   <Breite>           [ Value:    REAL]
   <Höhe>             [ Value:    REAL]
   <Länge>            [ Value:    REAL]
RULES
   <Kugel>            ::=  <Radius>:
   [
      <Kugel>.Volumen ←
         4/3π * <Radius>.Value * <Radius>.Value * <Radius>.Value
   ];
   <Quader>           ::=  <Breite><Höhe><Länge>:
   [
      <Quader>.Volumen ←
         <Länge>.Value * <Höhe>.Value * <Breite>.Value
   ];
   <Zylinder>         ::=  <Radius><Höhe>:
   [
      <Zylinder>.Volumen ←
         π * <.Radius>.Value * <.Radius>.Value * <Höhe>.Value
   ]
END;
```

Das Konzept der Mehrfachvererbung ist in diesem Ansatz noch nicht enthalten. Entsprechende Überlegungen sind allerdings Gegenstand der Forschung.

2.4 Explizite Bedingungen

Unter expliziten Integritätsbedingungen verstehen sich Vergleichsoperationen, die ausschließlich Objekteigenschaften betreffen. Sie gehören in das Datenbankschema und sind damit ein Teil der eigentlichen Typdefinition. Explizite Integritätsbedingungen lassen sich nicht nur zwischen Werten, sondern auch im allgemeineren Fall zwischen Objektidentifikatoren definieren.

Komplexere Bedingungen gehören im Rahmen abstrakter Datentypen auf die Ebene von Methoden, die als sehr mächtiges Konzept im Rahmen von Operationen zur Verfügung stehen und damit in den Bereich der eigentlichen Programmierung fallen.

Als besonders problematisch erweist sich diese Vorgehensweise in den folgenden beiden Punkten, die sehr eng zusammenhängen /Zhou, Baumann 90/.

o Kardinalitätsbedingungen auf heterogenen Mengen
o Schrittweise Generierung von Objekten

Entsprechend der Modellierung von Beziehungen in objektorientierten Systemen als eigenständiges Konstrukt /Chen 76/, durch die Aufnahme allgemeiner Relationen /Beeri 90/ oder durch Klassen selbst, werden Kardinalitätsbedingungen auf der Ebene von Beziehungen meist implizit im Datenmodell festgelegt. Die Granularität von Kardinalitätsbedingungen auf der Ebene von Mengen wird demgegenüber durch kompakte Intervalle bestimmt, deren obere bzw. untere Grenzen wählbar sind. Gerade die Angabe einer Mindestzahl kann sich dabei als problematisch erweisen, da dies Auswirkungen auf die Form der entsprechenden Update-Operation hat. Gleichzeitig sind solche Bedingungen normalerweise auf homogene Mengen, dh. Mengen des gleichen Typs beschränkt. Obwohl entsprechende Bedingungen in der Praxis für viele Anwendungen typisch sind, - ein Beispiel hierfür ist die Eulersche Regel innerhalb der Begrenzungsflächendarstellung- ist eine Verwendung auf heterogenen Objekt-Mengen nicht möglich.

Beispiel:
Innerhalb der Begrenzungsflächendarstellung, deren strukturelle Eigenschaften wir bereits betrachtet haben, sichert die Eulersche Regel die topologische Integrität des Körpers.
B + P - K = 2
mit
B = Anzahl der Begrenzungsflächen
P = Anzahl der Punkte
K = Anzahl der Kanten

DECLARE GRAMMARTYPE
    <Polyeder> ::= <Fläche>+
    <Fläche> ::= <Kante>+
    <Kante> ::= <Punkt><Punkt>
    <Punkt> ::= <REAL><REAL>

```
ATTRIBUTES
  <Polyeder>    [ Ok:       Boolean,                   ID:      Object_Identifier;
                  Flächen:  Set of Object_Identifier, Kanten:  Set of Object_Identifier,
                  Punkte:   Set of Object_Identifier]
  <Fläche>      [ ID:       Object_Identifier,         Kanten:  Set of Object_Identifier,
                  Punkte:   Set of Object_Identifier]
  <Kante>       [ ID:       Object_Identifier,         Punkte:  Set of Object_Identifier]
  <Punkt>       [ ID:       Object_Identifier]
RULES
  <Polyeder>  ::=  <Fläche>+:
    [
        <Polyeder>.ID       ←  new_Object_ID(),
        <Polyeder>.Ok       ←
          (COUNT(<Polyeder>.Flächen) - COUNT(<Polyeder>.Kanten)
            + COUNT(<Polyeder>.Punkte) = 2),
        <Polyeder>.Flächen  ←  UNION(<Fläche>.ID),
        <Polyeder>.Kanten   ←  UNION(<Fläche>.Kanten),
        <Polyeder>.Punkte   ←  UNION(<Fläche>.Punkte)
    ];
  <Fläche>    ::=  <Kante>+:
    [
        <Fläche>.ID        ←  new_Object_ID(),
        <Fläche>.Kanten    ←  UNION(<Kante>.ID),
        <Fläche>.Punkte    ←  UNION(<Kante>.Punkte)
    ];
  <Kante>     ::=  <Punkt><Punkt>:
    [
        <Kante>.ID         ←  new_Object_ID(),
        <Kante>.Punkte     ←  UNION(<Punkt>[0].ID,<Punkt>[1].ID)
    ]
END;
```

Die parameterlose Funktion new_Object_ID liefert bei jedem Aufruf eine neue Objektidentität.

In den meisten Datenmodellen existieren Beziehungen erst, wenn alle Referenzen der Typdefinition präsent sind. Dies erweist sich in Anwendungen, die eine schrittweise Realisierung von Beziehungen verlangen,-dazu gehören im besonderen Entwurfumgebungen - als gravierender Nachteil.

Ein Objekt oder eine Beziehung kann innerhalb einer attributierten Grammatik als vollständig angesehen werden, wenn ein entsprechender Boolescher Ausdruck den Wert TRUE annimmt. Ansonsten ist das Objekt weiterhin unvollständig. Ein Übergang des entsprechenden Wertes von FALSE auf TRUE kennzeichnet damit das Ende einer Entwurfstransaktion.

Da wir im Rahmen einer attributierten Grammatik die Mächtigkeit einer Programmiersprache zur Beschreibung von Konsistenzbedingungen zur Verfügung haben, ist es natürlich ebenso möglich, eine konsistente Numerierung von Abschnitten in Textstrukturen zu formulieren, wie in der Einleitung gefordert.

Zusammenfassend lassen sich objektorientierte Datenmodellierungskonzepte und ihre Realisierung im Rahmen attributierter Grammatiken in der folgenden Form gegenüberstellen.

Attributierte Grammatik	Objektorientiertes Datenmodell
Darstellung von Komponenten in der kontextfreien Grammatik	Komplexe Objekte
Verwendung von Attributen des Typs Object_Identifier	Objektidentität
Referenzierung von Objekten innerhalb einer Hierarchie durch Attribute vom Typ Object_Identifier.	Gemeinsame Unterobjekte
Darstellung von Alternativen in der Kontextfreien Grammatik	Generalisierungshierarchie
Realisierung der Beziehung zwischen Attributen, die vererbt werden, durch Aufstellung der entsprechenden Attributierungsregeln	Vererbung
Darstellung von Methoden als Berechnungsvorschriften für Attribute	Methoden

3. Anfragesprache

Nachdem in den bisherigen Überlegungen attributierte Grammatiken als eigenständiges Konzept zur Darstellung und Verwaltung von Datenobjekten eingeführt wurden, werden wir nun an einigen Beispielen versuchen, zumindest Grundzüge einer geeigneten, im wesentlichen PROLOG-orientierten Anfragesprache, vgl. /Abiteboul, Hull 86/ und /Bancilhon, Khoshafian 86/, zu entwerfen.

Im Mittelpunkt unserer Anfragesprache stehen dabei Restrukturierungsmechanismen, die die Transformation von Werten unterstützen. Sie beruhen auf der Formulierung logischer Regeln, die in sehr einfacher Weise die Manipulation typisierter hierarchischer Strukturen ermöglichen.

Wir betrachten dazu zunächst ein sehr einfaches Beispiel:

R1: [<Grundkörper>: X]X.Volumen= 5 → [<CSG-Objekt>: X]

Angewendet auf unser Ausgangsobjekt O ergibt sich, unter der Voraussetzung, daß das Volumen von X1 und X2 gleich 5 ist, als Ergebnis der Anfrage R1(O) die folgende zweielementige Objektmenge:

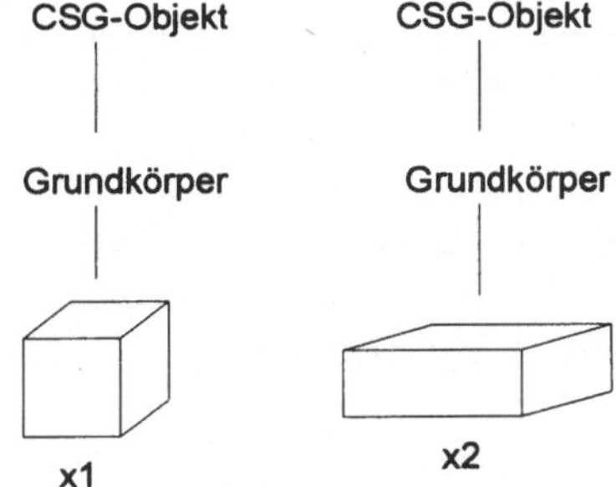

Das Ergebnis der Anfrage R1(O) läßt sich dabei intuitiv folgendermaßen verstehen. Für jede Belegung der Variablen X im Ausgangsobjekt O, für die der Anfrageausdruck wahr ist, erzeugt die Anfrage ein Objekt vom Typ <CSG-Objekt>. In der Anfrage wurde bewußt der Typ des Eingabeobjekts offen gelassen, dh. die Anfrage ist nicht beschränkt auf Objekte vom Typ <CSG-Objekt>. Dies erscheint sinnvoll insbesondere im Hinblick auf eine mögliche Verwendung im Rahmen interoperabler Systeme.

Das klassische Stücklistenproblem, nämlich die Selektion sämtlicher Grundkörper eines CSG-Objektes, ist ein Spezialfall der obigen Anfrage:

R2: [<Grundkörper>: X] $\rightarrow$ [X]

Für die meisten Anwendungen erübrigen sich damit die häufig relativ komplexen rekursiven Anfragen.

Da wir im Zusammenhang mit Vererbungsmechanismen von einer speziellen Klasse kontextfreier Grammatiken ausgegangen sind, soll zunächst eine einfache Regel unsere Ausgangsgrammatik in der geforderten Form erweitern:

DECLARE GRAMMARTYPE
    <CSG-Objekt>   ::= <Grundkörper> | **<Zus.-ges-Körper>**
    <Zus.-ges-Körper> ::= <CSG-Objekt><Mengenoperator><CSG-Objekt>
    <Grundkörper>   ::= <Kugel> | <Quader> | <Zylinder>
    <Mengenoperator>   ::= $\cap$ | $\cup$ | -
    <Kugel>   ::= <Radius>
    <Quader>   ::= <Breite><Höhe><Länge>
    <Zylinder>   ::= <Radius><Höhe>
    <Radius>   ::= <REAL>
    <Breite>   ::= <REAL>
    <Höhe>   ::= <REAL>
    <Länge>   ::= <REAL>
END

Die folgende Anfrage fügt das Zwischenobjekt <Zus.-ges-Körper> ein, dh. die linke Seite der Regel bezieht sich auf die ursprüngliche Grammatik, während sich die rechte Seite der Regel auf die neue Grammatik bezieht.

R: [<CSG-Objekt>[0]: X, <Mengenoperator>: Y, <CSG-Objekt>[1]: Z]]
    →
    [<CSG-Objekt>: [<Zus.-ges-Körper>: [<CSG-Objekt>[0]: X,
                    <Mengenoperator>: Y, <CSG-Objekt>[1]: Z]]]

Wiederum angewendet auf unser Ausgangsobjekt O stellt sich das Ergebnis R(O) wie folgt dar:

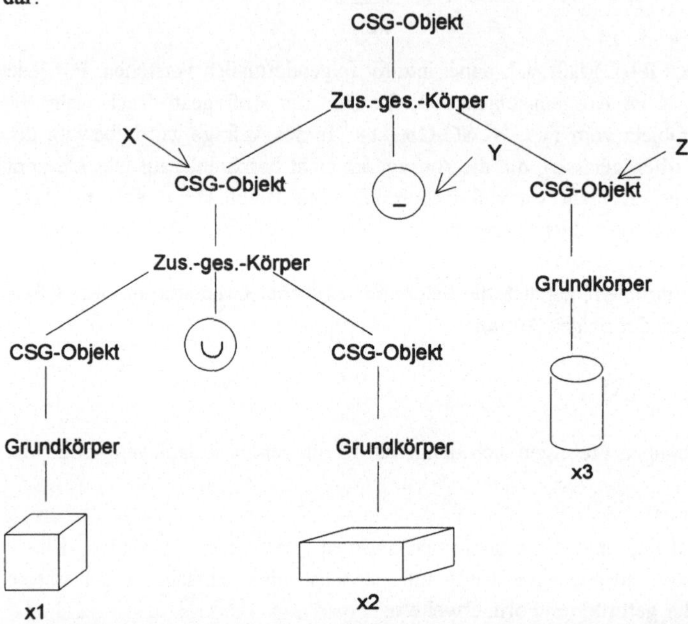

Die linke Seite einer Regel dient in dieser Weise der Selektion von Daten, die rechte Seite ihrer Restrukturierung. Sie beschreibt die Struktur der Objekte in der Ergebnismenge in Relation zu den Ausgangselementen. Im Rahmen der Verarbeitung hierarchischer Objektstrukturen lassen sich Restrukturierungsmechanismen in Form von Regeln damit als Grundlage eines flexiblen Sichtenkonzeptes verwenden.

4. Schlußbemerkung

Der Entwurf von abstrakten Modellen zur Repräsentation der in einer Anwendungsumgebung relevanten Bedeutungszusammenhänge ist ein zentrales Thema der Informatik. Ansätze dazu existieren -wenn auch weitgehend isoliert- in unterschiedlichen Bereichen. Während Programmiersprachen hierbei eine stärker algorithmische, prozedurale Sichtweise in den Vordergrund stellen, bevorzugen datenorientierte Modelle eine verstärkt deklarative Sichtweise. Es war das Ziel unserer Überlegungen zu zeigen, daß attributierte Grammatiken, obwohl sie eigentlich im Umfeld der Definition und Übersetzung von Programmiersprachen entstanden sind, grundlegende Mechanismen zur Darstellung von semantischen Objekteigenschaften enthalten, die eine Anwendung auch im Bereich der Datenmodellierung sinnvoll erscheinen lassen.

Von den eigentlichen objektorientierten Datenmodellen   unterscheiden sich attributierte Grammatiken allerdings in einem entscheidenden Punkt. Man beschränkt sich nicht auf eine Anzahl im Modell fest verdrahteter Repräsentationskonzepte, sondern stellt ein Werkzeug zur verfügung, das, reduziert auf ein wesentliches Konzept - das der Definition von syntaktischen und semantischen Eigenschaften unter der Verwendung von Regeln - die flexible Darstellung auch sehr komplexer Bedeutungszusammenhänge ermöglicht und Konsistenzbedingungen damit zu einer primären Eigenschaft des Objekts werden läßt.

Es wird das Ziel weiterer Überlegungen sein, attributierte Grammatiken im Rahmen einer geeigneten Anfragesprache auch zur Integration verschiedener Datenmodelle und damit zur einheitlichen Manipulation in interoperablen Systemen zu verwenden.

Danksagung

Die Autoren danken den anonymen Gutachtern für zahlreiche wertvolle Hinweise zur Verbesserung der Arbeit.

Literaturverzeichnis

/Abiteboul, Hull 86/: S. Abiteboul, R. Hull, Restructuring of Complex Objects and Office Forms, Proc. Int. Conf. On Database Theory, Rome, 1986

/Bancilhon, Khoshafian 86/: F. Bancilhon, S. Khoshafian , A Calculus for Complex Objects, PODS Boston, 1986, S 53-60

/Banerjee et al 87/: J. Banerjee, H.-T. Chou, J. Garza, W. Kim, D. Woelk, N. Ballou, Data model issues for object oriented applications ACM Trans. Office Information Systems, vol. 5, no. 1, 1987

/Barbic, Rabitti 84/: F. Barbic, F. Rabitti, The Type Concept in Office Document Retrieval, Proc. 11th Int. Conf. on Very Large Data Bases, Stockholm, 1985, S 34-48

/Beeri 90/: C. Beeri, A formal approach to object-oriented databases, Data & Knowledge Engineering 5, North-Holland, 1990, S 353-382

/Chen 76/: W. Chen, The Entity-Relationship Modell: Towards a Unified View of Data, ACM TODS, vol 1, no 1, 1976

/Gonnet, Tompa 87/: H. Gonnet, F. W. Tompa, Mind Your Grammar : A New Approach to Modelling Text, Proc. 13th Int. Conf. on Very Large Data Bases, Brighton, 1987, S 339-346

/Grosch, 90/: J. Grosch, Object-Oriented Attribute Grammars, Proc. 5th Int. Symp. on Computer and Information Sciences

/Gyssens et al 89/: M. Gyssens, J. Paredaens, D. Van Gucht, A Grammar-Based Approach Towards Unifying Hierarchical Dara Models, Proc. Int. Conf. on Management of Data, Portland Oregon, ACM SIGMOD RECORD vol. 18, no.2, 1989, S 263-272

/Harper 86/: R. Harper, Introduction to Standard ML, Laboratory For Foundations of Computer Science, Computer Science Department Edinburgh

/Hoare 75/: C. Hoare, Recursive Data Structures , Int. Journal of Computer and Information Science, vol 4, no. 2, 1975, S 105-132

/Kim et al 89/: W. Kim, Bertino, J. F. Garza, Composite Objects Revisted, Int. Conf. on Management of Data, Portland Oregon, ACM SIGMOD RECORD vol. 18, no.2, 1989, S 337-347

/Knuth 68/: D. Knuth, Semantics of context-free languages, Math. Systems Theory, vol. 2, no. 2, 1968

/Lamersdorf 85/: W. Lamersdorf, Semantische Repräsentation komplexer Objektstrukturen, Informatik-Fachberichte 100, Springer-Verlag, 1985

/Linnemann 80/: V. Linnemann, Kontextfreie Grammatiken und Ableitungsbäume als Hilfsmittel bei der Programmierung , Angewandte Informatik, 1980, S 60-66

/Linnemann 93/: V. Linnemann, Grammatiken und Syntaxbäume in Datenbanken, Tagungsband zur GI-Fachtagung: Datenbanken in Büro, Technik und Wissenschaft, Reihe "Informatik aktuell", Springer-Verlag, Braunschweig, 1993

/Meyer 88/: B. Meyer , Object-Oriented Software Construction, Int. Series in Computer Science, Prentice Hall, 1988

/Ridjanovic, Brodie 82/: D. Ridjanovic, M. L. Brodie, Defining Database Dynamics with Attribute Grammars, Informatin Processing Letters, vol. 14, no.3, 1982, S 132-138

/Salomaa 73/: A. Salomaa, Formale Sprachen, Springer-Verlag, 1973

/Ullman 93/: J. Ullman, Principles of database and knowledge systems, Computer Science Press, 1993

/Zhou, Baumann 90/: J. Zhou, P. Baumann, Evaluation of Complex Cardinality Constraints, Frauenhofer-Institut für Graphische Datenverarbeitung, Darmstadt, 1990

Systempufferverwaltung in
Multimedia-Datenbankverwaltungssystemen

Ulrich Marder[1] und Detlef Merten[2]

[1] TU Dresden, Fakultät Informatik, IBDR, 01062 Dresden
[2] Universität Erlangen-Nürnberg, IMMD VI,
Martensstr. 3, 91058 Erlangen

Zusammenfassung. Dieser Beitrag präsentiert Konzepte für den Entwurf und die Implementierung einer Systempufferverwaltung für Multimedia-Datenbanksysteme bzw. andere Multimedia-Systeme, die den Anwendungen eine datenunabhängige, d. h. geräte- und formatunabhängige Sicht auf Medienobjekte (und entsprechende Zugriffsmöglichkeiten) bieten. Solche Systeme müssen vor allem Ein- und Ausgabeoperationen (Medienobjekterzeugung, -präsentation) für alle Medienobjekttypen bereitstellen. Die Medienobjekte können beliebig groß und zusätzlich mit einer zeitlichen Dimension behaftet sein (Audio, Video), d. h. das System muß Zugriffe auf sehr große Datenobjekte unter Einhaltung von Fristen (Deadlines) durchführen können. In einer kurzen Übersicht werden diese Forderungen mit den Leistungsmerkmalen einiger bekannter Non-Standard-DBVS verglichen. Da die Forderungen nur unzureichend erfüllt werden, stehen im Mittelpunkt dieses Beitrags neue Pufferungskonzepte und der darauf basierende Entwurf einer Systempufferverwaltung, in die die aus der Echtzeitdatenverarbeitung bekannte Prefetching-Technik integriert wurde. Dieser Entwurf soll später den Kern einer MMDBVS-Systempufferverwaltung bilden.

1 Einleitung

Der Einzug von Multimedia in die Computerwelt eröffnet neue Wege, große Informationsmengen leicht verständlich und anschaulich zu präsentieren. Zudem werden Informationsverluste vermieden, die sonst bei der Konversion in die wenigen unterstützten Medien, z. B. Video $\rightarrow$ Text, zwangsweise entstehen würden.

Die mittlerweile in großer Zahl, auch kommerziell, verfügbaren Multimedia-Systeme sind jedoch nur für spezielle Anwendungen konzipiert, z. B. für Desktop Publishing (DTP), Computer-Based Training (CBT) oder für die Präsentation multimedialer Daten von CD-ROM (digitales Video, Computerspiele, Lexika, Touristik-Informationen, ...). Infolgedessen verwenden derartige Systeme speziell für die jeweilige Anwendung geeignete Datenformate und Speichergeräte, was dazu führt, daß die Datenbestände dieser Multimedia-Systeme für andere Anwendungen nur unter erheblichem Aufwand zugänglich gemacht werden können, z. B. durch Anlegen einer Kopie in wiederum anwendungsspezifischem Format.

Multimedia-Datenbanksysteme (MMDBS) [9, 7] sollen sich gegenüber den oben charakterisierten Multimedia-Systemen vor allem durch die Verfügbarkeit eines großen multimedialen Datenbestandes *für unterschiedlichste Anwendungen* auszeichnen. Zur Gewährleistung dieser Eigenschaft muß ein Multimedia-Datenbankverwaltungssystem (MMDBVS) multimediale Datenobjekte, kurz Medienobjekte oder MOs, anwendungsneutral und datenunabhängig verwalten können. Traditionelle DBVS leisten dies für Datentypen wie „Integer", „String" etc. mit Hilfe des *ADT-Konzepts*. Analog sind auch Medienobjekte als sog. *Medienspezifische Abstrakte Datentypen (MADT)* realisierbar, so daß man sich ein MMDBVS grundsätzlich als ein DBVS mit MADTs vorstellen kann.

Der Beitrag gliedert sich wie folgt: Im nächsten Kapitel wird das MADT-Konzept detaillierter vorgestellt und erörtert, welche Anforderungen daraus an das Speicherungssystem des MMDBVS resultieren. Das dritte Kapitel untersucht, inwieweit einige bekannte Non-Standard-DBVS in der Lage sind, diese Anforderungen zu erfüllen. Im vierten Kapitel werden neue, speziell für den Einsatz in MMDBVS konzipierte Pufferungskonzepte vorgestellt. Die Umsetzung dieser Konzepte in den Entwurf eines ersten Prototypen der Systempufferverwaltung skizziert Kapitel 5. Das abschließende sechste Kapitel bietet eine kurze Zusammenfassung der Ergebnisse dieses Beitrags und einen Ausblick auf künftige Entwicklungsaufgaben.

2 Anforderungen und Probleme

Nach dem MADT-Konzept [9, 7] besitzen Medienobjekte grundsätzlich die Datenkomponenten *Rohdaten* und *Registrierungsdaten*. Bei den Rohdaten handelt es sich um unformatierte Daten, genauer: um prinzipiell beliebig lange Sequenzen kleiner Datenelemente (Buchstaben, Bildpunkte, ...), die den Inhalt darstellen. Die Registrierungsdaten ermöglichen die korrekte Interpretation der Rohdaten. Bei einem Rasterbild enthalten sie u. a. Breite, Höhe, Pixeltiefe und die Farbtabelle (Colourmap). Als zusätzliche optionale Komponente werden die *Beschreibungsdaten* eingeführt, die durch aufwendige Berechnungen (z. B. Bildanalyse) oder manuelle Eingabe erzeugte redundante Informationen beinhalten und u. a. für inhaltsorientierte Suchoperationen herangezogen werden können.

Die MADTs definieren *Operationen* von hoher Funktionalität auf den MOs. Entsprechend dem ADT-Konzept dürfen Anwendungen nur über diese Operationen auf die Medienobjektdaten zugreifen. Folglich muß das MMDBVS für jeden MADT zumindest Operationen aus den Operationenklassen *Erzeugen* (aus einer Datei, aus Programmvariablen, von einem Eingabegerät) und *Ausgeben* (in eine Datei, in Programmvariable, auf ein Ausgabegerät) anbieten. Weitere mögliche Operationenklassen sind z. B. *Editieren, Auswerten, Verknüpfen.*

Ein MMDBVS hat vordergründig die Aufgabe zu erfüllen, die MOs datenunabhängig, d. h. geräte- und formatunabhängig, zu speichern und eine effiziente Implementierung der MADT-Operationen anzubieten. Als weitere wesentliche Aufgabe muß die Transaktionsunterstützung (Einbringen, Recovery, Zugriffsschutz) angesehen werden. Dieser Beitrag konzentriert sich darauf, Lösungskonzepte für den erstgenannten Aufgabenkreis aufzuzeigen. Die dabei zu bewältigenden Probleme lassen sich mit drei Schlagwörtern umreißen: **Größe** (MO-Datenvolumen), **Formatumwandlung** (Kodierung/Dekodierung, Formatkonvertierung, ...) und **Zeitsensitivität** (bei Präsentation/Erzeugung von Video, Ton und Animation). In den folgenden Absätzen werden diese Probleme näher betrachtet.

Für die **Größe** der MOs sind fast ausschließlich die Rohdaten verantwortlich. So beansprucht z. B. ein Rasterbild mit 1024×1024 Bildpunkten und 24 Bit Farbtiefe bereits 3 MB Speicher für die Rohdaten (unkomprimiert). Objekte dieser Größe muß das System in der für die jeweilige MADT-Operation geeigneten Weise im *Hauptspeicher* zwischenspeichern können. Geeignet heißt im Fall des Rasterbildbeispiels, daß etwa für die Ausgabe auf den Bildschirm die gesamten Rohdaten in einem kontinuierlichen Hauptspeicher-Adreßraum zu puffern sind. Bei noch größeren MOs, z. B. Videos, die i. a. gar nicht vollständig in den Hauptspeicher passen, müssen meist Teilstücke der Rohdaten, z. B. ein oder mehrere Einzelbilder, in dieser Weise gepuffert werden.

Weniger problematisch hinsichtlich der Pufferung im Hauptspeicher sind die Registrierungs- und Beschreibungsdaten: Da deren Volumen wesentlich geringer ist (i. d. R. sind Registrierungsdaten kleiner als die Blockgröße), wird ein Speicherungssystem, das die Rohdaten in der geforderten Weise puffern kann, keine spezielle Erweiterung benötigen, um auch die übrigen MO-Komponenten speichern und im Hauptspeicher bereitstellen zu können.

Formatumwandlungen zwischen internen und externen Datenformaten stellen in traditionellen DBVS kein besonderes Problem dar. Ganz anders verhält es sich bei Medienobjektdaten: Um Speicherplatz auf dem Externspeicher zu sparen und die Menge der über die I/O-Kanäle zu transportierenden Daten so gering wie möglich zu halten, werden für MO-Daten komprimierte Datenformate bevorzugt. Die Erzeugung (Kodierung) solcher internen Formate aus den externen Formaten, mit denen die Anwendungen arbeiten, ist i. d. R. mit einem hohen Bedarf an Rechenzeit und temporärem Puffer verbunden. Dasselbe gilt natürlich auch für die Wiedergewinnung der externen Formate (Dekodierung). Außerdem ist zu berücksichtigen, daß es mehrere verschiedene externe Formate für ein MO geben kann, z. B. GIF, TIFF, PCX, XImage, PixRect für Rasterbilder, und daß infolgedessen dasselbe MO nicht immer im selben externen Format angefordert wird, d. h. der Dekodierung schließt sich u. U. noch eine Formatkonvertierung an.

Da alle Formate und Komprimierungsverfahren mit einem hohem Kompressionsgrad nur für jeweils einen bestimmten Medienobjekttyp ausgelegt sind (und es auch nur sein können), müssen die Formatumwandlungsroutinen und deren optimale Auswahl konsequenterweise in den zugehörigen MADT-Modulen angesiedelt werden. Die Aufgabe der Systempufferverwaltung als Basisschicht muß es daher sein, den MADTs für diesen Zweck effiziente generische (d. h. MADT-unabhängige) Mechanismen und Adressierungsformen zur Verfügung zu stellen. Universelle Komprimierungsmethoden wie *Variable-Length-Encoding* (VLE) und *Lempel-Ziv-Welch-Kodierung* (LZW) jedoch sollten direkt innerhalb der Pufferverwaltung ablaufen und an deren Schnittstelle angeboten werden.

Die Medienobjekttypen Bewegtbild (Video, Animation) und Ton sind **zeit-sensitiv**. Das bedeutet, daß bei Operationen aus den Klassen *Erzeugen*und *Ausgeben*, z. B. „Ausgabe auf Ausgabegerät", die Daten(-Teilstücke) nur innerhalb eines bestimmten *Zeitfensters* im Hauptspeicher zur Verfügung stehen sollen. Sind die Daten zu früh im Hauptspeicher, so muß z. B. deren Ausgabe entsprechend verzögert werden und es werden Ressourcen verschwendet; sind sie hingegen zu spät im Speicher, kann die jeweilige Operation höchstwahrscheinlich nicht mehr korrekt ausgeführt werden. Der Anwender könnte dies z. B. als „Ruckeln", „Aussetzen" oder mangelhafte Synchronisation von Bild und Ton wahrnehmen.

Das Speicherungssystem soll solche zeitbezogenen Mängel unterbinden, indem es sog. *weiche Echtzeitanforderungen* an den Datentransfer zwischen Extern- und Hauptspeicher akzeptiert und deren Erfüllung überwacht. Im Gegensatz zur „harten Echtzeit" (z. B. Überwachung technischer Prozesse) gilt bei der „weichen Echtzeit" die Verletzung der Echtzeitanforderungen als begrenzt tolerierbar (zu spät gelieferte Daten für eine Multimedia-Präsentation sind zwar nutzlos und müssen übersprungen werden, die Präsentation kann aber i. d. R. fortgesetzt werden — natürlich mit verringerter Dienstgüte). Es sind u. a. die folgenden beiden Probleme zu lösen:

- Wegen des Mehrbenutzerbetriebs wird die Situation auftreten, daß mehrere zeitsensitive Operationen gleichzeitig bedient werden müssen. Zudem ist dafür zu sorgen, daß I/O-Anforderungen nichtzeitsensitiver Operationen, sog. asynchrone Transfers, nicht immer wieder zurückgestellt werden und infolgedessen „aushungern".
- Der Anwender hat i. d. R. die Möglichkeit, laufende Präsentationen interaktiv zu beeinflussen (Pause, Suchlauf, Zeitraffer, Zeitlupe, ...). Dadurch verschieben sich die Zeitfenster oft in unvorhersehbarer Weise, so daß das Speicherungssystem immer wieder gezwungen ist, seine I/O-Planung kurzfristig umzustellen.

3   Leistungen bekannter Non-Standard-DBVS-Speicherungssysteme

Nachdem im vorherigen Kapitel eine Reihe hoher Anforderungen an die Speicherungskomponente eines MMDBVS aufgestellt wurde, sollen diese nun mit den Leistungen einiger bekannter DBVS-Speicherungssysteme, die allgemein für die Speicherung großer Objekte konzipiert wurden, verglichen werden.

Die Non-Standard-DBVS **PRIMA** [6, 11] und **DASDBS** [15] speichern große Objekte in Seitenmengen. Dabei werden alle Seiten, die zusammen ein großes Objekt enthalten, über Verweise in einer Headerseite miteinander verkettet. Jede Seite enthält außer den Objektdaten auch interne Verwaltungsinformationen (Seitenheader). Aufgrund dieser Verkettungstechnik ist die maximale Größe der speicherbaren Objekte beschränkt (z. B. auf 2 MB bei PRIMA [11]).

Die Systempufferverwaltung dieser DBVS besitzt große Ähnlichkeit mit denen traditioneller DBVS. Wichtigster Unterschied ist, daß mit einem Funktionsaufruf eine ganze Seitenmenge referenziert werden kann [11]. Die einzelnen Seiten werden dann vom Seitenersetzungsalgorithmus über den seitenstrukturierten Systempuffer verstreut. Die Übergabe der Objektdaten erfolgt durch Kopieren in den Arbeitsbereich (Working Area) der Anwendung.

Die Systeme **EXODUS** [3], **ORION** [16], **Starburst** [8] und **EOS** [2] fassen große Objekte als Bytesequenzen auf. Außer bei ORION werden die Bytesequenzen auf dem Externspeicher in Clustern gespeichert. Spezielle Indexstrukturen (B^+-Bäume bei EXODUS und EOS, Listen bei ORION) ermöglichen die effiziente Durchführung von Änderungsoperationen auf dem Externspeicher. Die Anwendungen können beliebige Bytesequenzstücke in einem Objekt adressieren.

EXODUS puffert Bytesequenzen kontinuierlich (mit dynamischer Freispeicherverwaltung). Starburst puffert sog. lange Felder im System überhaupt nicht. EOS puffert nur bis zu einer Objektgröße von vier 4K-Blöcken. ORION besitzt einen blockstrukturierten Puffer und stellt eine Schnittstelle zum Lesen oder Schreiben eines Objekts als Blocksequenz zur Verfügung.

Weitere Konzepte für die Speicherung großer Objekte in Datenbanken bieten **POSTGRES** [13] mit seiner in die Anfragesprache integrierten Dateischnittstelle und der für den Aufbau eines *Virtual Memory Database System* entwickelte Speicherserver **WAKASHI** [1].

Alle bisher genannten DBVS-Speicherungssysteme sind zwar für die Speicherung großer Objekte konzipiert, jedoch erfüllt keines der Systeme die speziellen, in Kap. 2 definierten Anforderungen an ein MMDBVS-Speicherungssystem:

- Mit Ausnahme von EXODUS besitzt kein System eine Pufferverwaltung, die die kontinuierliche Pufferung prinzipiell beliebig großer Objekte erlaubt. MADT-Operationen, die eine solche Pufferung erfordern, würden daher eine lokale Pufferverwaltung benötigen.
- Kein System ermöglicht den Zugriff auf die Objekte unter (weichen) Echtzeitbedingungen.
- Kein System unterstützt Formatumwandlungen zwischen verschiedenen internen und externen MO-Formaten.

Das verteilte objektorientierte Multimedia-DBVS **AMOS** (Active Media Object Store) soll dagegen alle in Kap 2 aufgestellten Anforderungen erfüllen. AMOS basiert auf dem DBVS VODAK, das u. a. um den Interaction Manager zur Präsentation zeitsensitiver Daten erweitert wurde [14]. Jedoch sind den Autoren noch keine Veröffentlichungen über die Mechanismen innerhalb der Pufferverwaltung bekannt.

4 Pufferungskonzepte

In diesem Kapitel werden Pufferungskonzepte vorgestellt, die es ermöglichen, (prinzipiell) beliebig große Medienobjekte im Hauptspeicher zu puffern und dabei zwischen deren internem und externem Format zu konvertieren. Um auch zeitsensitive MOs in geeigneter Weise puffern zu können, sind die Pufferungskonzepte zudem für den Einsatz einer *Prefetching-Technik* [5, 12] ausgelegt. Zur

Reduzierung des Hauptspeicherbedarfs und Kopieraufwands werden Mittel zur Vermeidung von doppelter Pufferung (im System *und* beim Anwender) bereitgestellt.

Eine Besonderheit ist die Variier- und Kombinierbarkeit der Basiselemente. So ist es leicht möglich, für die Zugriffe auf MOs unterschiedliche Pufferungsstrategien bereitzuhalten und erst zur Laufzeit die endgültige Entscheidung für ein bestimmtes Konzept zu treffen. Selbst während des laufenden Zugriffs sind noch einige Variationen möglich, z. B. Veränderung der Anzahl der zu Beginn zugeteilten Puffer.

Die Pufferungskonzepte basieren auf einem Baukastenschema, dessen einziger Grundbaustein das sog. **Pufferobjekt** P ist. Die Pufferobjekte werden erst zur Laufzeit dem aktuellen Bedarf entsprechend angelegt. Ihre Größe soll beliebig aus dem Bereich zwischen der Blockgröße und mehreren Megabyte wählbar sein (die Obergrenze ist lediglich betriebssystemabhängig). So ist sichergestellt, daß z. B. Rasterbilder komplett in einem kontinuierlichen Adreßraum gepuffert werden können.

Die systemeigenen Pufferobjekte werden mit P^s bezeichnet, von Anwendungsprogrammen angelegte Pufferobjekte, die vom System direkt adressierbar sind (z. B. durch Anlegen als *Shared Memory*), werden zur Unterscheidung als P^a bezeichnet. Der Grund für die explizite Einführung der P^as ist die damit erreichbare Vermeidung der doppelten Pufferung, denn die unmittelbare Einbeziehung der P^as in die Systempufferverwaltung ersetzt das überflüssige und daher Rechenzeit und Hauptspeicher verschwendende Kopieren der Daten zwischen System- und Anwendungspuffer. Die Alternative, den Anwendungen direkten Zugriff auf den Systempuffer zu erlauben, wäre mit einem hohen Aufwand hinsichtlich Erteilung, Verwaltung und Überwachung der Zugriffsrechte verbunden. Diese Variante wurde daher nicht weiter verfolgt.

Es existieren vier verschiedene Operationen bzw. Operationenklassen, die die Inhalte von Pufferobjekten lesen oder verändern:

- *fetch*(P) füllt P mit Daten vom Externspeicher auf.
- *put*(P) schreibt den Inhalt von P auf den Externspeicher.
- *convert*(P_1, P_2) wandelt das Format der Daten in P_1 um und schreibt das neue Format in P_2.
- *access*(P) führt wahlfreie Zugriffe auf den Inhalt von P durch. Diese Operation ist entweder eine MADT-Operation oder, falls P ein P^a ist, Bestandteil der Anwendung.

4.1 Basiskonzepte

Es gibt zwei nützliche Basiskombinationen von zwei oder mehr Pufferobjekten: das **P-Paar** und den **P-Ring**. Ihre Funktion wird in den folgenden Abschnitten erläutert.

P-Paar für Formatumwandlung Das P-Paar ist für Formatumwandlungen vorgesehen. Ein Pufferobjekt übernimmt die Funktion des Quellpuffers, der das Quellformat enthält, und der andere die Funktion des Zielpuffers, der die Daten im Zielformat aufnehmen soll. Die Variante $P^s_{quell} : P^s_{ziel}$ ist für systeminterne Operationen, z. B. Präsentation, vorgesehen. Bei externen Operationen, z. B. Editieren der Daten durch die Anwendung, ist die Variante mit je einem P^s und einem P^a einzusetzen ($P^s_{quell} : P^a_{ziel}$ zum Erzeugen des externen Formats, $P^a_{quell} : P^s_{ziel}$ zum Erzeugen des internen Formats).

Eine genauere Betrachtung des Formatumwandlungsprozesses in Abb. 1 (a) (alle Abbildungen befinden sich am Ende des Artikels) zeigt, daß auf den beiden Pufferobjekten, d. h. dem Quell- und dem Zielpuffer, die drei beteiligten Operationen *fetch*, *convert* und *access* nacheinander ausgeführt werden. Wegen dieser Nacheinanderausführung der Operationen ist es nicht grundsätzlich erforderlich, daß tatsächlich *zwei* physische Puffer für die Formatumwandlung eingesetzt werden. Die Verwendung eines einzigen Puffers, der logisch betrachtet sowohl die Funktion des Quell- als auch die des Zielpuffers übernimmt, ist bei der Konzeptvariante mit zwei P^s (s. o.) möglich, wenn während der Formatumwandlung das Datenvolumen nicht anwächst und nicht Werteumgebungen (z. B. Nachbarpixel) zur Umwandlung benötigt werden. Das Anwachsen des Datenvolumens durch Formatumwandlung tritt jedoch auf jeden Fall bei der Dekomprimierung interner Formate auf.

P-Ring für Prefetching Mit einem P-Ring, bestehend aus mindestens zwei ringförmig verketteten Pufferobjekten, läßt sich die aus der Echtzeitdatenverarbeitung bekannte Prefetching-Technik [5, 12] realisieren. Da entsprechend dem MADT-Konzept alle zeitsensitiven Operationen systemintern realisiert werden (vgl. Kap. 2), wird im folgenden nur die Variante mit P^s betrachtet.

Beim Prefetching wird eine Datensequenz Stück für Stück vorausgelesen, wobei zuvor gelesene Datensequenzstücke immer wieder überschrieben werden (s. Abb. 1 (b)). So können Datensequenzen, die nicht komplett in den Hauptspeicher passen, kontinuierlich verarbeitet werden. Um zu erreichen, daß während der Verarbeitung eines Datensequenzstücks im Hauptspeicher bereits das darauffolgende Datensequenzstück vom Externspeicher geholt werden kann, müssen mindestens zwei Pufferobjekte verwendet werden. Auf diese greift abwechselnd ein schreibender Prozeß (Produzent) und ein lesender Prozeß (Konsument) zu, woraus die ringförmige Organisation der Puffer beim P-Ring-Konzept resultiert. Produzent und Konsument müssen aufeinander abgestimmt werden, da andernfalls z. B. Datenverlust durch Überschreiben noch nicht verarbeiteter Daten droht.

Prefetching wird für zeitsensitive Zugriffe eingesetzt, z. B. bei der Präsentation von Bildsequenzen (Video). Es funktioniert jedoch nur, wenn der Produzent im Durchschnitt (Schwankungen sind durch entsprechend große Puffer ausgleichbar) mindestens so schnell ist wie der Konsument, so daß der Konsument nie auf den Produzenten warten muß. Der entscheidende Richtwert für den Produzenten ist hierbei die sog. *Konsumrate*, die meist in KB/s angegeben wird. Aus der Konsumrate kann der Produzent den Zeitpunkt berechnen, bis zu dem er den Puffer mit Daten gefüllt haben muß. Dieser Zeitpunkt wird als *Deadline* bezeichnet.

In einem MMDBVS sind die einzelnen Produzentenprozesse i. d. R. erheblichen Schwankungen der momentan verfügbaren I/O-Kapazität ausgesetzt, so daß die Prefetching-Rate zeitweilig niedriger als die Konsumrate sein kann und nur im langfristigen Mittel auf dem Niveau der Konsumrate zu halten ist. Um derartige Geschwindigkeitsabweichungen auszugleichen, muß die Anzahl der Pufferobjekte im P-Ring erhöht werden. Dies kann sogar noch während eines laufenden Prefetching-Prozesses geschehen, falls geeignete Kommunikationsmittel für die Abstimmung zwischen Produzent und Konsument bereitstehen. Für die Anzahl der Ps gilt der Grundsatz: je höher die Anzahl der Ps, um so größere oder längerwährende Abweichungen sind kompensierbar (jedoch erhöht sich damit auch die Startverzögerung des Konsumentenprozesses).

Die Prefetching-Technik ist auch für das Schreiben von Datensequenzen auf den Externspeicher einsetzbar, z. B. Erzeugung von MO-Daten „in Echtzeit". Korrekterweise müßte es dann „Preputting" heißen. Da aber in beiden Fällen das gleiche P-Ring-Konzept zum Einsatz kommt, wird im folgenden nicht explizit zwischen Prefetching und Preputting unterschieden.

4.2 Komplexe Konzepte

Die komplexen Pufferungskonzepte demonstrieren die Kombinierbarkeit der bisher betrachteten Basiskonzepte „P-Paar" und „P-Ring". Damit soll eine *Vereinigung der Eigenschaften* beider Konzepte erreicht werden.

Der **P-Doppelring** ist eine solche Kombination. Er ist einerseits wie der einfache P-Ring für das Prefetching von Datensequenzen ausgelegt, andererseits jedoch auch für die Formatumwandlung der Datensequenz (s. Abb. 1(c)). Diese Kombination ist z. B. dann nützlich, wenn als internes Format einer zeitsensitiven Datensequenz ein komprimiertes Format gewählt wurde.

Wie beim Prefetching mit P-Ring gibt es beim Prefetching mit P-Doppelring einen Produzenten und einen Konsumenten. Der Produzent schreibt Daten (sequentiell und stückweise) in den Quell-P-Ring, und der Konsument liest Daten (ebenfalls sequentiell und stückweise) aus dem Ziel-P-Ring. Für die Umwandlung und Übertragung der Daten vom Quell- in den Ziel-P-Ring ist ein dritter Prozeß zuständig, der Konvertierungsprozeß. Dieser ist aus Sicht des Produzenten ein Konsument, aus Sicht des Konsumenten hingegen ein Produzent, und ist demgemäß in die Produzenten-Konsumenten-Synchronisation einzubinden.

Eine weitere sinnvolle Kombination der Basiskonzepte und ihrer Eigenschaften ist das **P-Ring + P**-Konzept, d. h. ein P-Ring ergänzt durch ein einzelnes, aber großes Pufferobjekt (s. Abb. 1(d)). Besonders geeignet ist es für die Formatumwandlung bei sehr großen Medienobjekten, z. B. Rasterbildern, die für den späteren Zugriff komplett in den Hauptspeicher geladen werden müssen. Die Formatumwandlung mit einem einzelnen P-Paar wäre in dieser Situation mit zwei Nachteilen behaftet:

1. Es müßten zwei sehr große Pufferobjekte angelegt werden, die jeweils das Objekt vollständig im internen bzw. externen Format aufnehmen können.
2. Der Formatumwandlungsprozeß könnte erst nach der Übertragung aller erforderlichen Daten in den Quellpuffer beginnen.

Die Nachteile könnten zwar mit dem P-Doppelring-Konzept behoben werden, jedoch müßte das externe Format nochmals vom Ziel-P-Ring in ein einzelnes, großes Pufferobjekt kopiert werden. Das P-Ring + P-Konzept vermeidet diesen zusätzlichen Kopierschritt und beseitigt auch die oben genannten Nachteile (unter der Voraussetzung, daß das Quellformat sequentiell konvertierbar ist). Zudem ist durch den Einsatz eines P-Rings als Quellpuffer, in den die Objektdaten nach und nach sequentiell eingelesen werden, der Hauptspeicherbedarf bei der Formatumwandlung großer MOs erheblich reduziert. Da I/O- und Konvertierungsprozeß miteinander verzahnt werden, ist außerdem zu erwarten, daß sich die Bereitstellung der konvertierten MO-Daten insgesamt beschleunigt. Beim Schreiben von MO-Daten mit diesem Konzept wird analog ein einzelnes Pufferobjekt als Quell- und ein P-Ring als Zielpuffer benutzt.

5 Entwurf der Systempufferverwaltung

Der Einsatz der oben beschriebenen Konzepte versetzt die Systempufferverwaltung in die Lage, große Medienobjekte im Hauptspeicher zu puffern sowie den Zugriff auf diese Objekte in weicher Echtzeit und deren Formatumwandlung zu unterstützen. Die Aufgaben einer solchen Systempufferverwaltung sind, verglichen mit denen traditioneller DBVS, wesentlich umfangreicher und komplexer. Davon betroffen sind z. B. die durch das Prefetching mit Deadlines sehr komplizierte Steuerung der Externspeicher-I/O sowie die Formatumwandlung und der MO-Datentransfer zwischen Pufferspeicher und den Aus- und Eingabegeräten (systemgesteuerte MO-Präsentation bzw. -Erzeugung).

5.1 Basis- und erweiterbare Systempufferschicht

Die genannten Aufgaben sind intern auf zwei verschiedene Komponenten bzw. Schichten der Systempufferverwaltung aufteilbar, denn die MO-Daten sollen an der Systempufferschnittstelle sowohl unkomprimiert als auch MADT-unabhängig komprimiert verarbeitet werden können: auf die Basisschicht setzt eine um beliebige universelle Komprimierungsverfahren wie VLE und LZW erweiterbare Schicht auf (s. Abb. 2).

Die Basis-Systempufferschicht stellt alle Funktionen bereit, die sich auf der Grundlage der MO-unabhängigen Adressierungseinheiten *Bytesequenz* und *Block* implementieren lassen. Dazu zählen vor allem die Externspeicher-I/O, die Bereitstellung und Verwaltung von Pufferobjekten sowie die Implementierung des Prefetching-Konzepts (P-Ring) einschließlich der erforderlichen Synchronisationsmechanismen und Steuerungs- bzw. Überwachungstechniken für die Einhaltung von Deadlines (Deadline-Scheduling).

Die Pufferung der Medienobjektdaten gemäß den Konzepten aus Kap. 4 findet nicht nur in den beiden Systempufferschichten statt, sondern durchdringt wegen der Einführung der P^as alle Systemschichten bis hin zu den Anwendungen. Die P^as durchwandern gewissermaßen die Hierarchie der Systemschichten, wenn Anwendungen sie der Systempufferverwaltung als Ersatz für systemeigene Puffer (P^s) zugänglich machen. Damit wird das aufwendige Kopieren der Daten zwischen Systempuffer und lokalem Arbeitsbereich der Anwendung überflüssig (vgl. Kap. 4). Voraussetzung ist jedoch, daß sowohl die internen Pufferverwaltungsstrukturen als auch die Schnittstellen für die Handhabung bzw. Übernahme der P^as ausgelegt werden.

Im folgenden sollen zwei der wichtigsten Komponenten der Systempufferverwaltung, und zwar die Pufferverwaltungsstrukturen und der I/O-Scheduler, genauer betrachtet werden.

5.2 Pufferverwaltungsstrukturen

Bei allen Pufferungskonzepten werden zwischen zwei oder mehr Pufferobjekten funktionale Beziehungen, die P-Paare und die P-Ringe, hergestellt (vgl. Kap. 4). Zu den wichtigsten Aufgaben der Pufferverwaltungsstrukturen gehören daher die Ermöglichung von P-Verknüpfungen und die Bereitstellung eines Synchronisationsmechanismus.

Um die Pufferobjekte frei von Verwaltungsinformationen zu halten, werden letztere in separaten Pufferkontrollblöcken (PKB) zusammen mit der Hauptspeicheradresse des zugehörigen Pufferobjekts abgelegt. Zur Herstellung der P-Verknüpfungen werden die entsprechenden PKBs miteinander verkettet. Dazu genügen zwei Zeiger in den PKBs, einer für die ringförmige Verkettung und einer für die paarweise Verkettung von Pufferobjekten.

Die Synchronisation der Prozesse, die auf die verknüpften Pufferobjekte zugreifen, kann mit Hilfe von Statusflags in den PKBs realisiert werden. Als Beispiel wird die Prozeßsynchronisation für ein Pufferpaar aus einem P-Doppelring betrachtet. Zur Synchronisation der drei auf dieses Pufferpaar zugreifenden Prozesse *fetch, convert* und *access* genügt ein Statusflag in den PKBs, das zwei verschiedene Pufferzustände anzeigen kann: *gültig* („Puffer enthält verarbeitbare Daten") oder *ungültig* („Puffer ist mit neuen Daten zu füllen oder wird gerade gefüllt") (s. Abb. 3).

5.3 I/O-Scheduling

Aus Sicht des I/O-Schedulers ist jedes Laden oder Ausschreiben auf Platte eines Pufferobjekts ein *I/O-Job*, der möglichst bald abzuarbeiten ist. In einem mehrbenutzerfähigen DBVS erreichen den I/O-Scheduler gewöhnlich sehr viele I/O-Jobs in unregelmäßigen Abständen, weshalb der Scheduler die ankommenden Jobs normalerweise nicht sofort bearbeiten kann.

Ein einfaches FIFO-Warteschlangensystem genügt — wie bei allen Multimedia-Systemen — für die hier entworfene Systempufferverwaltung jedoch bei weitem nicht, denn ein beträchtlicher Teil der von dieser Systempufferverwaltung generierten I/O-Jobs *muß* bis zu einem festgelegten Zeitpunkt bearbeitet sein, aber auch nicht zu früh. I/O-Jobs mit Deadline müssen somit Vorrang vor zeitunkritischen I/O-Jobs bekommen, was durch entsprechend gesetzte Prioritäten spezifiziert werden kann und als *Deadline-Scheduling* bezeichnet wird. Daß minder-privilegierte Jobs bei dieser Strategie „aushungern", kann durch eine stetige Erhöhung ihrer Priorität in Abhängigkeit von der Wartezeit verhindert werden.

Für das Deadline-Scheduling wird i. d. R. das in der Literatur unter dem Namen *Multilevel Feedback Queues* bekannte Warteschlangenmodell verwendet [4]. Im Detail birgt das I/O-Scheduling in MMDBVS aber ein neues Problem: die Prioritäten der I/O-Jobs können sich nicht nur durch die Verweilzeiten im Warteschlangensystem verändern, sondern auch durch interaktive Eingriffe der Anwender in die laufende Präsentation. Ein Lösungsansatz wäre, den I/O-Scheduler die Deadline-Berechnung für einen I/O-Job während dessen Verweilzeit in der Warteschlange bei solchen Ereignissen wiederholen zu lassen. Dafür müßte der I/O-Scheduler laufend über Veränderungen der Konsumraten informiert werden. Als Zwischenspeicher für derartige Informationen bieten sich die Pufferverwaltungsstrukturen an.

Der I/O-Scheduler sollte auch unbedingt durch eine *Externspeicherverwaltung mit Deadline-Disk-Scheduling-Strategie* [10] anstelle der normalen, nicht für zeitkritische Zugriffe optimierten Externspeicherverwaltung des Betriebssystems ergänzt werden.

6 Zusammenfassung und Ausblick

Ziel dieses Beitrags war es, Konzepte für die Pufferung von Medienobjekten in einem MMDBVS zu erarbeiten, die die in Kap. 2 beschriebenen Probleme *Größe, Formatumwandlung* und *Zeitsensitivität* lösen, und daraus einen Entwurf für die Systempufferverwaltung abzuleiten.

Aufgrund der Größe der Medienobjekte bilden sog. Pufferobjekte, die mehrere MByte groß sein können, den Grundbaustein der Pufferungskonzepte. Die paarweise Verknüpfung zweier Pufferobjekte (P-Paar) ermöglicht Formatumwandlungen, während ein Ring von zwei oder mehr Pufferobjekten (P-Ring für Prefetching) zeitsensitive Zugriffe erlaubt. Durch Kombination entstehen daraus komplexere Konzepte: einerseits für Formatumwandlungen bei zeitsensitiven Zugriffen (P-Doppelring) und andererseits für die Verringerung des Zeit- und Ressourcenbedarfs bei der Formatumwandlung großer MOs (P-Ring + P).

Die entworfene Pufferverwaltung gliedert sich in zwei Schichten: eine Basisschicht, die die genannten Pufferungskonzepte sowie Geräteunabhängigkeit bietet, und eine darauf aufsetzende, die universelle Komprimierungsmethoden zur Verfügung stellt.

Nach der Implementierung werden mit dieser Systempufferverwaltung bereits einige der wichtigsten Systempufferfunktionen für MMDBVS zur Verfügung stehen.

Bevor dieser Prototyp zu einer vollwertigen Systempufferverwaltung für ein MMDBVS reifen kann, müssen jedoch noch weitere Forschungsleistungen erbracht werden. An erster Stelle wäre hier die Integration eines Konzepts zur Transaktionsunterstützung (Einbringstrategie, Recovery, Zugriffsschutz) zu nennen, aber auch die Erweiterung der Systempufferverwaltung für die Realisierung von verteilten MMDBVS.

Danksagung

Wir danken den Herren Prof. Dr. Klaus Meyer-Wegener und Rolf Käckenhoff für die hilfreichen Hinweise zur Verbesserung dieses Beitrags.

Literatur

1. Guangyi Bai, Makinouchi Akifumi: Implementation and Evaluation of a new Approach to Storage Management for Persistent Data — Towards Virtual-Memory Databases. Proc. 2nd Far-East Workshop on Future Database Systems (April 26–28, Kyoto, Japan), World Scientific, 1992, pp. 211–220.
2. Alexandros Biliris: An Efficient Database Storage Structure for Large Dynamic Objects. Proc. 8th Int. Conf. on Data Engineering (Feb. 2–3, Tempe, Arizona), IEEE Computer Society Press, Los Alamitos, California, 1992, pp. 301–308.
3. Michael J. Carey, David J. DeWitt et al.: Object and File Management in the EXODUS Extensible Database System. Proc. 12th Int. Conf. VLDB, Kyoto, August 1986, pp. 91–100.
4. Harvey M. Deitel: An Introduction to Operating Systems. Reading, Massachusetts: Addison-Wesley 1990.
5. Jim Gemmel, Stavros Christodoulakis: Principles of Delay-Sensitive Multimedia Data Storage and Retrieval. ACM Transactions on Information Systems, Vol 10, No. 1, Januar 1992, pp. 51–90.
6. Theo Härder (Hrsg.): The PRIMA Project. Design and Implementation of a Non-Standard Database System. SFB 124, Report No. 26/88, Universität Kaiserslautern, März 1988.
7. Rolf Käckenhoff, Detlef Merten, Klaus Meyer-Wegener: Eine vergleichende Untersuchung der Speicherungsformen für multimediale Datenobjekte. In: W. Stucky, A. Oberweis (Hrsg.): Datenbanksysteme in Büro, Technik und Wissenschaft. GI-Fachtagung Braunschweig (3.–5. März 1993), Berlin: Springer 1993, S. 164–180.
8. Tobin J. Lehman, Bruce G. Lindsay: The Starburst Long Field Manager. Proc. 15th Int. Conf. VLDB, Amsterdam, 1989, pp. 375–383.
9. Klaus Meyer-Wegener: Multimedia-Datenbanken. Stuttgart: B. G. Teubner 1991.
10. A. L. Narasimha Reddy, Jim Wyllie: Disk Scheduling in a Multimedia I/O System. Proc. 1st ACM Int. Conf. on Multimedia (August 1–6, Anaheim, California), ACM Press, 1993, pp. 225–233.
11. Andrea Sikeler: Buffer Management in a Non-Standard Database System. In [6], pp. 37–67.

12. Richard Staehli, Jonathan Walpole: Constrained-Latency Storage Access. IEEE Computer, März 1993, pp. 44–53.
13. Michael Stonebraker, Michael Olson: Large Object Support in POSTGRES. Proc. 9th Int. Conf. on Data Engineering (April 19–23, Vienna, Austria), IEEE Computer Society Press, Los Alamitos, California, 1993, pp. 355–362.
14. Heiko Thimm, Thomas C. Rakow: Upgrading Multimedia Data Handling Services of a Database Managment System by an Interaction Manager. Arbeitspapiere der GMD Nr. 762, St. Augustin, Juli 1993.
15. Gerhard Weikum: Set-Oriented Disk Access to Large Complex Objects. Proc. 5th Int. Conf. on Data Engineering, IEEE Computer Society Press, Los Alamitos, California, 1989, pp. 426–433.
16. Darrell Woelk, Won Kim: Multimedia Information Management in an Object-Oriented Database System. Proc. 13th Int. Conf. VLDB (Sept. 1–4, Brighton, England), 1987, pp. 319–329.

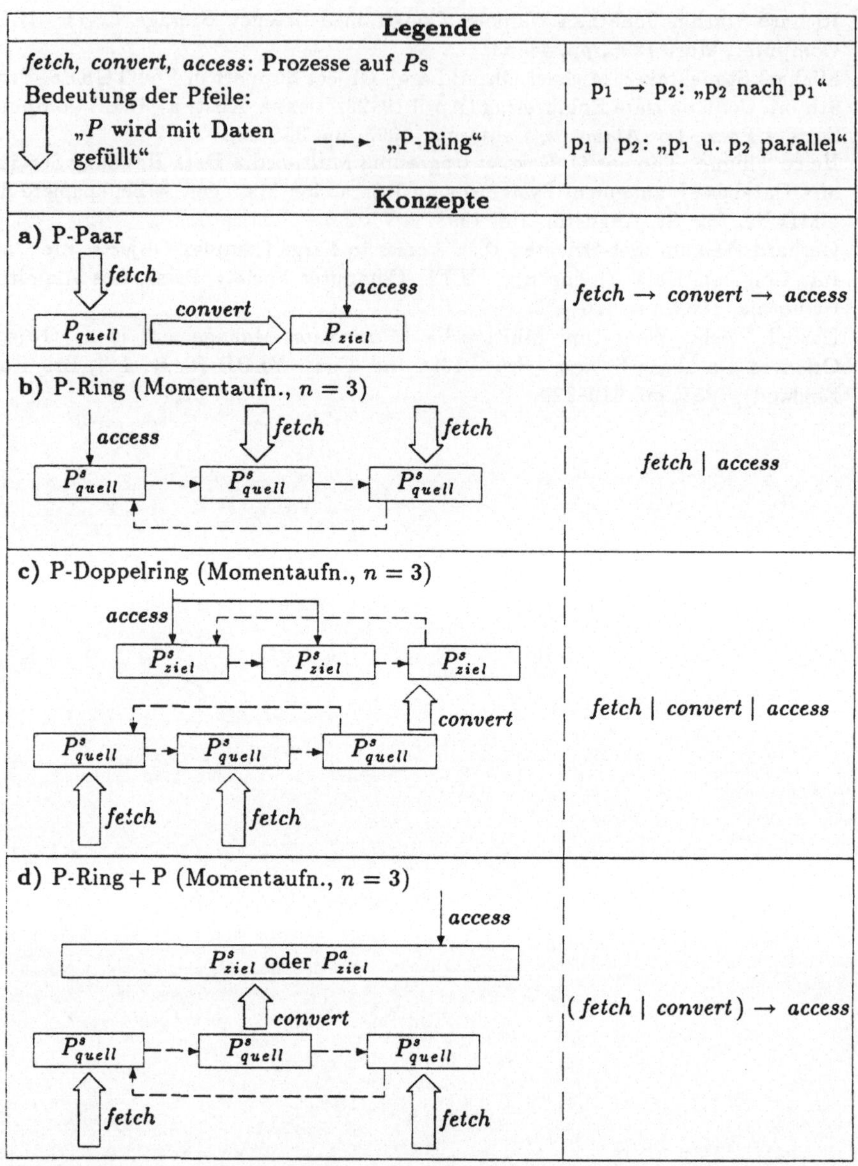

Abb. 1. Basis- und komplexe Pufferungskonzepte: Architektur und zeitliche Abfolge für lesende Zugriffe auf MO-Daten.

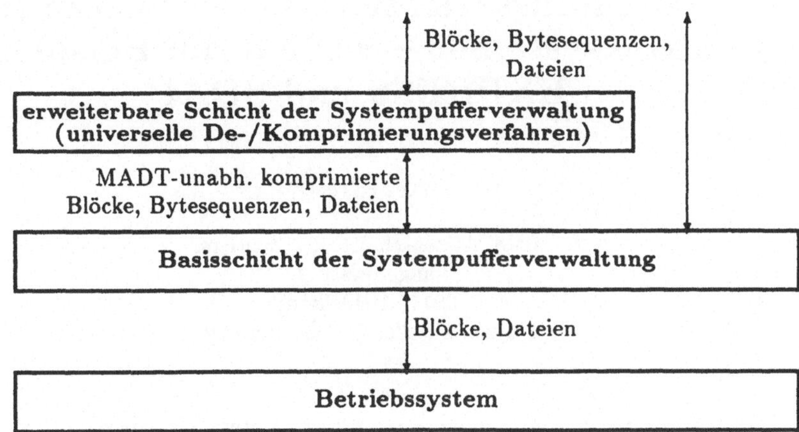

Abb. 2. Schichten der Systempufferverwaltung.

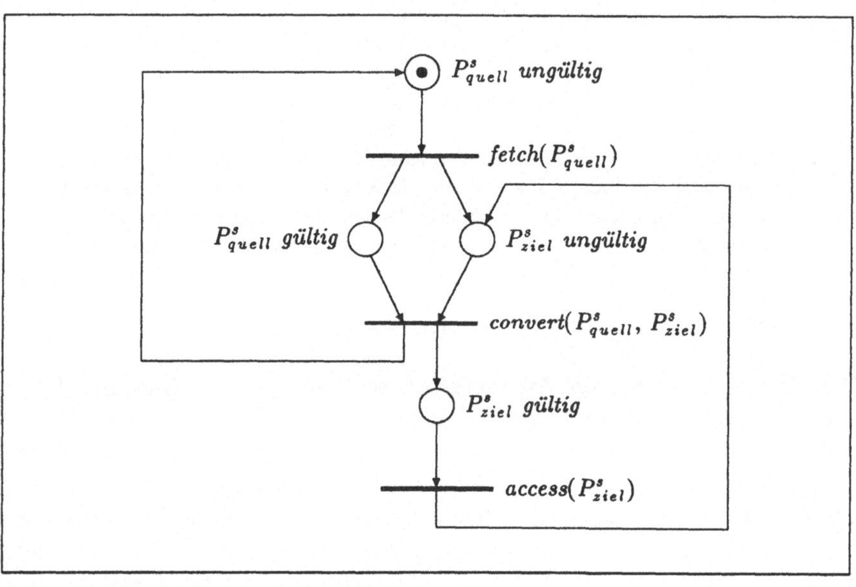

Abb. 3. Synchronisation der Prozesse auf einem P-Paar (innerhalb eines P-Doppelrings); Darstellung als Petri-Netz.

Anwendungsorientiertes Archivieren in Datenbanksystemen – vertieft am Beispiel von EXPRESS und SDAI

Axel Herbst*

IBM Wissenschaftliches Zentrum
Vangerowstr. 18
69115 Heidelberg
E-mail: aherbst @ vnet.ibm.com

Zusammenfassung. Zunehmend müssen Daten aus wirtschaftlichen und juristischen Gründen langfristig, kostengünstig und wiederverwendbar aufbewahrt werden. Während die elektronische Archivierung von Dokumenten eine etablierte Technik ist, wurde ein adäquater Datenbankservice bislang kaum untersucht. Auch in Datenbanksystemen belasten die Daten, mit denen längere Zeit nicht gearbeitet wird und die von "aktiven" Daten unterschieden werden sollen, unnötig das Sekundärspeichersystem. Tertiärspeicher werden nur unzureichend unterstützt. Dieser Beitrag stellt einen auf Datenbanksysteme bezogenen Archivierungsansatz vor, bei dem die zu archivierenden Daten auf der konzeptuellen Ebene der Datenbankanwendung (hier exemplarisch STEP/EXPRESS) bestimmt werden. Im Kontext der ISO-Norm EXPRESS bedeutet anwendungsorientiertes Archivieren eine Erweiterung der Zugriffsschnittstelle SDAI (Standard Data Access Interface). Aus unserer Spezifikation von SDAI–integriertem Archivieren leiten wir Anforderungen an Datenbanksysteme ab und zeigen verschiedene Implementierungsansätze auf.

1   Archivierung als Datenbankservice

Der Ursprung des Wortes *Archiv* (griechisch "archeion" = Rathaus) beeinflußt noch immer das Verständnis vom Archivieren als eine geordnete Aufnahme von Dokumenten und deren sichere Aufbewahrung auf Medien wie z.B. Papier, Microfilm oder optischen Platten. Neben dem traditionellen reinen Dokumentationscharakter eines Archivs tritt heute die *Wiederverwendbarkeit* der *kostengünstig* archivierten Daten immer mehr in den Vordergrund. Dies hat betriebswirtschaftliche Gründe [VS91] und kommt Forderungen des Gesetzgebers nach [Sam93]. Aktueller Forschungsgegenstand sind u.a. multimediale Archive, wobei hier die Verschiedenartigkeit der elektronisch zu archivierenden Dokumente (Video, Ton oder Bild) gemeint ist [RDMP94]. Beispiele für Dokumente im Konstruktionsumfeld sind technische Zeichnungen und Stücklisten. Aber auch sog. Geometriemodelle in Form von CAD–systemspezifischen Dateien oder in neutralen, standardisierten Austauschformaten zählen inzwischen dazu [HM94].

---

* auch: Universität Kaiserslautern, FB Informatik, AG Datenverwaltungssysteme

Mit dem Übergang zur Produktmodelltechnologie [GAP93] verschwimmt in diesem Anwendungsbereich der Dokument–Begriff: Produktdaten sind nicht länger nur inhaltstransparente Dateien, die ausschließlich über zusätzliche Beschreibungsattribute aufgefunden werden können. Produktdaten werden modelliert und feingranular *in Datenbanksystemen* gespeichert. Geblieben ist die Forderung nach ihrer Archivierung. Das Auslösen des Archivierungsvorgangs ist dabei nicht vom Alter der Daten abhängig, sondern wird durch andere "Reife"–Kriterien (z.B. Zeitpunkt der Freigabe) bestimmt. Eine derartige Archivierungsfunktionalität wurde erstmals in [EL90] von einer *Engineering Database* gefordert. Durch die wachsende Datenflut gewinnt die Archivierungsproblematik über technische Datenbanken hinaus an Brisanz. Neuartige Speichermedien motivieren zusätzlich, **anwendungsorientiertes Archivieren** als allgemeinen Datenbankservice mit folgender Semantik zu untersuchen:

– *Benutzerveranlassung*
  Das Datenbanksystem bietet dem Benutzer (ein Anwendungsprogrammierer oder auch Datenbankadministrator) Funktionen an, mit denen er bewußt die Archivierung auslöst. Nur aus den Anwendungen heraus ist bekannt, *welche Daten* langfristig aufbewahrt werden sollen. Vom Zeitpunkt der Archivierung an unterliegen diese Daten in aller Regel einem wesentlich anderen Zugriffsprofil (seltene, zeitunkritische, überwiegend lesende Zugriffe).

– *Abstraktionsebene Datenmodell*
  Datenbankanwendungen identifizieren die zu archivierenden Daten in der Terminologie und dem Granulat des jeweiligen Datenmodells. Im relationalen Fall sind dies etwa Tupel, Tabellen oder Sichten. Anwendungsorientiertes Archivieren kann aber auch auf Instanzen eines semantischen Datenmodells, das beispielsweise ein Konzept "Entity" definiert, übertragen werden.

– *Datenauslagerung*
  Die "weniger interessanten" Daten werden auf billigere, aber dafür langsamere Massenspeicher ausgelagert, um Platz für wichtigere, aktive Daten zu schaffen und die Anfrageauswertung nicht unnötig zu belasten. Angesichts Größenordnungen von mehreren 100 Terabyte werden verschiedene neue Tertiärspeicher – Speicher "unterhalb" von Magnetplatten in der Speicherhierarchie (z.B. optische Plattenroboter) – unumgänglich [KPCD⁺92].

Abstrahiert man von dem originären Ansatz in Verbindung mit dem Datenbankprototypen "PRODAT", stimmen wir in diesen Grundzügen mit [EL90] überein. Anders als in [EL90] nutzen und erweitern wir systemunabhängige Schnittstellen, die derzeit weltweit standardisiert werden und analysieren, inwieweit heutige Datenbanksysteme anwendungsorientiertes Archivieren unterstützen. Auf weitere Unterschiede verweisen wir im Verlauf des Beitrags. Unser Konzept grenzt sich aber schon jetzt deutlich von dem ab, was Datenbanksysteme üblicherweise zur Archivierung anbieten: ein Zusatzwerkzeug, das physische Datenbankgranulate (Seiten, Segmente, Log–Dateien) auf ein nicht weiter verwaltetes Speichermedium kopiert, um bei Ausfall des Sekundärspeichers eine Wiederherstellung der Datenbank (Recovery) zu ermöglichen. Auch in [MN93] gehen die Autoren von dieser *Backup–Semantik* aus.

Der Beitrag ist im weiteren wie folgt aufgebaut: Abschnitt 2 definiert unsere Abstraktionsebene für anwendungsorientiertes Archivieren, spezifiziert Archivierungsfunktionen und leitet Anforderungen an Datenbanksysteme ab. Abschnitt 3 klassifiziert Implementierungsansätze und untersucht, inwieweit relationale und objektorientierte Systeme unsere Spezifikation unterstützen. Wir illustrieren einen objektorientierten Ansatz an Hand unseres Prototyps in Abschnitt 4. Abschnitt 5 zieht Schlußfolgerungen und gibt einen Ausblick.

2 Anwendungsorientiertes Archivieren am Beispiel einer EXPRESS/SDAI–Datenbank

Wir wählen Teile von STEP (Standard for the Exchange of Product Model Data [Owe93]) aus drei Gründen als Kontext für anwendungsorientiertes Archivieren: Erstens sehen wir einen Bedarf für derartige Archivierungskonzepte in den aufkommenden STEP–Datenbanken [LRW93]. Zweitens sind die Modellierungssprache EXPRESS und die Zugriffsschnittstelle SDAI (Standard Data Access Interface) unabhängig vom primären Anwendungsbereich Produktdatenverwaltung [DHSV94, Her94, Wil94]. Schließlich versprechen die Standardisierung von EXPRESS und SDAI durch die ISO und die zunehmende weltweite Akzeptanz von STEP in der Industrie eine langfristigere Stabilität dieser beiden Teilnormen.

2.1 EXPRESS und SDAI aus Datenbanksicht

In [MSRD91] wurde EXPRESS unter dem Gesichtspunkt des Datenbankentwurfs analysiert[1]. Auch wenn die endgültige Veröffentlichung der Sprache als internationale Norm [ISO95] in einigen Punkten von der Darstellung in [MSRD91] abweicht, halten wir diese Analyse im wesentlichen für aktuell: Ein EXPRESS–Schema als Datenbankschema aufzufassen (und EXPRESS als DDL) bringt Probleme mit sich, die u.a. im komplexen Typsystem der Sprache liegen. Üblicherweise wählt man eine Abbildung von EXPRESS auf die DDL des zugrundeliegenden Datenbanksystems. Je nach Datenmodell ist diese Abbildung mehr oder weniger aufwendig (z.B. bei dem *SELECT*–Typ in EXPRESS, der ein Vereinigungstyp über Entities ist oder bei den vielfältigen Vererbungsbeziehungen, die zwischen Entities in Form von Super- und Subtypen spezifizierbar sind).

In [MSRD91] werden die globalen Regeln in EXPRESS noch als Datenbank–Integritätsbedingungen interpretiert. Inzwischen beantwortet die Schnittstellenspezifikation SDAI [ISO94] die Frage, wann diese Regeln zu überprüfen sind: bei expliziten Aufrufen aus Programmen heraus, die über SDAI auf Daten zugreifen, die durch das EXPRESS–Schema beschrieben werden.

---

[1] Wir verzichten daher auf eine detaillierte Vorstellung der Sprache. Eine umfassende Einführung findet man in [SW94]. Die Beispiele in Abschnitt 2.2 sollten auch dem Nicht-EXPRESS-Kenner einen ausreichenden Eindruck vermitteln. Vorerst genügt es festzuhalten, daß instanziierbare Entities das zentrale Modellierungskonzept sind. Entities haben Attribute (einfache und Entity–wertige Datentypen), erlauben Vererbung und werden syntaktisch zu EXPRESS-Schemata zusammengefaßt.

Neben den Operationen zur Regelauswertung enthält die SDAI–Spezifikation z.B. die folgenden, weitgehend selbsterklärenden Operationen für den Zugriff auf Instanzen von EXPRESS–Entities (bzgl. *model* siehe Abschnitt 2.2.):

```
CREATE_INSTANCE        <entity>, <model>
DELETE_INSTANCE        <instance>
PUT_ATTRIBUTE          <instance>, <attribute>, <value>
GET_ATTRIBUTE          <instance>, <attribute>
UNSET_ATTRIBUTE_VALUE  <instance>, <attribute>
GET_INSTANCE_TYPE      <instance>
```

Transaktionsklammern und einfache Anfragen (Selektion von Instanzen eines Entitys über einfache Prädikate) wurden erst vor kurzem in die Spezifikation aufgenommen. Dies liegt daran, daß SDAI nicht ursprünglich als Datenbankschnittstelle, sondern für Hauptspeicherzugriffe ohne Berücksichtigung eines Mehrbenutzerbetriebs konzipiert wurde.

Die verschiedenen sog. Language–Bindings der Spezifikation und die aktuell definierten Konformitätsklassen für SDAI–Implementierungen widersprechen nicht dem Prinzip, SDAI–Anwendungsprogramme weitgehend von dem zugrundeliegenden Speichersystem (Hauptspeicher, Dateisystem, Datenbanksystem) zu isolieren. SDAI ist damit zwar keine DML im strengen Sinne, aber doch *die* in der Standardisierung befindliche Schnittstelle, über die EXPRESS–Daten gelesen, modifiziert und unserer Meinung nach auch **archiviert** werden sollen.

2.2 Integration von Archivierungsfunktionalität in SDAI

Nachdem wir gerade die "Stelle SDAI" lokalisiert haben, an der Archivierungsdienste angeboten werden sollen, wollen wir diese zusätzliche Funktionalität genauer spezifizieren. Dabei gehen wir von der (konzeptionellen) Sicht des SDAI–Benutzers aus. Konkret ist dies die Person, die SDAI–Anwendungen entwirft und programmiert. Wir berücksichtigen gleichzeitig erste Implementierungsaspekte von *SDAI–integriertem Archivieren.*

SDAI–Metadatendefinitionen als Archivierungsgranulate. Das Abstraktionsniveau des SDAI-Benutzers, EXPRESS, spiegelt sich in Metadatendefinitionen wider, die ebenfalls Bestandteil von [ISO94] sind. Dazu zählen insbesondere das *SDAI Dictionary Schema* und das *Session Schema*, die wiederum in EXPRESS geschrieben sind. Beide Schemata sind ein geeigneter Anknüpfungspunkt für die Bestimmung der zu archivierenden Daten – interessanterweise auch aus Sicht des SDAI-Entwicklers: Um normkonform zu sein, muß die Funktionalität beider Schemata von einer SDAI-Implementierung bereitgestellt werden. Folglich entsprechen diese EXPRESS-Definitionen mehr oder weniger direkt Datenstrukturen der SDAI-Implementierungssprache.

Aus dem **Dictionary Schema** kann man z.B. ablesen, daß *schema, entity* und *attribute* anwendungsorientierte Dateneinheiten sind. Praktische Bedeutung als Granulat zum Archivieren besitzen jedoch nur die ersten beiden, da niemand langfristig auf eine Menge einzelner Attribut-Werte zugreift. Dagegen ist es vorstellbar, daß nur gewisse "archivierungswürdige" Entities aus einem Anwendungsschema ausgewählt werden sollen. Diese Auswahl ist eine Projektion auf der Ebene des Anwendungsschemas und entspricht der Selektion von Instanzen von Meta–Entities. Hierzu betrachte man den folgenden Ausschnitt aus dem Dictionary Schema, wo das (Meta–) Entity *entity_definition* vom (Meta–) Entity *schema_definition* referenziert wird:

```
ENTITY schema_definition;          ENTITY entity_definition;
 name: STRING;                      attributes: LIST OF attribute;
 entities: SET OF entity_definition; ...
 global_rules: SET OF global_rule; INVERSE parent_schema:
 ...                                 schema_definition FOR entities;
END_ENTITY;                        END_ENTITY;
```

Orthogonal zu der Auswahlmöglichkeit auf Typ– bzw. Schema–Ebene kann man die zu archivierenden Instanzenmengen gemäß den Definitionen aus dem **Session Schema** festlegen. In diesem Schema ist auch dokumentiert, wie SDAI die Anwendungen von der zugrundeliegenden Speichertechnologie isoliert: Ein sog. *SDAI Repository* ist der abstrakte Speicherort für sämtliche Daten, die von einer SDAI–Implementierung verwaltet werden.

```
ENTITY sdai_repository;            ENTITY sdai_repository_contents;
 name: STRING;                      models: SET OF sdai_model;
 contents: sdai_repository_contents; INVERSE repos:
 schemas: SET OF schema_definition;  sdai_repository FOR contents;
 ...                               END_ENTITY;
END_ENTITY;


ENTITY sdai_model;                 ENTITY schema_instance;
 underlying_schema: schema_definition; name: STRING;
 name: STRING;                      contents: SET OF sdai_model;
 contents: sdai_model_contents;     base_schema: schema_definition;
 repos: sdai_repository;            ...
 ...                               END_ENTITY;
END_ENTITY;
```

Hierbei steht *sdai_model_contents* für die Menge aller Instanzen eines *SDAI models*. Dies ist eine willkürliche Zusammenfassung von Instanzen, die zu beliebigen Entities aus genau einem EXPRESS–Schema gehören. Jede Instanz ist in genau einem *model* enthalten. In einem Repository werden in der Regel mehrere Schemata und die aktuell existierenden *models* verwaltet.

Das Entity *schema_instance*[2] hat einen sehr irreführenden Namen. Es steht für eine Menge von *models*, die den Gültigkeitsbereich für globale EXPRESS–Regeln und Referenzen zwischen (Entity–) Instanzen definiert. Letztere dürfen einander nur referenzieren, wenn sie in *models* enthalten sind, die in der gleichen *schema_instance* liegen.

---

[2] Dieses neue Konstrukt wurde in SDAI aufgenommen als man feststellte, daß der Gültigkeitsbereich *repository* "zu groß", aber *model* "zu klein" für Datenbankanwendungen ist.

Wir gehen davon aus, daß SDAI–Benutzer den Empfehlungen in [ISO94] folgen und semantisch zusammenhängende Daten in *model* und *schema_instance* gruppieren. Folglich bilden so zusammengefaßte Instanzen auch sinnvolle Mengen von Daten, die **als Ganzes** archiviert werden. Wenn Instanzen bestimmter Entities stets ausgeblendet werden sollen (etwa weil sie nicht archiviert werden brauchen), kann dies zusätzlich spezifiziert werden.

Neue SDAI Operationen. Mindestents zwei Operationen müssen in SDAI eingeführt werden, um anwendungsorientiertes Archivieren zu ermöglichen. Den Zugriff auf archivierte Daten klären wir anschließend.

1. **SELECT**

   Diese Operation bestimmt die zu archivierenden Daten. Im einfachsten Fall wird der Aufruf mit einem Verweis auf ein Granulat aus dem Session Schema parametrisiert. Zusätzliche Einschränkungen durch Vorgaben aus dem Dictionary Schema erhöhen zwar die Auswahlmächtigkeit, verlangen aber weitere Klarstellungen: Wie sollen z.B. offene Referenzen zwischen zu archivierenden und aktiven Daten behandelt werden, die entstehen können, wenn bestimmte Entities von der Archivierung ausgenommen werden? Das Auswahlvermögen der SELECT–Operation wäre noch höher, wenn Prädikate als Parameter zugelassen werden, wie sie auch in SDAI–Queries Verwendung finden. Auch eine deskriptive, EXPRESS–basierte Sichtbeschreibungssprache ist auf den ersten Blick eine wünschenswerte Erweiterung. Wir sehen jedoch keinen Bedarf für diese Funktionalität, da – wie bereits angesprochen – Daten langfristig nur grobgranular, also konkret in kompletten SDAI *schema_instance*s oder *model*s wiederverwendbar sind.

   Bereits das Archivieren ausgewählter *model*s ist nicht trivial: Neben den potentiellen offenen Referenzen kann im allgemeinen nicht davon ausgegangen werden, daß zuvor geltende EXPRESS–Integritätsbedingungen in Form globaler Regeln nach dem Archivieren immer noch erfüllt sind, da ihr Gültigkeitsbereich eine *schema_instance* ist. In diesem Fall kommt der SELECT–Operation die Aufgabe zu, die Korrektheit der Auswahl zu überprüfen. Dies führt zu einem iterativen Auswahlprozeß in Form einer Folge von SELECT–Aufrufen: Die Archivierungsanwendung wertet die Rückmeldungen des Archivierungssubsystems aus (Zurückweisungen von ausgewählten Granulaten oder Vorgaben zur Archivierung weiterer Daten, um einen referentiellen Abschluß zu erreichen) und setzt ggf. ein erneutes SELECT ab. Zusammenfassend halten wir fest, daß eine Folge von SELECT–Aufrufen die endgültige Menge der gewünschten und tatsächlich archivierbaren Daten festlegt. Als Granulate wählen wir vorzugsweise *schema_instance* und *model*.

2. **ARCHIVE**

   Entsprechend unserer Motivation löst ein SDAI–Anwendungsprogramm mit dieser Operation das Archivieren der zuletzt selektierten Daten aus. Ein Parameter identifiziert das zu verwendende Archiv. Dieser Vorgang wird aus Sicht der Anwendung synchron ausgeführt, so daß die betroffenen Daten im

Anschluß an den ARCHIVE–Aufruf im aktiven Repository nicht mehr sichtbar sind. Ihre tatsächliche Übertragung in das physische Archiv, d.h. das Auslagern auf Tertiärspeicher, sollte bei großen Datenmengen asynchron geschehen[3]. Auch bei weniger Daten ist es vorteilhaft, wenn man die Datenauslagerung auf Zeiten mit geringerer Systemlast verschieben kann.

Als Konsequenz aus der Trennung von *logischem Archivieren* und *asynchroner Datenmigration* kann sich eine "Zugriffslücke" derart ergeben, daß archivierte Daten zwar nicht mehr aktiv zugreifbar aber auch noch nicht in das Archiv migriert sind. Wenn eine SDAI–Implementierung vorliegt, die sämtliche Zugriffe auf Instanzen über logische Zugriffspfade abwickelt, kann dieses Problem in Analogie zu dem Vorschlag für logisches Archivieren von Dokumenten in [ZPD90] behandelt werden: Die ARCHIVE–Operation modifiziert die Zugriffspfade (Verweise, Indexe) so, daß die mittels SELECT ausgewählten Daten über die üblichen SDAI–Zugriffsoperationen nicht mehr erreichbar sind. Gleichzeitig wird ein Pfad eingerichtet, der nur vom Archivierungssubsystem zum Auffinden von Daten benutzt wird. Erst bei erfolgreicher *physischer Archivierung* werden diese Daten – ebenfalls von einem asynchronen Prozeß – in ihrem bisherigen Speicher freigegeben. Damit können archivierte, noch nicht migrierte Daten ebenso schnell über einen Archivzugriffspfad erreicht werden wie aktive Daten. Im allgemeinen halten wir die "Zugriffslücke" aber für nicht sehr kritisch: Beachtet man typische Arbeitsabläufe, so wird auf archivierte Daten erst nach geraumer Zeit zugegriffen.

Ein weiterer Aspekt bei dem Archivierungsvorgang ist die unterschiedliche Behandlung von Daten (Instanzen des Anwendungsschemas) und Metadaten (Instanzen des Dictionary und Session Schemas). Während den Daten eine *move*–Semantik unterliegt, wenden wir auf die Metadaten eine *copy*–Semantik an. Metadaten sicher *mit* den Anwendungsdaten zusammen zu archivieren (und nicht nur zu referenzieren!) ist unabdingbar für die Interpretation der Daten über Jahre oder sogar Jahrzehnte hinweg. Desweiteren erscheint es sinnvoll, Metadaten, die z.B. ein spezielles EXPRESS-Schema beschreiben, im aktiven Datenbestand zu halten, um das Schema sofort neu instanziieren zu können. Außerdem ist der Umfang der Metadaten im allgemeinen viel geringer als der der Anwendungsdaten, so daß die Auslagerung der Metadaten das Platzproblem nur unwesentlich entschärfen würde.

Eine Folge von SELECT– und einem ARCHIVE–Aufruf kann durch die vorhandenen SDAI–Transaktionsprimitive mit Datenbank–Transaktionssemantik (START_TRANSACTION..., COMMIT, ABORT) geklammert werden. Dieser Vorschlag berücksichtigt, daß SDAI SELECT und ARCHIVE in Schreibzugriffe des darunterliegenden Datenbanksystems und SDAI–Transaktionen in Datenbanktransaktionen umgesetzt werden. Potentielle Konflikte zwischen SDAI SELECT, ARCHIVE und anderen Datenbankzugriffen im Mehrbenutzerbetrieb werden so ohne zusätzlichen Aufwand durch die ohnehin vorhandene Synchronisationskomponente gelöst.

---

[3] Wir weisen an dieser Stelle auf den zusätzlichen Einsatz von Komprimierungsmethoden hin [RV93].

Abschließend stellt sich die Frage nach dem **Zugriff auf archivierte Daten**. Im Gegensatz zu [EL90] lassen wir uns von dem Vorgehen beim Archivieren und Zurückholen konventionell archivierter Dokumente leiten: Der Anwender sucht an einem anderen Ort (z.B. dem Zeichnungsarchiv), wendet dort aber die gleichen Techniken zum Wiederauffinden an. Analog dazu wollen wir die *logische Trennung* zwischen archivierten und aktiven Daten beibehalten und auch keine neuen SDAI–Zugriffsprimitive einführen.

Auch eine explizite **RESTORE**–Operation zum Zurückladen von Daten vor dem Zugriff sehen wir nicht vor. Zwar ist dadurch nicht das Installieren von ggf. *off-line* verwalteten Datenträgern gelöst, aber dies ist auch nicht Aufgabe eines SDAI-Anwendungsprogramms. Das gezielte Kopieren archivierter Daten in eine Speicherumgebung mit kürzeren Zugriffszeiten (**ELEVATE**) lohnt sich dann, wenn ein intensives Arbeiten mit diesen Daten geplant ist. Ein Umlagern archivierter Daten ist erforderlich, wenn Schreibzugriffe auf solche Daten beabsichtigt sind, die ausdrücklich als nicht modifizierbar klassifiziert und unter Umständen auf *read-only* Speichermedien ausgelagert wurden.[4]

Einführung von Archiv–Repositories. Die logische Trennung zwischen dem Archiv und dem aktiven Datenbestand sowie die Perspektive, auf archivierte Daten mit vertrauten SDAI–Operationen zugreifen zu können, sprechen dafür, in SDAI **Archiv–Repositories** einzuführen[5]. Wir erweitern deshalb das SDAI Session Schema wie folgt:

```
ENTITY sdai_session;
  known_servers:   SET OF sdai_repository;    -- zugreifbare Repositories
  archive_servers: SET OF archive_repository; -- neu! (siehe unten)
  active_servers:  SET OF sdai_repository;    -- geoeffnete Repositories
  ...
END_ENTITY;
```

In einer SDAI–Session stehen dem Anwendungsprogramm jetzt nicht nur "normale" Repositories, sondern auch Archiv-Repositories zur Auswahl. Wenn ein beliebiges Repository geöffnet wird, ist es (konzeptionell) auch in der Menge der *active_servers* enthalten. Anschließend sind grundsätzlich GET_ATTRIBUTE, SDAI QUERY usw. anwendbar.

Dieser Ansatz erlaubt es, spezielle Anforderungen an die Archivierung aus Anwendungssicht durch verschiedene Arten von Repositories auszudrücken:

- *read-only*   für Archive, die ausschließlich lesende Zugriffe unterstützen,
- *long-term*   für Archive mit extrem langen Aufbewahrungszeiten oder
- *vaulted*   für Archive, die in besonderem Maße gegen Umwelteinflüsse wie Feuer und Wasser geschützt werden sollen.

---

[4] Nicht alle Anwendungen sprechen gegen Updates in Archiven: Technische Zeichnungen werden oft lokal ("in place") korrigiert und mit einem Änderungsvermerk versehen.

[5] Wie Repositories *erzeugt* werden, ist nicht Gegenstand der Spezifikation [ISO94]. Deshalb haben wir auch keine Operation CREATE ARCHIVE eingeführt.

Wir spezifizieren diese Erweiterung auf der konzeptuellen Ebene des SDAI–
Benutzers und gehen davon aus, daß die Implementierung eines SDAI–Archivie-
rungsdienstes geeignete Tertiärspeicher als physische Grundlage der logischen
Archive vorsehen muß:

```
TYPE
  archive_type = ENUMERATION OF (read-only,long-term,vaulted,...);
END_TYPE;

ENTITY archive_repository
  SUBTYPE OF (sdai_repository);
  characteristics = SET OF archive_type;
END_ENTITY;
```

Eine Alternative zum Archiv-Repository-Ansatz ist die Kennzeichnung archivierter Daten (z.B. durch ein Status–Flag) unter Beibehaltung ihres bisherigen
logischen Speicherortes, d.h. des aktuellen SDAI-Repositorys. Gegen eine derart
uniforme Betrachtung spricht die wesentlich andere Qualität archivierter Daten
aus Sicht vieler Anwendungen. Beispielsweise werden Produktdaten einer abgeschlossenen Baureihe oder Bilanzen aus zurückliegenden Jahren nicht im operationalen Datenbestand erwartet. Das andere Zugriffsprofil (siehe Abschnitt 1)
und die erwartete Stabilität eines Archivs über lange Zeit rechtfertigen ebenfalls
dessen besondere, eigenständige Rolle – sowohl logisch als auch physisch.

2.3 Resultierende Anforderungen an Datenbanksysteme

Da wir SDAI in diesem Beitrag als eine Softwareschicht ansehen, die auf einem Datenbanksystem implementiert wird, leiten sich aus der spezifizierten Archivierungsfunktionalität Anforderungen an die zugrundeliegenden Systeme ab.
Bezüglich der Externspeicherebene haben wir bereits angedeutet:

- *kostengünstigere Speichermedien als Magnetplatten*
  Nicht nur rein magnetische Speicher unterliegen dem anhaltenden Preisver-
  fall. Neue, leistungsfähigere Laufwerke für magneto–optische (MO) Platten
  sind nur ein Beispiel für die attraktiver werdende MO-Technologie [NHVR93].
  In [GSSZ93] werden hohe Erwartungen in optische Bänder gesetzt.
- *Langzeitspeicherung*
  Sofern die Haltbarkeit von Datenträgern ohne Informationsverlust über Jahrzehnte nicht garantiert werden kann, müssen geeignete Refresh–Techniken
  oder Kopierverfahren dies kompensieren [Wal94].
- *ggf. WORM–Medien* [Zab90]
  Höchstens einmal beschreibbare Medien erhöhen die handels– und steuer-
  rechtliche Beweiskraft der Daten [Gei93]. Ein authentischer Nachweis liegt
  auch im Interesse von Herstellern, die für evtl. Produktfehler haften [Sam93].
- *ggf. "Electronic Vaulting"* [GR93]
  Die räumliche Unterbringung der Speichermedien erfolgt in entfernten, besonders abgesicherten Spezialräumen.

Methoden zur vollen Einbeziehung von Tertiärspeicher in Datenbanksysteme, d.h. als gleichrangige Externspeicheralternativen, die sich nur durch Zugriffszeit und Kapazität unterschieden, sind aktueller Forschungsgegenstand [CHL93, SS94]. Zu den ersten Produkten, die optische Platten(roboter) integrieren, zählen DB2, Illustra und Transbase/CD. Der Grad der Integration (z.B. nur Emulation einer Magnetplatten–Schnittstelle duch den Jukebox–Controller) und die Erweiterbarkeit um neue Speichermedien sind von System zu System verschieden. Beschränkungen findet man vor allem bezüglich folgender Anforderungen:

— Auswahl einschließlich Korrektheitskontrolle der Daten, die auf Tertiärspeicher archiviert werden sollen (Abbildung der selektierten SDAI–Granulate)
— Benutzerkontrolle der Archivierung (Abbilden der logischen ARCHIVE–Operation, Überprüfen der Zugriffsberechtigung)
— auslagerndes Archivieren (ggf. Nullwerte erforderlich, asynchrone Migration bzgl. "move data"/"copy metadata", Komprimierungsoption)
— effiziente Zugriffspfade für tertiärspeicherresidente Daten (Transformation von Indexen)
— Navigation durch / Anfragen an Daten, die nicht explizit auf Sekundärspeicher zurückgeladen werden (optimales Retrieval, Schreibzugriffe)
— Logging des Archivierungsvorgangs

3 Ausnutzung von Datenbanksystemen für SDAI–integriertes Archivieren

3.1 Ansätze im Überblick

Es überrascht nicht, daß es keine persistenten SDAI–Implementierungen auf der Basis von Netzwerk– oder hierarchischen Datenbanksystemen gibt. Verschiedene Systeme bilden EXPRESS auf das relationale Modell ab [Wil94], belassen es aber bei der systemeigenen DML (meist SQL) ohne eine zusätzliche SDAI–Schicht. In [RM94] wird argumentiert, daß das C++–Binding von SDAI die am erfolgversprechendste Variante ist, weil hier am ehesten EXPRESS–Semantik (insbesondere Vererbung) "gerettet" werden kann. Außerdem können viele Typüberprüfungen vom Compiler übernommen werden. Desweiteren wird C++ von den meisten objektorientierten Datenbanksystemen unterstützt. Wir gehen deshalb nur auf relationale und objektorientierte Systeme ein.

Die zweite Ebene unserer Klassifikation von Implementierungen anwendungsorientierter Archivierungsfunktionalität ist der Grad der Integration eines Archivierungssubsystems in ein Datenbanksystem. Wir geben im Rest des Abschnitts die markantesten bzw. einzig bekannten Beispiele für folgende Ansätze an:

a) Ausnutzung "üblicher" Schnittstellen, d.h. allgemein verfügbare oder standardisierte DDL/DML ohne systemspezifische Erweiterungen
b) Ausnutzung spezieller (Archivierungs–) Funktionen, die aber noch zur Anwendungsschnittstelle des Datenbanksystems gehören
c) Enge Integration von Archivierungskomponenten in das Datenbanksystem unter Ausnutzung interner Schnittstellen

3.2 (Erweitert) relationale Systeme

a) Systeme mit SQL–Schnittstelle. Die spezifizierte SDAI SELECT- und ARCHIVE–Operation kann in Markierungen durch tupelweises SQL UPDATE umgesetzt werden. Dazu muß das Datenbankschema so erweitert werden, daß die Basisrelationen zusätzliche Attribute erhalten oder ein vorhandenes Datenbank–Dictionary ausgenutzt wird. Auch die SDAI–Metadaten können um Statusinformationen angereichert werden. Diese sind in Anfragen auszuwerten. Die asynchrone Datenauslagerung in Archiv–Tabellen, die zuvor auf Tertiärspeicher angelegt worden sind, muß in separaten Transaktionen durch Folgen von SQL INSERT und SQL DELETE erfolgen.

b) Codd's Vorschlag für RM/V2. Codd schlägt in [Cod90] ein Kommando ARCHIVE vor, das unserer Spezifikation auf den ersten Blick ähnlich, aber im Detail weniger mächtig ist: Der Datenbankadministrator kann damit Relationen (komplette Basistabellen oder Sichten) synchron auslagern. Allerdings ist ein erneuter Zugriff darauf erst nach dem REACTIVATE-Kommando möglich. Bei dem Zurückladen werden evtl. existierende Relationen gleichen Namens überschrieben. Was im Fall einer Sicht passieren soll (Materialisierung von Basistabellen?) wird nicht näher beschrieben. Jegliche Implementierungshinweise fehlen. Da verschiedene Arten von Archiven nicht näher spezifizierbar und Anfragen an archivierte Daten nicht vorgesehen sind, wirkt dieser Ansatz eher wie ein tabellenbezogenes Backup/Restore. Datenbanksysteme, die diesen Vorschlag in die Praxis umsetzen, sind uns nicht bekannt.

c) Eingriffsmöglichkeiten in Postgres. Das erweitert relationale Datenbanksystem Postgres sah frühzeitig das Auslagern veralteter Sätze auf WORM-Datenträger vor [Sto87]. Der ursprüngliche *Vacuum Cleaner* überträgt die sich qualifizierenden Tupel einer Basis- in eine Archiv–Relation sofern der Modus *light-* oder *heavy-archive* angegeben ist.

Mit dem Einziehen einer Schnittstelle (*Storage Manager Switch*) zwischen dem Zugriffssystem (*Data Manager*) und den geräteabhängigen Speichersubsystemen (*Storage Device Manager*) wurde Postgres prinzipiell um beliebige Speicher erweiterbar [Ols92]. Neue Device Manager müssen sich an Postgres-Konventionen halten: Sie müssen z.B. Postgres–Relationen auf dem Speichermedium anlegen und in Blöcken von 8 KByte lesen und schreiben. Nach der wiederholten Übersetzung des gesamten Postgres(system)–Quelltextes werden die neuen Device Manager von den selben Zugriffsmethoden angesprochen.

Eine derart enge Integration bringt selbstverständlich Abhängigkeiten vom Datenbanksystem und damit eine geringere Autonomie des Archivierungssubsystems mit sich. Auch wenn man von Postgres-Spezifika wie z.B. der "no-overwrite"[6]-Speicherverwaltung absieht, kann das Vacuuming nur bedingt für SDAI–integriertes Archivieren ausgenutzt werden. So ist etwa das Kriterium,

---

[6] Tatsächlich erfolgen durchaus Updates in Blöcken, z.B. beim Setzen des Transaktionszustandes eines Tupels.

das zum Auslagern von Sätzen führt, anders zu fassen: Die SDAI SELECT–
Operation und nicht das Alter eines Tupels veranlassen dessen Archivierung.
Unabhängig vom Vacuuming ist das Granulat Relation für die (feste!) Zuordnung eines Speichermediums zu einer Relation sehr grob. Grundsätzlich ist aber
erst durch die Offenlegung des Storage Manager Switch die gleichrangige Einbeziehung von Tertiärspeicher möglich geworden.

Zu den inhärenten Problemen und Lösungsansätzen bei der Abbildung von
EXPRESS (ohne SDAI) auf das Datenmodell von Postgres verweisen wir auf
[Gud94]. In dieser Implementierung wurden viele Erweiterungen von Postgres gegenüber (rein) relationalen Systemen, wie z.B. benutzerdefinierte abstrakte Datentypen, bereits ausgenutzt. Die Modellierungsmächtigkeit (Datentypvielfalt,
Vererbungsbeziehungen) objektorientierter Systeme ist jedoch weitaus höher.

3.3 Objektorientierte Systeme

a) ODMG-93. Anders als im relationalen Fall unterscheiden sich die Konzepte
und Schnittstellen von objektorientierten Datenbanksystemen erheblich [Heu92].
Der Standardisierungsversuch in [Cat94] strebt eine Vereinheitlichung an, die im
Falle ihres Erfolgs eine geeignete Basis für die persistente Implementierung des
C++-Bindings von SDAI einschließlich Archivierung wäre. Für die gegenwärtige
Diskussion des Ansatzes "oberhalb ODBMS" ziehen wir ein konkretes System
vor: Wir besprechen unseren *ObjectStore*-basierten Prototyp in Abschnitt 4.

b) Archivierungs–Methoden in Versant. Versant ODBMS Release 3 bietet
dem Anwendungsprogrammierer eine Methode *archive()* an: Man kann Objekte
(Instanzen) spezifizieren, die in eine Archiv-Datenbank ausgelagert werden sollen. Dabei gibt es eine Reihe von Einschränkungen. Referenzen auf Objekte, die
nicht archiviert werden können (z.B. Schema–, Klassen–, System– oder versionierte Objekte), liefert die Methode zurück. Versant geht davon aus, daß die
Klasse, dem das Objekt entstammt (Schema–Objekt), mit der ggf. bereits archivierten Klasse gleichen Names kompatibel ist. In der aktiven Datenbank verbleiben Statusinformationen, sog. Stellvertreter oder *proxy objects*. Diese Funktionalität läßt sich prinzipiell für die Archivierung von Anwendungsobjekten
ausnutzen. Die SDAI Dictionary Instanzen müssen kopiert werden.

Der Aufruf der archive()-Methode muß in normale Transaktionsklammern
eingeschlossen werden, wodurch sich der Einfluß des Benutzers auf den Zeitpunkt
des tatsächlichen Datentransfers auf das Absetzen des Commits beschränkt. Dies
wirkt sich bei einer beabsichtigten separaten Implementierung von SDAI SE
LECT, SDAI ARCHIVE und asynchroner Datenauslagerung nachteilig aus.

Versant erzwingt vor dem Zugriff auf archivierte Objekte den Aufruf einer *restore()*-Methode. Dabei werden keine Kopien der Objekte zurückgeladen,
sondern die Objekte selbst, so daß sie anschließend nicht mehr in der Archiv-
Datenbank enthalten sind. Versant erhält somit streng die Identität eines Objekts – unabhängig von dessen Status bzw. Speicherort. Dieser Service ist für
SDAI–integriertes Archivieren dann von Vorteil, wenn die Auslagerung von Granulaten zugelassen werden soll, die zu offenen Objektreferenzen führen.

c) Storage–Manager–Klassen in ONTOS/DB. Wir wählen ONTOS/DB als Beispiel für die Verwendung "tiefer" bzw. interner Schnittstellen, weil dieses ODBMS bezüglich der Externspeicherverwaltung erweiterbar ist. Die Speicherverwaltung ist selbst als Menge von instanziierten Klassen implementiert und offengelegt. Ein Anwendungsprogramm kann **pro Objekt** eine *Storage Manager*-Instanz festlegen, über die das Anlegen, die Identifikation, das Auffinden und die Zugriffe auf das Objekt abgewickelt werden. Im Zusammenhang mit einem Archivierungssubsystem besteht die Idee darin, eigene Storage Manager unter Verwendung der Klasse "OC_ExternalSM" zu entwickeln, die Tertiärspeicher ansprechen (vgl. Device Manager in Postgres). Natürlich erfordert dies ein tiefes Systemverständnis, da viele virtuelle Methoden zur Sperrverwaltung, zur ONTOS–spezifischen Typregistrierung oder "Aktivierung" von Objekten neu zu implementieren sind.

Allerdings gibt es neben den allgemeinen Nachteilen bei der engen Integration eines Archivierungssubsystems (siehe 3.2.c) eine weitere konkrete Beschränkung: Die Zuordnung eines Storage Managers zu einem Objekt besteht für die gesamte Lebenszeit des Objekts. Die Auslagerung von Daten vom Sekundär- auf Tertiärspeicher im Zuge von SDAI ARCHIVE ist demnach nur über Kopieren, Zuordnen eines neuen Storage Managers und Löschen zu erreichen.

4 Implementierungsvariante "oberhalb ODBMS"

4.1 Prototyp eines EXPRESS/SDAI-Datenbanksystems

Unsere ersten praktischen Erfahrungen mit einem persistenten SDAI resultieren aus einem Prototyp, der sich an der Spezifikation des C++-Bindings von [ISO94] orientiert und die dort vorgegebenen Definitionen unter Ausnutzung des ODBMS ObjectStore implementiert. Abbildung 1 zeigt die vier Komponenten, die beim Anlegen und während des Zugriffs auf eine EXPRESS/SDAI-Datenbank zusammenspielen [Pri93, Her94].

1. *EXPRESS Parser*
   Wir wollten nach Möglichkeit auf existierende Softwarebausteine zurückgreifen und haben deshalb den frei verfügbaren Schema–Parser ausgewählt, der von NIST ("National Institute of Standards and Technology") in den USA entwickelt wurde. Dieser Parser ist mit einem Quelltex–Generator gekoppelt, der u.a. aus EXPRESS–Entities C++-Klassen mit attributbezogenen Zugriffsmethoden erzeugt.
2. *Präprozessor*
   Effiziente *awk*-Programme modifizieren den C++-Code so, daß SDAI–Konventionen strenger eingehalten werden. Der Präprozessor stellt auch sicher, daß persistente Objekte tatsächlich in der Datenbank und nicht durch herkömmliches *new* im Hauptspeicher angelegt werden.
3. *SDAI-Klassenbibliothek*
   Diese C++-Klassen sind unabhängig vom EXPRESS–Anwendungsschema. Sie realisieren das SDAI Dictionary- und Session Schema.

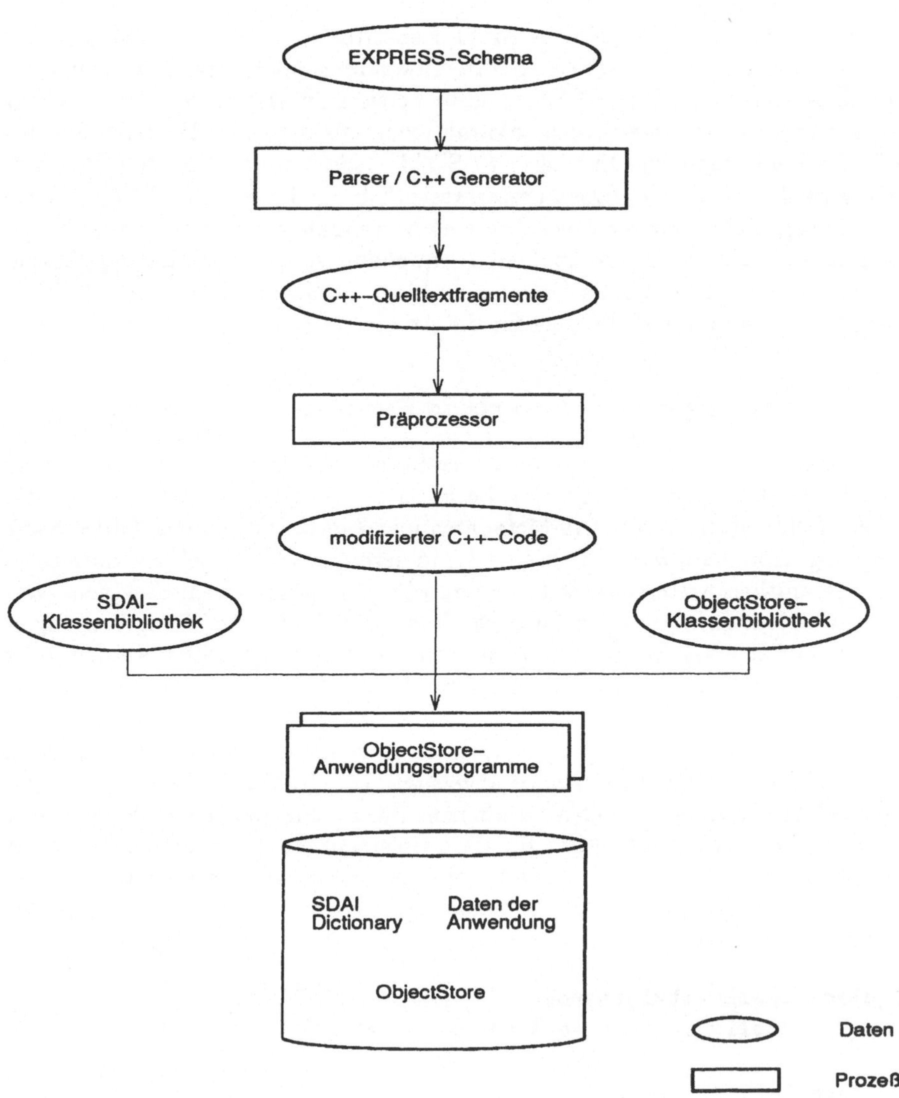

Abbildung 1. Komponenten unseres EXPRESS/SDAI–Datenbanksystems

4. *ObjectStore*

Die folgenden Eigenschaften dieses ODBMS lassen sich gut für die Implementierung des C++-Bindings ausnutzen:

- C++-Einbettung ("seamless integration")
- Persistenz orthogonal zum Typsystem
- Unterstützung für inverse EXPRESS Attribute (siehe Entities in Abschnitt 2.2)
- Kollektionsgebundene Anfragen

Auch wenn das Anlegen eines SDAI–Repositorys in [ISO94] nicht normiert ist (vgl. Fußnote 5), geht jedem SDAI–Anwendungsprogramm (*run time*) das Überführen eines EXPRESS–Schemas in persistente Daten des SDAI Dictionarys voraus (*build time*). Auch Informationen aus dem SDAI Session Schema (z.B. die Zuordnung von Instanzen zu SDAI *models*) werden im Datenbanksystem verwaltet. Dies verlangsamt zwar wesentlich die Schreibzugriffe, ermöglicht aber ein sog. *SDAI late binding* – also eine Anwendungsentwicklung, die weitgehend unabhängig von einem konkreten Anwendungsschema ist. Die langfristige Interpretierbarkeit der EXPRESS–Daten durch die SDAI–Metadaten ist gleichzeitig eine notwendige Bedingung für die Archivierung.

4.2 Erweiterungen des Prototyps in Richtung Archivierung

Unsere ersten Untersuchungen von ObjectStore hinsichtlich der Unterstützung von SDAI–integriertem Archivieren beziehen sich auf den Aspekt der gemeinsamen Archivierung von SDAI–Metadaten und Anwendungsdaten. ObjectStore kennt sog. *Konfigurationen*. Dies sind Gruppierungen von Objekten, die sich in ihrer Gesamtheit weiterentwickeln und dabei versioniert werden. Eine neue Version einer Konfiguration führt beim *check-in* zum "Einfrieren" ihrer Vorgängerversion. Auf alte Versionen kann dann nur noch lesend zugegriffen werden, oder es ist zuvor ein *check-out* erforderlich. Vereinfachend assoziieren wir *check-in* mit SDAI ARCHIVE.

Im SDAI C++–Binding sind Klassen für Anwendungsdaten und Metadaten von der Klasse *SdaiEntityInstance* abgeleitet. Um Konfigurationen von beliebigen SDAI–Granulaten bilden zu können, führen wir eine neue Wurzelklasse (ObjectStore's *os_configuration*) für die Implementierungshierarchie ein. Jetzt ist es möglich, *check-in* und *check-out* auf eine Konfiguration anzuwenden, die sowohl (Kopien der) EXPRESS-Schemainformationen als auch Anwendungsdaten umfaßt. Letztere gehören zum Extent der Klasse *SdaiAppInstance*:

```
class SdaiEntityInstance:
      public os_configuration { ... };


class SdaiAppInstance:
      virtual public SdaiEntityInstance { ... };
```

Allerdings deckt dieser Ansatz nur mit Einschränkungen die im Abschnitt 2.2 spezifizierte Funktionalität ab: Ein dynamisches SDAI SELECT, das erst zur Laufzeit des Anwendungsprogramms die Daten zur Archivierung auswählt, kann nicht unmittelbar realisiert werden, da Konfigurationen in folgendem Sinn statisch sind: Ein Objekt muß bereits bei seiner Erzeugung einer Konfiguration zugeordnet werden. Dies erzwingt wiederum das Markieren der zu archivierenden Daten bei SDAI SELECT und das Anlegen einer entsprechenden Konfiguration (z.B. durch Copy-Konstruktoren) während SDAI ARCHIVE. Die beabsichtigte Verringerung des aktiven Datenbestandes muß durch anschließendes explizites Löschen der Objekte erfolgen.

Aus einem anderen Grund kann unser konkretes Systemszenario den vollen Umfang von SDAI–integriertem Archivieren derzeit nur simulieren: Um die Idee eines tertiärspeicherresidenten SDAI–Archiv–Repositorys umzusetzen, bietet ObjectStore nur die Möglichkeit, **ganze** *ObjectStore–Datenbanken* auf einem Externspeicher zu plazieren. Dabei werden entweder *raw partitions* von Festplatten ausgewählter Hardwareplattformen unterstützt oder das UNIX–Dateisystem als geräteunabhängige Schnittstelle benutzt. Mit der Version 3.1 ist erstmalig ein *NFS mount* von nicht–lokalen (*remote server*) Dateisystemen erlaubt. Datengranulate, wie sie der ObjectStore–Server intern verwaltet (Seiten, Segmente) oder anwendungsbezogene Einheiten, die ein ObjectStore–Client kennt (Cluster, Versionen von Konfigurationen), können jedoch nicht selektiv auf Tertiärspeicher ausgelagert werden. Andererseits gewährleist eine "on–top"–Lösung im Vergleich zur Verwendung tieferer Schnittstellen eine größere Datenunabhängigkeit, die angesichts einer langfristigen Archivierung einen hohen Stellenwert besitzt.

5 Resümee

Wir sehen einen wachsenden Bedarf für anwendungsorientiertes Archivieren, wobei Fortschritte in der Massenspeichertechnologie neuartige Systemrealisierungen erst ermöglichen. Derzeit befindet sich die Erweiterbarkeit von Datenbanksystemen um eine integrierte Archivierungskomponente noch in den Anfängen. Aber auch eine lose Kopplung eines Datenbanksystems mit einem dedizierten Archivierungssystem (wie sie vergleichsweise im Zusammenhang mit einem Speichersystem für Multimediaobjekte in [KMMW93] konzipiert wurde) hat Vorteile, zu denen insbesondere Autonomie und Stabilität zählen [Her93].

Aus Sicht der spezifizierten Archivierungsfunktionalität kann durchaus auf die absolute Gleichberechtigung von Sekundär– und Tertiärspeicher ("1st class citizen" [CHL93]) zugunsten einer geräteunabhängigen Schnittstelle zu einem Archivierungssubsystem in einem Datenbanksystem verzichtet werden. Denn archivierte und aktive Daten unterscheiden sich grundlegend im Zugriffsprofil und dem tolerierbaren Zugriffszeitverhalten. Dies heißt jedoch nicht, daß der weitverbreitete einschlägige Datenbankservice – ein Backup/Restore – das benutzerveranlaßte, datenmodellbasierte und auslagernde Archivieren hinreichend unterstützt. Die angegebenen Vorschläge für höhere Archivierungskonzepte in relationalen und erste Realisierungen in objektorientierten Systemen decken sich ebenfalls nicht mit der von uns spezifizierten Semantik.

Wir haben in diesem Beitrag einen Ansatz gewählt, der auf Standards basiert. Wir betrachten EXPRESS und die sich in der Entwicklung befindliche SDAI–Schnittstelle über STEP hinaus als geeigneten Kontext für anwendungsorientiertes Archivieren. Notwendige Erweiterungen von SDAI sind die Operationen SELECT und ARCHIVE sowie die Einführung von Archiv–Repositories.

Unsere weiteren Arbeiten werden die Spezifikation und Implementierungsaspekte von SDAI–integriertem Archivieren detaillieren. Wir werden z.B. Tertiärspeicherzugriffe und Archivzugriffspfade simulieren müssen, solange wir auf Grenzen der internen Erweiterbarkeit von eingesetzten Datenbanksystemen stoßen.

Danksagung

Mein Dank gilt Herrn Prof. Dr. K. Küspert sowie den anonymen Gutachtern für die sorgfältige und hilfreiche Durchsicht des Manuskripts.

Literatur

[Cat94]   R. G. G. Cattell (Hrsg.). *The Object Database Standard: ODMG–93, Release 1.1*. Morgan Kaufmann, 1994.

[CHL93]   M. J. Carey, L. M. Haas, M. Livny. Tapes Hold Data, Too: Challenges of Tuples on Tertiary Store. In *ACM SIGMOD*, S. 413–417, Washington, 1993.

[Cod90]   E. F. Codd. *The Relational Model for Database Management: Version 2.* Addison–Wesley, Massachusetts, 1990.

[DHSV94]   M. Dach, N. Hoimyr, J. Saarela, J. Vuoskoski. Using EXPRESS in a High Energy Physics Research Environment. In *4th Int. EXPRESS Users Group Conf.*, Greenville, Oktober 1994.

[EL90]   J. Encarnacao, P. C. Lockemann. *Engineering Databases.* Springer–Verlag, Berlin Heidelberg New York, 1990.

[GAP93]   H. Grabowski, R. Anderl, A. Polly. *Integriertes Produktmodell.* Beuth–Verlag, Berlin, Wien, Zürich, 1993.

[Gei93]   I. Geis. Rechtliche Aspekte der elektronischen Dokumentenerarbeitung und -verwaltung. In *NormDOC'93*, Berlin, November 1993. Beuth–Verlag.

[GR93]   J. Gray, A. Reuter. *Transaction Processing: Concepts and Techniques.* Morgan Kaufmann, San Mateo, 1993.

[GSSZ93]   J. Gulbins, M. Seyfried, H. Strack-Zimmermann. *Elektronische Archivierungssysteme.* Springer–Verlag, Berlin, Heidelberg, New York, 1993.

[Gud94]   W. Guddat. Realisierung einer STEP–Produktdatenbank auf POST-GRES. Diplomarbeit, Friedrich-Alexander-Universität Erlangen–Nürnberg, Februar 1994.

[Her93]   A. Herbst. STEP–basierte Ansätze für Archivierungssysteme. Technischer Bericht TN 93.01, IBM WZH, Heidelberg, August 1993.

[Her94]   A. Herbst. Long-Term Database Support for EXPRESS Data. In *7th Int. Working Conference on Scientific and Statistical Database Management*, Charlottesville, September 1994.

[Heu92]   A. Heuer. *Objektorientierte Datenbanken: Konzepte, Modelle, Systeme.* Addison–Wesley, Bonn u.a., 1992.

[HM94]   A. Herbst, B. Malle. Perspektiven für die Archivierung von CAD–Daten in einer STEP–Umgebung. In *CAD'94*, Paderborn, März 1994. Hanser–Verlag.

[ISO94]   *ISO 10303-22: Product Data Representation and Exchange - Part 22: Standard Data Access Interface (CD)*. 1994.

[ISO95]   *10303-11: Product Data Representation and Exchange - Part 11: EXPRESS Language Reference Manual (IS)*. 1995.

[KMMW93]   R. Käckenhoff, D. Merten, K. Meyer-Wegener. Eine vergleichende Untersuchung der Speicherungsformen für multimediale Datenobjekte. In *Datenbanksysteme in Büro, Technik und Wissenschaft*, Braunschweig, März 1993. Springer–Verlag.

[KPCD+92] R. H. Katz, D. A. Patterson, A. Chervenak-Drapeau, J. Fine, E. Miller. An Approach to Cost-Effective Terabyte Memory Systems. In *COMPCON Spring'92*, San Francisco, Februar 1992.

[LRW93] H. Lührsen, T. Ruf, H. Wedekind. STEP-Datenbanken. *CIM Management*, 9(5):9–13, 1993.

[MN93] C. Mohan, I. Narang. An Efficient and Flexible Method for Archiving a Data Base. In *ACM SIGMOD*, Washington, 1993.

[MSRD91] U. Mehlhaus, S. Schneider, U. Rembold, R. Dillmann. Die Schemabeschreibungssprache EXPRESS des STEP-Standards und technische Datenbanksysteme — Eine Analyse. In *Datenbanksysteme in Büro, Technik und Wissenschaft*, Kaiserslautern, März 1991. Springer–Verlag.

[NHVR93] T. Nakagomi, M. Holzbach, R. VanMeter, S. Ranade. Re-Defining the Storage Hierarchy: An Ultra–Fast Magneto–Optical Disk Drive. In *12th IEEE Symposium on Mass Storage Systems*, Monterey, April 1993.

[Ols92] M. A. Olson. Extending the Postgres Database System to Manage Tertiary Storage. Master's thesis, Univ. of California, Berkeley, 1992.

[Owe93] J. Owen. *STEP - An Introduction*. Information Geometers, Winchester, 1993.

[Pri93] A. Primbs. STEP/EXPRESS-Datenverwaltung mit einem objektorientierten Datenbanksystem. Diplomarbeit, IBM WZH / Universität Mannheim, Dezember 1993.

[RDMP94] T. C. Rakow, P. Dettling, F. Moser, B. Paul. Development of a Multimedia Archiving Teleservice using the DFR Standard. In *Workshop on Advanced Teleservices and High Speed Communication Architectures*, Heidelberg, September 1994.

[RM94] T. Rando, L. McCabe. Issues in Implementing the C++ Binding to SDAI. *Computer Standards and Interfaces*, 16(4):331–340, 1994.

[RV93] M. A. Roth, S. J. VanHorn. Database Compression. *SIGMOD Record*, 22(3):31–39, September 1993.

[Sam93] U. E. Samel. Produkthaftungsgesetz und CAD-Archivierung. *CAD-CAM Report*, 9(5):138–144, 1993.

[SS94] S. Sarawagi, M. Stonebraker. Single Query Optimization for Tertiary Memory. Technischer Bericht Sequoia 2000, 94/45, University of California, Berkeley, 1994.

[Sto87] M. Stonebraker. The Design of the Postgres Storage System. In *13th VLDB*, S. 289–300, Brighton, 1987.

[SW94] D. A. Schenck, P. R. Wilson. *Information Modeling: The EXPRESS Way*. Oxford University Press, 1994.

[VS91] S. Vajna, W. Stenke. Wirtschaftliche Nutzung des digitalen Archivs. *CAD-CAM Report*, 7(5):143–149, 1991.

[Wal94] S. Wallace. Managing Mass Storage. *Byte*, 19(3):78–89, 1994.

[Wil94] P. R. Wilson. EXPRESS Tools and Services. Rensselaer Polytechnic Institute, Troy, August 1994.

[Zab90] P. Zabback. Optische und magneto–optische Platten in File- und Datenbanksystemen. *Informatik Spektrum*, 13:260–275, 1990.

[ZPD90] P. Zabback, J. B. Paul, U. Deppisch. Office Documents on a Database Kernel – Filing, Retrieval, and Archiving. In *5th Conf. on Office Information Systems*, S. 261–270, Cambridge, April 1990.

Die Nutzung mehrdimensionaler Zugriffsstrukturen für Anfragen über Standardattributen

Andreas Henrich[1] und Jens Möller[2]

[1] Universität Siegen, Fachbereich Elektrotechnik und Informatik, Praktische Informatik, D-57068 Siegen, henrich@informatik.uni-siegen.de
[2] FernUniversität Hagen, Fachbereich Informatik, Praktische Informatik 4, D-58084 Hagen, moeller@amundsen.fernuni-hagen.de

Zusammenfassung In den vergangenen Jahren hat es zahlreiche vielversprechende Ansätze zu mehrdimensionalen Zugriffsstrukturen gegeben. Dabei stand in der Regel die Anwendung im Hinblick auf geometrische Objekte im Mittelpunkt. In einigen Fällen wurde zwar behauptet, daß diese Strukturen auch eingesetzt werden können, um Selektionsbedingungen über mehreren Standardattributen zu unterstützen; Hinweise zur Lösung der damit verbundenen Probleme sucht man aber weitestgehend vergebens.

In diesem Papier beschreiben wir daher Lösungsansätze zu drei wesentlichen Problembereichen, die sich beim Einsatz mehrdimensionaler Zugriffsstrukturen über mehreren Standardattributen ergeben: (1) Wir schlagen ein Verfahren vor, mit dem sich die Selektivität der Zugriffsstruktur bezüglich der einzelnen Attribute gezielt steuern läßt. (2) Wir beschreiben einen Algorithmus mit dem auch Selektionsbedingungen berücksichtigt werden können, die mathematische Operationen wie '+', '−', '*' oder '/' enthalten. (3) Wir präsentieren ein Verfahren, mit dem Selektionsbedingungen bearbeitet werden können, die beliebige logische Verknüpfungen zwischen Teilbedingungen enthalten.

Mit Hilfe dieser Verfahren kann eine mehrdimensionale Zugriffsstruktur sehr gut an die Erfordernisse als Zugriffsstruktur über Standardattributen angepaßt werden, wie unsere Erfahrungen bei der Integration des LSD-Baumes in das Gral-System [Güt89] zeigen. Dabei bereitet auch die Bearbeitung von Selektionsbedingungen, die sich gleichzeitig auf geometrische Attribute und Standardattribute beziehen, keine Probleme.

1 Einleitung

In Anwendungen, in denen häufig Anfragen vorkommen, deren Selektionsbedingung sich auf mehrere Attribute bezieht, ist der Einsatz einer Multiattribut-Zugriffsstruktur dem Einsatz einer oder mehrerer Zugriffsstrukturen für einzelne Attribute tendenziell vorzuziehen. Ein Beispiel ergibt sich, wenn aus einer Patientendatenbank, in der zu jedem Patient seine Größe und sein Gewicht abgelegt ist, alle Patienten selektiert werden sollen, die Untergewicht haben[3]:

---

[3] Die in diesem Papier für Anfragen verwendete Syntax orientiert sich am Gral-System. Dabei wird zuerst der Name der Relation angegeben und im Anschluß der Selekti-

$$\text{Patient } \sigma[\texttt{Gewicht} < (\texttt{Größe} - 100) * 0,85]$$

Zu denken ist auch an die logische Verknüpfung von Teilbedingungen, wie z.B. bei der Suche nach jüngeren Patienten mit Bluthochdruck:

$$\text{Patient } \sigma[\texttt{Alter} \leq 30 \text{ and } \texttt{BlutdruckSystolisch} > 150]$$

Nun wurden in den vergangenen Jahren zahlreiche mehrdimensionale Zugriffsstrukturen vorgestellt (siehe z.B. [Rob81, NHS84, OMSD87, Fre87, LS89, HSW89b, SK90, KO91]). Die meisten dieser Strukturen wurden in erster Linie im Hinblick auf die Verwaltung geometrischer Objekte entwickelt. Einige – wie das Gridfile [NHS84] und der *hb*-Baum [LS89] – zielen aber vom Ansatz her auch auf den Einsatz als Zugriffsstruktur über mehreren Standardattributen und die meisten anderen Strukturen können ebenfalls in einem derartigen Umfeld eingesetzt werden. Dabei ergeben sich aber drei Problembereiche:

1. Die obigen Zugriffsstrukturen sind von ihrer Konzeption her symmetrische Zugriffsstrukturen, d.h. die Selektivität der Struktur ist in allen Dimensionen – und damit für alle betrachteten Attribute – gleich. Dies ist sinnvoll, sofern alle Attribute gleich oft als Selektionskriterium in Anfragen verwendet werden, gibt es aber Unterschiede, so kann es sinnvoll sein, die Selektivität bezüglich eines besonders oft in Anfragen vorkommenden Attributes zu Lasten der Selektivität bezüglich der anderen Attribute zu verbessern.
   Wir werden in Abschnitt 3.2 ein Verfahren vorstellen, mit dem die Selektivität mehrdimensionaler Zugriffsstrukturen hinsichtlich der einzelnen Attribute gezielt gesteuert werden kann.

2. Der Einsatz einer geometrischen Zugriffsstruktur zur Unterstützung von Selektionsanfragen über mehreren Standardattributen ist unproblematisch solange es für die Selektionsbedingungen über den Standardattributen eine geometrische Entsprechung gibt. Bei konjunktiv verknüpften Intervallbedingungen zu einzelnen Standardattributen ist dies der Fall. Hier erhält man ein achsenparalleles Rechteck oder einen achsenparallelen Quader als Anfragebereich. Liegen aber Selektionsbedingungen der Form $c_1 \cdot Attr_1 + c_2 \cdot Attr_2 \leq c_3$ oder $Attr_1 \cdot Attr_2 \geq c_1$ vor, so ist das Finden eines entsprechenden geometrischen Anfragebereiches wesentlich schwerer oder gar unmöglich[4].
   Mit einem Verfahren, das wir in Abschnitt 3.3 angeben werden, können aber auch derartige Selektionsbedingungen verarbeitet werden, und zwar ohne daß ein äquivalenter geometrischer Anfragebereich bestimmt werden muß.

3. Problematisch sind ferner logische Verknüpfungen wie *or*, *xor* oder *not* sowie *and*-Verknüpfungen zwischen Teilbedingungen, die keine einfache geometrische Entsprechung haben.

---

onsoperator σ mit der Selektionsbedingung als Parameter in eckigen Klammern.

[4] In Abschnitt 3.3 werden wir einige Beispiele für derartige Selektionsbedingungen angeben.

In Abschnitt 3.4 werden wir zeigen, wie die Bearbeitung von derartigen Selektionsbedingungen auf die Bearbeitung der einzelnen Teilbedingungen zurückgeführt werden kann. Dabei können ohne weiteres auch Teilbedingungen über geometrischen Attributen integriert werden (siehe Abschnitt 4).

Die in diesem Papier beschriebenen Verfahren können unmittelbar auf mehrdimensionale Zugriffsstrukturen angewendet werden, die eine Variante des k-d-Baumes als Directory verwenden (wie z.B. [Rob81, OMSD87, LS89, HSW89b, KO91]). Darüberhinaus ist die Adaption an andere Verfahren mit hierarchischem Directory möglich. In diesem Papier werden wir die Verfahren für den LSD-Baum als Beispiel für eine Zugriffsstruktur, die einen verallgemeinerten k-d-Baum als Directory verwendet, beschreiben.

2 Der LSD-Baum als geometrische Zugriffsstruktur

Bei geometrischen Objekten muß zwischen punktförmigen und ausgedehnten Objekten – wie z.B. Polygonen – unterschieden werden. Der LSD-Baum (Local-Split-Decision-Baum) [HSW89b] ist von seiner Konzeption her eine Zugriffsstruktur für punktförmige Objekte. Mit Hilfe des Transformationsansatzes, auf den wir am Ende dieses Abschnitts kurz eingehen werden, können in einem LSD-Baum aber auch ausgedehnte geometrische Objekte verwaltet werden.

Wenn geometrische Anfragen effizient bearbeitet werden sollen, müssen räumlich nah beieinanderliegende geometrische Objekte im Speicher gemeinsam abgelegt werden. Zu diesem Zweck unterteilt der LSD-Baum den Datenraum in disjunkte Teilräume. Diesen Teilräumen sind jeweils Speicherblöcke fester Größe zugeordnet, in denen die Punkte abgespeichert werden, die in dem Teilraum enthalten sind. Die Speicherblöcke werden im allgemeinen als Buckets und die zugehörigen Teilräume als Bucketregionen bezeichnet.

Um aufzuzeigen, in welcher Weise der Datenraum beim LSD-Baum in Bucketregionen aufgeteilt wird, betrachten wir das sequentielle Einfügen mehrerer Objekte in einen LSD-Baum:

Zunächst ist dem ganzen Datenraum genau ein Bucket zugeordnet. Tritt nach einigen Einfügungen die Situation ein, daß dieses Bucket aufgrund seiner beschränkten Kapazität das neue Objekt nicht mehr aufnehmen kann, wird eine achsenparallele Splitlinie bestimmt, auf deren Grundlage die Objekte über zwei Buckets verteilt werden. Nach weiteren Einfügungen wird der Fall eintreten, daß eines der beiden so entstandenen Buckets erneut überläuft. Dann bestimmt man eine Splitlinie, die die Bucketregion dieses Buckets aufteilt, und speichert die Objekte, die bisher in diesem Bucket abgelegt waren, in zwei Buckets ab. Dieses Verfahren wird dann in der gleichen Weise fortgeführt. Abbildung 1 zeigt eine auf diese Weise entstandene Aufteilung des Datenraumes.

Die Splitlinien werden in einem Directory verwaltet. Dazu wird ein verallgemeinerter k-d-Baum [Ben75] verwendet. Für jeden Split wird ein neuer Knoten in den Baum eingefügt, der die Splitlinie – charakterisiert durch Splitdimension und Splitposition – enthält. Die Blätter des Directory enthalten Verweise auf die Buckets, in denen die Daten abgelegt sind (siehe Abbildung 2).

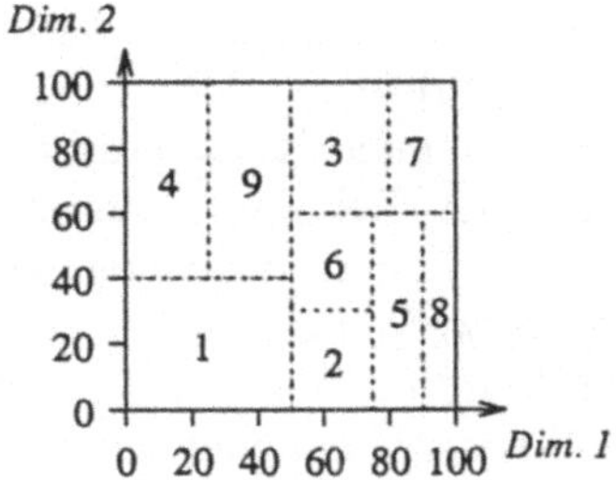

Abbildung 1. Aufteilung des Datenraumes in Bucketregionen durch einen LSD-Baum

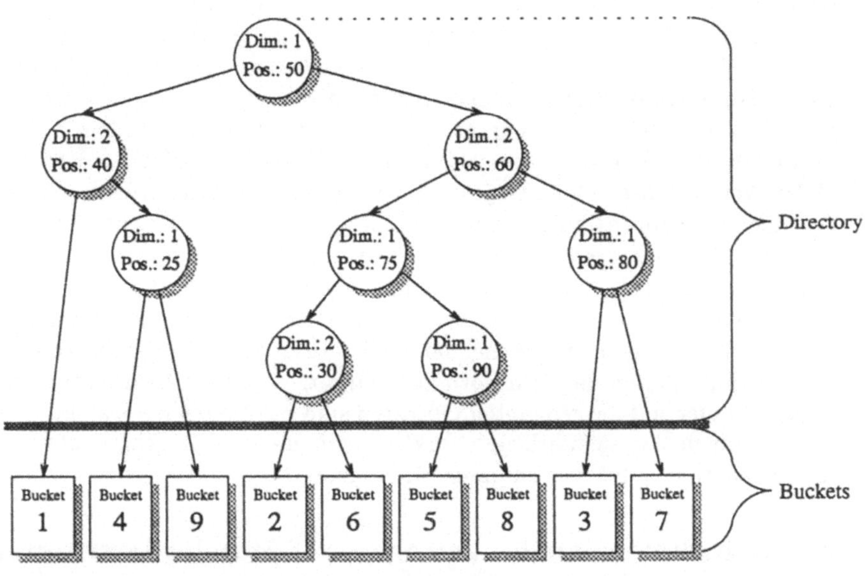

Abbildung 2. Zur Partitionierung aus Abbildung 1 gehörender LSD-Baum

Offensichtlich kann das Directory so groß werden, daß es nicht mehr vollständig im Hauptspeicher verwaltet werden kann. In diesem Fall werden Teilbäume auf externe Seiten ausgelagert, während der Teil des Baumes nahe der Wurzel weiterhin im Hauptspeicher verbleibt. Eine ausführliche Darstellung des Algorithmus, der diese *partielle Paginierung* realisiert, findet sich in [HSW89a].

Durch dir Verwendung eines verallgemeinerten *k-d*-Baumes als Directory kann wenn ein Bucket überläuft, die Splitlinie frei gewählt werden. Dazu können verschiedenste sogenannte *Splitstrategien* verwendet werden, die die Splitdimension und die Splitposition festlegen. Wir unterscheiden verteilungs- und datenabhängige Splitstrategien. Bei einer *verteilungsabhängigen Splitstrategie* wird die Splitposition gemäß einer Verteilungshypothese so festgelegt, daß die Wahrscheinlichkeit dafür, daß ein Objekt aus der Grundgesamtheit aller Objekte, das in der zu splittenden Bucketregion liegt, unterhalb oder oberhalb der Splitline liegt, jeweils gleich hoch ist. Bei einer datenabhängigen Splitstrategie wird die Splitposition aufgrund der in dem zu splittenden Bucket abgelegten Objekte festgelegt. Typischerweise verwendet man dabei den Median oder den Mittelwert über den entsprechenden Koordinatenwerten der Objekte. Eine ausführliche Diskussion verschiedener Splitstrategien findet sich in [HS91].

Eine Bereichsanfrage – bei der alle Objekte gesucht werden, die geometrisch in einem Anfragebereich (Rechteck, Kreis oder Polygon) liegen – wird auf einem LSD-Baum wie folgt bearbeitet:

Man beginnt bei der Wurzel des Directory und ermittelt durch Vergleiche mit dem Anfragebereich, ob nach links oder nach rechts verzweigt werden muß, oder ob beide Teilbäume untersucht werden müssen. Im letzteren Fall wird einer der beiden Teilbäume ausgewählt, während der andere zur späteren Bearbeitung auf einem Stack gespeichert wird. Das Verfahren wird dann rekursiv weitergeführt.

Zur Verwaltung ausgedehnter geometrischer Objekte in einem LSD-Baum verwendet man den sogenannten *Transformationsansatz* [Hin85, SK88, Hen90]. Dabei werden ausgedehnte Objekte durch minimale umschließende achsenparallele Rechtecke approximiert. Diese Rechtecke werden in Punkte überführt, indem man die Mittelpunkte und die halben Ausdehnungen in den einzelnen Dimensionen des Datenraumes als unabhängige Dimensionen im Bildraum betrachtet. Man gewinnt so aus k-dimensionalen ausgedehnten Objekten $2k$-dimensionale Punkte, die in einem entsprechenden LSD-Baum verwaltet werden können.

Die Einzelheiten des Transformationsansatzes und die Bearbeitung von Bereichsanfragen auf ausgedehnten Objekten sind in [Hen90] dargestellt. Dort findet sich auch ein ausführlicher Vergleich mit anderen Zugriffsstrukturen und insbesondere mit den Varianten des R-Baumes.

3 Mehrdimensionale Anfragen auf Standardattributen

In diesem Abschnitt zeigen wir am Beispiel des LSD-Baumes wie eine mehrdimensionale Zugriffsstruktur für geometrische Objekte als Zugriffsstruktur über mehreren Standardattributen eingesetzt werden kann.

3.1 Ein einführendes Beispiel

Gegeben sei eine Relation *dressmen*, in der eine Agentur die Daten der von ihr gemanagten Dressmen verwaltet. Diese Relation habe u.a. die Attribute *size* (INT) und *salary* (INT), die der Konfektionsgröße und der Gage pro Stunde entsprechen. Dann kann man mit folgender Anfrage alle Dressmen ermitteln, die die Konfektionsgröße 98 haben und deren Gage maximal 100 DM beträgt:

$$\text{dressmen } \sigma[\texttt{size} = 98 \text{ and } \texttt{salary} \leq 100]$$

In einer Datenbank, in der nur eindimensionale Indexstrukturen (wie z.B. der B-Baum) zur Verfügung stehen, können sich hier folgende Situationen ergeben:

1. *Weder zum Attribut 'size' noch zum Attribut 'salary' existiert ein Index:* In diesem Fall muß ein Scan über die Relation *dressmen* durchgeführt werden, bei dem für jedes Tupel die beiden Bedingungen überprüft werden.

2. *Zu genau einem der Attribute 'size' und 'salary' existiert ein Index und zum anderen existiert kein Index:* Dann wird mit Hilfe des Index eine entsprechende Suche durchgeführt und für jedes Tupel der Ergebnismenge die Bedingung über dem anderen Attribut überprüft.

3. *Zu den Attributen 'salary' und 'size' existiert jeweils ein Index:* In diesem Fall muß die günstigste Vorgehensweise in Abhängigkeit von verschiedenen Einflußfaktoren bestimmt werden. Zum einen ist dabei von Bedeutung, ob einer der beiden Indexe ein Primärindex[5] ist, oder ob es sich bei beiden Indexen um Sekundärindexe handelt, und zum anderen spielt die Selektivität der Bedingungen *size = 98* und *salary* $\leq$ 100 eine Rolle. Eine ausführliche Darstellung des zugehörigen Optimierungsprozesses würde den Rahmen dieser Arbeit sprengen (vgl. hierzu z.B. [LS87]). Hier sollen nur drei mögliche Arten der Anfragebearbeitung aufgeführt werden:

   (a) Ist einer der Indexe über die Attribute *size* bzw. *salary* der Primärindex, so sollte man bezüglich des entsprechenden Attributes eine Anfrage auf dem Primärindex durchführen und für jedes Tupel der Ergebnismenge die andere Bedingung überprüfen.

   (b) Handelt es sich bei beiden Indexen um Sekundärindexe, so kann man bezüglich der selektiveren Bedingung eine Anfrage auf der zugehörigen Indexstruktur durchführen und für jedes Tupel der Ergebnismenge die andere Bedingung überprüfen.

   (c) Alternativ kann man, sofern es sich bei beiden Indexen um Sekundärindexe handelt, auf beiden Indexen entsprechende Anfragen durchführen und die dabei ermittelten Tupelidentifikatormengen abgleichen, bevor man auf die Tupel selbst zugreift.

Steht auf der Relation *dressmen* hingegen ein LSD-Baum als Index zur Verfügung, bei dem die Attribute *size* und *salary* als Dimensionen eines mehrdimensionalen Datenraumes betrachtet werden, so kann zu der obigen Anfrage eine Bereichsanfrage mit dem Anfragebereich [98; 98] × [0; 100] auf diesem LSD-Baum durchgeführt werden. Der Effizienzvorteil durch den Einsatz des LSD-Baumes kann grob wie folgt verdeutlicht werden:

Sei $n_{dressmen}$ die Anzahl der Tupel in der Relation *dressmen* und sei $\alpha_{Präd}$ die Selektivität des Prädikates *Präd* (d.h. es gibt $n_{dressmen} \cdot \alpha_{Präd}$ Tupel in der Relation *dressmen*, die *Präd* erfüllen). Dann ist der Aufwand für die obige Anfrage bei der ausschließlichen Verwendung eindimensionaler Indexe größenordnungsmäßig im Bereich $n_{dressmen} \cdot \min\{\alpha_{[size=98]}, \alpha_{[salary \leq 100]}\}$ einzuordnen, während man bei Verwendung einer mehrdimensionalen Zugriffsstruktur den Bereich $n_{dressmen} \cdot \alpha_{[size=98]} \cdot \alpha_{[salary \leq 100]}$ erreichen kann.

In diesem Kontext dürfen aber zwei Probleme nicht übersehen werden:

---

[5] Wir wollen in diesem Papier unter einem Primärindex einen physisch clusternden Index verstehen, während bei einem Sekundärindex der Zugriff auf die Objekte über eine Indirektionsstufe (Tupelidentifikatoren) geschieht.

1. Die Selektivität einer mehrdimensionalen Zugriffsstruktur bezüglich der einzelnen betrachteten Attribute ist i.a. schlechter als bei einem eindimensionalen Index für das betreffende Attribut. D.h. sofern in der Selektionsbedingung einer Anfrage nur ein Attribut spezifiziert ist, kann man mit einem eindimensionalen Index i.a. eine bessere Performance erreichen.
2. Man kann zeigen, daß die Performance mehrdimensionaler Zugriffsstrukturen mit wachsender Zahl der Dimensionen schlechter wird [Hen90]. Diese Problematik führt offensichtlich dazu, daß es nicht sinnvoll sein kann, alle Attribute einer Relation bei der Ablage der Relation in einer mehrdimensionalen Zugriffsstruktur zu berücksichtigen. Vielmehr sollte man sich auf die Attribute konzentrieren, die häufig in Anfragen spezifiziert werden.

Wir wollen diese beiden Aspekte nun genauer betrachten und ein Verfahren vorschlagen, mit dem man die Selektivität eines LSD-Baumes bezüglich der einzelnen Attribute steuern kann.

3.2 Die Gewichtung einzelner Attribute

Zunächst beschreiben wir noch einmal kurz die Situationen, in denen der Einsatz einer mehrdimensionalen Zugriffsstruktur sinnvoll ist:

1. Auf einer Relation treten oft Anfragen auf, in deren Selektionsbedingung mehrere Attribute spezifiziert sind.
2. Gibt es zu einer Relation kein typisches Anfrageattribut, sondern mehrere Attribute, die ungefähr gleich oft in Anfragen spezifiziert sind, so müßte man bei Verwendung eindimensionaler Zugriffsstrukturen zwangsweise eines dieser Attribute herausgreifen und einen Primärindex über diesem Attribut errichten. Zu den anderen Attributen könnten nur Sekundärindexe erstellt werden. Dies würde bei Intervallanfragen auf den Attributen, zu denen nur Sekundärindexe existieren, zu einer schlechten Performance führen (vgl. zur Performance von Sekundärindexen bei Intervallanfragen [HHSW91]).

Es ist nun durchaus vorstellbar, daß man im voraus weiß, daß unter den im LSD-Baum berücksichtigten Attributen einzelne häufig und andere eher selten in Anfragen spezifiziert werden. Dem kann durch eine gezielte Wahl der Splitdimensionen (bzw. Splitattribute) Rechnung getragen werden.

Wir betrachten dazu ein Beispiel, in dem zwei Attribute berücksichtigt werden. Abbildung 3 zeigt drei verschiedene Möglichkeiten, den entsprechenden Datenraum in 16 Bucketregionen aufzuteilen. Im ersten Fall wurde immer nach *Attr1* gesplittet. Im zweiten Fall wurde auf einer Ebene des LSD-Baumes nach *Attr2* gesplittet, und im dritten Fall wurden *Attr1* und *Attr2* gleichberechtigt als Splitattribute verwendet. Die Verhältniszahl oberhalb der Aufteilungen gibt an, um wieviel feiner die Aufteilung des Datenraumes in der ersten Dimension im Vergleich zur zweiten Dimension ist. Zusätzlich sind je zwei Anfragebereiche dargestellt, die Anfragen entsprechen, bei denen für eines der beiden Attribute ein Anfrageintervall vorgegeben wurde, das ein Sechzehntel der Ausdehnung des Datenraumes umfaßt.

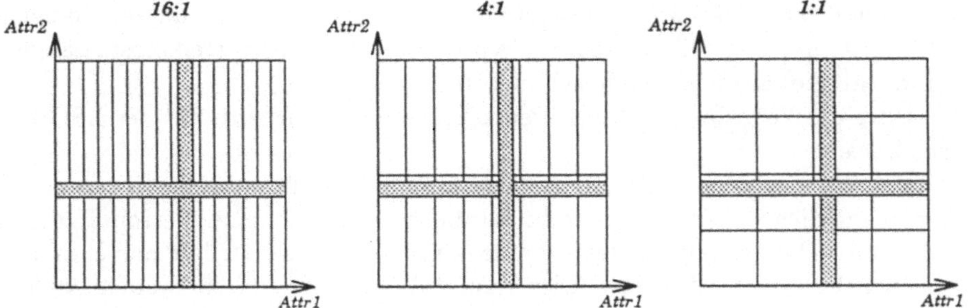

Abbildung 3. Alternativen zur Partitionierung bei zwei berücksichtigten Attributen

- Bei einem Verhältnis von *16:1* in der Datenraumaufteilung werden von einer solchen Anfrage, sofern *Attr1* spezifiziert ist, durchschnittlich 2 Bucketregionen geschnitten. Dagegen werden, sofern *Attr2* spezifiziert ist, immer 16 Bucketregionen geschnitten. Mit dieser Aufteilung des Datenraumes wird daher exakt die Performance erzielt, die auch mit einer eindimensionalen Zugriffsstruktur über *Attr1* erreicht würde.
- Bei der mittleren Datenraumaufteilung in Abbildung 3 werden, sofern *Attr1* spezifiziert ist, durchschnittlich ca. 3 Bucketzugriffe benötigt, während sich wenn *Attr2* spezifiziert ist, durchschnittlich ca. 9 Bucketzugriffe ergeben. Dabei wird die Selektivität in der zweiten Dimension auf Kosten der Selektivität in der ersten Dimension verbessert.
- Bei einer symmetrischen Aufteilung des Datenraumes (Abbildung 3 rechts) ist die Performance für Anfragen über *Attr1* weiter verschlechtert, während die Performance für Anfragen über *Attr2* weiter verbessert ist. In beiden Fällen werden durchschnittlich ca. 5 Bucketzugriffe benötigt.

Dieses Beispiel zeigt, daß eine Verbesserung der Performance für Anfragen über einem Attribut immer zu einer Verschlechterung der Performance bei Anfragen nach den anderen Attributen führt.

Um die Performance eines LSD-Baumes nun gezielt zu steuern, kann man den betrachteten k Attributen Prioritäten ψ_i ($1 \leq i \leq k$) zuordnen. Bei einem Bucketsplit muß die Splitdimension s_{Dim} dann im Hinblick auf die Anzahl der Splits auf dem Pfad von der Wurzel bis zu dem zu splittenden Bucket so gewählt werden, daß folgende Formel gilt:

$$\psi_{s_{Dim}} \cdot \frac{1}{2^{(\text{Anzahl der Splits in } s_{Dim})}} = \max\left\{\psi_i \cdot \frac{1}{2^{(\text{Anzahl der Splits in Dim. } i)}} \mid 1 \leq i \leq k\right\} \qquad (1)$$

Damit ist gewährleistet, daß das Verhältnis zwischen den Prioritäten immer näherungsweise der Feinheit der Zerlegung des Datenraumes in den einzelnen Dimensionen entspricht, wobei die Verteilung der Daten (bei einer datenabhängigen Splitstrategie) bzw. die Verteilungshypothese (bei einer verteilungsabhängigen Splitstrategie) automatisch beachtet wird.

Über die Vergabe der Prioritäten kann somit die Selektivität des LSD-Baumes gesteuert werden.

Eine Sonderbehandlung ist für Attribute erforderlich, zu denen es nur sehr wenige mögliche Ausprägungen gibt, wie beim Geschlecht einer Person. In diesem Fall muß sichergestellt werden, daß das entsprechende Attribut nur einmal als Splitattribut verwendet wird. Dies kann z.B. dadurch erreicht werden, daß ein Attribut nur dann als Splitattribut verwendet wird, wenn in dem zu splittenden Bucket verschiedene Ausprägungen dieses Attributes vorkommen.

3.3 Ein Verfahren für elementare Selektionsbedingungen

Im Hinblick auf die durch eine mehrdimensionale Zugriffsstruktur zu unterstützenden Selektionsbedingungen wollen wir vier Typen differenzieren.

Den ersten Typ bilden Selektionsbedingungen, bei denen mehrere Teilbedingungen, die sich jeweils nur auf ein Attribut beziehen, konjunktiv verknüpft sind. Anfragen mit solchen Selektionsbedingungen können, wie wir in Abschnitt 3.1 gesehen haben, effizient durch Bereichsanfragen mit einem rechteckigen Anfragebereich unterstützt werden. Sind einzelne Attribute nicht spezifiziert, so verwendet man für die entsprechenden Dimensionen als Anfrageintervall $[-\infty; \infty]$.

Der zweite Typ von Selektionsbedingungen kann dadurch charakterisiert werden, daß in einer Bedingung ohne *und*- und *oder*-Verknüpfungen mehrere Attribute auftreten. Betrachten wir z.B. eine Relation *projects* mit den numerischen Attributen *return* und *expense*. Um in dieser Relation die Projekte zu ermitteln, die mindestens 5 % Gewinn abwerfen, kann man folgende Anfrage stellen:

$$\text{projects } \sigma[\text{return} \geq (\text{expense} * 1.05)]$$

In Abbildung 4 ist auf der linken Seite zu sehen, wie diese Selektionsbedingung graphisch interpretiert werden kann.

Die Überführung dieser relativ einfachen Selektionsbedingung in einen entsprechenden polygonalen Anfragebereich für einen LSD-Baum, der als Index über die Standardattribute *return* und *expense* eingesetzt wird, würde noch keine größeren Probleme bereiten. Bei komplexeren Bedingungen wird aber deren Überführung in polygonale Anfragebereiche deutlich schwieriger und i.a. sogar unmöglich, womit wir zum dritten Typ von Selektionsbedingungen kommen. Ein Beispiel für eine solche Selektionsbedingung zeigt Abbildung 4, in der auf der rechten Seite eine Selektionsbedingung der Form $x \cdot y \geq 1$ dargestellt ist. Eine solche Selektionsbedingung könnte z.B. in folgendem Szenario sinnvoll sein:

Ein Industrieunternehmen verwaltet in einer Relation *products* die von ihm produzierten Produkte. Diese Relation habe die Attribute *pname* (Name des Produkts), *price* (Verkaufspreis), *daily_production* (Anzahl der pro Tag produzierten Einheiten) und *reject_rate* (Anteil fehlerhafter Produkte an der Gesamtproduktion).

Wenn nun alle Produkte gesucht werden, deren Tagesproduktion einen Wert von mehr als 100.000 DM hat, dann entspricht dies folgender Anfrage:

$$\text{products } \sigma[(\text{price} * \text{daily\_production}) > 100000]$$

Werden alle Produkte gesucht, für die der tägliche Ausschuß einen Wert von mehr als 1.000 DM hat, ergibt sich eine Selektionsbedingung, in der drei Attribute multiplikativ verknüpft werden:

$$\text{products } \sigma[(\text{price} * \text{daily\_production} * \text{reject\_rate}) > 1000]$$

Im Gegensatz zu linearen Bedingungen, bei denen nur mit Konstanten multipliziert wird (Typ 2), können nichtlineare Bedingungen wie die beiden obigen (Typ 3) nicht in einen polygonalen Anfragebereich überführt werden.

Noch komplexer wird das Problem wenn mehrere Teilbedingungen der Typen 2 und/oder 3 konjunktiv oder disjunktiv verknüpft werden (Typ 4). Ein Beispiel hierfür ist folgende Anfrage:

$$\text{products } \sigma[(\text{price} * \text{daily\_production} * \text{reject\_rate}) > 1000$$
$$\text{or } (\text{price} * \text{daily\_production}) > 100000]$$

Wir werden nun zunächst ein Verfahren vorstellen, mit dem sehr viele Selektionsbedingungen der Typen 2 und 3 bearbeitet werden können. Im Anschluß daran werden wir in Abschnitt 3.4 zeigen, wie die Bearbeitung von Selektionsbedingungen, die durch konjunktive und/oder disjunktive Verknüpfung einfacherer Teilbedingungen entstanden sind, auf die Bearbeitung der einzelnen Teilbedingungen zurückgeführt werden kann.

Für die folgenden Überlegungen benötigen wir den Begriff der *Datenregion*: Unter der Datenregion eines Buckets wollen wir dessen Bucketregion verstehen und unter der Datenregion eines Directory-Knotens die Vereinigung der Datenregionen seiner Söhne.

Bei Selektionsbedingungen der Typen 2 und 3 kann man nun folgende Vorgehensweise anwenden:

Statt im Verlauf einer Bereichsanfrage beim Abstieg durch das Directory die zu untersuchenden Datenregionen mit einem aus der Selektionsbedingung abgeleiteten Anfragebereich zu vergleichen, untersucht man für jeden Eckpunkt der betrachteten (rechteckigen) Datenregion, ob dieser die gegebene Selektionsbedingung erfüllt. Erfüllt keiner der Eckpunkte die Selektionsbedingung, so muß – sofern die Selektionsbedingung bestimmte Voraussetzungen erfüllt – der zugehörige Teil des LSD-Baumes nicht untersucht werden. Anderenfalls ist der entsprechende Teilbaum zu bearbeiten.

Welche Voraussetzungen müssen nun erfüllt sein, damit die beschriebene Vorgehensweise, die wir als *Eckentest* bezeichnen wollen, angewendet werden kann?

Satz 1: Wenn wir den Lösungsraum der gegebenen Selektionsbedingung mit Q bezeichnen, dann kann das oben beschriebene Verfahren genau dann angewendet werden, wenn für jeden Punkt $P = (p_1, \ldots, p_k)$ aus Q folgendes gilt $(1 \leq i \leq k)$:

$$
\begin{aligned}
&(\exists P' = (p_1, \ldots, p'_i, \ldots, p_k) \text{ mit } p'_i < p_i \wedge P' \notin Q) \Rightarrow \\
&\qquad (\forall P'' = (p_1, \ldots, p''_i, \ldots, p_k) \text{ mit } p''_i > p_i : P'' \in Q) \\
\wedge \; &(\exists P' = (p_1, \ldots, p'_i, \ldots, p_k) \text{ mit } p'_i > p_i \wedge P' \notin Q) \Rightarrow \\
&\qquad (\forall P'' = (p_1, \ldots, p''_i, \ldots, p_k) \text{ mit } p''_i < p_i : P'' \in Q)
\end{aligned}
\tag{2}
$$

(Diese Bedingung kann man informell wie folgt zusammenfassen: Wenn es auf einer "Seite" eines Punktes P, der in Q enthalten ist, einen Punkt P' gibt, der nicht in Q enthalten ist, dann müssen alle Punkte P'' auf der anderen "Seite" von P in Q enthalten sein.)

Beweis: *Wir zeigen zunächst, daß das beschriebene Verfahren zu einem Fehler führen kann, wenn Bedingung (2) nicht erfüllt ist:* Angenommen, Bedingung (2) sei nicht erfüllt. Dann gibt es mindestens einen Punkt $P = (p_1, \ldots, p_k)$ in Q, zu dem zwei Punkte $P' = (p_1, \ldots, p'_i, \ldots, p_k)$ und $P'' = (p_1, \ldots, p''_i, \ldots, p_k)$ mit $p'_i < p_i$ und $p''_i > p_i$ und $P' \notin Q$ und $P'' \notin Q$ existieren. Betrachtet man nun die degenerierte Datenregion $D = [p_1; p_1] \times \ldots \times [p'_i; p''_i] \times \ldots \times [p_k; p_k]$, so sind deren Eckpunkte (nämlich P' und P'') nicht in Q enthalten, obwohl der Punkt P, der ja auch in D enthalten ist, zu Q gehört[6]. Die oben beschriebene Vorgehensweise würde somit zu einem Fehler führen.

Wir zeigen nun, daß das beschriebene Verfahren nicht zu einem Fehler führen kann, wenn Bedingung (2) erfüllt ist: Angenommen Bedingung (2) sei erfüllt und das beschriebene Verfahren führe zu einem Fehler. Dann gibt es eine Datenregion $D = [l_1; u_1] \times \ldots \times [l_k; u_k]$, deren Eckpunkte alle außerhalb von Q liegen, und zu der es trotzdem mindestens einen Punkt $P = (p_1, \ldots, p_k)$ gibt, der in Q liegt, und für den außerdem $\forall i \in \{1, \ldots, k\} : l_i \leq p_i \leq u_i$ gilt. Wegen Bedingung (2) muß dann mindestens einer der Punkte $P'_1 = (l_1, p_2, \ldots, p_k)$ und $P''_1 = (u_1, p_2, \ldots, p_k)$ zu Q gehören. Daraus folgt wegen Bedingung (2), daß mindestens einer der Punkte $P'_2 = (l_1, l_2, p_3, \ldots, p_k)$, $P''_2 = (l_1, u_2, p_3, \ldots, p_k)$, $P'''_2 = (u_1, l_2, p_3, \ldots, p_k)$ und $P''''_2 = (u_1, u_2, p_3, \ldots, p_k)$ zu Q gehören muß, …

Diese Schlußweise kann man offensichtlich k-mal anwenden, wobei man am Ende die Aussage erhält, daß mindestens eine der 2^k Ecken der Datenregion D zu Q gehören muß. Nach dem obigen Verfahren würde der zugehörige Teilbaum des LSD-Baumes also untersucht. Dies steht aber im Widerspruch zu unserer Annahme, nach der das beschriebene Verfahren zu einem Fehler führen soll. $\qquad\Box$

---

[6] Die verwendete degenerierte Datenregion mag auf den ersten Blick künstlich wirken. Denkt man aber an diskrete Attributwerte, so ist relativ offensichtlich, daß derartige Datrenregionen entstehen können.

In Abbildung 4 sind zwei Selektionsbedingungen dargestellt, die Bedingung (2) erfüllen, und in Abbildung 5 sind zwei Selektionsbedingungen dargestellt, die Bedingung (2) nicht erfüllen. Der linke Lösungsraum in Abbildung 4 éntspricht allgemein einer Bedingung der Form $c_1 \cdot Attr_1 + c_2 \cdot Attr_2 \leq c_3$ und der rechte Lösungsraum einer Bedingung der Form $(Attr_1 + c_1) \cdot (Attr_2 + c_2) \geq c_3$.

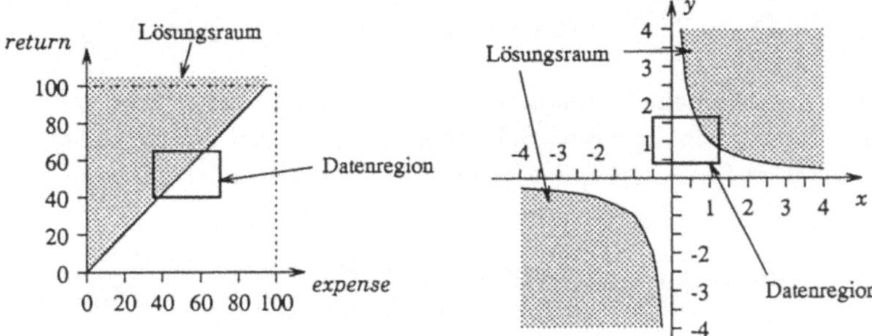

Abbildung4. Selektionen, bei denen der Eckentest angewendet werden kann

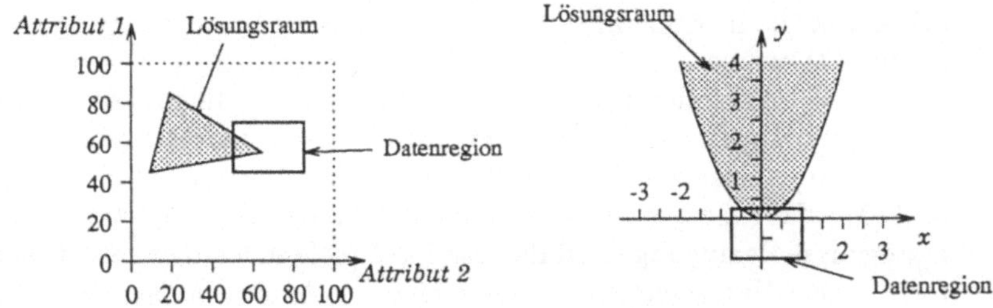

Abbildung5. Selektionen, bei denen der Eckentest zu einem Fehler führen kann

Wir wollen nun noch einen weiteren Aspekt betrachten. Man kann die Performance eines LSD-Baumes bei der Bearbeitung von Bereichsanfragen u.U. erheblich steigern, indem man beim Vergleich zwischen Datenregionen und Anfragebereich einen dreiwertigen Test vornimmt:

- Wenn für die Datenregion D eines Teilbaumes $D \cap Q = \emptyset$ gilt, muß der entsprechende Teilbaum nicht weiter verfolgt werden.
- Gilt für die Datenregion D eines Teilbaumes $D \subseteq Q$, so können alle in diesem Teilbaum abgelegten Objekte ohne einen weiteren Test der Lösungsmenge

hinzugefügt werden (was u.U. zahlreiche aufwendige Tests einspart), und
— lediglich wenn diese beiden Bedingungen nicht erfüllt sind, muß der entsprechende Teilbaum weiter einzeln untersucht werden.

Um die gleiche Vorgehensweise auch beim *Eckentest* anwenden zu können, wäre es nützlich, wenn man wie folgt schließen könnte:

1. Wenn keine Ecke der betrachteten Datenregion D in Q liegt, gilt $D \cap Q = \emptyset$.
2. Wenn alle Ecken der betrachteten Datenregion D in Q liegen, gilt $D \subseteq Q$.

Die in Satz 1 angegebene Bedingung (2) gewährleistet aber nur die erste Schlußfolgerung. Damit auch die zweite Schlußfolgerung korrekt ist, muß zusätzlich für jeden Punkt $P = (p_1, \ldots, p_k)$, der *nicht* in Q liegt, folgendes gelten ($1 \leq i \leq k$):

$$\begin{aligned}
(\exists P' = (p_1, \ldots, p_i', \ldots, p_k) \text{ mit } p_i' < p_i \wedge P' \in Q) \Rightarrow \\
(\forall P'' = (p_1, \ldots, p_i'', \ldots, p_k) \text{ mit } p_i'' > p_i : \; P'' \notin Q) \\
\wedge \; (\exists P' = (p_1, \ldots, p_i', \ldots, p_k) \text{ mit } p_i' > p_i \wedge P' \in Q) \Rightarrow \\
(\forall P'' = (p_1, \ldots, p_i'', \ldots, p_k) \text{ mit } p_i'' < p_i : \; P'' \notin Q)
\end{aligned} \tag{3}$$

Diese Bedingung kann informell wie folgt zusammengefaßt werden: Wenn es auf einer "Seite" eines Punktes P, der nicht in Q enthalten ist, einen Punkt P' gibt, der in Q enthalten ist, dann müssen alle Punkte P'' auf der anderen "Seite" von P außerhalb von Q liegen.

Der Beweis hierzu kann analog zu dem Beweis von Satz 1 geführt werden. Man beachte, daß die in Abbildung 4 dargestellten Selektionsbedingungen auch die Bedingung (3) erfüllen.

Der *Eckentest* eignet sich leider nicht für Selektionsbedingungen, in denen einzelne Teilbedingungen konjunktiv oder disjunktiv verknüpft sind. In diesen Fällen kann aus der Tatsache, daß die einzelnen Teilbedingungen die Bedingungen (2) und (3) erfüllen, nicht geschlossen werden, daß auch die gesamte Selektionsbedingung diese Bedingungen erfüllt. Zwei Beispiele sollen dies verdeutlichen. Nehmen wir an, ein Unternehmensberater wolle eine Analyse außergewöhnlicher Projekte erstellen und zu diesem Zweck all die Projekte betrachten, die entweder einen Ertrag von höchstens 100.000 DM oder einen Ertrag von mindestens 900.000 DM verursachen. Eine entsprechende Anfrage lautet:

$$\texttt{projects } \sigma[\texttt{return} \leq 100000 \texttt{ or return} \geq 900000]$$

Auf der linken Seite von Abbildung 6 wird diese Selektionsbedingung veranschaulicht. Der entsprechende Lösungsraum erfüllt offensichtlich nicht die Bedingung (3), obwohl die beiden Teilbedingungen jeweils die Bedingung (3) erfüllen.

Ein Beispiel für eine Selektionsbedingung, in der zwei Teilbedingungen konjunktiv verknüpft sind, bildet folgende Anfrage:

$$\texttt{projects } \sigma[\texttt{return} \geq 100000 \texttt{ and return} \leq 900000]$$

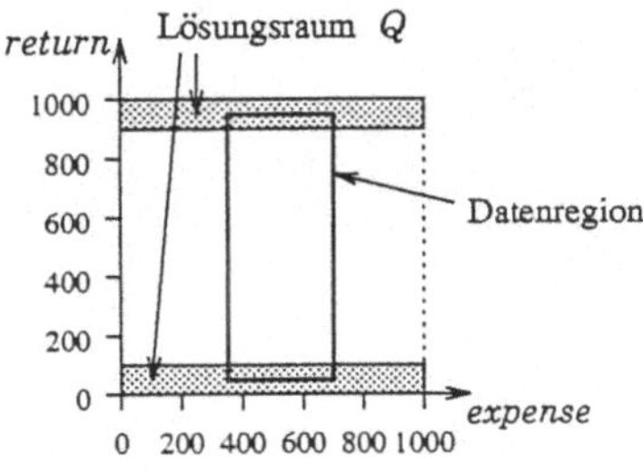
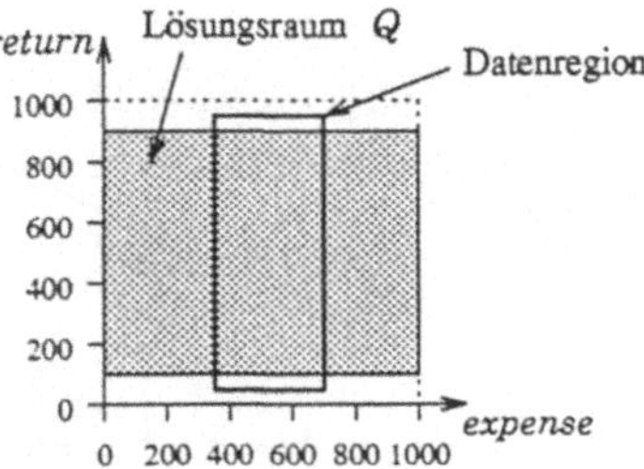

Abbildung6. Einfache Anfragebereiche, die dem Eckentest Probleme bereiten

Auf der rechten Seite von Abbildung 6 wird diese Selektionsbedingung veranschaulicht. Der Lösungsraum erfüllt die Bedingung (2) nicht, obwohl die beiden Teilbedingungen jeweils die Bedingung (2) erfüllen.

Dieses Beispiel, das einer einfachen Intervallanfrage entspricht, zeigt deutlich die Grenzen des *Eckentests* auf. Ein weiterer Nachteil des *Eckentests* ist, daß die Anzahl der Ecken, die betrachtet werden müssen, exponentiell in der Anzahl der Dimensionen des Datenraumes wächst. Der *Eckentest* ist somit kein Patentrezept. Er kann bei einigen Selektionsbedingungen relativ gut eingesetzt werden. So z.B. bei Selektionsbedingungen der Form $c_1 \cdot Attr_1 + c_2 \cdot Attr_2 \leq c_3$ oder der Form $(Attr_1 + c_1) \cdot (Attr_2 + c_2) \geq c_3$. Insbesondere bei konjunktiv und disjunktiv zusammengesetzten Selektionsbedingungen scheitert der *Eckentest* aber.

Aus diesem Grund schlagen wir als übergeordnete Vorgehensweise bei Selektionsanfragen die Aufspaltung zusammengesetzter Selektionsbedingungen in einfachere Teilbedingungen mit Hilfe eines Selektions-Baumes vor. Dabei können die einzelnen Teilbedingungen mit relativ einfachen Verfahren, wie z.B. dem *Eckentest* bearbeitet werden.

3.4 Ein Verfahren für zusammengesetzte Selektionsbedingungen

Zunächst benötigen wir eine grobe informelle Definition eines zu einer booleschen Bedingung gehörenden Selektions-Baumes:

1. Sei *Bed* entweder *true* oder *false* oder eine boolesche Bedingung, die weder *and*- noch *or*-Verknüpfungen enthält. Dann besteht der zugehörige Selektions-Baum nur aus einem Blatt, in dem *Bed* abgelegt ist.
2. Besteht eine Bedingung aus zwei Teilbedingungen *Bed1* und *Bed2*, die durch *and* oder *or* verknüpft sind, so enthält die Wurzel des zugehörigen Selektions-Baumes die entsprechende Verknüpfung, und die Söhne der Wurzel entsprechen den Selektions-Bäumen für die Teilbedingungen *Bed1* und *Bed2*.

Abbildung 7 zeigt einen solchen Selektions-Baum, für eine Selektionsbedingung der Form $((Bed1$ **or** $Bed2)$ **and** $(Bed3$ **or** $Bed4)) $ **or** $Bed5$.

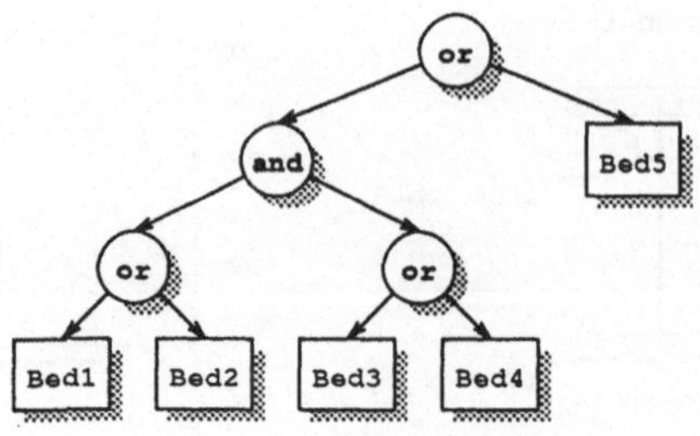

Abbildung7. Beispiel für einen Selektions-Baum

Die einzelnen Bedingungen *Bed1* bis *Bed5* können dabei z.B. Selektionsbedingungen der Form $Attr_1 \leq Attr_2$, $Attr_1 = c$ oder $Attr_1 \cdot Attr_2 > c$ sein.

Bei der Bearbeitung einer Anfrage mit zusammengesetzter Selektionsbedingung in einem LSD-Baum verfährt man nun im Prinzip genau wie bei einer Bereichsanfrage: Man beginnt in der Wurzel des Directory und ermittelt durch Vergleiche zwischen der Selektionsbedingung und den zu den Directoryknoten gehörenden Datenregionen, welche Teile des LSD-Baumes Tupel enthalten können, die der Selektionsbedingung entsprechen.

Bei den Vergleichen zwischen der Selektionsbedingung und den zu den Directoryknoten gehörenden Datenregionen können die Teilbedingungen in den Blättern des Selektions-Baumes, der die Selektionsbedingung repräsentiert, einzeln überprüft werden[7]:

Ist eine Teilbedingung für die gesamte Datenregion wahr, so wird das entsprechende Blatt im Selektions-Baum durch *true* ersetzt. Ist eine Teilbedingung für die gesamte Datenregion falsch, so wird das entsprechende Blatt im Selektions-Baum durch *false* ersetzt. Falls keiner der beiden obigen Fälle zutrifft, wird das entsprechende Blatt nicht verändert.

Nachdem jede Teilbedingung im Selektions-Baum in dieser Weise überprüft worden ist, wird der Baum so weit wie möglich vereinfacht. Diese Vereinfachung kann mit Hilfe der in Tabelle 1 angegebenen Regeln durchgeführt werden. In dieser Tabelle sind neben dem *logischen und* und dem *logischen oder* auch die *Negation* und die *Identität* berücksichtigt, um beispielhaft zu zeigen, daß beliebige boolesche Operatoren, analog behandelt werden können.

Nehmen wir z.B. an, bei einer Überprüfung des Selektions-Baumes aus Abbildung 7 habe sich herausgestellt, daß die Bedingung *Bed1* für die gesamte Datenregion wahr ist, während *Bed3* und *Bed5* für die gesamte Datenregion falsch sind. Für *Bed2* und *Bed4* kann keine eindeutige Aussage getroffen werden. Dann ergibt sich der neue Selektions-Baum in der in Abbildung 8 dargestellten Form.

---

[7] Dabei müssen jeweils nur die in der entsprechenden Teilbedingung vorkommenden Dimensionen der Datenraumes (= Attribute) berücksichtigt werden – was z.B. beim Eckentest zu einer erheblichen Vereinfachung der Überprüfung führen kann.

Bed1	Bed2	not Bed1	Bed1 or Bed2	Bed1 and Bed2	Bed1 $\equiv$ Bed2
true	true	false	true	true	true
true	false	false	true	false	false
true	unclear	false	true	Bed2	Bed2
false	true	true	true	false	false
false	false	true	false	false	true
false	unclear	true	Bed2	false	not Bed2
unclear	true	not Bed1	true	Bed1	Bed1
unclear	false	not Bed1	Bed1	false	not Bed1
unclear	unclear	not Bed1	Bed1 or Bed2	Bed1 and Bed2	Bed1 $\equiv$ Bed2

Tabelle1. Vereinfachungsregeln für den Selektions-Baum

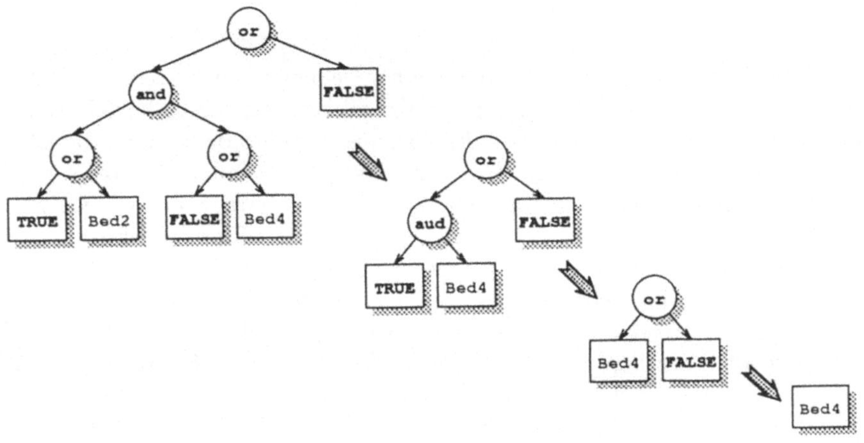

Abbildung8. Beispiel für die Vereinfachung eines Selektions-Baumes

Wenn es sich bei der betrachteten Datenregion um die Datenregion eines Directoryknotens gehandelt hat, muß jetzt – sofern in der Wurzel des vereinfachten Selektions-Baumes nicht *false* steht – mit dem vereinfachten Selektions-Baum bei den Söhnen fortgefahren werden. Handelt es sich bei der betrachteten Datenregion um die Datenregion eines Buckets, so sind folgende Fälle zu unterscheiden:

1. *In der Wurzel des vereinfachten Selektions-Baumes steht 'false':* Dann muß das Bucket nicht untersucht werden.
2. *In der Wurzel des vereinfachten Selektions-Baumes steht 'true':* Dann gehören alle Tupel, die in diesem Bucket abgelegt sind, zur Lösung der Anfrage.
3. *Der vereinfachte Selektions-Baum entspricht nicht den Fällen 1 oder 2:* Dann muß für jedes Tupel in diesem Bucket ein Test mit dem vereinfachten Selektions-Baum durchgeführt werden.

Das beschriebene Verfahren hat u.a. auch den Vorteil, daß man die einzelnen Teilbedingungen jeweils in einer geeigneten Form abprüfen kann. Dies wollen wir an drei Beispielen verdeutlichen:

1. Eine Teilbedingung der Form $Attr_i = c$ kann beim Test gegen eine Datenregion $D(w) = (w_{\lambda_1}; w_{v_1}] \times \ldots \times (w_{\lambda_k}; w_{v_k}]$ genau dann durch *false* ersetzt werden, wenn $c \notin (w_{\lambda_i}; w_{v_i}]$ gilt. Anderenfalls muß die Bedingung erhalten bleiben.

2. Eine Bedingung der Form $Attr_i \leq c$ kann genau dann durch *false* ersetzt werden, wenn $c \leq w_{\lambda_i}$ ist. Ist $c > w_{v_i}$ so kann die Bedingung durch *true* ersetzt werden, und nur wenn c im Intervall $(w_{\lambda_i}; w_{v_i}]$ liegt, kann die Bedingung nicht vereinfacht werden.

3. Bedingungen der Form $c_i \cdot Attr_i + c_j \cdot Attr_j \leq c$ oder $(Attr_i + c_i) \cdot (Attr_j + c_j) \geq c$ können mit Hilfe des *Eckentests* bearbeitet werden. Dabei müssen nur die Dimensionen des Datenraumes betrachtet werden, die in der Teilbedingung auftreten.

Neben diesen Standardverfahren können jederzeit auch weitere Verfahren ergänzt werden, wenn Teilbedingungen, die mit keinem dieser Verfahren gelöst werden können, häufiger auftreten. Ein Beispiel für eine Bedingung, die ein spezielles Testverfahren erfordern würde, ist $Attr_i^2 \leq c$. Andere Beispiele ergeben sich, wenn man an geometrische Attribute denkt. Darauf werden wir im folgenden Abschnitt eingehen. Zuvor soll noch ein kurzer Eindruck davon gegeben werden, wie das beschriebene Verfahren algorithmisch realisiert werden kann:

Zunächst wird die Selektionsbedingung in einen Selektions-Baum überführt. In jedem Blatt dieses Selektions-Baumes wird neben der entsprechenden Teilbedingung auch der Typ dieser Bedingung (*Gleichheitstest*, *Kleiner-Gleich-Test*, ..., *mathematische Bedingung*) abgelegt, aus dem der LSD-Baum schließen kann, welche Prozedur zum Testen der entsprechenden Bedingung verwendet werden muß. Die Teilbedingungen, die vom LSD-Baum nicht bearbeitet werden können, sei es, weil die entsprechenden Attribute im LSD-Baum nicht berücksichtigt sind, oder weil kein entsprechendes Verfahren implementiert ist, werden durch ein spezielles Flag gekennzeichnet.

Innerhalb des LSD-Baumes erfolgt dann der Test zwischen Anfragebereich (= Selektions-Baum) und den Datenregionen in der beschriebenen Weise, so daß sich der *"Anfragebereich"* beim Abstieg durch das Directory vereinfachen kann. Die gekennzeichneten Teilbedingungen, die vom LSD-Baum nicht bearbeitet werden können, bleiben dabei erhalten – es sei denn, sie können bei einer Vereinfachung des Selektions-Baumes eliminiert werden.

Der LSD-Baum liefert schließlich zu jedem gefundenen Tupel zusätzlich den Selektions-Baum zurück, gegen den dieses Tupel noch getestet werden muß. Der Test der einzelnen Tupel vollzieht sich dann außerhalb des LSD-Baumes.

Bei der Implementierung des Verfahrens ist zu berücksichtigen, daß bei jedem Knoten des Directory nur die Teilbedingungen aus dem Selektions-Baum überprüft werden müssen, die sich auf das im Vater dieses Knotens als Splitattribut verwendete Attribut beziehen, weil die Datenregion des Knotens in allen anderen Dimensionen der Datenregion seines Vaters entspricht, gegen die ja bereits getestet wurde.

Am Ende dieses Abschnitts sollen die Vorteile des beschriebenen Verfahrens kurz zusammengefaßt werden:

1. Eine Überführung der Selektionsbedingung in einen oder mehrere (geometrische) Anfragebereiche ist nicht erforderlich.
2. Auch Selektionsbedingungen, die nicht in einen oder mehrere Anfragebereiche überführt werden können, können mit dem beschriebenen Verfahren bearbeitet werden.
3. Bei der Überprüfung einer Teilbedingung müssen immer nur die Dimensionen des Datenraumes (= Attribute) berücksichtigt werden, die in dieser Teilbedingung betrachtet werden.
4. Bei jedem Knoten des LSD-Baumes müssen nur die Teilbedingungen überprüft werden, die sich auf das im Vater des Knotens abgelegte Splitattribut beziehen. Dadurch können i.a. sehr viele Tests eingespart werden.
5. Weil auch Teilbedingungen, die vom LSD-Baum nicht bearbeitet werden können, harmonisch in das beschriebene Verfahren integriert werden können, gibt es keine unangenehmen Sonderfälle.

4   Die Unterstützung gemischter Selektionsanfragen

Nachdem wir nun gezeigt haben, in welcher Weise eine geometrische Zugriffsstruktur bei Selektionsbedingungen über Standardattributen eingesetzt werden kann, wollen wir jetzt Anfragen betrachten, bei denen sowohl Standardattribute als auch geometrische Attribute spezifiziert sind. Nimmt man z.B. an, daß in der Konstanten *Schweiz* die Grenzen der Schweiz in Form eines Polygones abgelegt sind, dann bestimmt die folgende Anfrage alle Städte in der Schweiz mit mindestens 50.000 Einwohnern:

$$\text{cities } \sigma[\text{center } \textbf{inside Schweiz and } \text{cpop} \geq 50000]$$

Existieren zwei getrennte Indexe über den Attributen *center* und *cpop*, so steht man vor den schon im Abschnitt 3.1 beschriebenen Problemen. Es kann deshalb sinnvoll sein, über einen einzigen LSD-Baum sowohl die Standardattribute einer Relation als auch deren geometrische Attribute zu indizieren. Wenn man annimmt, daß neben einem k-dimensionalen geometrischen Attribut noch i Standardattribute berücksichtigt werden müssen, dann ergibt sich daraus entweder

1. eine $k+i$-dimensionale Struktur, wenn das geometrische Attribut punktförmig ist, oder
2. eine $2k+i$-dimensionale Struktur, wenn das geometrische Attribut ausgedehnt ist (z.B. bei Polygonen, die durch ein minimales umschließendes Rechteck approximiert werden).

Wenn wir das im vorhergehenden Abschnitt vorgestellte Verfahren zur Auflösung zusammengesetzter Selektionsbedingungen mit Hilfe eines Selektions-Baumes betrachten, dann wird deutlich, daß die Berücksichtigung geometrischer Teilbedingungen im Rahmen von Selektionsanfragen keine Probleme bereitet. Die Teilbedingung (oder die Teilbedingungen), die sich auf das geometrische Attribut beziehen, werden wie alle anderen Teilbedingungen auch in einem Blatt des Selektions-Baumes abgelegt. Dabei ist unerheblich, ob es sich um ein punktförmiges oder ein ausgedehntes Attribut handelt. Zum Vergleich einer geometrischen Teilbedingung mit einer Datenregion wird dann jeweils eine Testprozedur aufgerufen, die den Anfragebereich (Rechteck, Kreis, oder Polygon) mit den Dimensionen der $k+i$- oder $2k+i$-dimensionalen Datenregion vergleicht, die dem geometrischen Attribut zugeordnet sind.

5 Zusammenfassung und Ausblick

Wir haben in diesem Papier drei Verfahren vorgestellt, die wesentliche Problempunkte beim Einsatz mehrdimensionaler Zugriffsstrukturen über mehreren Standardattributen überwinden. Der LSD-Baum ist unter Verwendung dieser Verfahren als universelle Indexstruktur in das Gral-System [Güt89] integriert worden. Die dabei gemachten Erfahrungen bestätigen die praktische Anwendbarkeit der Verfahren.

Obwohl mit dem Eckentest die wesentlichen Selektionsbedingungen mit arithmetischen Operationen bearbeitet werden können, verbleiben hier zwei Problembereiche: Zum einen ist nicht leicht zu bestimmen, ob eine Selektionsbedingung mit Hilfe des Eckentests verarbeitet werden kann. Wir wenden derzeit eine einfache Heuristik an, die aber bei weitem nicht alle Selektionsbedingungen erkennt, die mit dem Eckentest verarbeitet werden können. Zum anderen gibt es Überlegungen zu aufwendigeren Verfahren, die eine größere Klasse von Selektionsbedingungen abdecken.

Neben der Anwendung mehrdimensionaler Zugriffsstrukturen über Standardattributen erscheint auch der Einsatz bei Information Retrieval Problemen interessant. Wenn Dokumente durch Beschreibungsvektoren repräsentiert werden, bietet es sich an, diese in einer mehrdimensionalen Zugriffsstruktur zu verwalten. Ein Problem stellt dabei die Anzahl der Dimensionen dar. Da aber zwischen den Gewichten in den einzelnen Dimensionen eine starke Korrelation besteht, erscheint es möglich, dieses Problem mit Hilfe einer Splitstrategie zu lösen, die die Splitdimension gezielt auswählt. Dann wäre die Unterstützung von Anfragen, die neben dem Beschreibungsvektor auch Standardattribute in der Selektionsbedingung betrachten, effizient möglich.

References

[Ben75]   J.L. Bentley. Multidimensional binary search trees used for associative searching. *Communications of the ACM*, 18(9):509–517, 1975.

[Fre87]   M. Freeston. The BANG file: a new kind of grid file. In *Proceedings of the ACM SIGMOD Int. Conf. on Management of Data*, pages 260–269, San Francisco, 1987.

[Güt89]   R.H. Güting. Gral: An Extensible Relational Database System for Geometric Applications. In *Proc. 15th International Conference on Very Large Data Bases*, pages 33–44, Amsterdam, 1989.

[Hen90]   A. Henrich. *Der LSD-Baum: eine mehrdimensionale Zugriffsstruktur und ihre Einsatzmöglichkeiten in Datenbanksystemen.* PhD thesis, FernUniversität Hagen, 1990.

[HHSW91] A. Henrich, A. Hilbert, H.-W. Six, and P. Widmayer. Anbindung einer räumlich clusternden Zugriffsstruktur für geometrische Attribute an ein Standard-Datenbanksystem am Beispiel von Oracle. In *Proc. GI-Fachtagung "Datenbanksysteme für Büro, Technik und Wissenschaft"*, Springer, Informatik-Fachbericht 270, pages 161–177, Kaiserslautern, Germany, 1991.

[Hin85]   K. Hinrichs. *The grid file system: implementation and case studies of applications.* PhD thesis, ETH Zürich, 1985. Dissertation Nr. 7734.

[HS91]   A. Henrich and H.-W. Six. How to split buckets in spatial data structures. In *Proc. International Conference on Geographic Database Management Systems*, Esprit Basic Research Series DG XIII, pages 212–244, Capri (Italy), 1991. Springer-Verlag.

[HSW89a] A. Henrich, H.-W. Six, and P. Widmayer. Paging binary trees with external balancing. In *Proc. 15th International Conference on Graph-Theoretic Concepts in Computer Science (WG'89)*, pages 260–276, Aachen, 1989.

[HSW89b] A. Henrich, H.-W. Six, and P. Widmayer. The LSD tree: spatial access to multidimensional point and non point objects. In *Proc. 15th International Conference on Very Large Data Bases*, pages 45–53, Amsterdam, 1989.

[KO91]   M.J. van Kreveld and M.H. Overmars. Divided k-d Trees. *Algorithmica*, 6:840–858, 1991.

[LS87]   P.C. Lockemann and J.W. Schmidt, editors. *Datenbank-Handbuch.* Springer-Verlag, Berlin, Heidelberg, 1987.

[LS89]   D.B. Lomet and B. Salzberg. A Robust Multi-Attribute Search Structure. In *Proc. IEEE 5th Int. Conf. on Data Engineering*, pages 296–304, 1989.

[NHS84]   J. Nievergelt, H. Hinterberger, and K.C. Sevcik. The Grid File: an adaptable, symmetric multikey file structure. *ACM Transactions on Database Systems*, 9(1):38–71, 1984.

[OMSD87] B.C. Ooi, K.J. McDonell, and R. Sacks-Davis. Spatial kd-Tree: An Indexing Mechanism for Spatial Databases. *IEEE COMPSAC*, pages 433–438, 1987.

[Rob81]   J.T. Robinson. The K-D-B-Tree: A Search Structure for Large Multidimensional Dynamic Indexes. In *Proceedings of the ACM SIGMOD Int. Conf. on Management of Data*, pages 10–18, 1981.

[SK88]   B. Seeger and H.-P. Kriegel. Techniques for design and implementation of efficient spatial access methods. In *Proc. 14th International Conference on Very Large Data Bases*, pages 360–371, 1988.

[SK90]   B. Seeger and H.-P. Kriegel. The buddy-tree: an efficient and robust access method for spatial data base systems. In *Proc. 16th International Conference on Very Large Data Bases*, pages 590–601, Brisbane, 1990.

Ein Kostenmodell der parallelen Anfragebearbeitung in Shared-Nothing-Datenbanksystemen

Robert Marek

Fachbereich Informatik, Universität Kaiserslautern
Postfach 3049, 67618 Kaiserslautern
e-mail: marek@informatik.uni-kl.de

Kurzfassung:

Zunehmend komplexe und datenintensive Benutzeranfragen auf Datenbanken verlangen parallele Verarbeitungsansätze. Vor allem Datenbanksysteme der Architekturklasse Shared-Nothing bieten derzeit eine geeignete Basis für die parallele Anfragebearbeitung. Im Hinblick auf den interaktiven Charakter komplexer Datenbankanfragen ist eine Verkürzung der Antwortzeit das vorrangige Leistungsziel paralleler Datenbanksysteme. Im Falle der heute weit verbreiteten mengenorientierten, relationalen Anfragesprachen erlaubt vor allem Intra-Operator-Parallelität eine effektive Antwortzeitverkürzung. Die Antwortzeit kann jedoch durch zunehmende Parallelisierung nicht beliebig verkürzt werden. Wird ein gewisser Parallelisierungsgrad überschritten, tritt eine Verschlechterung der Antwortzeit ein. Dieser Effekt liegt einerseits in einem beschränkten Parallelisierungspotential, andererseits in mit zunehmendem Parallelisierungsgrad steigenden Kooperations- und Kommunikationskosten begründet. Die Bestimmung des optimalen Parallelisierungsgrades ist daher von besonderer Bedeutung. Aus diesem Grunde haben wir ein analytisches Kostenmodell entwickelt, das die Antwortzeitentwicklung von Datenbankanfragen in Abhängigkeit vom Grad der Parallelisierung beschreibt. Anhand dieses Modells können wir grundsätzliche Trade-offs der parallelen Anfragebearbeitung untersuchen. Weiterhin kann das Kostenmodell zur Unterstützung des Optimierers bei der Anfrageparallelisierung sowie zur Bestimmung einer geeigneten Datenverteilung genutzt werden. Das Kostenmodell wurde mit Hilfe begleitender Simulationsversuche zur parallelen Bearbeitung von Anfragen validiert.

1 Einführung

In der Datenbankverarbeitung gewinnen komplexe Ad-hoc-Anfragen zunehmend an Bedeutung, was zum Teil durch die wachsende Verbreitung mächtiger Anfragesprachen und Benutzer-Tools bedingt ist. Doch auch die mächtigen Anfrage-, Manipulations- und Wartungsoperationen von DB-Anwendungen kommender Generationen wie Ingenieur-Anwendungen, VLSI-Entwurf, Multimedia-Anwendungen etc. vergrößern die Komplexität von DB-Anfragen deutlich [Silberschatz et al. 1991]. Für diesen Lasttyp steht eine Optimierung des Antwortzeitverhaltens im Vordergrund, um ein für den Dialogbetrieb akzeptables Antwortzeitverhalten gewährleisten zu können. Derartige Anfragen betreffen im allgemeinen große Datenvolumina und/oder führen aufwendige Berechnungen durch, so daß akzeptable Antwortzeiten nur durch den massiven Einsatz von Parallelität in der DB-Verarbeitung erzielt werden können [Pirahesh et al. 1990].

Parallele Datenbanksysteme sind daher heute für eine leistungsfähige Transaktions- und Anfragebearbeitung obligatorisch [DeWitt und Gray 1992, Valduriez 1993]. Derartige Systeme nutzen die Kapazität mehrerer lokal verteilter Verarbeitungsknoten, die über ein Hochleistungsnetzwerk miteinander verbunden sind. Die wichtigste Klasse paralleler Datenbanksysteme bilden derzeit *Shared-Nothing*-Architekturen [Stonebraker 1986, DeWitt und Gray 1992]. Zu den Parallelverarbeitung unterstützenden Shared-Nothing-Systemen gehören u.a. Produkte wie Tandem NonStop SQL [The Tandem Database Group 1989, Englert et al. 1990] und Teradata DBC/1012 [Neches 1986] sowie eine Reihe von Prototypen: Bubba [Boral et al. 1990], Gamma [DeWitt et al. 1990], EDS [Watson und Townsend 1991] und PRISMA/DB [Apers et al. 1992]. Shared-Nothing-Systeme bestehen aus mehreren funktional gleichwertigen Prozessorelementen (PE). Jedes PE verfügt über ein oder mehrere Prozessoren, lokalen Hauptspeicher sowie eigene Kopien der Anwendungs- und System-Software wie Betriebssystem und Datenbankverwaltungssystem (DBVS). Die Kommunikation zwischen den Prozessorknoten erfolgt in Shared-Nothing-Systemen nachrichtenbasiert - aus Leistungsargumenten i.d.R. über ein Hochgeschwindigkeitsnetzwerk. Die prägende Eigenschaft von Shared-Nothing-Systemen ist eine Auf- und Verteilung der Datenbank in sogenannte Partitionen derart, daß jedes PE eine eigene Partition der Datenbank "besitzt" (*Datenverteilung*). Transaktionen (Anfragen), die auf die Daten fremder PE zugreifen, starten auf den entsprechenden PE sogenannte Sub-Transaktionen, die den Datenzugriff stellvertretend für die eigentliche Transaktion durchführen.

Zur Verkürzung der Antwortzeit von Transaktionen bzw. Anfragen (Queries) wird Intra-Transaktionsparallelität benötigt - in Form von *Inter-* oder *Intra-DML-Parallelität*. Inter-DML-Parallelität bezeichnet die konkurrente Ausführung verschiedener DML-Befehle (DB-Operationen, Anweisungen der DBS-Anfrage- und Manipulationssprache) einer Transaktion. Aufgrund der im allgemeinen geringen Anzahl von DB-Operationen pro Transaktion sowie Vorgaben in der Ausführungsreihenfolge dieser Operationen ermöglicht diese Form der Parallelität i.d.R. nur eine eingeschränkte Parallelisierung. Als weiterer Nachteil erweist sich, daß der Anwendungsprogrammierer Inter-DML-Parallelität mit Hilfe geeigneter Sprachmittel explizit darstellen muß. Aus diesen Gründen unterstützen bestehende Systeme Intra-Transaktionsparallelität lediglich in Form von Intra-DML-Parallelität[1]. Ermöglicht wird die Nutzung von Intra-DML-Parallelität v.a. durch relationale Datenbanksysteme mit ihren deskriptiven, mengenorientierten Anfragesprachen (z.B. SQL) [DeWitt und Gray 1992]. Implementiert wird Intra-DML-Parallelität durch den DBVS-Anfrageoptimierer - vollkommen transparent für Benutzer und Anwendungsprogrammierer. Für jede DB-Operation erstellt der Optimierer hierzu einen (parallelen) Ausführungsplan. Dieser spezifiziert, in welcher Weise die Basisoperatoren (z.B. Scan, Filter, Join, etc.) der DB-Operation abzuarbeiten sind. Intra-DML-Parallelität kann in zwei Formen angeboten werden: *Inter-* und *Intra-Operator-Parallelität*. Inter-Operator-Parallelität bezeichnet die konkurrente Bearbeitung verschiedener Operatoren, wohingegen bei Intra-Operatorparallelität eine Parallelisierung einzelner Operatoren erfolgt. In beiden Fällen ist die Parallelisierung entscheidend von der gewählten Datenverteilung abhängig. Die Datenbank sollte derart auf Prozessorknoten verteilt werden, daß Operatoren oder Sub-Operatoren auf disjunkten Datenpartitionen parallel von verschiedenen PE bearbeitet werden können. Typischerweise werden hierzu Relationen *horizontal*, d.h. tupelweise, auf mehrere PE aufgeteilt.

Die Antwortzeit von Transaktionen hängt in hohem Maße von der Anzahl der PE ab, die für deren Bearbeitung eingesetzt werden: zusätzliche PE verkürzen prinzipiell die Antwortzeit, wobei idealerweise ein linearer Zusammenhang zwischen PE-Anzahl und Antwortzeitverbesserung besteht. In der Praxis kann diese lineare Beziehung jedoch nur begrenzt erzielt werden, und die Antwortzeit kann durch zunehmende Parallelisierung nicht beliebig verkürzt werden. Wird ein gewisser Parallelisierungsgrad überschritten, tritt vielmehr wieder eine Verschlechterung der Antwortzeit ein. Dieser Effekt liegt einerseits in einem beschränkten Parallelisierungspotential, andererseits in mit zunehmendem Parallelisierungsgrad steigenden Kooperations- und Kommunikationskosten begründet. Die Bestimmung des *optimalen* Parallelisierungsgrades ist daher von besonderer Bedeutung.

Im Einbenutzerbetrieb ist die Frage nach dem optimalen Parallelisierungsgrad äquivalent zu der Frage nach demjenigen Parallelisierungsgrad, der die geringste Antwortzeit bietet. Die Optimierungsentscheidung hängt in diesem Fall vorwiegend von statischen Parametern wie Datenverteilung, Relationengrößen, Zugriffsmethode und Schärfe von Selektionsprädikaten ab. Während im

---

1. Im Falle einer Ad-hoc-Anfrage beinhaltet eine Transaktion lediglich einen einzigen DML-Befehl. Intra-Transaktionsparallelität ist hier gleichbedeutend mit Intra-DML-Parallelität.

Einbenutzerbetrieb alle Betriebsmittel des DBS (CPU, Hauptspeicher, Datenobjekte,...) jeweils einer Anfrage exklusiv zur Verfügung stehen, zeichnet sich Mehrbenutzerbetrieb dadurch aus, daß die begrenzten Betriebsmittel geeignet zwischen konkurrenten Anfragen aufgeteilt werden müssen. Infolgedessen verlangt Mehrbenutzerbetrieb eine andere Definition des Optimalitätsbegriffs. Dort gilt es das Verhältnis zwischen Nutzen (Antwortzeitverkürzung) und Kosten (Kooperations- und Kommunikations-Overhead) der Parallelisierung in Abhängigkeit von der Systemauslastung zu optimieren mit dem Ziel, globale Antwortzeit- und Durchsatzvorgaben möglichst gut zu erfüllen. Der Parallelisierungsgrad im Mehrbenutzerbetrieb kann - je nach Systemauslastung - zum Teil deutlich von dem des Einbenutzerbetriebs abweichen [Marek und Rahm 1993, Rahm und Marek 1993].

Unser Ziel ist es, eine geeignete Unterstützung des Anfrageoptimierers bei der Bestimmung des optimalen Parallelisierungsgrades zu finden. Für den Einbenutzerbetrieb haben wir ein Kostenmodell entwickelt, das die Antwortzeitentwicklung in Abhängigkeit vom Parallelisierungsgrad beschreibt. Anhand dieses Modells können wir grundsätzliche Trade-offs der parallelen Anfragebearbeitung (z.B. Kommunikations-Overhead versus Parallelisierungsgewinn) untersuchen, ohne aufwendige Versuche basierend auf Simulationsmodellen oder Prototypimplementierungen paralleler DBS durchführen zu müssen. Mit Hilfe des Kostenmodells können wir in einfacher Weise den Einfluß signifikanter Systemparameter auf die Effektivität der Anfrageparallelisierung untersuchen. Das Kostenmodell kann ferner als Entscheidungshilfe zur Bestimmung einer geeigneten Datenverteilung genutzt werden.

Im folgenden Kapitel stellen wir ein abstraktes Modell der parallelen Anfragebearbeitung vor, aus dem wir das analytische Kostenmodell ableiten. Anhand einer detaillierten Betrachtung der parallelen Bearbeitung von unirelationalen Anfragen (*Scan-Anfragen*) schätzen wir in Kap. 3 die Koeffizienten des analytischen Kostenmodells ab. Daran anschließend wollen wir das Kostenmodell einschließlich der errechneten Koeffizienten anhand der parallelen Bearbeitung von Scan-Anfragen in Shared-Nothing-Systemen validieren. Dazu haben wir die parallele Bearbeitung von Anfragen mit Hilfe eines Simulationsmodells untersucht. Wir präsentieren in Kap. 4 die durchgeführten Versuche und bewerten das analytische Kostenmodell. In Kap. 5 werden wir die Übertragung des Kostenmodells auf Anfragen skizzieren, die zwei Relationen über einen Join-Operator miteinander verknüpfen.

2 Ein abstraktes Modell der parallelen Anfragebearbeitung

Zur Herleitung unseres Kostenmodells wollen wir uns auf ein einfaches Modell der parallelen Anfragebearbeitung stützen, das weitestmöglich von physischen Aspekten der Anfragebearbeitung abstrahiert. Wir unterstellen eine Shared-Nothing-Hardware bestehend aus n Knoten (PE), die über ein Kommunikationsnetzwerk miteinander verbunden sind. Das Parallelisierungsmodell besteht aus einer Verwaltungseinheit und einer Anzahl von Ausführungseinheiten. Die Ausführungseinheiten beschreiben diejenigen Teilaufgaben, die durch die Zerlegung einer parallel zu verarbeitenden (komplexeren) Aufgabe entstehen. Eine derartige Aufgabe kann beispielsweise die Bearbeitung eines DML-Befehles oder eines Operators (Scan, Join etc.) beinhalten. Die Verwaltungseinheit fungiert als Koordinator dieser Ausführungseinheiten. Sowohl die Verwaltungseinheit als auch die Ausführungseinheiten werden jeweils durch einen eigenen Prozeß repräsentiert und genau einem PE zugeordnet. Die Bearbeitung der gegebenen Aufgabe beginnt mit der Initialisierung der Ausführungseinheiten durch die Verwaltungseinheit. Dazu sendet der Verwalter Aktivierungsnachrichten an diejenigen PE, denen eine Ausführungseinheit zugeordnet werden soll. Wir unterstellen, daß diese Nachrichten sequentiell verschickt werden.

Mit Hilfe dieses Modells können wir sowohl Parallelität innerhalb einzelner Aufgaben als auch zwischen verschiedenen Aufgaben darstellen. Im letzteren Fall werden der Verwaltungseinheit mehrere Mengen von Ausführungseinheiten zugeordnet (Bild 1).

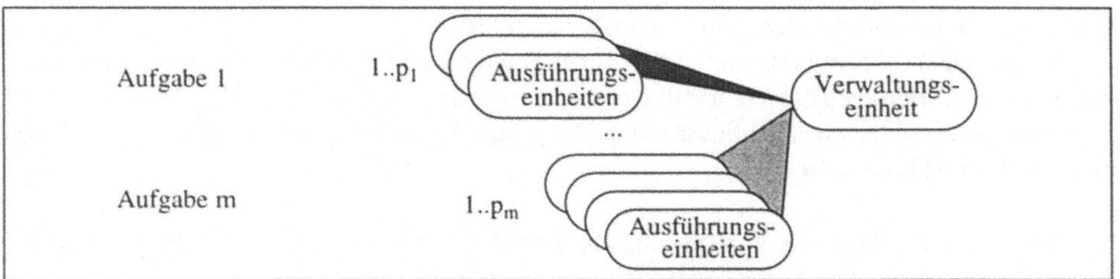

Bild 1: Ein abstraktes Modell der parallelen Anfragebearbeitung.

Wir wollen nun im folgenden untersuchen, wie sich die Bearbeitungszeit von Anfragen in Abhängigkeit von der Anzahl der Ausführungseinheiten verhält. Wir identifizieren dabei drei verschiedene Kostenanteile: ein konstanter (von der Anzahl der Ausführungseinheiten unabhängiger) Anteil, ein mit zunehmender Anzahl von Ausführungseinheiten abnehmender Anteil, sowie ein mit zunehmender Anzahl von Ausführungseinheiten steigender Kostenanteil. Im folgenden stellen wir eine allgemeine Betrachtung dieser Kostenterme vor und präzisieren den letztgenannten Kostenanteil (Parallelisierungsgewinn) in Abhängigkeit vom Speichermedium (Hauptspeicher bzw. Platte) der Operanden. Die Koeffizienten der Kostenformel werden wir auf analytischem Wege in Kap. 3 herleiten.

In [Wilschut et al. 1992] wurde ein ähnliches Kostenmodell vorgestellt. Im Gegensatz zu unserem Ansatz, der die Antwortzeit ganzer Anfragen (u.U. aus mehreren Operatoren bestehend) modelliert, beschränkt sich [Wilschut et al. 1992] auf einzelne Operatoren. Darüber hinaus wird in [Wilschut et al. 1992] der Einfluß des Speichermediums nicht explizit modelliert, und Operatoren mit superlinearen Verarbeitungskosten werden nicht berücksichtigt. Die Berechnung der Koeffizienten erfolgt in [Wilschut et al. 1992] auf Basis von Messungen an der Prototypimplementierung eines Hauptspeicher-DBS (*PRISMA/DB*). Wir wählen einen analytischen Ansatz (vgl. Kap. 3).

An dieser Stelle wollen wir hervorheben, daß das Kostenmodell auf einer weitreichenden Gleichverteilungsannahme basiert. Im Sinne einer praktikablen Kostenabschätzung berücksichtigen wir keine Streuung (*Skew* [Walton et al. 1991]) in den Verarbeitungskosten paralleler Ausführungseinheiten. Wir nehmen im folgenden an, daß Operanden zu parallelisierender Operatoren gleichmäßig auf alle Ausführungseinheiten verteilt werden und daß unter den parallelen Ausführungseinheiten keine Streuung in den Verarbeitungskosten pro Operand auftritt. Diese Annahmen implizieren beispielsweise eine gleichmäßige Datenverteilung der Basisrelationen auf Rechnerknoten, gleichmäßige E/A-Kosten pro Ausführungseinheit sowie einheitlich selektive Prädikate von Selektionsbefehlen verteilter Ausführungseinheiten. Sicherlich sollten weiterführende Arbeiten den Einfluß von Skew auf die Kostenentwicklung der Operatorparallelisierung berücksichtigen.

Konstanter Antwortzeitkostenanteil:

In der Antwortzeit sind im allgemeinen Kostenanteile enthalten, die von Parallelisierungsmaßnahmen unabhängig sind. Hierzu gehören vor allem Kosten für die Initialisierung der Anfrage sowie von der Parallelisierung nicht betroffene Operatoren. Beispielsweise erfordert die verteilte Berechnung einer Verbundoperation in der Regel das Mischen (*Merge*) der Treffertupel durch eine zentrale Instanz. Der Aufwand für die Merge-Operation hängt von der Anzahl der Treffertupel, nicht aber vom Parallelisierungsgrad des Verbundoperators ab. Derartige Kosten wollen wir mit einem konstanten Anteil a abschätzen.

Kooperations- und Kommunikationskosten:

Neben dem konstanten Kostenanteil ist in der Antwortzeit insbesondere auch der Aufwand für das Starten (und Beenden) der parallelen Ausführungseinheiten enthalten. Die hierbei anfallenden Kosten umfassen u.a. Aktivierungsnachrichten bzw. Quittungsmeldungen sowie Initialisierungskosten verteilter Ausführungseinheiten und sind proportional zur Anzahl der Ausführungseinheiten m:

(i) $$b \times m$$

Verkürzung der Bearbeitungszeit durch Parallelverarbeitung:

Im Falle relationaler Operatoren sind in der Regel Tupelmengen gegeben, auf die die Operatoren anzuwenden sind. Betragen die Verarbeitungskosten eines Operators pro Tupel c Zeiteinheiten und wachsen die Verarbeitungskosten linear mit der Tupelanzahl, so nimmt die sequentielle Verarbeitung aller M Tupel insgesamt

$$\text{(ii)} \qquad c \times M$$

Zeiteinheiten in Anspruch. Die Verarbeitung auf m Prozessorelementen dauert idealerweise lediglich

$$\text{(iii)} \qquad \frac{c \times M}{m}$$

Zeiteinheiten, wobei dieser Quotient gleichzeitig die Bearbeitungszeit einer jeden Ausführungseinheit angibt. Man spricht in diesem Falle von linearem *Speedup*. Der Speedup mißt die Verbesserung der Bearbeitungszeit einer Aufgabe durch Parallelisierung in m Ausführungseinheiten (bzw. PE) [Englert et al. 1990]. Dabei ist der Speedup definiert als Quotient der Bearbeitungszeit auf 1 PE und der Zeit, die für die Bearbeitung auf m PE benötigt wird (siehe unten).

Mit Hilfe der beschriebenen Kostenterme können wir nun abschätzen, wie sich die Parallelisierung von Operatoren mit linearen Verarbeitungskosten auf die Anfrageantwortzeit auswirkt. Für ein unirelationales SELECT beträgt die Anfrageantwortzeit R in Abhängigkeit vom Parallelisierungsgrad m des Scan-Operators

$$R(m) = a + b \times m + \frac{c \times M}{m}$$

Zeiteinheiten, wobei eine hauptspeicherresidente Speicherung der Eingaberelation angenommen ist. Wir können bei der parallelen Anfragebearbeitung eine Antwortzeitentwicklung beobachten, wie sie in Bild 2 dargestellt ist. Denjenigen Parallelisierungsgrad m_{opt}, der die geringste Antwortzeit erzielt, können wir ermitteln, indem wir die Ableitung der Kostenformel gleich Null setzen:

$$R'(m) = b - \frac{c \times M}{m^2} \qquad \text{und} \qquad R'(m_{opt}) = 0 \qquad \Rightarrow \qquad m_{opt} = \sqrt{\frac{c \times M}{b}}$$

Wir erkennen, daß dieser Parallelisierungsgrad unabhängig vom konstanten Kostenanteil a der Antwortzeit ist. Sind die Anzahl der von der Parallelisierung betroffen Tupel M, die Verarbeitungskosten c pro Tupel und die Initialisierungskosten b pro Ausführungseinheit bekannt, können wir nun mit Hilfe der Formel den optimalen Parallelisierungsgrad errechnen. Wir erkennen, daß dieser Parallelitätsgrad generell abhängig ist von dem Verhältnis zwischen Nutzarbeit $c*M$ und dem Parallelisierungs-Overhead b.

Die Effektivität der Operatorparallelisierung kann mit Hilfe des Antwortzeit-Speedups bewertet werden. In unserem Beispiel beträgt der Antwortzeit-Speedup:

$$\frac{R(1)}{R(m)} = \frac{a + b + c \times M}{a + b \times m + \dfrac{c \times M}{m}}$$

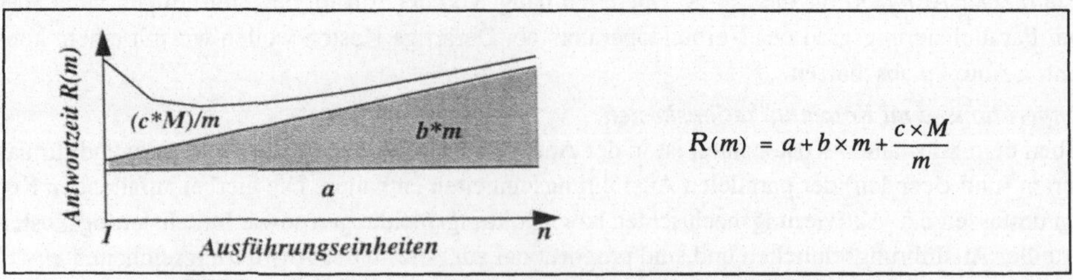

Bild 2: Einfluß der parallelen Anfragebearbeitung auf die Antwortzeit.

Im Gegensatz zum optimalen Parallelisierungsgrad ist die Effektivität der Anfrageparallelisierung vom konstanten Kostenanteil a abhängig. Ist dieser Anteil im Verhältnis zu den übrigen Kostenanteilen hoch, so hat die Operatorparallelisierung wenig Einfluß auf die Antwortzeitverbesserung der gesamten Anfrage (*die Operatorparallelisierung ist wenig effektiv*). Es sei bemerkt, daß linearer Speedup im Falle von $a=0$ und $b=0$ erzielt wird, d.h. wenn keinerlei Initialisierungskosten und Verzögerungen durch Nachrichten auftreten, so daß alle Ausführungseinheiten gleichzeitig beginnen.

Parallelisierung logarithmischer Operatoren:
Wie bereits erwähnt, liegt obigem Zusammenhang die Annahme linearer Verarbeitungskosten zugrunde, d.h., die Bearbeitungszeit verhält sich umgekehrt proportional zur Anzahl der eingesetzten PE. Wenngleich diese Annahme für einen Großteil der Implementierungen relationaler Operatoren erfüllt ist (z.B. unirelationale Selektion, Projektion ohne Duplikateleminierung, hash-basierte Join-Algorithmen etc.), unterliegen einige Algorithmen einer logarithmischen Kostenfunktion (z.B. Sortieralgorithmen, wie sie u.a. für die Implementierung von Sort-Merge-Joins benötigt werden). Der zugehörige Kostenterm läßt sich in analoger Weise zu linearen Kostenfunktionen beschreiben (vgl. Kap. 5).

Berücksichtigung von Platten-E/A:
Die bisher beschriebenen Kostenterme beinhalten diejenigen Operatorkosten, die beim Hauptspeicherzugriff der Operatoren auf deren Eingabetupel anfallen. Liegen die Eingabetupeln nicht im Hauptspeicher vor, so müssen die betreffenden Datenobjekte vom Sekundärspeicher (i.d.R. Platte) nachgeladen werden. Referenziert ein Operator während seiner Ausführung P Datenbankseiten, beträgt ferner die E/A-Kosten pro Seite io Zeiteinheiten und beträgt die Wahrscheinlichkeit, daß sich eine referenzierte Seite nicht im Hauptspeicher befindet f ($0 \leq f \leq 1$), so sind pro Ausführungseinheit zusätzlich zu den Hauptspeicherzugriffen

$$\text{(iv)} \qquad\qquad io \times \frac{P}{m} \times f$$

Zeiteinheiten für die Platten-E/A notwendig. Zu beachten ist hier, daß die Wahrscheinlichkeit für eine Fehlseitenbedingung, d.h. einen Plattenzugriff, von der Größe des verfügbaren Datenbankpuffers abhängig ist. Da der Datenbankpuffer wiederum mit der Anzahl m der Ausführungseinheiten zunimmt, verhält sich die Wahrscheinlichkeit für eine Fehlseitenbedingung umgekehrt proportional zur PE-Anzahl. Beträgt die Puffergröße eines PE B Seiten und umfaßt die referenzierte Relation D physische Seiten, so können wir (unter der Annahme, daß die Zugriffe auf alle DB-Seiten wahlfrei erfolgen und gleichverteilt sind) die Wahrscheinlichkeit f einer Fehlseitenbedingung mit folgender Annäherung abschätzen[2]:

$$\text{(v)} \qquad\qquad 1 - MIN\,(1, \frac{m \times B}{D})$$

Unter Berücksichtigung der Terme (iv) und (v) erkennen wir, daß mit zunehmender PE-Anzahl einerseits die Anzahl der Seitenreferenzen pro Ausführungseinheit abnimmt, andererseits aber auch die Fehlseitenwahrscheinlichkeit aufgrund wachsender Puffergröße abnimmt. Aus diesem Grunde können wir im Falle plattenallokierter Relationen im allgemeinen eine superlineare Antwortzeitverbesserung durch Anfrageparallelisierung erwarten [Marek und Rahm 1992].

In Kap. 4 werden wir die Koeffizienten der Kostenformel auf analytischem Wege ermitteln. Zu diesem Zweck wollen wir im folgenden Kapitel unsere Sicht der parallelen Anfrageverarbeitung präzisieren.

---

2. Dabei unterstellen wir Lokalität im Referenzierungsverhalten derart, daß Datenbankseiten einer Relation durch mehrere Benutzer bzw. Anfragen gemeinsam benutzt werden (*inter transaction locality* [Härder 1987]). Werden mehrere Relationen im gemeinsamen Puffer abgelegt, so vergrößert sich die Fehlseitenwahrscheinlichkeit entsprechend dem Umfang dieser Relationen. Liegt keinerlei Inter-Transaktions-Lokalität vor, so muß jede Anfrage im allgemeinen alle von ihr benötigten Datenbankseiten einlesen. Dies entspricht einer Fehlseitenwahrscheinlichkeit von 1.

3 Die Verfeinerung des Kostenmodells für Scan-Anfragen

Um nun die soeben hergeleitete Kostenformel effektiv nutzen zu können, müssen wir natürlich die Werte der bis jetzt noch unbekannten Koeffizienten der Formel kennen. Um zu einer adäquaten Abschätzung zu gelangen, werden wir unsere Sicht der parallelen Anfragebearbeitung präzisieren. Wir werden hierzu die Verarbeitungsschritte der parallelen Bearbeitung von Scan-Anfragen detailliert nachvollziehen und daraus eine Abschätzung der gesuchten Koeffizienten für Scan-Operatoren treffen.

3.1 Lastprofil

Die Anfragen, die wir hier zugrundelegen, verwenden den *Scan* als einzigen relationalen Basisoperator. Der Scan, ausgestattet mit einem Selektionsprädikat P, auf einer Relation A generiert einen relationalen Datenstrom als Ausgabe. Dazu liest der Scan alle Tupel der Eingaberelation, wendet das Prädikat P auf jedes Tupel an und fügt das Tupel zu der Ausgabemenge hinzu, falls es das Prädikat P erfüllt. Das Lesen aller Tupel der Eingaberelation (sog. Relationen-Scan) kann vermieden werden, wenn eine Indexstruktur (z.B. B*-Baum) den Zugriff nach dem Selektionsprädikat unterstützt. In diesem Fall werden, neben der Index-Information, nur die das Selektionsprädikat erfüllenden Tupel gelesen. Für die verteilte Anfragebearbeitung benötigen wir einen weiteren (Meta-) Operator: der sogenannte *Merge-Operator* "mischt" mehrere (sortierte) parallele Datenströme in einen sequentiellen Strom.

Wir wollen im folgenden untersuchen, wie sich die Anzahl der Ausführungseinheiten eines Scan-Operators auf die Gesamtkosten der Anfrage auswirkt. Dazu schätzen wir die Anzahl der notwendigen Instruktionen (Pfadlänge) bzw. Verzögerungen (Platten-E/A-Zeiten, Nachrichtenlaufzeiten) in Abhängigkeit von der Anzahl der Ausführungseinheiten in einer Näherung ab, die die wesentlichen Antwortzeitkostenanteile erfaßt.

Eine Anfrage wird in Form einer Transaktion ausgeführt, deren einziger DML-Befehl ein Selektionsbefehl auf einer Relation ist. Für unsere Kostenabschätzung wollen wir folgende Antwortzeitkomponenten heranziehen:

- Overhead für die Transaktionsverwaltung: d.h. Transaktions-Initialisierungskosten zu Beginn der Transaktion (BOT, Begin Of Transaction) sowie Kosten des verteilten Commit-Protokolls bei Ende der Transaktion (EOT, End Of Transaction),
- CPU-Kosten für den Zugriff auf Datenbankobjekte (Indexobjekte oder Tupeln von Basisrelationen bzw. temporären Relationen) im Hauptspeicher (z.B. Vergleich von Attributwerten oder Mischen von Eingabeströmen),
- CPU-Kosten für das Senden/Empfangen von Nachrichten sowie das Kopieren von Daten vom bzw. in den Hauptspeicher beim Senden/Empfangen von Aktivierungsnachrichten, Zwischenergebnissen und Commit-Nachrichten,
- Nachrichtenlaufzeiten über das Kommunikationsnetzwerk,
- sowie E/A-Kosten (CPU-Overhead, Kontroller-Belegungszeit, Seitenübertragungszeit sowie Plattenzugriffszeit) für Datenbankseiten, die nicht im Hauptspeicher verfügbar sind.

Die hier verwendeten Abkürzungen sind in Tabelle 2 aufgelistet.

3.2 Die parallele Verarbeitung von Scan-Anfragen

Im Falle eines unirelationalen Selektionsbefehls besteht die zugehörige Datenbankanfrage im wesentlichen aus einem Scan-Operator, der die Selektion auf der entsprechenden Basisrelation *i* ausführt. Der Grad an Intra-Operator-Parallelität wird durch die Datenverteilung statisch festgelegt, d.h., die Anzahl der Scan-Ausführungseinheiten entspricht im allgemeinen der Anzahl ($nrPE_i$) der Prozessorelemente, auf denen Partitionen der Relation allokiert sind (sofern einzelne PE - bei Über-

	Anzahl Instruktionen für:	m	Anzahl paralleler Operatorausführungseinheiten
bot	Initialisierung einer Transaktion	$kard_i$	Anzahl der Tupeln in Relation i
eot	Beendigung einer Transaktion	ts_i	Tupelgröße von Relation i (Bytes)
iscan	Initialisierung einer Scan-Ausführungseinheit	sel_i	Scan-Selektivitätsfaktor auf Relation i
		nrPE	Anzahl der involvierten PE
scan	Tupel- bzw. Indexreferenz beim Scan	$nrPE_i$	Anzahl PE, auf die Relation i verteilt ist
copy	Kopieren eines Bytes von/in Hauptspeicher	h_i	Höhe der Indexstruktur auf Relation i
		$block_i$	Blockungsfaktor von Relation i
merge * n	Mischen von n Tupeln	srs	Größe pro Scan-Ergebnistupel (Bytes)
receive	Empfangen einer Nachricht	buffer	Puffergröße pro PE (Seiten)
send	Senden einer Nachricht	mips	CPU-Leistung pro PE
nettime	Netzübertragungszeit pro Byte	io	E/A-Verzögerung pro Seite

Tabelle 2: Notation der Kostenabschätzung.

einstimmung von Verteilattribut der Relation und Selektionsattribut der Anfrage - nicht von der Anfrage ausgenommen werden können). Wir werden im folgenden betrachten, wie sich die Anzahl $nrPE_i$ der Scan-Ausführungseinheiten auf die Antwortzeit der Anfrage auswirkt.

Transaktionsverwaltungs-Overhead

Da wir uns hier v.a. auf Aspekte der Operatorparallelisierung konzentrieren, wollen wir eine einfache Modellierung der Transaktionsverwaltungskosten wählen. Die BOT-Kosten setzen wir als konstanten Anteil (*bot*) fest. Die EOT-Behandlung schließt die Ausführung des verteilten Zwei-Phasen-Commit-Protokolls [Mohan et al. 1986, Özsu und Valduriez 1991] ein, das alle PE ($nrPE_i$) betrifft, auf denen Ausführungseinheiten der Anfrage bearbeitet wurden. Die dabei entstehenden Kommunikationskosten berücksichtigen wir explizit. Legt man die in [Mohan et al. 1986] vorgeschlagene Optimierung zugrunde, bei der rein lesende Teilanfragen lediglich an der ersten Commit-Phase teilnehmen, so ist für die Scan-Anfrage nur eine Commit-Phase vonnöten. Die Verwaltungseinheit fordert alle beteiligten PE auf, die erste Commit-Phase einzuleiten (Sperrfreigabe), und wartet auf die Bestätigung der erfolgreichen Beendigung der verteilten Ausführungseinheiten, bevor die Transaktion endgültig beendet wird. Die Verwaltungseinheit sendet und empfängt somit $nrPE_i$ Nachrichten. Das Senden und Empfangen der Nachrichten in den verteilten Ausführungseinheiten wird überlappt durch diese Aktivitäten in der Verwaltungseinheit, so daß die Nachrichtenkosten der Ausführungseinheiten nicht in die Antwortzeit einfließen. Die lokalen EOT-Kostenanteile fassen wir in einem konstanten Anteil (*eot*) zusammen. Dieser Anteil umfaßt Kosten für lokales Logging sowie die Sperrfreigabe. Bei einer CPU-Leistung von *mips* MIPS pro PE ergibt sich folgende Bearbeitungszeit für die Transaktionsverwaltung:

$$(S1) \qquad TransManage = (bot + eot + nrPE_i \times (send + receive)) \times \frac{1}{mips}$$

Verarbeitung des Scan-Operators

Die Eingaberelation des Scans sei auf $nrPE_i$ Prozessorelemente verteilt. Für die Initialisierung der verteilten Scan-Ausführungseinheiten auf der Relation fällt pro Ausführungseinheit je eine Aktivierungsnachricht an. In jedem PE, dem eine Ausführungseinheit eines Scans zugeordnet ist, wird die Aktivierungsnachricht empfangen und die Ausführungseinheit initialisiert (*iscan*). Das Empfangen der Aktivierungsnachrichten und das Initialisieren der Scans erfolgt in den Ausführungseinheiten (durch das sequentielle Senden der Aktivierungsnachrichten zeitversetzt) parallel. Damit ergibt sich folgender Aufwand für die Initialisierung der Scans:

$$(S2) \qquad InitScan = (nrPE_i \times send + iscan + receive) \times \frac{1}{mips}$$

Bei der Berechnung der Kosten der verteilten Scan-Bearbeitung (Gleichung S3) gehen wir davon aus, daß die Tupelreferenzen eines Scans gleichmäßig auf die Ausführungseinheiten verteilt sind:

$$(S3) \quad ProcScan = \begin{cases} \left(\dfrac{kard_i}{nrPE_i}\right) \times \dfrac{scan}{mips} + io \times \left(\dfrac{kard_i}{block_i \times nrPE_i}\right) \times f_{rs} & \text{Relationen-Scan} \\[2em] \left(\dfrac{kard_i \times sel_i}{nrPE_i} + h_i\right) \times \dfrac{scan}{mips} + io \times \left(\dfrac{kard_i \times sel_1}{block_i \times nrPE_i}\right) \times f_{ind} & \text{Index mit Cluster-Bildung} \\[2em] \left(\left(\dfrac{kard_i \times sel_i}{nrPE_i}\right) \times 2 + h_i\right) \times \dfrac{scan}{mips} + io \times \left(\dfrac{kard_i \times sel_i}{nrPE_i}\right) \times f_{ind} & \text{Index ohne Cluster-Bildung} \end{cases}$$

Generell sind die Kosten der Scan-Ausführungseinheiten proportional zu der Anzahl der Tupel- bzw. Indexreferenzen. Im Falle von Relationen-Scans muß in jeder Ausführungseinheit jeweils die gesamte lokale Partition sequentiell durchlaufen werden ($kard_i/nrPE_i$ Tupeln). Dabei werden - entsprechend dem Blockungsfaktor $block_i$ der Relation - alle lokalen, d.h. genau $kard_i/(nrPE_i*block_i)$ Datenbankseiten referenziert. Die hierfür notwendigen E/A-Kosten schätzen wir mit io Zeiteinheiten pro Seite ab[3]. Diese Konstante umfaßt sowohl den CPU-Overhead einer E/A-Operation als auch die E/A-Verzögerungszeit (Plattenzugriffszeit, Übertragungszeit und Kontroller-Belegungszeit). Die Wahrscheinlichkeit, daß sich eine referenzierte Seite nicht bereits im Hauptspeicher befindet und von Platte gelesen werden muß (Fehlseitenbedingung), betrage dabei f_{rs} (siehe unten). Kann eine Indexstruktur für den Zugriff genutzt werden, so werden - neben den Referenzen auf die Indexstruktur - lediglich die das Selektionsprädikat erfüllenden Tupeln referenziert. In jeder Scan-Ausführungseinheit wird ein Anteil von sel_i der lokalen Tupeln als Treffer bestimmt. Im Falle einer Indexstruktur, die die Tupel nach dem Zugriffsattribut clustert (d.h. Tupel mit dem gleichen Attributwert in der selben physischen Seite ablegt), genügt ein einmaliger Durchlauf der Indexstruktur, d.h., jede Ebene wird einmal referenziert. Sind die Datenseiten untereinander verkettet, so fallen keine weiteren Indexreferenzen an, so daß die Index-Zugriffskosten proportional zur Höhe h_i der Indexstruktur sind. Liegt eine Clusterung der Datenbankobjekte nach dem Zugriffsattribut vor, so müssen lediglich $(kard_i*sel_i)/(nrPE_i*block_i)$ Datenbankseiten referenziert werden, wobei wir die Wahrscheinlichkeit einer Fehlseitenbedingung mit f_{ind} (siehe unten) beschreiben[4]. Bei einer Indexstruktur ohne Cluster-Bildung muß in der Regel die unterste Ebene der Indexstruktur vor jeder Tupelreferenz referenziert werden, da hier keine Verkettung der Datenseiten untereinander genutzt werden kann. Insgesamt werden somit $(kard_i*sel_i)/(nrPE_i)$ Einträge der Indexseiten und ebenso viele Tupel gelesen. Außerdem wird im allgemeinen bei jeder Tupelreferenz eine neue Datenbankseite referenziert, und es ist mit der Wahrscheinlichkeit f_{ind} eine E/A-Operation erforderlich. In diesem Fall sind daher $f_{ind}*(kard_i*sel_i)/nrPE_i$ E/A-Vorgänge notwendig. Für die Wahrscheinlichkeit einer Fehlseitenbedingung verwenden wir folgende Abschätzung:

$$f_{rs} = \begin{cases} 1 & \text{falls } buffer < kard_i/(block_i*nrPE_i) \\ & \quad\quad\quad\quad\quad\quad\quad\quad\quad\quad \text{Relationen-Scan} \\ 0 & \text{falls } buffer \geq kard_i/(block_i*nrPE_i) \end{cases}$$

$$f_{ind} = 1 - MIN\left(1, \frac{nrPE_i \times buffer \times block_i}{kard_i}\right) \quad\quad \text{Indexunterstützung}$$

Aufgrund des sequentiellen Referenzierungsmusters des Relationen-Scans sind keine Treffer zu erwarten ($f_{rs} = 1$), wenn die $kard_i/(block_i*nrPE_i)$ Datenbankseiten der $nrPE_i$ lokalen Partitionen der

---

3. Hier wird vereinfachend angenommen, daß Seitenzugriffe in wahlfreier und sequentieller Reihenfolge gleich teuer sind. Bietet das E/A-System kürzere Zugriffszeiten bei sequentiellem Zugriffsmuster (z.B. infolge kürzerer Plattenzugriffszeiten oder bei Unterstützung von Prefetching), so ist dies durch Definition zugriffsmusterspezifischer E/A-Kosten zu berücksichtigen.
4. Wir berücksichtigen an dieser Stelle keine E/A von Indexseiten. Indexseiten höherer Baumebenen können aufgrund ihrer hohen Referenzierungshäufigkeit zumeist von der Pufferverwaltung im Hauptspeicher gehalten werden. Für Blatt-Indexseiten kann der E/A-Aufwand analog zu den Datenobjekten abgeschätzt werden.

Basisrelation nicht in die lokalen Puffer (*buffer* Seitenrahmen) der PE passen. Sobald die lokalen Partitionen im Puffer Platz finden, ist keine E/A erforderlich ($f_{rs} = 0$). Im Falle des indexunterstützten Datenzugriffes nehmen wir eine Gleichverteilung der Seitenreferenzen auf die Datenbankseiten an, so daß die in Kap. 2 vorgestellte Formel für wahlfreie gleichverteilte Zugriffe zur Anwendung kommt. Die Gesamtanzahl der Datenbankseiten berechnet sich als Quotient aus Kardinalität und Blockungsfaktor der Relation[5].

Mischen der lokalen Scan-Ergebnisströme

Nach erfolgter Bearbeitung der lokalen Scan-Ausführungseinheiten müssen die verteilten Ergebnismengen gemischt werden. Dazu sendet jede Scan-Ausführungseinheit ihre Treffertupel in Verbindung mit einer Quittungsmeldung an die Verwaltungseinheit. Bei einer Gesamtanzahl von $kard_i{*}sel_i$ Ergebnistupeln nehmen wir $(kard_i{*}sel_i)/nrPE_i$ Ergebnistupel pro Scan-Ausführungseinheit an. Jede Ausführungseinheit sendet somit eine Nachricht und kopiert die $(kard_i{*}sel_i)/nrPE_i$ lokalen Treffertupel der Tupelgröße *srs* vom Hauptspeicher in das Kommunikationsmedium, wobei pro Byte ein Kopieraufwand von *copy* Instruktionen berechnet wird:

$$(\text{S4}) \qquad SendRes = \frac{send}{mips} + \frac{copy}{mips} \times \left(\frac{kard_i \times sel_i \times srs}{nrPE_i} \right)$$

Da die Ergebnisnachrichten recht umfangreich sein können, werden sie unter Umständen signifikant durch das Kommunikationsnetzwerk verzögert. Unterstellen wir eine hinreichend große Bandbreite des Netzwerkes, die eine weitestgehend kollisionsfreie Übertragung mehrerer Nachrichten erlaubt, und dauert die Übertragung eines Bytes *nettime*[6] Zeiteinheiten, so wird jede der $(kard_i{*}sel_i{*}\text{srs})/nrPE_i$ Bytes großen Ergebnisnachrichten um folgende Dauer verzögert:

$$(\text{S5}) \qquad Transmission = \left(\frac{kard_i \times sel_i \times srs}{nrPE_i} \right) \times nettime$$

Die Verwaltungseinheit empfängt pro Ausführungseinheit eine Nachricht und kopiert alle $kard_i{*}sel_i$ Treffertupeln in den lokalen Hauptspeicher:

$$(\text{S6}) \qquad ReceiveRes = \frac{receive}{mips} \times nrPE_i + \frac{copy}{mips} \times kard_i \times sel_i \times srs$$

Die Ergebnisströme werden schließlich mit linearem Aufwand gemischt, wobei dieser Aufwand nur bei $nrPE_i{>}1$ Ausführungseinheiten berechnet wird:

$$(\text{S7}) \qquad MergeRes = kard_i \times sel_i \times \frac{merge}{mips}$$

Der Gesamtaufwand - gemessen in Zeiteinheiten - für die Anfrage ergibt sich aus der Summe der Kostenterme (S1) bis (S7). Aus diesen Termen wollen wir nun die gesuchten Koeffizienten der Kostenformel aus Kap. 2 ermitteln.

Im allgemeinen Fall der parallelen Bearbeitung von Scan-Anfragen kommt die folgende Kostenformel zur Anwendung (vgl. Kap. 2), die die Anfrageantwortzeit in Abhängigkeit von der Anzahl $nrPE_i$ der Scan-Ausführungseinheiten beschreibt:

$$R(nrPE_i) = a + b \times nrPE_i + \frac{c \times M}{nrPE_i} + io \times \frac{P}{nrPE_i} \times f$$

---

5. In dieser Arbeit steht vor allem der Aspekt der Parallelverarbeitung im Vordergrund. Wir begnügen uns daher mit einer vergleichsweise einfachen Abschätzung lokaler Verarbeitungskosten (insb. Anzahl physischer Seitenzugriffe und Puffer-Trefferraten), welche für unsere Zwecke eine hinreichende Güte bietet. Ist eine detailliertere Berücksichtigung der E/A-Kosten erforderlich, so können diesbezüglich aus der Literatur bekannte Kostenabschätzungen integriert werden [Waters 1976, Yao 1977, Mackert und Lohman 1989].
6. In der Regel werden als Übertragungsgranulat Pakete fester Größe angeboten. Beispielsweise überträgt das Netzwerk der EDS-Maschine Datenpakete der Größe 128 Bytes (zzgl. Verwaltungsinformation) in 8 Mikrosekunden [Watson und Townsend 1991].

Indexobjekte wollen wir im folgenden als hauptspeicherresident annehmen. Sind auch die Daten-objekte hauptspeicherresident, so gilt für die Wahrscheinlichkeit f einer Fehlseitenbedingung $f=0$, so daß der letzte Term aus der Kostenformel herausfällt. Ist die Basisrelation auf Platten allokiert, so können die oben ermittelten Wahrscheinlichkeiten für Fehlseitenbedingungen f_{rs} und f_{ind} - in Abhängigkeit von der Zugriffsmethode - für f eingesetzt werden.

Die Anzahl M der Objektreferenzen pro Scan-Anfrage ist abhängig von der Zugriffsmethode und der Anfrageselektivität:

$$M = \begin{cases} kard_i & \text{Relationen-Scan} \\ kard_i \times sel_i & \text{Index mit Cluster-Bildung} \\ kard_i \times sel_i \times 2 & \text{Index ohne Cluster-Bildung} \end{cases}$$

Ohne Indexunterstützung muß die gesamte Relation gelesen werden ($kard_i$ Referenzen). Bei Index-unterstützung mit Cluster-Bildung kann direkt auf die Tupel, die das Selektionskriterium erfüllen ($kard_i * sel_i$), zugegriffen werden. Ohne Cluster-Bildung ist vor jedem Tupelzugriff anhand eines Zugriffs auf einen Eintrag der Indexstruktur festzustellen, in welcher Seite sich das gesuchte Tupel befindet, so daß insgesamt ($2 * kard_i * sel_i$) Referenzen zu bearbeiten sind.

Für die Anzahl P der Seitenreferenzen gilt entsprechend folgende Unterscheidung:

$$P = \begin{cases} \dfrac{kard_i}{block_i} & \text{Relationen-Scan} \\[2ex] \dfrac{kard_i \times sel_i}{block_i} & \text{Index mit Cluster-Bildung} \\[2ex] kard_i \times sel_i & \text{Index ohne Cluster-Bildung} \end{cases}$$

Bringt man nun die Kostenterme der Gleichungen (S1) bis (S7) in die Form der obigen Kostenfor-mel $R(m)$, so erhält man für die Koeffizienten a, b und c folgende Werte:

$$a_1 = \frac{bot + eot + iscan + receive + send + (copy \times kard_i \times sel_i \times srs)}{mips} + \begin{cases} \dfrac{h_i \times scan}{mips} & \text{Index} \\ 0 & \text{kein Index} \end{cases}$$

$$a = a_1 + \frac{merge}{mips} \times kard_i \times sel_i \quad \text{für } nrPE_i > 1$$

$$b = \frac{2 \times send + 2 \times receive}{mips}$$

$$c = \frac{scan}{mips} + \begin{cases} (\dfrac{copy}{mips} + nettime) \times sel_i \times srs & \text{Relationen-Scan} \\[2ex] (\dfrac{copy}{mips} + nettime) \times srs & \text{Index mit Cluster-Bildung} \\[2ex] (\dfrac{copy}{mips} + nettime) \times \dfrac{srs}{2} & \text{Index ohne Cluster-Bildung} \end{cases}$$

Werden die verteilten Ergebnisströme nur bei einer wirklichen Scan-Parallelisierung gemischt, so ergibt sich obige Unterscheidung zwischen $nrPE_i = 1$ (sequentielle Bearbeitung) und $nrPE_i > 1$ (pa-rallele Bearbeitung) Ausführungseinheiten für den Koeffizienten a.

Im Zuge der Simulationsversuche in Kap. 4 werden wir die Werte dieser Koeffizienten entspre-chend der Parametrisierung des Simulationssystems errechnen und die Kostenformel validieren.

4 Validierung des Kostenmodells paralleler Anfragebearbeitung

In diesem Kapitel untersuchen wir das Leistungsverhalten der parallelen Verarbeitung von unirelationalen Anfragen. Unser Ziel ist es zu überprüfen, wie gut das entwickelte Kostenmodell das beobachtete Leistungsverhalten annähert.

Für Leistungsanalysen der parallelen Anfragebearbeitung haben wir in einem umfassenden Simulationsmodell ein generisches Shared-Nothing-System hinsichtlich seiner Architektur und seiner Verarbeitungskonzepte modelliert. Dieses Modell wollen wir hier zur Validierung des Kostenmodells heranziehen.

In vorhergehenden Simulationsstudien ([Marek und Rahm 1992] und [Marek und Rahm 1993]) wurde bereits darauf verwiesen, daß das Simulationssystem das Verhalten realer Systeme hinreichend gut annähert, so daß wir von einer korrekten Modellierung des Simulationsansatzes ausgehen können. In [Marek und Rahm 1992; Marek 1993] wurden Versuche zur Parallelisierung von Scan-Anfragen durchgeführt. Insbesondere wurde die Effektivität der Parallelisierung in Abhängigkeit von den Einflußgrößen Zugriffsmethode und Anfrageselektivität betrachtet. Das beobachtete Verhalten deckt sich weitestgehend mit Ergebnissen von Messungen an dem (plattenbasierten) Shared-Nothing-System Gamma [DeWitt et al. 1990]. Die Gemeinsamkeiten zwischen unserem Simulationsansatz und den in Gamma gemessenen Werten beziehen sich u.a. auf den Antwortzeit-Speedup und das relative Antwortzeitverhalten von parallel bearbeiteten Scan-Anfragen beim Zugriff mit verschiedenen Zugriffsmethoden und Selektivitäten. Abweichungen sind in den absoluten Antwortzeitergebnissen gegeben - die absoluten Abweichungen sind jedoch ausschließlich eine Frage der Parametrisierung des Simulationssystems.

Insgesamt bietet das Simulationssystem somit eine hinreichend genaue Annäherung an das Verhalten realer Systeme bei der parallelen Anfragebearbeitung, so daß wir uns bei der nun folgenden Validierung des Kostenmodells auf unser Simulationssystem - stellvertretend für ein reales System - beziehen dürfen.

Wir geben in Abschnitt 4.1 einen Überblick über die Parametrisierung des Shared-Nothing-Modells und der Datenbankanfragen. Aus den Simulationsparametern berechnen wir die Koeffizienten der Kostenformeln für Scan- und Join-Anfragen und präsentieren schließlich in Abschnitt 4.2 die Ergebnisse der durchgeführten Simulationsversuche.

4.1 Parametrisierung der Simulationsversuche

Tabelle 3 faßt die wesentlichen Einstellungen der Datenbank- sowie der Anfrage- und Systemparameter zusammen. Die meisten Parameter sind selbsterklärend; einige werden wir bei der Diskussion der Ergebnisse erläutern. Die unirelationalen Anfragen führen je einen Scan auf der Eingaberelation A (250.000 Tupel) durch. Wir untersuchen, wie sich der Parallelisierungsgrad des Scan-Operators auf die Anfrageantwortzeit in Abhängigkeit von der Anfrageselektivität, der Zugriffsmethode sowie dem Speichermedium (Hauptspeicher bzw. Platte) auswirkt. Dazu variieren wir die Datenverteilung von Relation A zwischen 1 und 40 PE. Wir vergleichen den sequentiellen Zugriff (Relationen-Scan) mit einem index-unterstützten Zugriff. Für jede lokale Datenpartition nehmen wir einen B*-Baum mit je zwei Ebenen an. Wir untersuchen sowohl nach dem Zugriffsattribut geclusterte, als auch nach einem anderen als dem Zugriffsattribut geclusterte Zugriffsstrukturen. Wir betrachten hier Anfragen, die auf dem Anfrageprofil und dem Datenbankschema des Wisconsin-Benchmarks basieren [Gray 1991]. Dieser Benchmark wurde häufig für Leistungsanalysen paralleler Datenbanksysteme herangezogen [Englert et al. 1990, DeWitt et al. 1990, Wilschut et al. 1992].

Die Parameter des E/A-Systems wurden so gewählt, daß keine Engpässe auftraten (genügend große Anzahl von Platten und Kontrollern). Die Dauer einer E/A-Operation setzt sich zusammen aus der

Kontroller-Belegungszeit, der Platten-Zugriffszeit sowie der Übertragungszeit. Die Parameter des Kommunikationsnetzwerkes wurden entsprechend dem EDS-Prototypen [Watson und Townsend 1991] festgelegt.

4.2 Versuchsreihen zur parallelen Scan-Verarbeitung

In dieser Versuchsreihe untersuchen wir die Effektivität der parallelen Verarbeitung von Scan-Operatoren. Wir variieren den Parallelitätsgrad des Scan-Operators in Abhängigkeit von der Datenverteilung der Eingaberelation zwischen 1 und 40 PE. Insbesondere betrachten wir, wie sich die Koeffizienten der Kostenformel R in Abhängigkeit von Zugriffsmethode, Anfrageselektivität und Speichermedium der Eingaberelation verhalten. Wir gehen zunächst von einer hauptspeicherresidenten Speicherung der Eingaberelation aus, und untersuchen anschließend, wie sich die Plattenallokation auf die Anfrageparallelisierung auswirkt.

Im Falle von Scan-Anfragen unterliegt die Antwortzeit in Abhängigkeit von der Anzahl m der Scan-Ausführungseinheiten folgender Kostenformel (vgl. Kap. 3):

$$R(1) = a_1 + b + c \times M + io \times P \times f \quad \text{für } m = 1, \text{ und } \quad R(m) = a + b \times m + \frac{c \times M}{m} + io \times \frac{P}{m} \times f \quad \text{für } m > 1$$

Durch Einsetzen der Simulationsparameter in die zugehörigen Gleichungen aus Kap. 3 erhalten wir die Werte der Koeffizienten dieser Kostenformel. Tabelle 4 zeigt die Koeffizienten in Abhängigkeit

Zugriffsmethode	Selektivität [%]	M	a1 [ms]	a [ms]	b [ms]	c [ms]	P	io [ms]
Index (geclustert)	0.1	250	6.16	7.41	1.5	0.06875	7	16.55
	1.0	2500	20.225	32.725			63	
	10.0	25000	160.85	285.85			625	
Index (nicht geclustert)	0.1	500	6.16	7.41		0.05937	250	
	1.0	5000	20.225	32.725			2500	
	10.0	50000	160.85	285.85			25000	
Relationen-Scan	1.0	250000	20.125	32.625		0.05018	6250	

Tabelle 4: Koeffizientenwerte der Kostenformel R.

von Zugriffsmethode und Selektivität. Für die Wahrscheinlichkeit f einer Fehlseitenbedingung gilt $f=0$ im Falle einer hauptspeicherresidenten Allokation der Basisrelation. Ist die Basisrelation auf

Systemkonfiguration	Parameterwerte	Systemkonfiguration	Parameterwerte
Anzahl PE	40	**Pufferverwaltung:**	
CPU-Leistung pro PE	20 MIPS	Seitengröße	8 KB
		Puffergröße pro PE	250 Seiten (2MB)
Mittl. Anzahl Instruktionen:		**Kommunikationsnetzwerk:**	
BOT	25000	Paketgröße	128 Bytes
EOT	25000	mittlere Übertragungszeit	8 Mikrosekunden
Initialisierung von Scan-Ausführungseinheiten	25000	**Relation A:**	(50MB)
E/A	3000	Anzahl Tupel	250.000
Nachricht senden	5000	Tupelgröße	200 Bytes
Nachricht empfangen	10000	Tupeln pro Seite	40
Kopieren einer 8 KByte		Indextyp	B^*-Baum mit Cluster-Bildung
Nachricht in Hauptspeicher	5000	Höhe der Indexstruktur	2
Scan-Objektreferenz	1000	Speichermedium	Hauptspeicher/Platte
Mischen von n Tupeln	n * 100	PE-Zuordnung	1 bis 40
Plattengeräte:		**Scan-Anfragen**	auf Relation A
Kontroller-Belegungszeit	1 ms (pro Seite)	Zugriffsmethode	via Index/ sequentiell
Übertragungszeit pro Seite	0.4 ms	Selektivität	0.1%-10% der Tupel
mittl. Plattenzugriffszeit	15 ms	Scan-Ausführungseinheiten	1-40

Tabelle 3: Datenbank-, Anfrage- und Systemparameter.

Platten allokiert, so gilt in Abhängigkeit von der Zugriffsmethode:

$$f = \begin{cases} 1 & \text{falls } m < 25 \\ 0 & \text{falls } m >= 25 \end{cases} \qquad \text{für Relationen-Scans}$$

$$f = 1 - MIN\,(1, m \times 0.4) \qquad \text{bei Indexunterstützung}$$

Die lokale Puffergröße beträgt in unserem Versuchen 250 Seiten. Die Tupel von Relation A sind auf 6250 Seiten verteilt (Blockungsfaktor 40). Für 25 oder mehr PE paßt Relation A somit vollständig in die verteilten Puffer der PE, so daß die Tupelreferenzen ausschließlich durch Hauptspeicherzugriffe bearbeitet werden können. Die Zugriffskosten pro Datenbankseite betragen für alle Versuchsreihen konstant 16.55 ms.

Hauptspeicherresidente Allokation der Eingaberelation

Bild 3 zeigt die beobachteten Antwortzeiten der parallelen Scan-Verarbeitung in Abhängigkeit von der Zugriffsmethode und Anfrageselektivität und vergleicht sie mit den aus der Kostenformel R resultierenden Antwortzeitkurven. Wir erkennen, daß die Kostenformel für alle Versuchsreihen eine sehr gute Näherung der beobachteten Antwortzeiten bietet. Sowohl die qualitative Entwicklung der Antwortzeiten, als auch die absoluten Antwortzeitwerte stimmen weitgehend überein.

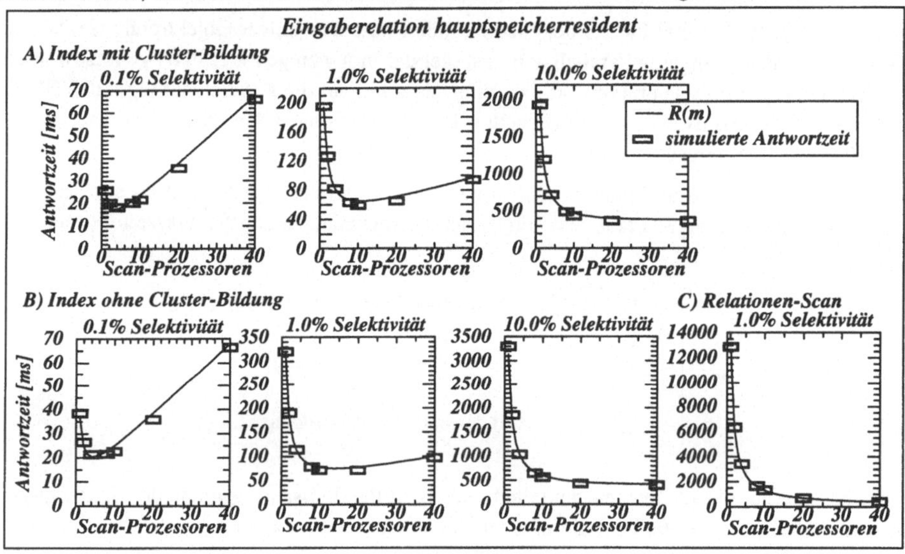

Bild 3: Einfluß von Zugriffsmethode und Anfrageselektivität auf die Effektivität der Parallelisierung von Scan-Operatoren bei hauptspeicherresidenter Speicherung der Eingaberelation.

Wir erkennen, daß die Anfrageparallelisierung v.a. für diejenigen Anfragen deutliche Antwortzeitverbesserungen bietet, die hohe Einprozessor-Antwortzeiten (sequentielle Verarbeitung) aufweisen. Ein geringes Parallelisierungspotential ist dagegen bei Indexunterstützung und hoher Anfrageselektivität vorhanden. In diesen Fällen erweist sich nur eine geringe Anzahl von Ausführungseinheiten als sinnvoll. Bei zu hoher Parallelisierung sind infolge des Kommunikations-Overheads sogar starke Antwortzeitverschlechterungen zu beobachten[7]. Dieses Verhalten schlägt sich auch in den zugehörigen Speedup-Kurven nieder (Bild 4). Lediglich im Falle des Relationen-Scans kann über eine große PE-Anzahl hinweg nahezu linearer Speedup erzielt werden (Speedup 19 bei

---

7. Eine detaillierte Diskussion findet der Leser in [Marek und Rahm 1992].

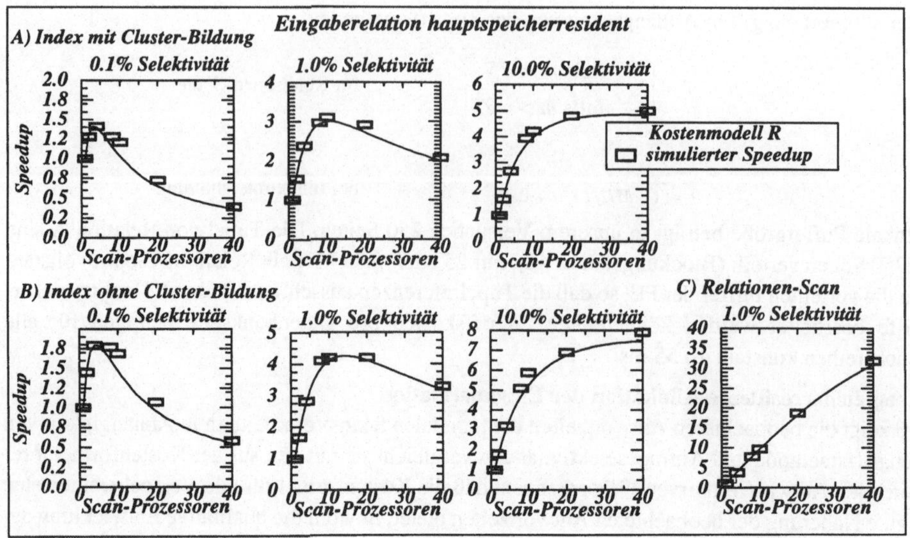

Bild 4: Einfluß von Zugriffsmethode und Anfrageselektivität auf den Antwortzeit-Speedup.

20 PE bzw. 31 bei 40 PE). Bei Indexunterstützung fallen weitaus weniger Objektreferenzen an, so daß hier aufgrund des geringeren Parallelisierungspotentials nur wenige PE effektiv genutzt werden können. Bei hoher Anfrageselektivität (0.1%) führt nicht einmal die Parallelisierung auf 2 PE zu einer linearen Antwortzeitverbesserung (Speedup 1.2 bei einem nach dem Zugriffsattribut geclusterten Index und 1.45 ohne Clusterung).

Mit Hilfe der ermittelten Koeffizienten können wir durch Ableitung der Kostenformel R für jede der Versuchsreihen denjenigen Parallelisierungsgrad m errechnen, der das Antwortzeitoptimum erzielt:

$$m_{opt} = \begin{cases} \sqrt{\dfrac{0.05018 \times M}{1.5}} & \text{Relationen-Scan (1.0\% Selekt.)} \\[2ex] \sqrt{\dfrac{0.06875 \times M}{1.5}} & \text{Index mit Cluster-Bildung} \\[2ex] \sqrt{\dfrac{0.05937 \times M}{1.5}} & \text{Index ohne Cluster-Bildung} \end{cases}$$

Tabelle 5 faßt die auf diesem Wege ermittelten optimalen Parallelisierungsgrade des Scan-Operators bei hauptspeicherresidenter Speicherung der Eingaberelation zusammen.

Zugriffsmethode	Selektivität [%]	M	m_{opt}
Index mit Cluster-Bildung	0.1	250	3
	1.0	2500	11
	10.0	25000	34
Index ohne Cluster-Bildung	0.1	500	5
	1.0	5000	14
	10.0	50000	45
Relationen-Scan	1.0	250000	91

Tabelle 5: Optimale Anzahl der Scan-Ausführungseinheiten in Abhängigkeit von Zugriffsmethode und Anfrageselektivität.

Ist das typische Anfrageprofil (Anfragetypen und deren Anteile an der gesamten Anfragelast) auf einer gegebenen Relation A bekannt, so können wir auf diese Weise eine Abschätzung eines geeigneten Datenverteilungsgrades für diese Relation treffen. Werden beispielsweise 40% der Anfragen auf Relation *A* durch einen nach dem Zugriffsattribut geclusterten Index, weitere 40% durch einen Index ohne Clusterung sowie 20% der Anfragen durch einen Relationen-Scan bearbeitet, und beträgt die Anfrageselektivität jeweils 1%, so bietet ein Datenverteilungsgrad (= Scan-Parallelisierungsgrad) von 28 eine im Mittel optimale Parallelisierung der Scan-Operatoren auf Relation *A* (vgl. Tabelle 6)[8].

Anfragetypen mit Zugriffsmethode	Selektivität [%]	Anteil an der Gesamtlast [%]	m_{opt}	m_{opt} (global)
Index (mit Cluster-Bildung)	1.0	40.0	11	0.4 * 11
Index (ohne Cluster-Bildung)	1.0	40.0	14	0.4 * 14
Relationen-Scan	1.0	20.0	91	0.2 * 91
				28

Tabelle 6: Optimale Anzahl der Scan-Ausführungseinheiten für einen Anfrage-Mix.

Zu beachten ist jedoch, daß lediglich ein im Mittel optimaler Datenverteilungsgrad bestimmt und ausgewählt werden kann. Auf Basis der gewählten Datenverteilung müssen alle Anfragen bearbeitet werden. Anfragen mit einem von diesem Datenverteilungsgrad abweichenden optimalen Parallelisierungsgrad werden unter Umständen stark benachteiligt. Bei großen Änderungen im Lastprofil ist daher im allgemeinen eine Reorganisation der Datenbank (im laufenden Betrieb) notwendig.

Plattenallokation der Eingaberelation
Zur Validierung der Kostenformel *R* für Scan-Operatoren bei Plattenallokation der Eingaberelation haben wir Versuche mit und ohne indexunterstütztem Datenzugriff bei einer Anfrageselektivität von 1.0% durchgeführt (Indexobjekte wurden als hauptspeicherresident angenommen).

Bild 5 zeigt die beobachteten Antwortzeiten der parallelen Scan-Verarbeitung im Falle der Plattenallokation in Abhängigkeit von der Zugriffsmethode im Vergleich zu den aus der Kostenformel *R* resultierenden Antwortzeitkurven. Die Kostenformel *R* bietet auch im Falle der Plattenallokation der Basisrelation eine gute Näherung der beobachteten Antwortzeiten.
Grundsätzlich sind gegenüber dem hauptspeicherbasierten Fall - je nach Anzahl der Seitenzugriffe - starke Antwortzeitverschlechterungen zu beobachten. Die Parallelisierung erlaubt jedoch stärkere Antwortzeitverbesserungen als sie im hauptspeicherbasierten Fall gemessen wurden. Anfragen mit vielen Seitenreferenzen (Relationen-Scan und Index ohne Cluster-Bildung) erlauben bis zu einer gewissen Anzahl von Ausführungseinheiten zum Teil sogar superlineare Antwortzeitverbesserungen. Ab 25 PE paßt die gesamte Relation in die verteilten Puffer (Trefferrate 100% ab 25 PE), so

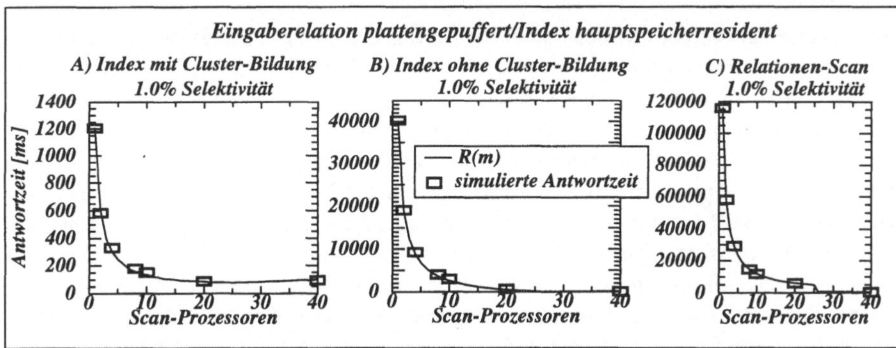

Bild 5: Einfluß von Zugriffsmethode und Anfrageselektivität auf die Effektivität der Parallelisierung von Scan-Operatoren bei Plattenpufferung der Eingaberelation.

---

8. Hierbei ist angenommen, daß das Optimum für den Anfragemix durch Linearkombination der einzelnen Optima berechnet werden kann. Im allgemeinen kann das Optimum z.B. durch ein Programm berechnet werden, welches für jeden möglichen Datenverteilungsgrad die Antwortzeit des Anfragemixes aus den Antwortzeiten der einzelnen Anfragetypen ermittelt.

daß die gemessenen Antwortzeiten denen des hauptspeicherbasierten Falles entsprechen. Während die Trefferraten bei Indexunterstützung bis 24 PE linear mit der PE-Anzahl wachsen, werden beim Relationen-Scan bis 24 PE keine Treffer im Puffer erzielt. Dies erklärt den Knick der Antwortzeitkurve zwischen 24 und 25 PE im Falle des Relationen-Scans.

Auch hier können wir nun durch Ableitung der Kostenformel diejenige Anzahl der Ausführungseinheiten bestimmen, die die niedrigste Antwortzeit ermöglicht. In Abhängigkeit von der globalen Puffergröße und der Anzahl der Datenseiten von Relation A beträgt R:

$$R(m) = \begin{cases} a + b \times m + \dfrac{c \times M}{m} + e \times \dfrac{P}{m} \times (1 - \dfrac{m \times B}{D}) & \text{Index-Scan} \quad \text{(i)} \\[2ex] a + b \times m + \dfrac{c \times M}{m} + e \times \dfrac{P}{m} & \text{Relationen-Scan} \quad \text{(ii)} \end{cases} \quad \text{falls } m < 25$$

$$a + b \times m + \dfrac{c \times M}{m} \qquad \text{falls } m >= 25 \qquad \text{(iii)}$$

Mit Hilfe der Steigungen der Teilfunktionen (i) bis (iii) können wir auch hier das Antwortzeitminimum der Kostenfunktion R errechnen. Tabelle 7 zeigt die errechnete optimale Anzahl von Ausfüh-

Zugriffsmethode	Selektivität [%]	M	P	m_{opt}
Index mit Cluster-Bildung	1.0	2500	63	25
Index ohne Cluster-Bildung	1.0	5000	2500	25
Relationen-Scan	1.0	250000	6250	91

Tabelle 7: Optimale Anzahl der Scan-Ausführungseinheiten in Abhängigkeit von Zugriffsmethode und Anfrageselektivität bei Plattenpufferung der Eingaberelation.

rungseinheiten für die durchgeführten Versuche. Grundsätzlich verschiebt sich das Antwortzeitoptimum gegenüber dem hauptspeicherbasierten Fall zu einer größeren Anzahl von Ausführungseinheiten. Ursache sind die E/A-Kosten für das Bereitstellen der Datenbankseiten, die die Zugriffskosten pro Tupel vergrößern. Mit zunehmender Anzahl der Ausführungseinheiten wächst jedoch der verfügbare Puffer. Ab 25 PE paßt die gesamte Relation in die verteilten Hauptspeicher, so daß keine E/A mehr notwendig ist und die Zugriffskosten pro Tupel denen des hauptspeicherbasierten Falles entsprechen.

5 Übertragung des Kostenmodells auf Join-Operatoren

In analoger Weise läßt sich das Kostenmodell auf Anfragen übertragen, die zwei Relationen miteinander über eine Verbundoperation (Join) verknüpfen. Der Join-Operator verknüpft zwei Eingaberelationen A und B anhand eines Join-Attributs und erzeugt eine neue Relation. Für jedes Tupel t_a in A werden alle Tupel t_b in B gesucht, deren Join-Attributwerte dem von t_a entsprechen (sog. Equi-Join). Hierzu sind beide Relationen zunächst mit Hilfe von Scan-Operatoren zu lesen. Die von den Scan-Operatoren generierten Ausgabemengen bilden die Eingaberelationen des Joins. Vor Ausführung des Joins ist im allgemeinen eine Umverteilung der Eingaberelationen zu den Join-Ausführungseinheiten erforderlich.

Die üblicherweise zur Anwendung kommende Methode ist die *symmetrischen Partitionierung*; sie wird u.a. bei Tandem, Gamma und Teradata angewandt. Bei der symmetrischen Partitionierung werden beide Eingaberelationen nach dem Verbundattribut auf mehrere Join-Ausführungseinheiten verteilt. Die wichtigste Eigenschaft ist, daß Tupel beider Eingaberelationen derart auf die Join-Ausführungseinheiten verteilt werden, daß alle Tupel mit dem gleichen Join-Attributwert der selben Join-Ausführungseinheit zugeordnet werden. Auf diese Weise wird die voneinander unabhängige Ausführbarkeit der Join-Ausführungseinheiten garantiert, da Verbundpartner nur innerhalb der Join-Ausführungseinheiten auftreten können. Das verwendete attributwertbasierte Verteilverfahren (i.d.R. Hash- oder Bereichspartitionierung) ist dabei unabhängig von der lokalen Join-Methode (z.B. Hash- oder Sort-Merge-Join). Bei Verwendung der symmetrischen Partitionierung können sowohl die Anzahl der Join-Ausführungseinheiten als auch deren Zuordnung zu Prozessorknoten frei gewählt werden; d.h. der Parallelitätsgrad kann dynamisch festgelegt werden und die Join-Bearbeitung kann an beliebigen Knoten erfolgen.

Wir haben in [Marek 1993] eine Kostenabschätzung der parallelen Join-Verarbeitung exemplarisch für eine Sort-Merge-Implementierung durchgeführt. Der Sort-Merge-Join basiert auf einem sukzessiven Lesen und Mischen beider Eingaberelationen (*Merging Scans*), wobei Sortierordnungen über den Verbundattributen beider Relationen ausgenutzt werden. Da im allgemeinen keine Sortierordnungen über den Verbundattributen vorliegen, müssen vor der Scan-Phase zunächst beide Relationen nach dem Verbundattribut sortiert werden. Nach erfolgter Sortierung werden Scans auf beiden Relationen eröffnet, die durch geeignetes Fortschalten für jeden Wert des Verbundattributes die zugehörigen Tupel liefern. Bei einem 1:n-Join genügt ein einmaliges Referenzieren jedes Tupels, bei einem n:m-Join müssen für jeden Join-Attributwert die n Tupeln der zweiten Relation m-fach referenziert werden[9]. In jedem Fall ist der Aufwand für diesen Teilschritt in Abhängigkeit von der Anzahl beteiligter Tupeln linear. Die CPU-Kosten des Sort-Merge-Joins setzen sich zusammen aus den Kosten für das Sortieren der Eingaberelationen (O(n log n)) und dem linearen Kostenanteil für das Mischen der sortierten Ströme.

Zur Antwortzeitabschätzung von Join-Anfragen in Abhängigkeit vom Parallelitätsgrad m des Join-Operators wurde in [Marek 1993] folgende Formel hergeleitet:

$$R\,(m)\ =\ a + b \times m + c_1 \times \frac{M_1}{m} + c_2 \times \frac{M_2}{m} + d_1 \times \frac{M_1}{m} \times \log\left(\frac{M_1}{m}\right) + d_2 \times \frac{M_2}{m} \times \log\left(\frac{M_2}{m}\right)$$

Der Parallelitätsgrad der Scan-Operatoren, die die Basisrelationen lesen, wurde dabei entsprechend der fest vorgegeben Datenverteilung als konstant angesehen. Der Antwortzeitanteil der Scan-Operatoren ist demzufolge in dem konstanten Antwortzeitanteil a enthalten. Die Kardinalität der Join-Eingaberelationen beträgt M_1 bzw. M_2.
Jede Join-Ausführungseinheit verarbeitet $1/m$ der am Verbund teilnehmenden Tupel. Die Koeffizienten d_i beschreiben den Aufwand für das Sortieren der Eingaberelationen je Join-Ausführungseinheit, die Faktoren c_i enthalten vor allem die Kosten für das Empfangen der Eingabemengen und das sukzessive Lesen und Mischen der sortierten Eingaberelationen. Die Kosten der Parallelverarbeitung (Initialisierung der Join-Ausführungseinheiten etc.) werden in dem Koeffizienten b berücksichtigt.
Auf eine detaillierte Koeffizientenbestimmung in Abhängigkeit von Anfrage- und Systemparametern sei an dieser Stelle aus Platzgründen verzichtet. Der interessierte Leser sei diesbezüglich auf [Marek 1993] verwiesen.

6 Zusammenfassung und Ausblick

Für die Anfrageparallelisierung im Einbenutzerbetrieb haben wir ein Kostenmodell vorgestellt, das die Antwortzeitentwicklung von Datenbankanfragen in Abhängigkeit vom Parallelisierungsgrad beschreibt. Mit Hilfe des Kostenmodells kann für Intra-Operator-Parallelität - die in praxi wichtigste Form von Intra-Query-Parallelität - derjenige Parallelitätsgrad bestimmt werden, der die Antwortzeit von Anfragen minimiert. Das Modell kann somit zur Unterstützung des Optimierers bei der Anfrageparallelisierung eingesetzt werden. Es kann sowohl als Entscheidungshilfe für die statische Bestimmung eines geeigneten Datenverteilungsgrades dienen, als auch für die dynamische

---

9. Bei einem m:n-Verbund (natürlicher Verbund) existieren zu jedem Tupel der äußeren Relation maximal m Verbundpartner in der inneren Relation; zu jedem Tupel der inneren Relation maximal n Verbundpartner in der äußeren Relation. Für m=1 spricht man von einem funktionalen Verbund.

Ermittlung des optimalen Parallelitätsgrades von Join-Operatoren genutzt werden. Insbesondere kann der Einfluß des Speichermediums (Hauptspeicher versus Platte) der Operanden berücksichtigt werden.

Wir haben drei unterschiedliche Antwortzeitanteile identifiziert, die sich bezüglich ihrer Abhängigkeit vom Parallelisierungsgrad voneinander unterscheiden. In der Regel enthält die Antwortzeit einer Anfrage einen Kostenanteil, der von der Operatorparallelisierung nicht betroffen ist, d.h. unabhängig vom Parallelisierungsgrad konstant ist. Diesem Anteil sind u.a. nicht-parallelisierte Operatoren und Query-Verwaltungsaktivitäten zuzurechnen. Der erwünschte Effekt der Anfrageparallelisierung (Nutzen), nämlich die Verkürzung der Anfrage- (bzw. Operator-) Bearbeitungszeit läßt sich in einem mit zunehmendem Parallelisierungsgrad abnehmenden Kostenanteil beschreiben. Die Reduktion der Operatorbearbeitungszeit ist dabei auf eine mit zunehmender Anzahl von Ausführungseinheiten abnehmenden Größe der Operandenmenge (Tupeln bzw. Datenbankseiten) pro Ausführungseinheit zurückzuführen. Die Beziehung zwischen Parallelisierungsgrad und Operatorbearbeitungszeit ist abhängig vom Operatortyp. Im Falle von Operatoren mit linearem Kostenverlauf erlaubt eine Vergrößerung des Intra-Operator-Parallelitätsgrads eine lineare Verbesserung dieses Kostenterms; im Falle logarithmischer Operatoren ist eine superlineare Beziehung gegeben. Dem letzten der drei Antwortzeitkostenanteile sind bei der Anfrageparallelisierung entstehenden Kommunikations- und Verwaltungskosten zuzurechnen. Diese Kosten wachsen linear mit zunehmendem Parallelisierungsgrad. Zur Bestimmung dieser Kostenanteile haben wir eine Abschätzung präsentiert, die auf einem detaillierten Modell der parallelen Anfragebearbeitung basiert.

Die Effektivität der Operatorparallelisierung (Speedup) ist von allen drei Kostentermen abhängig. Der optimale, die Antwortzeit minimierende Parallelitätsgrad ist hingegen unabhängig von dem konstanten Kostenanteil. Lediglich das Kosten-/Nutzenverhältnis der von der Operatorparallelisierung abhängigen Antwortzeitanteile in Verbindung mit der Größe der Operandenmenge bestimmt den optimalen Parallelitätsgrad im Einbenutzerbetrieb.

Zur Beurteilung der Güte des Kostenmodells wurde ein simulativer Ansatz gewählt. Für Leistungsanalysen der parallelen Anfragebearbeitung haben wir in einem umfassenden Simulationsmodell ein generisches Shared-Nothing-System hinsichtlich seiner Architektur und seiner Verarbeitungskonzepte modelliert. Das Simulationsmodell wurde anhand von Vergleichssimulationen zu realen Shared-Nothing-Systemen validiert. Auf Basis des Simulationsmodells durchgeführte Antwortzeitversuche zur Parallelisierung von Scan-Operatoren haben die Übereinstimmung von Kosten- und Simulationsmodell gezeigt. Wir haben gesehen, daß sich die beobachteten Antwortzeiten bei der parallelen Scan-Bearbeitung geeignet durch das vorgestellte Kostenmodell beschreiben lassen. Insbesondere liefern das Kostenmodell einerseits und die beobachteten Antwortzeitkurven andererseits den gleichen optimalen Parallelitätsgrad der Operatorparallelisierung. Ausgehend von der Validierung des Simulationsmodells gegen reale Systeme dürfen wir annehmen, daß das Kostenmodell eine gute Annäherung an das Verhalten realer Systeme bietet. Leistungsuntersuchungen von Datenbankanfragen im Einbenutzerbetrieb können daher mit Hilfe des analytischen Modells durchgeführt werden. Verglichen mit simulationsbasierten Untersuchungen ist ein analytischer Ansatz weitaus weniger aufwendig.

In zukünftigen Arbeiten wollen wir uns der Frage widmen, wie der Anfrageoptimierer bei der Operatorparallelisierung im Mehrbenutzerbetrieb geeignet unterstützt werden kann. Teilaspekte dieser Fragestellung sind eine von der aktuellen Lastsituation abhängige, dynamische Bestimmung des Operatorparallelitätsgrades sowie die Allokation von Ausführungseinheiten zu Prozessorelementen mit dem Ziel der Lastbalancierung. Erste Untersuchungen hierzu wurden bereits in [Rahm und Marek 1993] durchgeführt. Schließlich sollten in weiterführenden Arbeiten einige der bisher getroffenen Vereinfachungen aufgegeben werden. Im Hinblick auf realitätsnahe Anwendungslasten ist vor allem der Einfluß von Skew auf das Leistungsverhalten zu berücksichtigen.

7   Literatur

Apers, P.; van den Berg, C.; Flokstra, J.; Grefen, P.; Kersten, M.; Wilschut, A. 1992: PRISMA/DB: A Parallel, Main-Memory Relational DBMS. Memoranda Informatica 92-12, University of Twente, Enschede, The Netherlands.

Boral, H.; Alexander, W.; Clay, L.; Copeland, G.; Danforth, S.; Franklin, M.; Hart, B.; Smith, M.; Valduriez, P. 1990: Prototyping Bubba: A Highly Parallel Database System. *IEEE Trans. on Knowledge and Data Engineering* 2(1), 4-24.

DeWitt, D.J.; Ghandeharizadeh, S.; Schneider, D.A.; Bricker, A.; Hsiao, H.; Rasmussen, R. 1990: The Gamma Database Machine Project. *IEEE Trans. on Knowledge and Data Engineering* 2(1), 4-62.

DeWitt, D.; Gray, J. 1992: Parallel Database Systems: The Future of High Performance Database Processing. *Communications of the ACM* 35(6), 85-98.

Englert, S., Gray, J., Kocher, T., Shath, P. 1990: A Benchmark of NonStop SQL Release 2 Demonstrating Near-Linear Speedup and Scale-Up on Large Databases. *Proc. ACM SIGMETRICS Conf.*, 245-246.

Gray, J. (Hrsg.) 1991: The Benchmark Handbook. Morgan Kaufmann Publishers Inc.

Härder, T. 1987: Realisierung von operationalen Schnittstellen. In: Datenbank-Handbuch, Hrsg. P.C. Lockemann und J.W. Schmidt, Springer-Verlag.

Mackert, L.; Lohman, G. 1989: Index Scans Using a Finite LRU Buffer: A Validated I/O Model. *ACM Trans. on Database System* 14(3), 401-424.

Marek, R. 1993: Ein Kostenmodell der parallelen Anfragebearbeitung in Shared-Nothing-Datenbanksystemen. Technischer Bericht 3/93, Universität Kaiserslautern, Fachbereich Informatik, Mai 1993.

Marek, R.; Rahm, E. 1992: Performance Evaluation of Parallel Transaction Processing in Shared Nothing Database Systems. *Proc. 4th Int. PARLE Conference 1992*, Lecture Notes in Computer Science 605, Springer Verlag, 295-310.

Marek, R.; Rahm, E. 1993: On the Performance of Parallel Join Processing in Shared Nothing Database Systems. *Proc. 5th Int. PARLE Conference 1993*, Lecture Notes in Computer Science, Springer Verlag.

Mohan, C., Lindsay, B., Obermarck, R. 1986: Transaction Management in the R* Distributed Database Management System. *ACM Trans. on Database System* 11(4), 378-396.

Neches, P.M. 1986: The Anatomy of a Database Computer - Revisited. *Proc. IEEE CompCon Spring Conf.*, 374-377.

Özsu, M.T., Valduriez, P. 1991: Principles of Distributed Database Systems. Prentice Hall.

Pirahesh, H.; Mohan, C.; Cheng, J.; Liu, T.S.; Selinger, P. 1990: Parallelism in Relational Data Base Systems: Architectural Issues and Design Approaches. In *Proc. 2nd Int.Symposium on Databases in Parallel and Distributed Systems*, IEEE Computer Society Press.

Rahm, E.; Marek, R. 1993: Analysis of Dynamic Load Balancing Strategies for Parallel Shared Nothing Database Systems. *Proc. 19th Int. Conf. on Very Large Data Bases*, August 1993, Dublin, Ireland.

Silberschatz, A.; Stonebraker, M.; Ullman, J. 1991: Database Systems: Achievements and Opportunities. *Communications of the ACM* 34(10), 110-120.

Stonebraker, M. 1986: The Case for Shared Nothing. *IEEE Database Engineering* 9(1), 4-9.

The Tandem Database Group 1989: NonStop SQL, A Distributed, High-Performance, High-Availability Implementation of SQL. Lecture Notes in Computer Science 359, Springer-Verlag, 60-104.

Valduriez, P. 1993: Parallel Database Systems: Open Problems and New Issues. *Distributed and Parallel Databases 1* (1993), 137-165.

Walton, C.B; Dale A.G.; Jenevein, R.M. 1991: A Taxanomy and Performance Model of Data Skew Effects in Parallel Joins. *Proc. 17th Int. Conf. on Very Large Data Bases*, 537-548.

Waters, S.J. 1976: Hit Ratio. *Computer Journal* 19(1), 21-24.

Watson, P., Townsend, P. 1991: The EDS Parallel Relational Database System. In: Parallel Database Systems (*Proc. PRIMSA Workshop*), Lecture Notes in Computer Science 503, Springer-Verlag, 149-168.

Wilschut, A.; Flokstra, J.; Apers, P. 1992: Parallelism in a Main-Memory DBMS: The performance of PRISMA/DB. *Proc. 18th Int. Conf. on Very Large Data Bases*, 521-532.

Yao, S.B. 1977: Approximating Block Accesses in Database Organizations. *Communications of the ACM* 20(4), 260-261.

Architektur des parallelen Datenbanksystems MIDAS[1]

A. Listl, M. Pawlowski, A. Reiser, G. Bozas, R. Lehn

Institut für Informatik, Technische Universität München
Arcisstr. 21, D-80290 München
e-mail: {listl | pawlowsk | reiser | bozas | lehn}@informatik.tu-muenchen.de

Zusammenfassung. Durch den Einsatz von Mehrprozessorsystemen mit verteiltem Speicher als Hardware-Plattform zur Realisierung eines parallelen relationalen Datenbank-managementsystems wird sowohl die parallele Auswertung einzelner Datenbankanfragen als auch die parallele Ausführung einzelner relationaler Operatoren erreicht. Dies führt jedoch zu einer Reihe von Problemen. Bei der Untersuchung dieser Probleme entstanden in den einzelnen Bereichen eines parallelen Datenbanksystems jeweils Spezifikationen von Schichten und deren Komponenten. Eine hierauf basierende Integration der gewonnenen Einzelergebnisse führt zum Entwurf einer Gesamtarchitektur eines parallelen relationalen Datenbankmanagementsystems. Diese wird hier beschrieben und es wird gezeigt, wie die verschiedenen Parallelisierungsansätze, wie Intertransaktions- und Intraquery-Parallelität, in einem System vereinigt werden können.

1 Einführung

In den letzten Jahren haben relationale Datenbanksysteme eine weite Verbreitung erfahren. Gleichzeitig haben die Leistungsanforderungen an solche Systeme stark zugenommen. Um den damit verbundenen Anforderungen an die Rechenleistung gerecht werden zu können, erscheint der Einsatz von Mehrprozessorsystemen notwendig.

Wir untersuchen und entwickeln Grundlagen und Konzepte zur effektiven und effizienten Realisierung der Funktionen eines relationalen Datenbankmanagementsystems (RDBMS) in einer Mehrprozessorarchitektur mit verteiltem Speicher. Dabei werden folgende Parallelisierungsansätze [11] verfolgt:

- **Intertransaktions-Parallelität**. Die Idee dieses Parallelisierungsansatzes ist, Transaktionen nicht mehr nur quasiparallel auf einem Prozessor auszuführen, sondern durch Prozeßreplizierung auf mehrere Prozessoren eine echte Parallelausführung der einzelnen Transaktionen zu erreichen. Dadurch wird eine Steigerung der Transaktionsrate erzielt.

- **Intraquery-Parallelität**. Ziel dieses Parallelisierungsansatzes ist es, den Operatorbaum einer Datenbankanfrage (Query) parallel abzuarbeiten. Dies geschieht durch Zerlegung des Operatorbaums in Teilbäume und Verwendung paralleler relationaler Operatoren (Intraoperator-Parallelität). Dadurch wird eine Verkürzung der Antwortzeit erreicht.

Im Zuge dieser Parallelisierungsansätze wurden eine Reihe von Konzepten auf den verschiedenen Schichten eines RDBMS entwickelt. So lieferten z.B. Arbeiten aus den Bereichen der parallelen Query-Auswertung [12, 13] und der Datenbanksystempuffer-Verwaltung [8] neuar-

---

1. Diese Arbeit entstand im Rahmen des Projektes "Parallelisierung von Datenbanksystemen" unter der Leitung von Prof. R. Bayer, Ph.D., am Institut für Informatik der Technischen Universität München mit Unterstützung der DFG (SFB 342/B2).

tige Konzepte und Ergebnisse. Diese haben zur Spezifikation von Schnittstellen, Schichten und Komponenten eines parallelen RDBMS namens MIDAS (MunIch Parallel DAtabase System) geführt und bilden zusammen eine funktionelle Gesamtarchitektur für ein paralleles RDBMS.

In der vorliegenden Arbeit wird diese Gesamtarchitektur beschrieben und gezeigt, wie dadurch die gewonnenen Konzepte der einzelnen Parallelisierungsansätze in einem parallelen RDBMS auf einer Mehrprozessorarchitektur mit verteiltem Speicher realisiert werden können.

Diese Arbeit ist wie folgt aufgebaut: Nach der Einführung in diesem Abschnitt, wird im Abschnitt 2 ein Überblick über die Architektur des parallelen Datenbankmanagementsystems MIDAS gegeben. In den beiden darauffolgenden Abschnitten 3 und 4 findet sich dann eine ausführliche Beschreibung der einzelnen Komponenten. Abschnitt 5 bildet den Schluß dieser Arbeit, in dem die wichtigsten Punkte nochmal zusammengefaßt sind und ein Ausblick auf weitere geplante Arbeiten gegeben wird.

2 Architektur von MIDAS

In diesem Abschnitt wird die funktionelle Architektur von MIDAS beschrieben. Abbildung 1 zeigt diese Architektur schematisch.

MIDAS hat eine Client/Server Architektur. Der *MIDAS-Server* befindet sich auf einem Mehrprozessorsystem und bietet eine SQL-Schnittstelle, um auf den Inhalt der Datenbank (DB) effizient zugreifen zu können. Die Datenbank selbst ist auf einem Hintergrundspeicher untergebracht, auf den der Zugriff über die E/A-Schnittstelle durch ein vom Betriebssystem bereitgestelltes Dateisystem erfolgt.

Die *MIDAS-Clients* sind die DB-Anwendungen. Sie sind sequentielle Programme, welche den MIDAS-Server mit Transaktionen beauftragen. Jede Transaktion besteht aus einer Reihe von

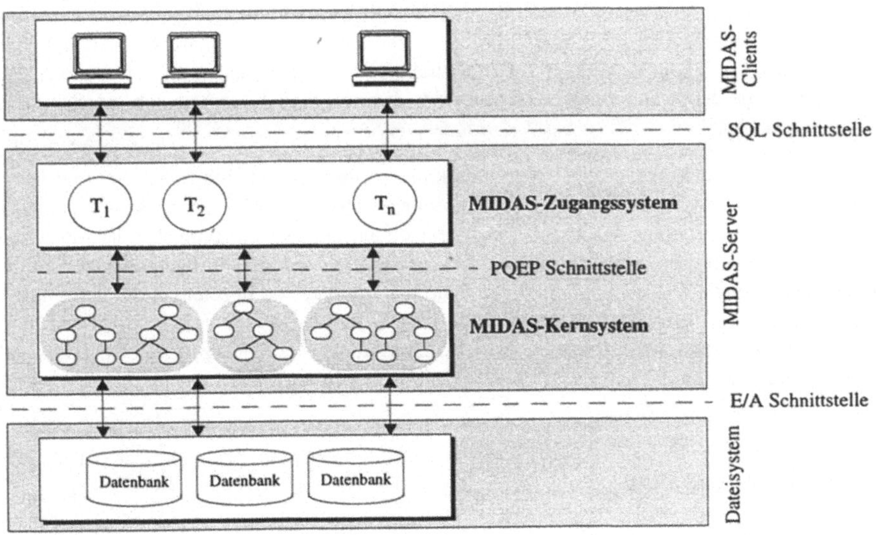

ABBILDUNG 1. Architektur von MIDAS

DB-Anfragen, welche auf den Inhalt der Datenbank zugreifen. Ein MIDAS-Client kann auf jedem (sequentiellen) Arbeitsplatzrechner (z.B. UNIX-Workstation bzw. Personal Computer) ausgeführt werden, der im Rahmen eines Netzwerks Zugriff auf den MIDAS-Server hat.

Zur Realisierung der oben beschriebenen Parallelisierungsansätze (siehe Abschnitt 1) ist der MIDAS-Server in zwei Hauptschichten unterteilt, dem *MIDAS-Zugangssystem* und dem *MIDAS-Kernsystem*, deren detaillierte Beschreibung in den Abschnitten 3 und 4 erfolgt.

Die Hauptaufgabe des MIDAS-Zugangssystems ist die Realisierung der Intertransaktions-Parallelität und die Vorbereitung der Intraquery-Parallelität. Ein wesentliches Ziel dabei ist, die Komplexität, die durch die Parallelisierung entsteht, vor den MIDAS-Clients zu verbergen. Es muß der gleichzeitige Zugriff mehrerer MIDAS-Clients ermöglicht, sowie die Parallelisierung einer sequentiellen SQL-Anfrage vorgenommen werden. Aus einer SQL-Anfrage wird ein paralleler Query-Execution-Plan (PQEP) erzeugt. Dabei möglicherweise auftretende Lastungleichheiten sind auszugleichen.

Das MIDAS-Kernsystem realisiert die Intraquery-Parallelität. Es empfängt vom MIDAS-Zugangssystem über die PQEP-Schnittstelle PQEPs, die parallel auf den zur Verfügung stehenden Rechnerknoten ausgewertet werden. Das Kernsystem stellt die Ausführungsmaschine für parallelisierte SQL-Anfragen dar. Parallelisierte relationale Operatoren werden dazu bereitgestellt. Außerdem wird zur Ausführung eines PQEPs ein effizienter Zugriff auf die physische DB realisiert, indem eine Synchronisations-, eine Datenbanksystempuffer- und eine Recovery-Verwaltung in das Kernsystem integriert sind.

Vergleicht man diese Architektur mit der klassischen Fünf-Schichten Architektur sequentieller relationaler Datenbanksysteme [6], so realisiert das Zugangssystem die Schicht *deklarativer Datenbankzugriff* und das Kernsystem die Schichten *navigierender Datenbankzugriff*, *physischer Satzzugriff* und *Systempuffer*. Die Schicht *Externspeicher* wird auf das Dateisystem des Betriebssystems abgebildet.

Der MIDAS-Server besteht selbst wieder aus einem System von Servern und Clients. Dabei sind *statische* und *dynamische* Komponenten zu unterscheiden. Die statischen Komponenten existieren während der Gesamtlaufzeit des MIDAS-Servers und bleiben in ihrer Anzahl konstant. Die dynamischen Komponenten hingegen existieren nicht dauerhaft. Ihre Anzahl ändert sich dynamisch und paßt sich dadurch den aktuellen Lastgegebenheiten an. Um hohe Anlaufkosten zu vermeiden, kann zur Realisierung der dynamischen Komponenten ein Serverpool verwendet werden.

Die in dieser Architektur benötigte Kommunikation unterscheidet sich in *externe* und *interne* Kommunikation. Als *extern* wird die Kommunikation zwischen einer Komponente des MIDAS-Servers und eines MIDAS-Clients bezeichnet. Da hier ein typisches Request-Reply Kommunikationsmuster auftritt, wird zur Realisierung der RPC-Mechanismus (RPC = Remote Procedure Call) verwendet. Die *interne* Kommunikation bezeichnet die Kommunikation zwischen den einzelnen Komponenten des MIDAS-Servers selbst. Sie wird durch spezielle Kommunikationsprimitive des Laufzeitsystems des Mehrprozessorrechners oder durch spezielle Message-Passing Programmierbibliotheken realisiert.

3 Das Zugangssystem

Zur Erfüllung der Anforderungen, die im Zusammenhang mit der Intertransaktions-Parallelität entstehen, besteht das MIDAS-Zugangssystem aus dem *MIDAS-Administrations-Server* und den *MIDAS-Anwendungs-Servern* (siehe Abbildung 2).

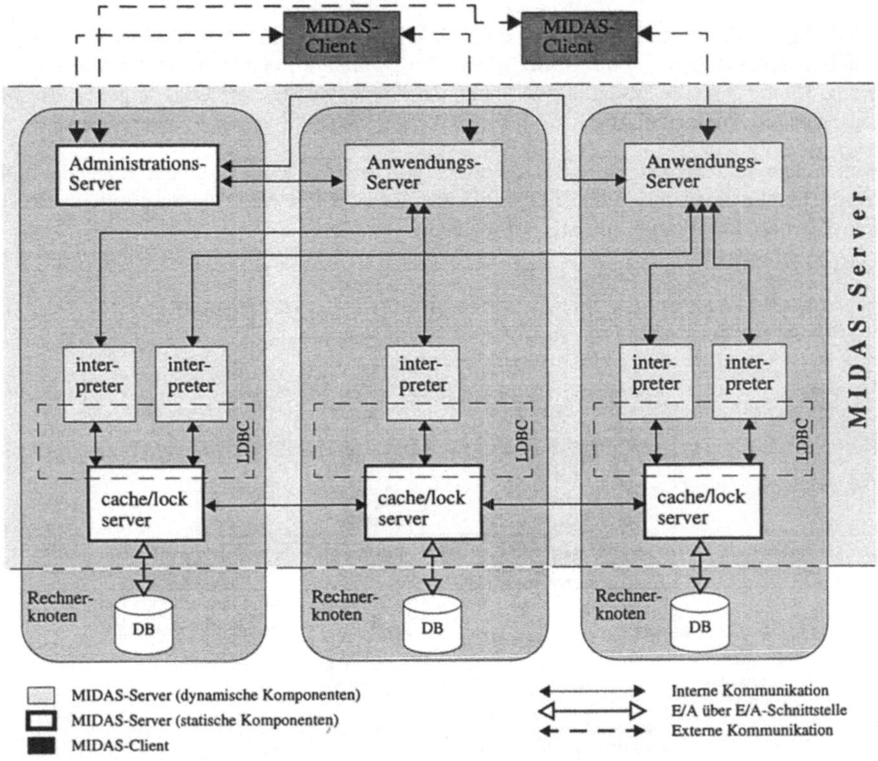

ABBILDUNG 2. MIDAS-Zugangssystem und MIDAS-Kernsystem

Der MIDAS-Administrations-Server ist eine statische Komponente des MIDAS-Servers. Er besitzt nur administrative Aufgaben. Dazu gehören das Kreieren, Löschen, Hochfahren und Herunterfahren von Datenbanken. Außerdem muß er Verbindungen zwischen MIDAS-Clients und dem MIDAS-Server einrichten (connect-request) und abbauen (disconnect-request). Daher kann der Administrations-Server als zentraler Server-Prozeß mit einer systemweit eindeutigen RPC-Adresse realisiert werden.

Auf Grund eines connect-requests eines MIDAS-Clients richtet der Administrations-Server einen neuen Anwendungs-Server ein, der dem Client exklusiv zugeordnet ist. Zusätzlich wird zwischen dem Client und dem Anwendungs-Server eine externe Kommunikationsverbindung aufgebaut, die es dem Client erlaubt, DB-Anfragen an den MIDAS-Server zu senden und die berechneten Ergebnisse von diesem zu empfangen. Dieser Anwendungs-Server existiert solange für diesen Client, bis diese Verbindung wieder abgebaut wird.

Der Anwendungs-Server ist eine dynamische Komponente des MIDAS-Servers und hat im wesentlichen folgende drei Aufgaben zu erfüllen:

1. Realisiert eine Verbindung zwischen der ihm zugeordneten DB-Anwendung (MIDAS-Client) und dem MIDAS-Server. Dadurch wird Intertransaktions-Parallelität erreicht.

2. Nimmt die von der Anwendung erzeugten DB-Anfragen entgegen, übersetzt, parallelisiert und optimiert diese und leitet sie zur Auswertung an das MIDAS-Kernsystem weiter

(PQEP-Schnittstelle). Dadurch wird Intraquery-Parallelität vorbereitet.

3. Leitet die vom Kernsystem berechneten Anfrageergebnisse zurück an den MIDAS-Client.

Zur Erledigung dieser drei Aufgaben ist ein Anwendungs-Server in fünf Module aufgeteilt, nämlich in den *Compiler*, den *Parallelisierer*, den *Optimierer*, den *PQEP-Scheduler* und den *Katalog-Manager* (siehe Abbildung 4), deren Zusammenwirken durch das folgende Beispiel veranschaulicht werden soll:

Angenommen, ein Anwendungs-Server erhält von seinem MIDAS-Client folgende SQL-Anfrage, welche die Namen aller Professoren und die Titel aller Vorlesungen ermittelt, die von den Professoren im Sommersemester 1994 gehalten worden sind:

```
select m.name, v.titel
from mitarbeiter m, durchfuehrung d, vorlesung v
where m.personalnr = d.veranstalter
        and d.vorlesung = v.nummer
        and d.semester = 'SS94'
```

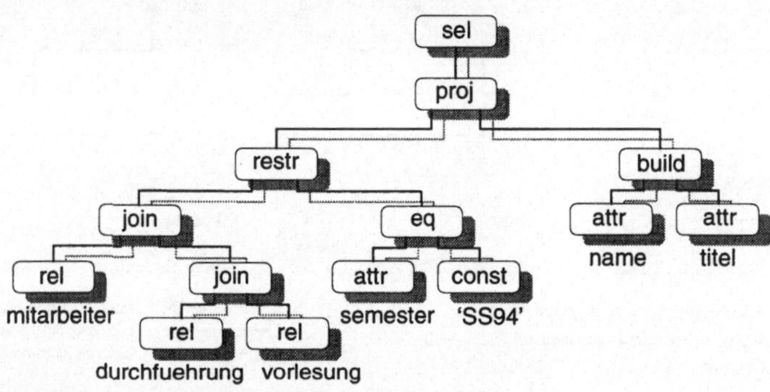

ABBILDUNG 3. **Sequentieller Operatorbaum (Beispiel)**

Der Compiler erzeugt aus dieser DB-Anfrage unter Verwendung der durch den Katalog-Manager verwalteten Systemtabellen einen sequentiellen Operatorbaum (siehe Abbildung 3). Dieser wird vom Parallelisierer gemeinsam mit dem Optimierer parallelisiert, wobei als Ergebnis eine Menge von Teilbäumen zusammen mit einem Ausführungsplan entsteht (siehe Abbildung 4). Dabei ergänzt der Parallelisierer den "klassischen" Optimierer um Aspekte der Verteilung. Der Ausführungsplan beschreibt zeitliche und örtliche Abhängigkeiten zwischen einzelnen Teilbäumen, die während der parallelen Ausführung existieren. So besagt z.B. der Ausführungsplan in Abbildung 4, daß der Teilbaum T4 erst ausgeführt werden kann, wenn die beiden Teilbäume T3 und T2 vollständig bearbeitet sind. Dabei können T3 und T2 nebenläufig ausgeführt werden, wobei T3 auf dem Rechnerknoten P2 und T2 auf dem Rechnerknoten P1 ausgeführt werden muß. Hingegen kann der Teilbaum T4 auf jedem Rechnerknoten des MIDAS-Servers ausgeführt werden.

Basierend auf den Informationen des Ausführungsplans werden die erzeugten Teilbäume vom PQEP-Scheduler mittels interner Kommunikation an das MIDAS-Kernsystem verteilt und das berechnete Ergebnis an den MIDAS-Client zurückgesendet. Die parallele Ausführung des PQEPs wird durch den PQEP-Scheduler dynamisch gesteuert.

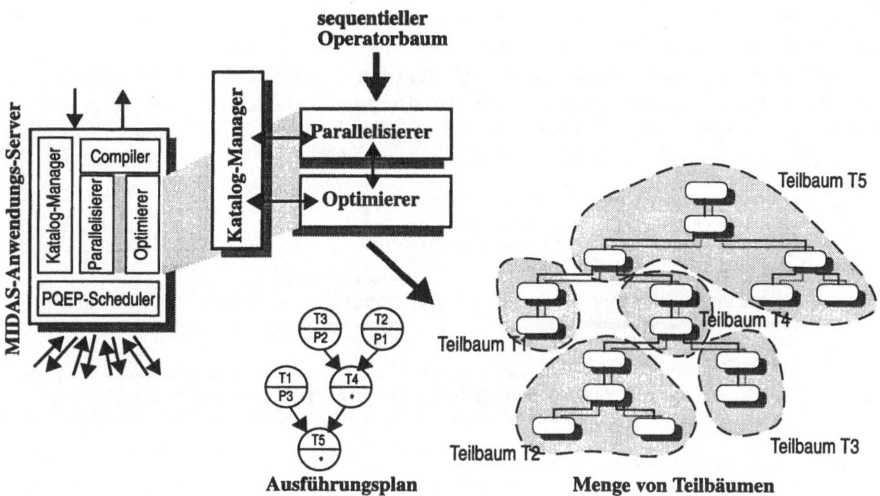

ABBILDUNG 4. Parallelisierung eines sequentiellen Operatorbaums

4 Das Kernsystem

Um die vom PQEP-Scheduler zugewiesenen Teilbäume parallel verarbeiten zu können, besteht das MIDAS-Kernsystem aus einer Menge von *Interpretern* und *Cache/Lock-Servern* (siehe Abbildung 2).

Die Interpreter werten die vom MIDAS-Zugangssystem erzeugten Teilbäume aus und stellen die Zwischenergebnisse eventuell anderen Interpretern zur Verfügung. Dazu werden die Interpreter vom PQEP-Scheduler auf Grund des vom Optimierer berechneten Parallelisierungsgrads zur Laufzeit bereitgestellt. Sie gehören also zum dynamischen Teil des MIDAS-Servers. Dadurch wird eine dynamische Anpassung des Kernsystems an die durch einzelne DB-Anfragen erzeugte Last erreicht.

Ein Interpreter arbeitet den ihm zugewiesenen Teilbaum ähnlich einem Operatorbaum in einem sequentiellen Datenbanksystem ab. Die Arbeitsweise innerhalb eines Teilbaums entspricht einer tupelorientierten Auswertung. Der Zugriff auf die zu verarbeitenden Eingabetupel und der berechneten Ergebnistupel ist mengenorientiert und wird über die Segmentschnittstelle des Cache/Lock-Servers abgewickelt. Ein Segment bildet einen linearen, seitenstrukturierten Adreßraum. Sowohl für den Zugriff auf die physische Datenbank als auch für die Kommunikation zwischen den einzelnen Interpretern werden Segmente verwendet. Dadurch erhalten wir einen einheitlichen Mechanismus. Kommunikation ist somit zwischen einzelnen Interpretern möglich, ohne daß in den Teilbäumen explizite Kommunikationsoperatoren (send, receive) verwendet werden müssen. Der Cache/Lock-Server stellt dafür folgende Segmenttypen zur Verfügung (siehe Abbildung 5):

- **Permanente Segmente**. Sie überdauern das Ende einer Transaktion und werden auf dem Hintergrundspeicher abgelegt. Sie dienen zur Aufnahme der Basisrelationen, deren Gesamtheit die Datenbank ausmacht.

- **Temporäre Segmente**. Sie sind lokal für eine Transaktion und werden an ihrem Ende gelöscht. Wir unterscheiden weiter in Zwischenergebnis- und Kommunikationssegmente.

Zwischenergebnissegmente sind rechnerknotenlokal und dienen zur Aufnahme großer Zwischenergebnisse (z.B. beim Sortieren).

Über *Kommunikationssegmente* können verschiedene Interpreter kommunizieren. Der sendende Interpreter schreibt das Kommunikationssegment, während der empfangende Interpreter das Kommunikationssegment liest. Es ist durch diesen Mechanismus nicht nur 1:1 sondern auch allgemeine n:m Kommunikation möglich [16].

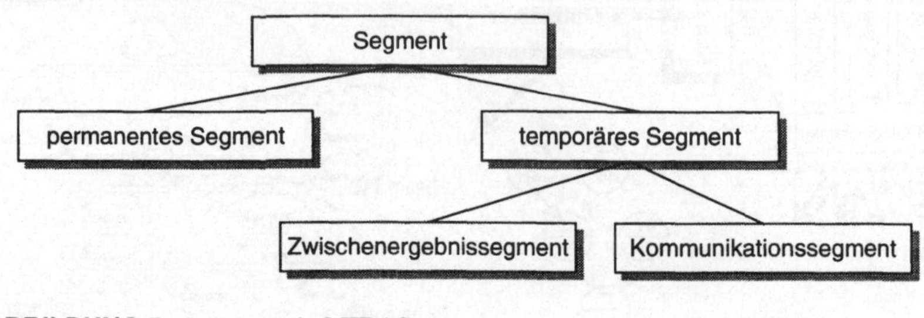

ABBILDUNG 5. **Segmente in MIDAS**

Wie bereits erwähnt, sind die Cache/Lock-Server für den Zugriff auf die physische Datenbank verantwortlich. Die Cache/Lock-Server werden beim Hochfahren einer Datenbank auf den Rechnerknoten des Mehrprozessorsystems vom MIDAS-Administrations-Server gestartet. Die Cache/Lock-Server zählen zu den statischen Komponenten von MIDAS, da deren Anzahl bzgl. einer Datenbank für die Dauer, in der sie hochgefahren ist, konstant bleibt. Allerdings ändert sich die Gesamtzahl der Cache/Lock-Server, die während der Laufzeit des MIDAS-Servers existieren, da für jede hochgefahrene Datenbank neue Cache/Lock-Server gestartet bzw. beim Herrunterfahren die entsprechenden Cache/Lock-Server beendet werden.

Die Cache/Lock-Server haben im wesentlichen folgende Aufgaben:

- Bereitstellen einer orts- und zugriffstransparenten Segmentschnittstelle,

- Durchführen des Zugriffs auf den Hintergrundspeicher und Pufferung von Seiten im Datenbanksystempuffer,

- Synchronisation nebenläufiger Datenbankzugriffe und

- Durchführung von Maßnahmen für die Recovery.

Für die Pufferung von Seiten wird in MIDAS der sogenannte virtuelle Datenbank-Cache (VDBC) verwendet [8, 9]. Der VDBC ist ein orts- und zugriffstransparenter Datenbanksystempuffer, der es jedem Interpreter erlaubt, lokal auf alle DB-Seiten zuzugreifen, egal auf welchem Rechnerknoten die Seiten tatsächlich liegen. Das dabei auftretende Kohärenzproblem, nämlich daß in mehreren Rechnerknoten verschiedene Versionen derselben Datenbank-Seite existieren können (dynamische Replikation der Daten), wird durch eine auf die Cache/Lock-Server verteilte Kohärenzkontrolle gelöst. Dabei kommunizieren die Cache/Lock-Server mittels interner Kommunikation untereinander und tauschen Zustandsinformationen sowie Seiten direkt miteinander aus.

In der Literatur sind eine Reihe von Verfahren zur Kohärenzkontrolle beschrieben (einen guten Überblick enthält [14]). Dabei ist all diesen Verfahren im wesentlichen gemeinsam, daß sie sich mit zwei Teilproblemen auseinandersetzen müssen:

- **Veralterungsproblem.** Der Zugriff auf veraltete Seiten muß verhindert werden.

- **Propagierungsproblem.** Die Änderungen in den Seiten müssen propagiert werden, um auf allen Rechnerknoten den aktuellen Inhalt der Seiten zu haben.

Das Veralterungsproblem wird in MIDAS durch Invalidierung gelöst, in dem am Ende einer Transaktion für jede geänderte Seite allen Knoten, die eine Kopie der Seite gepuffert haben, eine Nachricht geschickt wird, mit deren Hilfe die veralteten Kopien aus den Puffern entfernt werden können (broadcast invalidation). Das Propagierungsproblem wird in MIDAS durch eine Strategie gelöst, bei der ein Rechnerknoten als Besitzer (owner) einer Seite fungiert. Dabei versorgt der Besitzer einer Seite die anderen Rechnerknoten mit der jeweils aktuellen Version der Seite. Die Aufgabe des Owners kann für alle Seiten einem einzigen Rechnerknoten aufgetragen werden, was jedoch leicht zu Problemen der Fehlertoleranz und zu einem Leistungsengpaß führen kann. Daher wird in MIDAS eine verteilte Owner-Zuordnung verwendet, die dynamisch erfolgt, d.h. der Owner einer Seite kann sich ändern (dynamic ownership).

Zur Realisierung des VDBC verwaltet jeder Cache/Lock-Server auf seinem Rechnerknoten einen Speicherbereich, den sogenannten lokalen Datenbank-Cache (LDBC). Jeder LDBC ist in Kacheln unterteilt. Jede Kachel kann eine DB-Seite aufnehmen. Benötigt ein Interpreter während der Auswertung eines Teilbaums eine DB-Seite, so sendet er einen entsprechenden Auftrag an den Cache/Lock-Server auf seinem Rechnerknoten. Der Cache/Lock-Server lädt die angeforderte Seite in eine Kachel des LDBC und teilt dem Interpreter die Speicheradresse dieser Kachel mit. Damit der Interpreter auf diese Kachel zugreifen und den Inhalt der angeforderten Seite lesen bzw. verändern kann, muß sich der LDBC sowohl im Adreßraum des Cache/Lock-Servers als auch im Adreßraum des Interpreters befinden. Erreicht wird dies dadurch, daß ein LDBC als Shared Memory zwischen einem Cache/Lock-Server und den Interpretern auf demselben Rechnerknoten angelegt wird. Dies hat den Vorteil, daß mehrere Interpreter gleichzeitig auf die Seiten im LDBC zugreifen können, ohne daß die Seiten von einem Adreßraum in einen anderen Adreßraum mittels interner Kommunikation kopiert werden müssen.

Die Synchronisation nebenläufiger Zugriffe ist im MIDAS-Kernsystem Aufgabe einer auf die Cache/Lock-Server verteilten Sperrenverwaltung. Dabei verwendet die Sperrenverwaltung als Sperrgranularität die Seite. Dies hat den Vorteil, daß sowohl für die Kohärenzkontrolle als auch für die Synchronisation dieselbe Dateneinheit verwendet wird, was zu einer effizienten Integration von Sperrenverwaltung und Kohärenzkontrolle führt. Dadurch lassen sich Kommunikationskosten einsparen und die Leistungsfähigkeit des Datenbanksystems steigern [15].

Da die Maßnahmen der Recovery in Datenbanksystemen stark vom verwendeten Pufferungs- und Synchronisationsverfahren abhängen, ist die Recovery-Verwaltung Aufgabe der Cache/Lock-Server. Dabei ist die Kohärenzkontrolle für die Erzeugung der notwendigen Log-Dateien verantwortlich. Auf Grund der von der Pufferverwaltung verwendeten NOFORCE-Strategie[2] werden für die Recovery jeweils nur die von einer Transaktion geänderten DB-Seiten in Log-Dateien gesichert (physical after image logging [5]). Dies führt zu einem effizienten Restart-Verhalten und zu einem einfachen Abort von Transaktionen.

Für die bei der Aufgabenerfüllung der Cache/Lock-Server notwendigen Zugriffe auf den Hintergrundspeicher stellt das MIDAS-Kernsystem keine eigene Plattenverwaltung zur Verfügung, sondern stützt sich auf die vom Betriebssystem bereitgestellten Dienste ab (E/A-Schnittstelle). An dieser Stelle sei ausdrücklich darauf hingewiesen, daß die Architektur von MIDAS unverändert sowohl für Shared Disk als auch für Shared Nothing Systeme verwendet werden kann. Geringfügige Änderungen müssen allerdings in einigen Modulen vorgenommen werden: So berücksichtigen Optimierer, Parallelisierer und Katalog-Manager in einer Shared

---

2. NOFORCE: Geänderte Seiten müssen nicht während der Commit-Phase einer Transaktion in die Datenbank durchgeschrieben werden, sondern erst zu einem späteren Zeitpunkt, der hinter dem Commit-Zeitpunkt der Transaktion liegt [5].

Disk Umgebung die logische und in einer Shared Nothing Umgebung die physische Datenpartionierung. Der VBDC muß in einer Shared Nothing Umgebung zusätzlich berücksichtigen, daß die Zugriffe auf die Daten, die auf dem Peripheriespeicher liegen, nur noch lokal möglich sind. Das läßt sich durch unsere Architektur des VBDC leicht bewerkstelligen.

5 Zusammenfassung und Ausblick

In dieser Arbeit haben wir die Architektur des parallelen relationalen Datenbankmanagementsystems MIDAS vorgestellt und gezeigt, wie die Parallelisierungsansätze Intertransaktions- und Intraquery-Parallelität realisiert werden können. Dabei ist die Architektur von MIDAS so konzipiert, daß sie sich den Leistungsanforderungen in zweierlei Hinsicht dynamisch anpassen kann. Zum einen paßt sich das MIDAS-Zugangssystem dynamisch einer steigenden Anzahl von nebenläufig arbeitenden DB-Anwendungen an, und zum anderen ist das MIDAS-Kernsystem in der Lage, dynamisch auf die Anforderungen einzelner DB-Anfragen zu reagieren.

Zur Evaluierung der vorgeschlagenen Datenbankarchitektur wird MIDAS zunächst prototypisch auf einem Netz von Workstations implementiert [1]. Dabei wird als Implementierungsplattform PVM (Parallel Virtual Machine) verwendet. PVM erlaubt den Zusammenschluß von parallelen und seriellen Computern eines heterogenen Netzwerkes zu einem einzigen großen Parallelrechner mit verteiltem Speicher und bietet dem Programmierer als abstrakte Sicht eine Menge von Prozessen (PVM-Tasks), die untereinander Nachrichten austauschen können (message passing) [4].

Die Entscheidung, ein Netz von Workstations als Hardware-Plattform zu verwenden, begründet sich nicht nur auf eigenen Implementierungsansätzen auf einem Hypercube, sondern auch auf ähnlichen Erfahrungen, die bei der Implementierung von parallelen Datenbankprototypen in Karlsruhe (PANDA-Projekt [2]) und Wisconsin (GAMMA-Projekt [3]) gemacht wurden. Dabei erwies sich die Instabilität des jeweils verwendeten Parallelrechners als Hemmschuh der Entwicklung und Fortschritte.

Neben den oben erwähnten Eigenschaften zeichnet sich PVM noch durch sein dynamisches Verhalten und seinen hohen Grad an Fehlertoleranz aus. Das dynamische Verhalten von PVM ergibt sich aus der Fähigkeit, PVM-Tasks jederzeit zu erzeugen bzw. zu löschen. Diese Fähigkeit spielt bei der Implementierung von MIDAS eine zentrale Rolle, da dadurch ein skalierbares paralleles Datenbankmanagementsystem möglich ist, wobei mit skalierbar gemeint ist, daß sich das Datenbankmanagementsystem an verschiedene Leistungsanforderungen dynamisch anpassen kann [10]. Die Fehlertoleranz-Eigenschaft von PVM spielt ebenfalls eine wichtige Rolle bei der Implementierung paralleler Datenbanksysteme.

Auf Grund seiner guten Portierbarkeit und seiner weiten Verbreitung hat sich PVM zum de-facto Standard entwickelt. Daher läßt sich der Prototyp von MIDAS mit relativ geringem Aufwand auch auf "echte" Parallelrechner, wie z.B. die Paragon, übertragen.

Zum Schluß noch ein kurzer Ausblick auf die weiteren Arbeiten: Ausgehend vom Status Quo, den die Spezifikation der Architektur, sowie eine erste Implementierung einer Infrastruktur von MIDAS auf einem Netz von SUN SPARC-Workstations bildet, sollen in weiteren Arbeiten die Datenbank-Cache-Verwaltung, der MIDAS-Anwendungs-Server (hier vor allem der Parallelisierer und der PQEP-Scheduler), der Interpreter, sowie eine verteilte Synchronisation implementiert werden. Gleichzeitig werden mit Hilfe geeigneter Tools, wie z.B. XPVM [7] die implementierten Module analysiert und bewertet. Zusätzlich soll die Effektivität und Effizienz der gewonnenen Konzepte und Ergebnisse untersucht werden. Der Prototyp soll Erkenntnisse über Verträglichkeiten und Wechselwirkungen der einzelnen Konzepte untereinander liefern, welche sich auf Grund der hohen Komplexität des parallelen RDBMS nicht analytisch und auch nicht durch Simulation bestimmen lassen.

6 Literatur

[1] Bozas et al.: *Using PVM to Implement a Parallel Database System*. In Proc. of the First European PVM Users' Group Meeting, Rom, Italy, 1994.

[2] A.G. von Bültzingsloewen, A.R. Kramer: *PANDA: A Testbed for Investigating Strategies for Parallel Query Execution (Synopsis)*. In Proc. of PDIS'93, San Diego, CA, 1993.

[3] D. J. DeWitt et al: *The Gamma Database Machine Project*. IEEE Trans. on Knowledge and Data Eng., 2(1), 1990.

[4] A. Geist et al.: *PVM: Parallel Virtuel Machine*. MIT Press, Cambridge, MASS, 1994.

[5] T. Härder, A. Reuter: *Principles of Transaction-Oriented Database Recovery*. ACM Computer Surveys, 15(4), Seiten 287-317, 1983.

[6] T. Härder: *Realisierung von operationalen Schnittstellen*. In: P.C. Lockemann, J.W. Schmidt (Eds.) *Datenbank-Handbuch*, Seiten 163 - 335, Springer-Verlag, 1897.

[7] J.A. Kohl, G.A. Geist: *XPVM: A Graphical Console and Monitor for PVM*. PVM User's Group Meeting, Oak Ridge, TN, 1994.

[8] A. Listl: *Using Subpages for Coherency Control in Parallel Database Systems*. In Proc. of PARLE'94, Seiten 765-768, Athens, Greece, 1994.

[9] A. Listl, M. Pawlowski: *Parallel Cache Management of a RDBMS*. SFB-Bericht Nr. 342/18/92 A, Technische Universität München, 1992.

[10] A. Listl, T. Schnekenburger, M. Friedrich: *Zum Entwurf eines Prototypen für MIDAS*. SFB-Bericht Nr. 342/1/94 B, Technische Universität München, 1994.

[11] E. Loibl, H. Obermaier, M. Pawlowski: *Towards Parallelism in a Relational Database System*. SFB-Bericht Nr. 342/10/91 A, Technische Universität München, 1991.

[12] E. Loibl, M. Pawlowski, C. Roth: *PART: A Parallel Relational Toolbox as Basis for the Optimization and Interpretation of Parallel Queries*. SFB-Bericht Nr. 342/19/92 A, Technische Universität München, 1992.

[13] M. Pawlowski, R. Bayer: *Parallel Sorting of Large Data Volumes on Distributed Memory Multiprocessors*. In LNCS 732, Parallel Computer Architectures, Seiten 246-264, 1993.

[14] E. Rahm: *Concurrency and Coherency Control in Database Sharing Systems*. Technical Report 3/91, Institut für Informatik, Universität Kaiserslautern, 1991.

[15] E. Rahm: *Empirical Performance Evaluation of Concurrency and Coherency Control Protocols for Database Sharing Systems*. ACM TODS, 18(2), Seiten 333-377, 1993.

[16] M. Usner: *Kommunikation durch Segmente in parallelen Datenbanksystemen*. Diplomarbeit, Institut für Informatik, Technische Universität München, 1994.

Visualisierungstechniken
zur Exploration und Analyse sehr großer Datenbanken

Daniel A. Keim, Hans-Peter Kriegel

Institut für Informatik, Universität München

Leopoldstr. 11B, D-80802 München

e-mail: {keim, kriegel}@informatik.uni-muenchen.de

Zusammenfassung

Unser Ansatz zur Exploration und Analyse sehr großer Datenbanken basiert auf neuartigen Visualisierungstechniken für multidimensionale Daten. Die prinzipielle Idee dabei ist die gleichzeitige Darstellung möglichst vieler Datenobjekte am Bildschirm, wobei jeder Datenwert durch ein Pixel des Bildschirms repräsentiert wird. Die Farbe des Pixels entspricht dem Abstand des jeweiligen Datenwertes zum Anfragewert. Die Anordnung hängt von der Gesamtdistanz des Datensatzes in Bezug auf die Anfrage und von der gewählten Visualisierungstechnik ab. Durch ein graphisches Benutzerinterface kann der Benutzer seine Anfragen inkrementell ändern, wobei er durch das visuelle Feedback, das er bei Änderungen bekommt, in der Verfeinerung seiner Anfragen unterstützt wird. Ein zentrales Anliegen dieses Papiers sind Bewertung und Vergleich unserer Visualisierungstechniken. Bei der Bewertung von Visualisierungstechniken stehen nicht, wie sonst bei Leistungsvergleichen, die CPU-Zeiten oder die Anzahl der Zugriffe auf den Sekundärspeicher im Vordergrund, sondern die Wahrnehmbarkeit von Zusammenhängen und Eigenschaften der Daten. Analog zu den für Leistungsvergleiche von Datenbanksystemen entwickelten Benchmarks werden deshalb für die Evaluierung von Visualisierungstechniken künstlich erzeugte Testdaten mit vorgegebenen Eigenschaften verwendet.

Schlüsselwörter: Datenexploration und -analyse, Data Mining, Visuelle Anfrageunterstützung für Datenbanken, Visualisierung großer Datenmengen, Visualisierung multidimensionaler multivariater Daten

1. Einleitung

Bei Entscheidungen ist es wichtig, im richtigen Augenblick die richtigen Informationen zur Hand zu haben. Durch den schnellen technologischen Fortschritt steigt die Menge an Information, die in gespeicherter Form verfügbar und für die Entscheidungsfindung potentiell von Bedeutung ist, sehr schnell an. Nach neuesten Schätzungen verdoppelt sich die Menge an Information, die weltweit vorhanden ist, alle 20 Monate. Eine Ursache für die ständig ansteigenden Datenmengen ist die Automatisierung fast aller Vorgänge in Wirtschaft, Wissenschaft und Verwaltung. In der heutigen Zeit werden selbst einfache Vorgänge wie das Bezahlen mit Kreditkarte oder das Telefonieren durch Computer erfaßt. Versuchsreihen in Physik, Chemie und Medizin erzeugen große Mengen an Daten, die zumeist automatisch mit Hilfe von Sensoren gesammelt werden. Beobachtungssatelliten werden schon bald täglich Datenmengen im Terabytebereich sammeln und zur Erde übermitteln. Die gesammelten Daten gleichen Heuhaufen, in denen die Stecknadeln wichtiger Informationen versteckt sind. Die großen Mengen gespeicherter Daten stellen eine wichtige Informationsressource dar; es ist in den meisten Fällen aber recht schwer, die relevanten Informationen zu finden.

Die Speicherung großer Datenmengen erfolgt in der Regel mit Hilfe von Datenbanksystemen. Heute verfügbare Datenbanksysteme unterstützen den Benutzer bei der Speicherung und Verwaltung der Daten (RASIS: Reliability, Availability, Security, Integrity, Serviceability) sowie bei der Suche nach exakt spezifizierten Daten. Sie sind im allgemeinen aber ungeeignet, um die unexakt spezifizierte Suche nach interessanten Zusammenhängen sowie besonders 'heißen' Daten, den sog. 'data mining'-Prozeß, zu unterstützen. Zu 'Data Mining' (Datenexploration und Datenanalyse) gehören unter anderem die Suche nach Zusammenhängen, partiellen funktionalen Abhängigkeiten sowie Clustern von Daten mit ähnlichen Eigenschaften. Da in 'Data Mining'-Anwendungen typischerweise a priori nur wenig über die Daten, die Werteverteilung der Attribute und Zusammenhänge zwischen den Attributen bekannt ist, werden neue Anfragemechanismen benötigt. Wichtig sind zum Beispiel die Unterstützung von unscharfen (vage, fuzzy) Anfragen, von Datenanalysetechniken sowie von Techniken, die einen Überblick über die Daten liefern. Zu berücksichtigen sind Forschungsergebnisse aus den Bereichen

- multivariate Statistik - explorative Datenanalyse: Hauptkomponenten-, Faktor- und Cluster-Analyse sowie Multidimensionales Skalieren [DE 82, Hub 85],
- Knowledge Discovery: Decision Tree Inducers und Rule Discovery Techniques [FPM 91],
- Information Retrieval: Approximatives Matching (z.B. Techniken zur Gewichtung der Anfrageteile und zum Rangordnen der Ergebnisse [SB 88, FM 91]),
- Intelligente Datenbank-Benutzerschnittstellen (Kooperative Datenbank-Interfaces [GGM 92], Interfaces für unscharfe Anfragen [ABN 92] und intelligente Browser [Mot 90]).

In den genannten Bereichen wurden in den letzten Jahren beachtliche Ergebnisse erzielt. Mit wenigen Ausnahmen wurden die Techniken jedoch nicht für die Datenexploration und -analyse von sehr großen Datenbanken mit Hunderttausenden oder sogar Millionen von Datensätzen entworfen bzw. adaptiert. Erste Ergebnisse bei der Anwendung einiger Techniken auf großen Datenmengen zeigen, daß die Nutzung der Fähigkeiten des Computers allein nicht ausreichen, um überzeugende Ergebnisse bei der Datenexploration und -analyse zu erzielen. Verfahren, die erfolgreich auf großen Datenmengen arbeiten, nutzen zusätzlich zu der ernormen Verarbeitungsgeschwindigkeit des Computers auch die Fähigkeiten des menschlichen Benutzers, der beim Knowledge Discovery beispielsweise ein Ziel vorgeben oder beim Information Retrieval die Ergebnisse des ersten Suchlaufes bewerten kann.

Eine effektive Unterstützung von Datenexploration und -analyse ist derzeit nur unter Einbeziehung des Menschen und seiner Fähigkeiten möglich. Insbesondere die unübertroffenen Fähigkeiten der Wahrnehmung erlauben es dem Menschen, in kürzester Zeit komplexe Sachverhalte zu analysieren, wichtige Informationen zu erkennen und Entscheidungen zu treffen. Das menschliche Wahrnehmungssystem kann flexibel die verschiedensten Arten von Daten verarbeiten, wobei es automatisch ungewöhnliche Eigenschaften erkennt, bekannte Eigenschaften dagegen ignoriert. Menschen können leichter und besser mit vagen Beschreibungen und unscharfem Wissen umgehen als heutige Systeme, und ihr Allgemeinwissen erlaubt es ihnen, ohne geistige Anstrengung komplexe Schlußfolgerungen zu ziehen.

Das Ziel unseres Ansatzes der Datenexploration und -analyse ist deshalb, den Menschen in den 'Data Mining'-Prozeß mit einzubeziehen und seine Fähigkeiten auf die großen, in heutigen Computersystemen verfügbaren Datenbestände anzuwenden. Da weder Mensch noch Computer allein das Problem der Datenexploration sehr großer Datenbanken lösen kann, ist eine möglichst enge Kooperation zwischen Mensch und Computer erforderlich. Es gilt, die immense Speicherkapazität und Rechenleistung heutiger Computer mit Flexibilität, Kreativität und Allgemeinwissen des Menschen zu vereinen. Dabei ist die Entwicklung von Techniken wichtig, die den Menschen nicht einfach mit Daten überhäufen, sondern einen guten Überblick über die Daten ermöglichen. In diesem Zusammenhang müssen neue Darstellungsformen für große Mengen multidimensionaler Daten entwickelt werden, wobei alle Eigenschaften der visuellen Repräsentation, wie z.B. Anordnung und Farbe, zu berücksichtigen sind.

Unser Ansatz zur Datenexploration und -analyse großer Datenbanken basiert auf neuartigen Visualisierungstechniken für multidimensionale Daten. Die prinzipielle Idee ist die gleichzeitige Darstellung möglichst vieler Datenobjekte am Bildschirm, wobei jeder Datenwert durch ein Pixel des Bildschirms repräsentiert wird. Die Farbe des Pixels entspricht dem Abstand des jeweiligen Datenwertes zum Anfragewert. Die Anordnung hängt von der Gesamtdistanz des Datensatzes in Bezug auf die Anfrage und von der gewählten Visualisierungstechnik ab. Durch ein graphisches Benutzerinterface kann der Benutzer seine Anfragen inkrementell ändern, wobei er durch das visuelle Feedback, das er bei Änderungen bekommt, in der Verfeinerung seiner Anfragen unterstützt wird.

Da Datenvisualisierungstechniken nicht als allgemein bekannt vorausgesetzt werden können, soll im zweiten Abschnitt zunächst eine kurzer Überblick über Visualisierungstechniken für multidimensionale, multivariate Daten gegeben werden. In [KKS 94] wurde die prinzipielle Idee unserer Visualisierungstechnik sowie das interaktive Anfrage- und Visualisierungsinterface des ersten Prototypsystems vorgestellt. Inzwischen liegt eine vollständige Reimplementierung des Systems in C++ / MOTIF vor, die unter X-Windows auf HP 7xx Maschinen läuft. Die derzeitige Version ist um zusätzliche Visualisierungstechniken erweitert worden und ermöglicht einen direkten Vergleich der Techniken. Im dritten Abschnitt werden die Visualisierungstechniken, die durch die derzeitigen Version des Systems unterstützt werden, kurz vorgestellt. Der vierte Abschnitt beinhaltet einen detaillierten Vergleich sowie eine Bewertung der Visualisierungstechniken. Bei der Bewertung von Visualisierungstechniken stehen nicht, wie sonst bei Leistungsvergleichen, die CPU-Zeiten oder die Anzahl der Zugriffe auf den Sekundärspeicher im Vordergrund, sondern die Wahrnehmbarkeit von Eigenschaften der Daten. Für den Vergleich werden künstlich erzeugte Daten mit spezifischen vorgegebenen Eigenschaften verwendet. Abschnitt fünf faßt die Ergebnisse zusammen und erläutert zukünftige Forschungsvorhaben.

Bei unseren Betrachtungen gehen wir zunächst von einer einfachen Strukturierung der Daten, wie sie beim relationalen Modell vorhanden ist, aus. Dies ist für einen großen Teil der betrachteten Anwendungen adäquat, da sehr große Datenmengen heute zumeist mit Hilfe relationaler Systeme verwaltet werden. Unsere Visualisierungstechniken eignen sich jedoch ebenso für die Visualisierung großer Datenmengen, die in objekt-orientierten oder anderen Datenbanken gespeichert sind.

2. Visualisierung multidimensionaler Daten

In vielen Bereichen von Forschung und Industrie werden Visualisierungen von Daten, die eine inhärente zwei- oder drei-dimensionale Semantik haben, verwendet. Eine Übersicht über solche Techniken ist beispielsweise in den bekannten Büchern von Edward R. Tufte [Tuf 83, Tuf 90] zu finden. Bis vor kurzem gab es jedoch nur wenige Techniken, die eine Visualisierung multidimensionaler Daten ohne inhärente zwei- oder drei-dimensionale Semantik erlauben. Erste Ansätze sind Matrizen von X-Y-Diagrammen [And 72, Cle 93], die Chernoff'sche Gesichter-Darstellung [Che 73], und andere [And 57, Bri 79]. Durch die zunehmende Verfügbarkeit von Grafik-Workstations mit hoher Rechenleistung wurden in den letzten Jahren zahlreiche neue

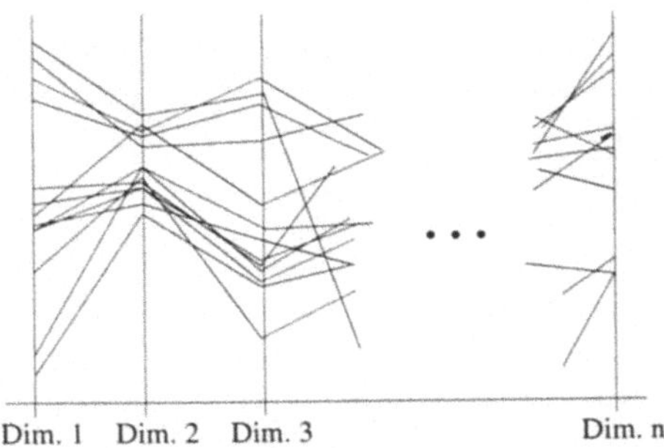

Abb. 1: Technik der Parallelen Koordinaten

Visualisierungstechniken entwickelt. In den bisher untersuchten Ansätzen ist die Anzahl der gleichzeitig visuell darstellbaren Datensätze noch stark begrenzt (100 - 1.000 Datensätze). Um einen Einblick in das Gebiet der Visualisierung multidimensionaler Daten zu geben, sollen im folgenden beispielhaft einige Techniken, die für die Visualisierung von Datenbanken geeignet sind, vorgestellt werden.

2.1 Geometrische Projektionen

Das Ziel geometrischer Projektionstechniken ist es, aussagekräftige Projektionen multidimensionaler Daten zu finden. Die Klasse der geometrischen Projektionen umfaßt Techniken aus der Statistik wie z.B. Hauptkomponenten-Analyse, Faktor-Analyse und multidimensionales Skalieren, die auch unter dem Begriff 'projection pursuit' zusammengefaßt werden [FT 74, Hub 85]. Da die Anzahl der Möglichkeiten, multidimensionale Daten mit hoher Dimension auf zwei Dimensionen abzubilden, sehr groß ist, versuchen 'projection pursuit'-Systeme (z.B. Grand Tour System [Asi 85]), automatisch aussagekräftige Projektionen zu finden oder wenigstens den Benutzer bei der Suche nach geeigneten Projektionen zu unterstützen.

Eine andere geometrische Projektionstechnik ist die Technik der Parallelen Koordinaten (parallel coordinates) [Ins 85, ID 90]. Diese Technik stellt den k-dimensionalen Raum mit Hilfe von k äquidistanten Achsen dar, die parallel zu einer der Bildschirmachsen liegen. Die Achsen entsprechen den Dimensionen und sind vom Minimum- bis zum Maximumwert der Dimensionen linear skaliert. Jeder Datensatz wird als polygonale Linie dargestellt, die jede Achse an dem Punkt schneidet, dessen Wert der jeweiligen Dimension entspricht (vgl. Abb. 1). Obwohl die Grundidee der 'Parallelen Koordinaten'-Technik einfach ist, ermöglicht sie das Erkennen eines weiten Spektrums von Datencharakteristika, wie z.B. verschiedene Datenverteilungen und funktionale Abhängigkeiten. Wegen der Überlappungen der Linien ist jedoch die Anzahl der Datensätze, die gleichzeitig visuell darstellbar ist, auf ca. 1.000 begrenzt.

2.2 Pixeldiagramme (Iconic Displays)

Eine andere Technik zur visuellen Darstellung multidimensionaler Daten sind Pixeldiagramme (iconic displays), bei denen jedes multidimensionale Datenelement durch ein Icon dargestellt wird. Erste Ansätze der 'iconic display' Technik sind die bereits erwähnten Chernoff'schen Gesichter [Che 73, Tuf 83], bei denen zwei Dimensionen durch die zwei Bildschirmdimensionen und die restlichen Dimensionen durch Merkmale des Gesichts (Form von Nase, Mund, Augen und des Gesichts selbst) dargestellt werden (vgl. Abb. 2). Die Chernoff'sche Visualisierungstechnik basiert auf der Fähigkeit des Menschen, Gesichter bzw. Gesichtszüge zu unterscheiden.

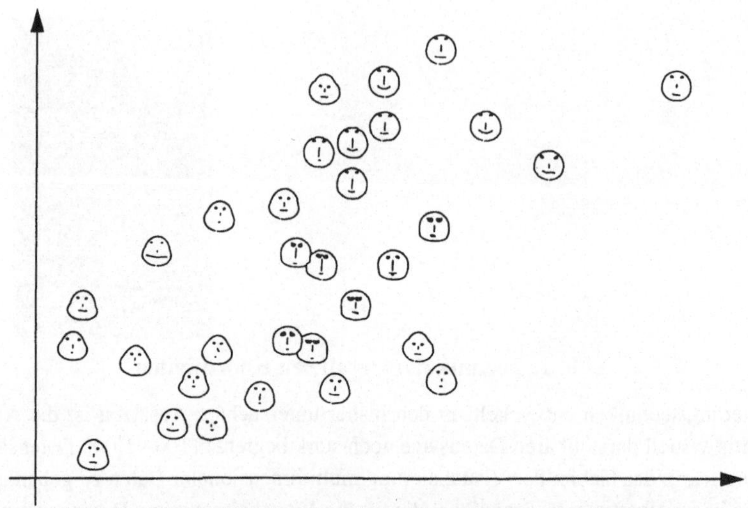

Abb. 2: Chernoff'sche Gesichterdarstellung (vgl. [Tuf 83])

Eine weitere bekannte Pixeldiagramm-Visualisierungstechnik ist die sog. Strichmännchen (stick figure)-Technik [Pic 70, PG 88]. Wie der Name bereits sagt, sind die verwendeten Icons eine Art Strichmännchen, wobei die Winkel und Strichlängen die Datendimensionen repräsentieren. Wenn die Datensätze im Bezug auf die Bildschirmdimensionen verhältnismäßig dicht beieinander liegen, zeigt die resultierende Visualisierung Strukturmuster, die gemäß der Datencharakteristika variieren. Als Strichmännchen können verschiedene Icons mit unterschiedlicher Dimensionalität verwendet werden (vgl. Abb. 3). In Abb. 4 ist eine Visualisierung von fünfdimensionalen Infrarot-Bildern der östlichen Großen Seen in den Vereinigten Staaten dargestellt, die mit Hilfe der Strichmännchen-Technik generiert wurde. An dieser Stelle sei angemerkt, daß sowohl bei der Strichmännchen-Technik als auch bei den Chernoff'schen Gesichtern die Anzahl der gleichzeitig darstellbaren Dimensionen begrenzt ist.

Anders ist dies bei der sog. 'shape coding' Technik [Bed 90]. Bei der 'shape coding' Technik wird jeder Dimension ein kleines Pixel-Array zugeordnet, wobei die Farbe bzw. Graustufe der Pixel dem Wert der Dimension entspricht. Die Pixel-Arrays, die zu den Dimensionen eines Datensatzes gehören, werden dann nacheinander in einem kleinen Quadrat oder Rechteck angeordnet. Die kleinen Quadrate oder Rechtecke, die den Datensätzen entsprechen, werden zeilenweise angeordnet.

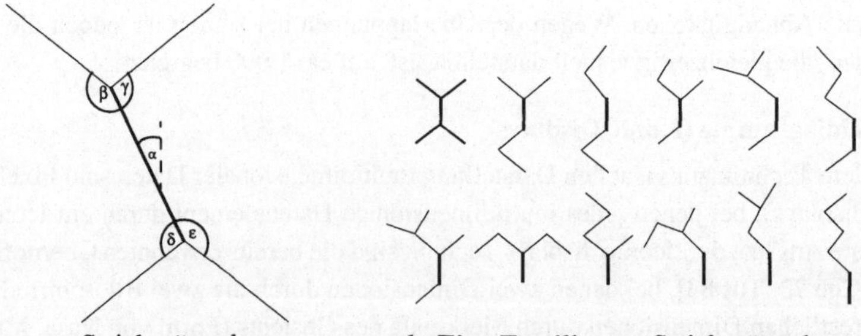

a. Strichmännchen   b. Eine Familie von Strichmännchen

Abb. 3: Strichmännchen Technik

Abb. 4: Strichmännchen-Visualisierung der östlichen Großen Seen (vgl. [SGP 91])

2.3 Hierarchische und Dynamische Techniken

Neben den Geometrischen Projektionen und Pixeldiagrammen gibt es noch zwei weitere Klassen von Visualisierungstechniken - die hierarchischen und dynamischen Techniken. Bei den hierarchischen Techniken sind insbesondere die n-Vision Technik (auch 'worlds within worlds' genannt) [BF 90], das dimensionale Stapeln (dimensional stacking) [LWW 90] und das hierarchische Zeichnen (hierarchical plotting) [MGTS 90] zu nennen. Beispiele für dynamische Techniken sind [MTS 91] und [MZ 92]. Hierarchische Techniken untergliedern den k-dimensionalen Raum und präsentieren ihn in einer hierarchischen Form. Beim dimensionalen Stapeln beispielsweise wird der k-dimensionale Raum in zweidimensionale Teilräume unterteilt. Da hierarchische Techniken hauptsächlich für die Visualisierung mehrdimensionaler Funktionen verwendet werden, unser Anliegen aber die Visualisierung von Datenbankinhalten ist, sollen sie an dieser Stelle nicht weiter behandelt werden.

3. Visualisierungstechniken zur Analyse sehr großer Datenmengen

In den bisher vorgeschlagenen und im letzten Abschnitt erläuterten Visualisierungstechniken für multidimensionale Daten ist die Anzahl der gleichzeitig am Bildschirm darstellbaren Datensätze auf maximal 100 bis 1.000 begrenzt. In diesem Abschnitt sollen kurz die von uns entwikkelten Visualisierungstechniken, die sich auch für sehr große Datenmengen (bis 1.000.000 Datensätze) eignen, vorgestellt werden.

Die Relationen einer relationalen Datenbank können als Mengen von Tupeln der Form $(a_1, a_2,..., a_k)$ angesehen werden, wobei $a_1, a_2,..., a_k$ die Attributwerte eines Datensatzes darstellen. Anfragen an relationale Datenbanken können als Anfrageregion(en) im k-dimensionalen Raum, der durch die k Attribute einer Relation aufgespannt wird, verstanden werden. Alle Datensätze, die innerhalb der Anfrageregion(en) liegen, stellen die Antwort auf die Anfrage dar und werden als

Ergebnis der Anfrage ermittelt. Die Menge der Antworten kann sehr groß, sie kann aber auch leer sein. In beiden Fällen ist es für den Benutzer schwierig, die Antwort zu verstehen und die Anfrage entsprechend zu modifizieren. Um dem Benutzer mehr Feedback auf seine Anfrage zu geben, werden durch unsere Visualisierungstechniken nicht nur die Datensätze visualisiert, die innerhalb der Anfrageregion(en) liegen und damit die Anfrage erfüllen, sondern auch solche, die 'in der Nähe' der Anfrageregion(en) liegen und damit die Anfrage nur approximativ erfüllen.

Unabhängig davon, ob ein Datensatz die Anfrage erfüllt oder nicht, kann für jedes Attribut der Abstand von dem vorgegebenen Anfragewert (oder -intervall) berechnet werden. Macht man dies für jedes Attribut, so erhält man Tupel $(d_1, d_2,..., d_k)$, die die Distanzen der Datenwerte bezüglich der Anfrage beinhalten. Verändert man die Anfrageregion, so ändern sich die Distanztupel entsprechend. Das Distanztupel kann um einen $(k+1)$-ten Werte erweitert werden, der die Gesamtdistanz des Datensatzes bezüglich der Anfrage darstellt. Der Wert von d_{k+1} ist '0', falls der Datensatz die Anfrage erfüllt; ansonsten gibt d_{k+1} den Abstand des Datensatzes bezüglich der Anfrage wieder. Die Menge der Distanztupel $(d_1, d_2,..., d_k, d_{k+1})$ wird nach dem Wert d_{k+1} (Resultat) aufsteigend sortiert, d.h. am Anfang stehen die Tupeln mit $d_{k+1} = 0$ (falls vorhanden) und am Schluß die Tupel mit den größten Distanzen.

Als nächstes werden den Distanzwerten Farben zugeordnet. Die Abbildung des Werteintervalls für jedes Attribut inklusive des Gesamtresultats wird dabei auf eine spezielle Farbskala abgebildet. Die Farbskala ist so entworfen, daß dem Distanzwert '0' die Farbe gelb zugeordnet ist; Distanzwerte größer '0' werden in aufsteigender Reihenfolge immer dunkler. Das Farbspektrum durchläuft die Farben hellgrün, blau, rot bis dunkelbraun. Die gelbe Farbe ist besonders hervorgehoben und zeigt an, daß der zugehörige Datenwert innerhalb des vorgegebenen Anfrageintervalls liegt; die übrigen Farben zeigen die relative Entfernung des Attributwertes von dem Intervall an. Für eine einfache Zuordnung von Datenwerten zu den Farbpixeln sorgt eine Option des interaktiven Interfaces: Durch Anklicken von Pixeln können die zugehörigen Datenwerte abgefragt werden. Details des interaktiven Interfaces sind in [KKS 94] und [Kei 94] beschrieben.

Die Verfahren zur Berechnung der Distanzen und ihre Kombination in die Gesamtdistanz sowie die Behandlung komplexer Anfragen, die aus einer beliebigen Boole'schen Verknüpfung von Anfragebedingungen (geschachtelte 'AND's und 'OR's) bestehen, mehrere Relationen betreffen oder aus einer Schachtelung von Teilanfragen bestehen, wurden in [KKS 94] vorgestellt und sollen deshalb an dieser Stelle nicht näher erläutert werden.

3.1 Spiralanordnung

Bei der Spiralanordnung wird jeder Distanzwert durch ein Pixel repräsentiert. Die Distanzwerte für die einzelnen Attribute sowie das Gesamtergebnis werden in separaten Fenstern dargestellt (vgl. Abb. 7). Die Anordnung der Pixel geschieht spiralförmig um die Mitte der Fenster herum (vgl. Abb. 5). Die Reihenfolge der Pixel entspricht dabei der Sortierung entsprechend der Gesamtdistanz. Im Fenster für das Gesamtergebnis sind in der Mitte die gelben Pixel; weiter nach außen verlaufen die Farben kontinuierlich von hellgrün bis dunkelbraun. Die Fenster für die einzelnen Attribute weisen keine kontinuierlichen Farbübergänge auf, da die Pixel der Attribute in derselben Reihenfolge angeordnet sind wie im Fenster für das Gesamtergebnis. Die Farben der Pixel sind von den Attributwerten abhängig und daher nicht gleichmäßig verteilt. Die Visualisierung der Datenbank besteht damit aus insgesamt $k+1$ Fenstern der gleichen Größe, wobei jedes Fenster eine Dimension des R^k (bzw. R^{k+1}) repräsentiert. Die Pixel, die zu den Attributwerten eines Datensatzes gehören, liegen in verschiedenen Fenstern. Da sie jedoch in jedem Fenster die

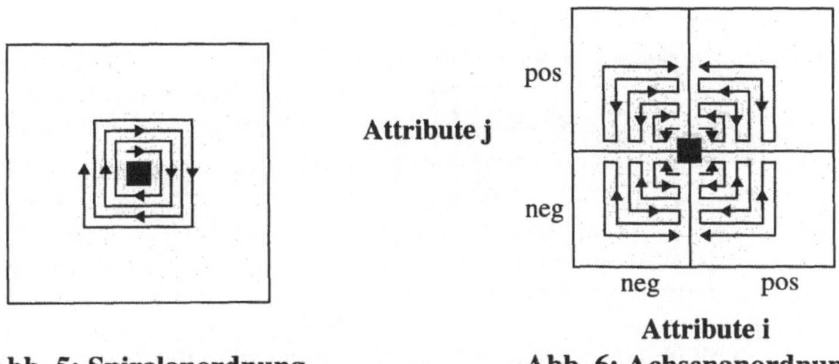

**Abb. 5: Spiralanordnung
eines Attributs**

**Abb. 6: Achsenanordnung
eines Attributs**

gleichen Koordinaten haben, können Zusammenhänge zwischen den Attributwerten eines Datensatzes hergestellt werden (vgl. Abb. 7).

3.2 Achsenanordnung

Die Achsenanordnung ist eine Weiterentwicklung der Spiralanordnung und beruht auf der Idee, die Daten entsprechend ihrer Distanz bezüglich zweier ausgewählter Attribute auf dem Bildschirm anzuordnen. Da Attributwerte im allgemeinen kleiner oder größer als das vorgegebene Anfrageintervall sein können, ergeben sich bei der Berechnung der Distanzen positive und negative Werte. Diese zusätzliche Information wird bei der Achsenanordnung ausgenutzt, um die Daten in vier Quadranten anzuordnen. Dazu werden zwei Attribute ausgewählt, und die Teilbilder für die Dimensionen bzw. die Gesamtdistanz durch zwei orthogonale Achsen in jeweils vier Quadranten aufgeteilt. Datensätze mit positiven Distanzen werden rechts bzw. oberhalb, Datensätze mit negativen Distanzen links bzw. unterhalb der jeweiligen Achse gezeichnet. Die Anordnung der Datensätze innerhalb der Quadranten erfolgt rechtwinklig um das Zentrum herum (vgl. Abb. 6). Die Datensätze, die die Anfrage erfüllen, liegen wie bei der Spiralanordnung im Zentrum der Achsen. Da die Quadranten bei der Achsenanordnung im allgemeinen nicht gleichmäßig gefüllt sind, können weniger Datensätze als bei der Spiralanordnung dargestellt werden. Dies ist aber der Preis für die größere Aussagekraft der entstandenen Visualisierungen, die in einigen Fällen Eigenschaften der Daten besser hervorheben (siehe Abschnitt 4).

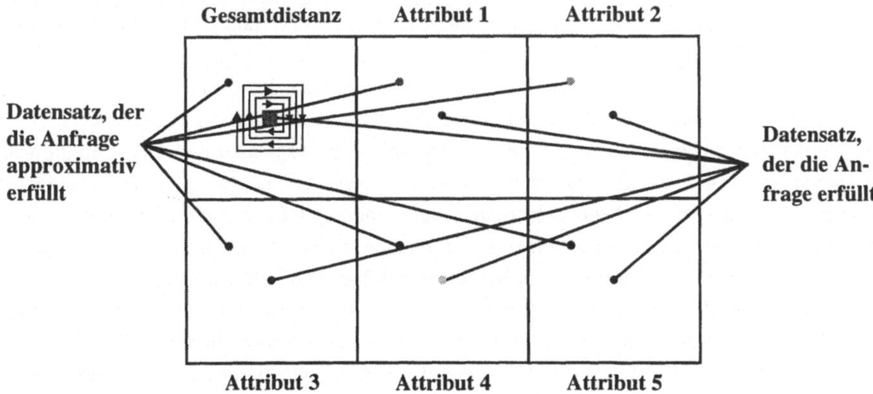

Abb. 7: Anordnung der Fenster bei der Visualisierung fünfdimensionaler Daten

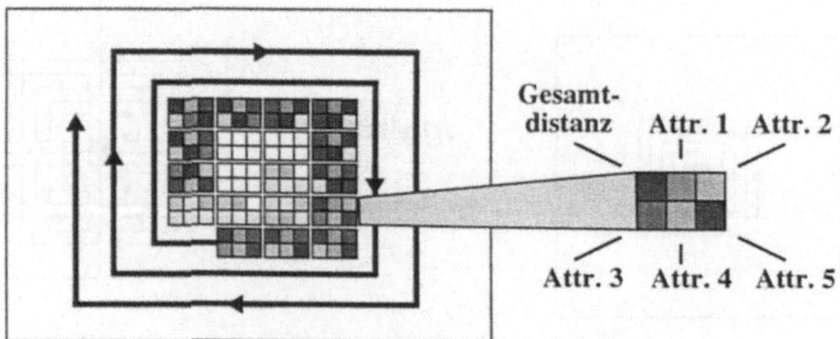

Abb. 8: Gruppenanordnung fünfdimensionaler Daten

3.3 Gruppenanordnung

Bei der Spiral- und Achsenanordnung sind die Pixel, die die Distanzen eines Datensatzes bezüglich seiner Attribute darstellen, in mehrere Teilbilder aufgeteilt. Im Gegensatz dazu werden bei der Gruppenanordnung die zu einem Datensatz gehörenden Distanzen in einem zusammenhängenden Bereich dargestellt (vgl. Shape Coding Technique in Abschnitt 2). Die Bereiche sind wie bei der Spiralanordnung spiralförmig um die Mitte des Fensters angeordnet. Im Gegensatz zur Spiralanordnung besteht die Visualisierung aus nur einem Fenster, das die Distanzwerte sämtlicher Datensätze darstellt, d.h. die Visualisierung ist nicht in Teilbilder für die Attribute und die Gesamtdistanz unterteilt. Die Gruppenanordnung benötigt wesentlich mehr Platz auf dem Bildschirm, da zum einen die Attributwerte nicht mehr mit nur einem Pixel dargestellt werden können (für die Erkennbarkeit einzelner Werte sind mindestens 2 x 2 Pixel erforderlich), zum anderen wird zusätzlich Platz für die Zwischenräume benötigt, damit die Datensätze voneinander unterscheidbar sind. Insgesamt können deshalb deutlich weniger Datensätze auf dem Bildschirm dargestellt werden (siehe Abschnitt 4).

3.4 Sequenzen von Visualisierungen

Bei den bisher vorgestellten Visualisierungstechniken ist die Anzahl der Datenwerte, die visualisiert werden können, durch die Anzahl der Pixel des Bildschirms beschränkt und liegt damit höchstens in der Größenordnung von einer Million Pixel; für die uns zur Verfügung stehenden 19 Zoll Bildschirme mit einer Auflösung von 1.024 x 1.280 sind es 1.3 Millionen Pixel. Um noch größere Datenmengen am Bildschirm darstellen zu können, müssen weitere Darstellungsdimensionen hinzugenommen werden. Naheliegend ist die Verwendung der Dimension 'Zeit'. Die prinzipielle Idee dabei ist, durch Verschieben der Anfrageregion im k-dimensionalen Raum Sequenzen von Visualisierungen zu erzeugen. Dadurch können zum einen größere Datenmengen visualisiert werden, zum anderen werden durch die Veränderung der Bilder aber auch Abhängigkeiten innerhalb der Daten besser wahrnehmbar. Bewegt man die Anfrageregion beispielsweise entlang einer Dimension des k-dimensionalen Raumes, so erhält man einen Überblick über die entsprechenden Veränderungen anderer Dimensionen. Die Verschiebung der Anfrageregion ist aber nicht auf einzelne Dimensionen beschränkt, sondern kann entlang eines beliebigen Pfades im k-dimensionalen Raum erfolgen. Der Bereich des k-dimensionalen Raumes, der durch die Visualisierungssequenz dargestellt wird, ist aber nicht nur vom Pfad sondern auch von der Verteilung der Daten im k-dimensionalen Raum abhängig. Die Ermittlung von Pfaden, die eine vollständige Überdeckung des gesamten k-dimensionalen Raumes garantieren, ist deshalb im allgemeinen ein schwieriges und bisher noch ungelöstes Problem.

4. Bewertung und Vergleich unserer Visualisierungstechniken

Ein zentrales Anliegen dieses Papers sind Bewertung und Vergleich unserer Visualisierungstechniken. Bei der Bewertung von Visualisierungstechniken stehen nicht, wie sonst bei Leistungsvergleichen, die CPU-Zeiten oder die Anzahl der Zugriffe auf den Sekundärspeicher im Vordergrund, sondern die Wahrnehmbarkeit von Zusammenhängen und Eigenschaften der Daten. Für die Bewertung und den Vergleich wurden sowohl reale als auch künstlich erzeugte Daten verwendet. Die Realdaten stammen aus einem Forschungsprojekt im Bereich der Molekularbiologie [EKSX 95]. Ziel des Projektes ist es, ein effizientes Durchsuchen von Proteindatenbanken nach potentiellen Dockingkandidaten und geeigneten Dockingstellen zu unterstützen. Um einen effizienten Zugriff auf potentielle Dockingkandidaten und -stellen zu gewährleisten, wurde in dem Projekt ein sogenannter 'Feature-Index' entwickelt, mit dessen Hilfe alle Proteine bzw. Regionen ermittelt werden können, deren Parameter zu den Oberflächenparametern des gegebenen Proteins komplementär sind [Ald 94]. Der Feature Index basiert auf einer Partitionierung der Proteinoberflächen in Regionen, die entsprechend eines oder mehrerer Oberflächenparameter vorgenommen wird. Bei der Partitionierung ist es wichtig, die richtigen Wertebereiche für die beteiligten Parameter sowie eine adäquate Gewichtung der Parameter bei der Verknüpfung zu finden. Für diese Teilaufgabe wurde unser Anfrage- und Visualisierungssystem erfolgreich eingesetzt, da es eine interaktive Veränderung der Anfragebereiche erlaubt und Feedback über die Verteilung der Daten bezüglich der Attribute liefert. Details sind in [Kei 94] beschrieben.

Ähnlich wie bei Untersuchungen der CPU-Zeit bzw. der Anzahl der Zugriffe auf den Hintergrundspeicher eignen sich reale Daten wegen ihrer schwer charakterisierbaren Eigenschaften jedoch nur bedingt zur Evaluierung von Visualisierungstechniken. Analog zu den, für Leistungsvergleiche von Datenbanksystemen entwickelten Benchmarks, haben wir deshalb für die Evaluierung von Visualisierungssystemen Teststrategien entwickelt, die künstlich erzeugte Daten mit vorgegebenen Eigenschaften verwenden und damit die Reproduzierbarkeit und Vergleichbarkeit der Ergebnisse gewährleisten. In folgenden werden die Teststrategien, das Testdaten-Generierungssystem sowie die Ergebnisse einiger Tests vorgestellt.

Für die Generierung künstlicher Daten wird die Testdatengenerierungsumgebung *'TestVis'* verwendet, die die Spezifikation eines breiten Spektrums von Datencharakteristika erlaubt. *TestVis* basiert auf einem Testdaten-Modell, das die Spezifikation verschiedener, für Visualisierungszwecke relevanter Datenmengen (z.B. statistische Daten oder Bilddaten) erlaubt [BKP 94].

Die in Datenbanken gespeicherten Daten können im allgemeinen am besten mit Hilfe statistischer Methoden beschrieben werden. *TestVis* erlaubt zu diesem Zweck die Spezifikation von Daten mit einer beliebigen Anzahl von Attributen (Dimensionen) und einer beliebigen Anzahl von Clustern. Für jedes Attribut kann die zugehörige Verteilungsfunktionen bzw. eine funktionale Abhängigkeit[1] von anderen Attributen festgelegt werden. Gleiches gilt entsprechend für die Cluster, wobei zusätzlich die Größe und Lage der Cluster festgelegt wird. Die funktionalen Abhängigkeiten, die mit Hilfe von *TestVis* spezifiziert werden können, sind von der Form

$$(1 + r \times \mathit{rf}) \times \left(\sum_{i=1}^{k} c_{i1} \times a_i^{c_{i2}} \right),$$

---

1. Mit funktionaler Abhängigkeit zwischen Attributen sind nicht nur Attributgleichheit sondern der allgemeinere Fall beliebiger mathematischer Zusammenhänge zwischen Attributen gemeint.

wobei

- c_{i1} und c_{i2} benutzer-definierte Konstanten sind,
- a_i die Attribute sind, von denen das spezifizierte Attribut funktional abhängig ist,
- r eine Zufallszahl im Bereich [-1, 1] und
- rf eine benutzer-definierte Zahl ist, die eine gewisse Zufälligkeit der Daten induziert.

Eine genauere Beschreibung des *TestVis*-Systems ist in [Kei 94] zu finden.

Im folgenden sollen Beispiele für generierte Testdaten mit spezifischen Eigenschaften gegeben sowie die zugehörigen Visualisierungen beschrieben werden. Die verwendeten Testdaten zeichnen sich durch einen großen, zufällig erzeugten Grunddatenbestand aus, der mindestens zwei Drittel der gesamten Daten ausmacht. In diesen Grunddatenbestand sind dann ein oder mehrere Cluster eingefügt, die eine unterschiedliche Dimensionalität haben bzw. unter Verwendung verschiedener Verteilungsfunktionen und funktionaler Abhängigkeiten definiert wurden. Aufgrund der hohen Anzahl an zufällig erzeugten Datensätzen führen mathematische und statistische Methoden für die betrachteten Testdaten nicht zu befriedigenden Ergebnissen. Aus Platzgründen verwenden wir für die Auswertung als Visualisierungstechnik nur die Spiralanordnung. Ein Vergleich von Spiral-, Achsen- und Gruppenanordnung wird anschließend vorgenommen.

4.1 Cluster mit unterschiedlicher Dimensionalität

In Abb. 9 sind Visualisierungen von sechsdimensionalen Testdaten dargestellt, die vier- bzw. fünfdimensionale Cluster enthalten. Die verwendeten Testdaten bestehen aus 15.000 Datensätzen, von denen zwei Drittel zufällig (im Bereich [0,100] für jede Dimension) generiert wurden. Das verbleibende Drittel besteht aus drei Clustern, die dadurch definiert sind, daß in vorgegebenen Wertebereichen für die Clusterdimensionen zusätzliche Datensätze generiert wurden. Abb. 9a zeigt die Visualisierung der Daten mit vierdimensionalen Clustern, Abb. 9b die Daten mit fünfdimensionalen Clustern. Als Anfrageregion wurde in beiden Fällen der Bereich [0, 10] für jede Dimension gewählt. Vergleicht man Abb. 9a und b, so fällt auf, daß die Wahrnehmbarkeit der Cluster mit kleiner werdender Dimension der Cluster deutlich abnimmt. Cluster mit kleiner Dimension können jedoch wahrnehmbar gemacht werden, indem der Gewichtungsfaktor eines Attributs auf einen Wert gesetzt wird, der deutlich höher ist als die Gewichtungsfaktoren der übrigen Attribute. Diese Technik führt insbesondere zu guten Ergebnissen, wenn das gewählte Attribut auch Clusterattribut ist. In Abb. 10a sind die Testdaten mit vierdimensionalen Clustern abgebildet, wobei Attribut zwei eine deutlich höhere Gewichtung als die übrigen Attribute hat. Sind die Gewichtungsfaktoren aller Clusterattribute höher als die der Nicht-Clusterattribute, so werden die Clusterregionen in der Visualisierung deutlicher und die Strukturen in den Fenstern für die Nicht-Clusterattribute verschwinden (c.f Abb. 10b).

Bei Experimenten mit ähnlichen Testdaten stellte sich heraus, daß die Ausdehnung der Cluster im multidimensionalen Raum nur einen kleinen Effekt auf die Visualisierung hat. Wichtiger hingegen ist die Anzahl der Datensätze, die zum Cluster gehören. Cluster, die nur aus wenigen Datensätzen bestehen, können nur wahrgenommen werden, wenn sie nahe an der Anfrageregion liegen und sich deutlich von den übrigen Datensätzen unterscheiden. Der Prozentsatz an Datensätzen, der zu einem Cluster gehören muß, damit es wahrnehmbar ist, hängt von der Unterschiedlichkeit zwischen Cluster und übrigen Daten, von der Dimension des Clusters im Vergleich zur Dimension der Daten, und von der Entfernung des Clusters von der Anfrageregion ab.

4.2 Cluster mit verschiedenen Datenverteilungen

In Abb. 11 sind Visualisierungen von Testdaten abgebildet, bei denen verschiedene Verteilungsfunktionen für die Clusterdefinition verwendet wurden. Der Grunddatenbestand von

10.000 Datensätzen ist im Bereich [-10000, 10000] gleichverteilt für jede Dimension. Das Cluster besteht aus 1.000 Datensätzen, wobei die Clusterdimensionen sich in der verwendeten Verteilungsfunktion sowie ihren Parametern unterscheiden. Die Parameter der Verteilungsfunktionen für die Dimensionen sind in folgender Tabelle zusammengefaßt:

	gleichverteilt			normalverteilt					
Dimension	1	2	3	4	5	6	7	8	9
Untere Grenze bzw. Mittelwert	-100	-1000	-10000	0	0	0	100	1000	5000
Obere Grenze bzw. Standardabweichung	100	1000	10000	10	100	1000	1000	1000	5000

Als Anfrageregion wurde der Bereich [0, 10] für jede Dimension benutzt. Da sich Anfrageregion und Cluster in den Dimensionen eins, zwei, vier und fünf überschneiden, ist das Cluster im Zentrum der entsprechenden Fenster gut erkennbar (vgl. Abb. 11a). Wird eine andere Anfrageregion verwendet, so ist es deutlich schwieriger das Cluster zu erkennen (vgl. Abb. 11b). Durch die Visualisierungen wird deutlich, daß für die Dimensionen mit einem großen Bereich bei der Gleichverteilung (Dimension drei) bzw. einer hohen Standardabweichung bei der Normalverteilung (Dimensionen sechs und neun) keine Clusterung vorhanden ist. Durch eine höhere Gewichtung einer Dimension wird dieser Effekt noch klarer (vgl. Abb. 11c).

4.3 Cluster mit funktionalen Abhängigkeiten

In Abb. 12 sind Visualisierungen von Testdaten zu sehen, bei denen verschiedene funktionale Abhängigkeiten für die Clusterdefinition verwendet wurden. Der Grunddatenbestand von 10.000 Datensätzen ist wieder gleichverteilt, diesmal allerdings in verschiedenen Bereichen: Für Dimension eins bis drei im Bereich [0, 1000], für Dimension vier bis sechs im Bereich [0, 2000], und für Dimension sieben bis neuen im Bereich [0, 1000000]. Das Cluster besteht aus 2.000 Datensätzen. Dimensionen eins bis drei des Clusters sind die unabhängigen Dimensionen, die im Bereich [0, 1000] gleichverteilt sind. Die funktionalen Abhängigkeiten der Clusterdimensionen sind in folgender Tabelle zusammengefaßt:

Dimension	1	2	3	4	5	6	7	8	9
funktionale Abhängigkeit	gleichverteilt im Bereich [0, 1000]			linear abhängig von Dimension			quadratisch abhängig von Dimension		
				1	2, 3	1, 2, 3	1	2, 3	1, 2, 3

Als Anfrageregion wurde der Ursprung des Koordinatensystems (Bereich [0, 0] für jede Dimension) benutzt. In Abb. 12a - c sind drei Visualisierungen der Daten abgebildet. Die drei Visualisierungen der Daten unterscheiden sich in den verwendeten Gewichtungsfaktoren. In Abb. 12a wird ein höheres Gewicht für Dimension eins verwendet, wodurch eine Strukturierung in den abhängigen Dimensionen vier und sieben sichtbar wird. In den Fenstern für die nicht von Dimension eins abhängigen Dimensionen fünf und acht dagegen ist keinerlei Strukturierung zu erkennen. Die Fenster für Dimensionen sechs und neun, die teilweise von Dimension eins abhängig sind, zeigen nur eine relativ schwach wahrnehmbare Strukturierung. In Abb. 12b wird ein höheres Gewicht für Dimension zwei und drei verwendet. Die entsprechenden abhängigen Dimensionen fünf und acht bzw. sechs und neun des Clusters sind zwar erkennbar, jedoch nicht so deutlich wie erwartet. Wird ein höheres Gewicht für die Dimensionen eins bis drei verwendet (vgl. Abb. 12c), so nimmt die Wahrnehmbarkeit der Abhängigkeiten weiter ab.

Um funktionale Abhängigkeiten sichtbar zu machen, entwickelten wir eine Technik, die wir 'Farbinvertierung' nennen [Kei 94]. Farbinvertierung bedeutet dabei, daß die Farbtabelle und damit die Zuordnung zwischen Farben und Distanzwerten invertiert wird. Die Auswirkungen der Farbinvertierungstechnik auf die Visualisierungen von Abb. 12 sind in Abb. 13 dargestellt.[1] Besonders auffällig ist die bessere Erkennbarkeit von Clusterdimensionen, die von mehreren Dimensionen abhängig sind.

4.4 Vergleich unserer Visualisierungstechniken

Für den Vergleich von Spiral- und Achsenanordnung verwenden wir vierdimensionale Testdaten mit mehreren Clustern, die sich an verschiedenen Stellen des k-dimensionalen Raumes befinden. Ein Ergebnis unserer Untersuchungen ist, daß die Cluster im allgemeinen bei der Achsenanordnung besser erkennbar sind als bei der Spiralanordnung. In Abb. 14 beispielsweise ist bei der Spiralanordnung keinerlei Strukturierung erkennbar, wohingegen die Achsenanordnung die Cluster recht deutlich zeigt. Die Wahl der Zuordnung von Attributen zu den Achsen hat bei der Achsenanordnung jedoch einen entscheidenen Einfluß auf die Erkennbarkeit der Cluster. Je nachdem, welche der Attribute den Achsen zugeordnet sind, sind die Cluster mehr oder weniger gut zu erkennen. Die Visualisierungen in Abb. 14b und Abb. 15 unterscheiden sich nur in der Zuordnung von Attributen zu den Achsen. Die Achsenanordnung bietet im allgemeinen mehr Information als die Spiralanordnung (vgl. Abb. 14), jedoch müssen zunächst geeignete Attribute für die Zuordnung zu den Achsen gefunden werden. Dies ist insbesondere bei Daten mit einer hohen Dimensionalität nicht immer einfach. Ein Nachteil der Achsenanordnung ist, daß die Anzahl der Datensätze, die visualisiert werden können im allgemeinen geringer ist. Im Extremfall sind zwei gegenüberliegende Quadranten leer (vgl. Abb. 16b), was bedeutet, daß nur halb so viel Datensätze wie bei der Spiralanordnung dargestellt werden können (Achsenanordnung in Abb. 16 ist verkleinert).

In Abb. 17 und Abb. 18 vergleichen wir alle drei Visualisierungstechniken. Zu diesem Zweck benutzen wir zwei achtdimensionale Testdatenmengen, die gleiche Clustereigenschaften haben, aber aus einer unterschiedlichen Anzahl an Datensätzen bestehen. Die in Abb. 17 visualisierten Testdaten bestehen aus 1.000 Datensätzen, die in Abb. 18 visualisierten aus 7.000 Datensätzen. Die Spiral- und Achsenanordnung in Abb. 17 und Abb. 18 sind vergrößert, wohingegen die Gruppenanordnung verkleinert ist (die Gruppenanordnung in Abb. 18 ist auf ca. 3% ihrer Originalgröße verkleinert). Durch die Größe der Visualisierungen wird bereits deutlich, daß die Gruppenanordnung nur für kleinere Datenmengen geeignet ist. Ein Vorteil der Gruppenanordnung ist jedoch, daß sie auch für Daten sehr hoher Dimension brauchbare Visualisierungen liefert. Bei der Spiral- und Achsenanordnung stehen die Pixel für die einzelnen Dimensionen nur durch ihre Position miteinander in Beziehung. Bei einer geringen Anzahl an Dimensionen ist es für den Menschen relativ leicht, die Fenster miteinander in Beziehung zu setzen. Je größer die Anzahl der Dimensionen jedoch wird, desto schwieriger wird es, die große Anzahl an Fenstern zu überblicken und Korrelationen zwischen den Fenstern zu erkennen. Bei der Gruppenanord-

---

1. Die Qualität der gedruckten Version unserer Visualisierungen ist relativ schlecht im Vergleich zur Qualität der Visualisierungen auf dem Bildschirm. Eigenschaften der Daten, die auf dem Bildschirm leicht zu erkennen sind, sind deshalb in der gedruckten Version zum Teil relativ schlecht erkennbar.

nung ist dies nicht notwendig und deshalb ist sie insbesondere für Daten höherer Dimension geeignet. Das blaue Cluster beispielsweise, das in der Gruppenanordnung von Abb. 17 deutlich erkennbar ist, ist in der Spiral- und Achsenanordnung nur relativ schlecht auszumachen. Eine weitere Beobachtung beim Vergleich der Visualisierungen von Abb. 18 ist, daß die Cluster im allgemeinen am deutlichsten in der Achsenanordnung zu erkennen sind. In vielen Fällen liegen die Cluster vollständig in einem der Quadranten (zum Beispiel das braune Cluster im Fenster für Dimension 8 in Abb. 18), was zusätzlich Rückschlüsse auf die Lage des Clusters bezüglich der den Achsen zugeordneten Attribute erlaubt.

Bei der Exploration unbekannter Daten ist es sinnvoll, zunächst mit der Spiralanordnung zu beginnen, um einen Überblick über die Daten zu bekommen. Hat man einen ersten Eindruck und insbesondere eine Idee, welche Dimensionen den Achsen zugeordnet werden sollen, so kann man mit Hilfe der Achsenanordnung eine detailliertere Analyse vornehmen. Die Gruppenanordnung kann dann in einem späteren Schritt für eine gezielte Analyse kleinerer Datenmengen verwendet werden. Datenexploration mit Hilfe unseres Anfrage- und Visualisierungssystems ist ein interaktiver Vorgang, der mit Hilfe von Abbildungen nur zum Teil beschrieben werden kann. Unser Datenbankvisualisierungssystem bietet zahlreiche Optionen, die die Interaktivität unterstützen. Beispiele sind die Optionen, die Datenwerte für ausgewählte Pixel oder Farbbereiche liefern, und die Slider zur Reduktion der Datenmenge. Details sind in [Kei 94], zum Teil auch in [KKS 94] zu finden.

Um die vorgestellten Datenexplorations- und Visualisierungstechniken möglichst effektiv nutzen zu können, ist es notwendig, eine globale Strategie zur Datenexploration zu haben. Einige aus der intensiven Benutzung des Systems stammenden Erfahrungen sollen im folgenden kurz beschrieben werden: Ist nichts über die Daten bekannt, so empfiehlt es sich, mit dem Ursprung des Koordinatensystems als Anfrageregion zu beginnen, wobei alle Dimensionen das gleiche Gewicht haben. Der folgende Datenexplorationsprozeß ist weitgehend durch das visuelle Feedback bestimmt, das der Benutzer durch die Visualisierungen erhält. Erhält der Benutzer nämlich Hinweise auf Korrelationen, funktionale Abhängigkeiten oder sonstige Cluster, so wird er versuchen, mit Hilfe des Systems diese Hypothesen zu überprüfen. Für diesen Zweck kann der Benutzer beispielsweise die Anfrageregion oder die Gewichtung der Dimensionen verändern. Falls in den Visualisierungen jedoch keine Hinweise auf interessante Eigenschaften der Daten erkennbar sind, so kann er einer beliebigen Dimension ein höheres Gewicht geben, die Farbinvertierungstechnik verwenden, den Prozentsatz der angezeigten Datensätze verändern oder eine andere Anfrageregion verwenden. In dieser Aufzählung wurden die Möglichkeiten, die unserer Erfahrung nach das beste Aufwand-Nutzen-Verhältnis haben, zuerst aufgeführt.

5. Zusammenfassung und Ausblick

Visualisierungstechniken können bei der Exploration und Analyse sehr großer multidimensionaler Daten hilfreich sein, um interessante Daten und ihre Eigenschaften zu finden. Unser Ansatz der Datenexploration zielt auf eine adäquate Unterstützung des Menschen durch den Computer ab und kombiniert Datenbankanfrage- und Information Retrieval-Techniken mit neuartigen Visualisierungstechniken. Die Anzahl der Datenwerte, die zu einem Zeitpunkt am Bildschirm dargestellt werden können, ist dabei nur durch die Auflösung des Bildschirms beschränkt. Verschiedene Varianten unserer Visualisierungstechniken unterstützen den Benutzer in den verschiedenen Phasen des Datenexplorations-Prozesses. Für Vergleich und Bewertung unserer Techniken werden künstlich erzeugte Testdaten verwendet, die entsprechend eines systematischen Testdaten-Modells generiert wurden.

Für die Entwicklung verbesserter Visualisierungstechniken ist eine systematische Analyse der existierenden Techniken im Hinblick auf ihre Möglichkeiten und Grenzen sowie ein detaillierter Vergleich der Techniken notwendig. Insbesondere ist ein Vergleich unserer Techniken mit anderen Visualisierungstechniken, die sich für größere Datenmengen eignen (z.B. die 'parallel coordinates'- und 'stick figure'-Technik), notwendig. Es ist beispielsweise zu untersuchen, welche Arten von Korrelationen, Clustern, funktionellen Abhängigkeiten, usw. in den durch die verschiedenen Techniken erzeugten Visualisierungen 'erkennbar' sind. Dabei spielen die betrachteten (realen oder künstlich erzeugten) Testdaten ebenso eine Rolle wie psychologische Fragen der Wahrnehmung (perception).

Ein weiterer Untersuchungsgegenstand ist die effiziente Unterstützung unseres Visualisierungssystems durch die unterliegenden Datenbanksysteme. Wie erste Untersuchungen zeigen [Kei 94], eignen sich heute kommerziell verfügbare Datenbanksysteme nur sehr beschränkt, Visualisierungstechniken wie die oben beschriebenen zu unterstützen. Datenbanksysteme unterstützen zwar hohe Transaktionsraten und die schnelle Suche nach exakt spezifizierten Daten, bieten aber nur unzureichende Performanz für Bereichsanfragen, die sich auf mehrere Attribute beziehen. Solche Anfragen erfordern eine schnelle multidimensionale Suche, die im allgemeinen nur unzureichend unterstützt wird. Ein weiteres Problem ist, daß in heutigen Datenbanksystemen jede Anfrage separat bearbeitet wird. Es gibt keine Möglichkeit, für eine Folge von Anfragen, die sich nur wenig von einander unterscheiden, nur den sich ändernden Teil der Antwortmenge zu erzeugen. Dies wirkt sich besonders negativ auf die Interaktivität unseres Visualisierungssystems aus. Zusätzlich ist es für unsere Visualisierungstechniken erforderlich, auf sämtlich Teilergebnisse für jedes Attribut bzw. für jede Teilanfrage zugreifen zu können. Auch dies wird von heutigen Datenbanksystemen nicht oder nur unzureichend unterstützt. Zusammenfassend kann man sagen, daß bei der Entwicklung einer sekundärspeicherbasierten Version des Systems, basierend auf einem kommerziell verfügbaren Datenbanksystem, noch eine Reihe interessanter Probleme gelöst werden müssen.

Referenzen

[ABN 92]   Anwar T. M., Beck H. W., Navathe S. B.: *'Knowledge Mining by Imprecise Querying: A Classification-Based Approach'*, Proc. 8th Int. Conf. on Data Engineering, Tempe, AZ, 1992, pp. 622-630.

[Ald 94]   Aldinger K., Ester M., Förstner G., Kriegel H.-P., Seidl T.: *'Datenbankunterstützung für das Protein-Protein-Docking: Ein effizienter und robuster Feature-Index'*, Proc. 2nd GI-Fachtagung 'Informatik in den Biowissenschaften', Jena, Germany, 1994.

[And 57]   Anderson E.: *'A Semigraphical Method For The Analysis of Complex Problems'*, Proc. Nat. Acad. Sci. USA, Vol. 13, 1957, pp. 923-927.

[And 72]   Andrews D. F.: *'Plots of High-Dimensional Data'*, Biometrics, Vol. 29, 1972, pp. 125-136.

[Asi 85]   Asimov D.: *'The Grand Tour: A Tool For Viewing Multidimensional Data'*, SIAM Journal of Science & Stat. Comp., Vol. 6, 1985, pp. 128-143.

[Bed 90]   Beddow J.: *'Shape Coding of Multidimensional Data on a Mircocomputer Display'*, Visualization '90, San Francisco, CA, 1990, pp. 238-246.

[BF 90]   Beshers C., Feiner S.: *'Visualizing n-Dimensional Virtual Worlds with n-Vision'*, Computer Graphics, Vol. 24, No. 2, 1990, pp. 37-38.

[BKP 94]   Bergeron R. D., Keim D. A., Pickett R.: *'Test Data Sets for Evaluating Data Visualization Techniques'*, in: Perceptual Issues in Visualization, Springer, 1994.

[Bri 79]   Brissom D.: *'Hypergraphics: Visualizing Complex Relationships in Art, Science and Technology'*, Amer. Association for the Advance of Science, Westview Press, Boulder, 1979.

[Che 73]   Chernoff H.: *'The Use of Faces to Represent Points in k-Dimensional Space Graphically'*, Journal Amer. Statistical Association, Vol. 68, pp 361-368.

[Cle 93]   Cleveland W. S.: *'Visualizing Data'*, AT&T Bell Laboratories, Murray Hill, NJ, Hobart Press, Summit NJ, 1993.

[DE 82]   Dunn G., Everitt B.: *'An Introduction to Mathematical Taxonomy'*, Cambridge University Press, Cambridge, MA, 1982.

[EKSX 95]   Ester M., Kriegel H.-P., Seidel T., Xu X.W.: *'Formbasierte Suche nach komplementären 3D-Oberflächen in einer Protein-Datenbank'*, Proc. GI-Fachtagung 'Datenbanken in Büro, Technik und Wissenschaft' (BTW), Dresden, Germany, 1995.

[FM 91]   Frei H. P., Meienberg S.: *'Evaluating Weighted Search Terms as Boolean Queries'*, Proc. GI/GMD-Workshop, Darmstadt 1991, in: Informatik-Fachberichte, Vol. 289, 1991, pp. 11-22.

[FPM 91]   Frawley W. J., Piatetsky-Shapiro G., Matheus C. J.: *'Knowledge Discovery in Databases: An Overview'*, in: Knowledge Discovery in Databases, AAAI Press, Menlo Park, 1991.

[FT 74]   Friedman J., Tukey J.: *'A Projection Pursuit Algorithm for Exploratory Data Analysis'*, IEEE Transactions on Computers, Vol. 23, 1974, pp. 881-890.

[GGM 92]   Gaasterland T., Godfrey P., Minker J.: *'An Overview of Cooperative Answering'*, Journal of Intelligent Information Systems, Vol. 1, 1992, pp. 123-157.

[Hub 85]   Huber P. J.: *'Projection Pursuit'*, The Annals of Statistics, Vol. 13, No. 2, 1985, pp. 435-474.

[ID 90]   Inselberg A., Dimsdale B.: *'Parallel Coordinates: A Tool for Visualizing Multi-Dimensional Geometry'*, Visualization '90, San Francisco, CA, 1990, pp. 361-370.

[Ins 85]   Inselberg A.: *'The Plane with Parallel Coordinates, Special Issue on Computational Geometry'*, The Visual Computer, Vol. 1, 1985, pp. 69-97.

[Kei 94]   Keim D. A.: *'Visual Support for Query Specification and Data Mining'*, Dissertation, Universität München, 1994.

[KKS 94]   Keim D. A., Kriegel H.-P., Seidl T.: *'Supporting Data Mining of Large Databases by Visual Feedback Queries'*, Proc. 10th Int. Conf. on Data Engineering, Houston, TX, 1994, pp. 302-313.

[LWW 90]   LeBlanc J., Ward M. O., Wittels N.: *'Exploring N-Dimensional Databases'*, Visualization '90, San Francisco, CA, 1990, pp. 230-239.

[MGTS 90]   Mihalisin T., Gawlinski E., Timlin J., Schwendler J.: *'Visualizing A Scalar Field on an N-dimensional Lattice'*, Visualization '90, San Francisco, CA, 1990, pp. 255-262.

[Mot 90]   Motro A.: *'FLEX: A Tolerant and Cooperative User Interface to Databases'*, IEEE Transactions on Knowledge and Data Engineering, Vol. 2, No. 2, 1990, pp. 231-246.

[MTS 91]   Mihalisin T., Timlin J., Schwegler J.: *'Visualizing Multivariate Functions, Data and Distributions'*, IEEE Computer Graphics and Applications, Vol. 11, No. 3, 1991, pp. 28-35.

[MZ 92]   Marchak F., Zulager D.: *'The Effectiveness of Dynamic Graphics in Revealing Structure in Multivariate Data'*, Behavior, Research Methods, Instruments and Computers, Vol. 24, No. 2, 1992, pp. 253-257.

[PG 88]   Pickett R. M., Grinstein G. G.: *'Iconographic Displays for Visualizing Multidimensional Data'*, Proc. IEEE Conf. on Systems, Man and Cybernetics, IEEE Press, Piscataway, NJ, 1988, pp. 514-519.

[Pic 70]   Pickett R. M.: *'Visual Analyses of Texture in the Detection and Recognition of Objects'*, in: Picture Processing and Psycho-Pictorics, Lipkin B. S., Rosenfeld A. (eds.), Academic Press, New York, 1970.

[SB 88]   Salton G., Buckley C.: *'Term-Weighting Approaches in Automatic Text Retrieval'*, Information Processing and Management, Vol. 24, No. 5, 1988, pp. 513-523.

[SGP 91]   Smith S., Grinstein G., Pickett R.: *'Global Geometric, Sound, and Color Controls for Iconographic Displays of Scientific Data'*, in: Extracting Meaning from Complex Data: Processing, Display, Interaction II, Vol. 1459, 1991, pp. 197-206.

[Tuf 83]   Tufte E. R.: *'The Visual Display of Quantitative Information'*, Graphics Press, Cheshire, CT, 1983.

[Tuf 90]   Tufte E. R.: *'Envisioning Information'*, Graphics Press, Cheshire, CT, 1990.

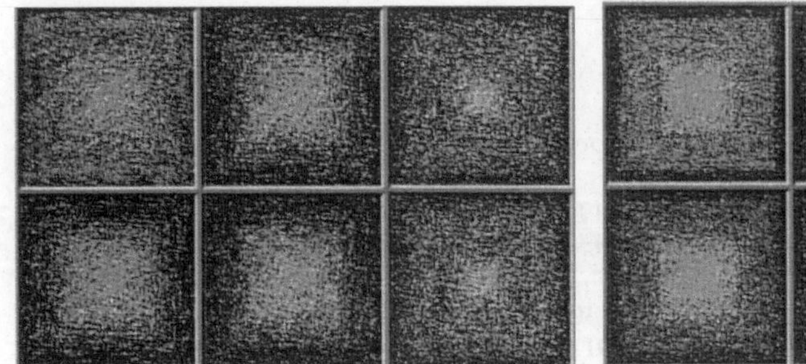

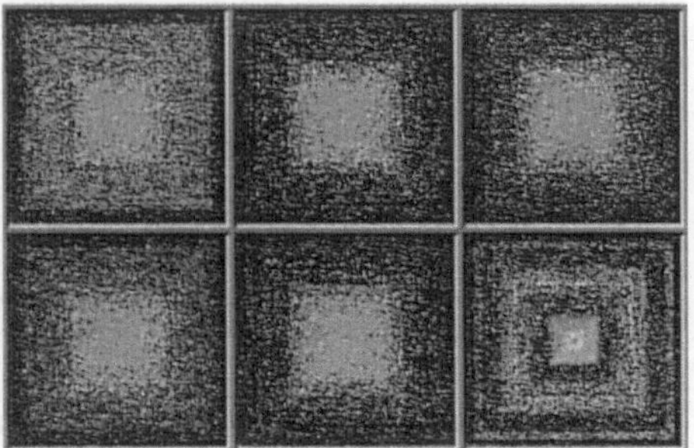

a. Vierdimensionale Cluster　　　　　　b. Fünfdimensionale Cluster

Abb. 9: Visualisierung von Clustern unterschiedlicher Dimensionalität

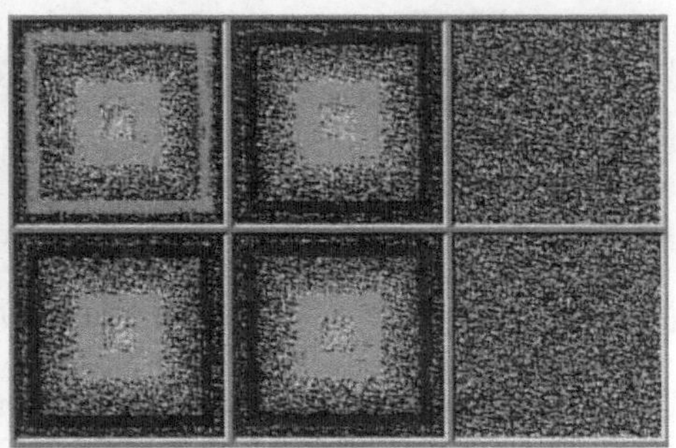

a. Höheres Gewicht für Attribut 2　　　　b: Höheres Gewicht für alle Clusterattr.

Abb. 10: Effekt geänderter Gewichtungsfaktoren

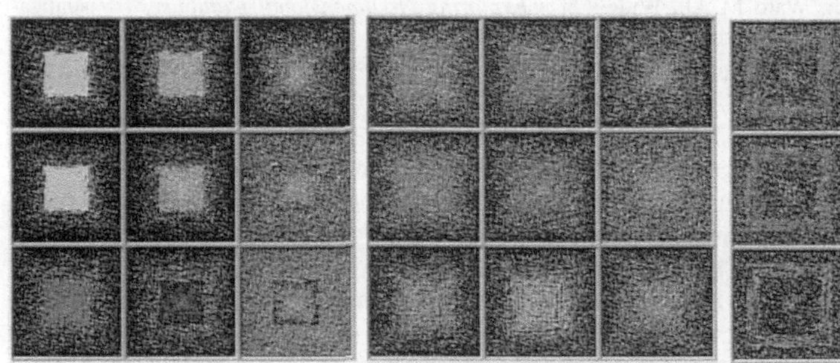

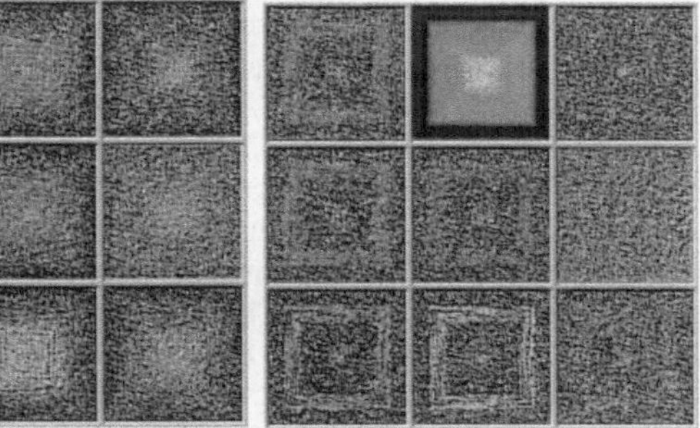

a. Anfrageregion [0, 10]　　b. Anfrageregion [4900, 5000]　c. Höheres Gewicht für Dim. 2

Abb. 11: Cluster mit verschiedenen Datenverteilungen

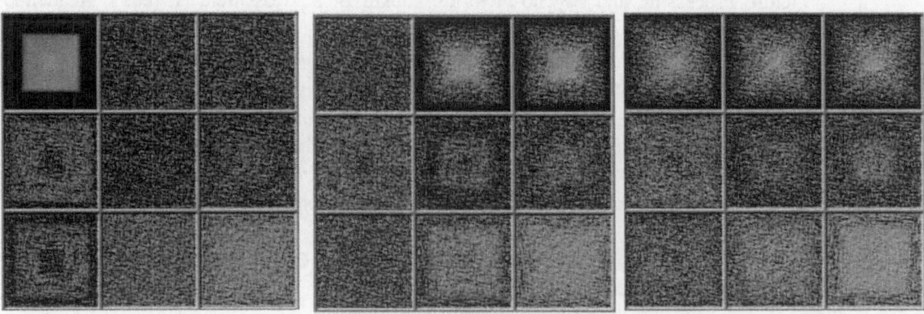

a. Höheres Gewicht auf Dim. 1　　b. Höheres Gewicht auf Dim. 2-3　c. Höheres Gewicht auf Dim. 1-3

Abb. 12: Cluster mit funktionalen Abhängigkeiten

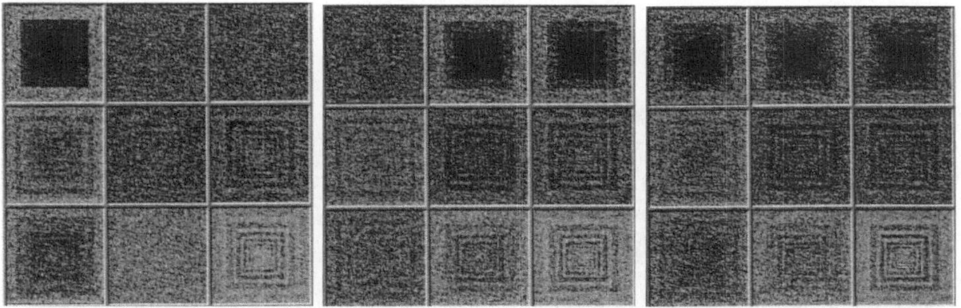

a. Höheres Gewicht auf Dim. 1   b. Höheres Gewicht auf Dim. 2-3   c. Höheres Gewicht auf Dim. 1-3

Abb. 13: Effekt der Farbinvertierung

a.

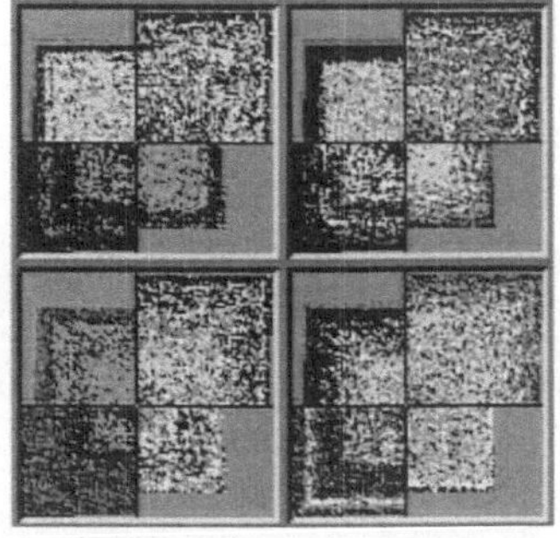

b.

Abb. 14: Vorteil der Achsenanordnung

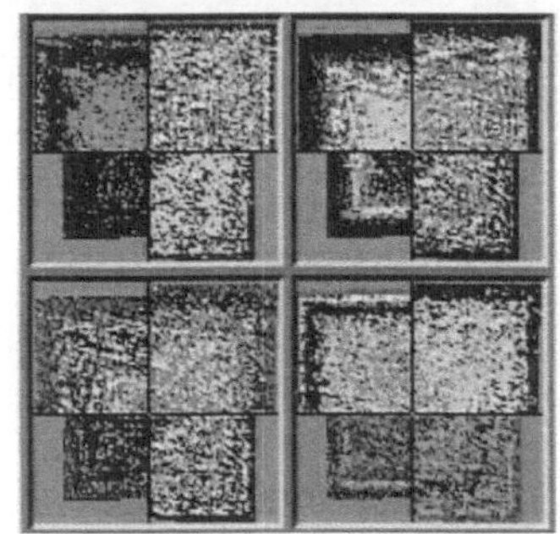

a.

b.

Abb. 15: Auswirkung verschiedener Zuordnungen von Attributen zu den Achsen

a.

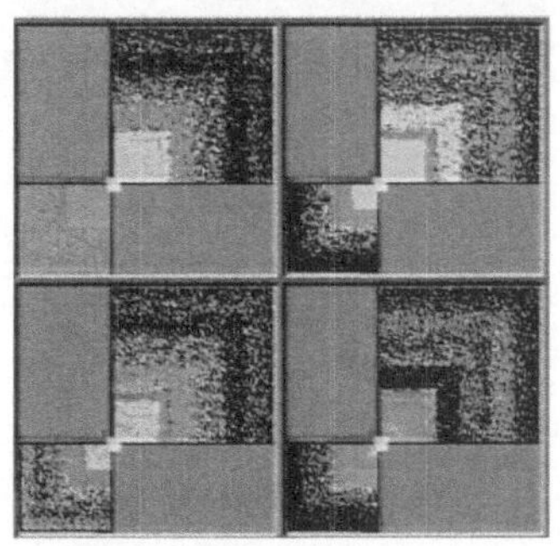

b.

Abb. 16: Nachteil der Achsenanordnung

a. Spiralanordnung

b. Achsenanordnung

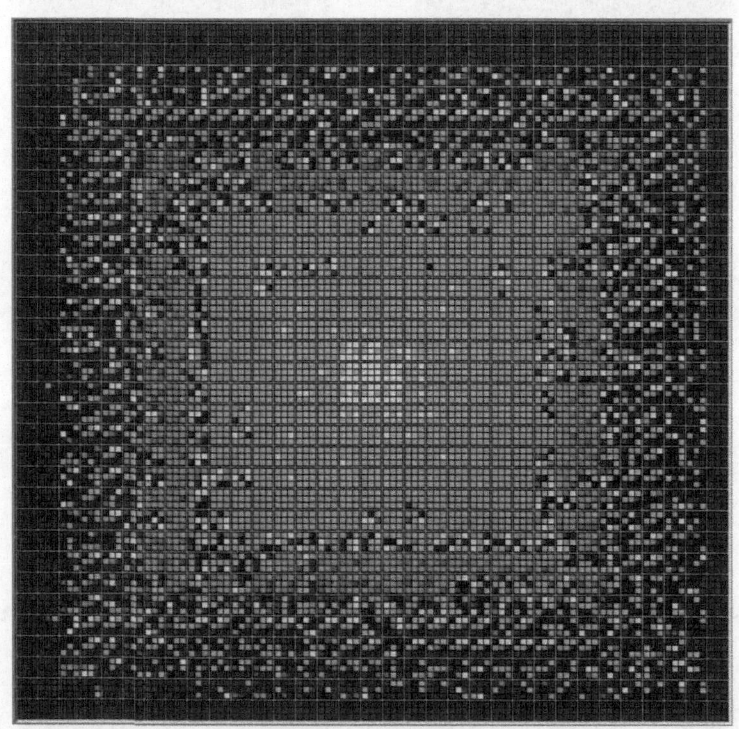

c. Gruppenanordnung

Abb. 17: Achtdimensionale Daten (1.000 Datensätze)

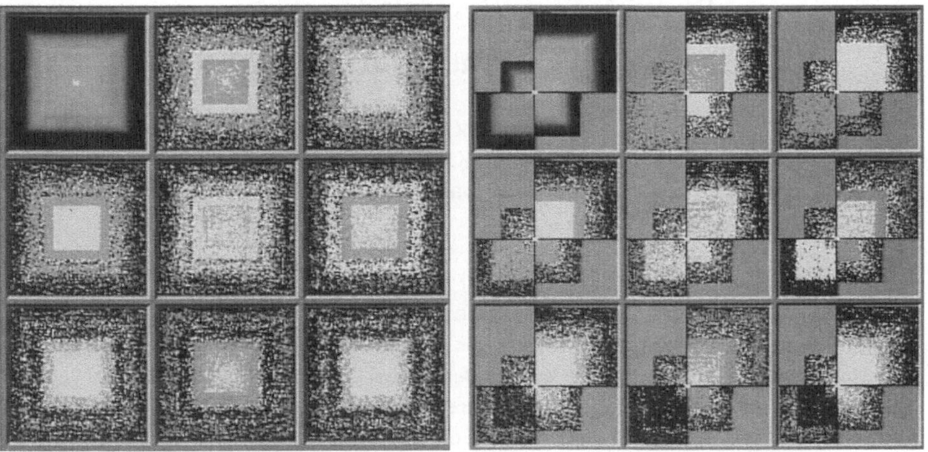

a. Spiralanordnung   b. Achsenanordnung

c. Gruppenanordnung

Abb. 18: Achtdimensionale Daten (7.000 Datensätze)

Strategien zum dynamischen Aufbau
komplexer Objekte in der Anfrageverarbeitung

Michael Gesmann
Universität Kaiserslautern
email: gesmann@informatik.uni-kl.de

Kurzfassung

Strukturell objektorientierte Datenbanksysteme bieten die Möglichkeit zur direkten Modellierung und Verarbeitung komplexer Objekte, die sich aus elementaren Objekten zusammensetzen. Ein wesentlicher Kostenanteil bei der Bearbeitung komplexer Objekte besteht aus der Interpretation und dem Verfolgen von Referenzen, welche Beziehungen zwischen elementaren bzw. komplexen Objekten modellieren. Eine grundlegende Basisoperation ist dabei der Aufbau einfach strukturierter Objekte, mit denen sich dann komplexere, z.B. rekursive oder netzwerkartige Objekte zusammensetzen lassen. Diese Basisoperation wird in der vorliegenden Arbeit am Beispiel des Non-Standard-Datenbanksystems PRIMA genauer untersucht. Ausgehend von sehr einfachen, aber auch ineffizienten Algorithmen wird ein erweitertes Verarbeitungsverfahren aufgestellt, das flexibel auf unterschiedliche Datenbankzustände und Anfrageformulierungen reagieren kann, um so eine optimale Ausführung zu gewährleisten. In dieses Verfahren werden unterschiedliche Aspekte der Zugriffspfadunterstützung, insbesondere die Clusterung komplexer Objekte, integriert. Darüber hinaus werden Probleme bei der parallelen Bearbeitung der Objekte untersucht.

1. Einleitung

Strukturell objektorientierte Datenbanksysteme (SODBS) haben sich in den vergangenen Jahren als geeignete Datenverwaltungssysteme in den sogenannten Non-Standard-Anwendungen erwiesen. Im Vergleich zu relationalen Systemen, die vor allen Dingen die konventionellen Anwendungsklassen durch eine effiziente Verarbeitung großer homogener Datenmengen unterstützen, bieten SODBS die Möglichkeit zur direkten Modellierung und Verarbeitung komplexer Objekte, wie sie z.B. in Entwurfsanwendungen und der Wissensverarbeitung benötigt werden.

Während für relationale Systeme eine fundierte Theorie sowie langjährige Implementierungserfahrung mit Verarbeitungsalgorithmen existieren, sind diese für SODBS nur ansatzweise vorhanden. Dies zeigt sich vor allem bei der Anwendungsunterstützung durch adäquate Anfragesprachen. Für relationale Systeme gibt es mit SQL eine standardisierte, mengenorientierte und deskriptive Anfragesprache. Bemühungen, eine solche Sprache für (strukturell) objektorientierte Systeme zu entwickeln und zu standardisieren, sind noch nicht abgeschlossen und Gegenstand der Forschung [HS91, AWS92, Ki93].

Einhergehend mit diesen Entwicklungen deskriptiver Sprachen treten Fragen nach angemessenen Verarbeitungsmodellen und geeigneten Umsetzungen der Anfragen in konkrete Verarbeitungspläne auf. Dabei sind Probleme der Optimierung und der Verarbeitungsunterstützung durch angemessene Speicherungsstrukturen sowie der Ausnutzung von Parallelität zu berücksichtigen. Aufgrund der direkten Modellierung von Beziehungen zwischen Objekten durch Referenzen ergeben sich im Vergleich zu relationalen Systemen andere Verarbeitungsmuster und Algorithmen.

In diesem Aufsatz werden verschiedene Algorithmen zum Aufbau komplexer Objekt aus elementaren Basisobjekten im SODBS PRIMA [Sch93] vorgestellt und bewertet. PRIMA bietet mit MQL eine deskriptive, mengenorientierte Anfragesprache, die, vergleichbar zu SQL, in der FROM-Klausel die Spezifikation des Typs der aufzubauenden komplexen Objekte, in der WHERE-Klausel die Einschränkung der Ergebnismenge sowie in der SELECT-Klausel die Projektion einzelner Teile der Ergebnisobjekte ermöglicht. In dieser Arbeit konzentrieren wir uns auf solche Anfragen, die in der FROM-Klausel nur baumartig strukturierte Objekttypen beschreiben. Anfragen diesen Typs lassen sich in einer Basisoperation des verwendeten Verarbeitungsmodells, dem AEM-Operator (Aufbau Einfacher Moleküle), berechnen. Die damit aufgebauten Objekte können in speziellen Operationen, die in diesem Aufsatz aber nicht weiter betrachtet werden sollen, zu komplexeren Objekten, z.B. rekursiver oder vernetzter Objekttypen zusammengesetzt werden.

Um einen notwendigen Begriffsapparat für die folgenden Diskussionen zur Verfügung zu stellen, wird im 2. Kapitel eine kurze Einführung in das PRIMA-System gegeben. Im 3. Kapitel werden der AEM-Operator, ein einfaches Verarbeitungsmodell sowie die Schwachpunkte dieses Modells diskutiert. In den folgenden Kapiteln werden diese Schwachpunkte durch ein Verarbeitungsmodell beseitigt, das durch eine an die gegebene Qualifikationsbedingung angepaßte Verarbeitung, durch Ausnutzung von Zugriffspfaden und durch parallele Verarbeitungsstrategien eine optimale Bearbeitung des AEM-Operators ermöglicht. Abschließend erfolgen eine Zusammenfassung unserer Ergebnisse sowie ein Ausblick auf weitere Untersuchungen.

Verwandte Arbeiten

Da die hier untersuchte Fragestellung schon in einer Reihe von Arbeiten betrachtet wurde, muß eine Einordnung und Abgrenzung erfolgen. Die Grundlage der vorliegenden Arbeit bilden die in [Sch94, Sch93] beschriebenen Probleme und deren Lösungsansätze bei der Anfrageverarbeitung in PRIMA. Von den dort erarbeiteten Strategien wird die Verarbeitung des AEM-Operators hier verfeinert und konkretisiert. Zusätzlich berücksichtigen wir hier die parallele Abarbeitung eines AEM-Operators. Es ist kein Ziel dieser Arbeit, ein Kostenmodell zu entwickeln, mit dem verschiedene Verarbeitungspläne bewertet werden können. Ein solches Modell wurde bereits in [Sch93] vorgestellt und müßte an die hier vorgestellten Erweiterungen angepaßt werden.

Im Gegensatz zum DASDBS [SPS90] werden hierarchische Strukturen in PRIMA nicht automatisch auch in den zugrundeliegenden Speicherungsstrukturen zusammenhängend abgespeichert. Während DASDBS ittels einer Single-Scan Schnittstelle versucht, hierarchische Objekte, mit einem einzigen Scan über diesen Speicherungsstrukturen zu lesen, kann diese Eigenschaft in PRIMA aufgrund der anderen Verarbeitungsalgorithmen und Speicherungsstrukturen nicht immer garantiert werden. Dies ist nur durch eine zusätzliche Speicherungsstruktur möglich, bei deren Nutzung sich für den AEM-Operator folglich eine Reihe von Ähnlichkeiten ergeben.

Eine Reihe von Arbeiten hat sich mit Speicherungsstrukturen, Zugriffspfaden und deren Anwendung bei der Verarbeitung komplexer Objekte beschäftigt [KM90, Be94, KVC88, JS90, TRS93, HT94, KD91]. Im Gegensatz zu diesen Arbeiten geht es hier um die algorithmische Beschreibung von Verarbeitungsstrategien. Selbstverständlich müssen dabei die vorhandenen Speicherungseigenschaften berücksichtigt werden, wobei wir uns auf die von PRIMA angebotenen Strukturen konzentrieren. Die in [KKW88] vorgestellten Verfahren zur Anfrageverarbeitung in OODBMS entsprechend weitgehend unseren einfachen, später verbesserten, Verfahren. Allerdings kommen wir durch eine detailliertere Betrachtung der Randbedingungen zu anderen

Heuristiken für die genaue Spezifikation. Im Vergleich zu [KGM91] und [KCB87], die ebenfalls Strategien zum Aufbau komplexer Objekte beschreiben, beruht unser System auf einer weitgehend datenflußgesteuerten Architektur, die insbesondere den parallelen Aufbau komplexer Objekte ermöglicht.

Die Umsetzung der Ausführung geschachtelter Anfragen oder Pfadausdrücke von Programmen mit geschachtelten Schleifen in eine Algebra, in der diese Konstrukte dann durch Verbund-Operationen aufgelöst werden können, wie z.B. in [SAB94], entfällt hier. In der Anfrageübersetzung und -optimierung wird direkt aus der MQL-Anfrage ein Operatorgraph mit den AEM-Operatoren als Basisoperatoren erzeugt. In dieser Arbeit wird diskutiert, welche Möglichkeiten dabei für die Spezifikation des AEM-Operators bestehen sollen.

2. PRIMA

In diesem Abschnitt wird ein kurzer Überblick über die für die folgende Diskussion wesentlichen Konzepte des PRIMA-Systems gegeben.

2.1 Datenmodell

PRIMA ist ein sogenanntes strukturell objektorientiertes Non-Standard-Datenbanksystem, das auf dem Molekül-Atom-Datenmodell (MAD) basiert [Mi88]. Es ermöglicht die direkte Verarbeitung von komplexen Objekten, den sogenannten **Molekülen**. Moleküle setzen sich aus einfachen Basisobjekten des Modells, den **Atomen**, die ihrerseits durch **Attribute** beschrieben werden, zusammen. Dabei besitzt jedes Atom einen systemweit eindeutigen Objektidentifier (kurz: **Identifier**) und gehört eindeutig zu einem **Atomtyp**. Beziehungen zwischen Atomen eines oder verschiedener Atomtypen werden in sogenannten **Referenzattributen** mit Hilfe der Identifier direkt modelliert. Dabei werden Referenzen grundsätzlich symmetrisch definiert, d.h., zu einem Referenzattribut vom Atomtyp A zum Atomtyp B gibt es immer auch ein entsprechendes Referenzattribut vom Atomtyp B zum Atomtyp A, so daß, wenn es eine Referenz vom Atom a1 vom Atomtyp A zum Atom b1 vom Atomtyp B gibt, es auf jeden Fall auch eine Referenz von b1 zu a1 gibt. Diese Symmetrie der Referenzen wird von PRIMA garantiert. Durch einen **Molekültyp** (kurz: MT) wird der strukturelle Aufbau von Molekülen, bestehend aus den beteiligten Atomtypen und Referenzattributen beschrieben. Jedes Molekül besitzt ein eindeutiges **Wurzelatom** vom ebenso eindeutigen **Wurzelatomtyp** des zugehörigen Molekültyps; beide zeichnen sich dadurch aus, daß sie die einzigen Atome/der einzige Atomtyp sind, die nicht von anderen Atomen/Atomtypen referenziert werden.

2.2 Verarbeitungsmodell

Die Anfrageverarbeitung in PRIMA läßt sich durch ein zweistufiges Modell beschreiben. Das Datensystem führt die Umsetzung der deskriptiven, molekülmengenorientierten Anfragen auf die atommengenorientierte Schnittstelle des Zugriffssystems aus. Dazu wird eine Anfrage in einen **Operatorgraphen** übersetzt, dessen Knoten Operationen der Verarbeitungsalgebra und dessen Kanten dem resultierenden Datenfluß zwischen den Operatoren entsprechen [Sch93]. Dabei bildet der **AEM-Operator** den Basisoperator der Algebra, der vom Zugriffssystem Atommengen anfordern kann und daraus Moleküle einfacher, d.h. baumartig hierarchischer Molekültypen aufbauen kann.

2.3 Zugriffspfadstrukturen

Das Zugriffssystem bietet eine atommengenorientierte Schnittstelle zum Lesen und Ändern von homogenen Atommengen. Durch auf diesen Atomen entscheidbare Qualifikationsbedingungen sowie durch eine Menge von Identifiern kann die Ergebnismenge von Leseanforderungen eingeschränkt werden. Neben einer **Basisspeicherungsstruktur**, die alle Atome eines Atomtyps zusammenhängend verwaltet (siehe Abb. 1), werden auch Zugriffspfadstrukturen wie **B*-Bäume** und **Sortierordnungen** zum effizienteren Lesen von Atomen angeboten. Eine Clusterbildung der Atome nach ihrer Zugehörigkeit zu Molekülen in der Basisspeicherungsstruktur, d.h., zu einem Molekül gehörende Atome eines Atomtyps werden auch dort zusammenhängend abgespeichert, ist im allgemeinen nicht möglich. Die dazu notwendige eindeutige Zuordnung eines Atoms zu einem Molekül ist in der Regel nicht gegeben ist, da ein Atom über verschiedene (oder gleiche) Referenzattribute zu unterschiedlichen Molekülen gehören kann.

Deshalb können für den effizienten Zugriff auf ganze Moleküle einfacher Molekültypen als zusätzliche Zugriffspfadstruktur **Atomcluster** definiert werden [SS89], die die redundante, zusammenhängende Abspeicherung aller Atome eines Moleküls von einem einfachen Molekültyp erlauben. Durch geeignete Retrievalfunktionen wird mit diesen Atomclustern der häufige Zugriff auf Moleküle des gleichen Molekültyps effizient unterstützt. Der **Atomcluster_Scan** ermöglicht das Lesen aller Atome einer angegebenen Menge von Atomtypen, die in einem konkreten Atomcluster vorhanden sind. Dabei können eine Projektionsliste für die Auswahl einzelner Attribute und eine Identifierliste zur Einschränkung der relevanten Atome angegeben werden. Zusätzlich ermöglicht der **Atomclustertyp_Scan** eine Auswertung komplexerer Bedingungen auf einem zusammenhängend abgespeicherten Molekül, so daß nur solche Moleküle aus dem Cluster in der weiteren Verarbeitung betrachtet werden müssen, die diese Bedingung erfüllen. Vergleichbar mit der Single-Scan-Schnittstelle des DASDBS-Projektes können mit diesen Operationen ganze Moleküle durch einen einzigen Scan über diese Speicherungsstruktur gelesen werden.

3. Der AEM-Operator

In diesem Abschnitt wird zunächst die Funktionalität des AEM-Operators vorgestellt. Anschließend wird ein erstes allgemeines Verarbeitungsmodell für denAEM-Operator eingeführt. Die konzeptionellen Schwächen dieses Modells werden in den folgenden Kapiteln behoben.

Der bereits im 2. Kapitel kurz vorgestellte AEM-Operator hat die Aufgabe, Moleküle aufzubauen, die durch Anfragen vom Typ "SELECT S(M) FROM M WHERE Q(M)" beschrieben werden. Dabei beschreiben M einen einfachen Molekültyp (**AEM-MT**), Q(M) eine auf Molekülen diesen Molekültyps entscheidbare Bedingung und S(M) die zu erfolgende Projektion. Beim Aufbau der Moleküle bedient sich der Operator der vom Zugriffssystem angebotenen Funktionen und Zugriffspfade, um die Atome aus den Speicherungsstrukturen zu lesen, die für

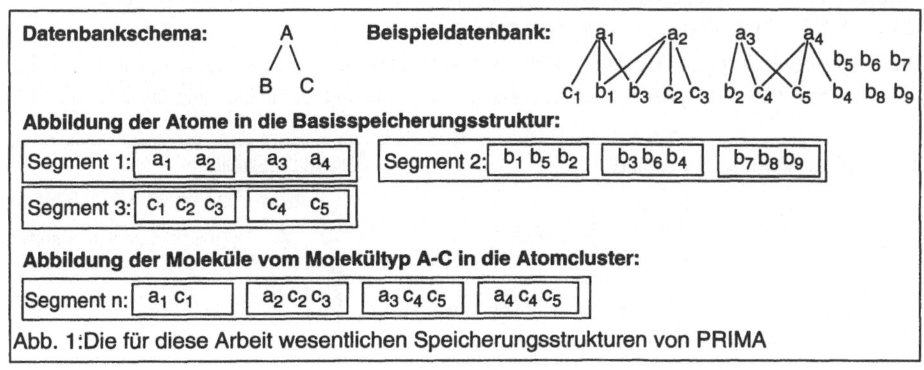

Abb. 1:Die für diese Arbeit wesentlichen Speicherungsstrukturen von PRIMA

die Bedingungsauswertung bzw. für den Aufbau der sich qualifizierenden Ergebnismoleküle benötigt werden.

Im Rahmen der Anfrageverarbeitung sind bei der Entwicklung von Verarbeitungsstrategien für diesen Operator folgende Ziele wesentlich:

- Die gesamte Molekülmenge soll möglichst schnell vollständig bestimmt werden, um eine möglichst kurze Antwortzeit für Anfragen zu erhalten.
- Die einzelnen Moleküle sollen möglichst schnell aufgebaut werden, damit sie in komplexeren Operatorgraphen durch ein Pipelining in den folgenden Operatoren möglichst früh zur weiteren Bearbeitung verfügbar werden [Sch93]. Für diese Art der Parallelität in der Anfrageverarbeitung ist es wichtig daß die AEM-Operatoren gleichmäßige Eingabeströme für die folgenden Operatoren erzeugen.

Die bisher erläuterten Begriffe und die Problemstellung der Aufgabe werden nun anhand eines einfachen Beispiels kurz erläutert. Mit Hilfe dieses Beispiels wird ein erstes, sehr einfaches Verarbeitungsmodell vorgestellt, das als Ausgangsmodell für weitere Verfeinerungen dient.

Es sei ein stark vereinfachter Ausschnitt aus einer Entwurfsdatenbank für den VLSI-Chip-Entwurf gegeben (siehe Abb. 2). Die Funktionalität einer Zelle Z wird durch ihre Spezifikation Sp formal beschrieben. Eine Dokumentation D enthält eine Beschreibung des Entwurfsprozesses. Sowohl die Spezifikation als auch die Dokumentation werden verantwortlich von (möglicherweise verschiedenen) Angestellten A erstellt. Die letztendlich gefertigte Zelle wird durch eine Realisierung R beschrieben, deren zellenunabhängige Fertigungsparameter, wie z.B. die Technologie T, explizit modelliert werden. Auf dieser Datenbank werde eine einfache Anfrage gestellt, die alle 2-Bit Addierer zusammen mit ihrer Dokumentation, Spezifikation und Realisierung sowie der dazu verwendeten Technologie extrahieren, sofern als Technologie MOSFETs benutzt werden.

Für den Aufbau der zu erzeugenden Moleküle sind eine Vielzahl von Algorithmen denkbar. Die einfachen Algorithmen lassen sich nach folgenden Kriterien klassifizieren:

- Anforderungsgranulat
  Einerseits können benötigte Atome vom Zugriffssystem einzeln, d.h. atomorientiert, angefordert werden. Andererseits berücksichtigen atommengenorientierte Algorithmen immer die Gesamtheit oder eine Teilmenge der zu lesenden Atome eines Atomtyps in einer Anforderung.
- Bearbeitungsgranulat
  Molekülorientierte Algorithmen bearbeiten aufzubauende Moleküle isoliert voneinander. Molekülmengenorientierte Verfahren betrachten gleichzeitig mehrere oder sogar alle Moleküle.
- Verarbeitungsreihenfolge
  Aufgrund der baumartigen Molekültypstrukturen können die üblichen Depth-first- und Breadth-first-Strategien unterschieden werden.

Die vorgestellten Kriterien sind zueinander orthogonal und allgemeingültig, d.h., sie können für jede konkrete Operatorspezifikation unabhängig voneinander betrachtet werden und sind für

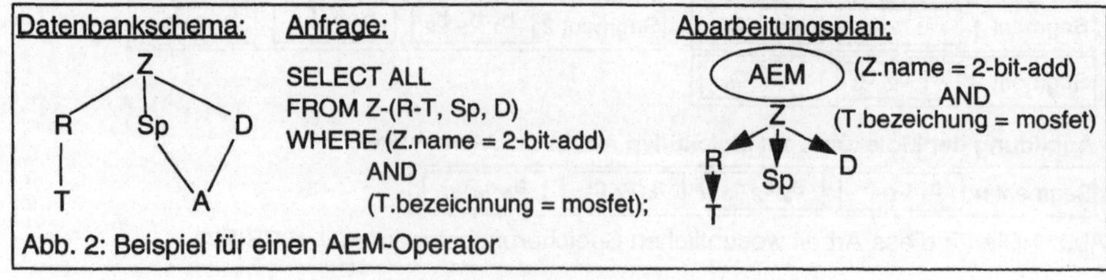

Abb. 2: Beispiel für einen AEM-Operator

alle möglichen AEM-MT anwendbar. Dabei entsprechen die molekülorientierten Verfahren der nested-loop Methode und die molekülmengenorientierten der sort-domain Methode aus [KKW88]. Die beiden übrigen Kriterien werden dort nicht berücksichtigt.

Allein nach diesen Kriterien entworfene Verarbeitungsstrategien genügen allerdings nicht aus, um ein gutes Leistungsverhalten zu erzielen. Dazu sind folgende Erweiterungen notwendig:

Die in der WHERE-Klausel spezifizierten Restriktionen, die bisher erst nach einem vollständigen Molekülaufbau ausgewertet werden, müssen besser berücksichtigt werden. Um den Molekülaufbau auf die unbedingt notwendigen Schritte einschränken zu können, sollte es möglich sein, den für die Bedingungsauswertung benötigten Ausschnitt der Moleküle beschreiben zu können, so daß bis zur endgültigen Qualifikation eines Moleküls nur dieser Ausschnitt berücksichtigt werden muß. Bei komplexeren Bedingungen kann es darüber hinaus sinnvoll sein, eine Reihenfolge festzulegen, in der Teilmoleküle aufgebaut werden. So erreicht man eine möglichst frühzeitige Disqualifikation des aktuell bearbeiteten Moleküls. Eine detaillierte Untersuchung hierzu erfolgt in Kapitel 4.

Selbstverständlich sollte es möglich sein, die Nutzung konventioneller Zugriffspfade wie auch der Atomcluster spezifizieren zu können. Dies wird in Kapitel 5 näher untersucht.

Um ein gutes Antwortzeitverhalten erreichen zu können, ist es notwendig, parallele Verarbeitungsstrategien zu nutzen. Kapitel 6 betrachtet diesen Problemkreis genauer.

4. Strategien zum Molekülaufbau

Dieser Abschnitt zeigt, wie an Bedingungen angepaßte Verarbeitungsalgorithmen einen effizienten Molekülaufbau ermöglichen. Grundsätzlich ist dabei folgender Zielkonflikt zu lösen. Einerseits soll möglichst wenig unnötige Arbeit geleistet werden, wenn sich Moleküle nicht qualifizieren, d.h. Teile, die nicht notwendig zur Entscheidung der Bedingung benötigt werden, sollen auch nicht bearbeitet werden. Andererseits sollen die Moleküle möglichst schnell aufgebaut werden, d.h., bei sich qualifizierenden Molekülen sollen unabhängige Teilmoleküle parallel aufgebaut werden. Um dieses Problem zu lösen, ist datenabhängig von Fall zu Fall zu unterscheiden, welche Strategien angewandt werden sollen. Als Grundlage für diese Entscheidung dienen dem Optimierer Statistiken über Werteverteilungen der Attribute und die Struktur der vorliegenden Bedingung.

Für eine weitere Betrachtung klassifizieren wir zunächst mögliche (Teil-) Bedingungen. Diese werden im folgenden Ausdrücke genannt, wenn nicht unterschieden wird, ob es sich um die ganze Bedingung oder um eine Teilbedingung handelt. **Einatomtyp-Ausdrücke** sind auf einem einzelnen Atomtyp im AEM-MT entscheidbar, z.B. (Atomtyp1.Attribut1 > 3) oder (EXISTS Atomtyp1). **Mehratomtyp-Ausdrücke** sind nicht auf Atomen eines einzelnen Atomtyps entscheidbar, sondern betreffen mehrere Atomtypen, z.B. (Atomtyp1.Attribut1 > Atomtyp2.Attribut1). Für alle Bedingungen gilt notwendigerweise, daß sie auf dem AEM-MT auswertbar sind. Sie werden existentiell abgeschlossen, d.h. vom Anwender nicht quantifizierte Atomtypen werden existentiell quantifiziert. Neben dem existentiellen Quantor (EXISTS) sind auch noch der universelle Quantor (FOR_ALL) sowie einige Spezialquantoren (EXISTS_AT_LEAST n, EXISTS_AT_MOST n und EXISTS_EXACTLY n) verfügbar. Der kleinste Ausschnitt aus einem Molekültyp, der alle in einem Ausdruck Q referenzierten Atomtypen umfaßt, wird im folgenden Ausdrucksmolekültyp (**AMT**) genannt. Der kleinste AMT, der die Wurzel des AEM-MT enthält, wird wurzelbasierter Ausdrucksmolekültyp (**wAMT**) genannt. Im Beispiel von Abb. 2 besteht der wAMT zum Ausdruck (T.bezeichnung = mosfet) aus den Atomtypen Z, R und T und den benutzten Referenzattributen.

4.1 Top-down-Strategie

Die einfachen Strategien zum Molekülaufbau können das unnötige Lesen für die Bedingungs-auswertung nicht benötigter Atome in Abhängigkeit von der Bedingung nicht vermeiden. Aus diesem Grund wird nun ein erweitertes Modell vorgestellt, das diese Forderung besser erfüllt. Dabei werden wie bisher, ausgehend von der Wurzel, Molekülteile aufgebaut, die zur Auswertung der Bedingung benötigt werden. Aufgrund des vom Wurzelatomtyp zu den Blättern gerichteten Molekülaufbaus wird dieses Verfahren Top-down-Strategie genannt.

Im Gegensatz zu den einfachen Strategien wird die Bearbeitungsreihenfolge für die einzelnen Atomtypen jetzt aber explizit durch eine Reihenfolgenummer im Molekültypgraphen festge-legt. Atomtypen mit der gleichen Nummer können gleichzeitig angefordert werden. Somit kennzeichnen die Nummern verschiedene Phasen des Molekülaufbaus. Eine Phase mit der Phasennummer (i+1) darf erst dann beginnen, wenn die Phase i beendet ist. Dabei ist eine Phase i dann beendet, wenn keine Atome von Atomtypen mit der Phasennummer i mehr zu lesen sind und die gegebene Bedingung ausgewertet wurde. Falls die Bedingung noch nicht entschieden ist, wird die Bearbeitung mit der nächsten Phase fortgesetzt. Ansonsten können die qualifizier-ten Ergebnismoleküle, bedingungsunabhängig fertiggestellt werden.

Ausgehend von der Wurzel, die die Phasennummer 1 bekommt, wird so eine Reihenfolge fest-gelegt, in der die Atomtypen bearbeitet werden. Dabei darf die Phasennummer eines referenzie-renden Atomtyps im Molekültyp nie größer sein, als die irgendeines seiner referenzierten Atomtypen. Zur Illustration enthält Abb. 3 für den einfachen AEM-MT aus unserem Beispiel verschiedene Verarbeitungsreihenfolgen, wobei a) die Breadth-first-Strategie, b) die Depth-first-Strategie und c) eine an die Bedingung angepaßte Reihenfolge festlegt. In c) werden in der ersten Phase die Z-Atome gelesen, die den ersten Teil der Bedingung (Z.name = 2-bit-add) erfüllen. In der anschließenden 2. Phase werden nur noch für diese Wurzelatome die Teilmole-küle R-T aufgebaut und der zweite Teil der Bedingung ausgewertet, so daß nur noch für die qualifizierten Moleküle in der abschließenden 3. Phase die noch fehlenden zum Molekül gehörenden Atome gelesen werden müssen.

4.1.1 Phaseneinteilung

Um für konkrete AEM-Operatoren gezielt Phaseneinteilung spezifizieren zu können, benötigen wir allgemeine Regeln, die im folgenden hergeleitet werden sollen. Dazu betrachten wir eine Qualifikationsbedingung Q, die aus mehreren Konjunktionen bzw. Disjunktionen von Ausdrük-ken Q_i besteht. Zu jedem Q_i gehört ein $wAMT_i$, der für die Auswertung aufgebaut werden muß. Die hier vorgenommene Untersuchung der Bedingung Q kann rekursiv auf die einzelnen Q_i übertragen werden, so daß das folgende Verfahren hierarchisch von der ganzen Bedingung bis zu nicht weiter zerlegbaren Ausdrücken angewandt werden kann. Deshalb spielt eine Normali-sierung der Bedingungen in eine Normalform für die weiteren Untersuchungen keine Rolle, da beide Verknüpfungsoperatoren betrachtet werden müssen. Aufgrund der unterschiedlichen Verknüpfungssemantik muß aber zwischen Konjunktionen und Disjunktionen unterschieden werden.

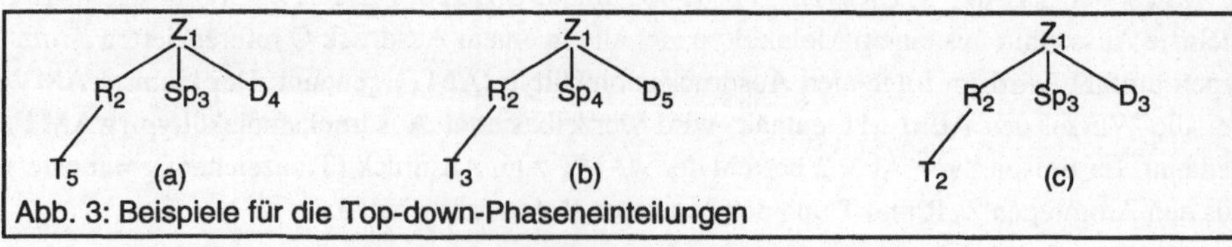

Abb. 3: Beispiele für die Top-down-Phaseneinteilungen

Bei einer Konjunktion von Ausdrücken kann die Auswertung abgebrochen werden, wenn einer der Ausdrücke nicht erfüllt ist. Es ist also sinnvoll, die einzelnen Ausdrücke sequentiell auszuwerten, d.h. die einzelnen AMT_i sequentiell aufzubauen und anschließend den Ausdruck Q_i auszuwerten. Zur Festlegung der Reihenfolge, in der die einzelnen Q_i bearbeitet werden sollen, muß der Optimierer für jeden Q_i dessen Selektivität S_{Qi}, also die Wahrscheinlichkeit, mit der Q_i zu FALSE ausgewertet wird, und die Kosten $K_{wAMTi'}$ für den Aufbau der Teilmoleküle vom $wAMT_i'$ (z.B. die Anzahl der zu lesenden Seiten) betrachten. Dabei ist zu berücksichtigen, daß in vorherigen Phasen bereits Teile des $wAMT_i$ aufgebaut worden sein können. Eine alleinige Berücksichtigung der Selektivitäten genügt nicht, da für die einzelnen Teilbedingungen in der Regel unterschiedlich große $wAMT_i$ aufgebaut werden müssen. Dies kann dazu führen, daß es günstiger ist, eine Teilbedingung mit geringerer Selektivität, die kostengünstig ausgewertet werden kann, einer anderen Teilbedingung mit höherer Selektivität aber sehr hohem Berechnungsaufwand vorzuziehen. Da es gilt, den Gesamtaufwand im Falle der Disqualifikation des Moleküls zu minimieren, wird ein Ausdruck Q_i vor einem Ausdruck Q_j ausgewertet, wenn $(S_{Qi}/K_{wAMTi'}) > (S_{Qj}/K_{wAMTj'})$. Die Bestimmung der S_{Qi} und $K_{wAMTi'}$ soll hier nicht weiter beschrieben werden, sie ist in [Sch93] enthalten.

Bei Disjunktionen ist diese Behandlung wesentlich einfacher. Da eine Bedingung erst dann zu FALSE entschieden wird, wenn alle Ausdrücke zu FALSE ausgewertet wurden, müssen dazu alle $wAMT_i$ aufgebaut werden. Aus diesem Grund können alle Ausdrücke und AMT_i parallel betrachtet werden. Selbstverständlich kann eine weitere Bedingungsauswertung entfallen, sobald ein Ausdruck zu TRUE ausgewertet wurde. Bei diesem Vorgehen kann allerdings noch unnötige Arbeit verrichtet werden, wenn in der Bedingungsauswertung vorkommende Molekülteile nicht projiziert werden. In diesem Fall ist ein zur konjunktiven Verknüpfung ähnliches Vorgehen notwendig, mit dem Unterschied, daß die Ausdrücke möglichst früh zu TRUE ausgewertet werden sollen. Sobald der Ausdruck zu TRUE ausgewertet wurde, brauchen die Molekülteile, die nicht ausgegeben werden, auch nicht mehr aufgebaut werden.

Eine nach diesen Kriterien erstellte Phaseneinteilung beschreibt eine Abarbeitungsreihenfolge, die nur in geringem Maße zu unnötiger Arbeit beim Aufbau von Molekülen führt, da die Disqualifikation bzw. Qualifikation früh entschieden werden und danach nur noch die auszugebenden Molekülteile aufzubauen sind. Allerdings erweist sich die strikte Trennung der Phasen, also die Ausführung von Phase i+1 erst nach vollständiger Beendigung der Phase i, als zu restriktiv. Aufgrund von Zusammenhängen in den Bedingungen, die bei der Phaseneinteilung verlorengehen, können Teile der Phase i+1 schon bearbeitet werden, nachdem bestimmte Teile der Phase i bearbeitet worden sind, aber die gesamte Phase i noch nicht beendet ist. Beispielsweise sei eine Bedingung der Form $((Q_1 \text{ AND } Q_2) \text{ OR } Q_3)$ gegeben. Q_1 habe eine höhere Selektivität als Q_2 und Q_3 habe einen höheren Berechnungsaufwand als Q_1 und Q_2 zusammen. Schließlich sollen alle für die Bedingungsauswertung benötigten Teilmoleküle auch projiziert werden. Mit den bisher vorgestellten Kriterien werden Q_1 und Q_3 in der ersten Phase und Q_2 in der zweiten Phase behandelt $((Q_1 \text{ AND } Q_2)$ parallel mit Q_3, Q_1 vor $Q_2)$. Mit der Bearbeitung von Q_2 wird also gewartet, bis auch Q_3 beendet ist. Dies ist aber nicht notwendig, da Q_2 schon nach Beendigung von Q_1 bearbeitet werden kann. Um dieses zu ermöglichen, werden diese Präzedenzbeziehungen (im Beispiel Q_2 nach Q_1) ebenfalls in die Strategiebeschreibung aufgenommen und die bisherige strikte Phaseneinteilung aufgehoben. Eine Phase i+1 kann nun bereits begonnen werden, wenn in der Phase i ein gemäß einer Präzedenzbeziehung festgelegter Atomtyp bereits vollständig bearbeitet wurde.

Insgesamt ergibt sich der in Abb. 4 dargestellte rekursive Algorithmus für die Phaseneinteilung in einem AEM-Operator. Eingabe sind der aktuell betrachtete Ausdruck Q sowie die Phasennummer, mit der dieser Ausdruck begonnen wird. Der Algorithmus vermerkt bei jedem Atomtyp im AMT dessen Phasennummer sowie die Präzedenzbeziehungen. Nach der vollständigen Ausführung des Algorithmus bekommen alle noch nicht behandelten Atomtypen die niedrigste, noch nicht vergebene Phasennummer; dabei handelt es sich um die Atomtypen, die nicht im wAMT der vollständigen Bedingung vorkommen. Diese abschließende Phase entspricht dem Vervollständigen der qualifizierten Moleküle um die noch fehlenden Atome. Zu beachten sind mögliche Überlappungen bei solchen Atomtypen, die in mehreren wAMT_i auftreten. In diesen Fällen werden die Atome in der Phase mit der niedrigsten auftretenden Phasennummer gelesen und zur Bedingungsauswertung benutzt (siehe Abb. 5 Beispiel 2).

```
PROCEDURE Definiere_Phaseneinteilung (     Q                 : Bedingung;
                                           phn               : Phasennummer;
                                 VAR   maximale_phn : Phasennummer);
BEGIN
   IF (Q nicht weiter zerlegbar) THEN
      alle Atomtypen des zu Q gehörenden wAMT werden in Phase phn bearbeitet, sofern sie nicht
         durch eine andere Teilbedingung bereits eine Phasennummer haben, die kleiner als phn ist.
      IF maximale_phn < phn THEN maximale_phn := phn END;
   ELSIF (Q zerlegbar in ODER-verknüpfte Qi) THEN
      Für alle Qi: Definiere_Phaseneinteilung(Qi, phn, maximale_phn);
   ELSE (* Q zerlegbar in UND-verknüpfte Qi *)
      für alle Qi:
         wähle Qj aus noch nicht behandelten Qi, so daß (SQj/KwAMTj') maximal;
         Definiere_Phaseneinteilung(Qj, phn, maximale_phn);
         kennzeichne Reihenfolge mit vorhergehendem wAMTj';
         phn := maximale_phn + 1;
   END;
END Definiere_Phaseneinteilung;
```
Abb. 4: Algorithmus zur Phaseneinteilung für den Top-down-Molekülaufbau

Das hier vorgestellte Verfahren zur Einteilung des Molekülaufbaus in verschiedenen Phasen kann noch an einigen Stellen weiter verfeinert werden. Beispielsweise werden bisher einzelne Konjunktionen völlig isoliert voneinander betrachtet. Sie können aber auch sinnvoll parallel berechnet werden, wenn die Ausdrücke nur eine geringe Selektivität aufweisen, so daß die Gesamtbedingung mit hoher Wahrscheinlichkeit zu TRUE ausgewertet wird.

4.1.2 Phasenabarbeitung

Die bisherige Phaseneinteilung orientiert sich ausschließlich an den von Bedingungen betroffenen Atomtypen und betrachtet noch nicht die Ausführung der einzelnen Phasen, sondern legt nur eine "Reihenfolge" fest, in der einzelne Teile des Molekültyps aufgebaut werden sollen. Gerade bei molekülorientierten Aufbaustrategien, die die Lokalität der Seitenreferenzen im Zugriffssystem stark verringern können, wenn Seiten mit Atomen für verschiedene Moleküle mehrfach angefordert werden, ist es deshalb wichtig, die Anzahl der Leseoperationen je Atomtyp zu minimieren. Falls also mehrere Atome referenziert werden, sollen nur die unbedingt benötigten gelesen werden. Dazu betrachten wir die Quantoren auf den betroffenen Atomtypen in einem Q_i.

Bei universell abgeschlossenen Ausdrücken Q_i kann jedes einzelne Molekül des AMT_i zur Disqualifikation des Moleküls führen. Deshalb kann hier der parallele Aufbau aller Moleküle erhebliche unnötige Arbeit verursachen. Aus diesem Grund wird in diesem Fall zunächst eine sequentielle Verarbeitung vorausgesetzt. Andererseits verlangsamen dieser streng sequentielle Aufbau und die Bedingungsauswertung nach jedem einzelnen Molekül des AMT die AEM-Operatorausführung. Um diesem, hier erneut auftretenden Zielkonflikt (schnelle Antwort gegen geringe Ressourcenbelastung) gerecht zu werden, muß hier ein Mittelweg zwischen möglicherweise überflüssigem Aufwand und dem Parallelitätsgrad beim Aufbau der Moleküle des AMT spezifizierbar sein. Dieser hängt wieder von der Selektivität der Bedingung ab; je höher sie ist, desto geringer ist der anzuwendende Parallelitätsgrad.

Bei existentiell quantifizierten Ausdrücken kann jedes einzelne Teilmolekül des betroffenen AMT zur Qualifikation des Ausdrucks führen. Deshalb müssen ggf. alle Teilmoleküle aufgebaut werden. Dies kann folglich wieder parallel geschehen, ohne daß viel unnötige Arbeit geleistet wird, wenn alle Teilmoleküle auch ausgegeben werden. Zuviel geleistete Arbeit im Falle einer späteren Disqualifikation (wenn dieser Ausdruck mit anderen Ausdrücken konjugiert wird, die in späteren Phasen bearbeitet werden) ist hier vernachlässigbar, da zunächst die Ausdrücke mit einer höheren Selektivität ausgewertet werden. (Die speziellen EXISTS-Quantoren werden hier nicht weiter betrachtet, da sie nur eine marginale Veränderung durch evtl. früher möglichen Abbruch des Molekülaufbaus bringen). Falls die Teilmoleküle nicht Bestandteil der Ergebnismoleküle sind, werden die Auswertung und der weitere Aufbau solcher Teilmoleküle unmittelbar nach der Qualifikation des gegebenen Ausdrucks beendet.

4.1.3 Beispiele

Abschließend werden in Abb. 5 einige Beispiele für die Spezifikation von Top-down-Strategien für den Molekülaufbau im AEM-Operator in Abhängigkeit von den angegebenen Bedingungen gezeigt. Die Indizes s bzw. p an den Atomtypen kennzeichnen, ob die betroffenen Teilmoleküle für die Bedingungsauswertung sequentiell bzw. parallel aufgebaut werden. Der Einfachheit wegen sei angenommen, daß die Kosten für den Aufbau der $wAMT_i$ immer gleich seien.

4.2 Bottom-up-Strategie

Eine inhärente Schwäche des Top-down-Molekülaufbaus ist, daß immer für alle Moleküle die Pfade von der Wurzel des Moleküls bis zu den Atomen, die für die Auswertung benötigt werden, aufgebaut werden müssen. Je länger diese Pfade sind und je weniger Atome auf diesen Pfaden für die Auswertung der Bedingung tatsächlich benötigt werden, umso größer ist der Zusatzaufwand, der für sich nicht qualifizierende Moleküle geleistet werden muß. Deshalb ist es sinnvoll, die Menge der möglichen Ergebnismoleküle bereits vorher einzuschränken.

Eine solche Einschränkung ist möglich, wenn man bei solchen Atomen mit dem Molekülaufbau anfängt, auf denen ein Ausdruck entschieden wird. Von dort ausgehend werden die Pfade zu den Wurzelatomen verfolgt. Die so bestimmte Wurzelatommenge schränkt den Suchraum für den weiteren Molekülaufbau ein. Wesentlich für dieses sogenannte Bottom-up-Verfahren ist, daß es mindestens alle Wurzelatome der Ergebnismolekülmenge liefern muß. Wenn diese Eigenschaft nicht zugesichert werden kann, ist es nicht sinnvoll anwendbar, da dann das Top-down-Verfahren trotz des Bottom-up-Verfahrens noch vollständig ausgeführt werden müßte, um die fehlenden Ergebnismoleküle zu bestimmen. In diesem Abschnitt werden dieses Verfahren sowie notwendige Voraussetzungen dazu im Detail erläutert.

Die grundlegende Idee ist, zunächst die Atome zu lesen, die eine Einatomtyp-(Teil-)Bedingung erfüllen. Aufgrund der Symmetrie der Referenzen ist es dann möglich, von diesen Atomen ausgehend die Pfade zur Wurzel des gegebenen AEM-MT zu verfolgen. Das Ergebnis ist eine Wurzelatommenge, die eine Teilmenge der existierenden Atome des Wurzelatomtyps ist. Für

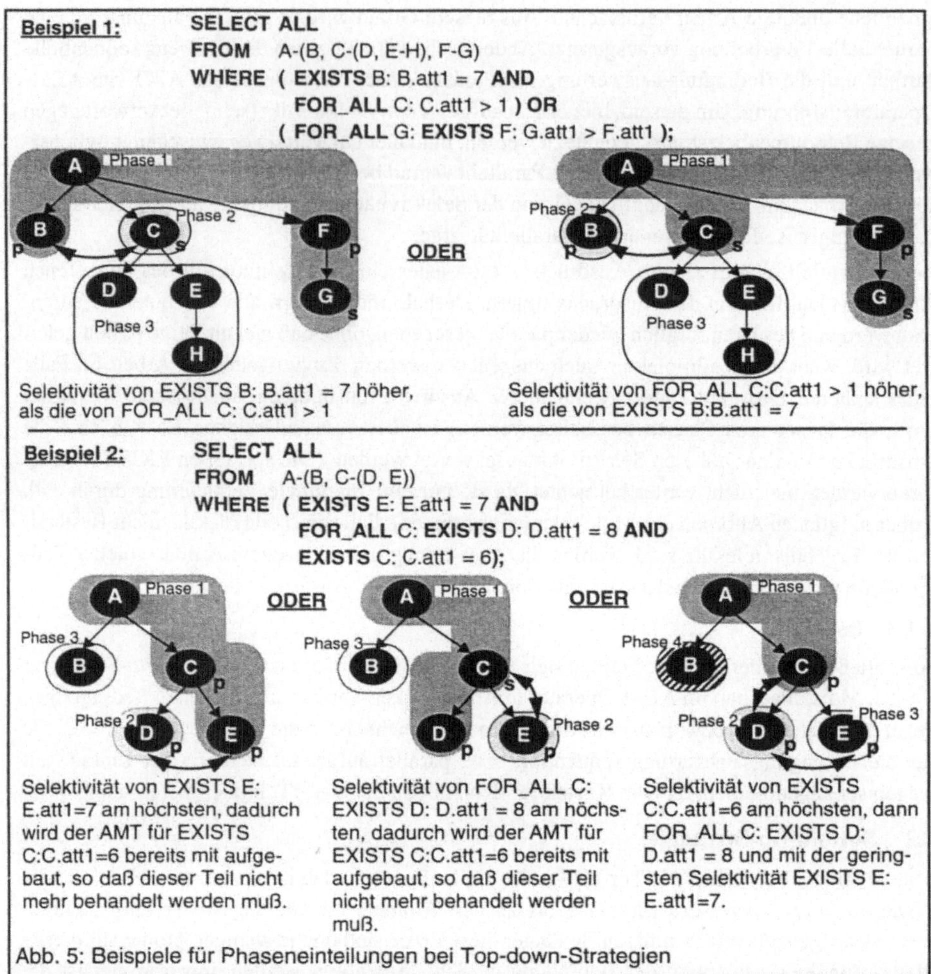

Abb. 5: Beispiele für Phaseneinteilungen bei Top-down-Strategien

die Atome dieser Wurzelatommenge müssen anschließend im Top-down-Verfahren die Moleküle um noch nicht gelesene Atome vervollständigt werden und noch nicht berücksichtigte Ausdrücke ausgewertet werden.

In Abb. 6 wird dieses Verfahren anhand eines einfachen Beispiels illustriert. Unter Ausnutzung eines Zugriffspfades für C.attr1 wird zunächst nur c3 gelesen. In der Bottom-up-Strategie werden über b3 und b4 die Pfade zu a2 und a3 verfolgt, um anschließend diese Moleküle zu vervollständigen. Ohne das Bottom-up-Verfahren müßten zur Auswertung der Bedingung alle Moleküle vom Molekültyp A-B-C aufgebaut werden.

Die möglichen Vorteile dieses Verfahrens werden durch das Beispiel deutlich. Eine genauere Betrachtung dieses Verfahrens zeigt allerdings, daß es aufgrund einiger Einschränkungen nicht immer sinnvoll bzw. überhaupt nicht anwendbar ist. Die notwendigen Voraussetzungen und die Grenzen des Verfahrens sollen im folgenden erläutert werden. Dazu werden mit **Startatomtyp/Startatomen** der Atomtyp/die Atome bezeichnet, von dem/denen das Bottom-up-Verfahren ausgeht, im Beispiel also C/(c1, .., c4).

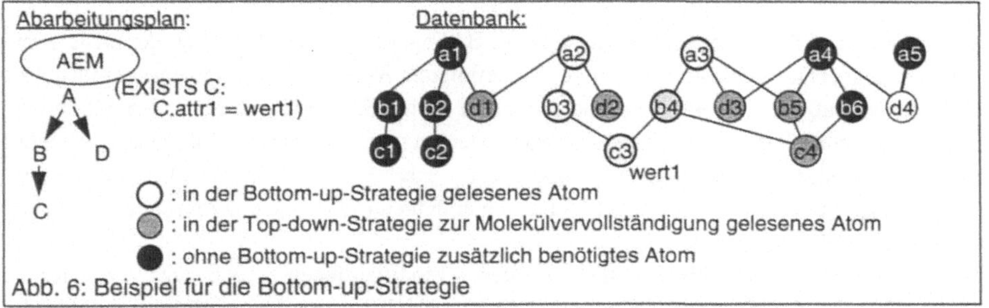

Abb. 6: Beispiel für die Bottom-up-Strategie

- Zunächst hängt die sinnvolle Anwendbarkeit der Bottom-up-Strategie von der Datencharakteristik der zugrundeliegenden Datenbank ab. Falls die Anzahl der Atome vom Startatomtyp sehr hoch ist, ohne durch Zugriffspfade sinnvoll eingeschränkt werden zu können, kann ein Scan über diesen Atomtyp teurer sein, als der Top-down-Aufbau der Moleküle. Dies wäre in Abb. 6 dann der Fall, wenn beispielsweise noch 10 weitere Atome vom Atomtyp C (kurz: C-Atome) existieren würden. Aber auch ein Zugriffspfad würde das Problem nicht lösen, wenn alle Atome im Attribut "attr1" den Wert "wert1" hätten. Auch dann müßten noch alle diese Atome gelesen werden, und ggf. weitere referenzierte B-Atome, selbst wenn es für diese dann keine Referenzen zu A-Atomen gibt.

Um über einen Einsatz der Bottom-up-Strategie zu entscheiden, muß also abgeschätzt werden, wieviel Aufwand mit der Bottom-up-Strategie im Vergleich zum Aufwand für die Top-down-Strategie verbunden ist. Dies ist von den Kardinalitäten der beteiligten Atomtypen, der Verteilung der Referenzen in den beteiligten Referenzattributen und den Werteverteilungen auf den zur Bedingungsauswertung benötigten Attributen abhängig [Sch93].

- Für den universellen Abschluß ist das Verfahren mit einer leichten Modifikation auch anwendbar. Nachdem alle C-Atome, die die Bedingung erfüllen, gelesen wurden (im Beispiel von Abb. 6 bei Ersetzung des EXISTS durch FOR_ALL: c3), werden alle referenzierten B-Atome (b3, b4) gelesen, aber nur noch diejenigen weiter berücksichtigt, die nur C-Atome aus der bereits gelesenen Menge referenzieren (b3). Dieses Verfahren kann über mehrere Stufen bis zu den Wurzelatomen angewandt werden. So werden nur solche Wurzelatome bestimmt, von denen keine Startatome erreicht werden, die die Bedingung nicht erfüllen. Dies entspricht der Umformung der Bedingung von (FOR_ALL x: Q(x)) in (NOT EXISTS x: NOT Q(x)).

Da ein universeller Abschluß zur Erfüllung der Bedingung die Existenz entsprechender Atome nicht fordert, werden solche Bedingungen offensichtlich auch von Molekülen erfüllt, die überhaupt keine Startatome enthalten (z.B. a5-d4). Um also eine vollständige Wurzelatommenge durch das Bottom-up-Verfahren in dieser Situation erzeugen zu können, darf in einem Molekül keine Referenz auf dem Pfad vom Wurzelatomtyp zum Startatomtyp leer sein, wie dies bei d4 der Fall ist. D.h., zu jedem Wurzelatom gibt es auch mindestens ein Startatom. Diese Eigenschaft des Pfades wird "sicherer Pfad" genannt. Wäre diese Bedingung nicht erfüllt, dann würde das Bottom-up-Verfahren nicht sicher eine vollständige Wurzelatommenge liefern und wäre somit nicht anwendbar. Die notwendigen Informationen sind in den Metadaten der Datenbank enthalten (Kardinalitätsrestriktionen in der Schemadefinition der Referenzattribute).

- Unabhängig von den gegebenen Quantoren muß in PRIMA gefordert werden, daß die Referenzattribute auf dem Pfad vom Wurzelatomtyp zum AMT keine undefinierten Werte aufweisen dürfen. Diese Eigenschaft wird "definierter Pfad" genannt. Sie ist notwendig, weil PRIMA zwischen einer sicheren Ergebnismenge und einer unsicheren Ergebnismenge unterscheidet

[Sch91]. Die sichere Ergebnismenge enthält die Ergebnismoleküle, die die gegebene Bedingung erfüllen, während die Auswertung dieser Bedingung bei den Molekülen der unsicheren Menge nicht entschieden werden konnte ("undefinierter Wert"). Für die Elemente der unsicheren Menge muß der Anwender entscheiden, ob sie weiter bearbeitet werden sollen oder nicht. Ohne die Eigenschaft des "definierten Pfades" würden im Bottom-up-Verfahren aber Wurzelatome der unsicheren Menge nicht gefunden (vgl. sicherer Pfad bei universellem Abschluß). Auch diese Informationen ist in den Metadaten enthalten (NOT_NULL-Klausel in der Schemadefinition der Attribute).

- Während der Algorithmus mit leichten Modifikationen auch die Quantoren EXISTS_AT_LEAST und EXISTS_EXACTLY behandeln kann, ist das Bottom-up-Verfahren für EXISTS_AT_MOST Quantoren überhaupt nicht anwendbar. Selbst wenn der Pfad sicher und definiert ist, kann es sein, daß vom Wurzelatom nur solche Startatome referenziert werden, die die Bedingung nicht erfüllen, im Beispiel z.B. das Molekül mit der Wurzel a1. Da solche Wurzelatome durch das Bottom-up-Verfahren aber nicht gefunden werden können, ist das Verfahren hier nicht anwendbar.

Die bisher gezeigten Einschränkungen gelten für einfache, nicht negierte Ausdrücke auf einzelnen Atomtypen. Eine Erweiterung zur Behandlung negierter Ausdrücke ist leicht möglich, da sie nach einfachen Regeln in nicht-negierte Ausdrücke umgeformt werden können (z.B. NOT EXISTS_AT_MOST n zu EXISTS_AT_LEAST n+1).

Neben den bisher betrachteten Ausdrücken können auch komplexere, d.h. konjunktiv oder disjunktiv verknüpften Bedingungen behandelt werden. In diesen Fällen wird die Bottom-up-Strategie für die einzelnen Ausdrücke getrennt angewandt, um so für jeden Ausdruck eine Wurzelatommenge zu bestimmen. Bei Disjunktionen wird dann eine Vereinigung, bei Konjunktionen eine Durchschnittsbildung dieser Wurzelatommengen durchgeführt. Dabei wird für die einzelnen Mengenoperationen die gleiche Reihenfolge eingehalten in der sie bei den entsprechenden logischen Operationen definiert sind. Auf der resultierenden Menge werden anschließend die weiteren Abschnitte des Molekülaufbaus im Top-down-Verfahren durchgeführt. Um eine vollständige Wurzelatommenge zu bestimmen, ist bei Disjunktionen wiederum notwendige Voraussetzung, daß alle disjunktiv verknüpften Ausdrücke bottom-up bearbeitet werden.

Weitere Optimierungen sind möglich; sie sollen hier aus Platzgründen aber nur kurz skizziert werden. Zunächst einmal muß die Durchschnittsbildung bei konjunktiv verknüpften Ausdrükken nicht notwendigerweise erst auf der Wurzelatommenge erfolgen. In Abhängigkeit von den gegebenen Ausdrücken kann diese auch bereits auf anderen gemeinsamen Atomtypen auf dem Pfad zum Wurzelatomtyp erfolgen. Bei existentiell quantifizierten Ausdrücken kann das Verfahren zusätzlich dadurch beschleunigt werden, daß die Wurzelatommenge bestimmt werden kann, ohne alle Atome auf dem Pfad dorthin lesen zu müssen. Dabei lassen sich die Symmetrie der Referenzen und ihre Modellierung mittels der Identifier ausnutzen. Diese ermöglichen es, ggf. nur Atome jeden zweiten Atomtyps lesen zu müssen. Sei beispielsweise auf dem Molekültyp A-B-C eine existentielle Bedingung auf C gegeben, seien ferner die betroffenen C-Atome gelesen und somit die referenzierten Identifier für die betroffenen B-Atome bestimmt. Dann müssen die B-Atome nicht unbedingt gelesen werden. Vielmehr können direkt die A-Atome gelesen werden, die Referenzen auf die identifizierten B-Atome besitzen. Dieses Verfahren ist insbesondere dann sinnvoll, wenn die B-Atome nicht mit ausgegeben werden oder wenn in einer anschließenden Top-down-Verarbeitung auch noch Ausdrücke ausgewertet werden müssen, so daß die B-Atome möglicherweise überhaupt nicht benötigt werden. Weitere Details und eine ausführlichere Diskussion dieser Optimierungen finden sich in [St94].

4.3 Vollständiges Verarbeitungsmodell

Die beiden bisher beschriebenen Teilmodelle zum Molekülaufbau werden jetzt in ein allgemeines Ausführungsmodell integriert. Jede Bearbeitung eines AEM-Operators beginnt, sofern möglich und sinnvoll, mit einer Bottom-up-Strategie, um die Menge der aufzubauenden Moleküle einzuschränken. Daher ist dieses Verfahren immer molekülmengenorientiert, d.h., es werden immer alle Atome eines Atomtyps zusammen angefordert und bearbeitet. Anschließend an das Bottom-up-Verfahren werden in einer in verschiedene Phasen zerlegten Top-down-Strategie die noch notwendigen Schritte zur endgültigen Auswertung der Bedingung ausgeführt. Dieses kann in Abhängigkeit von der durch den Optimierer erfolgten Spezifikation sowohl molekül- als auch molekülmengenorientiert geschehen. Dabei wird ein Molekül aus der Menge der zu bearbeitenden Moleküle entfernt, sobald seine Disqualifikation feststeht. Umgekehrt wird zum phasenunabhängigen parallelen Molekülaufbau übergegangen, sobald die Qualifikation des Moleküls feststeht. Abschließend wird das fertig konstruierte Molekül ausgegeben.

Die Bottom-up-Strategie erweist sich als besonders einfach, wenn als Ausgangspunkte nur einzelne Atomtypen betrachtet werden, auf denen Einatomtyp-Ausdrücke gegeben sind. Eine Verallgemeinerung dieses Verarbeitungsmodells läßt auch komplexere Ausdrücke auf Teilmolekülen zu. Dazu werden diese Teilmoleküle rekursiv unter Anwendung des beschriebenen Verarbeitungsmodells aufgebaut, und von den Wurzeln der so erhaltenen Teilmoleküle, die die gegebene Bedingung erfüllen, wieder die Bottom-up-Strategie angewandt. In diesem Fall übernehmen die Wurzelatome dieser Teilmoleküle die Rolle der Startatome für das Bottom-up-Verfahren. Allerdings entfällt bei den Teilmolekülen deren Vervollständigung, da diese erst ausgeführt werden soll, wenn sich das Molekül endgültig qualifiziert hat.

5. Zugriffspfade

Nun wenden wir uns der Frage zu, wie die in Kap. 2 vorgestellten Zugriffspfade in der bisher vorgestellte Verarbeitung genutzt werden können.

5.1 Ausnutzung konventioneller Zugriffspfade

Aus der bisherigen Darstellung des Molekülaufbaus geht hervor, daß der wertabhängige Zugriff auf einzelne Atome über Zugriffspfade nur zu Beginn der Verarbeitung notwendig ist, um so die Menge der aufzubauenden Moleküle effizient einschränken zu können. Dies gilt für Bedingungen auf dem Wurzelatomtyp beim Top-down- und auf den Startatomtypen beim Bottom-up-Verfahren. Darüber hinaus werden diese Zugriffspfade im Molekülaufbau nicht mehr benötigt, da der weitere Aufbau nur noch aus der Verfolgung von Referenzen besteht. Das entspricht einem vom Identifier abhängigen wertbasierten Zugriff, der aufgrund seiner Häufigkeit standardmäßig über Zugriffspfade (in PRIMA über Hashverfahren) unterstützt wird.

5.2 Ausnutzung von Atomclustern

Für häufig benötigte Molekültypen kann der Molekülaufbau durch Atomcluster unterstützt werden. Durch die zusammenhängende Abspeicherung der Atome eines Moleküls wird dabei die molekülorientierte Bearbeitung im AEM-Operator besonders unterstützt.

Aufgrund des hohen Speicheraufwandes durch die redundante Speicherung der Daten verbietet es sich, für jeden möglichen Molekültyp einen eigenen Clustertyp anzulegen. Deshalb ist genauer zu untersuchen, wie auch Teile von Atomclustertypen für Anfragen genutzt werden

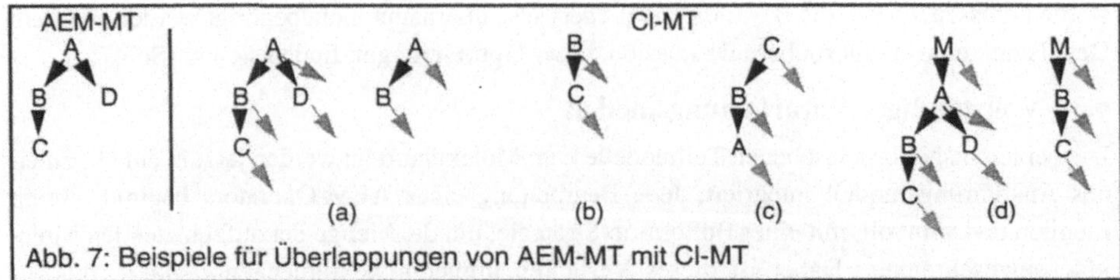

Abb. 7: Beispiele für Überlappungen von AEM-MT mit Cl-MT

können, deren Molekültypen nicht vollständig durch einen Atomcluster materialisiert werden. Dazu betrachten wir die Überdeckungen zwischen dem AEM-MT und dem im Atomcluster materialisierten Clustermolekültyp (**Cl-MT**), d.h., inwieweit Teile des AEM-MT im Cl-MT enthalten sind. Dabei kann der Cl-MT natürlich auch noch Teilmolekültypen umfassen, die mit dem AEM-MT nichts zu tun haben. Eine Diskussion aller möglichen Situationen würde hier zuweit führen. Zusammenfassend läßt sich jedoch feststellen, daß je genauer der AEM-MT im Cl-MT repräsentiert wird, umso besser kann der Cl-MT ausgenutzt werden (siehe Abb. 7):

- Falls der Cl-MT einen (Teil-) Molekültyp des AEM-MT enthält, wobei der Wurzelatomtyp des AEM-MT dem Wurzelatomtyp des Cl-MT entspricht (Abb. 7a), können die dort enthaltenen (Teil-) Moleküle direkt gelesen werden. Dies ist der denkbar günstigste Fall.
- Falls der Cl-MT einen Teilmolekültyp des AEM-MT ohne dessen Wurzelatomtyp enthält, aber der Wurzelatomtyp des betrachteten Teilmolekültypen dem des Cl-MT entspricht (Abb. 7b), können entsprechende Teilmoleküle direkt aus dem Cluster aufgebaut werden.
- Falls der Cl-MT Teile des AEM-MT enthält, wobei aber die Referenzen im Cl-MT in umgekehrter Richtung modelliert werden (Abb. 7c), ist eine Clusternutzung nur noch bedingt möglich, weil die Atome der aufzubauenden Moleküle nicht mehr vollständig in den Clustern enthalten sein müssen. Allerdings eignen sich diese Strukturen für die Bottom-up-Strategie.
- Falls die Wurzel des Cl-MT nicht gleichzeitig die Wurzel des (Teil-) Molekültypen des AEM-MT ist, der im Cluster bearbeitet werden soll (Abb. 7d), so enthalten die Cluster nicht mehr alle (Teil-) Moleküle, sondern nur noch solche, die von der Wurzel des Cl-MT über den Pfad zur Wurzel des (Teil-) Molekültyps erreichbar sind. D.h., die Atomclusternutzung verliert an Bedeutung, weil Teile des AEM-MT ggf. außerhalb der Atomcluster gelesen werden müssen.
- Ein Cl-MT, der auch Teilmolekültypen enthält, die nicht im konkreten AEM-Operator benötigt werden (Abb. 7a-d), läßt sich umso besser nutzen, je kleiner die nicht benötigten Teilmoleküle sind. Unnötige Teilmoleküle im Cluster führen zu unnötigen Seitenanforderungen während der Leseoperationen auf dem Cluster.

Bisher wurde nur die Eignung von Atomclustern zur Unterstützung von Lesevorgängen betrachtet. Bei ihrem tatsächlich Einsatz zeigen sich folgende Auswirkungen auf das bisher vorgestellte Verarbeitungsmodell:

(**1**) Die erweiterte Funktionalität mit der atomclusterinterne Auswertung von Bedingungen auf Molekülen ermöglicht vor allen Dingen eine effiziente Verarbeitung auch von komplexeren Bedingungen, z.B. zur Bestimmung von Startatomen für das Bottom-up-Verfahren.

(**2**) Atomclustertypen, die Teile eines oder den ganzen bottom-up zu verfolgenden Pfad materialisieren, ermöglichen ein schnelleres Bottom-up-Verfahren, weil als Startatome nur noch die Atome am Endpunkt dieses dort materialisierten (Teil-) Pfades gelesen werden müssen.

(**3**) Die bisher ermittelte Phaseneinteilung erfolgte unter ausschließlicher Berücksichtigung der Struktur der angegebenen Qualifikationsbedingung. Dabei wurde implizit angenommen, daß das Lesen von Atomen verschiedener Atomtypen unabhängig von der Phaseneinteilung immer mit dem gleichen Aufwand geschieht. Diese Annahme gilt bei der Ausnutzung von Atomclustern aber nicht mehr. Hier kann es sinnvoll sein, Atome, die bei einer nach den bisherigen Kriterien erstellten Phaseneinteilung nicht direkt in der gleichen Phase benötigt werden, trotzdem in dieser Phase zu lesen, weil die entsprechenden Seiten bei der Clusterverarbeitung bereits vorliegen. Dieses Vorgehen widerspricht zwar der Forderung aus 3.2, nur solche Atome zu lesen, die für den Molekülaufbau und die Bedingungsauswertung benötigt werden, bedeutet aber ggf. wesentlich weniger Zusatzaufwand als das wiederholte Einlesen der Seiten mit diesen Atomen.

6. Parallelität

Die bisherigen Betrachtungen zur Ausführung von AEM-Operatoren sind von Aspekten ihrer parallelen Verarbeitung unabhängig, da über die zeitliche Abfolge der Molekülbearbeitung nichts ausgesagt wurde. Alle Diskussionen zum Aspekt der Parallelität bezogen sich auf Anforderungen an das Zugriffssystem. Deshalb soll der Aspekt der parallelen Bearbeitung eines einzelnen AEM-Operators näher betrachtet werden. Dazu gehen wir zunächst auf die Vor- und Nachteile dieser Parallelität ein, ehe konkrete Realisierungsformen vorgestellt werden.

6.1 Beurteilung paralleler AEM-Operator-Ausführungen

Da der CPU-Bedarf zur Bearbeitung komplexer Objekte, deutlich höher ist, als der bei der Bearbeitung von Tupeln in relationalen Systemen (vgl. [SPS90]), kann das Zugriffssystem durch parallele Verarbeitungsstrategien mehr Atome produzieren, als sie von einer einzelnen Ausführungseinheit für den AEM-Operator verarbeitet werden können. Da AEM-Operatoren gleichzeitig auch sehr umfangreiche Molekülmengen bearbeiten, sind parallele Verarbeitungsstrategien sinnvoll, um kurze Antwortzeiten des Systems zu garantieren.

Die parallele Ausführung eines AEM-Operators bedeutet in unserer Umgebung, die aufzubauende Molekülmenge in verschiedenen Ausführungseinheiten des AEM-Operators zu konstruieren. Dabei ist die aufzubauende Molekülmenge eine Obermenge der auszugebenden Molekülmenge, weil auch die Moleküle, die sich gemäß der gegebenen Qualifikationsbedingung nicht qualifizieren, zu einem bestimmten Teil aufgebaut werden müssen. Bei der Untersuchung dieses Problems zeigen sich allerdings neben den immer auftretenden zusätzlichen Verwaltungskosten weitere Abhängigkeiten zu anderen Verarbeitungsparametern, z.B. zu den benutzten Speicherungsstrukturen, die bei der Implementierung berücksichtigt werden müssen.

Bei der unabhängigen Bearbeitung verschiedener Molekülteilmengen in unterschiedlichen Ablaufeinheiten eines AEM-Operators entstehen als Folge kontextfreie Aufträge an das Zugriffssystem. Wenn die benutzten Speicherungsstrukturen nicht an dieses Aufträge angepaßt sind, kann dies, wie bereits in 4.1.2 beschrieben, zu wiederholten Seitenanforderungen im Zugriffssystem führen, wenn verschiedene, unabhängige Leseoperationen unterschiedliche Atome in derselben Seite anfordern.

Weiterer Zusatzaufwand kann durch Überlappungen bei von verschiedenen Molekülen gemeinsam genutzten Teilmolekülen entstehen. Je größer diese Überlappungen sind, umso größer wäre auch der Zusatzaufwand durch wiederholten Aufbau der überlappenden Teilmoleküle. Deshalb muß dieses und damit das mehrfache Lesen von Atomen vermieden werden. Da mit Ausnahme der Wurzelatome die Anforderungen über die Referenzen (Identifier) erfolgen, können diese Überlappungen und die Tatsache, ob ein Atom bereits gelesen oder angefordert wurde, relativ einfach erkannt werden. Im Falle der parallelen Ausführung eines AEM-Operators in mehreren Ablaufeinheiten muß ein Protokoll für die Verwaltung entsprechender Informationsstrukturen eingehalten werden, das natürlich etwas komplizierter als bei der sequentiellen Verarbeitung ist.

Dieser Zusatzaufwand entfällt, wenn aufgrund der Datencharakteristik klar ist, daß diese Überlappungen nur in sehr geringem Maße existieren, so daß dieses Protokoll mehr Aufwand verursachen würde als die Mehrarbeit für den wiederholten Teilmolekülaufbau.

6.2 Realisierungsformen

Eine wertabhängige Partitionierung der Ergebnismolekülmenge, bei der jede Partition in einem
eigenen Operatoraufruf aufgebaut wird, eignet sich in der Regel nicht. In diesem Fall müßte sich
die Partitionierung wiederum an den Speicherungsstrukturen (z.B. Atomclustern) orientieren,
um die Lokalität der Seitenzugriffe nicht zu zerstören. Ohne die Atomcluster müßten die Atome
der Moleküle auch in der Basisspeicherungsstruktur nach ihrer Molekülzugehörigkeit zusammenhängend abgespeichert werden, was aufgrund der Zugehörigkeit von Teilmolekülen zu
mehreren Ergebnismolekülen nicht möglich ist (siehe 2.3). Aus diesem Grund wird die folgende
Strategie gewählt:

Nicht die konkrete Ergebnismenge sondern der zu bearbeitende Molekültyp wird in verschiedene Teilmolekültypen zerlegt, von denen jeder in einem eigenen Operator realisiert wird. Die
einzelnen Ergebnismoleküle werden anschließend durch einen Verbindungsoperator zu den
Endergebnissen zusammengesetzt (2. in Abb. 8). Mit dieser Zerlegung können die üblichen, in
[Ge95] beschriebenen Mechanismen zur Ausnutzung von Parallelität genutzt werden. Dies ist
zunächst die unabhängige Ausführung der Operatoren (Fall 1 in Abb. 9), die anwendbar ist,
wenn fast alle Submoleküle (C-Atome) des abgespaltenen AEM-Operators mit nicht leeren
Referenzattributen zum Wurzelmolekültyp tatsächlich benötigt werden. Im gegebenen Beispiel
gilt diese Voraussetzung. Wenn aber auf dem Molekültyp A-B eine selektive Bedingung angegeben wäre, würden auch weniger C-Atom benötigt. In diesem Fall bietet sich das Pipelining
zur Ausnutzung von Parallelität an. Die Submoleküle (C-Atome) werden dabei erst nach Erhalt
des Wurzelmoleküls im Verbindungsoperator angefordert (Fall 2 in Abb. 9) und während der
erste AEM-Operator weitere Wurzelmoleküle erzeugt, produziert der zweite AEM-Operator für
die bereits hergestellten Wurzelmoleküle die anzuhängenden Submoleküle.

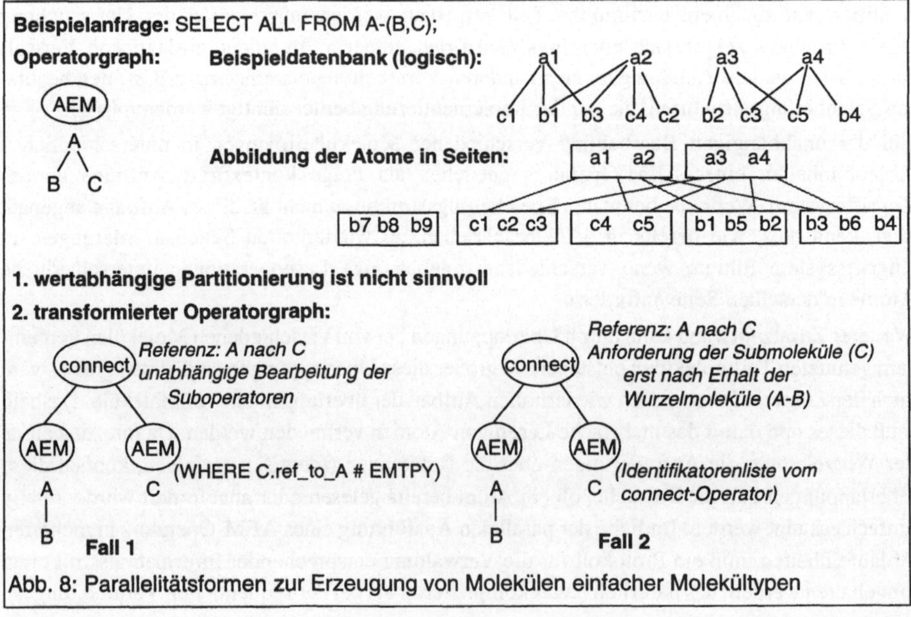

Abb. 8: Parallelitätsformen zur Erzeugung von Molekülen einfacher Molekültypen

Da solche Zerlegungen aber die Molekültypstruktur des ursprünglichen AEM-MT zerstören, muß sichergestellt werden, daß zur Bedingungsauswertung benötigte Atomtypen in den AEM-Operatoren auch zusammenhängend bleiben, da sonst die im Phasenmodell beschriebenen Strategien zur frühzeitigen Disqualifikation nicht mehr anwendbar sind. Eine Auswertung der Bedingung könnte erst nach dem Zusammensetzen der Teilmoleküle im Verbindungsoperator erfolgen. Zusätzlich muß sichergestellt werden, daß in Atomclustern genutzte Molekültypstrukturen bestehen bleiben, damit deren Nutzung überhaupt möglich ist.

7. Vollständige Spezifikation des AEM-Operators

Aus dieser Diskussion der für den Aufbau von Molekülen baumartig hierarchischer Molekültypen wesentlichen Faktoren ergibt sich folgendes Verfahren zur Bestimmung eines geeigneten Abarbeitungsplans.

Zunächst werden die gegebene WHERE-Klausel näher untersucht und eine entsprechende Phaseneinteilung erstellt. Dazu werden zunächst unter Berücksichtigung der verfügbaren konventionellen Zugriffspfade und Atomcluster die für das Bottom-up-Verfahren benötigten Teilmolekültypen, die durchzuführenden Bottom-up-Verfahren selbst sowie die Verknüpfung der einzelnen für den Wurzelatomtyp erhaltenen Identifiermengen spezifiziert. Anschließend wird das Top-down-Verfahren festgelegt. Dies umfaßt die Beschreibung der Reihenfolge, in der einzelne Atomtypen des AEM-MT behandelt werden, der bestehenden Abhängigkeiten sowie die Festlegung einer molekül- oder molekülmengenorientierten Verarbeitung der einzelnen Atomtypen.

Nachdem dieses Phasenmodell aufgestellt wurde, wird die Ausnutzung von Atomclustern für das Top-down-Verfahren definiert. Dazu werden zunächst die benutzbaren Atomcluster und die relevanten Teile des aufzubauenden Molekültyps identifiziert, ehe deren tatsächliche Nutzung festgelegt und die Phaseneinteilung des Top-down-Verfahrens überarbeitet werden.

Abschließend wird untersucht, ob durch eine Zerlegung des AEM-Operators ein äquivalenter kostengünstigerer Verarbeitungsplan erzeugt werden kann, in dem auch ein paralleler Aufbau verschiedener Molekülteile möglich ist.

8. Zusammenfassung und Ausblick

In der hier präsentierten Arbeit wurden Strategien zum Aufbau komplexer Objekte, wie sie für SODBS benötigt werden, diskutiert. Dabei wurden in der Datenbank vielfältige und komplexe Strukturen wie netzwerkartig und rekursiv verbundene Objekte angenommen, die sich nicht redundanzfrei in hierarchische Strukturen abbilden lassen. Von diesen Annahmen ausgehend, galt es, ein Modell zu finden, das es erlaubt, deskriptive, mengenorientierte Anfragen an das Datenbanksystem in optimale Abarbeitungspläne umzuformen. Aufgrund der Komplexität des Problems konzentrierte sich die Arbeit hier auf den Aufbau einfacher, d.h. baumartig hierarchischer Objektstrukturen. Dabei wurde das an der Universität Kaiserslautern entwickelte Non-Standard-Datenbanksystem PRIMA als Beispiel für die in der Diskussion angesprochenen Probleme genutzt. Dort übernimmt der AEM-Operator, als ein spezieller Operator des Verarbeitungsmodells, die vorgestellte Aufgabe.

Von sehr einfachen Algorithmen wie z.B. Depth-first-Strategien ausgehend wurden deren Schwächen identifiziert und anschließend durch verbesserte Strategien schrittweise behoben. Grundlegendes Ziel bei der Entwicklung war dabei zunächst, die Verarbeitungsschritte auf ein notwendiges Minimum zu reduzieren. Dazu wurden mögliche, auf den aufzubauenden komplexen Objekten entscheidbare Bedingungen untersucht und eine flexible Top-down-Strategie entwickelt, die an solche Bedingungen angepaßt werden kann. Dieses Verfahren spezifiziert einen zielgerichteten Molekülaufbau, so daß die gegebene Bedingung möglichst früh und ohne Ausführung unnötiger Bearbeitungsschritte entschieden werden kann. Ein dem Top-down-Verfahren vorgeschaltetes Bottom-up-Verfahren, in dem die resultierende Ergebnismenge frühzeitig eingeschränkt wird, vermeidet den Aufbau sich nicht qualifizierender Moleküle. Wie gezeigt wurde, hängt die Anwendbarkeit dieses Verfahrens allerdings von dem gegebenen Schema, der gegebenen Qualifikationsbedingung und der Datencharakteristik der zugrundeliegenden Datenbank ab.

Im Anschluß an die Darstellung dieses Verarbeitungsmodells wurde die Integration von Zugriffspfadstrukturen betrachtet. Es wurde gezeigt, daß neben den konventionellen Zugriffspfaden auch die Atomcluster sowohl in der Top-down- als auch in der Bottom-up-Verfahren einsetzbar sind. Ihre Nutzung hat allerdings Einfluß auf die Phaseneinteilung, so daß die in der Anfrageoptimierung ursprünglich festgelegte Phaseneinteilung bei einer Atomclusternutzung evtl. noch modifiziert werden muß.

Abschließend wurde die parallele Verarbeitung eines AEM-Operators untersucht. Es zeigte sich, daß diese grundsätzlich möglich, aber nicht immer tatsächlich sinnvoll einsetzbar ist. Eine wertbasierte Partitionierung der Ergebnismenge ist normalerweise nicht vorteilhaft, weil dazu nicht nur die Wurzelatommenge, sondern die ganzen Moleküle mit ihren Überlappungen angemessen auf die Speicherungsstrukturen abgebildet werden müßten. Daher erscheint es sinnvoller, den Molekültyp zu zerlegen, einen daran angepaßten Operatorgraphen zu erzeugen und bei dessen Verarbeitung die in [Ge95] vorgestellten Mechanismen zur Ausnutzung von Parallelität in Anspruch zu nehmen.

Die Ergebnisse dieser Arbeit, die hier am Beispiel von PRIMA ermittelt wurden, können auf andere objektorientierte DBMS übertragen werden. Für die auch dort notwendigen ad-hoc Anfragesprachen, z.B. [De90, Ca94] gilt, daß sie eine Ausdrucksmächtigkeit haben, die die vom AEM-Operator realisierte umfaßt. Hier sei nur ein sehr einfaches, selbsterkärendes Beispiel angegeben: Die MQL-Formulierung laute "SELECT Student(name) FROM Student.besucht_kurse-Kurs.gehalten_von-Professor WHERE Professor.fachgebiet = dbs;". Eine in ihrer Funktionalität ähnliche Formulierung, beispielsweise in OQL von ODMG [Ca94], sieht dann folgendermaßen aus: "select student.name from x in Studenten, y in x.besucht_kurse, z in y.gehalten_von where z.fachgebiet = dbs". Die für die Bearbeitung der MQL-Anweisung hier vorgestellten Verfahren können dort somit, bei einer entsprechenden Umsetzung der OQL-Anfrage in einen dem AEM-Operator ähnlichen Algebra-Operator vorausgesetzt, in ähnlicher Form angewandt werden. Ausnahmen stellen das Bottom-up-Verfahren, das auf der Symmetrie der Referenzen beruht, und die konkrete Nutzung von Zugriffspfaden, die systemabhängig überprüft werden muß, dar.

In weiterführenden Arbeiten gilt es nun, zu dem hier vorgestellten Verarbeitungsmodell ein Kostenmodell zu erarbeiten, das in Abhängigkeit der verschiedenen Parameter (Phasenzerlegung, Zugriffspfadnutzung, Parallelitätsnutzung) unterschiedliche Verarbeitungspläne für eine Anfrage bewerten kann. Dazu soll das in [Sch93] beschriebene Modell, das sich auf eine einfachere Realisierung des AEM-Operators bezieht, erweitert werden. Mit der Implementierung des hier vorgestellten Verarbeitungsmodells wird dann das Leistungsverhalten verschiedener, semantisch äquivalenter Operatorgraphen gemessen und mit den durch das Kostenmodell erfolgten Abschätzungen verglichen.

9. Literatur

AWS92 Ahmed, S., et al.: Object-oriented database management systems for engineering: A comparison, Journal of Object-Oriented Programming, pp. 27-44, 1992

Be94 Bertino, E.: A Survey of Indexing Techniques for Object-Oriented Database Management System, in: Freytag, J.C., Maier, D., Vossen, G.: Query Processing For Advanced Database System, Morgan Kaufmann Publishers, Inc., pp. 383-418, 1994

Ge95 Gesmann, M.: Parallel Query Execution in Hierarchically Layered Dataflow-Driven Complex Object DBMS, in Vorbereitung

HS91 Heuer, A., Scholl, M.: Principles of Object-Oriented Query Languages, Proc. BTW 1991, IFB 270, Springer-Verlag, pp. 178-197, 1991

HT94 Hua, K., Tripathy, C.: Object Skeletons: An Efficient Navigation Structure for Object-Oriented Database Systems, Proc. of 10th Conf. on Data Engineering, pp. 508-517, 1994

JS90 Jhingran, A., Stonebraker, M.: Alternatives in Complex Object representation : A Performance Perspective, Proc. of 6th Conf. on Data Engineering, pp. 94-102, 1990

Ki93 Kim, W.: Object-Oriented Database Systems: Promises, Reality and Future, Proc. of 19th VLDB Conference, pp. 676-687, 1993

KCB87 Khoshafian, S., Valduriez, P., Copeland, G.: Parallel Query Processing for Complex Objects, Proc. of 4th Conf. on Data Engineering, pp. 202-208, 1988

KD91 Keßler, U., Dadam, P.: Auswertung komplexer Anfragen an hierarchisch strukturierte Objekte mit Pfadindexen, Proc. BTW 1991, IFB 270, Springer-Verlag, pp. 218-237, 1991

KGM91 Keller, T., Graefe, G., Maier, D.: Efficient Assembly of Complex Objects, Research Report, University of Coloardo at Boulder, CU-CS-502-90, 1991

KKW88 Kim, K.-C., et al.: Acyclic Query Processing in Object-Oriented Databases, Proc. 7th Int. Conf. on the Entity/Relationship Approach, Roma, Italy, pp. 193-210, 1988

KM90 Kemper, A., Moerkotte, G.: Advanced Query Processing in Object Bases Using Access Support Relations, Proc. of 16th VLDB Conference, pp. 290-301, 1990

KVC88 Kim, W., Chou, H.-T., Banerjee, J.: Operations and Implementation of Complex Objects, Proc. of 3rd Conf. on Data Engineering, pp. 626-633, 1987

Mi88 Mitschang, B.: Ein Molekül-Atom-Datenmodell für Non-Standard-Anwendungen, IFB 195, Springer-Verlag, 1988

Sch91 Schöning, H.: Praktische Behandlung von Nullwerten - Realisierung im Molekül-Atom-Datenmodell, Proc. BTW 1991, IFB 270, Springer-Verlag, pp. 502-507, 1991

Sch93 Schöning, H.: Anfrageverarbeitung in Komplexobjekt-Datenbanksystemen, Deutscher Universitäts-Verlag, 1993

Sch94 Schöning, H.: Optimization of Complex-Object Queries in PRIMA - Statement of Problems, in: Freytag, J.C., Maier, D., Vossen, G.: Query Processing For Advanced Database System, Morgan Kaufmann Publishers, Inc., pp. 99-120, 1994

St94 Stratmann, O.: Realisierung verschiedener Strategien zum Aufbau einfacher Moleküle in PHOENIX, Diplomarbeit, Fachbereich Informatik, Universität Kaiserslautern, 1994

SAB94 Steenhagen, H., et al.: From Nested-Loop to Join Queries in OODB, Proc. of 20th VLDB Conference, pp. 618-629, 1994

SPS90 Schek, H.J., et al.: The DASDBS Project: Objectives, Experiences, and Future Prospects, IEEE Trans. on Knowledge and Data Engineering, Vol. 2, No. 1, pp. 25-43, 1990

SS89 Schöning, H., Sikeler, A.: Cluster Mechanisms Supporting the Dynamic Construction of Complex Objects, Proc. 3rd Int. Conf. on Foundations of Data Organization and Algorithms, FODO '89, pp. 41-46, 1989

TRS93 Teeuw, W. et al.: An Evaluation of Physical Disk I/Os for Complex Object Processing, Proc. of 9th Conf. on Data Engineering, pp. 363-371, 1993

Konsistenzüberwachung in Datenbanksystemen — Eine Anforderungsanalyse anhand der Entwurfsbereiche Architektur und Schiffbau

Karol Abramowicz [1*], Birgit Boss [1], Volkmar Hovestadt [2],
Jutta A. Mülle, Rose Sturm, Peter C. Lockemann [3]

[1] Forschungszentrum Informatik
an der Universität Karlsruhe (FZI)
Haid-und-Neu-Straße 10–14, 76131 Karlsruhe
e-mail: boss@fzi.de
[2] Institut für Industrielle Bauproduktion
Fakultät für Architektur und
[3] Institut für Programmstrukturen und Datenorganisation
Fakultät für Informatik
Universität Karlsruhe, 76128 Karlsruhe
e-mail: volkmar@ifib1.ifib.uni-karlsruhe.de,
[muelle|sturm|lockemann]@ira.uka.de

Zusammenfassung Im technischen Entwurfsbereich können große Teile von Anwendungsprogrammen, die für die Überprüfung der Datenkonsistenz zuständig sind, in das Datenbanksystem verlagert werden. Die Erweiterung von Datenbanksystemen um eine Konsistenzprüfungskomponente ermöglicht eine wesentliche Verkürzung der Überprüfungszeit. Dadurch kann der Datenaustausch zwischen den am Entwurfsprozeß beteiligten Partnern effizienter gestaltet werden. Dieses Papier analysiert anhand von zwei technischen Anwendungsbereichen, Architektur und Schiffbau, vielseitige Anforderungen an Konsistenzprüfungskomponenten in Datenbanksystemen.

1 Einleitung

Immer mehr finden Datenbanksysteme (DBS) Eingang in technische Bereiche, wie CAx-Systeme für Architektur, VLSI-Entwurf, Maschinen- oder Schiffbau, dies nicht zuletzt weil die gewünschte Funktionalität inzwischen nicht mehr durch mangelnde Leistungsfähigkeit behindert wird. Allerdings entstehen aufgrund der in diesen Anwendungsgebieten vorliegenden komplexen Daten und der zwischen ihnen bestehenden Querbezüge hohe Anforderungen nicht nur an eine adäquate Datenmodellierung, sondern auch an die Sicherstellung der Konsistenz. Diese zusätzlichen Anforderungen zu erfüllen, stellt eine besondere und in vielem immer noch neue Herausforderung an die Datenbanktechnik dar, sowohl

---

* inzwischen: AMS Management Systems (Deutschland) GmbH, Am Seestern 1, 40470 Düsseldorf, e-mail: Karol_W._Abramowicz@mail.amsinc.com

was die Funktionalität als auch die Leistungsfähigkeit angeht. Ziel des vorliegenden Beitrags ist es, diese Herausforderung deutlich zu machen. Wir wählen dazu zwei Anwendungsfelder, die nach unserer Erfahrung Anforderungen an die Konsistenzhaltung in besonders weitreichender und vielgestaltiger Weise stellen, weil es bei beiden um den Entwurf großer, komplexer Einzelprodukte, also den Einzelentwurf, geht.

Ein Hauptziel der Datenbanktechnik ist es, ein möglichst genaues Abbild der Realwelt in der Datenbank widerzuspiegeln. Ziel der Formulierung von Konsistenzbedingungen ist es, interessierende Sachverhalte der Realwelt, die nicht im Datenmodell erfaßt werden können, ausdrückbar und somit auch vom System abprüfbar zu machen.

Die Integration der Konsistenzbedingungen in das Datenbanksystem bietet viele Vorteile: Sie erzwingt einen einheitlichen Konsistenzbegriff sowohl für alle am Entwurfsprozeß beteiligten Partner als auch für unterschiedliche Werkzeuge. Dies eröffnet die Möglichkeit, daß mehrere Personen oder Werkzeuge koordiniert an einer gemeinsamen Aufgabe arbeiten. Durch die semantisch mächtigeren Ausdrucksmittel der Konsistenzdefinition wird es in einem relativ offenen System, wie es in Entwurfsumgebungen gefordert ist, überhaupt erst möglich, Daten verschiedener Partner gegenseitig nutzbar zu machen. Des weiteren können Konflikte hierbei frühzeitig erkannt und gemeldet werden, was für eine kooperative Arbeitsweise unumgänglich ist. Ein weiterer sehr wichtiger Aspekt ist die durch die Integration ermöglichte Optimierung der Konsistenzprüfung. Wenn die Überwachung der Konsistenz in einem Datenbanksystem stattfindet, läßt sich die Überprüfung auf die Dateneinheiten begrenzen, die nach dem letzten (vom Datenbanksystem) garantierten Konsistenzpunkt modifiziert wurden oder mit diesen in wohl definierter Beziehung stehen. Die Möglichkeit zur deklarativen Beschreibung von Konsistenzbedingungen erlaubt außerdem eine dynamische Anpassung der Überprüfungsstrategie abhängig vom aktuellen Datenbestand. Aus diesen Gründen verspricht die automatische Konsistenzprüfung in Datenbanksystemen für Entwurfsanwendungen eine erhebliche Verkürzung der Entwicklungszeiten und eine Erhöhung der Qualität der Entwürfe.

Die beiden erwähnten Anwendungen entstammen dem Architekturentwurf[1] und dem Schiffbau[2]. Anhand von Szenarien aus beiden werden im zweiten Kapitel Anforderungen aus Anwendersicht an die Konsistenzunterstützung, deren Gemeinsamkeiten und Unterschiede formuliert. Im darauffolgenden Kapitel werden diese Anforderungen in technische Maßnahmen in Datenbanksystemen übersetzt, und es wird diskutiert, auf welche Mechanismen man sich heute bereits abstützen kann und wo weiterer Forschungsbedarf für die Unterstützung komplexer Konsistenzanforderungen besteht. Eine Zusammenfassung und ein kurzer Ausblick auf unsere laufenden Projekte im Bereich von Konsistenzmechanismen in Datenbanksystemen beschließen den Beitrag.

---

[1] Gefördert im Rahmen des DFG-Projekts "Rechnerintegrierte Gebäudeplanung", Lo/11-1

[2] Gefördert im Rahmen des BMFT-Verbundprojekts ITiS 2b, 18S0057

2 Szenarien aus dem Architekturbereich und dem Schiffbau

2.1 Gemeinsame Charakteristika

Bei den betrachteten Anwendungsgebieten handelt es sich wie erwähnt um Einzelproduktionen. Eine Planung wird also jeweils spezifisch für ein Objekt durchgeführt. Hieraus folgt, daß die Planungskosten einen großen Bestandteil der eigentlichen Baukosten pro Objekt ausmachen, während im Gegensatz hierzu die Entwicklungskosten in der Serienproduktion auf sehr viele Objekte verteilt werden können.

Ein weiteres Charakteristikum der Serienproduktion ist, daß mehrere Prototypen, zum Teil im Maßstab 1:1, von dem Produkt erstellt und unterschiedlichen Tests unterzogen werden können, bevor ein Entwurf zur Produktion freigegeben wird. Im Schiffbau und im Architekturbereich ist es dagegen nicht möglich, einen vollständigen Prototyp des künftigen Schiffes bzw. Hauses zu bauen, das Schiff/das Haus selbst ist sozusagen der Prototyp. Die Entwerfer müssen vielmehr fast ausschließlich auf der vorliegenden Erfahrung mit früher gebauten Schiffen und Häusern aufbauen. "Abgemagerte" Prototypen sind allerdings möglich, so etwa im Schiffbau, wo verschiedene Versuche mit verkleinerten Prototypen durchgeführt werden, um z.B. das Strömungsverhalten zu testen. In vielen Bereichen jedoch wie z.B. der Verkehrssicherheit eines Schiffes haben verkleinerte Modelle nur sehr geringe Aussagekraft.

Wie alle Produktbereiche unterliegen auch unsere beiden Anwendungsgebiete einem zunehmenden Zeit–, Qualitäts– und Kostendruck. Ihm versucht man mit Arbeitskonzepten wie der "integralen Planung" zu begegnen [SGKG86, WiHS94]. Die Grundidee der integralen Planung ist es, das Planen zu parallelisieren und zeitlich zu komprimieren, anstatt die einzelnen Gewerke isoliert und sequentiell zu planen und nur deren Ergebnisse aufeinander abzustimmen. Durch die Bildung von interdisziplinären Planungsteams soll die Kommunikation zwischen den Beteiligten verstärkt, sollen frühzeitig Konflikte zwischen verschiedenen Spezialisten erkannt und dadurch bessere und schnellere Lösungen erzielt werden. Dieser Prozeß ist im Schiffbau stärker ausgeprägt als im Architekturbereich. Dies liegt insbesondere an der in weiten Teilen noch in handwerklicher Bautradition begründeten Planungsstruktur in der Achitektur. Jeder Spezialist (Haustechnikingenieur, Bauphysiker, Akustiker, Lichttechniker etc.) führt – meist unter der Leitung des Architekten als Treuhänder des Bauherrn und Gesamtkoordinator – die von ihm durchzuführenden Planungsschritte aus, ohne allzusehr auf die Belange der anderen Gewerke Rücksicht zu nehmen. Im Schiffbau ist dies durch einen relativ hohen Industrialisierungsgrad und dem Status der Werft als Generalunternehmen, welches einen Großteil der Planung und Fertigung unter einem Dach vereinigt, anders. So sind sowohl der Einsatz von CAx Systemen, als auch die Ansätze zur Integration von Werkzeugen auf einer gemeinsamen Datenplattform insgesamt im Schiffbau fortgeschrittener als in der Architektur.

Die These dieses Beitrags ist, daß man den geschilderten Problemen neben einem geeigneten Produktmodell als Basis durch eine Begrenzung der Entwurfsspielräume mittels Konsistenzbedingungen wirkungsvoll begegnen kann. Diese Begrenzung muß allerdings auf gewisse Eigenarten der hier behandelten Entwurfsprozesse Rücksicht nehmen. Sie lassen sich durch deren Nichtlinearität, Vielschichtigkeit und Individualität charakterisieren.

Nichtlinearität Die Nichtlinearität drückt sich in einem ständigen Navigieren zwischen alternativen Lösungen auch auf unterschiedlichen Maßstabsebenen aus. Teile eines Entwurfes können in ihrer Entscheidung zurückgenommen und auf einer anderen Maßstabsebene neu überarbeitet werden. Gerade in größeren Planungsteams entstehen so Teilbereiche der Planung mit unterschiedlicher Bearbeitungstiefe, die die gleiche Wichtigkeit im Gesamtkontext haben. In den verschiedenen Teilen des Entwurfes, die unter anderem räumlich und zeitlich beschrieben werden, können hierbei unterschiedliche Mengen von Konsistenzbedingungen gelten.

Die Menge der Konsistenzbedingungen kann darüberhinaus zeitlichen Änderungen unterliegen. So geht mit der Rücknahme von Entscheidungen eine Veränderung der Menge der Konsistenzbedingungen einher, die für einen bestimmten Entwurfsausschnitt gelten müssen. Kurzfristige Planungsentscheidungen wie die Auswahl eines bestimmten Bauteils oder Materials vor Ort, können ebenfalls Einfluß auf die Konsistenz haben.

Häufig muß man auch bei Zwischenentwürfen noch nicht auf allen Konsistenzbedingungen beharren, d.h. gegenüber dem endgültigen Entwurf können Verletzungen noch toleriert werden, ja Inkonsistenzen sind während des Entwurfsprozesses sogar der Normalfall.

Vielschichtigkeit Jeder am Entwurf Beteiligte hat seine eigene Sicht auf den Entwurf, die geprägt ist durch seine Erfahrungen und seine persönliche Geschichte. Dies äußert sich in einer eigenen Sprache und eigenen Modellen und erschwert so die Kommunikation zwischen den Beteiligten. Diese Vielschichtigkeit stellt an eine Formalisierung des Entwurfes etwa in einer gemeinsamen Datenbank besondere Anforderungen. Die Vielschichtigkeit läßt sich am Beispiel des Schiffbaus veranschaulichen. Bei der Konstruktion werden Teilaspekte (Außenhaut, Stahlkonstruktion, Rohr- und Elektroleitungen) separat entworfen - in einem Schiff müssen sie eine integrale Einheit darstellen.

Individualität Die zumeist unbewußte, unterschiedlich weitgehende Erfahrung aller Beteiligten im Umgang mit Planungsaufgaben im allgemeinen und der Planungsaufgabe im speziellen, ihre auf dieser Erfahrung basierende, nur schwer faßbare Intuition bei der Entscheidungsfindung macht diese im nachhinein für dritte schwer nachvollziehbar und bestimmt in entscheidendem Maße die Individualität und Einmaligkeit des Produktes.

Während die angeführten Anforderungen für beide Anwendungen gleichermaßen gelten, lassen sich doch eine Reihe von unterschiedlichen Merkmalen extrahieren. Diese werden im folgenden ausgeführt.

2.2 Architektur

Charakterisierung des Entwurfsvorgangs

Ziel Entwurfsziele werden dem Architekten durch den Bauherren aufgrund der geforderten Funktionalität des zu erstellenden Gebäudes vorgegeben. Die Erfüllung dieser Vorgaben ist sehr stark durch die vielfältigen Denkschulen beeinflußt: Ein Architekt versucht immer, eine für ihn ästhetisch zufriedenstellende Lösung zu finden.

Bau- und Planungsumfeld Die Rahmenbedingungen des architektonischen Bauprozesses hängen stark von einem individuell geprägten und meist wenig strukturierten Umfeld ab. Dieses Umfeld wird bei der Planung und Erstellung von Gebäuden im Gegensatz zur Serienproduktion, die auf festgefügte Produktionsstätten und Arbeitsteams zurückgreifen kann, zu großen Teilen für jedes Projekt neu definiert. Es besteht aus einem individuellen Ort, der dort anzutreffenden Infrastruktur und einer Vielzahl unterschiedlichster Bauausführender. Ihre Zusammensetzung ist für jedes Gebäude weitgehend unterschiedlich. Sie hängt ab von der Größe, der Art und dem Inhalt des Bauauftrages, sowie dem Ausgang der Ausschreibung der Planungs- und Bauleistungen. Bauträgergesellschaften und Generalunternehmer bilden hier in einigen Bereichen eine Ausnahme.

Die Charakteristika des individuellen Bauumfeldes lassen sich nur in Teilen auf die Zusammensetzung der Planungsteams übertragen. Hier ist der Architekt in der Auswahl der Fachplaner, die zur Planung hinzugezogen werden, relativ frei. So festigen sich über Projektgrenzen hinweg funktionierende Kooperationen, in denen die Kommunikation relativ eingespielt funktionieren kann.

Organisation und zeitlicher Rahmen Der gängige Ablauf der Bauplanung und -ausführung spielt sich innerhalb der Regeln der Baukunst und der gängigen Organisationsformen (VOB, HOAI) ab und läßt sich grob anhand der in der Honorarordnung für Architekten [HOAI91] festgelegten Phasen beschreiben.

Man unterscheidet Grundlagenermittlung, Vorplanung, Entwurfsplanung, Genehmigungsplanung, Ausführungsplanung, Vergabe, Bauausführung und Objektbetreuung mit Dokumentation, die wie Meilensteine die Planung strukturieren und ihr eine Richtung geben. Diese festgefügte Struktur, die die Planungsleistungen vor dem Hintergrund der Honorare regelt, ist immer noch ein großer Hemmschuh für eine weitgehende Parallelisierung der Planungsleistungen innerhalb einer Integralen Planung. Diese würde nämlich zu einer Verwischung der Grenzen zwischen den einzelnen Fachplanern, ihrer Zuständigkeitsbereiche und der allgemeinen Planungsphasen führen.

Automatisierungsgrad Es gibt zwar eine große Menge leistungsfähiger, jedoch spezialisierter und voneinander isolierter Software für die verschiedensten Bereiche des Bauens (CAD, Ausschreibungsprogramme AVA, Kosten- und Energiesimulationsprogramme etc.), aber die Bemühungen im Umfeld integrierter

Gebäudemodelle mit dem Ziel, eine gemeinsame Datenplattform für die verschiedenen Applikationen zu schaffen, haben bisher noch keinen durchschlagenden Erfolg gehabt (siehe auch [Fisc94]). Deshalb fehlen verläßliche Aussagen zu den Forderungen an Datenbanksysteme hinsichtlich Struktur und Volumen der Daten und Komplexität der Anfragen.

Charakterisierung der Bedingungen

Funktionale Bedingungen Die funktionalen Bedingungen beginnen mit der Definition der Bauaufgabe an einem bestimmten Ort, der Art des Gebäudes, seiner Funktion, seinem Volumen, den vorgesehenen Kosten, seinem gewünschten Energieverbrauch usw.. Diese Beschreibungen können z.B. in Form eines Pflichtenheftes oder Raumbuchs dem Architekten vorliegen. Darüber hinaus ist die architektonische Planung in ein Beziehungsgeflecht übergeordneter Planung, etwa der Stadt- und Regionalplanung, sowie in Gesetze und Verordnungen eingebunden. Hierzu zählen lokale Bebauungs- und Nutzungsvorschriften (Regionalplan, Flächennutzungsplan, Bebauungsplan mit Geschoßflächenzahl und Grundflächenzahl, Gestaltungssatzung, Denkmalpflege etc.), aber auch allgemeine Bauvorschriften mit Vorschriften zu Abstandsflächen, Fluchtwegen, Feuerwehrzufahrten u.a., die im Bundesbaugesetz oder den Landesbauordnungen geregelt sind.

Physikalische Bedingungen Mit dem Ort kommen weitere zumeist bindende Bedingungen hinzu. So hat jeder Ort eigene individuelle physikalische Bedingungen (Tragfähigkeit des Untergrundes, Höhe des Grundwassers etc.), sowie eine besondere Lage, Besonnung und Erschließung. Zur Erschließung zählen neben der Wegeanbindung der Zugang zu allen Medien wie Wasser, Abwasser, Gas, Elektrizität und Kommunikation.

Konstruktive Bedingungen Bei der Konstruktion eines Gebäudes gelten die sogenannten "Allgemein Anerkannten Regeln der Baukunst". Dies ist ein rechtlicher Begriff, der bei Streitfällen den Maßstab für die "richtige" Konstruktion liefert. Besonderheit ist, daß er nicht notwendigerweise mit dem formalisierbaren Wissen der Baukonstruktionslehrbücher oder den DIN-Normen der einzelnen Gewerke übereinstimmen muß. Die Baukonstruktion entwickelt sich unter dem Druck einer breiten dynamischen Bauindustrie mit einer Vielzahl von Produkten, Materialien und Konstruktionen ständig weiter, so daß das fixierte institutionalisierte Wissen nicht unbedingt auf dem aktuellen Stand ist. Gleichzeitig bedeutet dies, daß alle Konstruktionsweisen im individuellen Baukontext überprüft werden sollten. Das Gleiche gilt für die Bauphysik, die Statik und im Grunde alle anderen Vorgaben, z.B. des Bauherrn, wie Funktions–, Volumen– oder Gestaltvorgaben für das Gebäude. Viele der Bedingungen werden so im Laufe der Entwurfsdiskussionen neu definiert.

Juristische Bedingungen Die architektonische Planungspraxis ist gekennzeichnet durch eine Vielzahl kleiner individueller Verträge zwischen Auftraggebern, Planern und Ausführenden. Der Architekt und alle Fachplaner fungieren dabei als selbständige Unternehmer mit eigenem Haftungsrisiko, welches in der Regel zeitlich über die Haftung der Ausführenden weit hinausreicht. Dieses persönliche Planungsrisiko, welches durch keine Institution aufgefangen werden kann, wird bewußt und unbewußt zur Grundlage jeder Planungsentscheidung.

Individuelle Bedingungen Schwierigster Teil bei der Beschreibung der Rahmenbedingungen ist das gesellschaftlich kulturelle Umfeld, in dem die Bauaufgabe, der Architekt und der Bauherr stehen. Zu diesem Umfeld gehören kulturelle Aspekte, gestalterische Vorlieben und Ideologien, ein etwaiger Repräsentationsanspruch, die Einbindung in den baugeschichtlichen Kontext o.ä., die durchaus auf Gesetzmäßigkeiten basieren können. Ihre Gewichtung im architektonischen Planungsprozeß ist sehr unterschiedlich. Sie bestimmen mehr oder weniger die Ausprägung des Entwurfes und können je nach Bauaufgabe die übrigen oben beschriebenen Rahmenbedingungen als individuelle Bedingungen überdecken.

Überprüfungszeitpunkte Konsistenzbedingungen sollten im Architekturentwurf selektiv und ereignisgesteuert überprüfbar sein. Wird das Fernziel des "Integralen Planens" angestrebt, so müssen Konsistenzverletzungen frühzeitig an andere am Entwurf Beteiligten weiter geleitet werden können. Falls zum Beispiel zwei Fachplaner den selben Raum widersprüchlich verplanen, müssen sie unmittelbar benachrichtigt werden.

Ein anderer Aspekt ist durch die HOAI vorgegeben: zu bestimmten Meilensteinen müssen bestimmte Bedingungen erfüllt sein, damit der Architekt oder andere Fachplaner ihr Geld einfordern dürfen. Zu diesen Zeitpunkten müssen demnach die entsprechenden Bedingungen überprüft werden.

2.3 Schiffbau

Charakterisierung des Entwurfsvorgangs

Ziel Im Schiffbau geht es aufgrund harter zeitlicher Restriktionen und wegen der parallelen Arbeitsweise weniger darum, das "optimale" Schiff zu bauen, als vielmehr ein kostengünstiges, das jedoch trotzdem den Bedingungen z.B. in Hinblick auf die Verkehrssicherheit genügt [GL88]. Die Stahlbleche z.B. müssen bestellt werden, bevor der Optimierungsprozeß abgeschlossen werden kann. Je früher erkannt werden kann, ob eine Anforderung erfüllt ist oder nicht, desto besser für die Qualität des Entwurfs als auch für die Herstellungsdauer.

Bau- und Planungsumfeld Das Bau- und Planungsumfeld im Schiffbau ist im Gegensatz zur Architektur stabiler und stärker strukturiert. Bei der Konstruktion und Herstellung eines Schiffes sind zwar ebenfalls mehrere Partner wie Werften, Ingenieurbüros, Klassifikationsgesellschaften, Versuchsanstalten, Zulieferer und Reeder beteiligt, die sich jedoch von einem Auftrag zum nächsten in ihrer

Zusammensetzung in der Regel nicht grundlegend ändern. Darüberhinaus sind die Produktionsstätte, die Infrastruktur und die Produktionskapazität definiert, befinden sich größtenteils an einem Ort und sind damit eine berechenbare Größe.

In der Schiffbauindustrie werden fast alle Schiffe als Einzelstücke gebaut, sogar die Schwesterschiffe einer Baureihe unterscheiden sich voneinander durch wesentliche Ausstattungsmerkmale. Immerhin werden jedoch in Versuchsanstalten verschiedene Untersuchungen mit verkleinerten Prototypen durchgeführt, die es erlauben, Teilaspekte der Konstruktion zu überprüfen. Trotzdem spielt Erfahrung eine entscheidende Rolle, so etwa bei einem der wichtigsten Parameter des neuen Schiffes, seiner maximalen Geschwindigkeit. Sie kann nur grob berechnet werden, und auch die Ergebnisse der Tests mit einem verkleinerten Modell in einem Versuchsbecken können nur begrenzt übertragen werden.

Organisation und zeitlicher Rahmen Im Schiffbau ist es üblich, daß aus Termingründen schon in relativ frühen Entwurfszeiten begonnen wird, das Schiff auch wirklich zu bauen. Entwurfsentscheidungen, die sich schon im Produkt niedergeschlagen haben, können damit in der Regel nicht mehr revidiert werden und müssen als harte Bedingungen angenommen werden. Um die extrem kurzen Produktionszeiten (weniger als 18 Monate zwischen dem Vertragsabschluß und der Schiffübergabe) halten zu können, müssen bestimmte Teile und teilweise auch benötigtes Material im voraus bestellt werden. Beispielweise liegt der Bestellvorlauf beim Lieferanten der Hauptmaschine bei rund einem Jahr. Das bedeutet, daß die Hauptantriebparameter geschätzt werden müssen und die Stahlkonstruktion an den Antrieb angepaßt werden muß. Aus diesen Gründen heraus läßt sich im Schiffbau nicht eine so klare Einteilung in verschiedene Phasen finden wie dies in der Architektur der Fall ist.

Automatisierungsgrad Mit CAD-Systemen hat der Schiffbau schon lange Erfahrungen. Zudem hat man frühzeitig die Vorteile effizienter und standardisierter Datenaustauschmethoden erkannt, weil die Partner im Laufe der Zeit an mehreren Projekten zusammenarbeiten, was durch die Marktgegebenheiten (relativ kleine Anzahl der Werften, Zulieferer, Reederei usw.) bedingt ist [FDS91]. Die Leistungsanforderungen kennt man daher recht gut. Allein die Stahlkonstruktion wird durch mehrere hundert Klassen definiert. Für diese Klassen werden normalerweise einige hunderttausend Objekte erzeugt. Das Gesamtdatenvolumen liegt im Gigabyte-Bereich. Aus diesem Grund muß die Konsistenzprüfungskomponente in der Lage sein mit sehr großen Datenmengen effizient zu arbeiten, soll sie den Entwerfer frühzeitig auf mögliche Konsistenzverletzungen hinweisen können. Nur so kann die Qualität des Schiffes garantiert und die Abnahme beschleunigt werden.

Charakterisierung der Bedingungen

Funktionale Bedingungen Funktionale Bedingungen beschreiben im Schiffbau Bedingungen, die unmittelbar mit dem zu bauenden Schiff zusammenhängen. Es kommen, im Gegensatz zur Architektur, nur sehr wenig Bedingungen mit hinzu, die beispielsweise das Umfeld, in dem das Schiff eingesetzt werden soll, beschreiben. Funktionale Bedingungen betreffen z.B. Kostenvorgaben.

Physikalische und konstruktive Bedingungen Im Schiffbau kann nicht zwischen physikalischen und konstruktiven Bedingungen getrennt werden, da sie eng miteinander verknüpft sind. Ein Schiffentwurf oder ein bereits fertiges Schiff muß den Bedingungen z.B. im Hinblick auf die Verkehrssicherheit genügt. Hierunter fällt z.B. die gesamte Statik. Diese Bedingungen können z.B. in EXPRESS formuliert werden. Die entsprechenden Regeln betreffen teilweise das gesamte Schiff, manche nur einzelne Teile.

Juristische Bedingungen Eine Klassifikationsgesellschaft wird von Beginn an in die Planung mit einbezogen, um eine zügige Abnahme des Schiffes zu gewährleisten. Die Abnahme hängt von einer Reihe rechtlich festgelegter Richtlinien und Normen ab, die eingehalten werden müssen. Diese sind stark von dem Land abhängig, in dem das Schiff zugelassen werden soll.

Individuelle Bedingungen In einem Projekt im Schiffbau sind in der Regel eine hohe Anzahl von Personen involviert, die hochgradig parallel arbeiten. An einigen Projekten arbeiten sogar bis zu 70 Personen. Der Entwurf erfolgt auf mehreren Schichten (z. B.: Außenhaut, Stahlkonstruktion, Rohr- und Elektroleitungen), jede der Schichten wird in mehrere Teile aufgesplittet. Ein einzelnes Teil wird von einem Entwerfer auf einmal bearbeitet, wobei sich diese Teile so gut wie überhaupt nicht überlappen. Also lassen sich die Konsistenzbedingungen hier individuell zuordnen, allerdings auf rein objektiver und nicht subjektiver Grundlage.

Überprüfungszeitpunkt Die Personen, die die Konsistenzprüfung vornehmen, sind nicht notwendig identisch mit denjenigen, die das Produkt planen und erstellen. Die Klassifikationsgesellschaft überprüft z.B. das von anderen Partnern entworfene und gebaute Schiff zu bestimmten Meilensteinen. Sie arbeitet schon in frühen Entwurfsphasen relativ eng mit der Werft zusammen, um später eine möglichst schnelle Abnahme des Schiffes zu gewährleisten.

Aber natürlich ist es auch im Interesse der Entwerfer selbst, frühzeitig auf mögliche Konsistenzverletzungen hingewiesen zu werden, insbesondere wenn wie im Schiffbau angesichts der Verzahnung von Planung und Bau Revisionsmöglichkeiten als besonders restriktiv zu betrachten sind. Wichtig dabei ist, daß es nicht genügt, festzustellen, ob eine Bedingung gilt oder nicht, vielmehr sollte auch aufgezeigt werden können, warum eine Bedingung nicht gilt. Nur so kann der Fehler schnell behoben werden.

Die Überprüfung der Bedingungen ist zum Teil sehr zeitaufwendig, und durch die Überprüfung verursachte Arbeitsunterbrechungen sind für die Entwerfer nicht immer zumutbar. Hier sollte der Entwerfer selbst bestimmen können, wann Bedingungen geprüft werden. Beispielsweise könnten sie in "ruhige" Phasen, z.B. nachts, verlegt werden. Das sollte auf Wunsch auch automatisch erfolgen.

Zusätzlich sollte die Möglichkeit bestehen, bereits zu bestimmten Zwischenzeitpunkten einen gewissen Grad an Konsistenz einzufordern. Hierdurch läßt sich auch die Koordination von kooperierenden Experten leichter unterstützen. Im Schiffbau wird man wegen der fehlenden Revisionsmöglichkeiten sogar Zeitpunkte vorgeben müssen, zu denen bestimmte Konsistenzbedingungen erfüllt sein müssen, während andere durchaus noch offengelassen werden können.

3   Anforderungen an einen Konsistenzmechanismus

In diesem Kapitel werden nun die konkreten Anforderungen an einen Konsistenzprüfungsmechanismus in den oben vorgestellten Anwendungen beschrieben. Hierbei werden die einzelnen Anforderungen aufgestellt und jeweils durch die Anwendungen begründet. Anforderungen generell an Datenbanksysteme in Nicht–Standard–Anwendungen, um welche es sich bei den beiden hier betrachteten Bereichen handelt, wurden schon in zahlreichen Arbeiten der 80er Jahre, wie z.B. [LAB+85], behandelt. Jedoch gibt es bis heute insbesondere für den Bereich der Konsistenz keine umfassend zufriedenstellenden Lösungen. Teile dieser Anforderungen werden in Veröffentlichungen zu aktiven Datenbanksystemen behandelt, z.B. [AnMC93, BBKZ93, DiPG91, GaDi94a, GeJa91, Hans92, Jasp94, KoDM88, McDa89, SPAM91, StHP91, Wido92], einen vollständigeren Überblick geben [Jaeg94, Baye93, IEEE92, VoKe91, KiLS91]. Der Themenkreis wird ebenfalls in Wissensbankverwaltungssystemen (KBMS) (einen Überblick gibt z.B. [BoDa93]) behandelt. Bei der Beschreibung der Anforderungen gehen wir hauptsächlich auf die Aspekte näher ein, die unserer Meinung nach bislang noch nicht in ausreichendem Maße betrachtet wurden. Die Anforderungen werden jeweils durch Beispiele aus den von uns konkret betrachteten Anwendungsgebieten Architektur und Schiffbau veranschaulicht.

3.1   Sprachmittel zur Konsistenzbeschreibung

Bei der Betrachtung von Sprachmitteln für technische Bereiche müssen verschiedene Aspekte abgedeckt werden. Zum einen spielen Ausdrucksmächtigkeit und Formulierbarkeit durch den Benutzer eine wichtige Rolle, zum anderen sind Aspekte wie die entwurfsausschnittsbezogene und zeitliche Lokalität der Konsistenzbedingungen und Standardisierungsbemühungen von Bedeutung.

Ausdrucksmächtigkeit: Aufgrund der Komplexität der Anwendungsgebiete ist eine Vielzahl der verschiedensten Arten von Konsistenzbedingungen abzudecken. Neben sehr konkreten Angaben, wie etwa der maximalen Spannweite eines Trägers, existieren auch sehr vage Bedingungen, z.B. daß "das Kinderzimmer sehr groß und hell sein soll".

Um dieser Ausdrucksmächtigkeit Herr zu werden, ist die Unterstützung sowohl von *deklarativen* als auch von *prozeduralen* Konsistenzbedingungen notwendig. Deklarative Bedingungen sind im Anwendungsgebiet der Architektur beispielsweise die Gleichheit von Bauteilen oder auch Beziehungen der Form, wann ein Objekt neben einem anderen Objekt liegen soll. Prozedurale Bedingungen eignen sich demhingegen zur Beschreibung von komplizierteren Zusammenhängen wie Restriktionen, die die Luftaustauschrate eines Raumes erfüllen muß. Meistens wird eine Eigenschaft, die der fertige Entwurf haben soll, nicht durch einen einzelnen Wert beschrieben, sondern durch eine Menge von möglichen Werten, wobei jedoch gewisse Präferenzen zwischen den Werten bestehen. In der natürlichen Sprache sind solche Präferenzen implizit in vagen Begriffen wie "groß" etc. enthalten. Zusätzlich muß Unsicherheit bzgl. einer Bedingung ausgedrückt werden können, bzw. der Grad, zu dem man Abweichungen von der Bedingung tolerieren kann. In der natürlichen Sprache drücken wir solche Unsicherheiten mit Worten wie "soll", "muss", "sollte" aus. Da viele Konsistenzbedingungen als Entwurfsentscheidungen überhaupt erst im Laufe des Entwurfes entstehen und deshalb durch den Entwerfer selbst in das System eingebracht werden können sollen, muß sie oder er selbst die Ausdrucksform wählen können.

Eine vollständige Umsetzung dieser Anforderungen in einem Datenbanksystem ist uns nicht bekannt. EXPRESS [EXPR94], als Standardisierungsansatz, unterstützt im Ansatz die Formulierung sowohl von deklarativen als auch von prozeduralen Bedingungen. Allerdings ist hier die direkte Integration in die Datenbank noch nicht gelöst; die in EXPRESS formulierbaren Bedingungen sind so weit gefaßt, daß eine automatische Umsetzung in existierende Systeme nicht erfolgen kann, sondern entsprechende zusätzliche Programmierung erforderlich wird. Zur Unterstützung vager und unsicherheitsbehafteter Konsistenzbedingungen gibt es bislang kaum Arbeiten [Boss94].

Gültigkeitsbereich: Zusammen mit der Formulierung einer Konsistenzbedingung ist es notwendig, ihren Gültigkeitsbereich festzulegen. Gerade die vom Entwerfer dynamisch eingebrachten Bedingungen gelten nur für genau den durch den Benutzer definierten Entwurfsausschnitt und nicht für den gesamten Entwurf bzw. alle Objekte entsprechenden Typs. Da es für Entwurfsaufgaben typisch ist, daß Entwürfe in verschiedenen Ausschnitten unterschiedlich weit gediehen sind, gelten in den unterschiedlichen Ausschnitten aber auch unterschiedliche Mengen von Konsistenzbedingungen. Gefordert ist also eine sehr flexible Zuordnung von Entwurfsbedingungen zu spezifizierten Ausschnitten aus dem Gesamtentwurf.

Gültigkeitsbereiche können neben Entwurfsausschnitten natürlich auch einzelne Objekte oder Objekttypen sein. So muß es z.B. möglich sein, Restriktionen, die beispielsweise alle Stützen in einem Gebäude beschreiben, dem entsprechenden Objekttyp zuzuordnen. Andere Bedingungen dagegen betreffen genau einen Tisch, einen Raum oder die Brücke eines Schiffs.

Existierende Ansätze erlauben es i.d.R., Konsistenzbedingungen sowohl für einzelne Objekte als auch für Objekttypen zu formulieren. Nicht unterstützt wird eine Einschränkung des Gültigkeitsbereichs auf beliebige Ausschnitte des Gesamtentwurfs unabhängig von einer Objekt- bzw. Typbindung.

Formulierbarkeit durch den Benutzer: Ein Teil der Konsistenzbedingungen stellen einen integralen Bestandteil des Entwurfes dar und sind als Entwurfsentscheidungen aufzufassen. Deshalb muß es möglich sein, diese Bedingungen dynamisch zur Laufzeit in das DBS einfügen zu können. Das heißt u.a. auch, daß nicht eine speziell ausgebildete Person, z.B. der Datenbankadministrator, die Bedingungen formuliert, sondern die Entwerfer selbst. Dies stellt hohe Anforderungen an die Verständlichkeit der Sprache zur Formulierung der Bedingungen.

Wie schon zuvor beschrieben, müssen sowohl präzise als auch vage und unsichere Bedingungen beschrieben werden können. In beiden Fällen muß es dem Benutzer ermöglicht werden, möglichst intuitiv seine Bedingungen zu formulieren. Gerade bei den vagen Bedingungen wäre hier ein Ansatz wünschenswert, der dem Nutzer die Möglichkeit gibt, Bedingungen mithilfe von linguistischen Begriffen, die dem Entwerfer vertraut sind, zu formulieren. Ein solcher Ansatz könnte z.B. auf der Theorie der Fuzzy-Mengen basieren. In keinem der uns bekannten Ansätze ist es möglich, Bedingungen mittels linguistischer Begriffe in Datenbanken zu definieren. Wünschenswert wäre weiter eine Unterstützung durch adäquate Benutzeroberflächen und vordefinierte Sprachelemente.

Die meisten Ansätze legen den Schwerpunkt auf die Definition von globalen Bedingungen, d.h. Bedingungen, die zu Beginn einer Anwendung oder zur Schemadefinitionszeit definiert werden. Der Aspekt des dynamischen Definierens, Änderns und Entfernens von Bedingungen bzw. Bedingungsmengen steht in der Regel nicht im Mittelpunkt der Betrachtung, auch wenn dies zum Teil vom Konzept her möglich wäre. Entsprechend wird auch der Aspekt der benutzerabhängigen Prioritäten von Bedingungen nicht betrachtet. (Dagegen unterstützen mehrere Systeme global gültige Prioritäten zwischen einzelnen Regeln [AgCL91].)

Dem Anwender müssen auch Mittel an die Hand gegeben werden, die Gültigkeitsbereiche seiner Konsistenzbedingungen beliebig selber festzulegen. Hierbei ist es durchaus üblich, daß jede Konsistenzbedingung ihren eigenen Gültigkeitsbereich hat. Damit einher geht die Notwendigkeit, Konsistenzbedingungen explizit aktivieren und deaktivieren zu können, dies wiederum bezogen auf einen bestimmten Ausschnitt des Entwurfs.

Standards: Immer mehr gewinnen Standards Einfluß auf die verschiedenen Anwendungsdomänen. So wurden ein Teil der Konsistenzregeln im Schiffbau bereits in EXPRESS formuliert [IGR93]. Dementsprechend entsteht auch die Forderung, Konsistenzregeln, die in bestehenden Standards beschrieben sind, in ein Datenbanksystem zu integrieren.

3.2 Zeitpunkt der Überprüfung

In existierenden Ansätzen werden durchaus schon mannigfaltige Mechanismen zur Unterstützung flexibler Zeitpunkte zur Überprüfung von Konsistenzbedingungen angeboten, z.B. [CKAK94, GeJS92, GaDi94b]. Bezüglich des im Entwurf wichtigen Koordinations- und Kooperationsaspekts gibt es allerdings erst in jüngerer Zeit Arbeiten zu kooperierenden Transaktionen, z.B. [Duer94, JBK+93].

Bei einer wachsenden oder großen Anzahl von Bedingungen ist es sehr schwer für den einzelnen Entwerfer, den Überblick darüber zu behalten, welche Bedingungen zu welchem Zeitpunkt erfüllt sein müssen. Dies gilt noch verstärkt, wenn sie oder er den Zeitpunkt der Überprüfung selbst bestimmt. Hier sind Hilfestellungen z.B. in Form von Browsern nötig, um Informationen zu erhalten, welche Bedingungen zu welchem Zeitpunkt überprüft werden sollten. Eine gewisse Automatisierung ließe sich durch Einsatz von Methoden des Workflow Management und die Möglichkeit des Erkennes komplexer Ereignisse, die den Eintritt in eine neue Entwurfsphase einläuten, denken. Sie könnten auch dazu benutzt werden, Vorhersagen über die potentiell abzuarbeitenden Konsistenzbedingungen zu machen. Damit werden Vorarbeiten zur Sicherstellung einer schnellen Konsistenzprüfung möglich. Weiter könnte der Entwerfer in seiner Arbeit unterstützt werden, wenn Konsistenzbedingungen, von denen bekannt ist, daß sie in einem bestimmten Zustand erfüllt sein sollten, zu diesem Zustand automatisch aktiviert bzw. aufgerufen und abgearbeitet werden. Voraussetzung ist die Möglichkeit einer ereignisgesteuerten Überprüfung von Konsistenzbedingungen, wobei die Ereignisse sehr komplex sein können.

3.3 Partielles Rücksetzen und Revidieren von Entwürfen bzw. Entwurfsentscheidungen

Durch die Nichtlinearität des Entwurfs kommt es häufig vor, daß Entwurfsentscheidungen neu überdacht werden müssen. Manchmal möchte man in diesem Fall ganz konkret auf einen bestimmten Zustand zurücksetzen und noch einen Versuch starten. Im anderen Fall möchte man eine neue Entscheidung in das System einbringen, von der man weiß, daß sie eventuell zu anderen bereits zuvor getroffenen Entscheidungen in einem gewissen Konflikt stehen könnte. Diese müssen identifiziert und entsprechend modifiziert bzw. entfernt werden. Diesen beiden Fällen entsprechend unterscheiden wir zwischen Rücksetzen und Revidieren.

Rücksetzbarkeit: Es muß die Möglichkeit geben, einen Entwurf in einen beliebigen Ausschnitt eines beliebigen Zeitpunkts in der Vergangenheit zurückzusetzen, also alle Entwurfsentscheidungen in diesem Ausschnitt entsprechend zurückzunehmen. Wird nun davon ausgegangen, daß im Laufe des Entwurfes immer mehr Konsistenzbedingungen dynamisch zugeschaltet werden, so müssen diese ebenfalls mit zurückgesetzt werden. Es ergeben sich die folgenden Probleme für eine Konsistenzüberwachung :

- Für den zurückgesetzten Teil muß wiederum die Menge der Konsistenzbedingungen lokalisiert werden, die zu diesem Zeitpunkt in dem entsprechenden Bereich aktiviert waren. Da Inkonsistenzen zugelassen werden, ist auch in bezug auf diesen Aspekt auf den alten Zustand zurückzusetzen.
- Da andere Entwurfsausschnitte im neuen Zustand beharren, also der Gesamtentwurf nur partiell zurückgesetzt wurde, ist mit einer Fülle neuer Konsistenzverletzungen zu rechnen.

In bisherigen Ansätzen ist Rücksetzbarkeit immer mit Versionierung oder mit dem Begriff der langen Transaktionen verbunden. Im ersten Fall, der expliziten

Versionierung, gibt der Anwender an, in welchem Ausschnitt und zu welcher Zeit sie oder er eine bestimmte Version festlegen will. Im Rahmen von langen Transaktionen kann entweder auf den Zustand zu Beginn der Transaktion oder aber zu definierten Sicherungspunkten zurückgesetzt werden. Dieser Ansatz ist relativ flexibel, erlaubt das Zurückzusetzen allerdings nur innerhalb einer Transaktion und nicht über Transaktionsgrenzen hinaus. Beide Ansätze haben sich bisher nicht damit befaßt wie mit nicht lokalen Konsistenzbedingungen umgegangen werden soll.

Revidieren: Das Ziel einer Revision ist, daß möglichst wenig Änderungen in Bezug auf die Gesamtmenge der bereits getroffenen Entscheidungen bzw. Bedingungen vorgenommen werden müssen, die neu eingebrachte Bedingung jedoch nach der Änderung im System enthalten ist, also nicht zurückgewiesen wird, die Menge der Bedingungen nicht in sich inkonsistent ist und daß außerdem die Datenbasis mit diesen Bedingungen konform ist. Bedingungen und Daten also, die in einem nicht tolerierbaren Grad in Konflikt mit der neuen Bedingung stehen, müssen gelöscht bzw. entsprechend modifiziert werden. Ein Beispiel für eine Revision ist die Entscheidung, doch kein Tropenholz zu verwenden: Alle Entscheidungen für Verschalungen, die solches verwenden, werden durch diese neue Entscheidung hinfällig. Andere Entscheidungen werden jedoch davon nicht berührt. Eine Revision ist nicht immer erfolgreich, z.B. dann nicht, wenn Bedingungen höherer Priorität im System enthalten sind, die in Konflikt mit der neuen Entscheidung des Entwerfers stehen.

Das Revidieren von Entwurfsentscheidungen wird in bisherigen Mechanismen zur Überprüfung der Konsistenz nicht berücksichtigt. Das dürfte zu einem großen Teil daran liegen, daß die meisten Ansätze eher Bedingungen betrachten, die für sämtliche Entwürfe gelten, als solche, die nur für einen einzelnen Entwurf gültig sind. Aber selbst bei ersteren muß mit Revisionen von Zeit zu Zeit (wenn auch in größeren zeitlichen Abständen) gerechnet werden, insbesondere dann, wenn sich das Schema ändert.

3.4 Reaktion auf Konsistenzverletzung

Wie schon erwähnt, werden Inkonsistenzen bestimmter Regeln oder Regelmengen in bestimmten Entwurfsphasen bewußt in Kauf genommen. Dies ist unabhängig davon, ob eine Bedingung präzise oder vage formuliert oder von vornherein mit Unsicherheiten behaftet ist. Ein einfaches Deaktivieren der betroffenen Bedingungen in solchen Entwurfsphasen ist jedoch nicht immer ausreichend, da Reaktionen durchaus erwünscht sein können. Grob unterscheiden wir zwischen "harten" und "weichen" Konsistenzbedingungen, je nachdem ob die entsprechende Bedingung erfüllt sein muß oder Inkonsistenzen toleriert werden. Da dies von der Entwurfsphase abhängig ist, muß man eine Bedingung beliebig von "weich" auf "hart" und umgekehrt schalten können. Angenommen, ein bestimmter Raum solle 2 Türen haben. Zu Beginn der Planung ist diese Bedingung weich, da sie für den Architekten lediglich eine Art Merkfunktion darstellt. In der Phase, in der der Architekt diesen Raum genau spezifiziert, wird diese Bedingung hart und bleibt es auch, es sei denn der Entwerfer stößt einen Revisionsprozeß an oder setzt den Entwurf wieder zurück.

Ob eine Bedingung hart oder weich ist, hat Auswirkungen auf die mögliche Reaktion auf eine Verletzung. Bei harten Bedingungen wird erwartet, daß die Daten, die die Konsistenzverletzung verursachen, nicht so in den Entwurf aufgenommen werden. Bei weichen Bedingungen dagegen ist eine umfangreiche Palette möglicher Reaktionen denkbar. Dies reicht vom einfachen Warnen des Entwerfers, daß die Bedingung verletzt ist, bis zum Starten eines aufwendigen Kommunikationsprozesses, wie die Unstimmigkeiten behoben werden können, in den alle betroffenen Projektpartner einbezogen werden. Wenn Entwerfer Konsistenzverletzungen selbst beheben sollen, reicht das einfache Anzeigen, welche Bedingung mit welchen Belegungen verletzt ist, jedoch meist nicht aus. Vielmehr müssen auch die Ursachen dafür angegeben werden, soweit diese vom DBS erkannt werden können. Im Idealfall werden dem Entwerfer sogar Vorschläge für Reparaturen gemacht [MoLo91, Frie93].

Die Unterteilung in "Bedingung erfüllt" oder "Bedingung nicht erfüllt" ist sehr grob. Sie unterscheidet nicht zwischen Werten, die die Bedingung "fast" erfüllen und solchen, die sie mit Sicherheit nicht erfüllen. Ideal wäre eine weitere Unterteilung in verschiedene Grade der Konsistenz bzw. Inkonsistenz.

Die unterschiedlichen geforderten Reaktionen auf die Verletzung von Konsistenzbedingungen können teilweise durch aktive Datenbanken modelliert werden. Hier muß dann der entsprechende Implementierungsaufwand aufgebracht werden. Ein System, in dem auch explizit die Möglichkeit unterstützt wird, daß harte zu weichen Constraints werden und umgekehrt, wird z.B. in [EiWe93] diskutiert. Es gibt kaum Ansätze, die verschiedene Grade von Inkonsistenz unterscheiden: entweder wird (bezogen auf eine Regel) jegliche Inkonsistenz toleriert, oder gar keine. Manchmal wird der tolerierte Grad der Inkonsistenz oder die relative Konsistenz durch zeitliche Bedingungen und die Menge der sich in einem bestimmten Zeitraum geänderten Daten beschrieben [RuSK91, Datt94].

3.5 Leistung

Die Abarbeitung von Konsistenzbedingungen kann zum Teil recht zeitaufwendig werden, was abhängig ist von der Menge der Bedingungen, die zu prüfen sind, der Größe der Datenbasis bzw. der Menge der zu überprüfenden Objekte, sowie von der Komplexität der Bedingungen selbst. Die Leistungsanforderungen unterscheiden sich auch je nachdem, ob die Bedingungen zu einem bestimmten Zeitpunkt einmalig überprüft werden oder ständig im Hintergrund überwacht werden sollen. Im Hintergrund überwachte Bedingungen dürfen den Gesamtfluß des Entwurfs möglichst wenig beeinträchtigen. Bei einmaligen Überprüfungen kommt es nicht zuletzt auf die subjektive Einschätzung der Komplexität und der Gewichtung der Bedingungen durch den Entwerfer an, welche Wartezeiten in Kauf genommen werden. Für Bedingungen, für die gegenwärtig eine Person tagelang Berechnungen ausführt, bietet sich kaum eine Alternative zum System an, selbst wenn auch dort eine stundenlange Berechnung anfällt. Teilweise können

Verletzungen einer solchen Bedingung mit einem Blick auf eine Zeichnung schneller erkannt werden, jedoch ist bei dieser Vorgehensweise nicht gewährleistet, daß wirklich alle Fehler entdeckt werden. Bei wichtigen Bedingungen ist das nicht hinnehmbar, bei anderen dagegen wie z.B. der Festigkeitsprüfung ist eine intuitive Prüfung anhand der Zeichnung manchmal ausreichend. Folgt man etwa einem Workflow-Ansatz gemäß Abschnitt 3.2, so wird man daher unterscheiden wollen, ob eine systemrealisierte Überprüfung erfolgen soll oder der Entwerfer zu einer intellektuellen Überprüfung aufgefordert wird.

Verschiedene Arbeiten haben sich mit Leistungsaspekten befaßt. Einige beschäftigen sich mit der effizienten Abarbeitung einer kompletten Regelmenge (z.B. durch DB-adäquate Variationen des Rete-Algorithmus [EiWe93, FaRS93]), durch adäquate Transaktionsmechanismen, z.B. [DaRa93, SrHT90], oder durch algebraische Optimierung [Herz94], andere mit der effizienten Ausführung einer einzelnen Regel, z.B. [QiSm93, Alt94]. Insgesamt stellt aber bis heute das Problem der Leistungsoptimierung das größte Hindernis für einen breiten und flexiblen Einsatz von Konsistenzbedingungen dar.

4 Zusammenfassung und Ausblick

Der Beitrag ging von der These aus, daß Konsistenzbedingungen ein wesentliches Mittel sein können, um im Entwurfsprozeß Entscheidungen zu dokumentieren und in der Datenbasis durchzusetzen. Wir behaupteten darüberhinaus, daß diese Entscheidungen und damit die Bedingungen besonders hohe Ansprüche an ein Datenbanksystem stellen, wenn es sich um den Entwurf von Einzelprodukten handelt. Um diese Thesen zu belegen, untersuchte der Beitrag zunächst zwei Anwendungsfelder, in denen Einzelentwürfe dominieren. Diese Untersuchungen erfolgten ursprünglich völlig unabhängig voneinander. Die Tatsache, daß sich die jeweils gemachten Beobachtungen so stark überdeckten, war ein wesentliches Motiv für den vorliegenden Beitrag.

Es zeigte sich, daß derartige Anwendungen eine Vielfalt zum Teil recht ungewohnter Anforderungen an die Beschreibung und Überprüfung von Konsistenzbedingungen stellen, die u.a. die Präzision der Formulierung, die Gültigkeitsbereiche und -zeitpunkte, die Überprüfungszeitpunkte, die Reaktion auf Verletzungen, das dynamische Einbringen, Revidieren und das Rücksetzen betreffen. Ein kurzer Vergleich mit dem Stand der Technik machte deutlich, daß die Umsetzung der Forderungen an Datenbanksysteme noch zahlreiche neuartige Fragestellungen aufwirft.

Einige dieser Fragestellungen verfolgen wir derzeit in zwei Vorhaben. Das Projekt ArchE soll ein Framework zur Verfügung stellen, das den architektonischen Entwurfsprozeß von Beginn an, also schon bei der Erstellung der ersten Anforderungsanalysen, bis zum Gebäudeabriß unterstützt [HFH+93, LMSH94]. Insbesondere richten wir hierbei unser Augenmerk jedoch auf die frühen noch sehr schwach formalisierbaren Entwurfsphasen und auf das Ziel, die dort anfallenden Daten für Experten (Fachplaner [HoMS94, StLo94]), die erst in weiteren Entwurfsphasen hinzukommen, zu integrieren. Als Testumgebung für diese Aufgabenstellung haben wir die Fachplaner MIDI und Armilla ausgewählt. MIDI ist ein Stahlbausystem, das den Bau von mehrgeschossigen, hochinstallierten Gebäuden erlaubt. Armilla ist das hierzu passende allgemeine Installationsmodell, ein Regelbuch für die koordinierte Installationsführung in Gebäuden [Hall74, Hall85].

Ziel des ITiS-Projektes ist die Bereitstellung von Konsistenzprüfungsmechanismen für objektorientierte Datenbanksysteme im Schiffbau unter Verwendung der STEP/EXPRESS-Norm. Die Konsistenzbedingungen sowie Schemata sind in EXPRESS beschrieben. Ein besonderes Augenmerk wird auf die effiziente Bedingungsauswertung gelegt, da die Zeit einen besonders kritischen Faktor darstellt.

Danksagung

Wir möchten den anonymen Gutachtern für ihre zahlreichen Kommentare zu der ersten Version dieses Beitrages danken. Des weiteren danken wir unseren Kollegen Jochen Alt, Dr. Günter von Bültzingsloewen, Uwe Herzog und Dr. Ralf Kramer für weitere Anregungen und Korrekturen.

Literatur

[Alt94]   J. Alt, *Optimizing EXPRESS Rule Evaluation with Fine-grained, Dynamic Materialization in CAD Applications*, Proc. 4th Int. Conf. of EXPRESS Users Group, Greenville, South Carolina, Oct. 1994.

[AgCL91]   R. Agrawal, R.J. Cochrane, B.G. Lindsay *On Maintaining Priorities in a Production Rule System*, Proc. of 17th VLDB, Barcelona, 479-487, Sept. 1991.

[AnMC93]   E. Anwar, L. Maugis, S. Chakravarthy *A New Perspective on Rule Support for Object-Oriented Databases*, Proc. Int. Conf. on Management of Data, Washington D.C., 99-108, 1993.

[Baye93]   P. Bayer *State-of-the-art report on reactive processing in databases and artificial intelligence*, The Knowledge Engineering Review, Vol. 8:2, Cambridge University Press, 145-171, 1993.

[BBKZ93]   H. Branding, A. P. Buchmann, T. Kudraß, J. Zimmermann *Rules in an Open System: The REACH Rule System*, Proc. 1st Int. Workshop on Rules in Database Systems, Edinburgh, 111-126, Aug. 1993.

[BoDa93]   B. Boss, C. Danner *Rule Management in Expert Database Systems*, ESPRIT Project 736, Technical Report JCF/FZI/004-04/13-Feb-93, Feb. 1993.

[Boss94]   B. Boss *Handling of Vague and Uncertain Design Constraints in an Object Oriented Database*, ESPRIT Project 7364, Technical Report JCF/FZI/039-01/15-Nov-94, Nov. 1994.

[CKAK94]   S. Chakravarthy, V. Krishnaprasad, E. Anwar, S.-K. Kim *Composite Events for Active Databases: Semantics, Contexts and Detection*, Proc. of 20th VLDB, Santiago, Chile, 606-617, Sept. 1994.

[DaRa93]   C. Danner, M. Ranft *Transaction Management to Support Rule Based Database Applications*, Proc. 1st Int. Workshop on Rules in Database Systems, Edinburgh, 143-162, Aug. 1994.

[Datt94]   A. Datta *Research Issues in Databases for ARCS: Active Rapidly Changing Data Systems* SIGMOD RECORD, Vol. 23, no. 3, 8-13, Sept. 1994.

[DiPG91]   O. Diaz, N.W. Paton, P. Gray *Rule Management in Object Oriented Databases: A Uniform Approach*, Proc. of 17th VLDB, Barcelona, 317-326, Sept. 1991.

[Duer94]   M. Dürr *Koordinationsmechanismen für Teamarbeit: Modellbildung und Datenbank-Unterstützung*, VDI-Fortschrittsberichte, Reihe 10, Nr. 296, 1994.

[EiWe93]   C.F. Eick, P. Werstein *Rule-Based Consistency Enforcement for Knowledge-Based Systems*, IEEE Transactions on Data and Knowledge Engineering, Vol. 5, 52-64, Feb. 1993.

[EXPR94]   *EXPRESS Language Reference Manual*, ISO TC184/SC4/* WG5 N 55, Document N51, Part 11 of ISO 10303 International Standard, Jan. 1994.

[FaRS93]   F. Fabret, M. Regnier, E. Simon *An Adaptive Algorithm for Incremental Evaluation of Production Rules in Databases*, Proc. of 19th VLDB, Dublin, Ireland, 455-466, Aug. 1993.

[FDS91]   FDS Forschungszentrum des Deutschen Schiffbaus *Innovative Anwendungen der Informationstechnik im Schiffbau*, Abschlußbericht zur Projektdefinitionsphase, 1991.

[Fisc94]   R. Fischbach, *Architektur-CAD ist anders – Einzelstück*, iX, Vol. 5, 1994.

[Frie93]   G. Friedrich *Model-Based Diagnosis and Repair*, AI Communications, Vol. 6, No. 3/4, 187-206, Sept./Oct. 1993.

[GaDi94a]   S. Gatziu, K.R. Dittrich *SAMOS: An Active Object-oriented Database System*, IEEE Quarterly Bulletin on Data Engineering, 15(1-4), 23-26, Dec. 1992.

[GaDi94b]   S. Gatziu, K.R. Dittrich *Events in an Active Object-Oriented Database System*, Proc. 1st Int. Workshop on Rules in Database Systems, Edinburgh, 23-39, Aug. 1994.

[GeJa91]   N. Gehani, H.V. Jagadish *Ode as an Active Database: Constraints and Triggers*, Proc. of 17th VLDB, Barcelona, 327-336, Sept. 1991.

[GeJS92]   N. Gehani, H.V. Jagadish, O. Shmueli *Composite Event Specification in Active Databases: Model and Implementation*, Proc. of 18th VLDB, Vancouver, Britisch Columbia, Canada, 327-338, Aug. 1992.

[GL88]   Germanischer Lloyd *Vorschriften für Klassifikation und Bau von stählernen Seeschiffen*, Germanischer Lloyd, Hamburg, Okt. 1988.

[Hall74]   USM bausysteme Haller, *midi 1000, Tragwerk Planungsgrundlagen*, USM bausysteme Haller, 1974.

[Hall85]   F. Haller *Armilla – ein Installationsmodell*, Institut für Industrielle Bauproduktion, Universität Karlsruhe, 1985.

[Hans92]   E.N. Hanson *Rule Condition Testing and Action Execution in Ariel*, Proc. ACM SIGMOD Conf. on Management of Data, San Diego, California, 49-58, June 1992.

[Herz94]   U. Herzog *Eine Basis für schnelle Konsistenztests*, Tagungsband 6. Workshop "Grundlagen von Datenbanken", Bad Helmstedt, 61-65, Sept. 1994.

[HFH+93]   F. Haller, K. Friedrichs, V. Hovestadt, P. C. Lockemann, J. A. Mülle, R. Sturm *The Design Navigator*, Proc. 5th Int. Conf. Computing in Civil and Building Engineering, Anaheim, California, 335-340, 1993.

[HOAI91]   *HOAI: Verordnung über die Honorare für Leistungen der Architekten und Ingenieure*, Fassung der vierten Änderungs–Verordnung, Stand 1.1.1991, Düsseldorf, 1991.

[HoMS94]   V. Hovestadt, J. A. Mülle, R. Sturm *ArchE – Datenbankunterstützte Architektur–Entwurfsumgebung: Eine Anforderungsanalyse*, Technical Report No. 23, University Karlsruhe, 1994.

[IEEE92]   Bulletin of the Technical Committee on Data Engineering, *Special Issue on Active Databases*, Vol. 15, No. 1-4, Dec. 1992.

[IGR93]   *Integrated Generic Resources: Geometric and Topological Representation*, TCP 184/SC4/WG3, part 42 of ISO 10303 International Standard, May 1993.

[Jaeg94]   U. Jaeger, *Annotated Bibliography on Active Databases*, Humboldt-Universität zu Berlin, Dec. 1994, to be published.

[Jasp94]   H. Jasper *Active Databases for Active Repositories*, Proc. 10th Int. IEEE Conf. on Data Engineering, Houston, Texas, Feb. 1994.

[JBK+93]   S. Jablonski, S. Barthel, T. Kirsche, T. Rödinger, H. Schuster, H. Wedekind *Datenbankunterstützung für kooperative Gruppenarbeit*, it+ti, 35(1993)1, 34-44, 1993.

[KiLS91]   W. Kim, Y.-J. Lee, J. Seo *An Overview of Integrity Management in Object-Oriented Databases*, IEEE Bulletin of the Computer Society Technical Committe on Data Engineering, Vol. 14, No. 2, 38-42, June 1991.

[KoDM88]   A. Kotz, K.R. Dittrich, J. Mülle *Supporting Semantic Rules by a Generalized Event/Trigger Mechanism*, Proc. Int. Conf. on Extending Database Techn., Venice, 76-91, 1988.

[LAB+85]   P. C. Lockemann, M. Adams, M. Beuer, K. R. Dittrich B. Ferkinghoff, W. Gotthard, A. M. Kotz, R. P. Liedtke, B. Lüke, J. A. Mülle *Anforderungen technischer Anwendungen an Datenbanksysteme*, Proc. der GI-Fachtagung Datenbanken für Büro, Technik und Wissenschaft (BTW), Springer-Verlag, Heidelberg, Informatik Fachberichte Nr. 94, 1-26, 1985.

[LMSH94]   P. C. Lockemann, J. A. Mülle, R. Sturm, V. Hovestadt *Modeling and Integrating Design Data from Experts in a CAAD-Environment*, 1st. European Conference on Product and Process Modelling in Building Industry, Dresden, Germany, 1994.

[McDa89]   D. McCarthy, U. Dayal *The Architecture of an Active Data Base Management System*, Proc. 1989 ACM SIGMOD Conf. on Management of Data, Portland, Oregon, 215-224, June 1989.

[MoLo91]   G. Moerkotte, P. C. Lockemann *Reactive Consistency Control in Deductive Databases*, ACM Transactions on Database Systems, Vol. 16, No. 4, 670-702, Dec. 1991.

[QiSm93]   X.Qian, D.R. Smith *Integrity Constraint Reformulation For Efficient Validation* Proc. of 19th VLDB, Dublin, Ireland, 417-425, Aug. 1993.

[RuSK91]   M. Rusinkiewicz, A. Sheth, G. Karabatis *Specifying Interdatabase Dependencies in a Multidatabase Environment*, COMPUTER, 46-53, Dec. 1991.

[SGKG86]   P. Suter, R. Gfeller, N. Kohler, J. van Glist. *Haustechnik in der Integralen Planung*, Impulsprogramm Haustechnik 1986. Bundesamt für Konjunkturfragen, Bern, 1986.

[SrHT90]   J. Srivastava, K.-W. Hwang, J.S.E. Tan *Parallelism in Database Production Systems* Proc. 6th Int. Conf. on Data Engineering, LA, 121-128, Feb. 1990.

[SPAM91]   U. Schreier, H. Pirahesh, R. Agrawal, C. Mohan *Alert: An Architecture for Transforming a Passive DBMS into an Active DBMS*, Proc. of 17th VLDB, Barcelona, 469-478, Sept. 1991.

[StHP91]   M. Stonebraker, M. Hearst, S. Potamianos *A Commentary on the Post-gres Rules System*, SIGMOD Record 18, 14(7):897-909, Sept. 1989.

[StLo94]   R. Sturm, P. C. Lockemann *Bereichsdynamische Konsistenzüberwachung in Architekturdatenbanken*, Technical Report No. 24, University Karlsruhe, 1994.

[VoKe91]   M. H. van der Voort, M. L. Kersten, *Facets of database triggers*, Centrum voor Wiskunde en Informatica; Computer Science/Department of Algorithmics and Architecture; Report CS-R9122, March 1991.

[Wido92]   J. Widom *The Starburst Rule System: Language Design, Implementation, and Applications*, In [IEEE92], 15-18.

[WiHS94]   H.-J. Widmer, A. Hirsch, Th. Siodla *Neuartige Organisationsformen in der Konstruktion als Basis für die arbeitsorientierte Gestaltung des CAD-Referenzmodells* Proc. CAD'94 "Produktdatenmodellierung und Prozeß-modellierung als Grundlage neuer CAD-Systeme", Fachtagung der GI, Paderborn, 295-316, März 1994.

Specification and Implementation of Consistency Constraints in Object-Oriented Database Systems: Applying Programming-by-Contract

Andreas Geppert, Klaus R. Dittrich

Institut fuer Informatik, Universitaet Zuerich, Switzerland
{geppert l dittrich}@ifi.unizh.ch

Abstract

We describe an approach to the specification and implementation of consistency constraints in object-oriented database systems, adopting the programming-by-contract paradigm developed for object-oriented programming. We also investigate how consistency constraints specified in programming-by-contract can be transformed into production rules of an active, object-oriented database system.

Keywords: object-oriented database systems, consistency constraints, active database systems

1 Introduction

In addition to the tasks of modeling, storing, and retrieving data, a database system (DBS) has to prevent database states that do not represent legitimate models of the miniworld of interest. The DBS has to perform *consistency maintenance*, which comprises three tasks:

- the DBS has to provide means to *define* consistency constraints pertaining to the miniworld under consideration,
- inconsistent situations in the database have to be *detected*, and
- in case of inconsistencies, consistency has to be *enforced*.

We investigate these three tasks in the context of *object-oriented database systems* (ooDBSs). In this context, the requirements for consistency maintenance are as follows:

- consistency constraints should be defined in a declarative way instead of as code fragments,
- the approach to define consistency constraints should be well integrated with the object-oriented style of defining and manipulating classes and objects,
- the approach to define consistency constraints should take the behavior of objects into account,
- constraint maintenance should be applicable to persistent and volatile (non-persistent) objects (provided that applications access and manipulate both persistent and non-persistent objects),
- detection of consistency violations should be efficient,
- the concept should support efficient repairing of inconsistent situations.

In this paper, we adopt the Programming-by-Contract paradigm (PbC) [15] developed for object-oriented programming languages for consistency maintenance in object-oriented database systems. This approach will support implicit, dynamic (two-state transition) and a restricted form of behavioral consistency constraints.

We investigate the implementation of constraint violation detection and consistency enforcement on top of the active object-oriented database management system (aDBMS) SAMOS [8]. Since SAMOS is intended as a general platform for various functionalities that benefit from an active mechanism, it is also an interesting issue how well PbC can be implemented on top of SAMOS, or where potential limitations may be encountered.

The remainder of this paper is structured as follows. The next section describes the foundations for the paper: consistency constraints in database systems and the programming-by-contract principle. This section also introduces a running example. Section 3 describes how consistency constraints in an ooDBS are specified using the PbC paradigm. Section 4 shows how the specified consistency constraints are implemented through an active mechanism. Section 5 surveys related work, and section 6 concludes the paper. In Appendix A, we shortly investigate how our approach of consistency constraints checked at runtime can be combined with compile time transaction proofs.

2 Consistency Constraints in Database Systems and the Programming-by-Contract Paradigm

2.1 Consistency Constraints in Database Systems

The purpose of consistency constraints (CCs) is to restrict the database states (or sequences thereof) to those that are considered as legal. Therefore, constraints as present in the modeled miniworld have to be expressed in a formal way, i.e., must be made known to the DBS.

In general, consistency constraints can be classified according to where they are specified into *internal* and *external* consistency constraints.

Internal CCs are those that are known to and can be enforced by the DBS, while external CCs have to be expressed, checked, and enforced within application programs. Internal CCs can be subdivided into the following three types [7]:

- *inherent* consistency constraints: they are fixed for a given data model and therefore do not have to be specified (e.g., absence of cycles in inheritance relationships),
- *implicit* consistency constraints: they can be specified in the schema using specific constructs (keywords) of the data definition language (DDL), e.g., the identification of *unique* properties,
- *explicit* consistency constraints: they are formulated in a separate sublanguage of the DDL, the constraint definition language, either as predicates in a declarative language or by means of triggers. As an example, consider the typical consistency constraint that employees may not earn more than their manager.

Another classification of consistency constraints is based on whether only single database states or even database state transitions can be constrained [7]:

- *static* consistency constraints consider only single states of a database,
- *dynamic* CCs allow to constrain state transitions, i.e., they specify which transformations of database states into new ones are allowed. In the general case, dynamic CCs constrain arbitrary sequences of state transitions. Two-state transitions are a special case.

Finally, the third relevant classification of consistency constraints determines which properties of entities can be subject to constraints:

- *state* constraints specify conditions on the values (states) of entities,
- *behavioral* constraints further allow to constrain the behaviour of entities, e.g., specify correct semantics of methods.

Note that the last two classification dimensions are orthogonal to each other.

2.2 Programming by Contract

PbC [15, 16] is an approach to achieve correct and robust object-oriented, modular programs. In addition to the usual parts of class definitions, preconditions, postconditions, and class invariants are specified.

In PbC, preconditions define the conditions that must be fulfilled in order to execute a method correctly. Preconditions are formulas over the state of the receiver and the arguments of the message. Postconditions constrain the state of the receiver object after method execution as well as the results of the method. Postconditions are formulas over the final state, the initial state, and the output parameters. Note that in postconditions the old state of the receiver can be referred to, although the initial state might be modified by a method. Syntactically, the old value of an instance variable can be referred to through the keyword **old**. Together, preconditions and postconditions define a *contract*:

- the precondition defines the conditions the sender of a message has to obey,
- the postcondition defines what the receiver (the server) is obliged to produce.

Constraints that are not specific for a method but restrict the permissible states of any object of a class can be defined through *invariants*. An invariant is attached to its class and is guaranteed to hold at the end of each method execution for any instance of the class.

2.3 A Running Example

We consider the following mini world as a running example. The schema models a reuse-based CASE-environment. Modules are components that can be composed out of other components. Each module has as attributes an interface, a design, and an implementation. For designs, there can be different alternative design choices. DesignChoice in turn is a set of alternative designs. Designs of different designChoices can be related through the relationship incompatibilities, i.e., may not be used together within the same construction. Designs are realized through implementations. Implementations can be verified and tested. Each kind of artifact requires a documentation.

Example 1 shows the relevant class definitions. We restrict the schema to the parts necessary for subsequent examples (see also Figure 1 for the relevant classes).

```
class SWArtifact
        string        name;
        Person        author;
        Date          date;
        Docu          documentation;

class Module:SWArtifact
        Interface        interface;
```

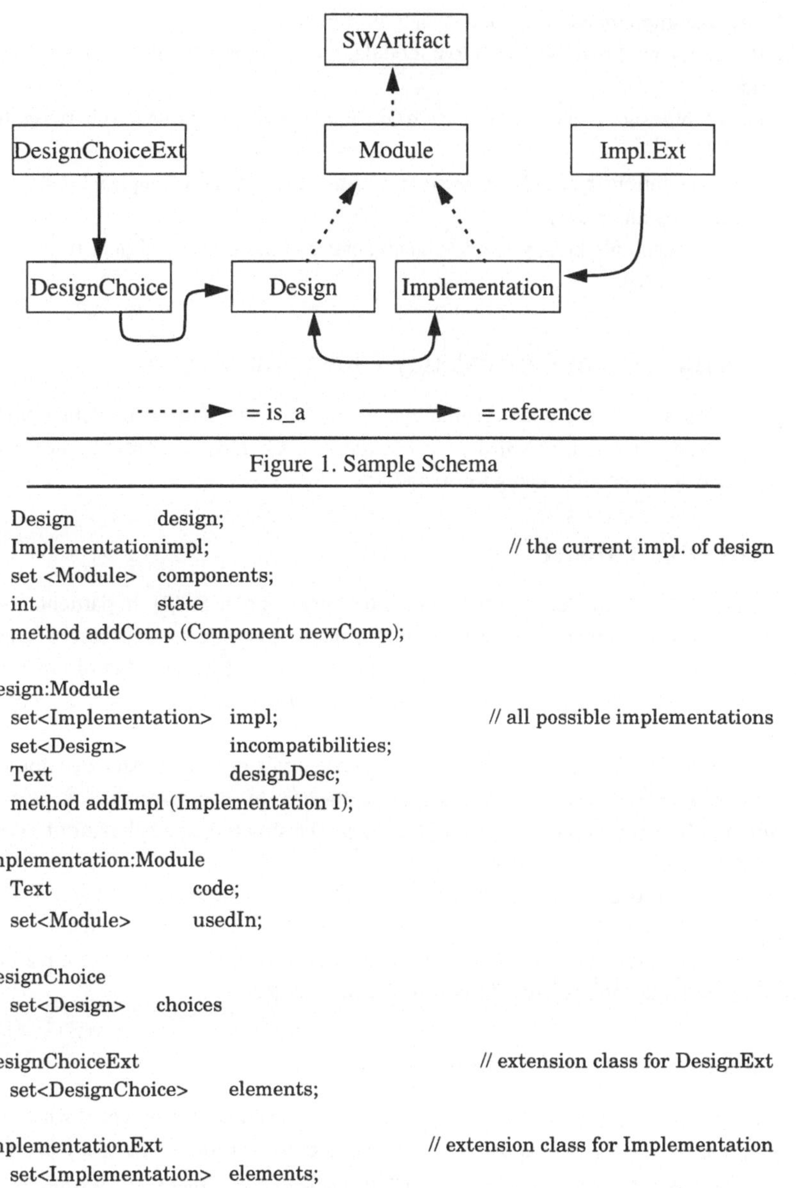

Figure 1. Sample Schema

```
Design          design;
Implementationimpl;                                    // the current impl. of design
set <Module>   components;
int            state
method addComp (Component newComp);


class Design:Module
       set<Implementation>   impl;                     // all possible implementations
       set<Design>           incompatibilities;
       Text                  designDesc;
       method addImpl (Implementation I);


class Implementation:Module
       Text            code;
       set<Module>     usedIn;


class DesignChoice
       set<Design>   choices


class DesignChoiceExt                                  // extension class for DesignExt
       set<DesignChoice>     elements;


class ImplementationExt                                // extension class for Implementation
       set<Implementation>   elements;
       method addImpl (Implementation I);
       method removeImpl (Implementation I);
```

Example 1.   Schema for Sample Class Definitions

In this context, we may define the following constraints:

CC1: Alternatives of different design choices may only be used within the same module if the
     alternatives are not related via the relationship incompatibilities.

CC2: Possible implementations for a design must be tested.

CC3: If a component is to be added to a module, the new component must have a documentation.

CC4: For each design choice, there have to be at least two alternatives (otherwise, there is no choice).

CC5: Implementations can only be removed from the extension of implementation if they are not used by any module.

CC6: Modules can only be approved by the manager of the author and only if the module is in the state tested.

3 Specification of Consistency Constraints

In this section, we introduce the assumptions we make for the underlying data model. We then introduce *Programming by Contract for Databases* (PbC-DB) and describe how consistency constraints can be specified using this paradigm.

3.1 The Object Model

We require an object model as provided by most current ooDBSs [2]. In particular, we assume that the definition of *classes* comprises a unique name, a type, a list of supertypes, and a set of method signatures. Each *method signature* defines a method name, a list of typed formal parameters, and possibly a return value. The database schema then consists of a set of class definitions.

Furthermore, the object model supports the concept of *extension*. An extension is a collection of *currently existing instances* of a specific class (or of subclasses thereof), while the class definition only specifies the *intension* of the class. The structure and behavior of extensions are in turn defined through classes.

We further consider database instances as collections of extensions. Each database has a unique schema assigned. We finally assume that the DBS also supports the definition and implementation of *application programs*. Throughout this paper, we require that method and application implementations obey the encapsulation of objects.

3.2 Requirements and Solution

In addition to the aforementioned requirements, additional ones are obtained when considering the granularity of CCs. It is apparently not sufficient to consider consistency just local to objects. CCs may also concern multiple, related objects (*inter-object CCs*). Moreover, it is not sufficient to just consider objects that are consistent one by one: each extension of an object class may require additional specific CCs. Finally, even if extensions and single instances are consistent, it may be the case that an application implements its purpose correctly only if specific conditions are valid. In particular, we want the database system to control consistency of entire databases and application programs (which is not possible, e.g., in relational systems). Hence, we obtain as a first requirement that consistency can be defined on the appropriate level: for objects, extensions, and entire databases/applications. In doing so, CCs can be kept local to the data they belong to.

Secondly, in order to provide for a "user-friendly" constraint definition language, CCs for objects, extensions, and applications must be specified in the same language.

Subsequently, we will define consistency maintenance mechanisms on three levels: the object level, the extension level, and the database level. Although these three levels are different from a semantic point of view, it turns out that constraints on all levels can be specified using the same language.

3.3 Constraints for Objects

3.3.1 Specification of Constraints

In PbC-DB, we express consistency constraints through invariants, pre- and postconditions.

Invariants are constraints that have to hold for all instances of a class. For classes, this means that their definition contains a further clause for the invariant namely:

invariant name formula [**repair** action] {, name formula [**repair** action] } ;[1]

Formulas are written as conjunctive forms. Each conjunct is a disjunction of predicates. Predicates can also contain range-restricted, quantified predicates. The only free variables permitted in formulas are the instance variables of the class. Methods are also permitted in formulas, as long as they do not perform modifications on the state of objects (i.e., only observers are allowed).

In formulas, it is also possible to refer to methods and instance variables of other objects of other classes if these objects are referenced. That is, we permit to violate encapsulation in constraint definitions[2]. Such *inter-object constraints* are necessary whenever a (real world) condition is not completely local to one object, but the consistency of one object depends also on the properties of other objects. Inter-object constraints require that the objects related by a constraint reference each other (i.e., inverse references must be defined).

The **repair** clause specifies an action to be performed whenever the invariant has been recognized to be violated. Actions are code fragments in the object model's data manipulation language. The user is responsible to specify only those repairs that lead to a consistent object state. Inconsistent object states resulting from a repair will be detected and will lead to further repairs, thus non-terminating repair cycles may happen in such a case.

Note that unlike in plain PbC, invariants are named here. An invariant can be equivalently written as several formulas (each with a distinct name), or as a large conjunction. Although this equivalence holds, it may be better in some cases to specify several clauses, especially if different repair actions are related to the formulas. Another reason for writing multiple invariants refers to the checking of invariants, to be discussed below.

---

invariant compat   // invariant in class Module
  forall components c, components d: ! (c.design in d.design.incompatibilities)

Example 2. Sample Invariant for class Module (CC1)

---

1. In syntax definitions, we use the following conventions: keywords are written in bold letters. A phrase enclosed in square brackets is optional, and a phrase in set brackets can be repeated arbitrarily many times (including zero). "!" stands for negation and "&&" for conjunction.
2. In this way, the schema designer is not forced to extend class interfaces only for the sake of CC definitions.

CCs that define a contract (i.e., requirements concerning the parameters of a method, semantics of method execution, and object states at the end of a method execution) are specified through pre- and postconditions. Similar to class definitions, method signatures are extended as well. In addition to the initial definition of methods, pre- and postconditions become a part of method definitions. They have a similar syntax to invariants:

require name formula [**repair** action] {, name formula [**repair** action] } ; // preconditions
ensure name formula [**repair** action] {, name formula [**repair** action] } ; // postconditions

---

require testedImpl   // precondition for method addImpl in Design
  (CC2)
  I.state == TESTED

ensure docExists   // postcondition for addComp in class Module (CC3)
  newComp.documentation != NULL

Example 3.   Sample Pre- and Postconditions for Methods

3.3.2   Semantics of Constraints

The semantics of constraints assigned to classes or methods are as follows.

Whenever a message m is sent to an object o, the precondition of the method named m assigned to the class of o is checked (see below how this check is performed). If none of the formulas in the precondition evaluates to false, the method body is executed. Suppose however that a set of formulas of the precondition evaluate to false; if any of them has no repair action defined, the method execution is aborted. In general, we assume that each method body is implemented as a transaction, so aborting the method means to abort the corresponding transaction. If all formulas evaluating to false have repairs defined, these repairs are executed after the condition check.

An alternative approach is taken in ODE [10], which allows two checking phases: after repairs have been executed, the constraints are checked again. If then one condition is still violated, the method is aborted. In our approach, however, constraint violations at the end of repairs lead to nested execution of repairs. Similarly, Starburst [4] allows multiple iterations, at the price of considering termination of multiple rules, whose repair actions may violate each others formula.

The same procedure for constraint checking and enforcement applies to postconditions and invariants. They are checked at the end of the method execution after the last statement of the method body (but before control leaves the method execution).

Invariants for classes and conditions for methods lead to the notion of *object consistency* (or class consistency). The specification and enforcement of these constraints results in legitimate states of objects and method executions (whereby the notion of legitimacy is user-defined). Still, constraints pertaining to the extensions or applications might be violated, although each object in the universe is consistent in itself. Therefore, the next two subsections describe how constraints can be specified for extensions and applications.

3.4 Constraints for Extensions

Constraints as defined above only refer to single instances of classes. However, it will usually also be necessary to constrain *extensions* of instances for a given class (and its subclasses).

Therefore, we apply the PbC-DB paradigm as outlined above to extensions, too. Recall that we assume that extensions are collection-valued objects and that they are defined by own classes. The role of the various constraints is the following:
- the constraints pertaining to the extensions in their entirety (instead of each single object) are formulated as part of the invariant of the extension,
- the constraints that an object and the extension have to obey in order to make the instance a member of the extension are expressed as preconditions of insertion methods,
- the circumstances under which an object can be legally removed from the extension are specified as postconditions of deletion methods.

As an example, consider the extension of DesignChoice (DesignChoiceExt). Only design choices that have at least two alternatives can be added to the extension. This is a precondition of the method addChoice of the extension class. Secondly, only implementations that have not been used in any module may be removed from the set of existing implementations: this is the postcondition of the method removeImpl of the extension class ImplementationExt.

---

require AlternativeChoices   // precondition for method addChoice (CC4)
   count (newChoice.choices) >= 2

ensure ImplNotUsed   // postcondition for method removeImpl (CC5)
   oldImpl.usedIn == NULL;

Example 4. Constraints for Extensions

Apparently, constraints for extensions are specified in the same way as constraints for objects/classes. They are also checked in the same way as described above. This leads to a second "level" of consistency: *extension consistency.* This property means that each extension in the database respects its invariants, and each method defined for an extension class obeys its pre- and postconditions. Note that extension consistency subsumes object consistency, since only consistent objects can be members of extensions.

3.5 Constraints for Databases and Applications

Extension and object consistency do not yet ensure that application programs behave in a consistent manner. Therefore, constraints for applications are required as well. To do so, we consider a database as a complex object and the applications operating on it as an equivalent to the methods of a class[3]. In other words, the "database object" has the extensions, possible other persistent variables, and the application programs as its properties.

Note that in this way the database system controls the consistency of applications, in addition to the consistency of database states. The types of constraints play the following role for databases and applications:

---

3. This is similar to the notions of "application" and "application program" in O_2 [7].

- constraints on the database states that are not already specified for extensions or classes can be formulated as invariants of the database object,
- constraints that have to hold in order to correctly execute application programs are specified as the precondition of the application,
- constraints that have to hold at the end of a program execution are defined in the postcondition of the application.

In Example 5, we consider an application program whose semantics are to approve a module mod and whose postcondition is given in CC6.

---

ensure Approval   // postcondition of application approve
    old mod.state == TESTED && approvingMgr == mod.author.manager &&
    mod.state == APPROVED

Example 5.   Constraints for Applications

Consistency constraints for databases/applications are checked in the same way as those for extensions or objects (i.e., at the begin and end of application transactions). This leads to the third level of consistency: *application consistency*. Note that application consistency subsumes extension consistency (and therefore also object consistency).

4   Implementation of Consistency Constraints and Consistency Enforcement

This section investigates how consistency maintenance in PbC-DB can be implemented. Similar to other authors [e.g., 4], we follow the approach to use an *active DBMS*. An aDBMS is able to detect events (and situations) in the database and beyond and to react accordingly. For consistency maintenance, the situations to be detected are the potential consistency violations.

We use the aDBMS SAMOS [8] for implementing PbC-DB. For the sake of comprehensiveness, we give a short survey of the active mechanism of SAMOS before we describe the transformation process of constraints into *production rules* (ECA-rules).

4.1   The Active Database System SAMOS

SAMOS [8] supports an active mechanism in addition to the usual features of an object-oriented database system. Active behavior is specified in terms of production rules. Each production rule consists of an event, a condition, and an action part. Events can be *primitive* (method events, value events, time events, transaction events) or *complex* (sequence, disjunction, negation and so forth) [9]. Method events can refer to the point of time before the method execution starts (expressed through the keyword **BEFORE**), or to the point in time after the method execution (**AFTER**). Transaction programs can be named, and the name can be referred to in transaction events. Such an event is then signalled only when an execution of the corresponding "transaction type" issues the transaction command.

The condition is a function expressed in the DML of the underlying ooDBS that returns a boolean value. Actions are also code fragments written in the DML.

SAMOS distinguishes between *class-internal* and *-external* rules. Class internal rules are part of the class definition, they can directly read or modify the instance variables of instances of the class they are defined for. They can only be defined by the class-implementor, not by any arbitrary user. Class-external rules have to respect encapsulation, and are therefore not permitted to read or modify instance variables directly.

The execution model is realized on top of the object-oriented database system ObjectStore [13] and uses the nested transaction model [17] of ObjectStore. The coupling mode for each rule defines when the rule is executed with respect to the triggering event: immediately (directly after the triggering event has been detected), deferred (before the triggering transaction commits), or decoupled (in a separate transaction). If multiple rules are defined for the same event, the execution order of the corresponding rules can be specified through priorities.

SAMOS supports nested rule execution: during the execution of a rule, new events may occur and trigger the execution of further rules.

4.2 Implementing Constraints through Production Rules

The General Translation Process

In principle, each constraint definition is translated into a production rule definition. All the generated production rules are class-internal. Furthermore, we assume that each method that performs modifications on the state of its receiver and that has constraints attached is realized as a transaction (i.e., as a subtransaction of the sender of the corresponding message).

For preconditions, the event (of the resulting production rule) is defined as a sequence of a message sending event and the begin of transaction (BOT) of the method body. In order to signal the BOT of the right transaction, the transaction event has as parameter the name of the transaction implementing the method (the concatenation of the class and the method name). Note that the message sending alone would not be sufficient as event specification. In this case, the transaction executing the method body has not yet started, and an abort would abort the transaction of the message sender. However, the message sending event is necessary in order to determine the "right" receiver of the message.

The condition is translated into a DML-fragment that computes the negated truth value of the constraint. The action is either the repair function, if one has been defined, or the abort command. The coupling mode is immediate.

The same translation applies to postconditions, with the exception that the rule has to be triggered after the execution of the method body (indicated through the transaction event **EOT**). Similar to the case of preconditions, message events (i.e., the SAMOS message event **AFTER**) are not appropriate, since the transaction can then already be committed, and an abort would rollback the transaction of the message sender. Therefore, events for production rules implementing postconditions are implemented as a sequence of a message event and a transaction event, too.

Production rules realizing invariants are triggered upon value events (i.e., any modification of some instance variable). Condition and action parts are determined in analogy to the case of pre- and postconditions. The coupling mode for invariants is deferred, as invariants may be violated during a method execution but have to hold at the end of the method execution.

Table 1 summarizes the translation rules. c denotes the name of a class for which a constraint is defined, and m a method for which pre- or postconditions are specified.

Kind of Constraint	Event	Condition	Action	Coupling Mode
precondition	BEFORE.c.m; BOT c_m	! (pre)	repair or abort	immediate
postcondition	BEFORE c.m; EOT c_m	! (post)	repair or abort	immediate
invariant	UPDATE (iv)	! (invariant)	repair or abort	deferred

Table 1. The Translation of Constraints into SAMOS Production Rules

```
ON   BEFORE.removeImpl ; BOT ImplementationExt_removeImpl
IF   ! (oldImpl.usedIn == NULL)
DO   abort;
```

Example 6.   Generated ECA-Rule for Postcondition CC5

Generation of ECA-Rules for Inter-Object Constraints

Events as defined above are sufficient for intra-object constraints. However, inter-object constraints (invariants) defined for the class of one object can be violated by methods executed for another object. Hence, whenever an invariant refers to other objects, the event definition of the generated ECA-rule has to reflect this possibility. Concretely, let an invariant I of class C refer to the related class C'. The compiler then generates an ECA-rule that triggers upon the modification of states of a C'-object. The condition checks whether the invariant I is violated, and the action eventually executes I's repair.

ECA-Rules for State-Transition Constraints

In PbC-DB, postconditions can refer to the state of the receiver as of the beginning of the method execution. Some systems such as Starburst or NAOS [6] support deltas (i.e., old and current states of objects), which are not provided by SAMOS. Therefore, old states have to be recorded by the generated *implementation* of condition evaluation functions. During the compilation of a postcondition, it is checked whether the postcondition refers to the old state. If yes, the object is copied at the beginning of the method execution, and this copy is supplied to the condition function as a parameter.

Optimization

Given the above translation, SAMOS would possibly execute the same rule multiple times for invariants. In fact, SAMOS would trigger one production rule for each modification of the instance variable iv within a method execution. A better solution using the event definition facilities of SAMOS [9] specifies that each invariant has to be checked only once during each method execution. Concretely, let iv_1 through iv_n be the instance variables referred to in one invariant constraint. The event of the production rule is then defined as

$$*(\text{UPDATE } (iv_1) \mid ... \mid \text{UPDATE}(iv_n)) : \text{same transaction}$$

The bars (|) define a disjunctive event. This disjunction specifies that the invariant production rule has to be triggered whenever one of the instance variables is modified. The asterisk (*) together with same transaction specifies that only the first occurrence of the disjunction within a method execution (read: transaction) is signalled, while each subsequent occurrrence is "forgotten". Figure 2 shows a sample method execution that contains three updates of two instance variables a and b (and therefore signals three value events). Using the *-operator, only the first event triggers the corresponding ECA-rule.

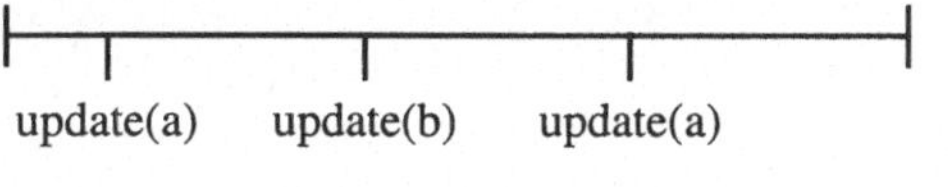

Figure 2. Sample Method Execution with Value Events

Termination

In general, it may occur that the execution of ECA-rules for constraint enforcement does not terminate. This is the case whenever the actions of one or more rules cyclically satisfy each others condition (i.e., the repairs violate each others constraint). This is a general problem of systems providing nested rule execution [e.g., 3, 4]. Although we would prefer a compile-time analysis of ECA-rules (which would then, e.g., determine whether termination is guaranteed), such an analysis tool is not yet available for SAMOS. It is therefore in the responsibility of the rule specifier that he/she ensures that no repair action violates any other constraint (i.e., it is a true repair). In this case, non-terminating rule execution during constraint enforcement cannot occur[4].

The current implementation of SAMOS allows to specify a maximum for the nesting depth of transaction trees. If this maximum is reached, SAMOS does not allow further subtransactions to begin execution. Albeit termination can be enforced in this way, it is still a brute-force solution, since once the nesting limit is reached no further rules can be executed (e.g., repairs).

4.3 Discussion

The above elaborations have shown that a powerful consistency constraint definition language such as PbC-DB can be implemented on top of a general-purpose active database system. The corresponding transformation benefits from powerful event definition facilities (value events, method events, transaction events, the *-operator, the *same transaction* keyword).

In general, the same functionality can be achieved by modifying the programming language and the language runtime system. The constraint maintenance mechanism is then a concept built into the language, for example as in Eiffel. However, using an aDBMS does not require to modify the programming language. Additionally, our approach can be used from different programming languages and query languages (which is not easily possible in the case of a tight integration with the programming language). Furthermore, since the active mechanism can also be used for further purposes, implementing constraints through ECA-rules contributes to the minimality of concepts needed in the DBMS [12].

Nevertheless, we have also recognized some possible deficiencies while developing the transformation process. First, an aDBMS useful for implementing (even simple) dynamic constraints should provide for deltas, while in SAMOS they must be implemented by the consistency constraint compiler. Second, it is still open how to determine termination and other

---

4. In the O_2 prototype, rules are deactivated during rule execution in order to prevent cycles [3]. Since the effects of rule execution are much harder to comprehend in this way, we do not follow this approach.

properties of ECA-rule executions in object-oriented aDBSs. If rule execution (say, for constraint maintenance) is not tailored to the needs of the application purpose (such as in ODE [10]), then a general-purpose active object-oriented database system needs tools to analyze sets of rules.

5 Related Work

The first approach that investigates a declarative language for the specification of constraints and production rules for implementation has been developed for Starburst [4]. A constraint specification defines a table list (the relations that are affected by the constraint) and an SQL predicate. Since the only possible events in Starburst are value events (in the SAMOS terminology), the set of possible *invalidating operations* has to be determined (the set of operations each of which potentially violates a constraint). Constraints are implemented through production rules, where invalidating operations are the triggering events. Special attention is needed to keep the set of invalidating operations (triggering events) small in order to trigger rules only if necessary. Repairs can be defined by users.

A logic-based constraint definition language for non-standard applications and structurally ooDBS is proposed in [12]. Similar to Starburst [4], constraints are transformed into trigger definitions. In this work, constraints are not related to class or ADT definitions.

Another constraint maintenance mechanism has been proposed for the O_2 prototype [3]. In this approach, constraints can be specified as predicates. Repairs are written in the database programming language of O_2. Constraints are implemented by the (active) rule management subsystem of O_2. Predicates are mapped into queries of the O_2 query language. As in Starburst, triggering events (which are method events in O_2) have to be determined during this transformation. Since the rule mechanism does not provide for value events, invariants are hard to implement efficiently.

The active ooDBS Ode also supports the specification of constraints [10]. Similar to our approach, they attach constraints to classes. *Hard constraints* have the same meaning as postconditions in PbC-DB. Furthermore, our approach is similar to Ode in that both allow the specification of repairs. Another kind of constraints in Ode are *soft constraints*: they are not checked at the end of method executions, but at the end of the issuing transaction. Ode does neither support preconditions nor invariants, and also cannot monitor state transitions of objects.

The TM data model supports the specification of constraints on three levels [11]: the object level, the class level (extension in our terminology), and the database object level. Constraints are specified as logic formulas over the states of objects. TM assumes the ACID transaction model, i.e., constraints are checked at the end of transactions, and transactions are rolled back whenever they would produce an inconsistent state otherwise. Hence, the unit of consistency is a rather coarse one, and the notion of method is not very well integrated with the consistency mechanism.

Chimera is a database language that supports the declarative specification of constraints [5]. Constraints in Chimera are deductive, set-oriented rules; they can be defined for single or multiple classes. Similar to PbC-DB, a restricted set of transitions can be constrained through referring to **old** states. Constraints are translated into production rules. Similar to Starburst [4], events of production rules are the potentially invalidating operations, i.e., database update operations. It is unclear from [5] how constraints (pre- and postconditions) can be related to methods as in PbC-DB or Ode.

Finally, while all approaches surveyed so far allow only two-state transitions, [14] allows to constrain general state transitions. To do so, the underlying logic is enhanced with special operators for referring to states (i.e., the current state and the next state), and temporal quantifiers (e.g., always, sometimes).

Summarizing, while some of the concepts used in PbC-DB have been proposed elsewhere, it at least exceeds existing approaches in the combination of the provided features:

- it not only supports constraints on states of objects, but also on object behavior and state transitions, as far as they can be represented as two-state transitions.
- It is integrated well with the underlying object-oriented paradigm, since it fosters a class-specific notion of consistency. It is in principle seamlessly applicable for persistent and volatile objects.
- When compared to database-wide consistency constraints, PbC-DB contributes to modularity of persistent object-oriented systems (whereby modularity is a prerequisite for reusability of classes). The notion of locality of consistency constraints is reflected by the three levels of consistency.

6 Conclusions

In this paper, we have developed a consistency maintenance mechanism for object-oriented database systems (PbC-DB). This approach supports the declarative specification of constraints. It is integrated well with the object-oriented paradigm and in its original form has been proven successful for object-oriented programming. It allows not only to constrain states of objects, but also the behavior of objects and simple forms of state transitions. In general, the proposed constraint maintenance mechanism is more powerful than existing ones, since it allows for invariants, preconditions, and postconditions.

We have shown that a powerful constraint definition language such as PbC-DB can be implemented on top of an active object-oriented DBMS. In doing so, we have also learned some lessons about benefits and a few shortcomings of the used active mechanism.

Nevertheless, some questions remain open for future work. First, we would prefer to specify repairs in the same declarative style as constraints, or to propose possible useful repairs. For repairs that are more complex than simple transaction abort, the problem is apparently the understanding of classes and methods.

Second, PbC-DB allows for a natural view of class-specific and method specific notions of consistency. Hence, specifying consistency constraints should be an integral part of database design. A design methodology is needed that considers not only structures and behavior of objects, but also the consistency constraints pertaining to objects and classes.

Third and most important, we conceive it as a drawback that constraint specifiers are responsible for the termination of constraint enforcement. One part of our future work will therefore focus on defining "nice" properties of rule sets in object-oriented aDBSs and on developing methods how to analyze rules with respect to these properties (comparable to [1] for the relational case).

Acknowledgements

We gratefully acknowledge the comments of our colleagues Stella Gatziu, Stefan Scherrer, and Dimitris Tombros on an earlier version of this paper.

References

1. A. Aiken, J. Widom, J.M. Hellerstein: *Behaviour of Database Production Rules: Termination, Confluence, and Observable Determinism.* Proc. ACM-SIGMOD Intl. Conf. on Management of Data, San Diego, June , 1992.

2. M. Atkinson, F. Bancilhon, D.J. DeWitt, K.R. Dittrich, D. Maier, S.B. Zdonik: *The Object-Oriented Database System Manifesto (a Political Pamphlet).* Proc. 1st Intl. Conf. on Deductive and Object-Oriented Databases, 1989.

3. C. Bauzer-Medeiros, P. Pfeffer: *Object Integrity Using Rules.* Proc. European Conference on Object-Oriented Programming, Geneva, Switzerland. LNCS 512, Springer 1991

4. S. Ceri, J. Widom: *Deriving Production Rules for Constraint Maintenance.* Proc. of the 16th Intl. Conf. on Very Large Data Bases, Brisbane, Australia, August 1990.

5. S. Ceri, P. Fraternali, S. Paraboschi: *Constraint Management in Chimera.* Bulletin of the IEEE Technical Committee on Data Engineering 17:2, June 1994.

6. C. Collet, T. Coupaye, T. Svensen: *NAOS: Efficient and Modular Reactive Capabilities in an Object-Oriented Database System.* Proc. of the 20th Intl. Conf. on Very Large Data Bases, Santiago, Chile, September 1994.

7. O. Deux: *The O2 System.* Communications of the ACM 34:10, 1991.

8. R. Elmasri, S.B. Navathe: *Fundamentals of Database Systems.* Benjamin/Cummings Publishing, 1989.

9. S. Gatziu, A. Geppert, K.R. Dittrich: *Integrating Active Mechanisms into an Object-Oriented Database System.* Proc. of the 3rd Intl. Workshop on Database Programming Languages (DBPL), Nafplion, Greece, August 1991.

10. S. Gatziu, K.R. Dittrich: *Events in an Active Object-Oriented Database System.* In N.W. Paton, H.W. Williams (eds): Proc. Workshop on Rules in Database Systems, Edinburgh, UK, September 1993 (Workshops in Computing, Springer-Verlag, 1994).

11. N. Gehani, H.V. Jagadish: *Ode as an Active Database: Constraints and Triggers.* Proc. 17th Intl. Conf. on Very Large Data Bases, Barcelona, Spain, September 1991.

12. P.W.P.J. Grefen, R.A. de By, P.M.G. Apers: *Integrity Control in Advanced Database Systems.* Bulletin IEEE Technical Committee on Data Engineering 17:2, June 1994.

13. A.M. Kotz: *Triggermechanismen in Datenbanksystemen.* IFB 201, Springer 1989.

14. C. Lamb, G. Landis, J. Orenstein, D. Weinreb: *The ObjectStore Database System.* Special Issue on Next-Generation Database Systems. CACM 34:10, 1991.

15. U.W. Lipeck, M. Gertz, G. Saake: *Transitional Monitoring of Dynamic Integrity Constraints.* Bull. IEEE Technical Committee on Data Engineering 17:2, June 1994.

16. B. Meyer: *Object-Oriented Software Construction.* Prentice Hall, New York, 1988.

17. B. Meyer: *Applying "Design by Contract".* IEEE Computer 25:10, 1992.

18. J.E.B. Moss: *Nested Transactions: An Approach to Reliable Distributed Computing.* MIT Press, 1985.

19. T. Sheard, D. Stemple: *Automatic Verification of Database Transaction Safety.* ACM Trans. on Database Systems 14:3, 1989.

Appendix: Consistency Constraint Checking vs. Transaction Proofs

Practical schemas can define a huge number of constraints, which all will be checked at certain points in time. Poor performance can be the result, although some constraints can be known to hold always. Therefore, it is not necessary to check them at runtime. On the other hand, deleting CCs from class and method definitions is not desirable, since these CCs still are beneficial for documentation purposes. We thus allow to switch single constraints on or off. Switching a constraint off means that it will no longer be checked at runtime, until it is switched on again. Note that even parts of invariants, pre- and postconditions can be deactivated, as these parts can be referred to via their name.

Syntactically, CCs can be switched on and off interactively with the commands:

```
assume name in class_name     // switch off consistency constraint checking for name
check name in class_name      // switch on consistency constraint checking for name
```

These two commands would be implemented through the **activate** and **deactivate** operations provided by SAMOS.

Note that in this way our PbC-based approach can be combined with approaches that perform *transaction verification* at compile time [e.g., 18, 11]. Application programs and methods can be successfully verified against the specified CCs, which can then be deactivated. Concretely, the following implementations have to be checked before the constraints can be switched off:

- after the precondition of a method (or application program) has been proven to be guaranteed by each client (sender of the corresponding message), the precondition can be deactivated,
- after the method has been proven to obey its postcondition, the postcondition of this method can be switched off,
- after each method implementation has been verified with respect to the invariant of the corresponding class, the invariant can be deactivated.

Ein Speichersystem für abstrakte Objekte

Lukas Relly   Stephen Blott

Institut für Informationssysteme, ETH Zürich, Schweiz
E-mail: {relly,blott}@inf.ethz.ch

Zusammenfassung Ein Hauptproblem bei der Benutzung von Datenbanksystemen für Nicht-Standard-Datenbankanwendungen besteht in der Abbildung des meist komplexen Anwendungsdatenmodells und der darauf definierten Operationen auf das Speichermodell des Datenbanksystems. Von den in den vergangenen Jahren vorgestellten Lösungsideen fanden folgende zwei grundsätzlich verschiedenen Ansätze besondere Beachtung: Einerseits wurden im Datenmodell des Datenbanksystems mächtigere Konstruktoren zur Verfügung gestellt, um komplex strukturierte Objekte abzubilden, anderseits wurden komplexe Objekte mit Hilfe extern definierter Typen abgebildet, welche dem Datenbanksystem bekanntgemacht wurden.
In diesem Beitrag stellen wir ein Speichermodell zur vereinheitlichten Behandlung dieser beiden Ansätze vor. Wir wenden dabei Techniken des physischen Datenbankdesigns und der Anfragebearbeitung einheitlich über intern wie extern definierte Typen an. Dies erlaubt einen möglichst nahtlosen Übergang von filebasierten zu datenbankbasierten Applikationen. Das hier vorgestellte Speichermodell kommt als Teil unserer Prototypentwicklung CONCERT zum Einsatz.

1 Einführung

Seit vielen Jahren stellen Nicht-Standard-Datenbankanwendungen, welche sich durch komplex strukturierte Objekte und anspruchsvolle darauf definierte Operationen auszeichnen, eine Herausforderung für die Datenbankforschung dar. Aufgabe eines Speichersubsystems ist die effiziente Verwaltung von Daten unter Berücksichtigung von Aspekten der Mehrbenutzerverwaltung. Die Effizienz ist dabei stark von einem adäquaten physischen Design abhängig. Systemkomponenten wie zum Beispiel RSS von System R [1] stellen Werkzeuge für das physische Design von *Standard*-Applikationen zur Verfügung. Analog dazu soll das hier vorgestellte Speichersubsytem Unterstützung bieten für *Nicht-Standard*-Datenbankanwendungen.

Viele der heute kommerziell erhältlichen Systeme im Bereich der Ingenieurapplikationen wie zum Beispiel Pro/ENGINEER oder Catia benutzen als Speichersystem direkt das Filesystem. Die komplexen Strukturen des Anwendungsdatenmodells werden hier als für das Speichersystem uninterpretierte grosse Objekte (BLOB) gespeichert: Die interne Struktur der Objekte bleibt dem Speichersystem verborgen. Das physische Design und der Datenzugriff haben somit vollständig in der Applikation zu erfolgen und lassen sich später nur mit unverhältnismässig grossem Aufwand ändern.

Datenbanken für *Standardanwendungen* trennen auf wohldefinierte Art die Anwendungsdaten und ihre Speicherrepräsentation voneinander. Um auch komplex strukturierte Objekte aus Nicht-Standard-Anwendungen in der gleichen Art und Weise von ihrer Speicherrepräsentation zu entkoppeln und damit effiziente Anfragebearbeitung durch das Speichersubsystem zu ermöglichen, wurden viele Vorschläge zur Erweiterung des Datenmodells diskutiert. Bekannt geworden sind insbesondere Speichermodelle für komplexe Objekte [15, 14, 3, 5, 8, 9].

Der Ansatz, komplex strukturierte Objekte durch ein erweitertes datenbankinternes Speichermodell zu realisieren hat zur Konsequenz, dass die Anwendungsoperationen, zum Beispiel die Konstruktion eines komplizierten Werkstücks in einer CAD/CIM-Umgebung, in diesem Speichermodell ausgedrückt werden müssen. Da dies oft unerwünscht ist, sind in den letzten Jahren viele Vorschläge zur Integration abstrakter Objekte in Datenbanksysteme vorgestellt worden [18, 6, 17, 7, 12]. In diesen Ansätzen wird das Typsystem um neue extern definierte Basistypen erweitert, die typischerweise als flache, uninterpretierte Objekte gespeichert werden. Physisches Design für solche Objekte ist nur limitiert möglich. Ein naheliegender Wunsch besteht nun darin, physisches Design für solche externen Objekte in der gleichen Art und Weise durchzuführen wie für komplexe datenbankinterne Objekte, ohne diese in ein datenbankinternes Format konvertieren zu müssen.

Über die letzten Jahre haben wir mit DASDBS ein Datenbankkernsystem realisiert, welches sowohl ein erweitertes Datenmodell zur Speicherung komplexer Objekte als auch das Konzept extern definierter Typen implementiert [14, 6, 16]. Die dabei gesammelte Erfahrungen wollen wir in einen neuen Prototypen einfliessen lassen, welcher insbesondere die angesprochene Schwachstelle bezüglich physischem Design von externen Objekten zu vermeiden sucht und darüber hinaus noch weitergehende Unterstützung für Nicht-Standard-Anwendungen enthält.

Anhand eines Beispieles zeigen wir, dass physisches Design externer Objekte mit bestehenden Ansätzen nur unbefriedigend möglich ist und in welcher Art unser Ansatz für die angesprochenen Probleme Lösungen anbietet. Am geographischen Institut der Universität Zürich wurden Daten erfasst, welche dem Standard des Geogr. Data Committee des U.S.G.S. genügen [4]. Dieser Standard beschreibt die Stuktur von Metadatenfiles zu digitalen raumbezogenen Daten. Jedes Datenfile enthält einige fest vorgegebene und bis zu einigen hundert optionalen Attributen, wobei einfach strukturierte, raumbezogene und unstrukturierte textuelle Attribute vorkommen. Ein Ausschnitt eines solchen Datenfiles findet sich in Abbildung 1.

Um solche Datensätze in einem System wie beispielsweise DASDBS [6] zu verwalten, stehen verschiedene Alternativen zur Verfügung. Die Tatsache, dass bereits Applikationen existieren, welche Datensätze dieses Formats bearbeiten, legt es nahe, den gesamten Datensatz im Sinne eines extern definierten Typs zu verwalten. Alternativ ist eine Speicherung des Datensatzes als NF^2-Tupel denkbar, wobei zum Beispiel die Wiederholungsgruppe `Theme_keyword` als Subrelation gespeichert wird. Das Textfeld `Data_set_description` und das Polygon `Data_set_G-polygon` können als EDT's behandelt oder ebenfalls als Subrelatio-

```
Data_set_identity     1:250,000 Hydrologic Cataloging Unit Boundaries
Identification_code   n/a
Data_set_description  This   data   set   was   derived   from   the
                      1:250,000-scale  source  by  the  U.S. Geological
                      Survey for the Land Use / Land Cover program ...
Theme_keyword         hydrologic unit
Theme_keyword         river basin
...
Data_set_G-polygon    inside(49.10,-123.27 49.15,-116.27 49.16,-104.06
                      49.40,-95.12 48.12,-88.40 ...)
...
```

Abbildung1. Ausschnitt eines Beispieldatenfiles

nen modelliert werden. Da die Struktur der Metadaten sehr komplex ist und die Anzahl Attribute vom Inhalt gewisser Feldwerte abhängig ist, sind beliebig viele weitere Designalternativen denkbar, wobei die optimale Repräsentation stark vom jeweiligen Verwendungszweck abhängt. Für die Speicherung in DASDBS muss eine Variante ausgewählt werden, welche sich zu einem späteren Zeitpunkt nur mit viel Aufwand ändern lässt.

In Nicht-Standard-Datenbankanwendungen ist es aber oft kaum vorhersehbar, welche Alternative schlussendlich am geeignetsten ist. Oft werden Daten für bisher nicht vorgesehene Zwecke eingesetzt und das Anforderungsprofil kann somit stark ändern. Unser Ansatz versucht, hier höhere Flexibilität zu ermöglichen, indem die physische Repräsentation von der Struktur der Objekte entkoppelt wird.

Für die Systemarchitektur hat sich in unserem eigenen wie auch in vielen andern Prototypen eine Systemkomponente als nützlich erwiesen, welche die allen Applikationen gemeinsame Verwaltung von Objekten implementiert. Verschiedene spezialisierte Datenmanager greifen auf die Dienste dieses Abstrakten Objektmanagers (AOM) zu. Abbildung 2 gibt einen Überblick über die Systemarchitektur und einige der von uns betrachteten möglichen Anwendungsgebiete. Das Kernsystem besteht aus drei Hauptkomponenten: Erstens einem Speichermanager, welcher transaktionsorientiert allgemeine Datenverwaltungsdienstleistungen anbietet, zweitens eine fixe Anzahl allgemeiner Zugriffsmethoden und drittens dem Abstrakten Objektmanager als Bindeglied zwischen diesen zweien. Zusätzlich lässt sich der Kern um applikationsspezifische abstrakte Objekte erweitern. In diesem Beispiel enthält das System vier eingebaute allgemeine Zugriffsstrukturen und wurde durch drei abstrakte Objekttypen eines GIS erweitert.

Der AOM implementiert für das physische Design und die Anfragebearbeitung eine Anzahl allgemein verwendbarer Zugriffsstrukturen wie Listen, Baumstrukturen und Komponenten zur Clusterbildung und Partitionierung. Im Sinne von EDT's lässt er sich um Datentypen und den darauf implementierten Opera-

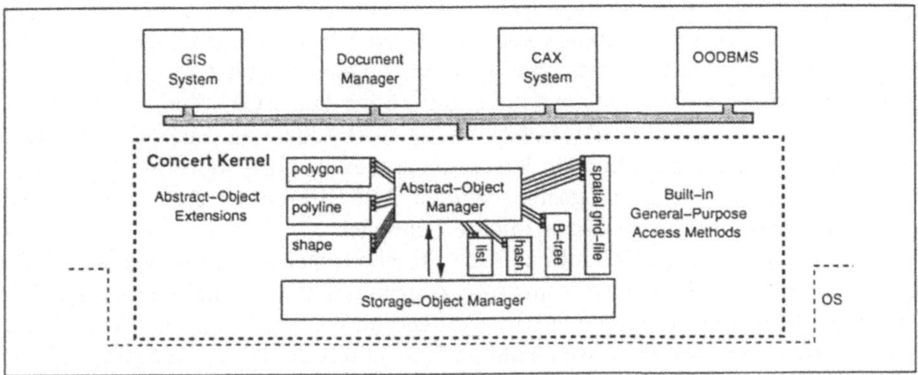

Abbildung 2. Die Systemarchitektur des CONCERT Kernsystems

tionen erweitern. Über diesen externen Datentypen können dann Zugriffsstrukturen aufgebaut werden.

Zusätzlich bietet der AOM ein Datenmodell an, in welchem komplex strukturierte Objekte modelliert und effizient verwaltet werden können. Während jedoch in bisherigen Systemen externe Objekte anders behandelt wurden als die internen, stellt unser Ansatz als Hilfsmittel eine sogenannte Ähnlichkeitsvereinbarung zur Verfügung, welche es erlaubt, einheitlich auf interne wie externe Objekte zuzugreifen. In kontrollierter Art und Weise wird die interne Struktur extern definierter komplexer Objekte dem Speichersystem bekanntgemacht, ohne dabei die Vorteile der abstrakten Repräsentation aufzugeben. Dadurch entsteht ein einfaches Modell für den Datenzugriff, wodurch besonders die Migration von filebasierten Lösungen nach Datenbanklösungen profitiert, weil nach einem ersten relativ kleinen Anpassungsschritt auf die externe Applikation gleich zugegriffen werden kann wie nach weiteren Integrationsschritten.

Im folgenden Abschnitt stellen wir das Objektmodell des AOM vor und gehen anschliessend im Abschnitt 3 detaillierter auf die Systemarchitektur ein.

2 Ein abstraktes Objektmodell

Die zentrale Aufgabe unseres Speichermanagers ist die Verwaltung abstrakter (extern definierter) Objekte, weswegen wir das Modell zu seiner Beschreibung abstraktes Objektmodell nennen. Das Modell besteht aus zwei Teilen: einer festen Menge sogenannt *konkreter* und einer Menge *abstrakter* Konzepte zur Bildung von Typen. Die **konkreten Konzepte**, im Wesentlichen *Basistypen*, *Record* zur Aggregation und *Liste* zur Assoziation, sind fest im AOM eingebaut und entsprechen somit in etwa dem NF^2-Modell [15, 10]. Auf das wichtige zusätzliche Konzept der *Punktmengen* gehen wir in 2.4 näher ein.

Das Neuartige an unserem Ansatz ist die Art, wie **abstrakte Typen** über ihre Ähnlichkeit auf konkrete zurückgeführt werden. Entscheidend ist dabei, dass physisches Design und Anfragebearbeitung ohne Kenntnis der exakten Stuktur abstrakter Objekte, lediglich aufgrund konzepttypischer Operationen durchgeführt werden kann. Ein abstrakter Typ kann zu einem konkreten Typ T *ähnlich* genannt werden (AT $\leadsto$ 'T'), wodurch gegenüber dem AOM *Konzepte* bekannt gemacht werden, ohne die *physische Stuktur* zu spezifizieren. Zusätzlich müssen dem AOM Implementationen der **konzepttypischen Operationen** für den abstrakten Typ zur Verfügung gestellt werden. Mit Hilfe dieser Operationen wird physisches Design für abstrakte Objekte ermöglicht.

Der AOM verwaltet Kollektionen von Objekten gleichen Typs. Diese Kollektionen werden durch eine oder mehrere Zugriffsstrukturen implementiert. Welche Zugriffsstrukturen implementiert werden können, ergibt sich direkt aus den zur Konstruktion des Typs verwendeten Konzepte und deren konzepttypischen Operationen.

Der AOM unterstützt **Prädikat- und Projektions-Anfragen** über Kollektionen. Grundsätzlich gilt, dass für jede Kollektion C, welche Objekte des Typs T enthält, die Form der Query über C durch die Struktur von T vorgegeben ist. Dies heisst, dass zum Beispiel für einen Record-Typ eine Prädikatanfrage als Anfrage in disjunktiver Normalform über seinen Komponenten gestellt wird, eine Projektionsanfrage wählt einzelne Felder des Records aus.

In den folgenden Unterabschnitten beschreiben wir die oben allgemein eingeführten **konkreten** und **abstrakten** Typen, **Operationen** und **Anfragen** für einige ausgewählte Konzepte. Eine umfangreichere und vollständigere Darstellung, welche den Rahmen dieses Beitrags sprengen würde, findet der an Details interessierte Leser in [13].

2.1 Basistypen

Bei den *konkreten* Typen BOOL, CHAR, INT und FLOAT handelt es sich um Basistypen, welche die bekannten Ordnungsprädikate (<, =, ...) unterstützen. Der Typ UNKNOWN ist ein unstrukturierter Basistyp, für welchen lediglich die beiden auf allen Typen vorhandenen Operationen, das bitmässige Kopieren und die Operation get_size definiert sind. Er erfüllt damit den gleichen Zweck wie der in andern Systemen häufig vorhandene Typ BLOB.

Ein einfaches Beispiel eines *abstrakten* Typs, welcher direkt auf einen Basistypen zurückgeführt wird, ist zeitpunkt $\leadsto$ 'INT'. Damit wird ausgedrückt, dass zeitpunkt ähnlich dem eingebauten Basistypen INT ist. Die zugehörige externe Repräsentation könnte eine ASCII-Repräsentation sein, zum Beispiel ,,22.3.95 14:15'', wie man sie Filedarstellungen findet. Typen, welche ähnlich zu einem Basistypen sind, müssen — analog zu diesem — Vergleichsoperatoren implementieren. Zusätzlich benötigen wir eine Operation, welche Werte des konkreten Typs in entsprechende abstrakte Werte umwandelt:

```
>, =, ... : zeitpunkt -> zeitpunkt -> BOOL
to-abstr : INT -> zeitpunkt
```

Die Operationen dieses einfachen Beispiels würde das Indizieren des Objektes mittels eines allgemeinen B-Baumes erlauben. Um die Lesbarkeit zu verbessern, erlauben wir, Typen mittels name $\rightarrow$ type zu benennen und den Typnamen anstelle seiner Definition zu verwenden.

2.2 Record-Typen

Record-Typen implementieren das Konzept der Aggregation seiner Komponenten. Wir schreiben dafür RT ::= (x_1:T_1, ..., x_n:T_n). Die konzepttypischen *Operationen* für Records sind die Record-Komposition (`compose`) und die Komponentenselektion (`project`). Analog zu den Basistypen kann ein extern definierter Typ als zu einem konkreten Record-Typen *ähnlich* bezeichnet werden. Betrachten wir als Beispiel nochmals das Datenfile in Abbildung 1. Ein solches Datenfile kann als *ähnlich* zu folgendem Record betrachtet werden:

      `usgs_file` ↝ `'(title: STRING, id: INT, contents: UNKNOWN)'`

Das heisst, dass das extern definierte File sich (abstrakt gesehen) aus den drei Komponenten `title,` `id` und `contents` zusammensetzt. Diese drei Komponenten sind dem AOM bekannt und er kann Anfragen über diese beantworten und entsprechende Zugriffsstrukturen aufbauen. Das gespeicherte File weist eine wesentlich komplexere Struktur auf, welche wir, um das Beispiel einfach zu halten, stark vereinfacht haben.

Diese Deklaration verlangt, sozusagen als Beweis der Ähnlichkeit zum konkreten Record-Typ, die Existenz der für die Aggregation konzepttypischen Operationen `compose` und `project` über dem Typ `usgs_file`. Um auch berechnete Attribute zu erlauben, ist zusätzlich die Information nötig, welche Komponenten zwangsläufig gespeichert werden müssen (`stored`), da sie sich nicht berechnen lassen. Über den syntaktisch gegebenen Operationen muss natürlich die Eigenschaft garantiert sein, dass für jeden abstrakten Record die Komposition seiner durch Projektion erhaltenen Komponenten wieder den Record erzeugen.

2.3 Listen-, Vereinigungs- und Referenz-Typen

So wie die oben beschriebenen Record-Typen der Aggregation dienen, stellt das Modell einen Listen-Typen (LT ::= [T]) zur Assoziation zur Verfügung. Seine konzepttypischen *Operationen* sind die Bildung von Listen aus Elementen des Typs T sowie der Zugriff respektive die Iteration über die Elemente der Liste. Vereinigungstypen (VT ::= (T_1 ∪ ⋯ ∪ T_n)) implementieren das Konzept heterogener Stukturen. Referenz-Typen (RT ::= ↑T) schliesslich implementieren das Konzept des Verweises. Ihre konzepttypische Operation ist die Materialisierung.

2.4 Punktmengen-Typen

Die bisher vorgestellten Konzepte entsprechen im Wesentlichen denjenigen, welche auch in vielen andern ähnlichen Systemen (z.B. [10]) vorhanden sind; Das hier vorgestellte Konzept der Punktmengen zur Modellierung von ausgedehnten Bereichen vermisst man hingegen. Wir nennen es `SPATIAL(T)` und charakterisieren damit einen ausgedehnten Bereich über dem Typ T. Man kann es sich somit als (potentiell unendliche) Menge von Objekten des Typs T vorstellen, welche zu einem neuen Objekt zusammengefasst werden. Instantiieren wir `SPATIAL` zum Beispiel über dem Typ (x: INT, y: INT), das heisst:

      `SPATIAL((x: INT, y: INT))`

so würden damit zweidimensionale Objekte wie Punkte, Linien und Flächen erfasst, wobei letztere zwei als unendliche Punktmengen zu verstehen sind. Der Name SPATIAL(T) deutet den primären Verwendungszweck im Bereich der raumbezogenen Informationssysteme an, das Konzept ist aber allgemeiner der generalisierte Konstruktor zur Modellierung von Nicht-Punkt-Daten wie temporale Daten, Zeitreihen, Frequenzspektren, Bilddaten und beliebig-dimensionale räumliche Daten. Diese Abstraktion ist ähnlich derjenigen in [11].

Die semantisch wichtigen Operationen über Punktmengen-Typen sind isempty, dem Test auf die leere Menge, interval, einer n-dimensionalen rechteckigen Approximation des Objektes, partition, welche diejenige Teilmenge des Objekts bestimmt, die ein bestimmtes Prädikat erfüllet, desweiteren compose, welche zwei Mengen vereinigt und schliesslich overlaps, welche entscheidet, ob die Schnittmenge der Elemente eines Objektes mit den Elementen eines n-dimensionalen Rechtecks leer ist. Zusätzlich existiert die Operation

```
mks : (lower:T, upper:T) -> SPATIAL(T),
```
welche eine einfache *konkrete* Punktmenge erzeugt.

Ein allgemeinerer zweidimensional räumlicher *abstrakter* Typ ist einer, welcher ähnlich ist zu einem Punktmengentyp über einem solchen Punkt:

```
Polygon ⤳ 'SPATIAL((x:FLOAT,y:FLOAT))'
```
Das heisst, ein extern definiertes Polygon wird (konzeptuell) als unendliche Punktmenge entlang seines Verlaufs betrachtet[1].

Viele Implementationen von räumlichen Objekten basieren auf geschachtelten Konstruktionen von Punkten und Listen. Es stellt sich die Frage, weshalb wir einen eigenen Typkonstruktor SPATIAL einführen, obwohl solche räumlichen Objekte genausogut mit Listen und Records modelliert werden könnten. Es geht uns *nicht* darum, eine neue *Repräsentation* für räumliche Typen einzuführen. Ziel unseres Modells ist, die Semantik der Typen dem Speichermanager bekanntzumanchen, ohne auf die Details der Speicherungsstruktur eingehen zu müssen. In dieser Beziehung unterscheiden sich räumliche Objekte grundlegend von verschachtelten Listen- und Recordstrukturen. Während sich bei letzteren die Operationen auf das Aufzählen und Anfragen individueller Komponenten der Struktur konzentrieren, sind Operationen über räumlichen Strukturen auf das Bilden respektive Vereinigen von Teilräumen angelegt. Dies sind denn auch genau die Operationen, welche von räumlichen Zugriffsstrukturen benötigt werden.

Wie andere Typen unterstützen Punktmengentypen Prädikat- und Projektionsanfragen. Prädikate sind dabei über die Mengenoperationen eines nicht-leeren Schnittes respektive der vollständigen Inklusion zwischen einem n-dimensionalen Anfragerechteck und einer Instanz des Punktmengentyps definiert. Projektion über Punktmengen bedeutet die Bildung der Schnittmenge der Punktmenge mit dem n-dimensionalen Projektionsrechteck. Um diese Anfragen zu beantworten werden die oben beschriebenen Operationen overlaps, interval und isempty verwendet.

---

[1] Die Implementation bleibt extern und ist sicher keine unendliche Punktmenge.

3   AOM Systemarchitektur

Nach Einführung der Grundlagen gehen wir im folgenden anhand eines Beispiels auf die Funktion des AOM als Bindeglied zwischen externen Objekten, internen Zugriffsstrukturen und dem Speichersubsystem ein. Eine Kollektion höhenlinien enthalte Objekte des Typs Höhenlinie:

```
form        ↝ 'SPATIAL((x:FLOAT,y:FLOAT))'
Höhenlinie → (e:INT,s:form)
```

Das heisst, eine Höhenlinie besteht aus ihrer Höhe (dargestellt als Wert des konkreten Typs INT) und ihrer abstrakten zweidimensionalen Form. Objekte dieser Art können zum Beispiel in einer Geodatenbank-Erweiterung Verwendung finden, welche auf dem CONCERT Speicherkernsystem aufsetzt. Der Entwickler einer solchen Erweiterung muss demzufolge die für den externen Typ form benötigten Operationen implementieren und dem AOM bekanntmachen.

In traditionellen Datenbanksystemen ist das Instantiieren von Zugriffsstrukturen relativ einfach: Ein Tupel besteht aus einer Menge von Attributen. Über einzelnen solchen Attributen oder Kombinationen davon können Indizes aufgebaut werden. In unserem Fall ist die Situation etwas komplizierter, einerseits wegen des zusätzlichen Konstruktors SPATIAL(T) und andererseits wegen der verschachtelten Typkonstruktion. Deshalb müssen wir exakter sein bei der Definition von Zugriffsstrukturen.

Allgemeine Zugriffsstrukturen erlauben nur ein Indizieren von Objekten mit bestimmten Eigenschaften. Ein B-Baum indiziert nur Objekte, über welchen eine Ordnung definiert ist, das Gridfile Objekte, die ähnlich dem Typ

```
'SPATIAL((dim1:FLOAT, ..., dimN:FLOAT))'
```

sind. Die konzepttypischen Operationen, welche dadurch dem AOM bekannt gemacht werden, sind exakt die Operationen, welche allgemeine Zugriffsstrukturen benötigen.

In den wenigsten Fällen entsprechen abstrakte Objekte genau den von den Zugriffsstrukturen verlangten Typen. Um dennoch Zugriffsstrukturen über solchen Kollektionen aufbauen zu können, benötigen wir sogenannte *Projektionsoperationen* vom Typen der Kollektion auf den durch die Zugriffsstruktur verlangten Typ. Wir schreiben T >> T' und bringen damit zum Ausdruck, dass eine (bedeutungstragende) Projektion von Objekten des Typs T nach Objekten des Typs T' existiert. Ein Beispiel einer solchen Projektion ist

```
Höhenlinie >> 'SPATIAL((dim1:FLOAT, dim2:FLOAT))'
```

womit jede Kollektion von Höhenlinien mittels einer zweidimensionalen Instanz eines Gridfiles indiziert werden kann.

Zwei Eigenschaften sind für Projektionen der Form T >> T' notwendig: Erstens muss es möglich sein, alle benötigten Operationen über dem Typ T' mittels den über dem Typen T definierten Operationen zu simulieren. Damit die Zugriffsstruktur nützlich ist, muss zweitens aus einer Anfrage über T eine korrespondierende Anfrage über T' generiert werden können. In [13] findet der an Details interessierte Leser eine umfassendere Darstellung.

Indem wir diese Regeln in das CONCERT Kernsystem einbauen und weil konkrete und abstrakte Objekttypen einheitlich behandelt werden, ist physisches Datenbankdesign und Anfragebearbeitung in unserem System einheitlich über abstrakte und konkrete Typen. Im Beispiel indizieren wir die Kollektion von Höhenlinien mittels eines zweidimensionalen Grid-Files. In gewissen Zusammenhängen, zum Beispiel beim Erstellen von Funkschattenkarten, wäre es allenfalls nützlicher, die Höhenlinien im dreidimensionalen Raum indizieren zu können. Das heisst, dass die Zugriffsstruktur den (abstrakten) räumlichen Anteil und die (konkrete) Höheninformation gemeinsam nutzen können muss. In unserm Fall kann das erreicht werden über die Projektion

```
Höhenlinie >> 'SPATIAL((dim1:FLOAT, dim2:FLOAT, dim3:FLOAT))',
```

indem die Komponenten e und s der Höhenlinie auf eine dreidimensionale Punktmenge projziert werden.

4 Zusammenfassung und Ausblick

In diesem Beitrag haben wir das abstrakte Objektmodell des CONCERT Speichermanagers vorgestellt, welcher allgemein bekannte und akzeptierte Konzepte der Speicherverwaltung zusammenbringt mit komplex strukturierten Objekten und extern definierten Typen. Während sich frühere Arbeiten über extern definierte Typen auf die Erweiterbarkeit der Benutzerschnittstelle konzentrierten, stellt unser Ansatz die Werkzeuge zur Verfügung, welche für eine gute Speicherverwaltung zwecks adäquatem physischem Design und einheitlicher Anfragebearbeitung nötig sind.

Unser Ansatz lässt sich wie folgt charakterisieren: Wie in vielen andern Speichersystemen enthält unser Ansatz ein allgemeingebräuchliches konkretes Speichermodell. Für den Fall, dass dieses fest eingebaute Modell ungeeignet ist, oder zur Einbringung von extern definierten Typen, lässt sich das Speichermodell um abstrakte Objekttypen erweitern, welche mit den gleichen Konzepten wie die eingebauten Typen behandelt werden.

Wir haben versucht, das Modell minimal zu halten. Es enthält lediglich die für das physische Design relevanten Komponenten. Wir sind der Meinung, dass es reichhaltig genug ist, Objekte aus unterschiedlichsten Anwendungsgebieten bezüglich ihres physischen Designs und bezüglich Anfragebearbeitung zu beschreiben. Ein interessantes Detail ist, dass unser Ansatz neben den bekannten Konzepten wie Listen und Records, welche auch in andern Ansätzen als Basiskonzepte eingeführt wurden, den Basistyp SPATIAL und damit das Konzept der Punktmenge als Basiskonzept eingeführt haben, da dieses sich nicht auf die andern im Modell vorhandenen Konzepte zurückführen lässt. Einige Aspekte der technischen Realisierung, so zum Beispiel die effiziente Verwaltung langer extern definierter Objekte, Heterogenität von Programm- und Maschinen-Umgebungen, Sicherheitsaspekte bei der Ausführung von fremdem Code, sind im Rahmen unserer Forschung ausführlich in [2, 16] behandelt worden und gelten auch für diesen Ansatz.

Danksagung: Wir möchten an dieser Stelle Prof. Hans-J. Schek, Gisbert Dröge, Andreas Wolf, Michael Rys und Helmut Kaufmann für ihre hilfreichen Kommentare und wertvollen Diskussionen herzlich danken.

Literatur

1. M. M. Astrahan et al. System R: Relational approach to database management. *ACM Transactions on Database Systems*, 1(2):97–137, June 1976.

2. S. Blott, H. Kaufmann, L. Relly, and H.-J. Schek. Buffering Long Externally-Defined Objects. In *Proceedings of the Sixth International Workshop on Persistent Object Systems (POS6)*, pages 40–53, Tarascon, France, September 1994.

3. T. Bode and A. B. Cremers. OMS - Ein erweiterbares Objectmanagementsystem. In R. Bayer, T. Härder, and P. Lockmann, editors, *Objectbanken für Experten*, Informatik Aktuell, pages 29–54. Springer-Verlag, 1992.

4. F. G. D. Committee. *Content Standards for Digital Geospatial Metadata*. U.S. Geological Survey, 590 National Center, Reston, Virginia 22092.

5. P. Dadam, K. Kuspert et al. A DBMS Prototype to Support Extended NF^2 Relations: An Integrated View on Flat Tables and Hierarchies. In *Procs. of the ACM SIGMOD Intl. Conf. on Management of Data*, pages 356–367, 1986.

6. G. Dröge, H.-J. Schek, and A. Wolf. Erweiterbarkeit in DASDBS. *Informatik Forschung und Entwicklung*, 5:162–176, 1990.

7. R. H. Güting. Gral: An Extensible Relational Database System for Geometric Applications. In *Proceedings of Fifteenth International Conference on Very-Large Database Systems*, pages 33–44, Amsterdam, Netherlands, 1989.

8. T. Härder, K. M. Wegner, B. Mitschang, and A. Sikeler. PRIMA – a DBMS Supporting Engineering Applications. In *Proceedings of Thirteenth International Conference on Very-Large Database Systems*, pages 433–442, Brighton, England, 1987.

9. A. Kemper, P. C. Lockmann, and M. Wallrath. An Object-Oriented Database System for Engineering Applications. In *Proceedings of the Annual ACM SIGMOD Conference*, pages 299–310, 1987.

10. K. Küspert, P. Dadam, and J. Günauer. Cooperative buffer management in the advanced information management prototype (AIM). In *Proceedings of the 13thInternational Conference on Very Large Databases*, pages 483–492, Brighton, 1987.

11. J. A. Orenstein and F. A. Manola. PROBE Spatial Data Modelling and Query Processing in an Image Database Application. *IEEE Transactions on Software Engineering*, 14(5):611–629, 1988.

12. B. Reinwald, S. Dessloch et al. Making Real Data Persistent: Initial Experiences with SMRC. In *Proceedings of the Sixth International Workshop on Persistent Object Systems (POS6)*, pages 194–208, Tarascon, France, Sept. 1994.

13. L. Relly and S. Blott. Ein Speichersystem für abstrakte Objekte. Technical Note (DBTN) 9, Database Research Group, ETH Zürich, Nov. 1994.

14. H.-J. Schek, H.-B. Paul, M. H. Scholl, and G. Weikum. The DASDBS Project: Objectives, Experiences, and Future Prospects. *IEEE Transactions on Knowledge and Data Engineering*, 2(1):25–43, March 1990.

15. H.-J. Schek and M. H. Scholl. The relational model with relation-valued attributes. *Information Systems*, 11(2):137–147, 1986.

16. H.-J. Schek and A. Wolf. From extensible databases to interoperability between multipel databases and GIS applications. In *Proceedings of the 3rd SSD*, Lecture Notes in Computer Science. Springer, June 1993.

17. M. Stonebraker, L. Rowe, and M. Hirohama. The implementation of POSTGRES. *IEEE Transactions on Knowledge and Data Engineering*, 2(1), Mar. 1990.

18. P. Wilms, P. Schwarz, H.-J. Schek, and L. Haas. Incorporating Data Types in an Extensible Database Architecture. In *Proceedings of the 3rd International Conference on Data and Knowledge Bases*, Jerusalem, June 1988.

Ein objektorientierter Ansatz
zur Restrukturierung
der betrieblichen Informationsverarbeitung

Günter Sauter[1], Joachim Thomas
Universität Kaiserslautern, FB Informatik
67653 Kaiserslautern
e-mail: thomas@informatik.uni-kl.de

Überblick

In vielen Unternehmen wird der aktuelle Datenbestand durch heterogene Datenbank- und Anwendungssysteme verwaltet. Die Restrukturierung der betrieblichen Informationsverarbeitung ist ein Weg, um dieses Altlastenproblem zu bewältigen. Im vorliegenden Aufsatz werden die Ergebnisse eines Projekts dargestellt, das ein Unternehmen der Versicherungsbranche (R+V-Versicherung[2]) in Zusammenarbeit mit der AG Datenverwaltungssysteme der Universität Kaiserslautern durchführte. Im Rahmen des Projekts wurde ein repräsentativer Ausschnitt der Informationsverarbeitung der R+V-Versicherung mit Methoden der objektorientierten Analyse strukturiert und mit Hilfe des Wissensbankverwaltungssystems KRISYS beispielhaft modelliert. Abschluß des Projekts war die Validierung der Ergebnisse hinsichtlich ihrer Adäquatheit für die Erfordernisse des Versicherungsunternehmens und für die konzeptionellen Umsetzung mittels kommerziell verfügbarer DBMS.

Stichworte: Altlastenproblem, Objektorientierte Analyse und Design, Reverse Engineering.

1. Einleitung

Die Restrukturierung der betrieblichen Informationsverarbeitung ist eine Aufgabe, die für viele Unternehmen immer mehr an Bedeutung gewinnt. Da der Einsatz von EDV noch bis vor wenigen Jahren mit sehr hohen Kosten verbunden war, gab es in den wenigsten Unternehmen ein umfassendes Konzept zur computergestützten Datenhaltung. Stattdessen wurden für ausgewählte Bereiche Einzelsysteme angeschafft. Der daraus resultierende hohe Grad an Heterogenität in der Datenverwaltung wurde zudem oft durch die Entwicklung der Unternehmen selbst (Expansion, Fusion mit anderen Firmen) bedingt.

Unmittelbare Konsequenz dieser Heterogenität sind hohe Betriebskosten. Sie entstehen zum einen aus der Notwendigkeit, unterschiedliche Systeme getrennt voneinander bedienen und warten zu müssen, zum anderen durch die im allgemeinen nicht zu vermeidende Redundanz der Daten, die zu höherem Speicherplatz- und Verwaltungsaufwand führt. Eine weitere Auswirkung, die unter Umständen weit größere finanzielle Einbußen verursacht, ist die Inflexibilität einer Ansammlung heterogener Anwendungssysteme. Systemübergreifende Zugriffe auf Daten sind im allgemeinen unmöglich, wodurch betriebliche Aufgaben erschwert bzw. verhindert werden. Durch die zunehmende Verfügbarkeit leistungsfähiger und kostengünstiger EDV-Lösungen verstärkt sich der Druck auf die Unternehmen, dieses *Altlastenproblem (legacy problem)* [BS93, EKPR92] zu bewältigen.

1.1 Alternative Ansätze zur Restrukturierung

Ein Ausweg aus dieser Situation ist die Restrukturierung der betrieblichen Informationsverarbeitung. Dabei lassen sich prinzipiell zwei Ansätze unterscheiden. Der idealtypische Weg ist die vollständige Neuentwicklung von Anwendungssystemen auf Basis eines unternehmensweiten Daten- und Funktionsmodells. Diese Lösung ist jedoch in den wenigsten Fällen praktikabel, zum einen, weil der finanzielle Aufwand sehr hoch ist (Reorganisation des gesamten Datenbestandes, Sperren des gesamten Datenbestandes während der Migrationsphase[3]), zum anderen, weil die zur Realisierung notwendigen person-

---

1. Daimler-Benz AG, Forschungszentrum Ulm, Produktionsinformatik (F3P), Postfach 2360, 89013 Ulm, e-mail: guenter.sauter@dbag.ulm.DaimlerBenz.COM
2. R+V Allgemeine Versicherung, Taunusstr. 1, 65193 Wiesbaden.
3. Komplexe Abbildungen zwischen den Schemata von Alt- und Neusystemen, ein hoher Grad an Redundanz, viele unterschiedliche Altsysteme, etc. führen zu einer unerwünscht langen Migrationsphase.

ellen Kapazitäten nicht ohne weiteres von den laufend anfallenden EDV-Aufgaben entbunden werden können [EKPR92].

Der alternative Weg zur Restrukturierung der betrieblichen Informationsverarbeitung besteht in der Integration von neuen und alten Systemen, wobei die bestehende Umgebung genutzt wird, um eine schrittweise und für den Benutzer transparente Migration von Anwendungs- und Datenverwaltungssystemen zu erreichen [RS94]. Diese Vorgehensweise wird durch *Föderierte Datenbanksysteme* [SL90] unterstützt. Kennzeichen dieses Architekturansatzes sind die gemeinsame Verwaltung möglicherweise heterogener Datenbanksysteme, die Autonomie integrierter lokaler (oder Alt-) Systeme und die Verteilung von Daten über mehrere Datenbanken der Föderation hinweg.

Ganz gleich, ob die Restrukturierung der betrieblichen Informationsverarbeitung durch Integration von Altsystemen oder durch Neuentwicklung erreicht werden soll, beiden Ansätzen muß ein *einheitliches Daten- und Funktionsmodell* zugrunde liegen, was aus der Analyse der unternehmensweiten Informationsstrukturen und Informationsflüsse gewonnen werden kann. Dieser Vorgang wird oft als *Reverse Engineering* bezeichnet [CC90].

1.2 Die Informationsverarbeitung der R+V-Versicherung

Anlaß zu diesem Projekt war die EG-weite Liberalisierung des Versicherungsmarkts zum 01.07.1994, die es Versicherungsunternehmen erlaubt, ihre Produkte innerhalb der gesamten EG zu vertreiben. Diese geänderten Rahmenbedingungen führen zu einer beträchtlichen Diversifikation der am Markt angebotenen Versicherungsprodukte. Dies betrifft einerseits standardisierte, einfache Produkte, andererseits werden Produkte benötigt, die individuell auf die Bedürfnisse einzelner Kunden abstimmbar sein müssen. Zusätzlich besteht die Notwendigkeit, auf eine geänderte Nachfrage schnell und kostengünstig reagieren zu können. Geeignete Anwendungssysteme müssen ein hohes Maß an Flexibilität aufweisen, um auf Änderungen des betrieblichen Regelwerks (z.B. die einer Versicherung zugrundeliegenden Tarife oder die von ihr abgedeckten Ereignisse) schnell und unkompliziert reagieren zu können. Diesen Ansprüchen werden die bestehenden Anwendungssysteme der R+V-Versicherung nicht mehr gerecht. Im Rahmen des Projekts sollte daher untersucht werden, inwieweit neuartige Datenmodelle und Modellierungstechniken zur Lösung der Anforderungen beitragen können.

Die Untersuchungen wurden für einen zentralen Bereich der Informationsverarbeitung der R+V-Versicherung, das Teilmodell *Produkt*, durchgeführt [R+V92]. Dieses Teilmodell wurde mit Methoden der objektorientierten Analyse (OOA) strukturiert. Die auf diese Weise ermittelten Informationsstrukturen und -flüsse wurden mit Hilfe von KRISYS [Ma91, DLMT93], einem an der Universität Kaiserslautern entwickelten Wissensbankverwaltungssystem (WBVS), beispielhaft modelliert. Die Vielfältigkeit des von KRISYS angebotenen Wissensmodells erlaubte dabei die direkte Umsetzung der in der OOA gewonnenen Eigenschaften des Teilmodells *Produkt*. Da KRISYS als prototypisches System nicht für den kommerziellen Einsatz konzipiert wurde, kann diese Implementierung nur als ein erster Schritt in Richtung objektorientiertes Design (s. Abschnitt 2.2) angesehen werden. So wurde, ergänzend zur Modellierung mit KRISYS, untersucht, inwieweit das aus der OOA gewonnene Daten- und Funktionsmodell auf ein kommerzielles (objektorientiertes) DBMS abgebildet werden kann.

1.3 Inhaltsübersicht

In Abschnitt 2 werden die grundlegenden Konzepte der objektorientierten Analyse und des objektorientierten Designs nach Coad/Yourdon vorgestellt. Anschließend wird in Abschnitt 3 die Realisierung des objektorientierten Entwurfs mit KRISYS diskutiert. Der Aufsatz schließt mit einer zusammenfassenden Bewertung der Ergebnisse des Projekts (Abschnitt 4).

2. Objektorientierte Analyse und Design nach Coad/Yourdon

Im Gegensatz zu klassischen strukturierten Analyse- und Entwurfsmethoden, die auf herkömmliche Programmiersprachen abgestimmt sind, bauen objektorientierte Verfahren auf der objektorientierten Programmierung auf [FK92]. Zentrale Bestandteile des Objektmodells sind [Bo94]:

- die *Abstraktion*, um die wesentlichen Eigenschaften eines Objekts zu erfassen und es klar von anderen Objekten zu unterscheiden,
- die *Kapselung*, um Details eines Objekts vor der Außenwelt zu verbergen, weil sie außerhalb des Objekts nicht relevant sind oder geheimgehalten werden sollen,
- die *Modularität*, die die Zerlegbarkeit eines Problemfelds in zusammenhängende aber dennoch klar abgegrenzte Teilbereiche beschreibt, sowie
- die *Bildung von Hierarchien* mit Hilfe von Generalisierung und Aggregation.

2.1 Objektorientierte Analyse

Es gibt eine Reihe von Verfahren zur objektorientierten Analyse [St93]. Im folgenden stellen wir den von Coad/Yourdon vorgeschlagene Ansatz vor [CY91a]. Die Autoren haben die Analyse in fünf Schritte unterteilt, welche allerdings mehr als Anhaltspunkte bei der Durchführung denn als feste Reihenfolge zu verstehen sind.

Finden von Klassen und Objekten

Ein Objekt im Sinne der Modellwelt ist eine Abstraktion eines Objektes der Problemumgebung, die es erlaubt, alle für das System relevanten Informationen zu halten und auf diese zuzugreifen. Eigenschaften und Verhalten des Objektes werden gekapselt. Eine Klasse ist definiert als die Beschreibung eines oder mehrerer Objekte mit gleichen Attributen und Methoden, wozu auch eine Beschreibung zur Generierung weiterer zur Klasse konformer Objekte gehören muß.

Strukturierung

Im zweiten Schritt werden die Klassen und Objekte zusammengefaßt, wobei die Abstraktionskonzepte Generalisierung/Spezialisierung und Aggregation verwendet werden können.

Modularisierung

Ein Modul ist ein (möglichst abgeschlossener) Teilbereich eines größeren Problemfelds, der unabhängig betrachtet und modelliert werden kann. Es gibt zwei Möglichkeiten nach Modulen einzuteilen: top-down und bottom-up. In großen Projekten wird man top-down vorgehen, d.h., man wird sich zunächst einen groben Überblick über die Problemumgebung verschaffen und sie dann in diverse Module einteilen. Diese werden dann an verschiedene Teams vergeben, die im Laufe der weiteren Analyse ggf. Teilmodule definieren. Im Gegensatz dazu steht die Bottom-Up-Methode: Sie sieht vor, zunächst einzelne Teilbereiche zu modellieren und diese dann zu größeren Modulen zusammenzufassen. Dabei wird gezielt nach semantisch zusammenhängenden Einheiten wie Generalisierungshierarchien oder Aggregationen gesucht. Je nach Bedarf ist es möglich, die beiden Vorgehensweisen zu kombinieren.[4]

Definition von Attributen

Ein Attribut ist eine Eigenschaft, die jedes Objekt einer Klasse besitzt. Die von Coad/Yourdon vorge-schlagene OOA sieht für Klassen keine Attribute vor. Klassen besitzen keine Eigenschaften, sondern reichen nur dort definierte Attribute an Subklassen weiter.

Die Auswahl der Attribute richtet sich nach deren Relevanz für die Problemumgebung. Prinzipiell sollte jedes Attribut so weit oben in der Generalisierungshierarchie stehen wie möglich, um die Vorteile der Vererbung weitestgehend ausnutzen zu können.

Definition von Methoden

Die Dynamik des Systems wird durch Methoden ausgedrückt. Mit Hilfe von Statusdiagrammen wird der Lebenszyklus jedes Objektes einer Klasse definiert. Die Detailliertheit des Statusdiagramms leitet sich

---

4. Wie wir später schildern werden, haben wir diesen Schritt an den Anfang der Analyse des Teilmodells Produkt gestellt, d.h., wir haben zunächst einen top-down-Entwurf verfolgt, sind aber im Verlauf des weiteren Entwurfs bottom-up vorgegangen.

aus Problemumgebung und dem zu modellierenden Zielsystem ab. Alle Attribute, die das Verhalten des Objektes beeinflussen, müssen darin aufgenommen werden. Im Anschluß daran werden die benötigten Methoden festgelegt. Danach wird sukzessive für jede Klasse, für die Methoden vorgesehen sind, geprüft, mit welchen anderen Objekten deren Objekte kommunizieren, d.h., Nachrichten versenden. Diese Kommunikationswege werden als Message-Connections bezeichnet. Im letzten Schritt werden die Methoden nun genauer spezifiziert mit Ein- und Ausgaben, sowie einem groben Flußdiagramm.

2.2 Objektorientiertes Design

Mit der Durchführung der OOA wurden alle relevanten Aspekte des zu modellierenden Ausschnitts der realen Welt in eine objektorientierte Darstellung übertragen. Das objektorientierte Design (OOD) [CY91b] füllt die Lücke zwischen OOA und einer konkreten Implementierung. Terminologie und Notation des OOD sind identisch mit der der OOA, wodurch der von klassischen Entwurfsmethoden bekannte Bruch zwischen Analyse und Design [FK92] vermieden wird.

Coad/Yourdon unterteilen das objektorientierte Design in vier Komponenten:

- Problemumgebungskomponente (*Problem-Domain-Component*):
  In dieser Komponente wird das Ergebnis der OOA nach Gesichtspunkten der Implementierbarkeit (im gewählten Zielsystem) untersucht und nach Kriterien wie Speicherplatzbedarf optimiert.

- Mensch-Maschine-Schnittstelle (*Human-Interaction-Component*):
  Hier werden Fenster, Eingabemasken und Ausgaben für die verschiedenen Benutzer des Systems spezifiziert.

- Datenverwaltungskomponente (*Data-Management-Component*):
  Diese Komponente ist für das Speichern/Laden von Objekten zuständig. Wie diese Komponente im einzelnen aussieht, hängt entscheidend von der Implementierungsumgebung ab (z.B. objektorientierte Programmiersprache oder objektorientiertes DBMS).

- Task-Manager (*Task-Management-Component*):
  Tasks sind Prozesse, auf die Methoden abgebildet werden. In einem großen System laufen in der Regel Tasks parallel ab (Multitasking), was durch den Task-Manager gesteuert wird.

Diese Komponenten werden als zusätzliche Problemfelder betrachtet, die, genau wie die Problemumgebung selbst, analysiert und modelliert werden müssen. Wie detailliert dies geschehen kann, ist allerdings sehr stark von der gewählten Implementierungsumgebung abhängig. Für das in diesem Aufsatz beschriebene Projekt handelt es sich dabei um das WBVS KRISYS.

3. Objektorientierte Repräsentation des Teilmodells Produkt

In diesem Kapitel stellen wir die Ergebnisse der objektorientierten Analyse des Teilmodells *Produkt* vor und skizzieren - aus Platzgründen gleichzeitig - deren Umsetzung mit Hilfe von KRISYS. Daher werden Objekte in einer Notation präsentiert, die inhaltlich der von Coad/Yourdon vorgeschlagenen Darstellung entspricht, allerdings bereits die spätere Umsetzung in KRISYS andeutet.

Wie schon in Abschnitt 2 bemerkt, haben wir, anders als im Ansatz von Coad/Yourdon, die Modularisierung an den Anfang der Analyse gestellt. Diese Vorgehensweise wird ebenfalls bei den STEP-Normierungsbemühungen verfolgt [ISO94]. Auch dort unterteilt man die reale Welt in einzelne Problemfelder, modelliert darin zunächst grundlegende anwendungsunabhängige Konzepte (*Integrated Resources*), bevor man eine detailliertere und anwendungsspezifische Aufschlüsselung der Problemfelder angeht (*Application Protocols*). Nach unseren Erfahrungen hat sich gezeigt, daß die nach der top-down-Untergliederung entstandenen Problemfelder nicht unabhängig voneinander modelliert werden können, sondern daß die bereits abgebildeten Teilausschnitte bei der weiteren Modellierung zu berücksichtigen sind (siehe z.B. Abschnitt 3.1.2). Dabei ist es sinnvoll, zunächst die Abhängigkeiten der Problemfelder untereinander festzustellen. Anschließend wird man zuerst das Problemfeld modellieren, von dem die meisten anderen Problemfelder abhängig sind

3.1 Modellierung der statischen Aspekte des Teilmodells Produkt

Für die gefundenen Problemfelder werden gemäß Coad/Yourdon zunächst Klassen und Objekte definiert, diese strukturiert und durch Attribute genauer spezifiziert. Es wird im folgenden deutlich, daß bereits definierte Objekte in diesen Prozeß mit einzubeziehen sind.

3.1.1 Produktkomponenten

Ein Produkt wird über eine baumartige Komponentenstruktur definiert. Produktkomponenten stellen dabei die einzelnen Bausteine dieser Struktur dar. Produktkomponenten erben ihre Attribute von der Klasse 'Prodkomp-Klasse', in der die Struktur aller Produktkomponenten zentral verwaltet wird und folglich auf einfache Weise für alle Objekte geändert werden kann.

Bei der Vollkaskoversicherung gibt es beispielsweise die beiden Produktkomponenten 'Vollkasko' und 'Teilkasko', die beide Instanzen von 'Produktkomp-Klasse' sind und über die Aggregationsbeziehungen 'hat-Prod-Komponente' bzw. 'Prod-Komponente-von' miteinander verbunden sind. Die Mehrfachverwendung von Produktkomponenten kann durch diese Art der Modellierung unterstützt werden.

3.1.2 Produkte

Unter einem Produkt wird ein Verkaufsobjekt im herkömmlichen Sinn verstanden. Eine Trennung von produkt- und produktkomponentenspezifischer Information ist wünschenswert. Es gibt für alle Produktkomponenten, die gleichzeitig Produkte sein können, eigene Objekte, die Instanzen von 'Produkt-Klasse' sind. Beispielsweise existiert für die Produktkomponente 'Teilkasko' das Objekt 'Teilkasko-Produkt'. Das jeweilige Produktobjekt ist über eine Aggregationsbeziehung mit den entsprechenden Produktkomponenten verbunden. Eine Alternative wäre die direkte Spezialisierungsbeziehung zwischen der 'Produkt-Klasse' und Produktkomponenten. Dies hätte allerdings zur Folge, daß untergeordnete Produktkomponenten (z.B. die Komponente Teilkasko bei der Vollkaskoversicherung) Produktinformationen beinhalten (durch die Vererbung), die bei der Betrachtung des übergeordneten Produkts (in dem obigen Beispiel die Vollkaskoversicherung) verborgen bleiben sollen.

3.1.3 Produktvereinbarung und Bestimmungsfaktoren

Die Produktvereinbarung dient zur Erfassung aller Daten, die bei einem Vertragsabschluß anfallen. Da ein Vertragsabschluß sich immer auf ein bestimmtes existierendes Produkt bezieht, ist die baumartige Produktomponentenstruktur zusammen mit dem Produkt-Objekt, im folgenden als Produktdefinitionsstruktur bezeichnet, Grundlage für die Produktvereinbarung. Die meisten Informationen, die bei einem Vertragsabschluß zu erfassen sind, können sogenannten Bestimmungsfaktoren zugeordnet werden. Andere Angaben sollen im folgenden außer Betracht gelassen werden.

Bestimmungsfaktoren

Die Komponenten (sowohl Produkt-, wie auch Vereinbarungs- oder Nutzungskomponenten, vgl. nachfolgende Abschnitte) unterscheiden sich jeweils voneinander durch den Versicherungsumfang, für den sie bestimmt sind. So deckt die Vollkaskoversicherung auch den selbstverschuldeten Schaden ab, der bei der Teilkaskoversicherung nicht inbegriffen ist. Demnach muß es möglich sein, für jede Komponente deren entsprechenden Versicherungsumfang zu repräsentieren. Dieser Umfang wird durch die drei sogenannten *Bestimmungsfaktoren* 'Ereignis', 'Schaden' und 'Leistung' festgelegt. Neben diesen Bestimmungsfaktoren, die gruppiert den Leistungsumfang definieren, gibt es auch solche, die jeweils einzeln Vereinbarungskomponenten zugeordnet werden können. So ist bei einem Vertragsabschluß beispielsweise ein 'Sachbearbeiter', der 'Versicherungsnehmer', etc. zu nennen. Um die Bestimmungsfaktoren voneinander unterscheiden zu können, werden sie durch eigene Klassen repräsentiert. Konkrete Bestimmungsfaktoren, die sogenannten *Bestimmungsfaktor-Objekte*, sind Instanzen dieser Klassen.

Bestimmungsfaktoren haben also zwei Aufgaben zu erfüllen, zum einen die detaillierte Beschreibung einer Produkt- und Vereinbarungskomponente, zum anderen die Festlegung des Leistungsumfangs für eine Produktkomponente. Nachfolgend wird die Modellierung von Bestimmungsfaktoren anhand dieser beiden Aufgaben besprochen.

Zur detaillierten Beschreibung einer Vereinbarungskomponente gehören u.a. der Name des Sachbearbeiters oder der Geltungsbereich der Vereinbarung. Entsprechend existieren die Bestimmungsfaktor-

Klassen 'Sachbearbeiter' und 'Geltungsbereich', sowie zum Beispiel das Bestimmungsfaktor-Objekt 'Sachbearbeiter_Hr_Maier'.

Die Bestimmungsfaktor-Objekte, die bei einem Vertragsabschluß für ein bestimmtes Produkt zu verwalten sind, werden durch Aggregationsbeziehungen mit den entsprechenden Vereinbarungskomponenten verbunden. Dabei gibt es für verschiedene Bestimmungsfaktoren-Arten auch unterschiedliche Aggregationsattribute.

Beispiel: Bei einer Teilkaskoversicherung sollen u.a. der Sachbearbeiter und der Geltungsbereich aufgeführt werden. Folglich bestehen jeweils zwischen Bestimmungsfaktor-Objekten der Klassen 'Sachbearbeiter' und 'Geltungsbereich' sowie der Vereinbarungskomponente 'Teilkasko-Vereinbarung' Aggregationsbeziehungen (dargestellt durch die Attribute 'Sachbearbeiter' bzw. 'Geltungsbereich').

Die Aggregationsattribute werden in sogenannten *Beziehungsobjekten* definiert und durch Instanziierung an die entsprechenden Vereinbarungs-Komponenten vererbt. Die Beziehungsobjekte haben den ausschließlichen Sinn, die Aggregationsattribute, welche Bestimmungsfaktor-Objekte mit Komponenten verbinden, zu definieren.

Beispiel: Bei einer Teilkasko-Vereinbarung ist als Bestimmungsfaktor das versicherte Objekt anzugeben. Also muß die Teilkasko-Vereinbarung Instanz des Beziehungsobjektes sein, in dem das Aggregationsattribut 'versichertes-Objekt' definiert ist. Dieses Attribut wird durch Instanziierung an 'Teilkasko-Vereinb' vererbt, so daß eine Beziehung zwischen 'Teilkasko-Vereinb' und dem entsprechenden Bestimmungsfaktor hergestellt werden kann.

Durch die Beziehungsobjekte wird eine zentrale Verwaltung der Aggregationsattribute und der für sie geltenden Integritätsbedingungen möglich.

Der Leistungsumfang für ein Produkt muß bei der Versicherungsvereinbarung vorgenommen werden. Er legt die Versicherungsleistungen fest, die für einen bestimmten Schaden, der wiederum durch ein gewisses Ereignis eingetreten ist, erbracht werden. Die Bestimmungsfaktoren 'Schaden', 'Ereignis' und 'Leistung' sind also, wie zu Beginn des Abschnitts erwähnt, zu einer Gruppe zusammenzufassen. Folglich werden die entsprechenden Bestimmungsfaktoren jeweils in einem *Paket* gruppiert, das als eigenständiges Objekt repräsentiert ist. Ein Paket und dessen zugehörige Bestimmungsfaktoren werden über Aggregationsbeziehungen verbunden. Ein Paket muß folglich Instanz der entsprechenden Beziehungsobjekte sein, um die jeweiligen Aggregationsattribute zu den entsprechenden Bestimmungsfaktoren zu erben.

Beispiel: Für eine Teilkaskoversicherung soll der Schaden "Verlust" durch das Ereignis "Diebstahl" versichert werden können, wobei als Leistungen "Anwalt-", "Mietwagen-" und "Wiederbeschaffungskosten" abgedeckt sind. Das Paket zu diesem Beispiel ist in Bild 1 gezeigt ('Auto-Diebstahl', 'Auto-Verlust', 'Anwalt-Leistung', 'Mietwagen-Leistung' und 'Wiederbeschaffungs-Leistung' sind die entsprechenden Bestimmungsfaktor-Objekte)[5]:

```
Verlust-durch-Diebstahl-Paket

INSTANCE-OF          (Ereignis-Bez-Objekt Schaden-Bez-Objekt Leistung-Bez-Objekt)

Ereignis             (Auto-Diebstahl)
    possible-values  (AND  (INSTANCE-OF Ereignis-Klasse)
                           (INSTANCE-OF Diebstähle))
    cardinality      [1 1]
Schaden              (Auto-Verlust)
    possible-values  (AND  (INSTANCE-OF Schaden-Klasse)
                           (INSTANCE-OF Verlust-Schäden))
    cardinality      [1 1]
Leistung             (Anwalt-Leistung Mietwagen-Leistung Wiederbeschaffungs-Leistung)
    possible-values  (AND  (INSTANCE-OF Leistung-Klasse)
                           (OR  (INSTANCE-OF Anwalt-Leistungen)
                                (INSTANCE-OF Mietwagen-Leistungen)
                                (INSTANCE-OF Wiederbeschaffungs-Leistungen)))
    cardinality      [1 3]
```

Bild 1:   Objektstruktur eines Paketes

Produktvereinbarung

Eine Produktvereinbarung entsteht durch Instanziierung einer Produktdefinitionsstruktur. Dadurch werden alle notwendigen Attribute automatisch in die Produktvereinbarung übernommen. Wie bereits erwähnt, werden Bestimmungsfaktoren durch Aggregationsattribute, die in Beziehungsobjekten definiert sind, mit Vereinbarungskomponenten verbunden. Da bereits bei der Produktdefinition festgelegt werden soll, welche Bestimmungsfaktoren von einer Vereinbarungskomponente aus referenziert werden dürfen, ist die entsprechende Produktkomponente Subklasse des Beziehungsobjektes (vgl. Bild 2).

Beispiel: *Bei der Definition des Produkts 'Teilkasko' wird festgelegt, daß bei einem später abzuschließenden Vertrag ein Sachbearbeiter, ein Geltungsbereich, etc. aufzunehmen ist. Dadurch, daß die Teilkasko-Produktkomponente (in Bild 2 'Teilkasko') Subklasse des Beziehungsobjektes ist ('Geltungsbereich-Bez-Objekt') erbt sie das Aggregationsattribut 'Geltungsbereich'. Dieses wird bei der Instanziierung der Produktkomponenten (während eines Vertragsabschlusses) an die entsprechende Vereinbarungskomponente weitervererbt. Somit kann bei einem Vertrag ('Teilkasko-Vereinb') der Geltungsbereich über das geerbte Aggregationsattribut 'Geltungsbereich' aufgeführt werden.*

Eine Produktaktion ist dafür verantwortlich, daß die Produktstruktur korrekt auf die Vereinbarungsstruktur übertragen wird, was allein durch die Instanziierung von Produktkomponenten nicht möglich ist. Auf Produktaktionen wird in Abschnitt 3.2 eingegangen.

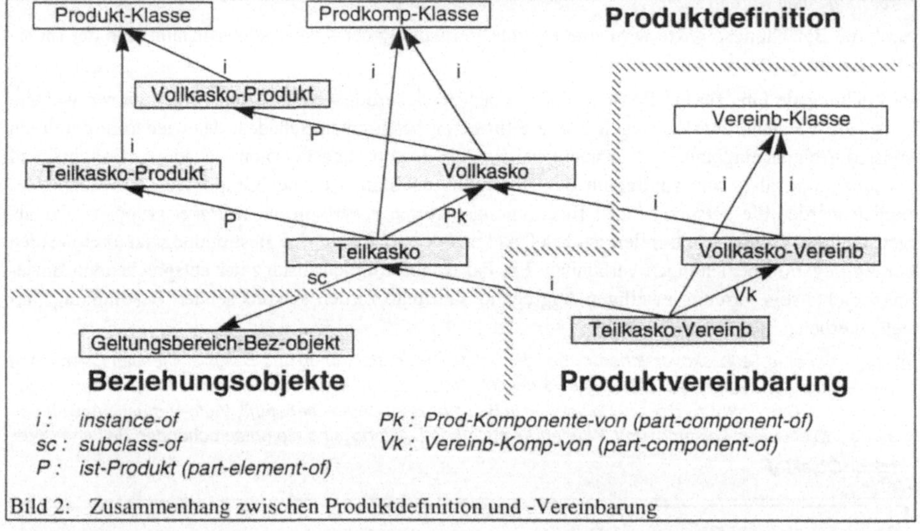

Bild 2: Zusammenhang zwischen Produktdefinition und -Vereinbarung

3.1.4 Produktnutzung

Im Rahmen der Produktnutzung werden Daten erfaßt, die bei einem bestimmten Vorfall aufgetreten sind. Sie betreffen die Bestimmungsfaktor-Pakete: welches Ereignis ist eingetreten (z.B. ein Diebstahl), zu welchem Schaden (z.B. dem Verlust) hat es geführt, usw. Anhand der Pakete, die in dem Vereinbarungsbaum aufgeführt sind, ist das Paket auszuwählen, das zu dem Vorfall "paßt", d.h., zur Aufnahme der Daten verwendet werden kann.

Im Gegensatz zur Vereinbarung muß bei der Nutzung nicht mehr der vollständige Produktbaum übertragen werden, denn in den meisten Fällen wird, wie beispielsweise bei einer Teilkaskoversicherung, nicht der volle Umfang des Produkts in Anspruch genommen. Daher wäre es ungünstig, bei der Produktnutzung den vollständigen Produktbaum verwalten zu müssen. Ebenso wie bei Produkt- und Vereinbarungskomponenten wird auch die Struktur von Nutzungskomponenten in einem Objekt

---

5. Dieses Bild zeigt schematisch die Instanziierung eines Beziehungsobjektes. In Bild 2 ist die korrekte Beziehung zwischen Vereinbarungskomponenten und Beziehungsobjekten dargestellt.

('Nutzung-Klasse') definiert. Als Modellierungskonstrukt für den Nutzungsbaukasten wird, wie bisher auch, die Aggregation verwendet (vgl. Bild 3).

Beispiel: *Im Rahmen einer Teilkaskoversicherung sei ein Verlust durch Diebstahl abzuwickeln. Hierzu wird das 'Verlust-Diebstahl-Vereinb-Paket' als Vorlage ausgewählt, da es sich zur Aufnahme der Daten am besten eignet. Indem eine Instanz des relevanten Bestimmungsfaktor-Pakets der Vereinbarung (also von 'Verlust-Diebstahl-Vereinb-Paket') erzeugt wird, kann zwischen dem generierten Nutzungspaket ('Teilkasko-Nutzung-01-01-94') und den Bestimmungsfaktoren, die den Vorfall betreffen ('Auto-Diebstahl', 'Auto-Verlust' und 'Anwalt-Leistung'), über das Nutzungspaket ('Verlust-durch-Diebstahl-Paket') eine Beziehung erzeugt werden.*

Bisher kann auf alle Nutzungskomponenten über das Objekt 'Nutzung-Klasse' zugegriffen werden. Es ist jedoch erwünscht, alle Nutzungen mit der Vereinbarung und dem Produkt zusammenzufassen. Dies wird durch den Produktnachweis ermöglicht.

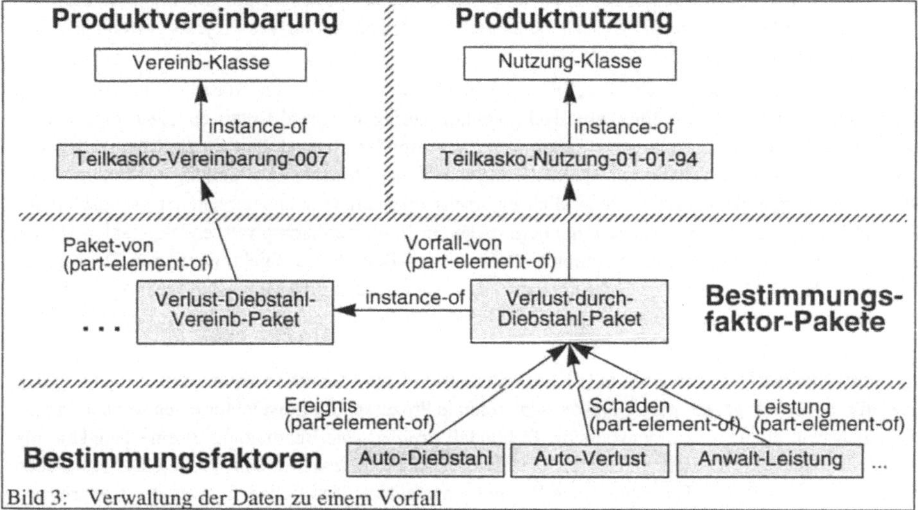

Bild 3: Verwaltung der Daten zu einem Vorfall

3.2 Modellierung der Dynamik

Dynamische Aspekte des Teilmodells *Produkt* sind der Aufbau der Produkt-, Vereinbarungs- und Nutzungsstrukturen. Da hierbei oft objektübergreifende Zugriffe durchzuführen waren, konnten die Methoden nicht immer einzelnen Objekten zugeordnet werden. Aus diesen Gründen modellierten wir die anwendungsspezifischen Methoden in eigenen Objekten, je eines für Produktgestaltung, Vertragsabschluß und Produktnutzung. Als Konsequenz daraus ergab sich eine zentrale Verwaltung aller Anwendungsprogramme mit einer dadurch verbundenen leichteren Wartbarkeit.

Die anwendungsspezifischen Methoden durchwandern rekursiv die zu bearbeitenden Baukästen (Produktkomponenten, Vereinbarungskomponenten, Nutzungskomponenten). Durch eine ständig aktualisierte grafische Repräsentation des gerade zu bearbeitenden Ausschnitts der Daten wird der Benutzer bei der Erzeugung komplexer Strukturen unterstützt.

Im Gegensatz zu allen anderen Produktaktionen ist die (versuchte) Inanspruchnahme durch Regeln realisiert. Der Hauptgrund hierfür ist die allgemeine Form der Inanspruchnahme, die aus einem Bedingungsteil (z.B. "Vertrag noch nicht gekündigt") und der Zahlungsanweisung besteht. Weil die Regeln zwischen verschiedenen Produkten stark variieren können, werden sie in produktbezogenen Regelmengen zusammengefaßt. Da Regeln in mehreren Regelmengen vorhanden sein können, wird die Mehrfachverwendung der gleichen Bedingung in mehreren Produkten unterstützt.

4. Zusammenfassende Bewertung

In den vorangehenden Abschnitten wurde die objektorientierte Analyse der Informationsverarbeitung der R+V-Versicherung am Beispiel des Teilmodells *Produkt* diskutiert und deren beispielhafte Implementierung mit Hilfe des WBVS KRISYS beschrieben. Abschluß und wesentlicher Bestandteil des Projekts war die Validierung der so erzielten Ergebnisse hinsichtlich ihrer Adäquatheit für die Erfordernisse der R+V-Versicherung und deren konzeptionelle Umsetzbarkeit mittels eines am Markt verfügbaren DBMS, da - wie schon in der Einleitung erwähnt - KRISYS als prototypisches System nicht den Leistungsanforderungen großer kommerzieller Anwendungen gewachsen ist. Im folgenden fassen wir die Ergebnisse dieser Bewertung zusammen.

Die objektorientierte Analyse erlaubte eine exakte und natürliche Beschreibung sowohl der statischen Aspekte als auch der dynamischen Aspekte der zu modellierenden realen Welt. Viele Details des Teilmodells *Produkt* konnten auf diese Weise berücksichtigt werden.

Das Ergebnis der objektorientierten Analyse spiegelte dementsprechend gut die Eigenschaften des Teilmodells *Produkt* wider und entsprach damit auch voll den zu Anfang des Projekts gestellten Anforderungen der R+V-Versicherung [R+V92].

Die aus der OOA resultierende Modellierung enthält eine Vielzahl von Klassen (für das gesamte Teilmodell 257 Klassen) mit einer zum Teil potentiell geringen Anzahl Instanzen. Zwar erfüllt diese Darstellung die an sie gestellten Anforderungen, insbesondere hinsichtlich Flexibilität, es ist aber fraglich, ob eine solch diversifizierte Modellierung sich in ein effizientes Anwendungssystem umsetzen läßt. Dieser Gegensatz zwischen Flexibilität einerseits und Effizienz andererseits ist grundsätzlicher Natur und hängt zunächst einmal nicht mit dem später zur Implementierung verwendeten realen System zusammen. Es erscheint uns daher durchaus sinnvoll, zu Beginn des objektorientierten Designs die Ergebnisse der OOA dahingehend zu untersuchen, wieviel Flexibilität zugunsten einer kompakteren Darstellung aufgegeben werden kann bzw. soll. Dieser Aspekt wird jedoch in vielen Ansätzen zur OOD nur unzureichend berücksichtigt [FK92].

Eine Schwäche des OOD, die auch in [FK92] kritisiert wird, sind die fehlenden Modellierungsmöglichkeiten für längerfristige, mehrere Objekte involvierende Prozesse. Ein Beispiel für einen solchen Prozeß ist die Bearbeitung eines Schadensfalls im Teilmodell *Produkt*. Die Bearbeitung ist eine Tätigkeit, die verschiedene Objekte betrifft und deren einzelne Bestandteile zwar mittels des OOD beschrieben werden können (z.B. das Erzeugen eines Bestimmungsfaktors 'Totalschaden', was der Generierung einer Instanz der Bestimmungsfaktor-Art 'Auto-Schaden' entspricht), die aber in ihrer Gesamtheit nicht darstellbar ist. Weil solche Methoden Instanzen mehrerer Klassen erzeugen, lassen sie sich nicht genau einem Objekt oder einer Klasse zuordnen. Eine entsprechende Erweiterung der Konzepte zum OOD wäre wüschenswert.

Betrachtet man die Ausdrucksmächtigkeit heute verfügbarer, kommerzieller OODBMS [Ca91], so wird deutlich, daß die Vielfalt objektorientierter Konzepte aus OOA und OOD mit keinem System vollständig abbildbar sind. So unterstützt beispielsweise kein System alle Abstraktionskonzepte, und viele Systeme bieten nur sehr eingeschränkte Möglichkeiten, Integritätsbedingungen zu formulieren. Aus diesem Grund läßt sich die für das Teilmodell *Produkt* gefundene Modellierung nicht direkt mit einem heute verfügbaren kommerziellen OODBMS umsetzen. Da dieses Teilmodell repräsentative Eigenschaften aufweist, kann diese Aussage wohl auf die gesamte Informationsverarbeitung der R+V-Versicherung ausgedehnt werden.

Für die Restrukturierung der Informationsverarbeitung bieten sich somit zwei Möglichkeiten. Die Maßnahmen könnten zum einen auf solche Bereiche beschränkt werden, die durch die Funktionalität eines heutigen kommerziellen OODBMS abgedeckt werden. Zum anderen könnte man eine objektorientierte Analyse der gesamten Informationsverarbeitung vornehmen und die praktische Umsetzung der so entstehenden, umfassenden Spezifikation an den Möglichkeiten heute verfügbarer OODBMS orientieren. Letztere Alternative hat den Vorteil, daß eine vollständige, in sich konsistente Strukturierung der Informationsverarbeitung vorliegt, die als mittel- bis langfristige Perspektive dienen kann. So könnte bei Verfügbarwerden semantisch mächtigerer Systeme sofort durch eine entsprechend weitergehende Umsetzung der Ergebnisse der OOA reagiert werden.

Nach unseren Erfahrungen ist die OOA eine geeignete Methode zur Restrukturierung der betrieblichen Informationsverarbeitung, die es erlaubt, alle relevanten Informationen und Aktionen exakt und einheitlich zu modellieren. Zwar muß eine praktische Umsetzung der Analyseergebnisse darauf abzielen, den Benutzern eine uniforme Sicht auf die zu bearbeitenden Daten zu bieten, unsere Untersuchungen bezüglich einer Implementierung haben jedoch gezeigt, daß eine ausschließlich objektorientierte Realisierung aus Effizienzgründen nicht wünschenswert ist. Stattdessen wäre es im Falle der R+V-Versicherung sinnvoll, die Daten je nach ihrer Struktur und Verwendung unterschiedlich zu verwalten: einfach strukturierte, große Datenmengen, auf denen nur elementare Operationen (wie Einfügen, Löschen oder Ändern von Einträgen) auszuführen sind, könnten in einem relationalen DBMS abgelegt werden, komplex strukturierte Daten mit operationalen Eigenschaften dagegen in einem OODBMS.

Solche Anforderungen können von einem föderierten Datenbanksystem erfüllt werden, in denen sich heterogene DBMS in einem globalen Schema zusammenfassen lassen. Eine Alternative bieten objektorientiert-relationale Systeme, wie sie von [SQL3] vorgeschlagen werden, die die Vorteile der relationalen und objektorientierten Repräsentationen verbinden.

Literatur

Bo94   Booch, G.: Object-Oriented Analysis And Design, Benjamin Cummings, New York, 1994.

BS93   Brodie, M., Stonebraker, M.: Incremental Migration of Legacy Data Base Applications, GTE Laboratories, Waltham, Mass., Technical Report 93-12, Januar 1993.

Ca91   Cattell, R. (ed.): Next Generation Database Systems, in: Special issue of Communications of the ACM, Vol. 34, No.10, 1991.

CC90   Chikofsky, E., Cross, J.: Reverse Engineering and Design Recovery: A Taxonomy, IEEE Software 7 (1), Januar 1990, 13-17.

CY91a   Coad, P., Yourdon, E.: Object-Oriented Analysis, Englewood Cliffs 1991.

CY91b   Coad, P., Yourdon, E.: Object-Oriented Design, Englewood Cliffs 1991.

DLM90   Deßloch, S., Leick, F.J., Mattos, N.M.: A State-oriented Approach to the Specification of Rules and Queries in KBMS, ZRI-Bericht 4/90, Universität Kaiserslautern, 1990.

DLMT93 Deßloch, S., Leick, F.J., Mattos, N.M., Thomas, J.: The KRISYS Project - A Summary of What We have Learned so far, in: Stucky, W., Oberweis, A. (eds.): Datenbanksysteme in Büro, Technik und Wissenschaft,, Springer (Informatik Aktuell), 1993, 124-143.

EKPR92 Eicker, S., Kurbel, K., Pietsch, W., Rautenstrauch, C.: Einbindung von Software-Altlasten durch integrationsorientiertes Reengineering, Wirtschaftsinformatik, 34. Jahrgang, Heft 2, April 1994, 137-145.

FK92   Fichman, R., Kemerer C.: Object-Oriented and Conventional Analysis and Design Methodologies, IEEE Computer 1992 Vol. 25, No. 10, 22-39.

HR85   Härder, T., Reuter, A.: Architektur von Datenbanksystemen für Non-Standard-Anwendungen, in: Proc. GI-Proc. GI Conf. on Database Systems for Office, Engineering and Scientific Applications, p.253-286, Karlsruhe, März 85, IFB 94, Springer Verlag, Heidelberg.

ISO94   ISO 10303-1: Product Data Representation and Exchange - Part 1: Overview and Fundamental Principles, ISO TC184 / SC4 N193, 1994.

Ma91   Mattos, N.M.: An Approach to Knowledge Base Management - Requirements, Knowledge Representation, and Design Issues -, Lecture Notes in Artificial Intelligence, Vol. 513 , Springer, 1991.

RS94   Radeke, E., Scholl, M.: Federation and Stepwise Reduction fo Database Systems, Proc. International Conference on Applications of Databases, Schweden, Juni 1994.

R+V92   R+V-Versicherung: Unternehmensmodell, Abschlußbericht, Wiesbaden, 1992.

Sa94   Sauter, G.: Modellierung eines flexiblen Baukastens für Versicherungsprodukte mit dem Wissensbankverwaltungssystem KRISYS, Diplomarbeit, Fachbereich Informatik, Universität Kaiserslautern, 1994.

SL90   Sheth, A.P. , Larson, J.A.: Federated Database Systems for Managing Distributed, Heterogeneous, and Autonomous Databases, ACM Computing Surveys, Vol. 22 , No. 3, September 1990, 183-236.

SQL3   ISO working draft Database Languages - SQL3, Februar 1993.

ST93   Stein, W.: Objektorientierte Analysemethoden - ein Vergleich, Informatik-Spektrum (1993) 16.

TK78   Tichritzis, D., Klug, A.: The ANSI/X3/SPARC DBMS Framework Report of the Study Group on Databasemanagement Systems, Information Systems, Vol. 3, 1978

Einsatz und Nutzen einer Metaebene für föderierte Datenbanksysteme am Beispiel der Molekularbiologie

Barbara Rieche, Klaus R. Dittrich

Forschungsbereich Datenbanktechnologie
Institut für Informatik, Universität Zürich
Email: {rieche, dittrich}@ifi.unizh.ch

Kurzfassung

Werden Daten aus mehreren, unterschiedlichen Datenhaltungssystemen benötigt, ist es sinnvoll, für deren Integration ein föderiertes Datenbanksystem (FDBS) einzusetzen. Dies gilt nicht nur für den kommerziellen Bereich, sondern ist ebenfalls für wissenschaftliche Anwendungsgebiete wie die Molekularbiologie interessant. In diesem Papier stellen wir im Rahmen des Projekts Moby Dick einen Ansatz vor, der die lokalen Systeme mit Hilfe einer Metaebene in das FDBS einbindet. Dadurch ermöglichen wir die explizite Darstellung der Zusammenhänge zwischen den Schemata der lokalen Systeme und demjenigen des FDBS, was einerseits die Arbeit des Datenbankintegrators (DBI), anderseits die Abfrageverarbeitung unterstützt. Ausserdem erfüllt die Metaebene zwei wichtige Anforderungen der Molekularbiologie: die Möglichkeit, das Datenmodell des FDBS zu erweitern und diejenige, anwendungsspezifische Metadaten und Metamethoden zu modellieren.

1   Einleitung

In vielen Anwendungen der Informatik werden heute Daten aus mehreren, unterschiedlichen Datenhaltungssystemen benötigt. Hierunter fallen einerseits Datenbanksysteme (relationale, netzwerkartige, objektorientierte usw.), anderseits aber auch Dateistrukturen. Diese Vielfalt stellt an die Entwickler hohe Anfordungen bezüglich der Kenntnisse über die einzelnen Systeme. Eine attraktive Lösung besteht darin, die existierenden (*lokalen*) Datenbanksysteme (DBS) in ein sogenanntes *föderiertes Datenbanksystem (FDBS)* zu integrieren. Der Vorteil eines solchen FDBS ist, dass dieses den (*globalen*) Anwendern eine einheitliche Schnittstelle zur Verfügung stellt, die ihnen den Eindruck eines homogenen DBS vermittelt. Dabei muss die Eigenständigkeit der lokalen DBS bewahrt bleiben, damit bereits vorhandene Anwendungen weiterhin lauffähig sind. In den letzten Jahren nahm daher die Forschung im Bereich der FDBS stark zu ([BHP92], [SL90]).

Im Zentrum der FDBS steht ein *globales Datenmodell*, das für die einheitliche Darstellung der Daten der lokalen DBS zuständig ist und somit die Heterogenität der *lokalen* Datenmodelle verbirgt. Die durch *lokale* Schemata beschriebenen Daten müssen also einerseits *homogenisiert*, d.h. mit Mitteln des globalen Datenmodells dargestellt werden. Anderseits müssen diese homogenisierten Schemata (*Komponentenschemata* genannt) zu einem *föderierten* Schema verbunden werden, wobei unter anderem Redundanzen und Konflikte zu erkennen und beheben sind. Mit unterschiedlichen lokalen Datenmodellen existieren auch verschiedene lokale Datenmanipulationssprachen (DML). Abfragen von globalen Anwendern werden in der DML des globalen Datenmodells gestellt, worauf sie — sind die benötigten Daten in verschiedenen DBS abgelegt — in mehrere Unterabfragen aufgeteilt werden, die dann mit Hilfe der lokalen DML auf die lokalen Datenbanken zugreifen.

Obwohl in den meisten Forschungsarbeiten im Gebiet der FDBS von kommerziellen Anwendungsgebieten ausgegangen wird (sofern überhaupt ein konkretes Gebiet betrachtet wird), treten die gleichen Probleme auch bei wissenschaftlichen Anwendungsgebieten auf. Die Datenhaltungssysteme, die hier bereits vorhanden sind, sind allerdings meist Dateien. In manchen Fällen werden auch Datenbanksysteme eingesetzt, die jedoch häufig Eigenentwicklungen sind und nicht die volle Datenbankfunktionalität anbieten. Hier gilt es, Dateien, die als Eingabe für vorhandene Programmpakete dienen, wie auch etwaige relationale Systeme weiterhin zu unterstützen, aber überdies Mittel (z.B. objektorientierte DBS) zur Verfügung zu stellen, um in Zukunft die doch recht komplexen wissenschaftlichen Daten auf geeignetere Art und Weise abzuspeichern ([FJP90], [Jone91]). Bei Wissenschaftlern, die meist Laien im Gebiet der Informatik sind, ist es dabei besonders wichtig, eine einheitliche Schnittstelle zu allen vorhandenen Daten anzubieten. Folglich ist auch in wissenschaftlichen Anwendungsgebieten der Einsatz von FDBS durchaus sinnvoll.

Im Projekt Moby Dick[1] ([RD94]) gehen wir von einer existierenden molekularbiologischen Arbeitsumgebung aus. Ein zentraler Teil des Projekts ist die Integration der dort vorhandenen Daten durch ein FDBS, das die sogenannte *Datenhaltungskomponente* bildet. Im Gegensatz zu heutigen Ansätzen für FDBS, in denen die Zusammenhänge der lokalen Schemata mit den Komponentenschemata und dem föderierten Schema in der Kopplungssoftware meist fest implementiert sind ([Ahme91], [Härt94]), modellieren wir in unserem Ansatz diese Zusammenhänge explizit auf einer Metaebene. Für jedes lokale DBS wird ein Metaschema, dessen Instanzen die lokalen Schemata sind, mittels eines *Metamodells* erstellt. Gleichermassen wird für das FDBS ein Metaschema kreiert, welches die Komponentenschemata und das föderierte Schema als Instanzen enthält. Mit Hilfe von sogenannten *Abbildungsbeziehungstypen* definieren wir explizit die Zusammenhänge zwischen diesen Metaschemata und somit zwischen den lokalen Schemata, den Komponentenschemata und dem föderierten Schema. Das verwendete Metamodell weist die wichtigsten objektorientierten Eigenschaften ([ABDD89]) auf; wir sprechen hier von *Metatyp, Metaattribut, Metamethode* usw. Ein Metatyp ist dann beispielsweise `MAttribute`, welcher alle im föderierten Schema oder in den Komponentenschemata vorkommenden Attribute beschreibt. Unser Metamodell unterstützt eine deklarative Metadatendefinitions- und -manipulationssprache (*MDDL, MDML*), welche dem Datenbankintegrator (DBI) erlaubt, einerseits Metaschemata für neue lokale DBS zu definieren, anderseits sich über frühere Integrationen zu informieren, ohne Programmcode lesen zu müssen. Weiter unterstützt die Metaebene die Implementierung der DML des globalen Datenmodells durch die Objektorientierung des Metamodells: DML-Operationen wie die Auffindeoperation werden als *Verhalten* der Metatypen aufgefasst und daher als deren Metamethoden implementiert. Die Abfrageverarbeitung erfolgt dann durch das Verschikken von *Nachrichten* zwischen Metaobjekten, d.h. den Instanzen der Metatypen.

Die Metaebene bringt allerdings nicht nur einen Nutzen für das FDBS, sondern erfüllt gleichzeitig auch wichtige Anforderungen der Molekularbiologie an die Datenverwaltung. Erstens erlaubt die MDDL, das globale Datenmodell zu erweitern, indem neue Konzepte als Metasubtypen eingefügt werden. Eine solche Erweiterung ist dann notwendig, wenn die molekularbiologische Forschung in eine Richtung vordringt, die Daten einer neuen Komplexität hervorbringt (z.B. dreidimensionale Proteinstrukturen), welche mit Konzepten des aktuellen globalen Datenmodells nicht mehr vernünftig modelliert werden können. Zweitens verlangen wissenschaftliche Anwendungen im allgemeinen, dass anwendungsspezifische Metadaten wie z.B. Masseinheiten abgelegt werden können. Solche Metadaten können ebenfalls durch die MDDL definiert und durch die MDML gesetzt werden. Und schliesslich wird es durch die Metaebene möglich, Funktionen, die auf Mengen von Objekten operieren, diesen und nicht den einzelnen Objekten zuzuordnen.

---

[1] Molecular biology federated DBMS-based integrated computer-supported working environment

Der Beitrag des vorliegenden Papiers ist somit der folgende: Es wird gezeigt,

- wie durch die Einführung einer Metaebene sowohl die Zusammenhänge zwischen den lokalen und den Komponentenschemata, als auch zwischen den Komponenten- und dem föderierten Schema gleichermassen explizit dargestellt werden können,

- wie diese explizite Darstellung und die objektorientierten Eigenschaften des Metamodells die Implementierung von DML-Operationen und deren Verarbeitung unterstützen, und

- welchen Nutzen eine solche Metaebene für eine wissenschaftliche Anwendung wie die Molekularbiologie hat.

Nach einer kurzen Einführung in das Projekt Moby Dick, in der insbesondere auf die Schemaarchitektur und das globale Datenmodell eingegangen wird, beschreibt Abschnitt 3 die Metaebene. Im Vordergrund stehen deren Architektur und die Abbildungsbeziehungen. In Abschnitt 4 werden die auf dem Metamodell definierten Sprachen (MDDL und MDML) eingeführt und deren Einsatz dargelegt. Abschnitt 5 beschäftigt sich dann mit der DML des globalen Datenmodells. Hier wird hauptsächlich auf deren Implementierung und Verarbeitung eingegangen. Verwandte Arbeiten werden in Abschnitt 6 diskutiert und mit unserem Ansatz verglichen. Das Papier schliesst mit einer Zusammenfassung und einem Ausblick.

2   Einführung in Moby Dick

Im Zentrum der Molekularbiologie steht heute unter anderem die Erforschung von DNS- (und Protein-) Sequenzen (DNS = Desoxyribonukleinsäure, enthält die Gene eines Lebewesens oder einer Pflanze). Diese werden in Experimenten aus Chromosomen extrahiert und mit Hilfe von Anwendungsprogrammen analysiert, die einerseits dazu dienen, eine gefundene Sequenz mit bereits bekannten zu vergleichen, anderseits dazu, die Eigenschaften einer Sequenz oder der durch sie beschriebenen Gene herauszukristallisieren. Bis heute werden die in Experimenten anfallenden Daten (Sequenzen) und deren Auswertungsdaten in Dateien abgespeichert, deren Format je nach Experiment unterschiedlich sein kann. Hinzu kommen Daten aus verschiedenen Quellen, wie beispielsweise anderen Forschungseinrichtungen, die in die Analyse der Experimentdaten miteinbezogen werden müssen. Die "Verwaltung" dieser Daten erfolgt in der Regel über spezielle Anwendungsprogramme, die häufig angepasst oder gar neu geschrieben werden müssen, da sich das Format der Dateien ändert, beziehungsweise andere Information aus den Daten herausgelesen werden soll. Durch technologische Fortschritte in der Labortechnik werden zudem immer kompliziertere und automatisiertere Instrumente benutzt, die mehr und mehr Daten in kürzerer Zeit produzieren. Nur selten werden DBS (meist relationale oder selbstentwickelte) eingesetzt. Es erstaunt daher nicht, dass die Molekularbiologen sich nur mit Mühe eine Übersicht über die Daten und die Zugriffsmöglichkeiten darauf verschaffen können.

Moby Dick trägt durch geeignete Integration der vorhandenen Daten und Anwendungsprogramme zu einer Verbesserung dieser Situation bei. Mittelpunkt von Moby Dick ist dabei die *Datenhaltungskomponente*, ein föderiertes Datenbanksystem, welches alle vorhandenen Daten zentral verwaltet, unabhängig davon, ob diese in Dateien oder DBS gespeichert sind, und dem Benutzer eine einheitliche Sicht auf diese Daten erlaubt. Im Vordergrund des vorliegenden Papiers steht die Einführung einer Metaebene für die Kopplung der Schemata lokaler DBS mit dem föderierten Schema der Datenhaltungskomponente. Zuvor ist es jedoch nötig, auf die Schemaarchitektur der Datenhaltungskomponente und das von uns verwendete globale Datenmodell näher einzugehen. Für eine detailliertere Übersicht über die gesamte Architektur von Moby Dick sei auf [RD94] verwiesen.

2.1 Schemaarchitektur

Die Schemaarchitektur des FDBS von Moby Dick[2] basiert auf der in [SL90] vorgestellten Referenzarchitektur. Während dort allerdings fünf Ebenen von Schemata unterstützt werden, sind für uns nur deren drei relevant: lokale Schemata, Komponentenschemata und das föderierte Schema. Unter *lokalen Schemata* versteht man die Schemata der lokalen DBS, die in deren Datenmodell definiert worden sind. Durch die *Homogenisierung* wird jedes lokale Schema in ein *Komponentenschema* transformiert, indem die lokalen Schemata mit den Mitteln des *globalen Datenmodells* dargestellt werden[3]. Diese Komponentenschemata werden in einem zweiten Schritt, der *Schemaintegration*, zu einem *föderierten Schema* zusammengefügt. Dieses wird ebenfalls durch das globale Datenmodell dargestellt und bietet somit dem Benutzer eine einheitliche, integrierte Sicht auf die verschiedenen lokalen Schemata.

Beide Schritte können schwerlich voll automatisiert werden, da die in einem lokalen Schema dargestellten Daten nach dem individuellen Verständnis der Benutzer modelliert wurden. Der DBI muss unter Umständen Rücksprache mit den Benutzern halten. Im Vordergrund dieses Papiers steht somit nicht die *volle* Automatisierung der obigen Schritte, sondern die *Unterstützung* des DBI durch geeignete Darstellung der Schemazusammenhänge im FDBS, um Entscheidungshilfen zu geben und eine Teilautomatisierung zu erreichen.

2.2 Das globale Datenmodell

Das globale Datenmodell lehnt sich an die in [ABDD89] vorgeschlagenen Richtlinien für objektorientierte Datenmodelle an. Es ist zudem erweiterbar in dem Sinne, dass zusätzlich neue Konzepte, die für die Molekularbiologie wichtig sind, definiert werden können. Auf die Erweiterbarkeit wird in Abschnitt 4.1 kurz eingegangen. Hier sollen vorerst die Konzepte des Kerns des globalen Datenmodells erwähnt werden, die zu einem besseren Verständnis der folgenden Abschnitte nötig sind:

- Eine Datenbank besteht aus *Objekten*, die durch einen Zustand und ein Verhalten charakterisiert sind. Jedes Objekt besitzt zudem eine *Identität*, die durch einen eindeutigen Identifikator ausgedrückt wird. Dieser Identifikator wird vom Datenbanksystem vergeben und während der gesamten Lebensdauer eines Objekts nicht geändert.

- Der Zustand (*Attribute*) und das Verhalten (*Methoden*) der Objekte ist in *Typen* beschrieben, während die eigentlichen Objekte in *Objektbehältern* enthalten sind. Ein Typ entspricht somit der *Intension*. Pro Typ können mehrere Objektbehälter existieren, wobei einer davon alle real vorhandenen Objekte des Typs, d.h. dessen *Extension*, verwaltet.

  Typen sind in einer (zyklenfreien) *Typhierarchie* beliebiger Tiefe angeordnet. Ein Typ erbt immer alle Eigenschaften seiner direkten und indirekten Supertypen. Jeder Subtyp enthält allerdings weitere, in den Supertypen nicht unbedingt vorhandene Eigenschaften. Objektbehältern können sogenannte *Objektbehältermethoden* zugeordnet werden, die über alle im Objektbehälter enthaltenen Objekte Werte berechnen (z.B. Durchschnittswert eines Attributs).

  Objektbehälter können ebenfalls in einer Hierarchie angeordnet sein, wobei ein Unter-Objektbehälter immer auch eine Untermenge des Ober-Objektbehälters darstellt. Vererbung kommt auch hier zum Zuge: Objektbehältermethoden eines Ober-Objektbehälters werden an die Unter-Objektbehälter vererbt.

---

[2] Im folgenden verwenden wir den Ausdruck FDBS auch stellvertretend für die Datenhaltungskomponente.
[3] Im Falle von Dateien existieren keine in einer DDL formulierten lokalen Schemata. Die Komponentenschemata werden daher aus der Struktur der Dateien abgeleitet.

- Der Wertebereich eines Attributs kann ein *primitiver Typ* (z.B. integer, string, boolean) sein oder aber eine *Assoziation* zu einem anderen Typ bilden. Dabei unterscheiden wir zwei Arten von Assoziationen: *Referenzen* und *Unterobjektbeziehungen* (*is-part-of* Beziehungen). Der Unterschied liegt darin, dass im Falle von Referenzen der Wert des Attributs ein Zeiger auf ein eigenständiges Objekt ist, während bei Unterobjektbeziehungen das Objekt als Teil des Attributobjekts, als sogenanntes *Unterobjekt*, betrachtet wird. Das Objekt, das Unterobjektbeziehungen aufweist, wird dann *komplexes Objekt* genannt. Zudem kann Attributen mit Hilfe von Konstruktoren wie *Menge, Liste, Tupel* auch mehr als ein Wert zugewiesen werden.

3 Architektur der Metaebene

Analog zur oben beschriebenen Schemaarchitektur wird auch die Metaebene in drei Teile unterteilt. Jeder Teil beschreibt die jeweiligen Schemata einer Ebene (Abb. 1). Die Mittel für diese Beschreibungen sind für alle Teile die gleichen, nämlich die des *Metamodells*. Dieses ist von gängigen objektorientierten Datenmodellen abgeleitet und unterstützt daher Konzepte wie Typen, Attribute, Methoden, Vererbung und Einkapselung. Um einer Begriffsverwirrung vorzubeugen, setzen wir vor die obigen Begriffe den Prefix "Meta", wenn von der Metaebene die Rede ist.

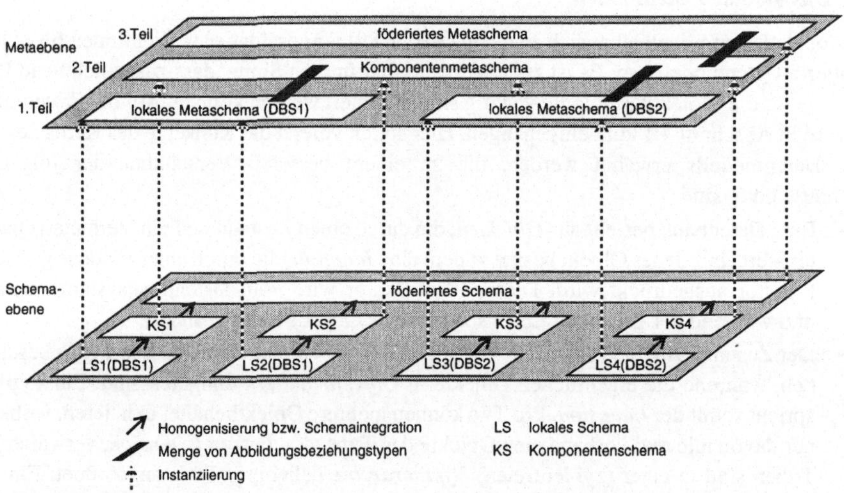

Abb. 1: Zusammenhänge Schemaebene — Metaebene

Es wäre naheliegend, für das Metamodell die gleichen Konzepte wie die des globalen Datenmodells zu verwenden, so dass das globale Datenmodell selbstbeschreibend wird. Die Gründe, warum in Moby Dick kein selbstbeschreibendes Datenmodell übernommen wird, sind die folgenden: Einerseits enthält das globale Datenmodell Konzepte, die zwar in bezug auf die Datenmodellierung für die Molekularbiologie wichtig sind (z.B. Objektbehälter), aber nicht für die Modellierung von Metadaten. Anderseits werden auf Metaebene Konzepte wie Abbildungsbeziehungstypen eingeführt, die einzig auf Metaebene benötigt werden und für den molekularbiologischen Datenbankentwurf keinen Sinn machen. Metamodell und Datenmodell werden daher separat betrachtet, wenn auch die Kernkonzepte übereinstimmen.

Im folgenden wollen wir zuerst auf die einzelnen Teile der Metaebene zu sprechen kommen, um dann auf deren Beziehungen untereinander näher einzugehen und das Vorgehen bei der Homogenisierung zu betrachten.

3.1 Arten von Metaschemata

Pro lokales DBS wird ein Metaschema gebildet, dessen Instanzen jeweils die lokalen Schemata des DBS sind. Diese *lokalen Metaschemata* bilden den ersten (lokalen) Teil der Metaebene. Für jedes Konzept des lokalen Datenmodells wird ein Metatyp gebildet, während die Zusammenhänge zwischen den Konzepten als Metabeziehungstypen dargestellt werden. Bei einem lokalen DBS mit relationalem Datenmodell werden beispielsweise die Relationen und Attribute als Metatypen `RRelation` bzw. `RAttribute` repräsentiert, die Namen der Relationen als Metaattribut von `RRelation` usw.

Während im ersten Teil der Metaebene noch mehrere Metaschemata (pro lokales DBS eines) existieren, besteht der zweite Teil nur aus einem Metaschema, dem *Komponentenmetaschema*. Dieses enthält für jedes Konzept des <u>globalen</u> Datenmodells einen Metatyp, wobei die Zusammenhänge zwischen diesen Konzepten wiederum durch Metabeziehungstypen dargestellt werden. Beispielsweise werden die Objektbehälter durch den Metatyp `MObjContainer`, die Typen durch den Metatyp `MType` beschrieben. Die Metadaten, die durch das Komponentenmetaschema beschrieben werden, entsprechen hier den Komponentenschemata.

Der dritte Teil der Metaebene schliesslich enthält die Beschreibung des föderierten Schemas, das *föderierte Metaschema*. Wiederum liegt hier das globale Datenmodell zugrunde. Für die Implementierung ist daher nur ein Metaschema für die Komponentenschemata und das föderierte Schema notwendig. Da wir die Konzepte der Metaebene hier allerdings vom logischen Gesichtspunkt aus betrachten, unterscheiden wir zwischen Komponentenmetaschema und föderiertem Metaschema.

3.2 Abbildungsbeziehungstypen

In einem FDBS und somit auch in Moby Dick müssen typischerweise die Beziehungen zwischen globaler und lokaler Ebene festgehalten werden, damit beispielsweise bei einer globalen Abfrage bestimmt werden kann, auf welchen lokalen Systemen sich die Daten befinden. Wir führen hierzu sogenannte *Abbildungsbeziehungstypen* zwischen den einzelnen Teilen der Metaebene ein. Wir verstehen darunter spezielle Beziehungen, die nicht innerhalb eines Metaschemas definiert werden, sondern, im Gegenteil, die Metaschemata der verschiedenen Teile der Metaebene verbinden (siehe Beispiel 1).

BEISPIEL 1:   Bei der Homogenisierung eines relationalen Schemas muss entschieden werden, in welche Konzepte des globalen Datenmodells die Relationen, Attribute, Primär- und Fremdschlüssel transformiert werden. Gegeben seien die folgenden Relationen, welche Sequenzen mit ihrem Entdecker und den in ihr enthaltenen Genen darstellen:

    SEQUENZ(<u>S#</u>, Name, Organismus, Länge, *F#*)

    GEN(<u>G#</u>, Name, Funktion, *S#*)

    FORSCHER(<u>F#</u>, Name, Adresse)

Natürlich kann jede Relation in einen Typ transformiert werden, und jedes Attribut ein Attribut bleiben. Das heisst, eine Möglichkeit wäre es, einen Abbildungsbeziehungstyp zwischen den Metatypen `RRelation` und `MType` zu bilden. Allerdings ist es offensichtlich, dass das mächtigere globale Datenmodell eine semantisch reichhaltigere Darstellung desselben Sachverhalts erlaubt. So sind die Gene Teile der Sequenz und können daher mit Hilfe der *part-of*-Beziehung als Unterobjekte modelliert werden, wodurch der Fremdschlüssel S# in GEN überflüssig wird. Die andere Fremdschlüsselbeziehung (F#) entspricht einer normalen Beziehung und kann daher als Referenz dargestellt werden.

Die Abbildungsbeziehungstypen zwischen dem Komponenten- und dem föderierten Metaschema sind naturgemäss einfacher, da beiden Metaschemata das gleiche Datenmodell, nämlich das globale, zugrunde liegt. Erstes Ziel ist es somit, das Komponentenschema möglichst unverändert in das föderierte Schema zu übernehmen. Selbstverständlich treten auch hier Komplikationen auf, wenn beispielsweise ein Komponentenschema den Organismus (Beispiel 1) als Referenz auf ein eigenes Objekt modelliert hat, während ein anderes ihn nur als Zeichenkette darstellt. Auf die Problematik der Schemaintegration soll hier nicht weiter eingegangen werden. Zu Konflikten bei der Schemaintegration siehe beispielsweise [KS91] oder [DH84].

3.3 Transformationsfunktionen

Obwohl die obigen Beispiele noch recht einfach sind, wird bereits klar, dass die Abbildungsbeziehungstypen als Mittel für die Darstellung der Zusammenhänge der einzelnen Teile der Metaebene nicht genügen. Vielmehr muss auch festgehalten werden, auf welche Art und Weise zum Beispiel ein relationales Attribut zu einer Referenz wird. Hierzu werden den einzelnen Instanzen der Abbildungsbeziehungstypen sogenannte *Transformationsfunktionen* zugeordnet, hinter denen sich der Code für die Umwandlung verbirgt. Transformationsfunktionen treten immer paarweise auf, da pro Abbildungsbeziehung zwischen zwei Metaobjekten jeweils eine Transformationsfunktion benötigt wird, um die Daten von globaler auf lokale Ebene zu konvertieren (*export*) und umgekehrt (*import*). In manchen Fällen können die Transformationsfunktionen auch wegfallen, z.B. wenn ein integer auf lokaler Ebene in einen integer auf globaler Ebene umgewandelt werden soll und auf beiden Ebenen derselbe Typ integer unterstützt wird.

Wenn wir es mit Metaobjekten zu tun haben, die wiederum andere Metaobjekte enthalten, wird es schwieriger zu entscheiden, ob Transformationsfunktionen nötig sind oder nicht. Das Konzept solcher *komplexen Metaobjekte*, welches es erlaubt, ein Metaobjekt mit all seinen Unterobjekten zu betrachten und zu bearbeiten, spielt hier eine äusserst wichtige Rolle: Bei der Prüfung, ob Transformationsfunktionen für die Abbildungsbeziehung zwischen zwei komplexen Metaobjekten nötig sind, muss jeweils das *ganze* komplexe Metaobjekt betrachtet werden. Die Abbildungsbeziehung kann genau dann auf Transformationsfunktionen verzichten, wenn nicht nur die Metaobjekte, sondern auch sämtliche Unterobjekte von ihnen (rekursiv!) gleich sind, d.h. eins zu eins aufeinander abgebildet werden können.

3.4 Vorgehen bei der Integration

Soll ein zusätzliches DBS integriert werden, so erstellt der Datenbankintegrator (DBI) ein lokales Metaschema, welches das Datenmodell des DBS beschreibt. Ebenfalls legt er die auf den Metatypen des neuen lokalen Metaschemas ausführbaren Operationen als Metamethoden fest und definiert die Abbildungsbeziehungstypen zwischen dem lokalen und dem Komponentenmetaschema. Als Hilfsmittel benutzt er eine Metadatendefinitionssprache (siehe Abschnitt 4).

Für die Integration eines lokalen Schemas definiert der DBI die Schemadaten als Metadaten, d.h. als Instanzen des lokalen Metaschemas. Hierzu verwendet er eine Metadatenmanipulationssprache (siehe Abschnitt 4)[4]. Die Homogenisierung des lokalen Schemas wird durch die bei der

---

[4] Hier wäre auch eine Unterstützung durch geeignete Werkzeuge angebracht, deren Betrachtung den Rahmen dieses Papiers allerdings sprengen würde.

Integration des DBS definierten Abbildungsbeziehungstypen unterstützt, indem das FDBS Möglichkeiten für ein Komponentenschema anhand der Abbildungsbeziehungstypen aufzeigt. Nimmt der DBI diese Vorschläge an, können zumindest Teile der Komponentenschemata automatisch erzeugt werden. Bei der Schemaintegration wird entsprechend vorgegangen.

4 Sprachen der Metaebene

So wie jedes Datenmodell Operationen für die Definition und Manipulation von Daten zur Verfügung stellt, werden auch auf der Metaebene entsprechende Möglichkeiten benötigt (siehe Abschnitt 3.4). Der Datendefinitionssprache (DDL) entspricht hier die *Metadatendefinitionssprache (MDDL)*, der Datenmanipulationssprache (DML) die *Metadatenmanipulationssprache (MDML)*. Im folgenden soll auf diese beiden Sprachen näher eingegangen werden. Die verwendete Syntax lehnt sich an diejenige von NO^2 ([GDGS93]) und Zoo_{IFI} ([Härt94]) an.

4.1 Die Metadatendefinitionssprache

Die Metadatendefinitionssprache dient einerseits der Definition der Metaschemata (Beispiel 2) und der Abbildungsbeziehungstypen zwischen ihnen, anderseits aber auch der Erweiterung des Datenmodells, was für die Modellierung von speziellen (Nicht-Standard-) Anwendungsdaten nötig werden kann. Ein Beispiel für eine Datenmodellerweiterung sind zeitabhängige Daten, die mit vorhandenen Konzepten des globalen Datenmodells nicht modelliert werden können und somit einer Erweiterung bedürfen[5].

BEISPIEL 2:   Die Relationen und ihre Attribute sollen durch die Metatypen `RRelation` und `RAttribute` verwaltet werden. Die Definition des entsprechenden lokalen Metaschemaausschnitts erfolgt folgendermassen:

```
METATYPE RRelation
      name: STRING;
      attr: SET(RAttribute);
END RRelation
METATYPE RAttribute
      name: STRING;
      rel:  RRelation;
END RAttribute
```

Ebenfalls kann das föderierte Metaschema mit Hilfe der MDDL derart erweitert werden, dass auch anwendungsspezifische Metadaten hinzugenommen werden können:

BEISPIEL 3:   In einer Experimentierumgebung kommen typischerweise viele Messdaten vor, d.h. Daten, die durch Angabe einer Masseinheit quantifiziert werden. Statt für jeden einzelnen Messwert die Masseinheit abzuspeichern, genügt es, diese ein einziges Mal für das Attribut, deren Werte diese Messwerte sind, abzulegen. Die Metaebene und die MDDL erlauben es nun, eine neue Art von Attribut, welche als Metaattribut die Masseinheit mitführt, hinzuzunehmen. Dies kann mit Hilfe der MDDL folgendermassen formuliert werden:

```
METATYPE MmeasAttr METASUPERTYPE MAttribute
      unit_of_meas: STRING;
END MmeasAttr
```

---

[5] Eine Datenmodellerweiterung ist jedoch nur dann sinnvoll, wenn auch entsprechende Unterstützung in der Datenverwaltung (z.B. Speicherstrategien) zur Verfügung gestellt werden.

Der Metatyp `MmeasAttr` erbt hiermit die Struktur und das Verhalten von normalen Attributen (beschrieben durch den Metatyp `MAttribute`), besitzt aber ein zusätzliches Metaattribut `unit_of_meas` für die Masseinheit.

Zur Vermeidung von Problemen, wie sie von der Schemaevolution her bekannt sind, erlauben wir vorerst keine Metaschemamanipulationen wie Löschen oder Ändern.

4.2 Die Metadatenmanipulationssprache

Die Datenmanipulationssprache der Metaebene dient dem DBI zum einen dazu, Schemata als Metadaten zu erfassen. Zum andern gibt sie ihm die Möglichkeit, sich über den Inhalt der Metadatenbanken in Kenntnis zu setzen, d.h. sich über bereits integrierte lokale Schemata, deren Komponentenschemata und das föderierte Schema zu informieren.

Weiterhin hat der Molekularbiologe durch die MDML die Möglichkeit, anwendungsspezifische Metadaten abzufragen und anwendungsspezifische Funktionen auf Mengen von Objekten, also auf Objektbehältern, zu definieren. Ein Beispiel für eine solche Funktion ist das Berechnen von Durchschnitten der Werte alle im Objektbehälter enthaltenen Objekte.

Grundsätzlich könnten durch die Metadatenmanipulationssprache auch Schemaänderungen durchgeführt werden. Wir erlauben in Moby Dick allerdings nur Schemamanipulationen, die auf der Hinzunahme von Schemaelementen beruhen. In der Molekularbiologie kann vorausgesetzt werden, dass das Löschen von Schemaelementen nicht relevant ist: Alle Information, die einmal festgehalten wird, darf weder geändert noch gelöscht werden, denn es kann davon ausgegangen werden, dass die zusammengetragene Information möglicherweise ungenau, aber nie falsch ist.

4.2.1 Erzeugen von Metadaten

Wegen der Autonomie der lokalen DBS sind die Datendefinitionssprachen (DDL) der lokalen Datenmodelle vom FDBS entkoppelt und erzeugen daher auch keine Metadaten für die lokalen Metaschemata. Wird also auf lokaler Ebene ein neues Schema entworfen, so merkt davon das FDBS nichts. Vielmehr muss der Benutzer, falls er dieses Schema in das FDBS integriert haben möchte, dies dem DBI angeben. Für eine solche Integration erzeugt der DBI als erstes aus dem lokalen Schema Metadaten und stellt sie durch das lokale Metaschema dem FDBS zur Verfügung. Hierzu benötigt er entsprechende Metadatendefinitionsoperationen:

BEISPIEL 4:

```
        INSERT INTO RRelation
            [rname =   "Sequenz",
              attributes ={(INSERT INTO RAttribute
                         [    aname = "Name",
                              atype = "STRING" ]),
                        ( INSERT INTO RAttribute
                         [    aname = "Organismus",
                              atype = "INTEGER" ]) }   ]
```

Hier wird die Relation `Sequenz(Name, Organismus)` als Instanz von `RRelation` eingefügt, wobei für jedes Attribut der Relation wiederum eine Instanz von `RAttribute` erzeugt wird.

Auf gleiche Art und Weise werden auch die Metadaten nach der Homogenisierung und Schemaintegration in das Komponentenmetaschema bzw. das föderierte Metaschema eingefügt. Hier kann das FDBS insofern Unterstützung anbieten, als dass es durch vorgegebene Abbildungsbeziehungstypen zwischen den Metaschemata Vorschläge macht und — falls der DBI diese annimmt — die Instanzen des Komponenten- und föderierten Metaschemas automatisch erzeugt.

Wird von einem globalen Benutzer das föderierte Schema erweitert, so geschieht dies durch die Datendefinitionssprache des globalen Datenmodells. Da dieses als Teil des FDBS betrachtet wir, schliesst seine Semantik ein, dass die nötigen Metadaten des föderierten Metaschemas automatisch erzeugt werden.

4.2.2 Abfrage von Metadaten

Der Abfrageteil der MDML umfasst Operationen, die es erlauben, Schemainformation abzufragen. Dabei wird nicht nur die Inspektion des föderierten Schemas erlaubt, sondern auch diejenige der Komponenten- und lokalen Schemata und deren Zusammenhänge, also der Abbildungsbeziehungen. Ebenfalls können mit Hilfe der MDML anwendungsspezifische Metadaten abgefragt werden. Abfragen von Metadaten werden also einerseits vom DBI benötigt, damit er sich bei der Homogenisierung und Schemaintegration über bestehende Metadaten informieren kann. Anderseits muss ein Teil der Operationen auch dem wissenschaftlichen Benutzer zur Verfügung gestellt werden, damit er auf anwendungsspezifische Metadaten zugreifen kann und sich über das föderierte Schema informieren kann. Die dem wissenschaftlichen Benutzer zugänglichen Funktionen sind somit eine Untermenge der dem DBI zur Verfügung stehenden.

BEISPIEL 5:   Den Benutzer interessiert die Masseinheit, in der die Temperatur in einem Experiment gemessen wird. Die Temperatur ist als messbares Attribut (vgl. Beispiel 2) namens "Temperature" abgelegt. Die Abfrage lautet also folgendermassen:

```
SELECT unit_of_meas
FROM MmeasAttr
WHERE aname = "Temperature"
```

Da wissenschaftliche Benutzer meist Laien auf dem Gebiet der Informatik sind, werden die ihnen zur Verfügung stehenden Operationen durch eine graphische Benutzeroberfläche unterstützt. Aus Platzgründen kann an dieser Stelle jedoch nicht näher auf diese eingegangen werden.

5   Unterstützung der Abfrageverarbeitung durch die Metaebene

Die wichtigsten Funktionen einer Datenmanipulationssprache sind bekanntlich die Erzeugung, das Auffinden, die Änderung und das Löschen von Daten. Ausserdem unterstützt die globale DML von Moby Dick den Aufruf von objekttypspezifischen Methoden innerhalb einer Anfrage sowie Operationen wie das Verschieben von Objekten von einem Objektbehälter in einen anderen, die Gruppierung der Objekte in einem Objektbehälter, usw.

Betrachten wir diese Funktionen genauer, stellen wir fest, dass sie sich in solche, die direkt auf Objekten ausgeführt werden, und solche, die auf Typen oder Objektbehältern aufgerufen werden, unterteilen lassen. Während eine objektspezifische Methode für ein (oder mehrere) Objekt(e) ausgeführt wird, wird beispielsweise das Auffinden von Objekten auf Mengen von Objekten, also auf Objektbehältern durchgeführt. Im folgenden wollen wir zeigen, wie die Metaebene und das objektorientierte Metamodell die Implementierung und Verarbeitung von DML-Operationen auf Typen und Objektbehältern unterstützen. Als Beispiele sollen die Erzeugung von neuen und das Auffinden von existierenden Objekten dienen. Die Änderung und das Löschen spielen im wissenschaftlichen Umfeld kaum eine Rolle, da prinzipiell davon ausgegangen werden muss, dass erlangte Forschungsdaten vielleicht ungenau, aber nicht falsch sind und daher auch nicht geändert oder gelöscht werden dürfen.

5.1 Implementierung von DML-Operationen

Durch die explizite Darstellung von Typen und Objektbehältern auf der Metaebene liegt es nahe, Operationen auf diesen als Metamethoden zu implementieren. Beispielsweise ist das Auffinden von Objekten eine Operation, die auf einer Menge von Objekten, in unserem Fall also auf einem Objektbehälter ausgeführt wird. Der Metatyp `MObjContainer`, welcher diese Objektbehälter repräsentiert, besitzt dafür eine Metamethode `Find`, der als Parameter eine Bedingung übergeben wird und die als Resultat die gewünschten Objekte liefert. Da das Ergebnis wiederum eine Menge von Objekten ist, wird es als neuer, nicht-persistenter Unter-Objektbehälter des Objektbehälters, auf dem die Abfrage ausgeführt wurde, aufgefasst:

BEISPIEL 6:   In einem Objektbehälter `Experiment` sollen alle Objekte (also Experimente) gefunden werden, die bei einer Temperatur von 20 Grad durchgeführt wurden:

```
Experiment.Find("Temperature = 20");
```

Das Resultat ist ein Unter-Objektbehälter von `Experiment`, der nur die gesuchten Experimente enthält.

Eine weitere DML-Operation, die auf Metaebene implementiert ist, ist die Objekterzeugung. Der Metatyp `MType` enthält hierzu eine Metamethode `CreateObj`, der als Parameter ein Objektbehälter übergeben werden kann, in den das neue Objekt eingefügt werden soll. Wird kein Parameter spezifiziert, gilt als Standardwert der Objektbehälter, der die Extension des Typs darstellt. Die Initialisierung des Objektwerts wird als Methode des Typs implementiert und von `CreateObj` aufgerufen.

5.2 Verarbeitung von DML-Operationen

In Abschnitt 5.1 haben wir gezeigt, wie die explizite Darstellung des globalen Datenmodells als Metaschema der Implementierung von DML-Operationen entgegenkommt. Ausserdem muss auch die Weiterleitung der Operationen zu den lokalen DBS betrachtet werden. Dabei nutzen wir wiederum den Umstand aus, dass unser Metamodell objektorientiert ist, und somit den Metatypen in den lokalen Metaschemata ebenfalls ein Verhalten zugeordnet werden kann, welches diese Operationen implementiert.

Für eine Auffindeoperation sieht das im einzelnen so aus, dass die Metatypen der lokalen Metaschemata ebenfalls eine Metamethode zum Auffinden von Daten besitzen, deren Implementierung lokalen Verhältnissen angepasst ist. Im relationalen Fall enthält der Metatyp `RRelation` die Metamethode `RFind`, deren Implementierung z.B. eingebettetem SQL entspricht. Die Kopplung zwischen der Metamethode `Find` des Metatyps `MObjContainer` und der entsprechenden Metamethode `RFind` des Metatyps `RRelation` soll an einem sehr stark vereinfachten Beispiel gezeigt werden:

BEISPIEL 7:   Eine globale Anfrage ruft für einen Objektbehälter `Experiment` die Metamethode `Find` auf. Daraufhin stellt das FDBS anhand der Abbildungsbeziehungen (föderiertes Schema → Komponentenschema(ta) → lokale(s) Schema(ta)) fest, welches lokale System (evtl. auch mehr als eines) die entsprechenden Daten enthält, und hinter welcher Schemakomponente sie sich verbergen. Angenommen sie befinden sich in einem relationalen Datenbanksystem, und zwar besteht eine Abbildungsbeziehung zwischen dem Objektbehälter `Experiment` im föderierten Schema und dem gleichnamigen Objektbehälter in einem Komponentenschema und zwischen diesem und der Relation `Exp` eines lokalen Schemas. Die Metamethode `Find` von `Experiment` ruft dann die Metamethode `RFind` von `Exp` auf. Das Resultat von `RFind` — in Form einer temporären Relation — wird darauf mit den entsprechenden Transformationsfunktionen auf globale Ebene importiert (konvertiert) und als Elemente eines neuen temporären Unter-Objektbehälters von `Experiment` dem Benutzer angezeigt.

Betrachten wir die Erzeugung von neuen Objekten, muss zuerst festgestellt werden, in welchem lokalen DBS diese abgelegt werden sollen. Auch hier wird auf die Abbildungsbeziehungen und deren Transformationsfunktionen zurückgegriffen. Der globale Benutzer bestimmt den Typ des neuen Objekts und gegebenenfalls auch einen Objektbehälter. Aufgabe von `CreateObj` ist es dann, über die Abbildungsbeziehungen vom föderierten zum Komponentenschema und von dort zum lokalen Schema festzustellen, in welchem Datenbanksystem ein Objekt erzeugt werden soll. Die vom Benutzer auf globaler Ebene eingegebenen Initialisierungsdaten werden dann durch die zur Abbildungsbeziehung gehörende Transformationsfunktion `export` in das lokale Format konvertiert und in einer Datenbank abgelegt.

6 Verwandte Arbeiten

Wegen der Vielfalt der Forschungsarbeiten im Gebiet der FDBS würde es den Rahmen dieses Papiers sprengen, eine umfassende Übersicht zu geben. Wir greifen uns daher einige Beispiele heraus, die ebenfalls ein Datenmodell mit objektorientiertem Charakter als globales Datenmodell unterstützen. Eine ähnlich explizite Darstellung der Zusammenhänge zwischen den Ebenen von Schemata, wie sie unser Ansatz unterstützt, wird unseres Wissens allerdings nur in einer Arbeit angeboten ([UW91]).

Pegasus

Pegasus ([Ahme91], [CL88]) basiert auf einem funktionalen, objektorientierten Modell als globalem Datenmodell. Es handelt sich hier um eine Erweiterung des IRIS-Datenmodells ([FABC88]). Pro lokales DBS und somit pro lokales Datenmodell existiert ein separater Kopplungsmodul, mit dem die Abbildungen zwischen dem lokalen und dem globalen Datenmodell definiert werden. Dieser Kopplungsmodul übernimmt auch die Übersetzung globaler Abfragen in solche, die in der jeweiligen lokalen DML formuliert sind.

Pegasus lässt sich kaum mit unserem Ansatz vergleichen. Es ist jedoch ein gutes Beispiel für ein System, das sowohl die Beziehungen zwischen lokalen und föderiertem Schema als auch die Abfrageverarbeitung fest implementiert hat. Der DBI muss sich hier mit der Durchsicht von Programmcode befassen, wenn er sich über zurückliegende Integrationsschritte informieren möchte. Wie die Schemata mit den Kopplungsmoduln interagieren, wird aus obigen Papieren nicht klar. Die Integration eines neuen lokalen Schemas — selbst wenn andere Schemata desselben lokalen Systems bereits integriert wurden — könnte bedeuten, dass der entsprechende Kopplungsmodul umgeschrieben werden muss.

Das COMANDOS-Integrationssystem

Bei der Integration heterogener Datenhaltungssysteme wird im COMANDOS-Integrationssystem (CIS) ([Ahme91], [BNPS89]) für jedes lokale System eine objektorientierte Sicht mit Hilfe des globalen objektorientierten Datenmodells erstellt. Dabei wird für jeden lokalen Typ eine *abstrakte Klasse* definiert. Für jede abstrakte Klasse wird dann wiederum eine sogenannte *Implementierungsklasse* erstellt, welche die Implementierungen aller Operationen der globalen DML für diese Klasse in Termini der lokalen DML enthält. Dadurch entstehen viele unterschiedliche Implementierungen für jede globale Operation. Beim Aufruf einer solchen Operation sucht CIS sich die zu benutzende heraus und führt sie über dem lokalen System aus.

Dieser von [BNPS89] "operational mapping" genannte Ansatz unterscheidet sich von anderen Ansätzen (z.B. [Motr87]) dadurch, dass globale Abfragen nicht durch ein Übersetzungsmodul in lokale Abfragen übersetzt werden, sondern die Implementierungen für die lokalen Systeme vorgegeben (vom DBI implementiert) werden, so dass bei einer Abfrage auf die dem lokalen System entsprechende Implementierung zurückgegriffen werden kann. Zu dieser Art Ansatz kann auch unsere Arbeit gezählt werden. Im Unterschied zu CIS erfassen wir allerdings die lokalen Schemata in Metaschemata, was uns die Möglichkeit gibt, DML-Operationen als Verhalten der Metatypen zu implementieren. Dadurch wird jede Operation genau einmal pro DBS und nicht pro Typ implementiert. Der Aufwand für die Integration weiterer lokaler Schemata, die von demselben DBMS verwaltet werden, wird somit stark verringert, da Implementierungen für die DML-Operationen bereits existieren.

ZOO$_{IFI}$

ZOO$_{IFI}$ ([Härt94]) vereinfacht die Integration lokaler Schemata durch einen sogenannten Integrationsrahmen. Dieser bietet den globalen Anwendern ein objektorientiertes globales Datenmodell in Form einer Klassenhierarchie als Schnittstelle an. Diese Klassen realisieren einerseits die globale Objektidentität, anderseits sind die generischen Operationen des globalen Datenmodells hier als Methoden implementiert. Als Schnittstelle zu den lokalen Systemen existiert eine zweite Klassenhierarchie, deren Klassen auf die lokalen Systeme zugeschnittene Implementierungen der generischen Operationen erlauben. Die Klassen eines Komponentenschemas werden in einer Metadatenbank erfasst, worauf für sie Unterklassen der ersten Klassenhierarchie generiert werden, sodass die Klassen des Komponentenschemas aufgrund der Objektorientierung die Objektidentität und die generischen Operationen erben. Die Zusammenhänge zwischen der Metadatenbank und der zweiten Klassenhierarchie müssen vom DBI implementiert werden, wobei dieser weitere Unterklassen innerhalb dieser Hierarchie bilden kann, um die Implementierung der generischen Operationen für die lokalen Systeme zu spezialisieren.

Im Gegensatz zu unserem Ansatz werden die Zusammenhänge zwischen den lokalen und den Komponentenschemata hier nicht explizit dargestellt. Für die Komponentenschemata existiert zwar ein Metaschema, nicht aber für die lokalen Schemata. Die Zusammenhänge sind als Erweiterungen des Metaschemas fest implementiert. Der Aufruf einer globalen Abfrage, bzw. einer globalen Operation bewirkt, dass die Implementierung des Metaschemas die entsprechende lokale Operation aufruft.

Ansatz von [UW91]

Wie bereits oben erwähnt, ist [UW91] unseres Wissens der einzige Ansatz, der ebenfalls eine Metaebene für die explizite Darstellung von Schemazusammenhängen unterstützt. Es wird ein semantisches Datenmodell, das Spezialisierung/Generalisierung sowie mehrwertige Attribute unterstützt, als globales Datenmodell verwendet. Ausserdem dient es gleichzeitig als Metamodell, so dass die Metaschemata, die das föderierte und die lokalen Schemata beschreiben, in gleicher Weise durch dieses semantische Datenmodell definiert werden. Die Zusammenhänge zwischen dem föderierten und einem lokalen Schema werden analog zu unserem Ansatz durch Abbildungsbeziehungstypen auf Metaebene beschrieben. Diesen Beziehungen werden ebenfalls Prozeduren für die Datenkonvertierung angehängt. Auf die Abfrageverarbeitung wird in [UW91] nicht weiter eingegangen. Da das semantische Datenmodell allerdings die Modellierung von Verhalten in Form von Methoden nicht weiter unterstützt, ist unser Ansatz für die Abfrageverarbeitung nicht realisierbar. Ebenfalls nicht angesprochen wird, mit welchen Mitteln (d.h. welchen Sprachen) die Metaschemata definiert werden können.

7 Zusammenfassung und Ausblick

Im Vordergrund dieses Papiers stand die Einführung einer Metaebene für ein FDBS, wobei von einer wissenschaftlichen Anwendung, der Molekularbiologie, ausgegangen wurde. Nach einer kurzen Einführung in das Projekt Moby Dick sind wir auf die Architektur der Metaebene eingegangen und haben gezeigt, wie durch die Metaebene die Zusammenhänge zwischen den lokalen, den Komponenten- und dem föderierten Schema explizit dargestellt werden können. Weiter haben wir die auf der Metaebene definierten Sprachen und ihre Anwendungsbereiche betrachtet sowie die Abfrageverarbeitung diskutiert. Es wurde gezeigt, dass die Konzepte der Metaebene nicht nur den DBI unterstützen, sondern auch den Anforderungen der Molekularbiologie entgegenkommen. Der Nutzen der Metaebene ist im einzelnen der folgende:

- *Unterstützung bei der Homogenisierung:* Da in lokalen Schemata häufig nicht die volle Semantik der Daten dargestellt ist, sondern stattdessen in Anwendungsprogrammen steckt, muss der Entwerfer des lokalen Schemas in den Homogenisierungsprozess miteinbezogen werden. Die Homogenisierung kann somit nicht voll automatisch erfolgen, sondern höchstens vom FDBS unterstützt werden. In unserem Ansatz erhält der DBI durch die Abbildungsbeziehungstypen Unterstützung. Er kann sich vom FDBS einen Vorschlag unterbreiten lassen, wie das lokale Schema in ein Komponentenschema transformiert werden könnte. Es liegt dann im Ermessen des DBI, diesen Vorschlag (oder Teile desselben) zu akzeptieren oder nicht und gegebenenfalls die Homogenisierung manuell mit Hilfe der MDML durchzuführen.

- *Unterstützung bei der Abfrage von Informationen über bestehende Integrationen:* Der DBI kann sich über existierende Metadaten und die Zusammenhänge zwischen den Schemata und somit über bestehende Integrationen informieren. Dies wird unter anderem durch die Metadatenmanipulationssprache (MDML) und die explizite Darstellung der Abbildungsbeziehungen unterstützt. Wären diese fest implementiert, könnte auch keine deklarative Sprache zu deren Abfrage definiert werden und der DBI müsste sich in den Programmcode vertiefen.

- *Unterstützung bei der Abfrageverarbeitung:* Durch die Verwendung eines operationalen Ansatzes für die Abfrageverarbeitung müssen globale Abfragen nicht in die lokale DML übersetzt werden. Zudem werden die objektorientierten Eigenschaften des Metamodells ausgenützt, indem DML-Operationen auf Metaebene als Verhalten von Metatypen implementiert werden (sowohl im föderierten Metaschema als auch in den lokalen Metaschemata) und deren Aufruf dem Verschicken von Nachrichten entspricht.

- *Unterstützung für die Erweiterung des globalen Datenmodells:* Da auch auf Metaebene eine Datendefinitionssprache (MDDL) definiert ist, kann das globale Datenmodell erweitert werden. Solche Erweiterungen sind dann nötig, wenn existierende Datenmodellkonzepte den wechselnden Anforderungen der Molekularbiologie nicht mehr genügen. Sie werden durch Hinzunahme von neuen Metatypen oder -beziehungen im föderierten Metaschema realisiert, was der Erweiterung der DDL und — durch die Metamethoden der neuen Metatypen — einiger DML-Operationen entspricht. Selbstverständlich genügt dies allein nicht; vielmehr müssen auch entsprechende Erweiterungen der Speicherkonzepte zur Verfügung gestellt werden, was im Rahmen dieses Papiers allerdings nicht weiter betrachtet wurde.

- *Unterstützung der Modellierung anwendungsspezifischer Metadaten und Funktionen:* Ebenfalls durch die MDDL wird es möglich, anwendungsspezifische Metadaten wie die Masseinheit auf Metaebene zu modellieren. Die Zuweisung eines Wertes erfolgt dann mit

Hilfe der MDML. Ebenfalls mit MDML können Funktionen auf Objektbehältern (also auf Mengen von Objekten) statt nur auf einzelnen Objekten definiert werden.

Momentan arbeiten wir an der Implementierung der beschriebenen Konzepte auf ObjectStore ([Obje92]). Das Metaschema für die Komponentenschemata und das föderierte Schema (wie in Abschnitt 3.1 erwähnt, genügt für die Implementierung *ein* Metaschema) wurden bereits implementiert, ebenso dasjenige für ObjectStore und die Abbildungsbeziehungstypen dazwischen. Unter die zukünftigen Arbeiten fällt die Integration von Oracle als zweites DBS, die Entwicklung von Schemaparsern, deren Eingabe lokale Schemata sind und die als Ausgabe die entsprechenden Metadaten liefern, sowie ein Test mit realen molekularbiologischen Daten.

Literatur

[ABDD89] Atkinson, M., Bancilhon, F., DeWitt, D., Dittrich, K.R., Maier, D., Zdonik, S., "The Object-Oriented Database System Manifesto", *Proceedings of DOOD*, Kyoto, December 1989

[Ahme91] Ahmed, R., et al., "The Pegasus Heterogeneous Multidatabae System", *IEEE Computer*, Vol. 24, No. 12, December 1991

[Bert88] Bertino, E., et al., "The COMANDOS Integration System: an Object-Oriented Approach to the Interconnection of Heterogeneous Applications", *Proceedings 2nd International Workshop on Object-Oriented Database Systems (OODBS)*, Bad Münster am Stein-Ebernburg, Germany, September 1988

[BHP92] Bright, M.W., Hurson, A.R., Pakzad, S.H., "A Taxonomy and Current Issues in Multidatabase Systems", *IEEE Computer*, March 1992

[BNPS89] Bertino, E., Negri, M., Pelagatti, G., Sbattella, L., "Integration of Heterogeneous Database Applications through an Object-Oriented Interface", *Information Sciences*, Vol. 14, No. 5, 1989

[CL88] Connors, T., Lyngbaek, P., "Providing Uniform Access to Heterogeneous Information Bases", *Proceedings 2nd International Workshop on Object-Oriented Database Systems (OODBS)*, Bad Münster am Stein-Ebernburg, Germany, September 1988

[DH84] Dazal, U., Hwang, H.-Y., "View Definition and Generalization for Database Integration in a Multidatabase System", *IEEE Transactions on Software Engineering*, Vol. SE-10, No. 6, November 1984

[FABC88] Fishman, D.H., Annevelink, J., Beech, D., Chow, E.-C., Connors, T., Davis, J.W., Hoch, C.G., Kent, W., Lyngbaek, P., Mahbod, B., Neimat, M.-A., Risch, T., Ryan, T.A., Shan, M.-C., Wilkinson, W.K., "Overview of the Iris DBMS", Hewlett-Packard Laboratories, P.O. Box 10490, Palo Alto, California 94303-0971, 1988

[FJP90] French, J.C., Jones, A.K., Pfaltz, J.L., "Summary of the Final Report of the NSF Workshop on Scientific Database Management", *SIGMOD RECORD*, Vol. 19, No. 4, December 1990

[GDGS93] Geppert, A., Dittrich, K.R., Goebel, V., Scherrer, S., "The NO^2 Data Model", Technical Report No. 93.09, Institut für Informatik, Universät Zürich, April 1993

[Härt94] Härtig, M., "Objektorientierte Integration von autonomen Datenhaltungssystemen", Dissertation, Institut für Informatik, Universität Zürich, 1994

[Jone91] Jones, A.K., "The Scientific Data Decade", *COMPUTER*, September 1991

[KS91] Kim, W., Seo, J., "Classifying Schematic and Data Heterogeneity in Multidatabase Systems", *IEEE Computer*, Vol. 24, No. 12, December 1991

[Motr87] Motro, A., "Superviews: Virtual Integration of Multiple Databases", *IEEE Transactions on Software Engineering*, Vol. 13, No. 7, 1987

[Obje92] ObjectStore User Guide, Release 2.0, ObjectDesign, Inc., Burlington, USA, October 1992

[RD94] Rieche, B., Dittrich, K.R., "A Federated DBMS-Based Integrated Environment for Molecular Biology", *Proceedings of the 7th SSDBM*, Charlottesville, Virginia, September 1994

[SL90] Sheth, A.P., Larson, J.A., "Federated Database Systems for Managing Distributed, Heterogeneous, and Autonomous Databases", *ACM Computing Surveys*, Vol. 22, No. 3, pp. 183-235, September 1990

[UW91] Urban, S.D., Wu, J., "Resolving Semantic Heterogeneity through the Explicit Representation of Data Model Semantics", *ACM SIGMOD RECORD*, Vol. 20, No. 4, December 1991

Formbasierte Suche nach komplementären 3D-Oberflächen in einer Protein-Datenbank[1]

Martin Ester, Hans-Peter Kriegel, Thomas Seidl, Xiaowei Xu

Institut für Informatik, Universität München
Leopoldstr. 11B, D-80802 München
{ ester | kriegel | seidl | xu }@informatik.uni-muenchen.de

Zusammenfassung:
Die Komplementarität der 3D-Oberflächen von Proteinen ist neben den physikochemischen Eigenschaften ein entscheidendes Kriterium dafür, ob und an welchen Stellen zwei Proteine miteinander wechselwirken, d.h. docken, können. Anders als in Geo-Datenbanksystemen, die Anfragen nach Objekten mit einer gegebenen räumlichen Lage und Ausdehnung unterstützen, werden deshalb beim Protein-Docking Objekte aufgrund ihrer Form gesucht. Wir beginnen mit einer Darstellung der Anforderungen dieser neuen Anwendung an Datenbanksysteme. Zur effizienten Anfragebearbeitung übernehmen wir die in Geo-Datenbanksystemen bewährte Technik der mehrstufigen Anfragebearbeitung, die den Kreis der potentiellen Dockingkandidaten sehr schnell einengt. Der Filterschritt benutzt eine Beschreibung der geometrischen Oberflächencharakteristik mit Hilfe rotations- und translationsunabhängiger Kennzahlen. Ein mehrdimensionaler Join liefert Dockingpartner, die Oberflächenpunkte mit komplementären Kennzahlwerten besitzen. Im Verfeinerungsschritt werden selektierte Oberflächenpunkte mit ihren Nachbarn zu 3D-Regionen erweitert und deren Komplementarität gemessen. Die mehrstufige Anfragebearbeitung wird in ein Docking-System integriert, das auf einem kommerziellen objektorientierten Datenbanksystem basiert.

Schlüsselwörter: Anfragebearbeitung in Geo-Datenbanksystemen, Datenbanken in der Biologie, Dockingsuche in Protein-Datenbanken, Ähnlichteilsuche, 3D-Formbeschreibungen.

1 Einleitung

Die Funktion eines Proteins besteht in der Interaktion mit anderen Biomolekülen, etwa wieder Proteinen, DNA oder auch kleineren Partnern. Da die Interaktionen eine Anlagerung der betroffenen Partner aneinander darstellen, bezeichnet man sie als *Docking*. Wir entwickeln ein Protein-Docking-Datenbanksystem, das für ein vorgegebenes Anfrageprotein mögliche Interaktionspartner in einer Datenbank von Proteinen finden soll. Neben den physikochemischen Eigenschaften der Moleküle spielt die Geometrie der Moleküloberfläche an der Interaktionsstelle eine zentrale Rolle beim Docking. Das Datenbanksystem muß deshalb Anfragen nach Proteinen mit ähnlichen bzw. komplementären Oberflächen beantworten.

Geo-Datenbanksysteme dienen der Verwaltung von räumlich ausgedehnten Objekten in Anwendungen wie CAD-Datenbanken, geographischen Informationssystemen oder Bild-Datenbanken. Typische Anfragen in Geo-Datenbanksystemen suchen Objekte mit einer definierten räumlichen Lage, z.B. liefert eine Region-Query alle Objekte, die eine gegebene Anfrageregion schneiden und ein Spatial Join [BKSS 94] alle Paare von Objekten, die in einer gegebenen räumlichen Beziehung zueinander stehen. Zur effizienten Anfragebearbeitung in Geo-Datenbanksystemen haben wir neben räumlichen Zugriffsstrukturen Methoden der Approximation, der Dekomposition und der Clusterung [BK 94] entwickelt. Zur Beantwortung von Anfragen

1. Das diesem Bericht zugrundeliegende Vorhaben wird mit Mitteln des Bundesministeriums für Forschung und Technologie unter dem Förderkennzeichen 01 IB 307 B gefördert. Die Verantwortung für den Inhalt dieser Veröffentlichung liegt bei den Autoren.

nach Objekten mit gleicher oder ähnlicher Form unabhängig von der räumlichen Lage, wie in unserer Anwendung erforderlich, sind bisherige Algorithmen der Anfragebearbeitung in Geo-Datenbanksystemen jedoch nicht geeignet.

Es gibt in der Literatur einige Vorschläge, Geo-Datenbanksysteme zur Unterstützung von Anfragen nach der Form von Objekten zu erweitern. Zwei Ansätze werden dazu verfolgt:

- Normierung der Lage im geometrischen Raum
  [Jag 91] und [MG 93] beschreiben die Form der Objekte durch eine geordnete Menge von Punkten bzw. Rechtecken, deren Lage im Raum normiert wird. Die Punkte bzw. Rechtecke werden in Punkte eines höherdimensionalen Raums transformiert und mit Hilfe einer der bekannten Punktzugriffsstrukturen abgespeichert. Die Suche nach einem Objekt mit gegebener Form wird dann als Region-Query formuliert. Beide Artikel betrachten 2D-Objekte. [SKSH 89] behandelt die Ähnlichteilsuche für rotationssymmetrische CAD-Bauteile. Die 3D-Bauteile werden durch ihre zweidimensionale Kontur repräsentiert. Die Lage der Konturen im Raum wird geeignet normiert und für die Suche genutzt.
- Abstraktion von der Lage mit Hilfe von geometrischen Kennzahlen
  Die Form eines Objekts wird nicht direkt durch seine Geometrie, sondern mit Hilfe von Kennzahlen beschrieben, die die Charakteristik der Geometrie in lageunabhängiger Weise beschreiben. Solche Kennzahlen können z.B. mit Hilfe einer diskreten Fourier-Transformation gewonnen werden, wie sie in [AFS 93] und [FRM 94] für eine Datenbank von Zeitreihen reeller Zahlen eingesetzt wird.

Alle obigen Verfahren arbeiten jedoch im 2D und sind somit für dreidimensionale Protein-oberflächen nicht direkt geeignet. Unser Lösungsansatz basiert auf der in Geo-Datenbanksystemen üblichen Architektur einer mehrstufigen Anfragebearbeitung (vgl. [BHKS 93], [KSB 93]). Im Filterschritt verwenden wir, wie auch in der Molekularbiologie vorgeschlagen, geometrische Kennzahlen zur Abstraktion von der Lage. Im Verfeinerungsschritt normieren wir die Lage der Objekte, um die 3D-Geometrie von Dockingkandidaten miteinander vergleichen zu können.

Der Artikel gliedert sich wie folgt: Kapitel 2 beschreibt die wichtigsten Anforderungen an Datenbanksysteme, die die Anwendung des Protein-Protein-Docking stellt. In Kapitel 3 wird die Architektur unserer Anfragebearbeitung vorgestellt. Definition, Berechnung und Komplementierung der Oberflächenkennzahlen werden in Kapitel 4 dargestellt. In Kapitel 5 werden der Filterschritt und der Verfeinerungsschritt der Anfragebearbeitung behandelt. Kapitel 6 faßt die Ergebnisse zusammen und gibt einen Ausblick.

2 Anforderungen des Protein-Protein-Docking an Datenbanksysteme

Die Vorhersage von Dockingvorgängen zwischen zwei Molekülen ist ein aktueller Forschungszweig in der Molekularbiologie, in dem neuartige Anforderungen an Datenbanksysteme auftreten. Unsere Aufgabenstellung im Projekt BIOWEPRO (Biomolekulare Wechselwirkungen von Proteinen) [Ald 94] besteht darin, für ein vorgegebenes Anfrageprotein mögliche Interaktionspartner in einer Datenbank von Proteinen zu finden. Zusätzlich soll die relative Position eines Antwortmoleküls zum Anfrageprotein angegeben werden, deren sechs Freiheitsgrade sich mit drei Translations- und drei Rotationsparametern beschreiben lassen. Ein Tupel (Protein, Protein, relative Position) bezeichnen wir als *Konstellation*. Alle Autoren stimmen darin überein, daß beim Protein-Protein-Docking neben den physikochemischen Eigenschaften der Moleküle die Geometrie der Moleküloberfläche an der Interaktionsstelle eine große Rolle spielt.

Als Datengrundlage stehen die kristallographisch ermittelten Atomkoordinaten von Proteinen und Proteinkomplexen in der Brookhaven Protein Data Bank (PDB) zur Verfügung [Ber 77]. Die PDB enthält derzeit knapp 3.000 Proteine, Enzyme und Viren [PDB 94] und wächst ständig. Die PDB ist eine Sammlung von Files, in denen jeweils die Daten eines Proteins als Text enthalten sind. Ein Datenbankmanagementsystem im Sinne von [Ull 88] ist nicht vorhanden.

Ein *Protein* besteht aus mehreren Ketten, die sich wiederum aus Aminosäuren und diese aus (insgesamt mehreren hundert bis tausend) Atomen zusammensetzen. Die Atome besitzen je nach Typ verschiedene Radien, Ladungen etc. und eine Position im 3D-Raum, gegeben durch die Koordinaten ihres Zentrums. Mit Hilfe der Eigenschaften der Atome lassen sich die physikochemischen Eigenschaften des Proteins an jedem 3D-Punkt berechnen. Proteine sind also sowohl sehr große als auch sehr komplex strukturierte Objekte.

Die *Oberfläche* eines Proteins wird als diejenige Fläche definiert, die für eine Probenkugel mit gegebenem Radius zugänglich ist [Ric 77]. Sie setzt sich aus konkaven, sattelförmigen und konvexen Flächenstücken zusammen (siehe das Beispiel in Abbildung 1).

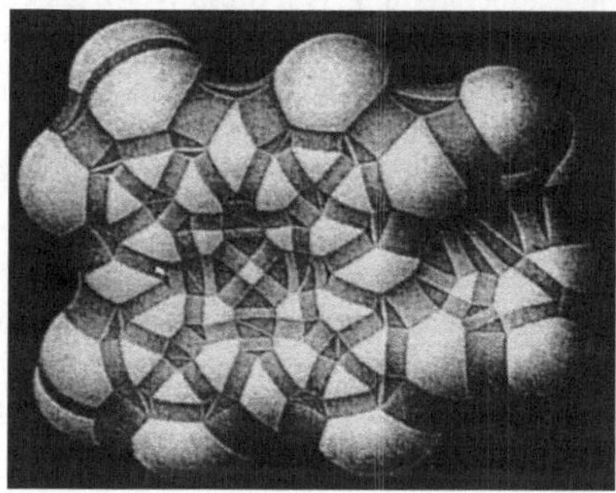

Abb. 1: Oberfläche einer Teilgruppe von Hämoglobin [Con 83].

Diese analytische Repräsentation ist z.B. für die Berechnung des Normalenvektors eines Oberflächenpunkts geeignet. Durch eine möglichst gleichmäßige Verteilung von Punkten erhält man eine gepunktete Repräsentation der Oberfläche, die z.B. für die Berechnung von geometrischen Oberflächeneigenschaften benötigt wird. Die Anwendung erfordert also eine Mehrfachrepräsentation der Proteinoberflächen in der Datenbank.

Auf den oben skizzierten Objekten der Datenbank arbeiten Dockingalgorithmen, deren zentrales Problem die enorme Größe des Suchraums aller möglichen Konstellationen ist. Die PDB enthält derzeit ca. 2500 Proteine, die in der von uns gewählten Auflösung durchschnittlich 2000 Oberflächenpunkte besitzen. Das ergibt ca. $2500 * 2000 * 2000 = 10^{10}$ verschiedene Konstellationen, die für die Bearbeitung einer Anfrage relevant sind. Die bisherigen Verfahren beschränken sich alle auf das 1:1-Docking, d.h. auf die Interaktion eines Paares von Proteinen. Wir untersuchen daher im folgenden (Übersicht siehe Abbildung 2) Algorithmen aus der Literatur auf ihre Anwendbarkeit für das 1:n-Docking, d.h. die Interaktion eines Proteins mit allen Proteinen der Datenbank.

Referenz	Verfahren	Laufzeit	Anzahl Beispiele, Erfolg (+ / −)
[Kat 92]	gitterbasierte Suche, diskrete FFT	Ø 7,5 Std.	3+, 4−
[PD 93]	Simulated Annealing	Ø 30 Std.	3+
[Con 86b]	Matchen von Punkten ("knobs and holes")	17 Std.	1+
[BMH 92]	Matchen von Profilen; nur 2D, kein 3D	0,3 Std.	1 ?
[HT 94]	Matchen von Schnitten	3 - 24 Std.	3+, 1−
[FNNW 93]	Matchen von Dreiecken im 3D	0,5-0,75 Std.	1+, 1−

Abb. 2: Vergleich von ausgewählten Dockingverfahren

Bei den Verfahren in [Kat 92] und [PD 93] werden für zu untersuchende Proteinpaare alle Schritte der Dockingsuche jedesmal neu durchlaufen. Es ist keine Vorverarbeitung möglich, so daß sich die Ansätze nicht für das 1:n-Docking eignen. Solche Verfahren eignen sich also besser für Verfeinerungsschritte als für die erste Suche nach Dockingpartnern und -stellen. Wegen der immensen Größe des Suchraums eignen sich für den ersten Filterschritt einer Datenbanksuche besser solche Methoden, die eine Vorbearbeitung der Moleküle durchführen. Die Ermittlung charakteristischer Formbeschreibungen sowie eine translations- und rotationsinvariante Darstellung ermöglichen eine Indexunterstützung für die Suche.

In der Literatur finden sich dazu einige Anregungen. [Con 86b] berechnet auf der Protein-oberfläche "knobs and holes" als Punkte mit lokal extremen Werten für "Solid Angle" (vgl. Kapitel 4). Diese Punkte charakterisieren Aus- und Einbuchtungen auf der Oberfläche und eignen sich für die paarweise Gegenüberstellung. Auf diese Weise lassen sich erfolgversprechende Dockingkonstellationen ohne vollständiges Durchlaufen eines Rasters ermitteln. [BMH 92] und [HT 94] beschreiben die Formen von Molekülen durch 2D-Schnittkonturen mit Hilfe von Polygonen, auf denen in der Anfragebearbeitung ähnliche Ausschnitte ermittelt werden. Die Verallgemeinerung von 2D auf 3D ist dabei noch nicht zufriedenstellend gelöst. [FNNW 93] arbeitet mit Distanzmatrizen und "geometrischem Hashing" und ist leider nicht ausreichend robust.

Ein allgemeiner Algorithmus zur Lösung des Protein-Dockingproblems ist derzeit noch nicht absehbar. Die "Korrektheit" von Algorithmen wird in der Regel nur an wenigen bekannten Beispielkomplexen überprüft. Diese Prüfung ist ein grundlegendes Problem, da die Korrektheit einer Vorhersage für unbekannte Dockingpartner nur im biochemischen Laborexperiment nachgewiesen werden kann und sehr zeitaufwendig ist.

Zusammenfassend läßt sich feststellen, daß das Protein-Protein-Docking eine große Herausforderung für Datenbanksysteme darstellt. Folgende *Anforderungen* sind zu erfüllen:

- Verwaltung komplexer Objekte
- Verwaltung von 3D-Freiformflächen
- effiziente 3D-Ähnlichkeitssuche.

Im Rahmen dieses Artikels konzentrieren wir uns auf Ansätze zur Erfüllung der letzten Anforderung.

3 Architektur der Anfragebearbeitung

Die enorme Größe des Konstellationsraums, die in Kapitel 2 skizziert wurde, legt eine Anfragebearbeitung in mehreren Schritten nahe, um akzeptable Laufzeiten zu erreichen. Wegen der anfänglich sehr großen Menge potentieller Konstellationen wird in den ersten Schritten auf ihre genaue Untersuchung zu Gunsten geringerer Filterkosten pro Konstellation verzichtet. Wir arbeiten nicht auf der komplexen 3D-Oberfläche, sondern auf einer Abstraktion mit Hilfe geometrischer Oberflächenkennzahlen. Wegen der immer kleiner werdenden Menge von potentiellen Dockingstellen dürfen die späteren Schritte mit höheren Kosten pro Dockingkandidat verbunden sein und können deshalb auf der 3D-Oberfläche selbst arbeiten.

Da bisher kein Algorithmus existiert, der mit Sicherheit feststellt, ob eine Konstellation dockt, müssen die vom Dockingsystem gelieferten Resultate letztendlich vom Molekularbiologen im Experiment überprüft werden. Im Unterschied zu Geo-Datenbanksystemen, die evtl. schon im Filterschritt Antworten finden können, kann es in allen Schritten unserer Anfragebearbeitung deshalb nur darum gehen, nicht in Frage kommende Konstellationen zu verwerfen.

Abbildung 3 stellt die Architektur der Anfragebearbeitung dar, die aus folgenden Schritten besteht:

Filterschritt
Berechnung der Oberflächenkennzahlen für das Anfrage-Protein
Auswahl der Extrempunkte unter den Oberflächenpunkten
Join für die ausgewählten Punkte von Datenbank und Anfrage

Verfeinerungsschritt
Erzeugen von Regionen aus den Extrempunkten
Übereinanderlegen zweier Regionen
Bewertung der Ähnlichkeit der 3D-Regionen

Physiko-chemische Bewertung

Abb. 3: Architektur der Anfragebearbeitung

- *Filterschritt mit geometrischen Kennzahlen*
  Für jeden Oberflächenpunkt der Proteine in der Datenbank werden verschiedene Kennzahlen berechnet, die die charakteristischen Eigenschaften der Geometrie in lageunabhängiger Weise darstellen. Von der großen Menge der Oberflächenpunkte werden diejenigen ausgewählt, bei denen die Oberflächenkennzahlen einen lokalen Extremwert annehmen. Bei Auswahl von ca. 50 von durchschnittlich 2000 Oberflächenpunkten eines Proteins erreichen wir eine Einschränkung des Konstellationsraums um den Faktor $40 * 40 = 1600$, es verbleiben noch $6.25 \cdot 10^6$ potentielle Dockingkonstellationen. Die Kennzahlen der ausgewählten Punkte werden komplementiert und mit einem Verweis auf den Punkt abgespeichert. Zur eigentlichen Anfragebearbeitung werden die Kennzahlen für ein gegebenes Anfrageprotein berechnet. Der Filterschritt liefert mit Hilfe eines mehrdimensionalen Joins Paare aus je einem Punkt eines Proteins aus der Datenbank und einem Punkt des Anfrageproteins, deren Kennzahlen mindestens eine vorgegebene Ähnlichkeit besitzen.

- *Verfeinerungsschritt mit der 3D-Geometrie*
  Zum Vergleich der 3D-Geometrie werden räumlich ausgedehnte Objekte benötigt. Deshalb werden die vom Filterschritt gelieferten Extrempunkte beider Dockingpartner mit ihren Nachbarn und den verbindenden Kanten der Triangulierung zu Regionen zusammengefaßt. Die 3D-Geometrie der Regionen eines Kandidatenpaares wird nun miteinander verglichen, wofür die beste relative Position der zu vergleichenden Regionen im 3D zu bestimmen ist. Ergebnis des Verfeinerungsschritts sind Konstellationen von zwei Proteinen.

- *Bewertung der Konstellationen nach physikochemischen Eigenschaften*
  In den ersten beiden Schritten der Anfragebearbeitung werden nur die geometrischen Kriterien für Dockingkandidaten überprüft. Die fürs Docking ebenfalls relevanten physikalischen und chemischen Eigenschaften der Dockingregionen werden erst im letzten Schritt einbezogen, weil sie von der relativen Position zweier Proteine abhängen, die erst im Verfeinerungsschritt bestimmt wird.

4 Geometrische Oberflächenkennzahlen

Der Filterschritt der Anfragebearbeitung benutzt eine Beschreibung der geometrischen Oberflächencharakteristik mit Hilfe verschiedener Kennzahlen. Die Kennzahlen werden für jeden Punkt der Oberfläche berechnet und drücken geometrische Eigenschaften der Umgebung des Punktes aus. In der Literatur finden sich verschiedene Vorschläge für Kennzahlen. Für erste

Untersuchungen haben wir *Solid Angle* (SA) aus [Con 86a] sowie *Local Shape Index* (LSI) aus [Koe 90] gewählt, da sie sich in den Experimenten als gute Formbeschreibung erwiesen haben und einfach zu komplementieren sind. Die Auswahl einer für die Dockingsuche wirklich gut geeigneten Kombination von Kennzahlen ist eine wichtige, noch offene Frage.

Bei der zählenden Ermittlung des SA legt man eine Meßkugel K zugrunde, auf deren Oberfläche man eine bestimmte Anzahl n von Punkten gleichmäßig verteilt. Diese Kugel K legt man nun um P und zählt dann diejenigen Punkte auf K, die nicht im Inneren des Moleküls liegen (vgl. Abbildung 4). Teilt man das Ergebnis durch n und normiert es auf 4π, so erhält man ein Maß für den 3D-Öffnungswinkel ("Solid Angle") des Moleküls im Punkt P. Über den Radius der Meßkugel K hat man eine Skalierungsmöglichkeit für diese Kennzahl.

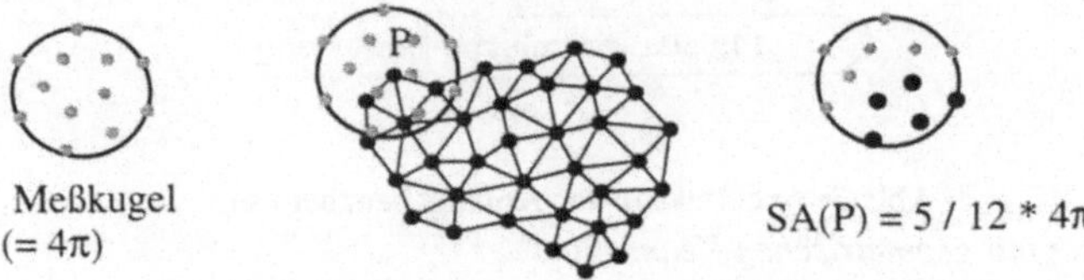

Abb. 4: Berechnung des SA für den Punkt P

Der LSI ist eine skalare Größe und beschreibt die Form der Oberfläche in der Umgebung eines Punktes P. Er kann als Maßzahl für die Konkavität bzw. Konvexität der Umgebung von P verstanden werden. Seine Werte liegen zwischen -1 und +1, die zugehörigen Formen sind in Abbildung 5 veranschaulicht.

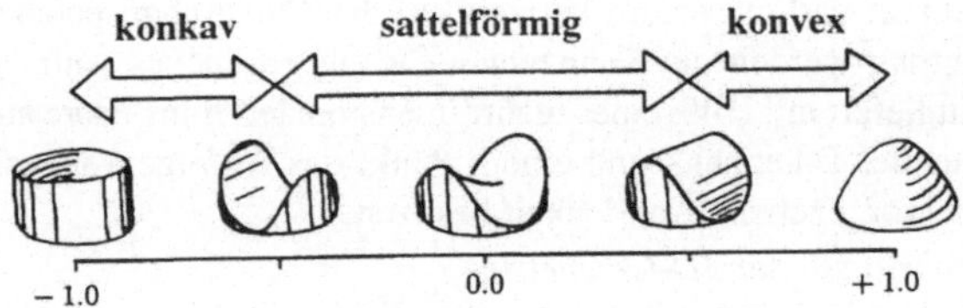

Abb. 5: Bedeutung des LSI (aus [Koe 90], S. 322)

Zur Berechnung des LSI am Punkt P wird ein elliptisches bzw. hyperbolisches Paraboloid in die Umgebung von P auf der triangulierten Oberfläche eingepaßt. Dann ermittelt man die beiden Hauptkrümmungen k_{min} und k_{max} als Eigenwerte der Hessematrix, die die zweiten Ableitungen des Paraboloids enthält, und faßt diese Krümmungswerte nach [Koe 90] zusammen.

Ein wichtiger Parameter für LSI ist der Selektionsabstand ("Radius") r, über den wir bestimmen, welche Nachbarn von P zum Einpassen berücksichtigt werden. Wir messen r entlang der Dreieckskanten und wählen dadurch neben den direkten Nachbarn eines Knotens auch weiter entfernt liegende Stützpunkte aus. Dadurch haben wir ein Maß, wie lokal oder regional die Form der Umgebung von P bestimmt werden soll. Für unsere Untersuchungen haben wir für r Werte zwischen 3 Å und 8 Å gewählt (Abbildung 6).

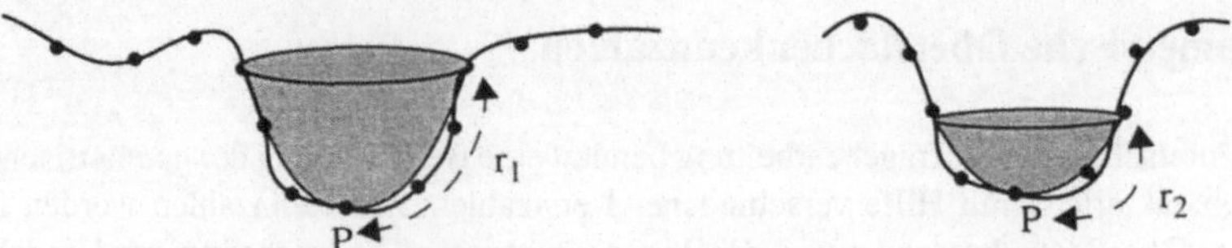

Abb. 6: Berechnung des LSI mit Selektionsabstand r_1 bzw. r_2

Für das Protein-Protein-Docking benötigen wir nicht Oberflächen, die ähnlich sind, sondern solche mit einer komplementären Form. Zur Vorbereitung der Anfragebearbeitung speichern wir die Kennzahlen der in der Datenbank gespeicherten Proteine komplementiert ab. Bei Annahme eines vernachlässigbaren Abstands der beiden Proteine an einer Dockingstelle können die Kennzahlen folgendermaßen komplementiert werden:

- Solid Angle: das Komplement erhält man als Differenz zum Maximalwert 4π.
- Local Shape Index: das Komplement ergibt sich durch Wechsel des Vorzeichens.

Mit SA und LSI haben wir nun zwei geometrische Kennzahlen, die die Form einer Oberflächenregion beschreiben und sich einfach komplementieren lassen. Sie werden im Filterschritt der Anfragebearbeitung eingesetzt, die im nächsten Kapitel beschrieben wird.

5 Die Schritte der Anfragebearbeitung

Der Filterschritt der Anfragebearbeitung, der auf den geometrischen Kennzahlen arbeitet, soll eine wesentliche Reduktion der Menge potentieller Konstellationen bewirken, ohne jedoch tatsächliche Dockingstellen auszuschließen. Zur effizienten Unterstützung des Filterschritts setzen wir eine mehrdimensionale Zugriffsstruktur, den R*-Baum [BKSS 90], ein. Beim Einfügen eines Proteins in die Datenbank wird folgende *Vorverarbeitung* durchgeführt:

- *Berechnung der Oberflächenkennzahlen.* Für jeden Oberflächenpunkt des in der Datenbank abzuspeichernden Proteins werden die Werte der Kennzahlen SA und LSI berechnet.
- *Auswahl der Extrempunkte der Oberfläche.* Alle Punkte der triangulierten Oberfläche, die bezüglich des SA in einer Umgebung von 6Å minimal oder maximal sind, werden ausgewählt. Dieses Vorgehen beruht auf der Annahme, daß die geometrisch signifikanten Regionen (konvexe oder konkave) beim Docking bedeutsam sind.
- *Update des R*-Baums für die Protein-Datenbank.* Die Kennzahlen der ausgewählten Punkte werden komplementiert. Die erhaltenen Punkte im k-dimensionalen Raum der Kennzahlen werden in einem R*-Baum abgespeichert und mit einem Verweis auf das Protein und die geometrische Lage innerhalb des Proteins versehen.

Die eigentliche *Anfragebearbeitung* läuft folgendermaßen ab:

- *Aufbau eines R*-Baums für das Anfrageprotein.* Für ein Anfrageprotein werden wie beim Einfügen in die Datenbank die Kennzahlen berechnet, die analog in einem zweiten R*-Baum verwaltet werden.
- *Join zwischen Datenbank und Anfrageprotein.* Ein mehrdimensionaler Join auf den beiden R*-Bäumen liefert alle Paare von je einem Punkt eines Proteins aus der Datenbank und einem Punkt des Anfrageproteins, deren Distanz im Kennzahlenraum kleiner als ein gegebenes ε ist. ε ist als minimaler Wert zu wählen, bei dem die bekannten Dockingstellen noch sicher gefunden werden.

Der Filterschritt wurde implementiert und mit Proteinen aus der PDB getestet. Dazu wurden Proteinkomplexe ausgewählt, die aus zwei oder mehreren Proteinen im gedockten Zustand bestehen. Sie wurden in ihre Teile zerlegt und in der Datenbank abgespeichert. Die Teilproteine wurden dann als Anfragen an die Datenbank gestellt. Diese Anfragen müssen in ihren Antwortmengen die aus der PDB bekannten Dockingpartner enthalten.

Abbildung 7 stellt die Anzahlen gefundener Punktpaare für die beiden Proteine 2ptc (Trypsin mit Trypsin Inhibitor) und 2pab (Präalbumin) bei verschiedenen Werten für ε dar.

Der Filterschritt mit allen Oberflächenpunkten hat erwartungsgemäß eine viel zu niedrige Selektivität, man erhält als Antwort etwa 20% aller Paare von Oberflächenpunkten. Bei Beschränkung auf die Extrempunkte der Oberfläche verbessert sich die Selektivität des Filterschritts um den Faktor 1000 bis 2000, was der Reduktion der Anzahl der Oberflächenpunkte um den Faktor 20 bis 40 etwa entspricht.

Protein	ε	Alle Punktepaare	Suche auf allen Punkten	Suche auf Extrempunkten	Punktepaare auf Dockingstelle
2ptc	1.5		$0.53 \cdot 10^6$	236	1
	2.0	$2.77 \cdot 10^6$	$0.73 \cdot 10^6$	341	2
	3.0		$1.17 \cdot 10^6$	545	2
2pab	1.5		$0.46 \cdot 10^6$	617	0
	2.0	$3.16 \cdot 10^6$	$0.66 \cdot 10^6$	760	1
	3.0		$1.13 \cdot 10^6$	1022	4

Abb. 7: Anzahlen gefundener Antwortpaare

Im Fall von 2pab wird die Dockingstelle bei $\varepsilon = 1.5$ nicht als Antwort geliefert, so daß man mit einem ε von mindestens 2.0 arbeiten muß. Eine Ursache für dieses relativ große ε liegt im bisherigen einfachen Verfahren zur Auswahl der Extrempunkte. Es treten nämlich Fälle auf, in denen die auf beiden Dockingpartnern gewählten Extrempunkte und damit auch ihre Kennzahlen relativ weit voneinander entfernt sind.

Der Filterschritt der Anfragebearbeitung liefert Paare von Punkten, die mit ihren Umgebungen für komplementäre Regionen stehen. Im Verfeinerungsschritte sind die Konstellationen explizit zu bestimmen sowie die geometrische Komplementarität der beiden Partner zu bewerten. Dazu sind folgende Aufgaben zu bearbeiten: Die Bildung von Regionen, die Normierung der Lage im Raum, die Bestimmung der relativen Positionen und die Berechnung einer Maßzahl für die Komplementarität.

Wir definieren die *Region* zu einem Punkt P als Menge von Oberflächenpunkten aus der Umgebung von P. Dazu wählen wir diejenigen Punkte aus, die von P aus über Kanten der Triangulierung innerhalb eines vorgegebenen Abstandes zu erreichen sind.

Die Region werden nun in eine normierte Lage gebracht, d.h. es wird eine Darstellung bestimmt, die translations- und rotationsinvariant ist. Für diese Normierung benötigen wir den Referenzpunkt R, den Normalenvektor N und eine Hauptachse H der Region. Alle drei Parameter werden durch die gewählten Approximationen zur Verfügung gestellt. Die Lage einer Region läßt sich durch sechs Parameter beschreiben: drei Koordinatenwerte für die Translation und drei Winkelwerte für die Rotation. Im ersten Schritt der Normierung werden die drei Freiheitsgrade der Translation bestimmt, im zweiten Schritt zwei Freiheitsgrade der Rotation. Zum Schluß wird eine Hauptachsentransformation durchgeführt, wodurch der dritte Freiheitsgrad der Rotation festgelegt wird (vgl. Abbildung 8).

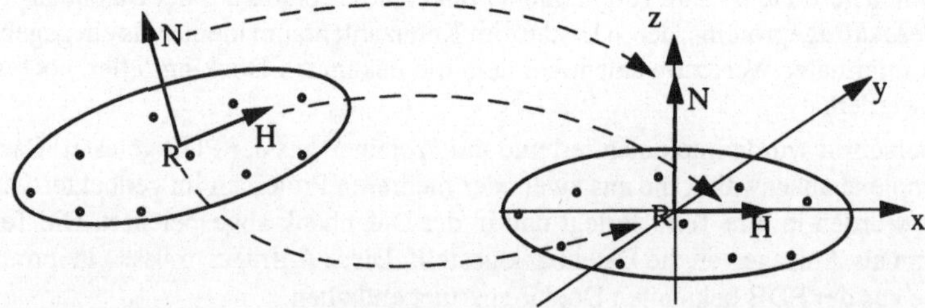

Abb. 8: Normierung der Lage einer Region

Mit Hilfe der normierten Lage wird die Konstellation genau bestimmt, d.h. die beiden Interaktionspartner werden zu einem Komplex zusammengesetzt. Dies geschieht dadurch, daß die beiden Regionen in ihrer normierten Lage übereinandergelegt werden.

6 Zusammenfassung und Ausblick

Das Protein-Docking ist eine Aufgabenstellung mit neuartigen Anforderungen an Datenbanksysteme. Die Objekte sind Körper im 3D mit komplexen Oberflächen. Das wesentliche Suchkriterium ist die Form der Objekte. Die absolute Lage und Orientierung der Objekte im Raum spielt—anders als bei herkömmlichen Anwendungen von Geo-Datenbanksystemen—für die Anfragebearbeitung im Dockingsystem keine Rolle.

Der prinzipiell unendlich große Suchraum für die Dockinganfrage eines Proteins an die Proteindatenbank wird durch die triangulierte Repräsentation der Oberflächen diskretisiert. Durch die Vorauswahl von Extrempunkten als potentielle Dockingstellen reduziert sich der gesamte Suchraum aller Punktpaare nochmals. Zur weiteren Einschränkung des Suchraums benutzen wir die bewährte Technik der mehrstufigen Anfragebearbeitung. Für den Filterschritt verwenden wir abstrakte Formbeschreibungen durch Kennzahlen. Die ausgewählten Punkte aller Proteine sowie diejenigen eines Anfrageproteins werden jeweils mit Hilfe eines R*-Baums verwaltet. Ein mehrdimensionaler Join liefert alle Paare von Punkten, deren Abstand im Kennzahlenraum eine vorgegebene Toleranz ε nicht überschreiten. Die Antworten aus dem Filterschritt sind Paare von Punkten, die im Verfeinerungsschritt zu Regionen erweitert werden. Diese Regionen werden in der Lage normiert und dann übereinandergelegt, um einfache Komplementaritätsprüfungen auf der 3D-Geometrie durchzuführen. Eine experimentelle Untersuchung des Filterschritts wurde beschrieben, für den Verfeinerungsschritt wird sie derzeit durchgeführt.

Wir haben verschiedene Komponenten des Dockingsystems vorgestellt, das wir zusammen mit unseren Partnern aus Braunschweig, Bielefeld und Göttingen im BMFT-Verbundprojekt BIOWEPRO entwickeln. Die Basis des Systems bildet ein kommerzielles objektorientiertes Datenbanksystem, das wir mit den Proteinen aus der PDB laden. Die Algorithmen zur Berechnung der Oberflächenrepräsentation, der Oberflächenkennzahlen und der potentiellen Dockingstellen sowie die Module der mehrstufigen Anfragebearbeitung werden zusammen mit den Bausteinen unserer Projektpartner zu einem Gesamtsystem integriert.

Danksagung

Wir danken unserem Kollegen Ralf Schneider für intensive und fruchtbare Diskussionen. Unseren Partnern im Projekt BIOWEPRO verdanken wir insbesondere die Einführung in die biologische Problemstellung.

Literaturhinweise

[AFS 93] Agrawal R., Faloutsos C., Swami A.: *'Efficient Similarity Search in Sequence Databases'*, Proc. 4th. Int. Conf. on Foundations of Data Organization and Algorithms, Evanston, ILL, in: Lecture Notes in Computer Science, Vol. 730, Springer, 1993, pp. 69-84.

[Ald 94] Aldinger K., Ester M., Förstner G., Kriegel H.-P., Seidl T.: *'Datenbankunterstützung für das Protein-Protein-Docking: ein effizienter und robuster Feature-Index'*, Proc. 'Bioinformatik – Computereinsatz in den Biowissenschaften', 2. GI-Fachtagung 'Informatik in den Biowissenschaften', 05.-07.09.94, Jena, 1994.

[Ber 77] Bernstein F. C., Koetzle T. F., Williams G. J., Meyer E. F., Brice M. D., Rodgers J. R., Kennard O., Shimanovichi T., Tasumi M.: *'The Protein Data Bank: a Computer-based Archival File for Macromolecular Structures'*, Journal of Molecular Biology, Vol. 112, 1977, pp. 535-542.

[BHKS 93] Brinkhoff T., Horn H., Kriegel H.-P., Schneider R.: *'Eine Speicher- und Zugriffsarchitektur für effiziente Anfragebearbeitung in Geo-Datenbanksystemen'*, Proc. GI-Fachtagung Datenbanksysteme in Büro, Technik und Wissenschaft, Braunschweig, 1993, in: Informatik aktuell, Springer, 1993, pp. 356-374.

[BK 94]   Brinkhoff T., Kriegel H.-P.: *'The Impact of Global Clustering on Spatial Database Systems'*, Proc. 20th Int. Conf. on Very Large Data Bases, Santiago, Chile, 1994.

[BKSS 90]   Beckmann N., Kriegel H.-P., Schneider R., Seeger B.: *'The R*-tree: An Efficient and Robust Access Method for Points and Rectangles'*, Proc. ACM SIGMOD Int. Conf. on Management of Data, Atlantic City, NJ, 1990, pp. 322-331.

[BKSS 94]   Brinkhoff T., Kriegel H.-P., Schneider R., Seeger B.: *'Efficient Multi-Step Processing of Spatial Joins'*, Proc. ACM SIGMOD Int. Conf. on Management of Data, Minneapolis, MN, 1994, pp. 197-208.

[BMH 92]   Badel A., Mornon J. P., Hazout S.: *'Searching for geometric molecular shape complementarity using bidimensional surface profiles'*, Journal of Molecular Graphics, Vol. 10, 1992, pp. 205-211.

[Con 83]   Connolly M. L.: *'Solvent-Accessible Surfaces of Proteins and Nucleic Acids'*, Science, Vol. 221, 1983, pp. 709-713.

[Con 86a]   Connolly M. L.: *'Measurement of protein surface shape by solid angles'*, Journal of Molecular Graphics, Vol. 4, No. 1, 1986, pp. 3-6.

[Con 86b]   Connolly M. L.: *'Shape Complementarity at the Hemoglobin $\alpha_1\beta_1$ Subunit Interface'*, Biopolymers, Vol. 25, 1986, pp. 1229-1247.

[FNNW 93]   Fischer D., Norel R., Nussinov R., Wolfson H. J.: *'3-D Docking of Protein Molecules'*, Proc. 4th Annual Symposium on Combinatorial Pattern Matching (CPM '93), Padova, Italy, in: Lecture Notes in Computer Science, Vol. 684, Springer, 1993, pp. 20-34.

[FRM 94]   Faloutsos C., Ranganathan M., Manolopoulos Y.: *'Fast Subsequence Matching in Time-Series Databases'*, Proc. ACM SIGMOD Int. Conf. on Management of Data, Minneapolis, MN, 1994, pp. 419-429.

[HT 94]   Helmer-Citterich M., Tramontano A.: *'PUZZLE: A New Method for Automated Protein Docking Based on Surface Shape Complementarity'*, Journal of Molecular Biology, Vol. 235, 1994, pp. 1021-1031.

[Jag 91]   Jagadish H. V.: *'A Retrieval Technique for Similar Shapes'*, Proc. ACM SIGMOD Int. Conf. on Management of Data, Denver, CO, 1991, pp. 208-217.

[Kat 92]   Katchalski-Katzir E., Shariv I., Eisenstein M., Friesem A. A., Aflalo C., Vakser I. A.: *'Molecular Surface Recognition: Determination of Geometric Fit between Proteins and their Ligands by Correlation Techniques'*, Proc. National Academy of Science USA, Vol. 89, 1992, pp. 2195-2199.

[Koe 90]   Koenderink J. J.: *'Solid Shape'*, MIT Press, Cambridge, MA, 1990.

[KSB 93]   Kriegel H.-P., Schneider R., Brinkhoff T.: *'Potentials for Improving Query Processing in Spatial Database Systems'*, invited talk, Proc. 9emes Journées Bases de Données Avancées (9th Conference on Advanced Databases), Toulouse, France, 1993.

[MG 93]   Mehrotra R., Gary J. E.: *'Feature-Based Retrieval of Similar Shapes'*, Proc. 9th Int. Conf. on Data Engineering, Vienna, Austria, 1993, pp. 108-115.

[PD 93]   Pellegrini M., Doniach S.: *'Computer Simulation of Antibody Binding Selectivity'*, Proteins: Structure, Function, and Genetics, Vol. 15, 1993, pp. 436-444.

[PDB 94]   Protein Data Bank: *'Quarterly Newsletter No. 70 (October 1994)'*, Brookhaven National Laboratory, Upton, NY, 1994.

[Ric 77]   Richards F. M.: *'Areas, Volumes, Packing, and Protein Structure'*, Annual Reviews in Biophysics and Bioengineering, Vol. 6, 1977, pp. 151-176.

[SKSH 89]   Schneider R., Kriegel H.-P., Seeger B., Heep S.: *'Geometry-based Similarity Retrieval of Rotational Parts'*, Proc. Int. Conf. on Data and Knowledge Systems for Manufacturing and Engineering, Gaithersburg, ML, 1989, pp. 150-160.

[Ull 88]   Ullman J. D.: *'Principles of Database and Knowledge-Base Systems (Volume 1)'*, Computer Science Press, Rockville, ML, 1988.

SDAI auf DBS implementieren und anwenden

U. Nink

Fachbereich Informatik, Universität Kaiserslautern,
Postfach 3049, 67653 Kaiserslautern
e-mail: nink@informatik.uni-kl.de

Abstract: Der internationale Standard zum Austausch von Produktdaten, STEP, erlaubt die elektronische Verwaltung aller während des gesamten Lebenszyklus eines Produktes anfallenden Daten. Mit SDAI wird in STEP eine Zugriffsschnittstelle standardisiert, die von konkreten Datenbanksystemen (DBS) abstrahiert. Wir stellen ein Projekt vor, das zum einen die Eignung von relationalen und objektorientierten Datenbanksystemen (RDBS bzw. OODBS) zur Implementierung von SDAI-Schnittstellen untersucht. Zum anderen soll die Eignung von SDAI zur Implementierung von DB-Anwendungen geprüft werden. Dabei identifizieren wir wichtige Aspekte aus Sicht des SDAI- und des Anwendungsprogrammierers. Während die Implementierung der SDAI-Schnittstelle auf einem OODBS aufgrund der ähnlichen Datenmodelle und der Unterstützung einfacher Zugriffsfunktionen nahtloser ist, bieten RDBS bessere Adaptions- und Optimierungsmöglichkeiten für verschiedenste Anwendungen.

1. Einleitung

STEP (Product Data Representation and Exchange, ISO 10303 [1]) ist eine Norm zum Austausch von Produktdaten, die die Abbildung sämtlicher Merkmale eines Produktes während seines gesamten Lebenszyklus erlaubt. Zur Modellierung der Produktdaten wird die objektorientierte Datenmodellierungssprache EXPRESS [14] als Teil 11 und zentraler Knotenpunkt des Standards vorgegeben. Ein weiterer wichtiger Teil dieses Standards ist die Zugriffsschnittstelle SDAI (Standard Data Access Interface [15], Teil 22), die den Zugriff auf durch EXPRESS beschriebene Daten unabhängig von der verwendeten Datenhaltung erlaubt. Neben dem Austausch der Produktdaten gewinnt in zunehmendem Maße auch deren Verwaltung in Datenbanksystemen (DBS) an Bedeutung, da dadurch typische DBS-Eigenschaften wie Persistenz, Konsistenz und Konkurrenz verfügbar werden. Aus diesem Grunde sind Bemühungen im Gange, SDAI auf DBS abzustimmen und aufzusetzen. In Abb. 1 ist eine typische Architektur für SDAI/DB-Anwendungen skizziert. Es sind zwei verschiedene DBS dargestellt, auf denen jeweils eine eigene SDAI-Schnittstelle liegt. Ausgehend von einem gemeinsamen EXPRESS-Schema werden DBS-abhängig die jeweiligen DB-Schemata erzeugt (schwarz durchgezogene Pfeile). Der Zugriff einer Applikation auf eine Datenbank (helle Pfeile) erfolgt über SDAI. Damit kann dieselbe Anwendung auf unterschiedlichen DBS, ob relational (RDBS) oder objektorientiert (OODBS [6]), ohne größere Anpassungsmaßnahmen laufen. Bislang erfolgt der Datenaustausch zwischen verschiedenen DBS über Dateien in einem in STEP standardisierten Format, wobei DBS-spezifische "Prozessoren" das Lesen und Schreiben solcher Dateien übernehmen (gestrichelte Pfeile). Alternativ dazu kann in jede SDAI-Schnittstelle eine entsprechende File-Schnittstelle integriert werden, sodaß ein DBS-unabhängiger Prozessor implementiert werden kann.

Wir untersuchen in einem laufenden Projekt zwei grundlegende Fragen. Die erste beschäftigt sich mit den Auswirkungen der Wahl eines DBS auf die Implementierung der SDAI-Schnittstelle. Wir diskutieren dazu für objektorientierte und relationale DBS Modell-, Architektur- und Realisierungsaspekte. Die zweite Frage beschäftigt sich mit der Eignung von

SDAI für die Implementierung von Datenbankanwendungen. Hierzu diskutieren wir im wesentlichen Mächtigkeit, Handhabung und Effizienz der SDAI-Schnittstelle. Wir haben aufbauend auf einer gegebenen Implementierung der SDAI-Schnittstelle [5] auf einem objektorientierten Datenbanksystem [11] die Erstellung eines experimentellen Prototyps einer Stücklistenverwaltung für den Automobilbau begonnen, wobei wir die Architektur in Abb. 1 anstreben. Da ein Produkt (Fahrzeug) oft in vielen Varianten (bzgl. Motor, Karosserie, Farbe, Sonderausstattung) erzeugt werden kann, ist es sinnvoll, diese Information in varianten Stücklisten zu repräsentieren. Die verschiedenen Variationen, die für ein Bauteil existieren, sind spezifizierbar. Auf oberster Ebene bedeutet dies, daß ein Kunde Wünsche äußert (Klimaanlage, Servolenkung). Auf tieferen Ebenen qualifiziert ein solcher Wunsch eine Menge von Bauteilen mit jeweils zugehöriger Variante für den Einbau. Bei der Ableitung ist zu beachten, daß die Qualifikation eines Bauteils (transitiv) entscheidend für die Qualifikation anderer Bauteile sein kann (britisches Exportmodell impliziert Rechtslenker). Wir verwenden für die Ableitungsvorschrift einen regelbasierten Ansatz. Diese Anwendung ist genügend komplex, um repräsentative Aussagen zu ermöglichen. Wir erläutern unsere bisherigen Erkenntnisse und Erfahrungen bei deren Umsetzung.

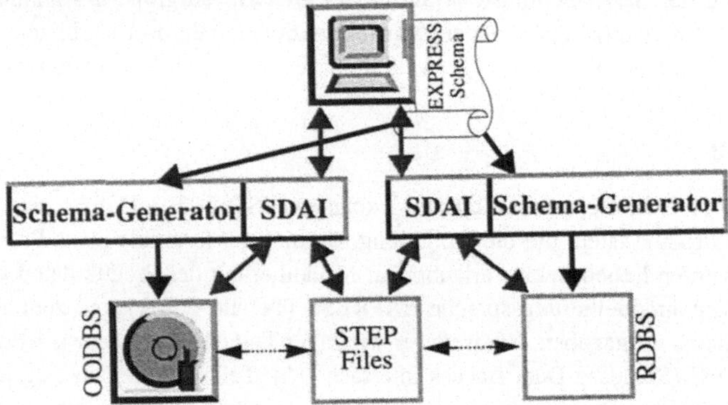

Abb. 1: Architektur für SDAI/DB-Anwendungen

In den folgenden beiden Abschnitten stellen wir zunächst Teil 11 (EXPRESS) und Teil 22 (SDAI) des STEP-Standards vor. Anschließend diskutieren wir die Implementierung von SDAI auf verschiedenen DBS und die Implementierung von DB-Anwendungen mit SDAI. Das Papier schließt mit einem Ausblick auf zukünftige Arbeiten.

2. Modellierung mit EXPRESS

Die wichtigste Voraussetzung für den Austausch von Daten zwischen verschiedenen Programmen auf unterschiedlichen DBS und Rechnerarchitekturen ist das Schaffen einer gemeinsamen Basis in Form eines einheitlichen abstrakten Datenmodells. Der zentrale Knotenpunkt des STEP-Standards ist deshalb die Modellierung der Produktdaten. Dies geschieht über eine Sprache (EXPRESS), die im folgenden kurz vorgestellt wird.

Vergleichbar mit einer Data Definition Language (DDL) in DBS werden einfache Datentypen und Konstrukte zum Aufbau komplexer Datentypen zur Verfügung gestellt. Wichtigster Baustein ist das *Entity*, das aus einer Menge von Attributen schon bekannter Datentypen aufgebaut wird. Da damit der Begriff Entity-Typ assoziiert ist, ersetzen wir im folgenden Entity durch Entity-Typ und bezeichnen dessen Ausprägungen als Instanzen. Neben einfachen, varianten, benannten, Enumerations- und Aggregattypen sind auch Entity-Typen als Attributtypen nutzbar. Letztere erlauben die Definition von (symmetrischen) *Beziehungen*; wir sprechen dann auch von Entity-wertigen Attributen. Aggregierte Entity-wertige Attribute ermöglichen die Modellierung von 1:n und n:m Beziehungen, die zusätzlich über Kardinalitätsrestriktionen verfeinert werden können. Eine Menge von Typdefinitionen läßt sich modular zu einem *Schema* zusammenfassen. In Abb. 2 sind zwei Entity-Typen "Position" und "Variante" dargestellt, die zur Verwaltung von Einbaupositionen von Bauteilen in einem Produkt und den an jeweils einer Position einbaubaren Varianten eines Bauteils dienen. Position besitzt ein Attribut für textuelle Informationen ("info"). Seine restlichen Attribute repräsentieren folgende Beziehungen: (1) Es sollen bis zu zehn verschiedene Varianten an einer Position einbaubar sein ("moeglich"); (2) das eingesetzte Baukastenprinzip soll über eine Hierarchie von Positionen ("besteht_aus") ausgedrückt werden. Durch das Schlüsselwort INVERSE wird für eine bestehende Beziehung ("FOR besteht_aus") die Rückwärtsrichtung ("teil_von") eingerichtet. Die Beziehung ist damit symmetrisch und gewährleistet referentielle Integrität.

```
SCHEMA Stueckliste;                              ENTITY Variante;
  ENTITY Position;                                 nr: INTEGER;
     info: STRING;                                 info: STRING;
     moeglich: LIST[0:9] OF Variante;            WHERE
     besteht_aus: SET OF Position;                 Bereich: 1 <= SELF.nr <= 10;
  INVERSE                                        END_ENTITY;
     teil_von: Position FOR besteht_aus;        END_SCHEMA;
  END_ENTITY;
```

Abb. 2: Ausschnitt aus einem EXPRESS-Schema

Weiter können *Regeln*, interpretierbar als Integritätsbedingungen, aufgestellt werden. Zu deren Definition sind aus Programmiersprachen bekannte Konstrukte (Zuweisung, Operationen, Variablen, Funktionen und Prozeduren) verwendbar. Da diese jedoch nicht zur Verhaltensbeschreibung von Entity-Typen herangezogen werden können, ist EXPRESS nicht voll objektorientiert sondern "nur" strukturell objektorientiert. Im Beispiel schränkt die WHERE-Klausel den "Bereich" der gültigen Variantennummern ein. Zur Verfeinerung von Entity-Typen ist (multiple) *Vererbung* einsetzbar. Vererbt werden Attribute und Regeln. Abweichend von gängigen Vererbungskonzepten sind Vererbungsbeziehungen weiter einschränkbar, was wir an einem Beispiel erläutern. Ausgehend von einem Entity-Typ "Motor" gebe es die Subtypen "Turbo" und "Einspritzer"; Motoren können nun mit einem Turbolader, einer Einspritzanlage oder aber beidem ausgestattet sein. In einer ersten Umsetzung definieren wir zu Motor die Subtypen Turbo, Einspritzer und TurboEin - letzteren als Subtyp von Turbo und Einspritzer. In EXPRESS ist die Definition von TurboEin nicht notwendig, da mit "ENTITY Motor SUPERTYPE OF (Turbo ANDOR Einspritzer)" die aufgeführten Subtypen gemeinsame Instanzen haben dürfen. Anstelle von "ANDOR" erzwingt man mit "ONEOF" und "AND" die Zugehörigkeit einer Instanz zu genau einem bzw. zu allen der angegebenen Entity-Typen.

Aus diesem kurzen Überblick über EXPRESS wird deutlich, daß bei der Umsetzung auf das Datenmodell eines DBS einige Probleme auftreten. Wir kommen darauf noch zurück. Wie Instanzen erzeugt und manipuliert werden, beschreibt der Standard mit dem Teil 22, der Zugriffs- und Manipulationsschnittstelle SDAI.

3. Zugriff über SDAI

Ein weiterer wichtiger Punkt für die Unterstützung des Austauschs von Produktdaten ist neben einem einheitlichen Datenmodell eine einheitliche Zugriffsschnittstelle, die vom darunterliegenden DBS abstrahiert. Während EXPRESS das Datenmodell in STEP festlegt, beschreibt SDAI diese Schnittstelle. Für ihre Spracheinbettung werden verschiedene Einbettungsvorschriften (Language Bindings) für jede der vorgesehenen Zielsprachen C, Fortran und C++ standardisiert. Anbindungen an Sprachen wie C oder Fortran weisen aufgrund fehlender objektorientierter Konzepte einen deutlichen Reibungsverlust auf. Eine optimale Unterstützung für die SDAI-Schnittstelle bietet in unseren Augen nur die Anbindung an C++, auf die wir uns im folgenden beschränken. Es wird zwischen *Early* und *Late Binding* unterschieden, was nicht mit den Begriffen frühes und spätes Binden in objektorientierten Programmiersprachen verwechselt werden sollte, da keine Übereinstimmung sondern nur eine Überlappung mit letzteren besteht. Zur besseren Abgrenzung ersetzen wir die SDAI-Begriffe im folgenden durch E- und L-Binding und erklären sie genauer. Im L-Binding sind alle SDAI-Operationen, die dem Programmierer zur Verfügung stehen, schemaunabhängig spezifiziert; alle Hinweise auf beteiligte EXPRESS-Konstrukte erfolgen über Eingabeparameter. Das E-Binding ist sehr viel spezieller; es stellt nur eine Teilmenge der Operationen (bspw. fehlt der Datenzugriff über Schemainformation) zur Verfügung; Hinweise auf EXPRESS-Konstrukte sind weitgehend in die Namen der Operationen integriert. So gibt es z.B. für ein Attribut einer Instanz "pos" des Entity-Typs Position zwei verschiedene Zugriffsmethoden: "pos->info()" und "pos->GetAttr("info")". Die zweite Methode, die nur im L-Binding definiert ist, erlaubt im Gegensatz zur ersten auch den Zugriff auf erst zur Laufzeit bekannte Attribute. In C++ können aber beide Methoden sowohl früh als auch spät gebunden werden, das ist der jeweiligen Implementierung überlassen. Dies hat natürlich erheblichen Einfluß auf die Effizienz, zumal eine Reihe weiterer SDAI-Operationen hiervon betroffen ist.

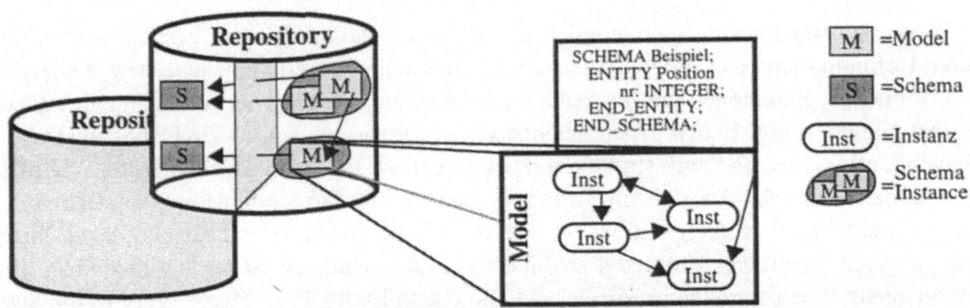

Abb. 3: Datenorganisation in SDAI

SDAI führt nun folgende Abstraktionen für Datengranulate und -operationen ein. Instanzen werden in gröberen Datenbehältern, *Model* genannt, gesammelt (Abb. 3). Ein Model ist einem *Schema* zugeordnet, das Metainformationen für Instanzen bereitstellt. Eine Menge von Schemata und Models wird zu einem *Repository* zusammengefaßt. Abweichend von der zum Zeitpunkt der Erstellung dieses Papiers offiziellen Norm, in der Transaktionen mit Repositories verwoben waren, gehen wir von einer orthogonalen Modellierung eines Transaktionskonzeptes wie in [15] aus. Auf dort ebenfalls neu vorgestellte Konzepte, wie *Schema Instance* (eine Menge von sich auf das gleiche Schema beziehende Models als Gültigkeitsbereich von Beziehungen und Regeln) oder *SDAI-Query* (erlaubt assoziative Extraktion einer Teilmenge eines Aggregats) konnten wir jedoch nicht eingehen. Die folgende Auflistung zeigt die wichtigsten Arten von Operationen (ohne Schemadienste) ihren verschiedenen Bereichen zugeordnet:

- Kontrollfluß (Open Session, Begin Transaction, ...)
- Repository (Open, Close)
- Model (Create, Delete, Get Entity Extent, Validate Global Rule, ...)

- Instanz (Get Attribute, Put Attribute, Get Type, ...)
- Aggregat (Add, Remove, Iteratoren, ...)

Nach dieser Einführung in die Modellierungssprache EXPRESS und die zugehörige Zugriffsschnittstelle SDAI gehen wir nun zur Diskussion der Implementierung von SDAI auf unterschiedlichen DBS über. Im darauf anschließenden Kapitel stellen wir unsere bisherigen Erkenntnisse in Bezug auf die Implementierung von DB-Anwendungen mit SDAI vor.

4. Implementierung von SDAI auf Datenbanksystemen

Im folgenden zeigen wir, welchen Einfluß verschiedene DBS auf die Implementierung einer SDAI-Schnittstelle haben. Die betrachteten Punkte sind unabhängig von der verwendeten SDAI-Implementierung gültig. Für die Diskussion schien uns die Einordnung der jeweils als wichtig empfundenen Aspekte in die Bereiche *Modell-* (objektorientiert, relational, SDAI), *Architektur-* (Page-, Object-, Query-Server [4, 7]) und *Realisierungsaspekte* (Synchronisation, Pufferung, Speicherungsstrukturen) sinnvoll.

4.1 Modellaspekte

Da EXPRESS das für SDAI zugrundeliegende Datenmodell ist - alle Strukturen der SDAI-Spezifikation liegen in EXPRESS vor - hängt die Implementierung von SDAI von der Abbildung von EXPRESS auf das Datenmodell des DBS ab. [13] beschreibt eine Abbildung von EXPRESS auf das *Relationenmodell*. Probleme bereitet die Umsetzung objektorientierter Modellierungskonzepte, wie komplexe Typen oder Vererbung (impedance mismatch). Im wesentlichen werden für jeden Entity-Typ und für jedes komplexe Attribut (aggregiert oder Entity-wertig) eigene Relationen und Sichten erzeugt. Jede Instanz erhält eine eigene Identität (ID), über die die Beziehung zu komplexen Attributen und damit auch anderen Instanzen realisiert wird. Bei der Abbildung auf *objektorientierte* DBS gibt es weniger Reibungen. Wir legen im folgenden das Datenmodell von C++ zugrunde. Jeder Entity-Typ wird auf eine eigene Klasse abgebildet, wobei jedes seiner Attribute ein C++-Attribut, genannt "Element", der Klasse definiert. Einfache Attribute können ohne Indirektion integriert werden. Für komplexe Attribute werden Container-Klassen bereitgestellt. So können Beziehungen zu anderen Entity-Typen nahtlos auf Instanz- bzw. Zeiger-auf-Instanz-wertige Klassenelemente übertragen werden. Starre Abbildungsvorschriften können jedoch ein Nachteil sein. Gerade alternative Möglichkeiten bei der Umsetzung von z.B. symmetrischen Beziehungen (Suchfunktion oder Materialisierung der Rückwärtsrichtung) bieten Optimierungsmöglichkeiten. Für eine SDAI-Operation wie "FindEntityInstanceModel" (suche zur Instanz das zugehörige Model) bspw., die eher selten verwendet wird, ist die Bereitstellung einer Suchfunktion angebracht.

Einige Punkte bereiten sowohl RDBS als auch OODBS Probleme. Eine nahtlose Abbildung des Vererbungskonzeptes von EXPRESS erfordert, daß die Zugehörigkeit einer Instanz zu mehreren Entity-Typen instanzabhängig gesteuert werden kann. In den Datenmodellen von C++ und anderen kommerziellen Systemen ist dies nicht möglich. Im C++-Binding von SDAI wird dafür multiple Vererbung herangezogen, jedoch muß jede (in EXPRESS implizite) Kombination von Entity-Typen explizit als eigene Klasse modelliert werden. Da die Zahl der Kombinationen sehr stark mit n wächst (bei n mit ANDOR verknüpften Entity-Typen $O(2^n)$), ist eine automatische Generierung aller Klassen nicht sinnvoll. Man nutzt stattdessen den Template-Mechanismus von C++, mit dem die benötigten Klassen über Instantiierung erzeugt werden. Damit muß aber im Anwendungprogramm codiert werden, welche Kombinationen auftreten dürfen. Das bedeutet, daß schon bei der Erzeugung einer Instanz entschieden wird, zu welcher Kombination sie gehört; jede nachträgliche Änderung der Zugehörigkeit impliziert zumindest die Migration der Instanz in eine andere Klasse. Ein weiteres Problem stellen die in EXPRESS definierbaren Regeln dar, die die Gültigkeit von Instanzen festlegen; wir verstehen sie als Integritätsbedingungen. Die Verantwortung für deren Einhaltung überträgt SDAI dem Anwendungsprogrammierer. Da aber in vielen DBS Integritätsbedingungen spezifiziert und automatisch überwacht werden können, sollte eine Möglichkeit zur Nutzung dieser Fähigkeiten angestrebt werden. Bei automatischer Überwachung ist getrennt von der EXPRESS-Schemabeschreibung eine Einteilung der Bedingungen in *direkt* oder *verzögert auszuwerten* effizienzsteigernd einsetzbar. Dies führt zu einem eigenen Integritätssubsystem. Auch die Gleichheitssemantik in SDAI hat Auswirkungen auf die Effizienz. Es wird zwischen *IsSame* und *IsEqual* unterschieden. Bei ersterem werden die Identitäten zweier Instanzen, bei letzterem jeweils die Werte der einfachen Attribute der Instanzen und rekursiv ihrer referenzierten Instanzen verglichen. Ein spezieller Algorithmus fängt im zweiten Fall etwaige Zykel ab. Da dieser "tiefe" Vergleich mitunter sehr zeitaufwendig werden kann und ohnehin oft nicht der Gleichheitssemantik der Benutzer entspricht, wären benutzerdefinierte Vergleichsvorschriften, die schon bei der Datenmodellierung definiert werden können, hier vorzuziehen. So ließen sich z.B. für den Vergleich zweier Varianten die allgemeinen Informationen (info) ihrer zugehörigen Positionen heranziehen, ohne die Attribute der Varianten berücksichtigen zu müssen.

4.2 Architekturaspekte

Um architekturunabhängig zu bleiben, kann SDAI dem Anwendungsprogrammierer kaum direkte Mittel zur Optimierung bieten. Dies muß damit eine wesentliche Aufgabe der Schnittstellenimplementierung sein. Optimierungsspielraum sehen wir insbesondere bei der Wahl des Anforderungs- bzw. Nachladegranulats und in der Cluster-Bildung. Mit der Einführung von einfachen Anfragen [15] kann man darüberhinaus auf Anfrageoptimierung zurückgreifen. Zur Verdeutlichung der Diskussion zeigt Abb. 4 die Architektur von SDAI-Schnittstellen auf unterschiedlichen Server/Workstation-DBS-Architekturen [4, 7]. Diese DBS-Architekturen erhalten ihre Bezeichnung Page-, Object- bzw. Query-Server nach dem Datenaustauschgranulat zwischen Server- und Workstation-Komponente (S- bzw. WS-DBS). Gestrichelte Pfeile repräsentieren Schnittstellenaufrufe, durchgezogene Pfeile, deren Dicke die Menge der auf eine Anforderung hin übertragenen Daten suggerieren soll, den Datenfluß.

Der Aufruf einer SDAI-Operation führt für Page- und Object-Server zum Aufruf einer oder weniger Operationen der WS-DBS-Schnittstelle. Und jede Anforderung einer Instanz eines Entity-Typs führt evtl. zur Anforderung einer Seite bzw. eines Objektes aus der Datenbank. Navigation führt in der Regel zu weiteren Seiten- bzw. Objektanforderungen. Diese Nachladevorgänge geschehen automatisch, und angeforderte Seiten bzw. Objekte werden in einem vom WS-DBS verwalteten Cache auf der Workstation gepuffert. Mit Objectstore [11] als Page-Server ist es weiter möglich, eine Seitenmenge, die mindestens eine und maximal alle Seiten eines Segmentes enthält, auf einmal übertragen zu lassen. Mit Versant [17] als Object-Server kann man Objektmengen übertragen, im Extremfall das gesamte Model auf einmal. Ontos [2] erlaubt als adaptierbares System, die Übertragung objekt-, seitenbezogen oder sogar gemischt zu gestalten. In allen Architekturen ist die Größe des Transfergranulates anpassbar.

Während für Page- bzw. Object-Server das Transfergranulat eine Seite bzw. ein Objekt ist, sollte es beim Query-Server zur Minimierung der Kommunikation das Model oder ein größerer Teil davon sein. Bei relationalen Systemen, die wir als Spezialfall des Query-Server auch als Relationen-Server bezeichnen, wären es mehrere Instanzenmengen (abhängig von der Zahl

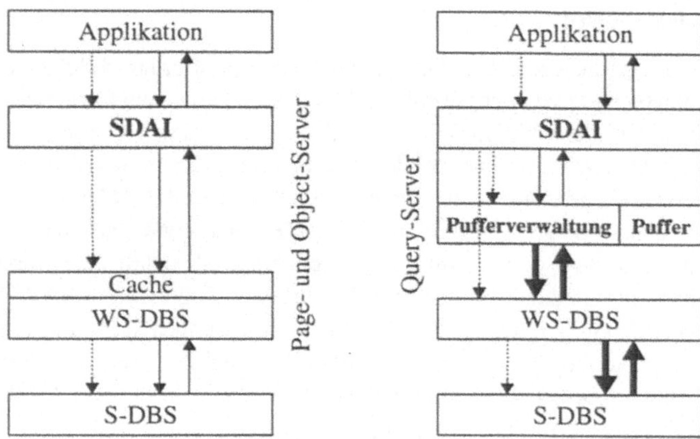

Abb. 4: Architektur von SDAI-Schnittstellen auf WS/S-DBS-Architekturen

der Entity-Typen im Model). Wir unterstützen dies, indem wir einen Puffer verwalten (siehe rechten Teil der Abbildung) und beim Öffnen eines Model eine Anfrage ausführen lassen, die den Inhalt des Model oder einen Teil davon in diesen Puffer lädt. Anschließende SDAI-Operationen, die sich auf das im Puffer befindliche Model beziehen, können dann ohne den Zugriff über das DBS allein auf dem Puffer abgewickelt werden. Da der Zugriff auf ein Entity-wertiges Attribut (Dereferenzierung) eine Instanz aus einem anderen Model liefern kann, ist u.U. auch hier ein Nachladen notwendig. Dies muß explizit in der SDAI-Schnittstelle kodiert werden, was jedoch im Gegenzug einen großen Optimierungsspielraum bietet, da das Transfergranulat kontextabhängig von der einzelnen Instanz bis hin zum kompletten Model reicht. Eine solche kontextabhängige Entscheidung kann über die SDAI-Operation "Get_Attribute" realisiert werden, da jede Dereferenzierung über diese Operation erfolgen muß. Geschieht das Nachladen über die Anfrageschnittstelle des DBS, so sind einzelne Objekte als Transfergranulat zu vermeiden; vielmehr ist wieder das gesamte Model oder ein Teil davon nachzuladen.

Innerhalb eines *Page-Server* ist ein Model auf ein Cluster, also auf eine zusammengehörige Menge von Seiten z.B. ein Segment, abzubilden. Models, die aufgrund vieler Model-übergreifenden Referenzen ihrer Instanzen eine starke indirekte Verbindung aufweisen, sind möglichst in das gleiche Segment abzulegen, um Verwaltungsaufwand oder nachfolgende Zugriffe einzusparen bzw. zu optimieren. Allgemein gilt, daß die Wahl der Cluster-Bildung größten Einfluß auf die Effizienz eines Page-Server hat. Wir können dies in der erforderlichen Kürze nicht ausreichend erklären und verweisen deshalb auf [7]. Für *Object-Server* kann Cluster-Bildung eingesetzt werden, um auf Server-Seite eine Einsparung von Transfers vom Server-Seitenpuffer zur Platte und zurück und eine bessere Server-Pufferausnutzung zu erzielen. Diese Verbesserung gilt auch für *Query-Server*. Hier gilt weiter, daß die Kommunikation zwischen Server und Workstation durch mengenweises Zusammenstellen von Instanzen zur Übertragung minimiert wird, und zwar unabhängig von jeglicher Cluster-Bildung.

Der für unser Projekt verwendete SDAI-Prototyp setzt auf Objectstore, einem Page-Server, auf und folgt der Architektur im linken Teil der Abb. 4. Ein Model ist dabei genau einem Segment zugeordnet, und das Laden von Daten geschieht seitenweise. Ursprünglich beabsichtigten wir, das kommerzielle Produkt ST-Developer 1.3 von Step Tools Inc. [16] einzusetzen. Dieses erwies sich jedoch als ungeeignet, da es keine SDAI-Schnittstelle für Objectstore bereitstellte. Die Alternative, Daten zunächst aus der Datenbank in eine Datei auszulesen und dann über SDAI (gegeben als L-Binding für C) zu bearbeiten, schien uns kaum sinnvoll.

4.3 Realisierungsaspekte

Die im folgenden betrachteten Aspekte Synchronisation, Pufferung und Speicherungsstrukturen sind eher unabhängig von der jeweiligen Architektur. Bei einem Page-Server ist im Sinne der *Synchronisation* die Abbildung jedes Model auf ein eigenes Cluster in Erwägung zu ziehen, da so Instanzen verschiedener Models nicht in der gleichen Seite liegen können, was den konkurrierenden Zugriff auf Instanzen unterstützt. Bei Einsatz adaptiver Locking- und Callback-Mechanismen [3] zur Unterstützung variabler Sperr- und Pufferaustauschgranulate benötigt man diese vorbeugende Maßnahme nicht. Dies gilt somit auch für Object- und Query-Server, denn diese können Sperren auf Objekt- bzw. Tupelebene halten. Zur Minimierung der Sperrverwaltung und der Anzahl der Sperranforderungen spielen über Repräsentanten sperrbare komplexe Objekte eine große Rolle. Der Idealfall ist dann die Abbildung eines Model auf <u>ein</u> komplexes Objekt. Um komplexe Objekte oder allgemein Anfrageergebnisse eines Query-Server auf Seite der Anwendung bereitzustellen, ist dort das Einrichten eines *Puffers* sinnvoll. Zusätzlich zu den hierzu in 4.2 erfolgten Überlegungen betrachten wir einige weitere Aspekte. Die Pufferung ist durch Quelltextanalyse oder Programmiererangaben steuerbar; ersteres ist sehr aufwendig, letzteres einfach und zumutbar bspw. über SQL. Diese Flexibilität erfordert die Unterstützung verschiedener Austauschgranulate, welche von einzelnen Instanzen über Mengen von Instanzen eines Entity-Typs bis hin zu vollständigen Models reichen können. Bei Page- und Object-Server sind deren implizite Caching-Mechanismen nutzbar. So muß zwar eine auf das jeweilige System angepaßte Abbildung erfolgen, die Implementierung der SDAI-Schnittstelle ist jedoch einfacher als auf einem Query-Server, da sie keinen Puffer explizit verwalten muß. Die Implementierungen sollten unterschiedliche *Speicherungsstrukturen* für Daten auf Platte und Hauptspeicher zur Verfügung stellen [12], da beim Zugriff auf Externspeicher der I/O-Overhead und im Hauptspeicher der Rechenaufwand wesentlich die Effizienz bestimmen. Da EXPRESS lediglich abstrakte "Container" vorgibt, ist dies leicht zu verbergen. Applikationsabhängige Anpassungen sollten möglich sein, um ein mglw. bekanntes Zugriffsverhalten auszunutzen. Ebenso kann im Hauptspeicher Pointer-Swizzling [8], das im wesentlichen eine Transformation der DB-Referenzen auf Hauptspeicheradressen darstellt, entscheidende Effizienzgewinne bringen.

5. Implementierung von DB-Anwendungen mit SDAI

Eine leichte Portierbarkeit einer Anwendung auf unterschiedliche DBS erfordert, daß sich der Programmierer an die Möglichkeiten von SDAI hält. Wir wollen dazu im folgenden unsere Erfahrungen mit der Implementierung der Stücklistenanwendung berichten. Wir diskutieren, welche Möglichkeiten SDAI zur Anwendungsprogrammierung bietet, welche Einschränkungen sich ergeben und welche Erweiterungen sinnvoll sind. Wir beschränken uns darauf, daß die Anwendung auf nur einem Repository arbeitet - diese Sichtweise führt zu einer einfachen Handhabung ohne die wesentlichen Punkte einzuschränken. Die abgeleiteten Aussagen sind meist allgemein gültig und auch in anderen Anwendungen nachvollziehbar; sprachliche Aspekte sind auf Sprachen mit ähnlichen Eigenschaften wie C++ übertragbar.

Abbildung der Anwendungsdaten auf Models Zunächst liegt die Abbildung einer kompletten Stückliste auf ein Model nahe. Dagegen spricht die Existenz von Abhängigkeiten zwischen Stücklisten in der Art, daß in der Regel gemeinsame Teile (Motor oder andere Konstruktionsgruppen) auftreten, die oft logische Einheiten für sich darstellen. Diese sind zu identifizieren und getrennt abzubilden. Weiter soll nach Möglichkeit der konkurrierende Zugriff minimal behindert werden. Grundsätzlich ist die Wahl des Sperrgranulats aber Aufgabe des zugrundeliegenden DBS, und Models sollten für den Anwender lediglich eine abstrakte Strukturierungshilfe für die Ablage, die Verwaltung und das Anfordern von Daten sein.

Mächtigkeit der SDAI-Sprachschnittstelle SDAI ist bislang vom Aufgabenumfang der einzelnen Funktionen eine recht einfache Schnittstelle, die dem Anwender die ganze Last der Vorgehensweise bei der Bearbeitung der Daten eines Repository aufbürdet. Läßt man die Schemadienste außen vor, so gibt es grob gesprochen drei Arten von Verarbeitungsschritten beim "Durchstöbern" eines Repository:

a) Finden von Einstiegspunkten über einen vorher vergebenen Namen (GetModel).

b) Navigieren von Instanz zu Instanz (GetAttr).

c) Iterieren über eine Menge von Instanzen (Beginning, Next, Previous, End).

Ob diese Operationen für eine effiziente Verarbeitung ausreichen, ist von der jeweiligen Anwendung abhängig. Da STEP wohl insbesondere in großen heterogenen Systemen zum Einsatz kommen soll, werden aber sehr verschiedenartige Anwendungen beteiligt sein. Aus diesem Grund muß die SDAI-Schnittstelle möglichst allgemein sein. So sind selbst einfache Erweiterungen nützlich. Bspw. war schon die Erweiterung der Iteration um "Previous" für Stücklistenanwendungen effizienzsteigernd. Im wesentlichen genügten die von SDAI bereitgestellten Möglichkeiten zur Realisierung unseres Projektes. Vermißt wurden jedoch assoziative Zugriffsmöglichkeiten, wie z.B. auf Aggregatelemente über die Spezifikation eines Attributwertes. Die unjüngst eingeführten SDAI-Queries befriedigen prinzipiell diese Anforderung. Jedoch ist eine Leistungssteigerung erst mit dem Einsatz von Indizes (nicht von EXPRESS und SDAI abgedeckt) zu erwarten. Kommt ein Puffer zum Einsatz, sodaß die Anfrageverarbeitung auch auf dem Hauptspeicher abläuft, ist zu beachten, daß gegenüber der externspeicherbezogenen Verarbeitung die Effizienz durch ganz andere Faktoren bestimmt wird (siehe 4.3). Jeweils zugeschnittene Speicherungs- und Zugriffsstrukturen und auch Satzformate können hier wesentliche Effizienzgewinne bringen.

Benutzung der Entity-Typen in der Anwendung Wir haben für die Implementierung das E-Binding für C++ benutzt. Die Klassen, die die Entity-Typen modellieren, möchte man in der Regel um anwendungsbezogene Funktionalität erweitern. Dies wird von EXPRESS nicht direkt unterstützt (es gibt jedoch auch hier anderweitige Bemühungen [9]). In SDAI erhält man stattdessen für jeden Entity-Typ eine C++-Klasse mit der in SDAI allgemein festgeschriebenen Basisfunktionalität. Eine naheliegende Lösung zur Erweiterung der Funktionalität ist der Einsatz von Vererbung: es werden bspw. nur um Methoden erweiterte Klassen von den generierten Klassen abgeleitet. So kann ein wichtiger Aspekt für Sprachintegration erfüllt werden: möglichst natürlich zusätzliche Fähigkeiten in eine Sprache zu integrieren.

Ausnutzung von Verarbeitungskontexten Das Wissen um Verarbeitungskontexte ist für Optimierungen und Vereinfachungen ausnutzbar. Oberhalb der SDAI-Schnittstelle kann dies nur durch die Abbildung der Anwendungsdaten auf SDAI-Models geschehen. Da sich aber das Zugriffsverhalten innerhalb eines Model und auch die Verarbeitungskontexte verschiedener Anwendungen oft sehr unterscheiden, muß man bei der Abbildung Kompromisse eingehen. In SDAI integrierte Anfragemöglichkeiten wären zur dynamischen Kontextspezifikation nutzbar, wodurch eine Abbildung auf Models prinzipiell überflüssig würde.

6. Ausblick

Neben der Mächtigkeit der SDAI-Schnittstelle ist die Einschätzung ihrer Performanz aus Anwendersicht besonders wichtig. Offensichtlich muß man bei der Verwendung von SDAI mit Effizienzeinbußen rechnen. Die Frage ist, ob diese vertretbar bzw. zu verkraften sind. Mit der Prototypimplementierung sollen die Voraussetzungen geschaffen werden, detaillierte Messungen in dieser Richtung zu unternehmen. Gleichzeitig soll auch die Umsetzung von Benchmarks, die gegenüber unserer Beispielanwendung anwendungsunabhängig sind oder sich zumindest auf einen größeren Anwendungsbereich beziehen, Aufschluß über die Effizienz von SDAI geben. Wir erhoffen uns durch den direkten Vergleich einer Anwendung oder eines Benchmarks mit und ohne Nutzung der SDAI-Schnittstelle Resultate, die uns zeigen, wie man mit geschickter Implementierung von SDAI etwaige Effizienzverluste weitgehend ausschalten oder diejenigen Konzepte erkennen kann, die für diese Verluste verantwortlich sind. Weitere Einbußen werden erkauft, wenn der Zugriff auf Instanzen über Schemainformation erfolgt. Interessant wäre es, zu sehen, welche Einbußen allein durch das Ersetzen der E-Binding Funktionen durch die äquivalenten L-Binding Funktionen in einer Anwendung anfallen und in welchem Verhältnis diese Einbußen zum Overhead von SDAI stehen.

Wir wollen ebenfalls unsere SDAI/DB-Anwendung auf unterschiedlichen Datenhaltungssystemen realisieren. Hierbei interessieren wir uns nicht nur für Laufzeitunterschiede, sondern auch für evtl. auftretende Schwierigkeiten bei der Portierung. Erst die Umsetzung auf ein anderes System wird zeigen, wo der Standard noch Probleme aufweist. Der nächste und letzte Schritt in diese Richtung ist dann, eine Applikation über eine SDAI-Schnittstelle auf zwei oder mehr unterschiedlichen DBS laufen zu lassen, sodaß innerhalb eines Prozesses Daten aus beiden Systemen manipuliert und ausgetauscht werden.

7. Literatur

[1]   R. Anderl: STEP - Grundlagen der Produktmodelltechnologie. In W. Stucky, A. Oberweis (Ed.), GI-Fachtagung für Büro, Technik und Wissenschaft, 1993, pp. 33-53.

[2]   M. J. Carey, D. J. DeWitt, J. F. Naughton: The OO7 Benchmark. In ACM SIGMOD, 1993, pp. 12-21.

[3]   M. J. Carey, M. J. Franklin, M. Zaharioudakis: Fine-Grained Sharing in a Page Server OODBMS. In ACM SIGMOD 1994, pp. 359-370.

[4]   D. J. DeWitt, P. Futtersack, D. Maier, F. Velez: A Study of Three Alternative Workstation-Server Architectures for Object Oriented Database Systems. In VLDB 1990.

[5]   A. Herbst: Long-Term Database Support for EXPRESS Data. In Proc. 7th Int. Working Conf. on Scientific and Statistical Database Management, Charlottesville, Virginia, 1994.

[6]   A. Heuer: Objektorientierte Datenbanken: Konzepte, Modelle, Systeme. Addison-Wesley, 1992.

[7]   T. Härder, B. Mitschang, U. Nink, N. Ritter: Workstation/Server-Architekturen für datenbankbasierte Ingenieuranwendungen. Bericht 26/93, SFB 124, Univ. Kaisersl., 1993.

[8]   A. Kemper, D. Kossmann: Adaptable Pointer Swizzling Strategies in Object Bases. Proc. Int. Conf. on Data Engineering, Vienna, Austria, 1993, pp. 155-162.

[9]   M. Koethe, A. Nieva, F. Schönefeld: Product Data Exchange in Open Systems: The PISA Approach. In STAK, Ilmenau, Deutschland, März 1994, pp. 101-119.

[10] F. Leymann: Towards The STEP Neutral Repository. In Proc. of the 4th Int. Conference on CALS and Information Management in Europe, Berlin, Deutschland, 1993.

[11] C. Lamb, G. Landis, J. Orenstein, D. Weinreb: The ObjectStore Database System. Communications of the ACM, 34(10), Oktober 1991, pp. 50-63.

[12] T. J. Lehman, E. J. Shekita, L.-F. Cabrera: An Evaluation of Starburst's Memory-Resident Storage Component. Report RJ 8919, IBM Almaden Research Center, 1992.

[13] K. C. Morris: Translating Express to SQL: A Users's Guide. National Institute of Standards and Technology, U.S. Department of Commerce, 1990.

[14] ISO TC184/SC4/WG5: Product Data Representation and Exchange - Part 11: EXPRESS Language Reference Manual, ISO TC184/SC4/WG5 N55, Januar 1994.

[15] ISO TC184/SC4/WG7: Product Data Representation and Exchange - Part 22: Standard Data Access Interface, ISO TC184/SC4/WG7 N370 Committee Draft, November 1994.

[16] ST-Developer 1.3 Reference Manuals. Step Tools Inc. 1994.

[17] VERSANT Release 2 System Reference Manuals. July 1993.

Unscharfe Anfragen an eine Grenzwert-Datenbank

– Software-Architektur, Anfragebearbeitung und Leistungsoptimierung –

Ralf Kramer[*]
Forschungszentrum Informatik (FZI)
Haid–und–Neu–Str. 10–14, D–76131 Karlsruhe
kramer@fzi.de

Zusammenfassung

Grenzwerte, die dem Umweltschutz dienen, sind in einer Vielzahl von Richtlinien, Gesetzen und Verordnungen für einzelne Bundesländer, Staaten, aber auch für Ländergemeinschaften wie die EU und die UN festgelegt. Diese Richtlinien unterscheiden sich u.a. in ihrer Terminologie und in den Details ihrer Festlegungen (z.B. Grenzwert für einzelne Schwermetalle oder aber für schwermetallhaltige Verbindungen insgesamt). Werden Grenzwerte aus unterschiedlichen Quellen in Datenbanksystemen erfaßt, sollten daher insbesondere auch mit der Materie nur wenig vertraute Benutzer ohne langwieriges Reformulieren von Datenbankanfragen die gesuchten Ergebnisse erhalten.

In diesem Beitrag wird ein Modul zur Realisierung benutzerkonfigurierbarer, unscharfer Datenbankanfragen auf der Basis eines klassischen, relationalen Datenbanksystems vorgestellt. Neben anwendungsspezifischen Suchbesonderheiten werden insbesondere auch unscharfe Datenbankanfragen auf der Grundlage von Fuzzy Sets unterstützt. Diese Anfragen werden innerhalb des Datenbankservers in einer Client-/Server-Architektur bearbeitet. Das System wurde für die übergreifenden Komponenten des Umweltinformationssystems Baden-Württemberg entwickelt und realisiert, das Implementierungskonzept ist jedoch auch für andere Anwendungen, insbesondere auch als Ergänzung zur konventionellen Bearbeitung präziser Anfragen, anwendbar.

1 Einführung

Die heute kommerziell verfügbaren relationalen und objektorientierten Datenbanksysteme unterstützen lediglich deklarative Anfragen, die der klassischen booleschen Logik genügen. Insbesondere dann, wenn komplexe Sachverhalte modelliert und in Datenbanksystemen erfaßt werden sollen, ist diese Situation wenig zufriedenstellend, da die Formulierung der Suchprädikate in solchen präzisen Anfragen sehr schwierig werden kann. Wird eine Anfrage zu sehr einschränkend formuliert, besteht die Gefahr, daß keine Ergebnisdatensätze gefunden werden und daraus fälschlicherweise der Schluß gezogen wird, die gesuchten Informationen lägen nicht vor. Wird das gesuchte Ergebnis hingegen nicht hinreichend eingegrenzt, wird der Anwender mit einer unstrukturierten Ergebnismenge konfrontiert. In solchen Situationen müssen Datenbanksystemnutzer ihre Anfragen daher mehrfach umformulieren und neu stellen, bis sie das tatsächlich gesuchte Ergebnis erhalten.

---

[*]Teilweise finanziert durch das Umweltministerium Baden-Württemberg, Vertragsnr. U 15-93.01, und die Landesanstalt für Umweltschutz, Karlsruhe, Vertragsnr. 96239.

Ein Ansatz, die beschriebenen Probleme zu lösen, besteht darin, nicht nur den exakt angefragten Wert, sondern auch Werte in seiner Umgebung als Anfrageergebnis mit auszugeben. Derartige Umgebungen können sowohl problemspezifisch durch die Berücksichtigung der bei der Datenmodellierung in Erscheinung getretenen Besonderheiten als auch durch eine suchattributspezifische Festlegung von Ähnlichkeiten definiert werden. Zur Festlegung solcher Ähnlichkeiten sowie zu ihrer späteren Auswertung in der Anfragebearbeitung eignen sich Fuzzy Sets.

Ein solcher Ansatz wird in der übergreifenden Grenzwert-Datenbank [Kra93, KS93, KS94, Kra94a] des Umweltinformationssystem (UIS) Baden-Württemberg [BaW91, MF93] verfolgt. Schwerpunkt dieses Beitrags sind die Beschreibung und Analyse der Anfragebearbeitung im Suchmodul sowie die gegenüber der ersten Version inzwischen realisierten Verbesserungen [Kra94b]. Im folgenden 2. Abschnitt beschreiben wir zunächst kurz den Hintergrund der Anwendung. Im 3. Abschnitt gehen wir auf unscharfe Datenbankanfragen ein. Abschnitt 4 beschreibt die Software-Architektur sowie die Nutzungsmöglichkeiten des realisierten Systems. Die Bearbeitung unscharfer Anfragen in dieser Architektur ist Gegenstand von Abschnitt 5. Ein kurzes Resümee sowie ein Ausblick auf zukünftige Arbeiten beschließen das Papier in Abschnitt 6.

2 Grenzwert-Datenbank im UIS

Aktuelle Meßwerte, Umweltbeobachtungen und -analysen bilden eine wesentliche Grundlage für eine moderne, vorsorgende Umweltpolitik. Zur informationstechnischen Unterstützung dieser Aufgaben wird vom Umweltministerium Baden-Württemberg gegenwärtig ein fachübergreifendes Umweltinformationssystem (UIS) aufgebaut. Um gemessene Umweltdaten bearbeiten, bewerten und interpretieren zu können, werden in zahlreichen Komponenten dieses Systems Grenzwerte aus verschiedenen Quellen verwendet. Insbesondere in den ressortübergreifenden Berichtssystemen UFIS (Umwelt-Führungsinformationssystem) [Hen93] und TULIS (Technosphäre- und Luft-Informationssystem) [Koh93] ist es erforderlich, bei der Darstellung von Meßwerten kontextabhängig (beispielsweise abhängig von konkreten Umweltthemenbereich, dem gemessenen Parameter sowie dem Meßzeitraum) auf Grenzwerte zuzugreifen. Für diese übergreifenden Systeme wird das relationale Datenbanksystem Oracle eingesetzt, dessen Verwendung daher auch für die Grenzwert-Datenbank vorgegeben war.

Die Datenmodellierung der in [Lan92] erfaßten Richtlinien erfolgte auf der Basis des Entity-Relationship-Modells. Ergebnis der für sämtliche möglichen Arten von Grenzwerten (Grenzwerte, Richtwerte, Leitwerte, Warnwerte, ...) einheitlichen konzeptuellen Modellierung ist ein ER-Diagramm mit knapp 25 Entitytypen, die um den für die Aufgabenstellung zentralen Entitytyp **Grenzwert** gruppiert sind [Kra93, KS93]. Berücksichtigt werden u.a. Werte für Immissionen und Emissionen, zeitliche Beschränkungen der Gültigkeit von Grenzwerten (Verschärfungen), Parametersynonyme, richtlinienspezifische Festlegungen von Parametergruppen (z.B. „schwermetallhaltige Verbindungen") sowie die Fortschreibung von Richtlinien durch andere.

3 Unscharfe Datenbankanfragen

3.1 Beispiele

Die zu Beginn der Einführung gemachten Aussagen hinsichtlich der Schwierigkeiten, Datenbankanfragen im Sinne der intendierten Antwort korrekt zu formulieren, kann man nun mit einfachen Beispielen aus der vorliegenden Anwendung Grenzwert-Datenbank illustrieren. Diese Beispiele untermauern die Forderung zur Unterstützung unscharfer Anfragen, wie sie in [Fuh90b, Fuh94] speziell für Umweltinformationssysteme erhoben wurde.

Hinsichtlich der rechtlichen Verbindlichkeit sind verschiedene Arten von Grenzwerten zu unterscheiden. Es gibt *Grenzwerte*, deren Einhaltung von den Betroffenen zwingend gefordert wird, ferner u.a. *Richtwerte, Leitwerte, Orientierungswerte* und *Vergleichswerte*. Für den Laien sind diese zunächst subtilen Unterscheidungen kaum nachzuvollziehen und von Experten kaum vollständig zu überblicken. Die Schwierigkeiten, ohne Mehrfachformulierung einer Anfrage zum benötigten Ergebnis zu gelangen, sind offensichtlich.

Weitere Beispiele finden sich beim Gültigkeitsbereich, d.h. bei der Region, für den ein bestimmter Grenzwert gültig ist. So verläuft die Suche nach einem Grenzwert für Jahresmittelwerte von Schwefeldioxid mit Gültigkeitsbereich Baden-Württemberg ergebnislos. In diesem Fall relevant wäre der entsprechende Grenzwert der Europäischen Union; ein entsprechender Wert auf Bundesebene existiert hingegen nicht. Verzichtet man nun aber völlig auf die Angabe eine Gültigkeitsbereichs, erhält man eine sehr umfangreiche Ergebnismenge mit allen vorhandenen Einträgen zu Schwefeldioxid, aus der man sich dann manuell den hier relevanten der EU heraussuchen muß.

3.2 Lösungsansätze

Im Hinblick auf Unschärfe in Datenbanksystemen wird üblicherweise (s. z.B. [Mot90]) zwischen der Fähigkeit, mit unpräzisen Daten oder aber mit unpräzisen oder vagen Anfragen umgehen zu können, unterschieden. Für das hier zu lösende Problem, unscharfe Anfragen gegen eine präzise Datenbasis auszuführen, sind aus der Literatur verschiedene Lösungsansätze bekannt.

Bei Verwendung von Metriken, die auf dem aus dem Information Retrieval bekannten *Vektorraummodell* basieren und wie sie beispielsweise in VAGUE verwendet wurden [Mot88], ist es erforderlich, daß der Benutzer komplexe Verknüpfungsmetriken zur Definition von mehrdimensionalen Ähnlichkeiten zwischen den Werten unterschiedlicher Attribute explizit angibt. *Probabilistische Ansätze* [Fuh90a] basieren auf der Wahrscheinlichkeitstheorie. Sie unterliegen daher deren Restriktionen, insbesondere den Kolmogoroffschen Axiomen (Positivität, Normiertheit, Additivität) [HEK91]. Die hieraus unmittelbar resultierende Annahme der paarweisen Unabhängigkeit von Ereignissen ist (nicht nur) bei der vorliegenden Anwendung nicht erfüllt; beispielsweise hängt die Art des Grenzwerts von der Richtlinie ab. Mittels der *Fuzzy Set Theorie* [DPY93, KGK93, Zim91] ist es hingegen möglich, Ähnlichkeiten zunächst in einzelnen Suchdimensionen bzw. -parametern, also unabhängig voneinander, zu formulieren und diese dann (systemintern) miteinander zu verknüpfen. Die Fuzzy Set Theorie kommt damit der menschlichen Fähigkeit, in monokausalen Wirkungsketten, nicht aber in komplexen Wirkungsnetzen denken zu können [D. 92], entgegen. Fuzzy Sets bilden daher den geeigneten Ausgangspunkt. Sie erlauben darüberhinaus eine Benutzerkonfiguration in einzelnen Suchattributen.

Die zur Anfragebearbeitung benötigten Ähnlichkeiten werden explizit formuliert. Diese Ausdrücke entsprechen Entities im konzeptuellen Datenmodell bzw. Attributwerten im logischen Datenmodell. Gegenwärtig wird eine Ähnlichkeitssuche bei 6 Entitytypen (Suchparametern) unterstützt. Für diese existieren jeweils entsprechende Ähnlichkeitsrelationen, deren Aufbau dem allgemeinen Muster `zu ersetzendes Entity, ersetzt durch Entity, Ähnlichkeit` folgt. Für ein zu ersetzendes Entity können so ein oder beliebig viele Ersatz-Entities angegeben werden. Für die Ähnlichkeiten sind Werte zwischen $0,9$ („sehr ähnlich") und $0,1$ („wenig ähnlich") zulässig. Ähnlichkeiten werden also jeweils für ein Paar von Entities definiert.

Durch die Berücksichtigung von Ähnlichkeiten hat sich die ausschließlich konjunktive

Gültigkeits-bereich	ersetzt durch	Ähnlich-keit	Werttyp	ersetzt durch	Ähnlich-keit
Deutschland	Baden–Württemberg	0.9	Grenzwert	Richtwert	0.9
Deutschland	Europäische Union	0.7	Grenzwert	Leitwert	0.7
Deutschland	Vereinte Nationen	0.5	Grenzwert	Schätzwert	0.5
Deutschland	Schweiz	0.3	Grenzwert	Orientierungswert	0.3
Deutschland	Schweden	0.1			

Tabelle 1: Ähnlichkeitsrelationen für Gültigkeitsbereiche und Werttypen

zu ersetzender Parameter	ersetzt durch	Ähnlichkeit
Schwefeldioxid (SO_2)	Sulfat (SO_4)	0.9
Schwefeldioxid	Schwefel	0.8
Schwefeldioxid	Schwefelwasserstoff (H_2S)	0.5
Schwefeldioxid	Isotop Schwefel–32	0.2

Tabelle 2: Ähnlichkeitsrelation für Parameter

Verknüpfung der Suchprädikate als ausreichend erwiesen; die Ähnlichkeiten ersetzen quasi Oder-Verknüpfungen. Zur konjunktiven Verknüpfung benötigt wird eine sog. t-Norm T [KGK93], die die Bedingungen Monotonie ($a \leq b \Rightarrow \mathsf{T}(a,c) \leq \mathsf{T}(b,c)$), Kommutativität ($\mathsf{T}(a,b) = \mathsf{T}(b,a)$) und Assoziativität ($\mathsf{T}(a,\mathsf{T}(b,c)) = \mathsf{T}(\mathsf{T}(a,b),c)$) erfüllt, und für die es ferner ein neutrales Element ($\mathsf{T}(a,1) = a$) gibt.

Beispiele aus unserer Anwendung bestätigten Ergebnisse empirischer Studien [Zim91], nach denen die Min-/Max-Operatoren (für Konjunktion bzw. Disjunktion) häufig nicht ausreichen, „da beide nur eine sehr grobe Annäherung an die Bewertungsweise menschlichen Denkens darstellen" [KGK93]. Daher wurde als t-Norm zunächst [KS93, KS94] die Verknüpfung mittels Multiplikation, d.h. $\mathsf{T}_{\mathrm{prod}}(x,y) := x * y$, gewählt. Im folgenden Abschnitt gehen wir auf die Auswahl einer geeigneteren t-Norm ein, die inzwischen in unserem System eingesetzt wird.

3.3 Auswahl geeigneter t-Normen

Zur Auswahl geeigneter t-Normen für konjunktive Verknüpfungen dient eine Anfrage, die mit den Suchprädikaten Gültigkeitsbereich = Deutschland, Werttyp = Grenzwert und Parameter = Schwefeldioxid die typischerweise verwendeten Suchattribute umfaßt. Die Tabellen 1 und 2 zeigen die zugehörigen Ähnlichkeitsrelationen, Tabelle 3 die verwendeten Beispieltupel.

Bei der Festlegung bzw. Auswahl einer geeigneten t-Norm hat man zwei Möglichkeiten [Zim91]: Beim *klassischen und* ist für die Ordnung der Tupel das Minimum der Argumentwerte entscheidend, bei gleichem Minimum bestimmen die übrigen Werte die Reihenfolge.

Tupel–ID	Gültigkeitsbereich (GB)	Werttyp (WT)	Parameter (P)	...
t0	Deutschland	Grenzwert	Schwefeldioxid	...
t1	Baden–Württemberg	Richtwert	Sulfat	...
t2	Baden–Württemberg	Leitwert	Sulfat	...
t3	Vereinte Nationen	Schätzwert	Schwefelwasserstoff	...
t4	Europäische Union	Orientierungswert	Schwefel	...
t5	Schweiz	Schätzwert	Isotop Schwefel–32	...
t6	Schweden	Orientierungswert	Schwefel	...

Tabelle 3: Relevante Ausschnitte der Beispieltupel zur Auswahl von t-Normen

Tpl. ID	Ähnlichkeiten			Produkt	Hamacher–Produkt	Hamacher–Operator	Dombi–Operator
	GB	WT	P				
t0	1.0	1.0	1.0	1.000	1.000	1.000	1.000
t1	0.9	0.9	0.9	0.729	0.750	0.750	0.839
t2	0.9	0.7	0.9	0.567	0.606	0.606	0.687
t3	0.5	0.5	0.5	0.125	0.250	0.250	0.366
t4	0.7	0.3	0.8	0.168	0.249	0.250	0.295
t5	0.3	0.5	0.2	0.030	0.120	0.120	0.174
t6	0.1	0.3	0.8	0.024	0.079	0.079	0.097

Tabelle 4: Ergebnisse der konjunktiven Verknüpfung mit verschiedenen t–Normen

Beim *kompensatorischen und* wird dagegen ein niedriger Wert in einem Argument durch hohe Werte in den anderen Argumenten innerhalb eines gewissen Bereiches ausgeglichen.

Bei der Richtlinienwertsuche gibt der Benutzer Werte für die für ihn relevanten Suchparameter an. Ziel ist es, diejenigen Tupel in der Datenbasis zu finden, die in den entsprechenden Attributen möglichst gut mit den Anfragewerten übereinstimmen. Erfüllt ein Tupel die vorgegebenen Suchattribute nur zum Teil, so sollte dieses Tupel nur mit einem geringen Ähnlichkeitswert belegt werden. Dies entspricht eher einer klassischen, nicht-kompensatorischen Auffassung der Und–Verknüpfung. Von den aus der Literatur bekannten Operatoren [GQ91] verhalten sich das Hamacher–Produkt, der Hamacher–Operator (für $\lambda = 1000$) und der Dombi–Operator (für $\lambda = 2$) entsprechend. Tabelle 4 zeigt die mit ihnen im Beispiel erzielten Werte. Ein Vergleich mit dem anfangs eingesetzten Produktoperator, der sich kompensatorisch verhält, zeigt die Unterschiede in der Reihenfolge bei den Tupeln t3 und t4.

Der Hamacher–Operator scheidet aus, da er bei komplizierterer Berechnung fast die gleichen Werte wie das Hamacher–Produkt liefert. Der Dombi–Operator liefert höhere Werte als das Hamacher–Produkt, was bei der Verknüpfung von mehreren Werten von Vorteil ist. Ferner gehen die sich ergebenden Ähnlichkeiten auch bei vielen Argumenten weniger schnell gegen Null und die Ergebniswerte sind auch bei nur geringfügig differierenden Argumentwerten und geringerer Rechengenauigkeit unterscheidbar. Als konjunktiver Verknüpfungsoperator gewählt wird daher der Dombi–Operator mit dem Parameterwert $\lambda = 2$:

$$\top_D^2(x,y) = \begin{cases} 0 & \text{falls x=0 oder y=0,} \\ \dfrac{1}{1+\sqrt{(\frac{1}{x}-1)^2+(\frac{1}{y}-1)^2}} & \text{sonst.} \end{cases}$$

4 Software-Architektur

4.1 Realisierungsalternativen

Für die Realisierung der im vorherigen Abschnitt vorgestellten Suchfunktionalität gibt es in einer Client-/Server-Umgebung im wesentlichen die folgenden drei Möglichkeiten: Implementierung als Teil einer interaktiven Endbenutzeranwendung, Realisierung separat davon als eigenständiger Modul und schließlich Realisierung so, daß die Anfragen im Datenbank-Server bearbeitet werden. Bewertet werden müssen diese Alternativen hinsichtlich der Kriterien Nutzbarkeit durch mehrere Anwendungen, Portabilität zwischen unterschiedlichen Datenbanksystemen sowie Kommunikationsaufwand zwischen Datenbank-Server und Modul für Zwischenergebnisse.

Tabelle 5 faßt die Bewertungen zusammen. Es wird deutlich, daß der Bearbeitung im Datenbank-Server insbesondere dann der Vorzug zu geben ist, wenn die Portabilität zwischen unterschiedlichen Datenbanksystemen keine Anforderung darstellt. Bei den hier

Kriterium	Teil der Anwendung	separates Anwendungsprog.	Bearbeitung im Datenbankserver
Nutzung durch mehrere Anwendungen	–	(+) (Vor.: Präcompiler-Appl.)	+
Portabilität zwischen Datenbanksystemen	+	(+) (Vor.: SQL-Standard)	–
Kommunikationsaufwand für Zwischenergebnisse	–	–	+

Tabelle 5: Bewertung der Realisierungsalternativen

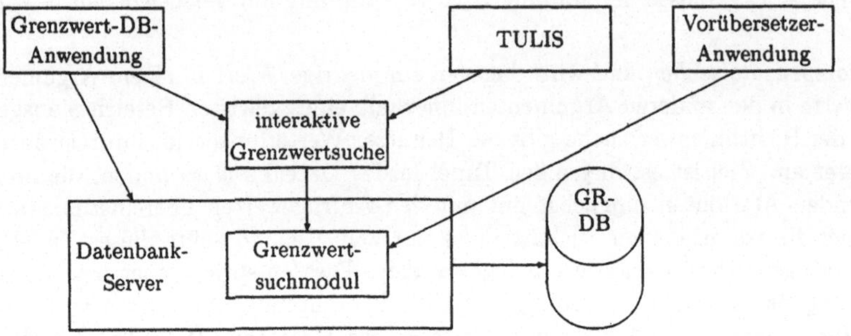

Abbildung 1: Systemarchitektur mit Aufrufhierarchie und Nutzungsmöglichkeiten

relevanten relationalen Systemen hat das vollständige Fehlen der Portabilität seine Ursache in der fehlenden Standardisierung der prozeduralen SQL-Erweiterungen [MS93]. Da Portabilität bei der Grenzwert-Datenbank nicht gefordert wurde, fällt die Entscheidung zugunsten einer Realisierung der Suchfunktionalität als sog. Package, das die erforderlichen Stored Procedures zusammenfaßt [Ora92].

4.2 Systembeschreibung

Das für eine Client-/Server-Umgebung konzipierte System besteht im wesentlichen aus der eigentlichen Datenhaltung im Oracle-Datenbanksystem (Version 7), einem Modul zur Grenzwertsuche, einer interaktiven Oberfläche für diesen Modul sowie einer ebenfalls interaktiven Gesamtanwendung. Abbildung 1 zeigt die Software-Architektur des realisierten Systems.

Die Prozeduren des in PL/SQL, der herstellerspezifischen prozeduralen SQL-Erweiterung [Ora92], realisierten Moduls für die Grenzwertsuche ermöglichen sowohl die gezielte Suche nach Grenzwerten als auch eine erweiterte Suche unter Berücksichtigung von Ähnlichkeitskriterien. Einzelne Suchattribute werden i.d.R. auf mehrere Attribute der Relationen abgebildet. Die Prozeduren können auch unter Verzicht auf die interaktive Schnittstelle aus beliebigen Programmen unter Verwendung eines SQL-Vorübersetzers verwendet werden. Interaktiven Endbenutzer- und Administrator-Schnittstellen werden neben der Grenzwertsuche auch das Erfassen neuer Richtlinien (-Werte), die Konfiguration der Ähnlichkeitssuche sowie die Benutzeradministration ermöglichen. Die interaktive Grenzwertsuche kann auch als Unterprogramm aus anderen Programmen wie TULIS [Koh93] heraus aufgerufen werden, wobei Anwendungskontexte als Vorbelegung der Suchparameter übernommen werden können.

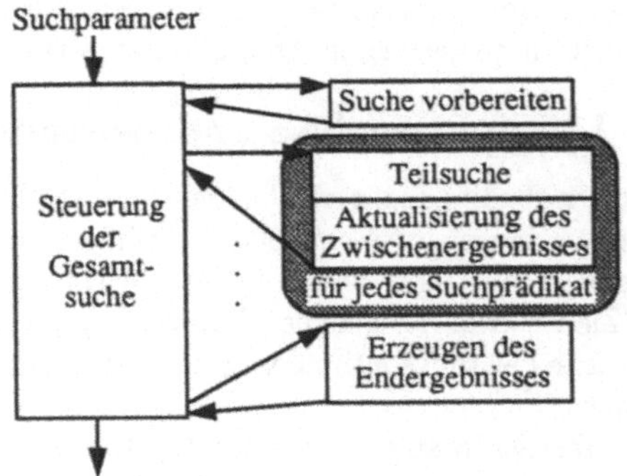

Abbildung 2: Ablauf der Gesamtsuche im Suchmodul

5 Anfragebearbeitung im Suchmodul

5.1 Randbedingungen

Für die Anfragebearbeitung im Suchmodul gelten – u.a. aufgrund der in Abschnitt 4 getroffenen Entscheidungen – eine Reihe von Randbedingungen. Die Suche wird nicht über eine SQL-Anfrage, sondern über eine entsprechende Prozedur gestartet. Das Endergebnis der Suche muß als Relation materialisiert werden, um das vorgegebene Tool (Oracle Forms4) zur Realisierung der interaktiven Benutzeroberfläche nutzen zu können. Ergebnisse können aufgrund der Wahlmöglichkeiten bei der Ähnlichkeitssuche (aktivieren/deaktivieren für einzelne Suchattribute, Benutzerkonfiguration [KS93, KS94]) nicht vorausberechnet werden, sie müssen anfragespezifisch ermittelt werden. Temporäre Relationen werden nicht unterstützt, die Sprachkonstrukte von PL/SQL unterstützen nicht die mengenorientierte Bearbeitung im Hauptspeicher. Für Zwischenergebnisse werden daher persistente Relationen verwendet. Innerhalb von PL/SQL wird dynamisches SQL (noch) nicht unterstützt (s.a. Abschnitt 6.2). Aufgrund dieser Randbedingungen haben wir den im folgenden Abschnitt vorgestellten Modulaufbau entwickelt und realisiert.

5.2 Modulaufbau und generelle Bearbeitungsstrategie

Abbildung 2 zeigt die generell Vorgehensweise bei der Anfragebearbeitung im Suchmodul. Aus der Gesamtsuche wird nach einem Vorbereitungsschritt für jedes Suchprädikat eine entsprechende Teilsuche aufgerufen, in der sämtliche Richtlinienwerte selektiert werden, die die jeweilige Suchbedingung unmittelbar erfüllen oder die sich aufgrund der definierten Ähnlichkeiten qualifizieren. In diesen Teilsuchen werden – ebenfalls auf Benutzeranforderung – auch die in der Einleitung angesprochenen anwendungsproblemspezifischen Suchbesonderheiten berücksichtigt. So kann bei der Suche nach einem bestimmten Parameter (z.B. Blei) zugleich auch nach Parametersynonymen und nach Parametergruppen gesucht werden. Die Verschärfung von Grenzwerten erfolgt zum einen innerhalb der Richtlinie, in der der Grenzwert festgelegt wird; ein solcher niedrigerer Grenzwert, der ab einem bestimmten Datum gelten soll, wird durch die Berücksichtigung des Datums bei der Anfrage mit erfaßt. Zum anderen werden aber auch existierende Richtlinien durch neue Richtlinien modifiziert, so daß statt der ursprünglichen Richtlinie nunmehr auch die neue anzufragen ist. Dies geschieht auf Benutzeranforderung in der entsprechenden Teilsuche, ggf. auch über mehrere Änderungen einer Richtlinie hinweg.

Am Ende jeder Teilsuche wird das Zwischenergebnis, d.h. die bislang qualifizierten

Richtlinienwerte mit zugehörigen Ähnlichkeiten, aktualisiert. Schließlich wird das Endergebnis materialisiert und nach absteigenden Ähnlichkeiten sortiert.

5.3 Analytische Leistungsanalyse und Leistungsoptimierung

Aus dem sich durch die Randbedingungen ergebenden Implementierungskonzept sind bei umfangreicheren Relationen (beispielsweise 50.000 Richtlinienwerte aus 1.000 Richtlinien) Leistungsprobleme zu erwarten. Daher wurde in [Sto94] ein analytisches Kostenmodell entwickelt, bei dem als Zielfunktion primär die Minimierung der Anzahl logischer Seitenzugriffe verfolgt wurde. Zur Leistungsoptimierung ergeben sich aufgrund dieser Analyse die folgenden Maßnahmen.

Die Richtlinienwerte-Relation besteht neben den eigentlichen Richtlinienwerten im wesentlichen aus den Fremdschlüsseln anderer Relationen. Für diese Fremdschlüsselattribute lohnt es sich, entsprechende Zugriffspfade (nicht-geclusterte Indices) anzulegen, um die Zugriffe auf die Richtlinienwerte-Relation in den einzelnen Teilsuchen zu beschleunigen. Nicht lohnend ist hingegen ein Index auf der Zwischenergebnisrelation, um diese bereits in den Teilsuchen zur Überprüfung der weiteren Qualifikation der Tupel einzusetzen.

Schließlich kann die Kernidee zur Anfrageoptimierung in (Monoprozessor-) Datenbanksystemen, möglichst früh möglichst kleine Zwischenergebnisse zu erzielen, auf die Anfragebearbeitung im Suchmodul übertragen werden. Erreicht wird dies durch eine Festlegung der Bearbeitungsreihenfolge der Teilsuchen in Abhängigkeit von den zu erwartenden Selektivitäten zur Laufzeit innerhalb der Gesamtsuche. Von dieser Änderung der Steuerung der Gesamtsuche (s. Abb. 2) bleiben die Implementierungen der einzelnen Teilsuchen unberührt, die Schnittstelle der Gesamtsuche zur Anwendung ändert sich ebenfalls nicht.

Insbesondere die letzte Maßnahme – die Realisierung eines Schedulers, der die Gesamtsuche steuert – führt zu einer deutlichen Reduktion der Anzahl logischer Seitenzugriffe. Da sich aber der weitaus überwiegende Anteil der logischen Seitenzugriffe auf die Zwischenergebnisrelation beziehen (in einer Beispielanfrage über 80%), wirkt sich diese Reduktion der Anzahl logischer Seitenzugriffe in einer Reduktion der Pfadlänge, nicht aber notwendigerweise auch in einer ebenso deutlichen Reduktion der Anzahl zu erwartender physischer Blockzugriffe aus. Da sich diese physischen Blockzugriffe aber auf die eigentlichen Nutzdaten beziehen, sind sie – zumindest bei den Blockungsmöglichkeiten relationaler Systeme – unvermeidbar. Das Optimierungspotential an dieser Stelle ist daher zunächst ausgeschöpft.

6 Zusammenfassung und Ausblick

6.1 Resümee

In diesem Beitrag wurde anhand der Grenzwert-Datenbank des UIS Baden-Württemberg ein Konzept vorgestellt, unscharfe Datenbankanfragen auf der Basis eines unveränderten relationalen Datenbanksystems zu implementieren. Ausführlich wurde auf die Berechnung von Ähnlichkeiten sowie die Leistungsoptimierung eingegangen, die derzeitigen Grenzen des Ansatzes (Portierbarkeit, Leistung im Falle umfangreicher Datenbestände) wurden aufgezeigt. Das vorgestellte Realisierungskonzept ist nicht auf die Grenzwert-Datenbank oder auf ein bestimmtes (relationales) Datenbanksystem beschränkt. Vielmehr ist der Ansatz auch in anderen Systemen und Anwendungen, insbesondere auch als Ergänzung zur konventionellen Bearbeitung präziser Anfragen, verwendbar.

Von anderen Ansätzen, in denen unscharfe Datenbankanfragen ebenfalls auf der Basis der Fuzzy Set Theorie realisiert wurden (z.B. [Zem89]), unterscheidet sich unser System vor allem durch die Nutzung der aktuellen Datenbanktechnologie. Im Gegensatz zu anderen Systemen, die ebenfalls Grenzwerte für den Umweltschutz beinhalten (z.B. [Lan93]), werden Grenzwerte aus den unterschiedlichsten Bereichen einheitlich modelliert; ferner werden unscharfe Anfragen unterstützt. Eine ausführlichere Diskussion konkurrierender Ansätze und Systeme findet sich in [KS93, KS94].

6.2 Weiterführende Arbeiten

Auf der Grundlage der bislang bereits gemachten Erfahrungen bieten sich u.a. die folgenden Punkte für weitere Arbeiten an.

Die Einführung von Schwellwerten für die minimal zu erfüllende Ähnlichkeit (s. z.B. [PF93]) in den Teilsuchen bietet ebenfalls einen Ansatz, den Umfang von Zwischenergebnissen möglichst schnell zu verringern. Da im Gegensatz zur Verwendung des Minimum-Operators die resultierenden Ähnlichkeitswerte beim Produkt- und Dombi-Operator von der Anzahl der Verknüpfungen abhängen (s.a. Tabelle 4), muß bei diesem Ansatz sinnvollerweise eine Abbildung von durch den Anwender vorgegebenen Begriffen wie *sehr ähnlich* auf quantitative Werte in Abhängigkeit von der Anzahl der Verknüpfungen erfolgen.

Ein neues Oracle Release wird die Möglichkeit bieten, auch in PL/SQL dynamisches SQL einzusetzen [Ofe94]. Damit ergeben sich völlig neue Möglichkeiten zur Optimierung der Anfragebearbeitung innerhalb des Suchmoduls, wobei als zusätzliche Kosten die der Anfrageübersetzung zu berücksichtigen sind.

Der Umfang der Implementierung des Suchmoduls resultiert primär aus dem mangelnden Sprachumfang der prozeduralen SQL-Erweiterung und der in SQL fehlenden Typisierung von Relationen. Interessant wäre es daher, die Suchfunktionalität als Methoden in einem objektorientierten Datenbanksystem, das die Speicherung der Methoden gemeinsam mit den Objekten im Datenbanksystem, also *nicht* lediglich nur als Teil der Anwendung, unterstützt, zu realisieren.

Die einzelnen Suchparameter sind nicht in allen Fällen voneinander unabhängig. Dies kann für einen entsprechenden Dialog mit dem Benutzer oder aber für eine semantische Anfrageoptimierung innerhalb des Suchmoduls ausgenutzt werden.

Danksagungen: Herrn Dr. Horst Spandl von der Landesanstalt für Umweltschutz (LfU), Karlsruhe, danke ich für die gute Zusammenarbeit in diesem Projekt. Meinen Kolleginnen und Kollegen am FZI, Birgit Boss, Dr. Günter von Bültzingsloewen und Dr. Mechtild Wallrath, danke ich für konstruktive Anmerkungen zu einer früheren Version des vorliegenden Papiers.

Literatur

[BaW91]   Umweltinformationssystem Baden-Württemberg. Reihe Verwaltung 2000, Band 6, Hrsg.: Innenministerium und Umweltministerium, Stuttgart, 1991.

[D. 92]   D. Dörner. *Die Logik des Mißlingens – Strategisches Denken in komplexen Situationen*. Rowohlt, Reinbek. 1992.

[DPY93]   D. Dubois, H. Prade und R.Y. Yager (Hrsg.). *Readings in Fuzzy Sets for Intelligent Systems*. Morgan Kaufmann, San Mateo, California, USA. 1993.

[Fuh90a]   N. Fuhr. A Probabilistic Framework for Vague Queries and Imprecise Information in Databases. In *Proc. 16th VLDB Conf., Brisbane, Australia*, 1990, Seite 696–707.

[Fuh90b]   N. Fuhr. Anfragefunktionen für Umweltinformationssysteme. In W. Pillmann und A. Jäschke (Hrsg.), *Informatik für den Umweltschutz; Proc. 5. Symposium, Wien, Austria, September 1990*. Springer, 1990, Seite 27–37.

[Fuh94]   N. Fuhr. Umweltinformationssysteme aus der Sicht des Information Retrieval. In B. Page und L.M. Hilty (Hrsg.), *Umweltinformatik: Informatikmethoden für Umweltschutz und Umweltforschung*, Nr. 13.3 der Handbuch der Informatik, Kapitel 7, Seite 127–141. Oldenbourg, 1994.

[GQ91]   M. M. Gupta und J. Qi. Theory of T-norms and fuzzy inference methods. *Fuzzy Sets and Systems* Band 40, 1991, Seite 431–450.

[HEK91]   J. Hartung, B. Elpelt und K.-H. Köster. *Statistik – Lehr- und Handbuch der angewandten Statistik*. R. Oldenbourg Verlag, München, Wien. Ausgabe 8, 1991.

[Hen93]   I. Henning. Von Sachdaten zur Führungsinformation - Das Umwelt-Führungsinformationssystem Baden-Württemberg. In Jäschke u.a. [JKPR93], Seite 349–358.

[JKPR93]   A. Jäschke, T. Kämpke, B. Page und F. J. Radermacher (Hrsg.). *Informatik für den Umweltschutz, Proc. 7. Symposium GI–FA 4.6*, Berlin Heidelberg, 1993. Springer.

[KGK93]   R. Kruse, J. Gebhardt und F. Klawonn. *Fuzzy-Systeme*. Teubner, Stuttgart. 1993.

[Koh93]   J. Kohm. Das Technosphäre- und Luft-Informationssystem als Instrument für die Entscheider der Umweltschutzverwaltung. In Jäschke u.a. [JKPR93], Seite 369–380.

[Kra93]   R. Kramer. *Grenzwert-/Richtwert-Datenbank für UIS (Gesamtdokumentation)*. Forschungszentrum Informatik (FZI), Karlsruhe, Germany, November 1993.

[Kra94a]   R. Kramer. Scharfe Grenzwerte unscharf angefragt – Fuzzy-Set-basierte Bearbeitung von Datenbankanfragen. In Fachausschuß 1.2 Inferenzsysteme Gesellschaft für Informatik e.V. (Hrsg.), *Fuzzy-Systeme '94 – Klassifikation, Entscheidungssupport und Control; Workshop, 20.–21.10.1994, München*, Oktober 1994.

[Kra94b]   R. Kramer. Unscharfe Anfragen an eine Grenzwert-Datenbank – Software-Architektur, Anfragebearbeitung und Leistungsoptimierung – . FZI-Bericht 8/94, Forschungszentrum Informatik (FZI), Karlsruhe, Germany, Dezember 1994. URL: http://www.fzi.de/divisions/dbs/publications/overview.html.

[KS93]   R. Kramer und H. Spandl. Limits Database for an Environmental Information System – A Fuzzy Set based Querying Approach. FZI Report 25/93, Forschungszentrum Informatik (FZI), Karlsruhe, Germany, Dezember 1993.

[KS94]   R. Kramer und H. Spandl. Limits Database for an Environmental Information System – A Fuzzy Set based Querying Approach. In W. Litwin und T. Risch (Hrsg.), *Applications of Databases; First International Conference, ADB-94; Vadstena, Sweden; Proceedings*, Nr. 819 der LNCS. Springer, 1994, Seite 158–171.

[Lan92]   Landesanstalt für Umweltschutz Baden Württemberg and L. Roth. *Grenzwerte – Kennzahlen zur Umweltbelastung in Deutschland und in der EG, Tabellenwerk*. Ecomed Fachverlag, Landsberg. 1992.

[Lan93]   Landesanstalt für Immisionsschutz Nordrhein-Westfalen. *Organismen- und Stoffliste*, 1993. Version 3.1.

[MF93]   R. Mayer-Föll. Das Umweltinformationssystems Baden-Württemberg – Zielsetzung und Stand der Realisierung. In Jäschke und andere [JKPR93], Seite 313–337.

[Mot88]   A. Motro. VAGUE: A user interface to relational database that permits vague queries. *ACM Transactions on Office Infomation Systems* 6(3), Juli 1988, Seite 187–214.

[Mot90]   A. Motro. Accomodating Imprecision in Database Systems: Issues and Solution. *ACM SIGMOD Record* 19(4), Dezember 1990, Seite 69–74.

[MS93]   J. Melton und A. R. Simon. *Understanding the New SQL: A Complete Guide*. Morgan Kaufmann Publishers, San Mateo, California, USA. 1993.

[Ofe94]   U. Ofer. Oracle Release 7.1: Nur ein Maintenance Release? *Datenbank Fokus* Band 05/06, 1994, Seite 46–51.

[Ora92]   Oracle Corporation, 500 Oracle Parkway, Redwood City, CA 94065, USA. *PL/SQL User's Guide and Reference – Version 2.0*, Dezember 1992.

[PF93]   U. Pfeifer und N. Fuhr. Aufwandsabschätzung für die Prozessierung vager Anfragen auf der Basis des Datenstromansatzes. In W. Stucky und A. Oberweis (Hrsg.), *Datenbanksysteme in Büro, Technik und Wissenschaft; GI-Fachtagung, Braunschweig, 3.-5. März 1993*. Springer, 1993, Seite 375–392.

[Sto94]   M. Stockwald. Fortentwicklung und Leistungsbewertung Fuzzy-Set-basierter Datenbankanfrage-Bearbeitungsstrategien. Diplomarbeit, Universität Karlsruhe, Fakultät für Informatik, Karlsruhe, Germany, Juli 1994.

[Zem89]   M. Zemankova. FIIS: A Fuzzy Intelligent Information System. *IEEE Data Engineering* 12(2), 1989, Seite 11–20. Special Issue on Imprecisions in Databases.

[Zim91]   H. J. Zimmermann. *Fuzzy Set Theory and its Applications*. Kluwer Academic Publisher, Boston/Dordrecht/London. Ausgabe 2, 1991.

Design and Implementation of Advanced Knowledge Processing in the KBMS KRISYS

S. Deßloch[1], N. Mattos[1], B. Mitschang, J. Thomas

Department of Computer Science
University of Kaiserslautern
67653 Kaiserslautern, Germany
e-mail: {thomas | mitsch}@informatik.uni-kl.de

Abstract

Advanced data models and knowledge models together with their powerful query and manipulation languages have already proven to be essential for systems that support non-standard applications such as engineering and knowledge-based application systems. In order to raise their usability and acceptability, it is overly important to provide adequate implementation techniques that guarantee extensible and efficient processing for this advanced DBMS scenario. In this paper we present design alternatives and implementation techniques for such kinds of advanced DBMS, strongly focussing on query and knowledge processing in client/server architectures. To discuss our considerations and implementation technologies, we refer to the knowledge-processing framework of the KBMS KRISYS, although our ideas are generally applicable to (advanced) DBMS.

Keywords: Implementation Issues, Knowledge Processing, Query Processing, Constraint Enforcement, Client/Server Architectures, DBMS, KBMS

1. Introduction

In the last years, the modeling and querying facilities required by advanced applications have consolidated, and standardizations like SQL3 [ISO94] and ODMG [ODMG93] have emerged. Consequently, current research must not focus on data models and their languages only, but should pay increasing attention to improving system performance through adequate processing models and implementation technologies. Prominent examples adhering to that direction come from the area of object-oriented databases, as mentioned in, e.g., [OHMS92], knowledge base management systems (KBMS), e.g. [In84, Ma91, KL89], or other post-relational DBMS, as for example mentioned in [HS93, Gr94, LLPS91, LVZZ94, CR94].

KRISYS (Knowledge Representation and Inference System), a KBMS developed at the University of Kaiserslautern, features an object-oriented knowledge model and a set-oriented, declarative query language as user interface. At the last BTW conference, we reported experiences with the first implementation of KRISYS, which were based on a number of applications modeled with this KBMS [DLMT93]. While the object model turned out to be sufficiently expressive, the lack of an adequate concept for modeling semantic integrity constraints became apparent. Regarding the processing model and implementation of KRISYS, we learned that, for performance reasons, we needed a better adaptation of processing to the workstation/server architecture KRISYS has been conceived for. Application-oriented processing should be performed at the workstation, relying on a buffer for exploiting locality of reference.

As a result we started a major redesign of KRISYS We put special emphasis on knowledge-processing techniques, especially on query processing and constraint management. In this paper we report on the design decisions and implementation techniques that guided the development of advanced knowledge processing in the new version of KRISYS.

---

1. IBM Database Technology Institute, Santa Teresa Laboratory, 555 Bailey Ave., San Jose, CA, 95161 USA, e-mail: dessloch@almaden.ibm.com, mattos@stlvm14.vnet.ibm.com.

From a knowledge-modeling point of view, the representational framework for semantic integrity constraints resembles the major improvement in the new KRISYS version. Concerning knowledge-processing techniques, the new KRISYS is conceived for client/server environments with most application-oriented processing being done in main-memory at the client side. Consequently, a client infrastructure for efficient and effective knowledge processing close to the application is indispensable. KRISYS supports main-memory query-processing which asks for run-time optimization to dynamically exploit the client buffer contents at run time to achieve efficient overall query processing. In addition, this framework for advanced knowledge-processing supports extensibility at different levels of query processing to cope with later extensions either of the query interface (shifting more application-oriented semantics into the scope of query processing) or of evaluation methods (such as improved join algorithms) [TD93]. Moreover, a new, flexible mechanism for supporting integrity constraints is added to the system features and realized within the same framework.

Another major design decision has been made to improve the interaction between client and server components. The object-server approach, which turned out to be a performance bottleneck in the first KRISYS implementation, is replaced by a query-server architecture that supports the delegation of subqueries. In contrast to traditional query servers, this approach allows to exploit existing buffer contents at the client and improves the overall balance of processing across the client-server architecture. Moreover, it supports set-oriented retrieval of objects from the server, yet avoiding some of the drawbacks encountered with page-server approaches, such as [LLOW91], whose effectiveness strongly relies on appropriate object-clustering mechanisms.

All these design and implementation decisions are thoroughly motivated by the lessons learned from the first implementation of KRISYS [DLMT93] and therefore do not need to be restated in this paper, which is organized as follows. Sect. 2 provides a brief overview of the KRISYS object model and its query language, giving the conceptual starting point for our re-implementation of KRISYS as being described in Sect. 3. A basic understanding of the tasks of each component relevant to knowledge processing is provided and the interaction of these components is demonstrated using a small example. The main motivation for this presentation is to establish a framework for the detailed discussion of architectural components and the subsequent steps of query optimization and processing in Sect. 4. Finally, Sect. 5 sums up the major results of the paper, discusses related work, and gives a brief outlook to future work.

2. The Object Model and Query Language of KRISYS - A Brief Review

In this chapter, we summarize the main features offered by the object model of KRISYS, as adopted from the first version of KRISYS. The model extensions related to integrity constraints will be discussed in Sect. 4.4.

The KOBRA (KRISYS Object Representation) object model supported by KRISYS is comparable to object-oriented data models [Ca91]. An object is uniquely identified by a name (i.e., object identifier), and contains a set of attributes to describe its characteristics. Attributes can be of two kinds: slots are used for representing properties of an object and for modeling relationships to other objects, methods are used for expressing object behavior. Moreover, attributes can be further described by aspects, defining, e.g., the cardinality of a slot. KRISYS supports the abstraction concepts of classification, generalization, association, and aggregation [Ma91] whose semantics (e.g., inheritance along the classification and generalization relationships) is automatically enforced by the system. Objects are typically organized in hierarchies or lattices defined via those abstraction concepts. For the generalization and classification relationships, this means that both multiple inheritance and multiple instantiation (i.e., an object is a direct instance of more than one class) are supported. In addition, the object model of KRISYS provides various other features, as, e.g., integrity constraints and rules, not usually found in object-oriented models [Ma91, De93].

KOALA (KRISYS Object Abstraction Language) [Ma91], a descriptive, set-oriented language, constitutes the user and application interface of KRISYS. KOALA features two powerful operations, ASK to query the KB, and TELL to change the state of the KB. For example, the ASK statement given in Fig. 1 selects all furnishings costing more than US$1,000, which are suitable for rooms located at the south side of the house. Please note that, using the MESSAGE predicate, a method 'is-suitable-for' is invoked for determining suitability. For reference purposes, we numbered the lines of the query. We assume a KB containing generalization hierarchies for *rooms* and *furnishings*. Symbols with a leading question mark are query variables, similar to tuple variables in SQL. They may appear in the qualification clause and the projection clause. In our example, the projection clause states that the complete objects retrieved constitute the result of that query. The query refers to the abstraction concept of classification and reads as follows: Firstly, *instances of rooms* (direct as well as indirect ones, indicated by the asterisk behind the class' name) are retrieved and bound to query variable ?X (line (1.1)). The resulting set of objects is further restricted by the condition that attribute *orientation* contain value 'South' (line (1.2)). In addition to instances of *rooms*, the query also refers to instances of *furnishings* which must have a price higher than US$1000, represented by the value of attribute 'price' (lines (1.3), (1.4)). Finally, a method is called to check which furnishings are suitable for which rooms (line (1.5)).

<table>
<tr><td>(1.0)(ASK ((?X)(?Y))</td><td>} projection clause</td></tr>
<tr><td>(1.1)   (AND (IS-INSTANCE ?X rooms *)</td><td></td></tr>
<tr><td>(1.2)   (EQUAL South (SLOTVALUE orientation ?X))</td><td></td></tr>
<tr><td>(1.3)   (IS-INSTANCE ?Y furnishings *)</td><td>} qualification clause</td></tr>
<tr><td>(1.4)   (> (SLOTVALUE price ?Y) 1000)</td><td></td></tr>
<tr><td>(1.5)   (MESSAGE is-suitable-for ?Y ?X)))</td><td></td></tr>
</table>

Fig. 1:　Sample ASK statement.

3. The New KRISYS Architecture and Processing Model

In the following, the new architecture, as shown in Fig. 2, will be presented to give a basic understanding of the tasks of each system component and to demonstrate the interaction of the components using a small example. The main motivation for this presentation is to establish a framework for the detailed discussion of architectural components in subsequent sections, thus providing the background for understanding the role of each component in a global context.

3.1 Overview of the Architecture

The server part, resembled by the *PRIMA kernel* [HMMS87], concentrates on an efficient and reliable KB management. At its interface, it features a composite-object data model, the MAD (Molecule-Atom Data) model, and its query and manipulation language MQL, for application-independent data management. The workstation side of KRISYS is partitioned into several components organized on three hierarchical layers. The Working Memory is seen as a passive application buffer controlled by the Context Manager, which is keeping a declarative description of the Working-Memory contents and is responsible for loading and unloading sets of objects into or from the Working Memory. To transfer objects between server and workstation, the Context Manager interacts with the Mapping System, which transforms objects from MAD to KOBRA structures and vice versa. This component is also responsible for generating appropriate mapping schemes for the processing phases of an application. At the next layer, the Constraint Manager appears as an additional component besides the KOBRA component. It performs all activities related to checking or processing the constraints of the KB. The topmost layer, the KOALA Processing System, provides the user (and application system) interface. Its task is to prepare and control the processing of KOALA queries.

In the following, we will give an overview of the tasks of each component located at the workstation side. Moreover, we will sketch the overall processing model of the new architecture by showing the interaction of the different parts of the system during query processing.

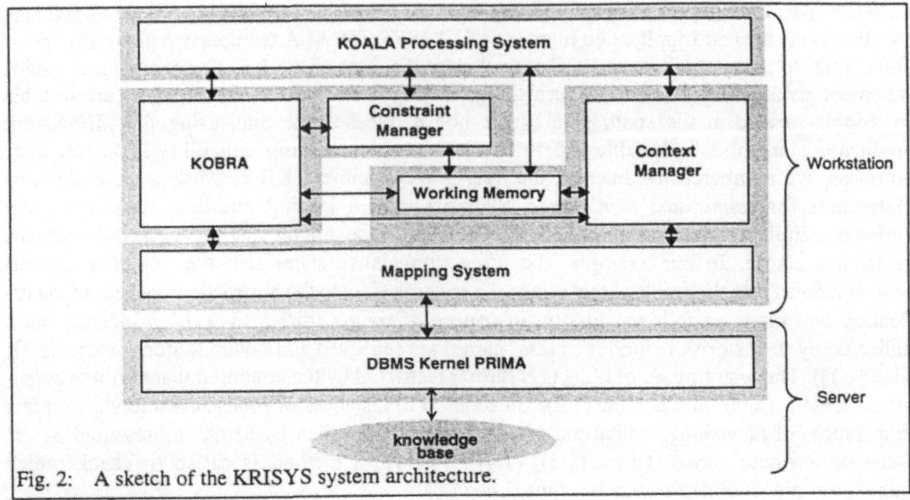

Fig. 2:   A sketch of the KRISYS system architecture.

Mapping System

The *Mapping System* provides KOBRA objects as uniform knowledge-representation format for the workstation-based components of KRISYS. Thus it isolates workstation-based knowledge processing from representational aspects of the current server DBMS. Moreover, the Mapping System allows the generation of optimized, application-dependent mapping schemes and their utilization during application processing. Such a mapping allows us, for example, to combine several interrelated classes in a single (PRIMA) table or to split one class across several tables in order to improve the performance of critical DML operations. This task can be divided into the following independent subtasks [Su91]:

- generation of an optimized mapping for a specific application,
- transformation of delegated KOALA subqueries into queries of the PRIMA kernel, and
- adaptation of the mapping in case of changes in the KB structure.

These tasks are accomplished by the following internal components of the Mapping System.

- The *MAD-Schema Generator* establishes an efficient mapping tailored to the needs of the applications [Su91]. It is activated after the design of the KB has been completed, and produces a mapping scheme based on the KB structure as well as processing characteristics.

- According to the mapping information produced by the Schema Generator, the *Mapping Component* handles the delegation of KOALA (sub-)queries [Sch91]. It produces appropriate MQL queries, which are evaluated by the PRIMA kernel, and transforms the corresponding results into the data structures of the Working Memory.

- Operations like the definition or deletion of classes, attributes, etc., which are usually regarded as schema-evolution operations, may induce changes on the mapping produced by the Schema Generator. These changes, as well as transformations of data into the new representation, are accomplished by the *Transformation Component* [Kr93].

Working Memory

The general task of the Working Memory is to support the concept of *near-by-the-application locality of processing* when KOBRA objects are referenced during query and constraint processing. In order to accomplish this task, the Working Memory

- provides data structures and operations for representing and effectively manipulating objects in a format directly reflecting the semantics of the knowledge model,

- allows efficient set-oriented processing of objects by the KOALA Processing System through so-called *Access Structures* (AS), combining functions similar to DB scan-operations with main-memory index facilities, and
- supports pointer-like navigational access or traversal of objects in abstraction hierarchies to optimize the processing of model-inherent constraints.

Transformations of the object format take place whenever objects are transferred from the server and stored in the Working Memory. Such transformations include swizzling pointers representing inter-object and abstraction relationships, construction of appropriate Access Structures, etc. [La91].

While the Working Memory provides basic functions for modifying its contents, buffer management is performed by the Context Manager introduced later in this paper.

KOALA Processing System

The *KOALA Processing System* accepts a KOALA statement, transforms it into an algebra graph, performs rewrite optimizations, and generates a plan-operator graph (i.e. execution plan), which is then compiled and executed [TMMD93].

Obviously, the evaluation of a query should exploit the Working-Memory contents as far as possible. To reach this goal, the KOALA Processing System closely interacts with the Context Manager as well as with the Constraint Manager to identify which parts of the query should be performed at the workstation side and which parts are to be delegated to the server. This decision is reflected by different types of plan operators in the execution plan (e.g. 'Buffer-SELECT' and 'DBMS-SELECT').

Context Manager

During the generation of an execution plan, the KOALA Processing System has to find out which parts of the query may directly be executed on the buffer contents, because the required objects are already present in the Working Memory. A buffer description based on object identifiers is not sufficient for accomplishing this task [De93, DLMT93]. Instead, a declarative description is required.

It is the major task of the *Context Manager* to maintain such a declarative buffer description. It can be incrementally constructed from the subqueries that are delegated to the server since the selection conditions of these queries perfectly describe the results (i.e. the contexts) that are loaded into the Working Memory. To provide the required information for the KOALA Processing System, the Context Manager performs special context-inferencing operations comparing parts of a query to the contexts of the buffer and producing a declarative description of those object sets that must be fetched from the server.

KOBRA

The KOBRA component provides the other components, mainly the KOALA Processing System, with a basic set of functions for modifying and retrieving information in the Working Memory on a 'per object' basis. This functionality, which includes reading/changing attribute values, object creation/deletion, connection/disconnection of abstraction relationships, method execution, etc., incorporates the semantics of the KOBRA knowledge model.

Constraint Manager

The task of maintaining KB consistency according to the given constraints is fulfilled by an additional component, the *Constraint Manager* [De93]. Based on events reported by the KOALA Processing System or the KOBRA component (e.g., atomic write/read operations, begin/end of composed activities, etc.), the Constraint Manager initiates actions to ensure consistency, or stores the events for later, deferred activation. Moreover, the creation, deletion, or modification of constraints is reported to this component.

Additionally, the Constraint Manager provides information about certain types of constraints to the KOALA Processing System necessary for rewriting purposes during query optimization.

3.2 Interaction of System Components During Query Processing

To illustrate the interactions and dependencies between the different system components of the new KRISYS architecture, we sketch the evaluation of a simple example query. We refer to the query already presented in Fig. 1.

After having been submitted to the KOALA Processing System (Fig. 3 ①), the statement is transformed into an algebra graph, on which algebraic optimizations are performed (Fig. 3 ②). These involve query rewrites commonly applied in relational DBMS, such as subquery to join transformation, selection-push-down, etc.

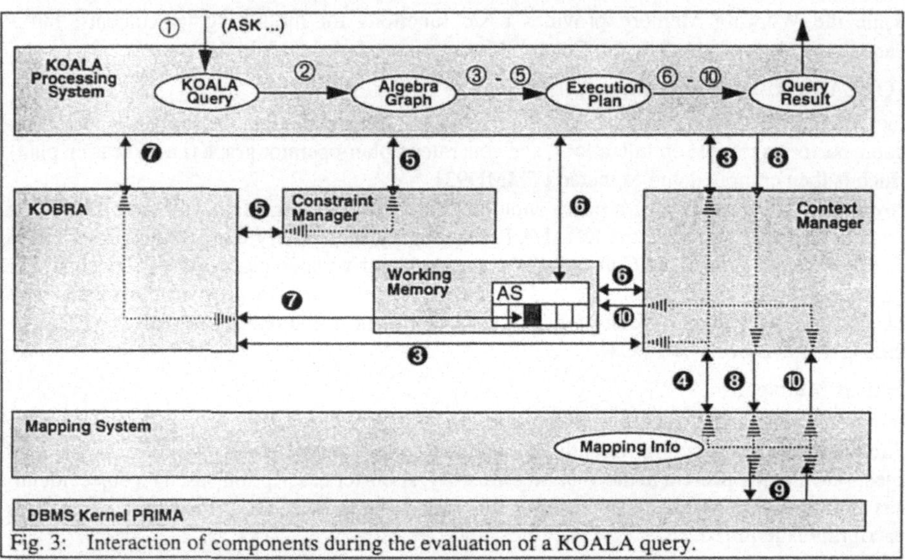

Fig. 3: Interaction of components during the evaluation of a KOALA query.

In the next step, an appropriate execution plan will be generated. At this stage of processing, the KOALA Processing System will interact with the Context Manager (Fig. 3 ❸) to determine which parts of the query can be executed on the Working-Memory contents and which have to be delegated. Not all parts of the query are considered for delegation. For example, all operations involving method calls, like the join operation of rooms and furnishings resulting from the activation of method 'is-suitable-for', can only be performed at the workstation side [De91]. To provide the required objects, the Context Manager analyzes the descriptions of the contexts already installed in the Working Memory. There may, for example, be no context containing rooms, so that an appropriate answer is given to the KOALA Processing System, which will then consider the delegation of the corresponding subquery. It will, however, not always be that easy. In many cases there will be contexts that somehow overlap with the set of objects requested by the subquery. For this purpose, the Context Manager supports specialized inference capabilities that allow to determine a declarative description of those objects that are still missing and consequently have to be fetched from the server.

In our example, the Context Manager would return the answer that the selection subquery involving furnishings can completely be supported by an existing context. Using the information provided by the Context Manager, the KOALA Processing System produces an appropriate execution plan. For this task, the KOALA Processing System additionally needs an estimation of execution costs. Here, the mapping scheme chosen for the current application plays a very important role. To provide the required cost estimations, the Context Manager therefore enriches its description of execution alternatives with cost information provided by the Mapping System, before passing it to the KOALA Processing System (Fig. 3 ❹). Depending on cost information, the KOALA Processing System may even choose not to exploit some of the inferences drawn by the Context Manager.

Additionally, the KOALA Processing System must interact with the Constraint Manager (Fig. 3 ❺)[2]. This is necessary because the evaluation of predicates in the selections to be delegated might involve the activation of constraints, which cannot be performed by the server [De91]. For example, the attribute 'price' of *furnishings* may be involved in a constraint relating it to the additional features of the furnishing. Depending on how the KB designer has chosen to represent this constraint (e.g., defining the price of *furnishing* as a virtual attribute, whose value is computed on demand), additional rewrite operations may be necessary.

Let us assume that the subqueries chosen for delegation do not require the activation of constraints, so that the execution plan generated by the KOALA Processing System is confirmed and can be compiled and executed (steps ❻ - ❿). The execution of Working-Memory plan operations is based on Access Structures containing sets of object tuples (Fig. 3 ❻). Working-Memory operators appearing as leaves of the plan-operator graph rely on contexts residing in the Working Memory. To this end, the Context Manager provides initial access to the associated contexts organized in particular Access Structures managed by the Context Manager. In our example, an Access Structure containing the furnishings is provided. Each operator can be understood as producing a temporal Access Structure to be consumed by its successor. The functionality required to implement the operations performed on each element of the Access Structure during the execution of a plan operator (e.g., accessing the attribute 'price' of the instances of *furnishings*) is provided by the KOBRA component (Fig. 3 ❼).

The execution of DBMS plan-operators is performed in several steps. First, the Mapping System is consulted to produce an equivalent server DML operation based on the actual mapping scheme (Fig. 3 ❽). This DML operation is sent to the server and executed (Fig. 3 ❾). The result of the query is then returned to the Mapping System, which transforms it into the Working-Memory representation (i.e., KOBRA objects). Finally, the resulting objects are inserted into the Working Memory and collected in a new Access Structure (Fig. 3 ❿). This last step is performed by the Context Manager, which registers the result of the delegated subquery as a new context and provides it as an Access Structure to subsequent plan operators.

Plan execution is continued in the above described manner and completed by returning the result of the query to the user or application.

4. Knowledge Processing in KRISYS

4.1 Working Memory

As described above, processing of the Working-Memory contents is not performed 'directly' by the application program, but is carried out through the KOALA Processing System, the Constraint Manager, and KOBRA. The Working Memory therefore must provide functionality for efficiently supporting the processing requirements of these components [La91].

Efficient access of information on a 'per-object' basis

An important processing requirement is the fast localization of objects based on their identifiers. This is achieved through an object hash-table. Moreover, efficient access to information about the objects (i.e., attribute information, aspect information, etc.) is also supported. Such access usually occurs repeatedly to different attributes of the same object, or to different aspects of the previously accessed attributes, and can therefore be seen as a kind of 'navigation within the object'. For example, an update operation involves the localization of the object, the write

---

2. Please note that points ❸ - ❺ are not necessarily executed in the sequential order chosen above for illustrating the interactions.

access on an attribute within the object, and additional accesses to aspect information associated with the attribute in order to record events and notify the constraint affected by the update.

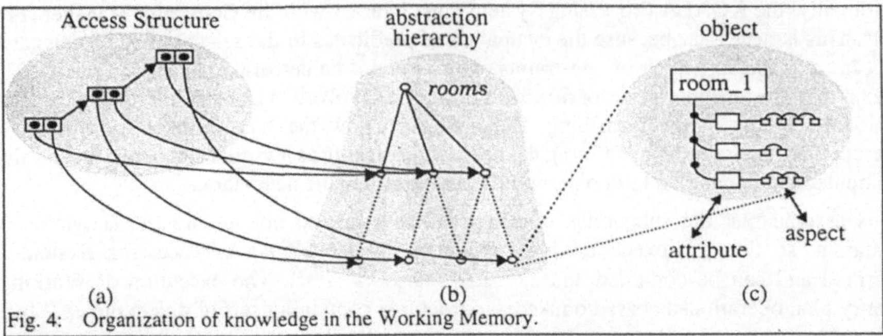

Fig. 4: Organization of knowledge in the Working Memory.

The different internal representational levels (object, attribute, and aspect) are directly reflected in the Working-Memory representation (Fig. 4 c), and are linked via main-memory pointers. The pointers allow an efficient retrieval of attribute and aspect information based on the data structure of the object. In Fig. 4 c, we have sketched this representation for the object *room_1*.

The chosen representation has the additional advantage to support the structural heterogeneity of objects in a single, uniform data structure for accessing object information. For example, even objects belonging to the same class may have varying structures because they belong to structurally different subclasses. Moreover, some objects might be instances of multiple classes, or some attributes may have been defined only for individual objects. Due to the above representation scheme, information about objects can be retrieved and modified on a uniform basis without having to access additional meta information (e.g. class descriptions) in order to interpret the data structures.

Moreover, the Working Memory offers functions for creating and deleting data structures for objects, attributes, and aspects, as well as for read/write access.

Fast navigation across abstraction hierarchies

It is important to speed up the retrieval of objects via abstraction relationships (e.g., all 'transitive' instances of a class) and provide means for efficiently guaranteeing model-inherent integrity constraints. For example, the creation of a new attribute in a class requires the traversal of the class hierarchy to perform inheritance. Consequently, the abstraction relationships between objects are materialized as main-memory pointers. This materialization has been depicted in Fig. 4 b for the generalization/classification hierarchy of *rooms*.

Besides operations for establishing/deleting abstraction links among objects, the Working Memory offers additional functionality to traverse abstraction hierarchies and perform operations on the traversed objects. These functions, which are mainly used for maintaining model-inherent integrity, can be supplied with parameters that determine the relationships to be followed, specify a search strategy for the traversal (e.g., breadth-first), or denote operations to be performed at each node during the traversal. For example, attribute inheritance was easily implemented as a breadth-first traversal following the *subclass-of* and *instance-of* relationships, performing the creation of a data structure for an attribute every time a node is reached, and testing for possible inheritance conflicts which will determine the next step in the traversal.

Direct support of set-oriented processing of Working-Memory objects

For set-oriented processing of objects, the Working Memory allows the KOALA Processing System to create, maintain, and exploit collections of objects organized as Access Structures (cf. Fig. 4 a). In order to be suitable for the purposes of the KOALA Processing System, an Access Structure must contain items that match the internal format used during query processing, the so-called KOALA tuple-format, which will be described in detail in section 4.2.2 and basically consist of a single object or several associated objects.

As shown in Fig. 4 a, these tuples do not contain copies of Working-Memory objects, but are associated with the objects via main-memory pointers. In this example, the Access Structure contains pairs of objects resulting from a join. This ensures that during query processing no redundancies are introduced by the KOALA Processing System. Intermediate results are produced by employing a sophisticated concept for sharing object information even at the attribute and aspect level, using multiple pointers to the same information.

The Working Memory provides the following functionality for exploiting Access Structures.

- Creation and deletion of Access Structures.

- Opening and closing cursors for Access Structures, which allow to scan Access Structures in forward or backward direction. Multiple cursors can be defined for the same Access Structure, so that an intermediate query result can be exploited by several 'threads' of the query execution simultaneously.

- Functions for reading, inserting, removing, and replacing tuples of Access Structures relative to the cursor position.

In its basic form, an Access Structure is organized as a list of KOALA tuples. In addition, Access Structures can also be organized as trees or hash tables, thereby supporting the maintenance of main-memory indices. In such a case, additional information must be provided at the creation of Access Structures, describing the key attributes of objects to be indexed, and the associative access to the contents of Access Structures is supported through additional functionality. With these facilities, the KOALA Processing System may fully exploit the contents of the Working Memory during query processing. Further optimizations are provided through the usage of Access Structures as main-memory indices, which may be introduced dynamically or temporarily (i.e., in the scope of a single query) during query processing.

In summary, the Working Memory directly and effectively supports the requirements of the other system components concerning the processing of object information, thereby providing a suitable basis for knowledge processing in the workstation component of KRISYS.

4.2 Query Processing

Query Processing is performed by the KOALA Processing System. To guarantee a semantically clear and streamlined system design, we partitioned its overall tasks into a processing framework and a part responsible for knowledge-model semantics. While the processing framework is based on an algebraic model that allows conventional (relational) algebraic optimizations to be used to a large extent, knowledge-model semantics is founded on the functionality provided by KOBRA. In the following, we will discuss both issues in more detail.

4.2.1 Knowledge-Model Semantics

Except for the notion of object structures, the processing framework of the KOALA Processing System is completely independent of knowledge-model semantics which is introduced via *base predicates*. Base predicates represent an intermediate level between KOALA and KOBRA. While KOALA expressions are declarative, state-oriented, and set-oriented, base predicates operate object-wise, however still being declarative and state-oriented. Since base predicates resemble assertions on single objects, they can be easily mapped to the procedural level of KOBRA. Fig. 5 depicts the different representational levels and their processing characteristics. To the right side of Fig. 5, we sketched how an example KOALA statement is translated to base predicates and the KOBRA level. We use a TELL asserting that all corridors (being instances of that class, denoted by query variable ?C) are adjacent to any room ?R lying in the same private area ?A. Let us have a look at the way the assertion is translated to base predicates. The assertion to be met is that a qualifying corridor ?C is a value of attribute 'neighboring-rooms' of any adjacent room of that private area. It is translated into a piece of code at the KOBRA level that reads the actual value of attribute 'neighboring-rooms' and adds the current value of ?C to the attribute values if it is not yet included.

level	processing	example

KOALA	declarative *set-oriented* state-oriented	(TELL (IS-IN ?C (SLOTVALUES neighboring-rooms ?R))
		WHERE (EXIST ?A
		         (IS-INSTANCE ?A private-areas *)
		         (IS-INSTANCE ?C corridors *)
		         (IS-INSTANCE ?R rooms *)
		         (IS-AGGREGATION ?A has-rooms ?C)
		         (IS-AGGREGATION ?A has-rooms ?R)))

base predicates	declarative *object-wise* state-oriented	**Conditions:** is-inst(?A, private-areas), is-inst(?C, corridors), is-inst(?R, rooms) is-aggr(?A, has-rooms, ?C), is-aggr(?A, has-rooms, ?R) **Assertions:** has-attval-member(?R, neighboring-rooms, ?C)
KOBRA	procedural object-wise *state-dependent*	..... actval:= read-attr(?R, neigboring-rooms) (if not(member (?C, actval)) add-attr-value(?R, neighboring-rooms, ?C) ......

Fig. 5:   Mapping of KOALA to KOBRA.

4.2.2 Processing Framework

The overall steps of query processing proceed in a similar fashion as those in relational DBMS [HFLP89]: first, an algebra graph is generated and subsequently optimized, i.e., rewritten; thereafter, a plan-operator graph is constructed; finally, executable code is assembled, and the query is actually evaluated. Fig. 6 gives an overview of the steps and representational levels of query processing. We will discuss them more concisely in the following.

Algebra Level

Algebra operators work on data streams consisting of sets of n-tuples which they accept as input and also produce as output. A data stream can be seen as a table made up of n columns bound to query variables. A table is represented as an Access Structure in Working Memory, and each n-tuple (table entry) represents an Access-Structure entry and comprises n elements, each featuring object level, attribute level, and aspect level. The elements of a column may be unnested on the attribute level and/or the aspect level, depending on the operations to be performed on that column. Fig. 7 depicts an example table consisting of 2-tuples and demonstrates the effects of unnesting/nesting the first column on the attribute level[3].

KOALA algebra consists of three kinds of operators. The first kind comprises operators that are responsible for handling columns or object structures (e.g., COL-COPY, COL-PROJECT, COL-UNION, NEST, UNNEST). The operators of the second kind provide functionality comparable to conventional relational algebras, e.g., EXIST, FORALL, JOIN, PRODUCT, or SELECT. The third kind is responsible for modifications of the KB. As described above, KOALA algebra employs state-oriented base predicates for realizing knowledge-model semantics. Consequently, the algebra level need not consider the actual state of the KB, and needs only a single operator, ASSERT, to carry out modifications. In relational algebras, however, where state-orientation is not known, several operators are required to carry out changes in the database (e.g., UPDATE, INSERT, DELETE).

To illustrate how a query is translated into an algebraic representation, we refer to the sample TELL statement and the way it is decomposed into base predicates shown in Fig. 5. First, an algebra graph is constructed (cf. step ❶ from Fig. 6). It is shown in Fig. 8 (a). Firstly, instances

---

3. Nesting and unnesting of attributes is used, for example, during projections.

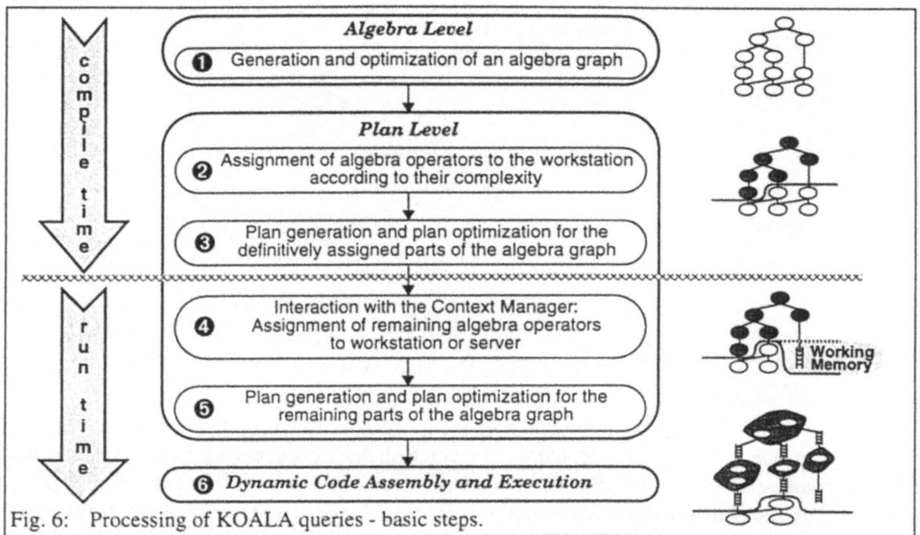

Fig. 6:   Processing of KOALA queries - basic steps.

of *areas* are selected. Since relevant rooms and corridors must be components of some private area, the corresponding object identifiers can be retrieved from attribute *has-rooms* of each selected area. To access this attribute, each area object must be unnested on the attribute level. Thereafter, all objects referenced by attribute *has-rooms* of a given area can be retrieved. Since such an evaluation of object references is quite a frequent operation, a special operator FOLLOW-UP has been added to the KOALA algebra. After the FOLLOW-UP, rooms and corridors are selected separately. Those belonging to the same private area are joined and provided as input to the assertion part of the TELL statement.

4.2.3 Plan Level

Our plan-operator approach involves the concepts shown in Fig. 9. We briefly recapitulate the salient features of the plan level; for a detailed description we refer to [TD93, TGHM94]. Plan-operator templates realize a *simple processing paradigm for plan operators*, as well as *extensibility at the plan-operator level*. Knowledge-model semantics is introduced into plan-operator processing via base predicates supplied as parameters to the plan operators. This guarantees *extensibility of the query language* without affecting existing plan operators. Subgraphs of a plan-operator graph are combined to units of execution, called *blocks*. Blocks are constructed such that intra-block processing works in a pipelining mode, i.e. tuple-wise, without the need for intermediate result materialization. The concept of *LAS* (logical Access Structures) provides an adequate data structure for this kind of internal data flow. Data streams between blocks are

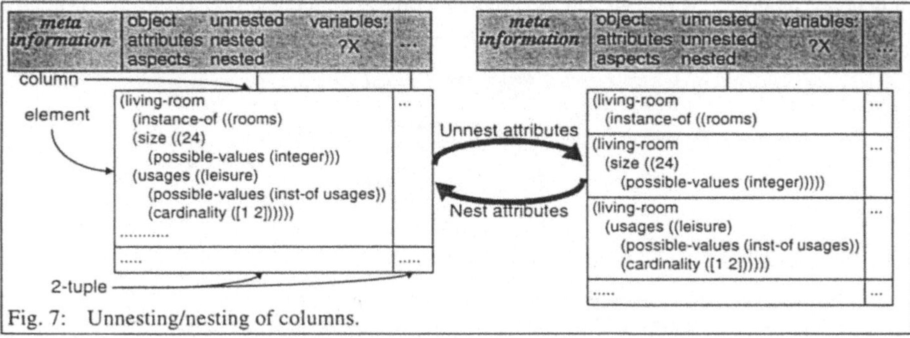

Fig. 7:   Unnesting/nesting of columns.

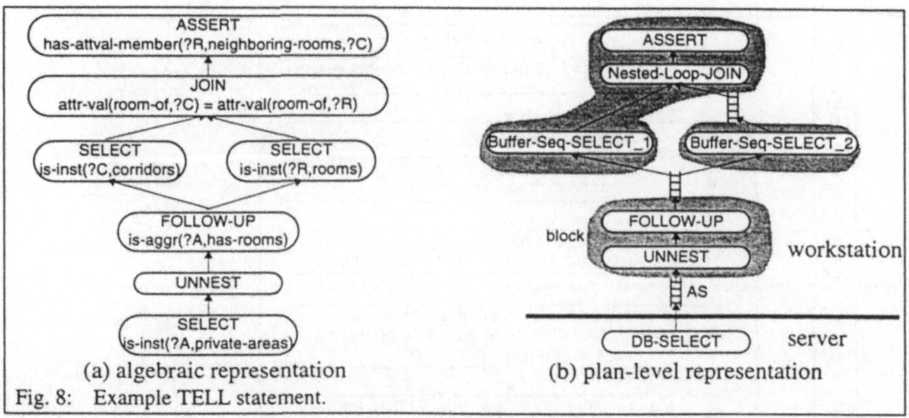

(a) algebraic representation   (b) plan-level representation

Fig. 8:   Example TELL statement.

materialized in the Working Memory and mapped to Access Structures, thus ensuring *efficient data flow between blocks*. Moreover, the way in which all these concepts are combined warrants *efficient dynamic query optimization* and the construction of *flexible units of execution* even at run time. These characteristics were achieved by a modular design and realization of the plan level.

Due to the workstation/server environment in which query processing is performed, determining the evaluation site of each algebra operator is a crucial issue (step ❷ in Fig. 6). By delegating operations to the server, the amount of data to be transferred into Working Memory can be reduced. This also results in less objects to be installed in Working Memory allowing a better exploitation of its storage capacities. Deciding on the evaluation site of each operator is based upon two criteria. Firstly, those algebra operators must be assigned to the workstation that are either too complex to be evaluated by the server DBS or that cannot be transformed into queries to the server due to the current mapping to the server DBMS.[4] Secondly, for performance reasons, the KOALA Processing System must exploit the contents of the Working Memory (including indices, sort orders, etc.).

The first criterion can be tested at compile time so that a preliminary borderline between workstation-based and server-based operations can be drawn (cf. Fig. 6, right side). Depending on the contents of the Working Memory at run time, the operators below the borderline may be assigned to workstation or server. Hence, plan-level manipulations can be definitively completed only at run time, yet preliminary plan optimizations may be performed for those operators definitively assigned to the workstation to save run-time effort (step ❸ in Fig. 6).

At run time, the KOALA Processing System interacts with the Context Manager to compare the actual contents of the Working Memory to the information referred to by the query at hand. If the input to an operator already resides in Working Memory (as an Access Structure), the producing subgraph[5] is pruned and replaced by a pointer to the appropriate Access Structure.

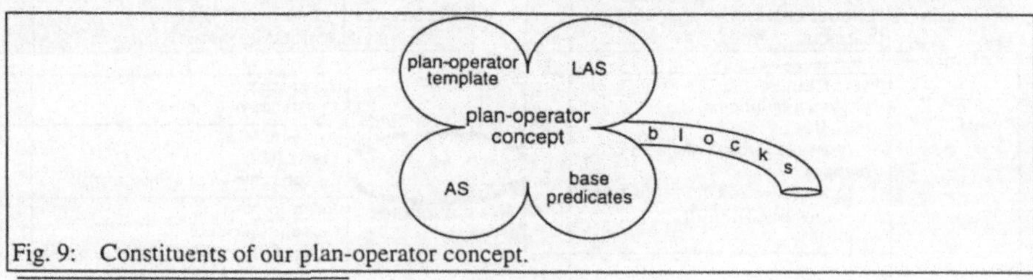

Fig. 9:   Constituents of our plan-operator concept.

---

4. For simplicity reasons, we shall not consider this aspect in this paper.
5. Consisting of one or more plan operators.

While this applies to operators above as well as below the preliminary borderline, for the latter it also implies that these operators are assigned to the workstation, i.e., the borderline is moved downward, and less operators must be delegated to the server (sketched in Fig. 6, right side). For those subgraphs not yet assigned to workstation or server, two further situations may arise. If the Working Memory does not contain any required input for a subgraph, the whole subgraph must be evaluated at the server DBMS[6], and the border between workstation and server remains where it has been put at compile time. The second situation occurs if only part of the required input is residing in Working Memory, and the rest must be fetched from the server. In this case, basically two processing strategies are possible: to completely delegate the query to the server, requiring to previously write back to the database the potentially updated portion of knowledge installed in Working Memory, or to only complement the Working-Memory contents such that the query can be performed in Working Memory. To solve this optimization problem, the KOALA Processing System interacts with the Context Manager (step ❹ in Fig. 6). This interaction and its outcome for our example query will be described in Sect. 4.3. Fig. 8 (b) shows the resulting plan-operator graph[7] assuming that no instance of *area* is residing in Working Memory. Hence, the corresponding selection must be executed in the server and is transformed into a server plan-operator (DB-SELECT). Since the subsequent UNNEST operator refers to object structures of the knowledge model, it must be carried out at the workstation side. Consequently, all its successors must be executed there as well, although evaluating the FOLLOW-UP operator may result in additional queries to be sent to the server. Since making assertions over the KB may involve the full functionality of the knowledge model, algebra operator ASSERT is always transformed into a workstation-based plan-operator (of the same name).

The resulting plan-operator graph can be further optimized (step ❺ in Fig. 6).

4.2.4 Dynamic Code Assembly and Execution

These tasks complete overall query processing (step ❻ in Fig. 6). The plan-level representation of a query is transformed into a graph made up of *blocks* (sketched in Fig. 6, right side) which are the units of execution in our query-processing approach. Blocks rely on the plan-operator level, both conceptually and concerning their implementation [TGHM94]. Just like plan operators, blocks accept one or more input streams and produce a single output stream. Blocks are constructed based on the processing characteristics of plan operators to minimize the amount of materialized intermediate results during query processing. Fig. 8 (b) shows the blocks constructed from the plan-operator graph at hand. The UNNEST and FOLLOW-UP operators can work in a pipelining fashion, and are therefore combined into a single block. The same holds for the Buffer-Seq-SELECT_1 (alternatively Buffer-Seq-SELECT_2), NESTED-LOOP-JOIN and ASSERT operators.[8]

Evaluating a query means executing the corresponding blocks. The most straightforward way is to perform blocks in a sequential order defined by the inter-relationships of the block-structured graph. Additionally, our query-processing approach also permits parallel execution of blocks [TMMD93].

Opposed to conventional query-processing systems requiring *strict compilation*, we assemble executable code by putting together precompiled functions, yet we may still choose to compile a query, e.g., for complex queries or large amounts of data to be processed. We call this approach *dynamic code assembly* [TGHM94], allowing to assemble executable code using fully compiled functions by data structures containing function pointers.

---

6. Note that it has already been checked at compile time that all operators below the borderline can be evaluated at the server.
7. For simplicity, we did not repeat the base predicates for the plan operators.
8. Note that, for this block being able to operate as a pipeline, the complete results of Buffer-Seq-SELECT_2 must be computed previously. Only in this case, the NESTED-LOOP-JOIN can directly process any new result being piped from Buffer-Seq-SELECT_1.

4.3 Context Management

It is the task of the Context Manager to provide the KOALA Processing System with information about the Working-Memory contents during plan generation. Due to the declarative query interface to the server component, the Context Manager should maintain its description of the Working-Memory contents in a declarative form as well. The Context Manager perceives the Working Memory as a collection of *contexts*. A context represents a set of Working-Memory objects being the complete extension of a logical condition, the *context description*.

Contexts directly correspond to the results of (sub-)queries that have been delegated to the server and whose results have been brought into Working Memory. For each set of query results received from the server, the Context Manager keeps the query condition as a context description and maintains an Access Structure that contains the set of result objects.[9] The language for context descriptions is therefore equivalent to the subset of KOALA that can appear as a condition of a DB-SELECT plan operator. In the following, we will illustrate the main activities performed by the Context Manager in coordination with the KOALA Processing System using the example query already introduced above.

Context Description

Let us assume, that a previous query retrieved from the server all instances of *areas* having more than three rooms. The Context Manager has therefore registered the following context description.

```
((?X)                                                    <------------- projection
    (IS-INSTANCE ?X areas *)            <----------- variable definition
    (> (SLOTVALUE no-of-rooms ?X) 3))   <------ selection
```

The description is divided into three parts. The *variable definition part* (V) characterizes the domain of the context's objects in terms of predicates referring to the abstraction concepts, while the *selection part* (S) states further selection conditions applying to the context. The *projection part* (P) completes the description, listing those attributes that have been brought into the Working Memory.

Context Comparison

When consulting the Context Manager, the KOALA Processing System submits a description of a 'wanted' context, resembling the subquery currently under consideration. The Context Manager compares the wanted context W with a 'given' context G, i.e., with a context available in Working Memory. To this end, we developed an algorithm that basically compares the different parts of W with the corresponding parts of G. For our example query, the KOALA Processing System will ask the Context Manager about contexts available for supporting the selection on *private-areas*. The result of the involved context comparison is depicted in Fig. 10.

First of all, the projection parts of the contexts are compared. Since both projection parts preserve the complete object structure, they turn out to be equivalent. Next, the variable definitions are compared. To determine the result, the Context Manager will at this point have to inspect the abstraction relationships defined in the KB. Since *areas* is known to be a superclass of *private-areas*, the result of the comparison is the set inclusion $V(G) \supseteq V(W)$. Finally, the selection parts are compared. Since no additional selection is defined for W (i.e., all *private-areas* are contained in the context), the comparison results in the set containment $S(G) \subseteq S(W)$.[10] The comparison of predicates in both the selection and the variable-definition parts relies on the interpretation of set relationships as logical relationships, where set containment is equivalent to logical implication.

---

9. The Access Structure can later be handed to the KOALA Processing System for accessing the context.
10. If several predicates are involved in a selection (or a variable-definition) part, each predicate of G must be compared with each one of W. For complex selection conditions (involving disjunctions, etc.), a disjunctive variant of the algorithm is supplied in addition to the above described (conjunctive) version.

G(iven)	Rel.	W(anted)
P: (?X)	$\equiv$	P: (?X)
V: (IS-INSTANCE ?X areas *)	$\supseteq$	V: (IS-INSTANCE ?X private-areas *)
S: (> (SLOTVALUE no-of-rooms ?X) 3)	$\subseteq$	S: 'true'
context G	'O'	context W

$G \cap W$: SELECT
    (IS-INSTANCE ?X private-areas *)
    FROM G

$W \setminus G$: LOAD
    (?X)
    (AND (IS-INSTANCE ?X private-areas *)
    (NOT (> (SLOTVALUE no-of-rooms ?X) 3))

Fig. 10: Context comparison (example).

To obtain the overall relationship between G and W, the individual comparison results for P, V, and S must be combined. In our example, the relationship 'G overlaps with W', (denoted by 'O') is achieved, because we have obtained two 'inverse' set inclusions in V and S. The 'overlap' result means that we can exploit the context existing in the Working Memory for answering the query. However, we still need to query the server for those objects not covered by the context. Therefore, the Context Manager additionally produces descriptions how to filter the existing context for the required result set (i.e., how to obtain $G \cap W$ from G), and how to retrieve the remaining objects from the server (i.e., how to retrieve $W \setminus G$). These results are passed to the KOALA Processing System for modifying the query plan accordingly. Moreover, a pointer to the AS containing G is passed on to make it accessible for the KOALA Processing System.

In our example, the KOALA Processing System chooses not to consider the private areas already in the Working Memory but to fetch all instances of *private-area* from the server. Before executing the query, however, the Context Manager must write back to server all private areas residing in the workstation buffer. Analogously, the Context Manager is asked about contexts available for rooms and corridors, the other classes involved in the example query. For reasons of simplicity we assume that these subqueries can be fully supported by contexts at the workstation component. The resulting query execution plan is depicted in Fig. 8 (b).

The above algorithm, which is outlined in detail in [De93], exhibits polynomial time complexity w.r.t. the number of predicates involved in the comparison. It is important to note that, although we retrieve only objects in $W \setminus G$ from the server, we might well retrieve objects that are already in the Working Memory. For example, other contexts might be present there that overlap with W, but are not exploited for the query because the 'amount of overlap' is not promising enough. The Working Memory is capable of handling this situation simply by ignoring already installed objects (i.e., no additional copies are introduced into the Working Memory).

Additional Tasks of the Context Manager

Although maintaining and comparing context descriptions can be seen as the central task of the Context Manager, additional activities are performed by this component to realize consistent buffer management based on the notion of contexts.

For instance, the Context Manager is involved in the process of *update propagation* to the server component. Before a query is delegated to the server, updates that have occurred on Working-Memory objects must be propagated to the server. Otherwise, inconsistencies between server DB and Working Memory may result in wrong query results. Using the Context Manager, we can realize a partial update delegation approach, i.e., not all updates, but only those updates (or a relatively small superset) that are needed to guarantee a correct query result are propagated.

Additional activities are required by the Context Manager to keep context extensions 'up-to-date' after updates, and for discarding contexts from the Working Memory. A more detailed discussion of these tasks can be found in [De93].

4.4 Constraint Management

In this paper, we can only briefly outline the modeling and processing concepts involved with integrity constraints. An elaborate description can be found in [De93].

Constraint Modeling

KRISYS supports a layered approach for representing constraint characteristics at different abstraction levels. The central part of a constraint is its condition, i.e., a logical condition that has to be valid in a consistent KB state. At the operational level, the constraint is described in terms of adjustments telling the system how to correct inconsistencies. For a single constraint, multiple, alternative adjustments can be specified, which are selected and executed according to various criteria. At the realization level, the 'implementation' of a constraint is described in terms of event patterns, whose occurrence will lead to the execution of particular checking and adjustment operations. Among other things, the constraint designer may choose either a data-driven realization (i.e., where violating actions trigger corrections), or a demand-driven semantics (i.e., 'dependent' information is recomputed each time it is needed).

An example illustrating the layered approach is depicted in Fig. 11 showing a constraint stating that for all rooms ?X that have a corridor ?Y as a neighboring room, ?Y must have ?X as one of its accessible rooms (i.e., the corridor allows access to room ?X). One of the adjustments defined for this constraint states that for pairs of rooms and corridors violating the constraint, the room should be added as an attribute value of 'accessible-rooms' of the corridor. Essentially, KOALA is used (in a slightly modified form) for specifying constraint conditions and adjustments. The user may define constraints by specifying logical formulas with both existential and universal quantification. Moreover, user-defined methods can be evaluated in the query and constraint language environment, and can therefore be used for checking consistency and for carrying out reactive operations. At the realization level, a data-driven implementation was chosen, meaning that the adjustment will be performed on occurrence of an update event on the 'neighboring-rooms' attribute of a room. Alternatively, a demand-driven implementation would have been possible, which is also depicted in Fig. 11.

Along the specification of the constraint, the system shields the user as far as possible from (event-oriented) realization details by automatically determining constraint characteristics at the realization level. For our example constraint, only the condition and the adjustment (in the syntax presented in Fig. 11) were actually specified by the user. This support allows a high-level, implementation-independent constraint specification. Determining event-patterns describing in which situations an adjustment should or should not be applied is performed by the system based on the assumption that adjustments should always be conflict-avoiding. This means that an adjustment should, if possible, not contradict (or undo) user operations that caused the inconsistency. If this assumption does not hold, the person having defined the constraint may replace the event-patterns produced by the system, thereby specifying his own 'implementation'.

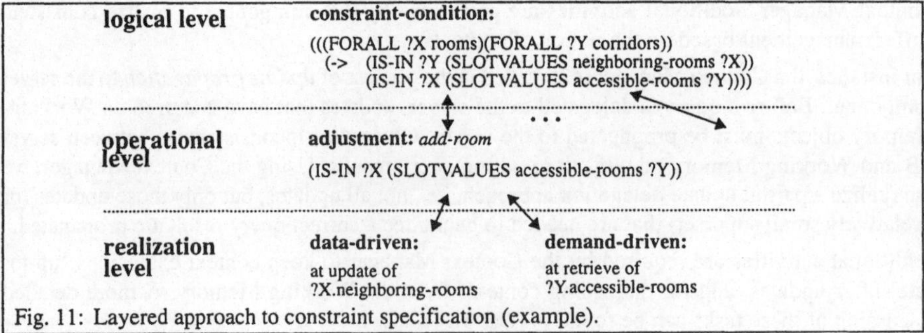

Fig. 11: Layered approach to constraint specification (example).

Additional aspects of the constraint mechanism can only be briefly listed here. We refer to [De93] for details.

- Methods in KRISYS are executed in a nested-transaction scheme. Both methods and integrity constraints can be associated with integrity levels describing certain degrees of partial consistency to be guaranteed by methods executing on that level.

- Constraint violations can be tolerated and defined as exceptions. This is especially important for long-running activities, such as design applications, where a rollback of work is not desirable.

- Constraints can be specified not only for classes, but also for individual object instances. This allows, for example, to represent design goals specific to a product under development as constraints.

- Method calls can be used in both conditions and adjustments, allowing to employ procedures for testing consistency and implementing corrections.

- Constraints are represented as objects in the KRISYS knowledge representation framework, allowing them to be organized using abstraction concepts and queried using KOALA.

- Constraint templates allow the definition of parameterized constraints, thereby permitting constraints to be tailored to application-specific needs.

Constraint Monitoring

Constraint monitoring, being essential for achieving effective and efficient integrity control for the applications KRISYS is intended for, is performed at the workstation side. Consequently, constraint monitoring activities can be realized in the knowledge representation framework of KRISYS, i.e., they are implemented in a natural way as the 'behavior' of the objects (such as constraint, adjustment, and integrity-level objects) used for constraint modeling. Moreover, the processing concepts, such as the processing of KOALA and the functionality of the Working Memory can be directly employed.

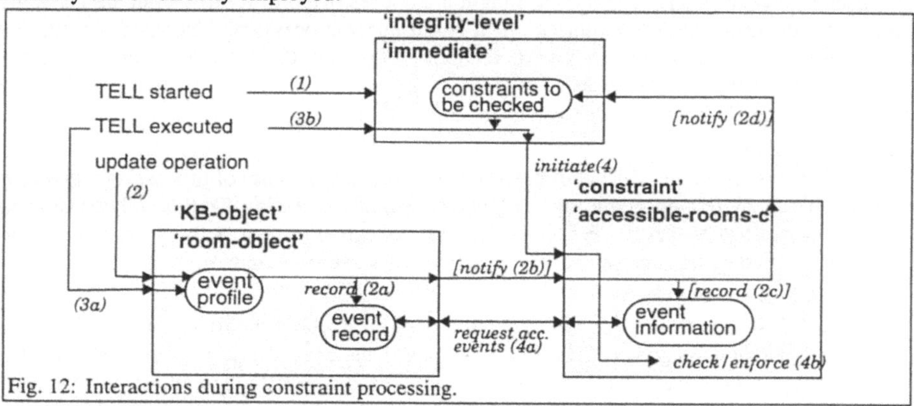

Fig. 12: Interactions during constraint processing.

As shown in Fig. 12, constraint-monitoring activities are distributed across three major components. *Event management* is integrated into the regular KB objects by

- keeping an event profile for each object that contains information about the events to be recorded and about the constraints that are affected, and

- storing an event record with the objects, thereby supporting local event accumulation.

These activities are initiated by base predicates responsible for updating an object in the Working Memory (see Sect. 4.2.1). After the initiation of a TELL is reported to the appropriate integrity-level object (Fig. 12, step 1), the execution of the base predicate (Fig. 12, step 2) modifying attribute values will cause the appropriate event description to be stored with each object added to class *rooms*. Moreover, the constraint object representing the constraint defined in Fig. 11 will be notified.

Constraint scheduling is performed by those integrity-level objects responsible for initiating the processing of individual constraints in an appropriate order. For example, the object representing the 'immediate' integrity-level will be directly activated after the TELL statement is executed (Fig. 12, step 3), but before the transaction associated with the statement is committed. It will then schedule constraint monitoring according to a priority scheme, if multiple constraints need to be activated, and in turn activate the constraint objects (Fig. 12, step 4).

Constraint enforcement is realized by the individual constraint objects. They have the task to check the constraint condition according to the event information supplied by the event management and take the appropriate actions to handle the occurring violations. In our example, the constraint object will try to use the single adjustment defined for it to correct the violations, and will be able to apply the adjustment because it does not contradict the operation performed by the user (i.e., it will not undo the effects of the TELL statement). The adjustment is again realized as a TELL statement that exploits the event information passed to the constraint object for adjusting only inconsistent objects. This TELL statement has been generated by the system by specializing the adjustment supplied by the user to specific event patterns.

5. Conclusions

In this paper we described the design and implementation of advanced knowledge processing in the KBMS KRISYS. The most important issues to be addressed by this framework are the workstation/server environment as well as its impact on overall knowledge processing resulting in main-memory-based query processing. The processing framework of KRISYS founds on the KOBRA knowledge model and benefits from well-known query-processing techniques, especially from the areas of relational, main-memory, object-oriented, and parallel database systems [HFLP89, IEEE92, Ca91, MPTW94]. The applicability of our approach as well as of the mechanisms necessary for implementing it are not restricted to KRISYS but are generally valid for (advanced) DBMS requiring client-based query processing. Therefore, we see our knowledge-processing framework and its implementation, i.e. KRISYS, as a valuable contribution to current research in advanced DBMS.

Our approach can be best characterized by its major components

- Working Memory
  Its task is to support the concept of near-by-the-application locality of processing when KOBRA objects are referenced during query and constraint processing. To this end, the Context Manager guarantees that the Working-Memory contents is exploited for query processing, thus reducing data transfer between workstation and server to a minimum.

- KOALA Processing System
  The query language KOALA is processed following an algebraic approach that is sufficiently flexible to adapt to language extensions. Along the same lines, the plan-operator concept for client-based query processing has been designed to be extensible and to allow run-time optimizations.

- Constraint Manager
  A new mechanism for integrity management has been outlined and integrated into the knowledge-processing framework of KRISYS.

Although object-oriented DBMS aim at the same application domains as KRISYS, to the best of our knowledge, there are no such systems that offer comparable concepts for optimizing and processing arbitrary queries on the workstation's buffer. ObjectStore [OHMS92], for example, provides simple search arguments (path expressions) for navigating the buffer. Selecting appropriate indices handling simple search arguments and execution are interleaved. This optimization measure differs from our approach of employing run-time optimization before execution.

Run-time optimizations may be motivated either by the desire to flexibly adjust execution strategies, as pursued by Volcano [Gr94], or by the desire to dynamically exploit buffer contents, as proposed for ADMS [CR94]. ADMS integrates matching and query optimization. The query graph is reduced by those parts that match cached query results stored in a cache space and organized by a specific data structure called *logical access-path schema*. In our case, representations of buffered and intermediate (cached) data coincide. Hence, matching and optimization operate on a single representation, thus simplifying query-processing implementation.

Re-implementation of KRISYS started with the Working-Memory representation, Access Structures, and their functionality. This provided the basis for the KOBRA model and its internal interface which have been fully operational since 1993 as well. At the same time, the Mapping System had been completed so that we could start implementing the KOALA Processing System. The transformation of a KOALA query into an algebraic representation and the subsequent rewrite are already realized, as well as all constituents of the plan-operator level, including blocks and the corresponding functionality. Currently, the KOALA Processing System allows to sequentially execute block-structured queries.

The availability of query-processing facilities opens up a range of research activities we are currently working on or which will be part of our future work:

- implementing the Context Manager to practically investigate the interplay between the knowledge referenced by queries and the costs and benefits of context maintenance,

- realizing the Constraint Manager starting from the basic functionality linking query processing and constraint management, i.e., event management, constraint scheduling, and constraint enforcement,

- considering non-algebraic optimization, i.e., establishing a cost model for query processing taking into account features of the knowledge model (method calls, transitive closure operations like inheritance, etc.), context management and mapping information.

References

Ca91   Cattell, R. (ed.): Next Generation Database Systems, in: Special issue of Communications of the ACM, Vol. 34, No.10, 1991.

CR94   Chen, C.M., Roussopoulos, N.: The Implementation and Performance Evaluation of the ADMS Query Optimizer: Integrating Query Result Caching and Matching, in: Advances in Database Technology - EDBT '94, Jarke, M., Bubenko, J. (eds.), Lecture Notes in Computer Science 779, Springer-Verlag, 1994, 323-336.

De91   Deßloch, S.: Handling Integrity in a KBMS Architecture for Workstation/Server Environments, in: Proc. of the GI-Fachtagung "Datenbanksysteme in Büro, Technik und Wissenschaft", Kaiserslautern, März 1991, Hrsg. H.-J. Appelrath, Informatik-Fachberichte 270, Springer-Verlag, S.89-108.

De93   Deßloch, S.: Semantic Integrity in Advanced Database Management Systems, Doctoral Thesis, Dept. of Computer Science, University of Kaiserslautern, Sept. 1993.

DLMT93 Deßloch, S., Leick, F.J., Mattos, N., Thomas, J.: The KRISYS Project - A Summary of What We have Learned so far, in: Stucky, W., Oberweis, A. (eds.): Datenbanksysteme in Büro, Technik und Wissenschaft,, Springer (Informatik Aktuell), 1993, 124-143.

Gr94   Graefe, G.: Volcano, an Extensible and Parallel Query Evaluation System, in: IEEE Transactions on Knowledge and Data Engineering, Vol.6, No.1, 1994, pp. 120-135.

HFLP89 Haas, L. Freytag, J., Lohman, G., Pirahesh, H.: Extensible Query Processing in Starburst, in: Proc. ACM SIGMOD Int. Conf. on Management of Data, Portland, 1989, 377-388.

HMMS87 Härder, T., Meyer-Wegener, K., Mitschang, B., Sikeler, A.: PRIMA - A DBMS Prototype Supporting Engineering Applications, in: Proc. of the 13th Int. VLDB Conf., Brighton, UK, 1987, pp. 433-442.

HS93   Hong, W., Stonebraker, M.: Optimization of Parallel Query Execution Plans in XPRS, Distributed and Parallel Databases, Vol. 1, 1993, 9-32.

IEEE92   Eich, M. (ed.): IEEE Transactions on Knowledge and Data Engineering, Special Issue on Main-Memory Databases, Vol. 4, No. 6, 1992.

In84   IntelliCorp Inc.: The Knowledge Engineering Environment, IntelliCorp, Menlo Park, CA, 1984.

ISO94   ISO/IEC JTC1/SC21/WG3: ISO/ANSI working draft Database Languages - SQL3, American National Standards Institute, 1430 Broadway, New York, NY 10018, Sept. 1994.

KL89   Kifer, M., Lausen, G.: F-Logic, a Higher-Order Language for Reasoning about Objects, Inheritance and Schema, Proc. of the ACM SIGMOD Int. Conf. on Management of Data, 1989, pp. 134-146.

Kr93   Krivokapic, N.: Schema Evolution in KRISYS (in German), Diploma Thesis, University Kaiserslautern, 1993.

La91   Langkafel, D.:A Component for Graph-oriented Management of Knowledge-base Excerpts (in German), Undergraduation Final Work, Dept. of Computer Science, University Kaiserslautern, 1991.
LLOW91   Lamb, C., Landis, G., Orenstein, J., Weinreb, D.: The ObjectStore Database System, in: Communications of the ACM, special issue on next-generation database systems, vol. 34, no. 10, 1991, pp. 50-63.
LLPS91   Lohman, G. Lindsay, B., Pirahesh, H., Schiefer, B.: Extensions to Starburst: Objects, Types, Functions, and Rules, in: CACM, Vol. 34, No. 10, 1991, pp. 94-109.
LVZZ94   Lanzelotte, R. Valduriez, P., Zait, M., Ziane, M.: Industrial-Strength Parallel Query Optimization: Issues and Lessons, in: Information Systems, Vol. 19, No. 4, 1994, pp.311-330.
Ma91   Mattos, N.: An Approach to Knowledge Base Management, in: LNCS 513, Springer-Verlag, 1991.
MPTW94   Mohan, C., Pirahesh, H., Tang, W., Wang, Y.: Parallelism in relational database management systems, in: IBM System Journal, Vol.33, No. 2, 1994, pp. 349-371.
ODMG93   Cattell, R. (ed.): The Object Database Standard: ODMG-93, Morgan Kaufmann, CA, 1993.
OHMS92   Orenstein, J., Haradhvala, S., Margulies, B., Sakahara, D.: Query Processing in the ObjectStore Database System, Proc. of the 1992 ACM SIGMOD Conference, 403-412.
Sch91   Schulte, D.: Flexible mapping of Knowledge Models to Data Models exemplified using the knowledge Model KOBRA and the Relational Model (in German), Diploma Thesis, University Kaiserslautern, 1991.
Su91   Surjanto, B.: Design and Implementation of a Knowledge-based System Generating Application-specific KB schemata for KRISYS (in German), Diploma Thesis, University Kaiserslautern, 1991.
TD93   Thomas, J., Deßloch, S.: A Plan-Operator Concept for Client-Based Knowledge Processing, Proc. 19th VLDB Conference, Dublin, Ireland, August 1993.
TGHM94   Thomas,J., Gerbes, T., Härder, T., Mitschang, B.: Implementing Dynamic Code Assembly for Client-Based Query Processing, submitted for publication.
TMMD93   Thomas, J., Mitschang, B., Mattos, N., Deßloch, S.: Enhancing Knowledge Processing in Client/Server Environments, Proc. 2nd Int. Conf. on Information and Knowledge Management, Washington, D.C., 1993, 324-334.

Managing Temporal Knowledge Using a Deductive Constraint Database System

Roman Gross and Robert Marti

Institut für Informationssysteme
ETH Zentrum, CH-8092 Zürich
Switzerland
(gross,marti)@inf.ethz.ch

Abstract. This paper describes how the technology of deductive constraint database systems and constraint query languages can be used to represent and reason with partially incomplete temporal knowledge. First, we summarize our approach to solving constraints over reals within deductive database systems. This approach is based on the compile-time rewriting of clauses which are not necessarily range-restricted. Then, we show how the timestamping of facts and rules in temporal databases can be mapped to constraints over reals. Subsequently, we present a more efficient and elegant approach which is based on a special temporal constraint solver. Finally, we show how problems such as periodically recurring events can be elegantly modeled and solved within our framework.

Keywords: temporal databases, temporal reasoning, deductive databases, constraint satisfaction, constraint query languages, constraint logic programming

1 Introduction

Current database management systems ultimately return a set of ground substitutions for the variables occurring in a query, that is, equations of the form $X = c$ where X is a variable and c is a constant. In other words, every answer corresponds to a tuple of constant values, typically of type integer, real or string. However, many real-world problems can not be solved by associating constant values to all of the variables e.g. because insufficient information is available in order to compute a precise answer. Instead, some variables may take part in constraints in the form of complex equations or inequalities, or they may even be completely free. Problems which naturally give rise to such "partial" answers which are subject to certain constraints include configuration tasks, circuit design and temporal reasoning.

In a similar vein, conventional database systems typically fail to answer queries if at least one of the subqueries has infinitely many solutions. Hence, the answer set cannot be enumerated as it would be in ordinary systems. Typical problems of this kind are periodically recurring events such as the weekly departure of a particular flight.

FlightNr	*DepartDay*	*DepartTime*
'SR100'	1994/12/10	13:05
'SR100'	1994/12/10	13:05
⋮	⋮	⋮

However, the infinitely many solutions may be subject to certain conditions which can be represented as a finite collection of constraints. The tuples in the example above have in common that the *DepartTime* is equal to 1994/12/10 modulo 7 days.

FlightNr	*DepartDay*	*DepartTime*
'SR100'	1994/12/10 mod 7 days	13:05

Jaffar et al. have successfully merged constraint solving techniques to deal with the above mentioned problems with logic programming [JL87]. In the last few years, many systems based on the approach of constraint logic programming (CLP) have been implemented, e.g. CLP($\mathcal{R}$). All of them are main memory based and hence are limited to handle large amount of data. Therefore, [KKR90] have proposed the concept of a constraint query language (CQL) in order to represent and handle constraints in deductive databases. CQLs are similar to CLP-languages in that they support the management of non-ground facts and non-allowed rules as well as non-ground answers. However, to the best of our knowledge, no complete and reasonably efficient implementation of a CQL exists with the exception of our own DeCoR[1] system ([GM93, GM94b], see below).

During the same period, a lot of research has been done in the areas of temporal databases (see e.g. [TCG$^+$93, Böh94]) and temporal reasoning. Temporal databases not only contain information about the present state of the real world, but also the history leading up to this state and/or possible future developments. Most of these efforts are based on the relational model and SQL.

In this paper, we argue that the constraint satisfaction technology of DeCoR can elegantly be applied to managing temporal information, providing the functionality associated with typical temporal database systems. Moreover, temporal information which is incomplete and/or potentially infinite can be represented by the system.

The paper is structured as follows: Section 2 gives an overview of DeCoR and how it deals with constraints. Section 3 sketches how temporal knowledge can be represented in the existing DeCoR system, using constraints over reals. Section 4 presents a more elegant approach which relies on building a special purpose constraint solver which can deal with constraints over both time points (instants) and time intervals.

---

[1] DeCoR stands for DEductive database system with COnstraints over Reals.

2 Overview of DeCoR

The DeCoR system is a prototype of a deductive constraint database system implemented as a strongly coupled front-end (written in Prolog) running on top of an SQL-based commercial database product (Oracle). As a result of this architecture, the DeCoR system features full database functionality (i.e., concurrency control, logging and recovery, authorization and physical data independence).

A DeCoR database consists of a set of clauses (facts and rules) which are mapped to SQL base tables and views in a straightforward way. Rule bodies and queries are translated into SQL statements which can be executed by the underlying relational database system (DBMS). The queries are evaluated in a bottom-up fashion in an attempt to minimize the calls to the DBMS. In addition to these parts of usual deductive database systems, the DeCoR system contains components to store and handle constraints.

2.1 Deductive Database with Constraints

In the following we assume familiarity with deductive database systems, as e.g. described in [MWW89, CGT90, VRK$^+$91, Bur92, RSSS93]. These systems usually handle equations and inequalities $(=, \neq, <, \leq, >, \geq)$ on arithmetic terms (with $+, -, *$) only if the variables occurring in these expressions are ground and therefore the arithmetic expressions can be evaluated. DeCoR generalizes the treatment of arithmetic relations by allowing variables to be non-ground. Hence, these built-in predicates can be viewed as constraints on potential values for those variables.

Definition 1. A *constraint* is a relation $(t_1 \Theta t_2)$ where t_1, t_2 are arithmetic terms and the symbol Θ represents any of the symbols $(=, \neq, <, \leq, >, \geq)$.

Definition 2. A *generalized clause* is an implication of the form

$$p_0(\mathbf{X}_0) \leftarrow p_1(\mathbf{X}_1), \ldots, p_n(\mathbf{X}_n), c_1(\mathbf{X}_{n+1}), \ldots, c_m(\mathbf{X}_{n+m}).$$

where p_i are user defined predicates and c_j are constraints. The $\mathbf{X}_k$ are vectors of variables. A generalized clause does not have to be range-restricted.

This definition follows that given by Kanellakis et al. [KKR90] for a generalized fact.

Definition 3. A system of generalized clauses form a database with constraints, called a *constraint database*.

Formulas in the DeCoR system may contain conjunctions (,), existential quantifiers ($\exists$) as well as negation ($\neg$). Disjunctions have to be represented by multiple clauses. Without loss of generality we assume in the following that clauses and queries are in standard form, where all arguments in atoms are variables and each variable occurs at most once in an user-defined predicate, c.f. [GM94b, JM94].

426

Example 1. The standard form of the clause $p(X, Y) \leftarrow q(X, 5), r(X, Y, Y)$. will be written as

$$p(X, Y) \leftarrow q(X_1, Z), r(X_2, Y_1, Y_2), X = X_1, X_1 = X_2, Y = Y_1, Y_1 = Y_2, Z = 5.$$

2.2 Types of Constraints

In deductive database systems which demand allowedness, all variables become ground during bottom-up evaluation [CGT90]. This is no longer guaranteed in constraint database systems because some variables might be only constrained by inequalities or even completely free. Therefore, two types of variables are distinguished according to their groundness which is determined in a bottom-up fashion.

Definition 4. A variable X in the body of a clause is *ground* $\langle g \rangle$ if

- X is bound to a constant c.
- X can be bound to a term $f(Y_1, \ldots, Y_n)$ by solving the constraints of the clause. (For this to be possible, the Y_i have to be ground.
- X appears in a user-defined predicate at an argument position which is ground. (The groundness of the arguments is determined by the groundness patterns of the body predicates, see below).

Otherwise the variable is *non-ground* $\langle n \rangle$.

The arguments in the head of a clause inherit the groundness information from the body. The groundness of the arguments in turn determines the groundness patterns of the predicates.

Example 2. The groundness pattern $\langle ggng \rangle$ for a predicate determines that the first, second and fourth arguments are ground whereas the third argument is non-ground.

Based on the groundness information of the variables, constraints can be separated into evaluable and non-evaluable ones.

Definition 5. A constraint C is *evaluable* if

- C is an equation which can be transformed into $X = f(Y_1, \ldots, Y_n)$ where each Y_i is ground.
- C is an inequality not containing any non-ground variable.

Otherwise, the constraint is *non-evaluable*.

It can easily be seen that evaluable constraints correspond exactly to those allowed in "ordinary" deductive database systems. As shown e.g. in [CGT90, Bur92] these constraints can be translated into selection conditions in relational algebra in a straightforward way. This is not the case with non-evaluable constraints which have to be manipulated separately.

2.3 Constraint Lifting Algorithm

The constraint database system DeCoR delays the evaluation of non-evaluable constraints until they become evaluable (if ever). For that purpose, the clauses are rewritten at compile-time in such a way that at run-time, only evaluable parts have to be dealt with [GM93, GM94b]. This is achieved by propagating non-evaluable constraints into dependent clauses. This process is denoted as *constraint lifting (CL)*.

The constraint lifting algorithm (CLA) consists of the following 5 steps which are applied iteratively on each clause C in a bottom-up fashion on the reduced dependency tree.

1. Rewrite clause C into standard form. In doing so, all equality constraints become explicit.
2. For each literal in the body of C, lift the non-evaluable constraints occurring in its respective definitions into C.
3. Simplify (solve) the resulting conjunction of constraints.
4. Split the simplified constraints into evaluable and non-evaluable ones.
5. Fold the evaluable parts (user-defined predicates and evaluable constraints) into a unique auxiliary predicate which contains as arguments the variables of the non-evaluable part (non-evaluable constraints).

Step 3 of the CLA depends on a domain-specific constraint solver which has to meet some special requirements [GM94a]. For example, it must be able to deal with variables for which it is only known whether or not they will become ground at run-time. The DeCoR system contains a solver for constraints over reals based on Kramer's rule and Fourier elimination.

The following example shows the abilities of the CLA in the DeCoR system.

Example 3. Given a set of ground facts $tax\_rate(Low, Up, Rate)$ which contain the tax rate applicable to specific income ranges, e.g. $tax\_rate(0, 5\,000, 0)$. $tax\_rate(5\,000, 25\,000, 0.05)$. $tax\_rate(25\,000, 55\,000, 0.1)$.

$$tax(Inc, Tax) \leftarrow$$
$$tax\_rate(Min, Max, Rate), Min \leq Inc, Inc < Max, \qquad (1)$$
$$Tax = Rate * Inc, Min < 10\,000.$$

Steps 1 to 3 of the CLA do not affect the rewriting of this clause because tax_rate is a base predicate. Steps 4 and 5 result in

$$tax(Inc, Tax) \leftarrow$$
$$tax\_aux(Inc, Tax, Min, Max, Rate), Min \leq Inc, Inc < Max, \qquad (2)$$
$$Tax = Rate * Inc.$$
$$tax\_aux(\_, \_, Min, Max, Rate) \leftarrow \qquad\qquad\qquad\qquad\quad (3)$$
$$tax\_rate(Min, Max, Rate), Min < 10\,000.$$

(2) contains the non-evaluable parts of the original clause and (3) the evaluable ones.

The query $?\text{--}\,tax(I,T)$ is also rewritten by the CLA. In step 2, the body of (2) is lifted into the query and replaces the predicate tax_rate. The resulting query

$$?\text{--}\,tax\_aux(I,T,Min,Max,Rate), Min \leq I, I < Max, T = Rate * I.$$

does not have to be processed further and can be answered by

I	T	$Constraints$
	0	$0 \leq I, I < 5\,000$
		$5\,000 \leq I, I < 25\,000, T = 0.05 * I$

As a consequence of this approach, the run-time query evaluation mechanism of the DeCoR system only has to deal with the evaluable parts of the clauses and hence can be realized using well known techniques developed for deductive databases. In particular, the usual optimization techniques developed for standard bottom-up evaluation (e.g. Magic Template [Ram88], Constraint Pushing [SS94]) can be combined with the CLA.

3 Managing Temporal Knowledge in DeCoR

Managing temporal knowledge can be considered as an application of the general-purpose constraint database system DeCoR. Such an application should support time points (following [JCE$^+$94], we will use the term instant) and time intervals as well as relations between objects of these types. The DeCoR system provides the functionality to implement most of the typical features of temporal databases.

In this paper we restrict ourselves to relations with only one temporal argument which can be considered as the valid-time of a tuple. Nevertheless, our ideas can easily be generalized to relations with multiple temporal arguments such as bitemporal relations.

In the following, familiarity with temporal databases as e.g. described in [TCG$^+$93, Böh94] is assumed. Moreover, we attempt to adhere to the terminology introduced in [JCE$^+$94]. In order to improve readability, a special notation for temporal terms is used: Instant variables (event variables) will be denoted by $\mathcal{E}_1, \mathcal{E}_2, \ldots$ whereas interval variables will be denoted by $\mathcal{T}_1, \mathcal{T}_2, \ldots$. The start (end) point of a time interval $\mathcal{T}$ will be denoted by $\mathcal{T}^s$ ($\mathcal{T}^e$). A concrete instant is represented as e.g. /1994/5/22~13:40:13.6. An instant such as /1994/6/15~00:00:00 will be abbreviated to /1994/6/15. Finally, time intervals are considered as closed at the lower bound and open at the upper one. The format for such an interval is [/1994/6/15 – /1994/6/23].

3.1 Temporal Datatypes and Relations

While the DeCoR system supports the datatypes string, integer and real, only constraints over reals can currently be solved. To pass the constraint solving ability on temporal terms, an instant $\mathcal{E}$ is mapped to a value of type real. This is done by calculating the number of seconds between $\mathcal{E}$ and a reference point, e.g. /1970/1/1.

Example 4. The predicate *rate* shows the instant and the exchange rate between two currencies

$$rate(/1993/4/23 \sim 13{:}45{:}12.4, \text{'DM'}, \text{'SFR'}, 86.6)$$
$$\Updownarrow$$
$$rate(7.251183e + 08, \text{'DM'}, \text{'SFR'}, 86.6)$$

A consequence of the above mapping is that the best precision is obtained for instants near the reference point. This is usually not a problem because most databases contain instants within a few decades only or do not need a temporal granularity smaller than microseconds.

In historical databases, each fact is typically timestamped with a valid time interval which represents the knowledge that the fact is true at every instant within this interval. The distinction between a valid time interval and all the instants within the interval leads to two different representations of intervals in the DeCoR system. The *implicit* representation emphasizes the validity of the fact at every instant in the interval. The *explicit* representation emphasizes the time interval and gives direct access to the borders of the interval.

Definition 6. The *implicit representation* of a fact $p(\mathbf{X})$ valid in the interval $[T^s\text{–}T^e]$ is
$$p(\mathbf{X}, \mathcal{E}) \leftarrow T^s \leq \mathcal{E}, \mathcal{E} < T^e.$$
The *explicit representation* of the same fact is
$$p(\mathbf{X}, T^s, T^e).$$

The advantage of the implicit representation is that the temporal conjunction $(p(\mathbf{X}, \mathcal{E}), q(\mathbf{X}, \mathcal{E}))$, which requires the intersection of the valid times associated with p and q, can be directly performed by the constraint solver of the constraint database system. On the other hand, it is not possible to extract the bounds of the interval. Hence, it is not possible to calculate e.g. the duration of the interval. This drawback disappears if the intervals are explicitly represented. However, this representation requires that the temporal relations such as *before* have to be defined explicitly too. The advantages and disadvantages of these two representations are similar to those of time intervals respectively instants. (We refer to [Böh94] for the discussion of time intervals versus instants and further references.)

As opposed to "ordinary" deductive database systems, the temporal relations can easily be represented in a constraint database system such as DeCoR. As a consequence, the explicit representation of time intervals is preferred.

The following three examples give an impression how the temporal relations can be realized.

Example 5. The interval $[T_3^s-T_3^e]$ is the (non-empty) *temporal intersection* of the intervals $[T_1^s-T_1^e]$ and $[T_2^s-T_2^e]$

$$
\begin{aligned}
&/*\,intersect(T_1^s,T_1^e,T_2^s,T_2^e,T_3^s,T_3^e).\,*/\\
&intersect(T_1^s,T_1^e,T_2^s,T_2^e,T_1^s,T_1^e) \leftarrow T_1^s \geq T_2^s, T_1^e \leq T_2^e.\\
&intersect(T_1^s,T_1^e,T_2^s,T_2^e,T_1^s,T_2^e) \leftarrow T_1^s \geq T_2^s, T_1^e > T_2^e.\\
&intersect(T_1^s,T_1^e,T_2^s,T_2^e,T_2^s,T_1^e) \leftarrow T_1^s < T_2^s, T_1^e \leq T_2^e.\\
&intersect(T_1^s,T_1^e,T_2^s,T_2^e,T_2^s,T_2^e) \leftarrow T_1^s < T_2^s, T_1^e > T_2^e.
\end{aligned}
$$

Example 6. The relation $[T_1^s-T_1^e]$ *before* $[T_2^s-T_2^e]$ can be written as

$$
before(T_1^s,T_1^e,T_2^s,T_2^e) \leftarrow T_1^e < T_2^s.
$$

Example 7. The *duration* D of an interval T is calculated in seconds and can be written as

$$
duration(T^s,T^e,D) \leftarrow D = T^e - T^s.
$$

The temporal relations can be used as ordinary user-defined predicates. This can be seen at the following example adapted from [Böh94].

Example 8. The timestamped relation $works\_in(EmpNo, DepNo, T^s, T^e)$ has to be defined. The query: "When ($[T3s, T3e]$) and how many days (D) did the persons with the employee number 1354 and 245 work in the same department (Dep)?" will be written as:

$$
\begin{aligned}
?-\ &\exists\, T1s, T1e, T2s, T2e, S\\
&(works\_in(1354, Dep, T1s, T1e),\\
&\ works\_in(245, Dep, T2s, T2e),\\
&\ intersect(T1s, T1e, T2s, T2e, T3s, T3e),\\
&\ duration(T3s, T3e, S),\\
&\ S = 86400 * D).
\end{aligned}
$$

The last constraint $S = 86400 * D$ is necessary because the predicate *duration* calculates the difference of $T3s$ and $T3e$ in seconds (S) and not in days (D) as demanded in the query.

If the predicate *works_in* contains ground facts only, all variables in the query will be ground and hence all constraints lifted from *intersect* and *duration* turn out to be evaluable. However, this query will possibly give a partially instantiated answer if there is a person for whom only the starting point of his or her employment in a department is known. Such an answer cannot be returned by conventional temporal database systems because they do not have a constraint component.

Example 9. If the ground fact $works\_in(1354, \text{'Sal'}, /1994/4/1, /1994/10/1)$ and the partially instantiated fact $works\_in(245, \text{'Sal'}, /1994/2/1, \_)$ are stored in the database, the answer to the query of Example 8 is

$T3s$	$T3e$	D	$Constraints$
/1994/4/1	/1994/10/1	240	$works\_in(245, \text{'Sal'}, /1994/2/1, \mathcal{E})$, $\mathcal{E} \geq /1994/10/1$
/1994/4/1	$\mathcal{E}$	$D1/86400$	$works\_in(245, \text{'Sal'}, /1994/2/1, \mathcal{E})$, $\mathcal{E} < /1994/10/1$, $duration(/1994/4/1, \mathcal{E}, D1)$

3.2 Temporal Reduction (Coalescing)

As pointed out e.g. in [BM93, BM94, Böh94], it is necessary to coalesce time intervals for value-equivalent facts (facts which are identical with the exception of their temporal arguments). They refer to this operation as *temporal reduction.*

Of course, we have to perform temporal reduction in our representation of a temporal database as well. Because the reduction operator is second order and because it is not integrated in the underlying DeCoR system, the reduction has to be programmed explicitly for every user-defined predicate.

In the following, the reduction scheme for a generic predicate $p(\mathbf{X}, T^s, T^e)$ is presented. The reduction requires two additional relations. $p\_clos(\mathbf{X}, T^s, T^e)$ contains the transitive closure obtained by pairwise coalescing the intervals pertaining to value-equivalent tuples. The relation $p\_red(\mathbf{X}, T^s, T^e)$ contains the temporally reduced facts.

$$p\_clos(\mathbf{X}, T^s, T^e) \leftarrow p(\mathbf{X}, T^s, T^e).$$
$$p\_clos(\mathbf{X}, T_1^s, T_2^e) \leftarrow p(\mathbf{X}, T_1^s, T_1^e), p\_clos(\mathbf{X}, T_2^s, T_2^e),$$
$$T_1^s < T_2^s, T_2^s \leq T_1^e, T_1^e < T_2^e.$$

$$p\_red(\mathbf{X}, T^s, T^e) \leftarrow p\_clos(\mathbf{X}, T^s, T^e),$$
$$\neg \exists T_1^s, T_1^e (p\_clos(\mathbf{X}, T_1^s, T_1^e),$$
$$T_1^s \leq T^s, T^e \leq T_1^e, \neg(T_1^s = T^s, T^e = T_1^e)).$$

3.3 Assessment

The typical functionality associated with temporal database systems can be implemented as an application of the DeCoR system. Moreover, the possibility to manipulate partially instantiated facts and answers as supported by the DeCoR system can be exploited nicely as shown in Example 9.

Unfortunately, this approach has some serious drawbacks. First, it is not very efficient because the CLA has to lift many constraints. In particular, each temporal conjunction results in the lifting of four constraint parts. This overhead is not acceptable for such a frequent operation. Second, as seen in the examples above, it is clumsy to explicitly write two arguments for every time interval.

Both drawbacks are primarily due to the facts that time intervals are represented by two points and that the database system knows nothing about the special semantics of these two arguments as interval bounds.

4   A Temporal Extension of DeCoR

The drawbacks mentioned above disappear if certain temporal knowledge is not only represented in a database but directly built into the underlying database system. Therefore, the TDeCoR system is an extension of the constraint database system DeCoR. The extensions consist of temporal datatypes, constraints relating temporal and non-temporal variables and the incorporation of the reduction algorithm. The two main goals are improving (1) the efficiency of the evaluation of temporal queries and (2) the readability of temporal clauses and queries.

4.1   Constraints over Temporal Domains

The DeCoR system is extended by the two datatypes "instant" and "interval". Constants of one of these types are denoted as described at the beginning of Section 3. In contrast to the ChronoLog system [BM93, Böh94], there is no special syntax for temporal arguments. However, as shown below, the unification of temporal arguments has a special semantics. We mention in passing that this design decision supports the definition of multiple temporal arguments, e.g. to represent valid and transaction time.

Table 1. interval × interval constraints

T_1 *precedes* T_2
T_1 *follows* T_2
T_1 *contains* T_2
T_1 *equals* T_2
T_1 *overlaps* T_2

Similar to the constraints $(=, \neq, >, <, \geq, \leq)$ between terms of type real currently supported in the DeCoR system, we introduce the temporal constraints shown in Tables 1 and 2 (as suggested in [All93]). As seen in Table 2, some constraints are overloaded in the sense that they represent relations between two intervals as well as between an instant and an interval. For example, the constraint *starts* can not only be used to relate intervals with the same start point, but also to extract or set the start point of an interval.

Table 2. interval × interval or instant × interval constraints

T_1 before T_2	$\mathcal{E}$ before T
T_1 starts T_2	$\mathcal{E}$ starts T
T_1 during T_2	$\mathcal{E}$ during T
T_1 ends T_2	$\mathcal{E}$ ends T
T_1 after T_2	$\mathcal{E}$ after T

Table 3. instant × integer constraints

$year(\mathcal{E},\ I)$	
$month(\mathcal{E},\ I)$	
$day(\mathcal{E},\ I)$	Ith day of the month
$weekday(\mathcal{E},\ I)$	Ith day of the week
$hour(\mathcal{E},\ I)$	
$minute(\mathcal{E},\ I)$	
$second(\mathcal{E},\ I)$	

In addition to the above constraints, we introduce relations to extract different properties of an instant (see Table 3).

Note that constraints are relations rather than functions and can therefore be used in a bidirectional way.

Example 10. In the query "in which month is Peter born" the instant argument $\mathcal{E}$ is the given argument for predicate *month*

$$?-\ \exists \mathcal{E}\ birthday('Peter',\mathcal{E}), month(\mathcal{E}, Month).$$

whereas in the rule "Paul has to present the progress of his work every Monday" the integer argument I is the given one:

$$duty('Paul', 'present\ work', \mathcal{E}) \leftarrow weekday(\mathcal{E}, 1).$$

As seen in the example above, it is possible to express periodical knowledge in the TDeCoR system. (Indeed, the constraints listed in Table 3 are somewhat similar to the modulo relations of [TCR94].)

The constraint *duration* (interval × integer × unit) calculates the duration of an interval. The third argument which has to be given determines the granularity in which the duration is measured.

Example 11. The constraint *duration* can be used to add a span e.g. 6 months to an instant $\mathcal{E}$ in the following way

$$\mathcal{E}\ starts\ T, duration(T, 6, month), \mathcal{E}_1\ ends\ T$$

The constraint *intersect(T_1,T_2,T_3)* determines the intersection T_3 of two time intervals T_1 and T_2.

In addition to the above datatypes and constraints, special syntax expresses which parts of a formula have to be temporally coalesced. The TDeCoR system does not make an implicit reduction because in some cases, the user does not want to perform a reduction. Moreover the system is more efficient if the coalescing is performed only on demand. Following [Böh94], the formula F which has to be coalesced must be enclosed by braces {}. (If multiple temporal arguments are present the user has to specify which ones have to be reduced by supplying a second argument within the braces)

Example 12. The query "Who worked in our company for more than 25 years" needs coalescing

$$?- \exists\, T, Y\; (\{(\exists DepNo\; works\_in(EmpNo, DepNo, T)), T\},$$
$$duration(T, Y, year), Y \geq 25).$$

The reduction algorithm realized in the TDeCoR system is similar to the approach described in [BM93]. In addition, it is extended in a straightforward way to temporally reduce facts with multiple temporal arguments in each user specified direction. This is for example necessary to reduce bitemporal relations.

4.2   Handling of Temporal Constraints

The constraint lifting algorithm presented in Sect. 2.3 is not restricted to constraints over variables of type real. Indeed, similar to the CLP scheme [JL87], the CLA depends on a concrete domain. Ultimately, the constraint solver invoked in step 3 of the CLA only determines which constraints can be simplified and solved. The integration of the constraint solver of DeCoR with a temporal constraint solver will be investigated in the next section.

In order to apply the CLA on clauses with temporal constraints, it is necessary to define (1) the standard form of a temporal formula and (2) when a temporal constraint is evaluable.

Non-temporal formulas are rewritten into standard form by replacing the second and every further occurrence of a variable X by a new unique variable X_i and a constraint $X = X_i$ (see Example 1).

However, if a variable of type time interval occurs multiple times in a formula, this transformation is not so useful since it imposes the constraint that the two intervals be exactly the same. In temporal databases, it is usually much more interesting to merely impose the constraint that time intervals associated with different facts *overlap* (i.e., have a non-empty intersection). As a result, multiple occurrences of variables denoting time intervals are related via the *intersect* constraint. (Note that this strategy corresponds to the notions of temporal join respectively temporal conjunction.)

Example 13. The temporal formula

$$emp(ENo, Name, T), work\_in(ENo, \_, T), salary(ENo, Sal, T)$$

will be rewritten in standard form as

$$emp(ENo, Name, T), work\_in(ENo_1, \_, T_1), salary(ENo_2, Sal, T_2),$$
$$ENo = ENo_1, ENo = ENo_2, intersect(T, T_1, T_3), intersect(T_3, T_2, \_)$$

As a consequence of this approach, the readability is improved. As a case in point, consider the above example: "When and how many days did the persons with the employee numbers 1354 respectively 245 work in the same department?"

$$works\_in(1354, Dep, T), works\_in(245, Dep, T), duration(T, D, day).$$

In order to define the evaluability of a temporal constraint, the definition of the groundness of a variable has to be extended. The terms ground or non-ground given in Def. 4 do not allow to adequately categorize variables bound to partially instantiated intervals.

Definition 7. A *partially instantiated interval* is an interval with one bound ground and the other non-ground.

Definition 8. A variable X bound to the partially instantiated interval T is *start-ground (s)* if the start point of T is ground. If the end point of T is ground then the variable X is *end-ground (e)*. A ground interval variable is both start-ground and end-ground.

Example 14. A variable bound to the interval $[/1994/8/23{\sim}12{:}24{:}13.8 - \mathcal{E}]$ is start-ground whereas a variable bound to the interval $[\mathcal{E} - /1996/1/1]$ is end-ground.

Table 4 shows which minimal groundness tags are required for every argument of a temporal constraint in order to guarantee its evaluability. (Note that the following partial order holds for groundness tags: $n < s$, $n < e$, $s < g$, $e < g$. Also, instant variables can only be ground or non-ground.)

These groundness tags make it possible for the constraint lifting algorithm to manipulate temporal constraints just like constraints over reals. In particular, temporal constraints can be split into evaluable and non-evaluable ones. This is important for efficiency reasons because only non-evaluable constraints must be lifted further into depending clauses.

4.3 Constraint Solving

The CLA is applicable even if no constraint simplification takes place in step 3 at all. However, as indicated above, the recognition of as many evaluable constraints as possible is a key parameter to efficiency.

For space reasons, the specification of a temporal constraint solver can not be given in this paper. However, a general specification for a solver in a constraint

Table 4. Groundness patterns for evaluable temporal constraints

before	$\langle es \rangle$
after	$\langle se \rangle$
precedes	$\langle en \rangle, \langle ns \rangle$
follows	$\langle sn \rangle, \langle ne \rangle$
during, contains	$\langle gg \rangle$
equals	$\langle gn \rangle, \langle se \rangle, \langle es \rangle, \langle ng \rangle$
starts	$\langle sn \rangle, \langle ns \rangle$
ends	$\langle en \rangle, \langle ne \rangle$
overlaps	$\langle eg \rangle$
year, month ...	$\langle gn \rangle$
duration	$\langle gn \rangle, \langle sg \rangle, \langle eg \rangle$
intersect	$\langle ggn \rangle, \langle sge \rangle, \langle egs \rangle, \langle ngg \rangle, \langle gse \rangle, \langle esg \rangle, \langle ges \rangle, \langle seg \rangle, \langle gng \rangle$

database system is given in [GM94a]. Nevertheless, a temporal constraint solver can not simply be added to the existing non-temporal one. Instead, the two solvers have to collaborate by passing information about freshly bound variables between them. This is illustrated in example 15.

Example 15. In the query "at which instant would John have worked twice as long in the sales department as in the engineering department?"

$$?-\ \exists\, T, T_1, M, M_1$$
$$(works\_in(\text{`John'}, \text{`Sal'}, T),$$
$$works\_in(\text{`John'}, \text{`Eng'}, T_1),$$
$$duration(T_1, M, month),$$
$$M_1 = 2 * M,$$
$$duration(T, M_1, month),$$
$$\mathcal{E}\ ends\ T).$$

the temporal variable $\mathcal{E}$ (the result we are looking for) depends on the non-temporal variable M_1. M_1 depends on M which in turn depends on the interval variable T_1.

The first call of the temporal constraint solver determines that the constraint $duration(T_1, M, month)$ is evaluable so that M becomes ground. The temporal constraint $duration(T, M_1, month)$ remains non-evaluable because the first argument is only start-ground and the second argument is non-ground. In the next step, the non-temporal solver determines $M_1 = 2 * M$ as evaluable and therefore M_1 as ground. Now the temporal constraint solver can deduce that $duration(T, M_1, month)$ and $\mathcal{E}\ ends\ T$ are evaluable.

This example shows that it is necessary to iterate steps 3 and 4 of the constraint lifting algorithm until no further variables are determined to be ground. A variable can only become ground if the solver determines some constraints as evaluable. Because these constraints are subsequently removed from the constraint set, it follows that this iterative process eventually terminates.

437

4.4 Extended Example

In the following, we illustrate some of the expressive power of the query language of the TDeCoR system. In particular we show how the integration of the temporal aspects into a constraint database system leads to a natural formulation of periodic knowledge.

We consider that in the flight database the time table of departing flights is present. Special flights which are scheduled only once are represented as ground facts.

$$/* \; depart(FlightNr, DepartureTime) \; */$$
$$depart(`AR125', /1994/10/8 \sim 10{:}24).$$
$$depart(`BL358', /1994/10/8 \sim 15{:}12).$$
$$depart(`IR931', /1994/11/2 \sim 20{:}02).$$

Regular flights, which depart periodically, are represented by temporal constraints. For example, the Swissair flight from Zurich to New York departing every day at 13:05 is represented as

$$depart(`SR100', Dep) \leftarrow hour(Dep, 13), minute(Dep, 5).$$

Most temporal database systems do not support such periodical knowledge at all. Even if they do, the evaluation of some queries may not terminate because periodical knowledge is typically represented by recursive rules involving function symbols such as

$$depart(`SR100')@/1994/1/1 \sim 13{:}05.$$
$$depart(`SR100')@T + 1day \leftarrow depart(`SR100')@T.$$

which give rise to infinite extensions (see e.g. [Böh94]).

The implicit representation of the TDeCoR system avoids this problem because the knowledge is represented using a finite number of constraints so that there is no need to compute the extension.

With the following clause the user can retrieve all flights ($FlightNr$) which depart at a specific date ($\mathcal{E}$).

$$depart\_at\_day(FlightNr, \mathcal{E}) \leftarrow \exists \, \mathcal{E}_1, T \; (depart(FlightNr, \mathcal{E}_1),$$
$$\mathcal{E} \; starts \; T,$$
$$duration(T, 1, day),$$
$$\mathcal{E}_1 \; during \; T).$$

Note that the interval T which contains all the instants within one day is calculated in the body of the clause. (Remember that the notation /1994/10/2 is only an abbreviation for the instant /1994/10/2$\sim$00:00:0)

The query ?– $depart\_at\_day(FlightNr, /1994/10/2)$ will be answered by:

FlightNr
'AR125'
'BL358'
'SR100'

In addition to the above relation we assume that the flight database contains also the tables $flight(FlightNr, From, To)$ and $flight\_time(From, To, Hours)$. This allows us to write a clause which calculates the arrival time for a flight.

$$arrival(FlightNr, \mathcal{A}) \leftarrow \exists\ From, To, \mathcal{E}, \mathcal{E}_1, T\ (depart(FlightNr, \mathcal{E}),$$
$$flight(FlightNr, From, To),$$
$$flight\_time(From, To, \mathcal{E}_1),$$
$$\mathcal{E}\ starts\ T,$$
$$duration(T, \mathcal{E}_1, hour),$$
$$\mathcal{A}\ ends\ T).$$

To consider an example, we suppose that the flight 'SR100' from Zurich to New York takes 8 hours and 15 minutes and that these facts are known in the database. With this knowledge, the query $?-\ arrival('SR100', Arr)$ will return the answer:

Arr	*Constraints*
	$hour(Arr, 21), minute(Arr, 20)$

This answer contains a conjunction of constraints because the flight 'SR100' is scheduled to arrive at that time every day. The system would calculate an exact arrival time for the flights which are scheduled only once.

5 Conclusions

In this paper, we have first shown how the constraint solving techniques developed in artificial intelligence can be integrated into deductive database systems. Subsequently, we have demonstrated that constraints over reals can in principle be used to represent the timestamping information typical of temporal databases. Finally, we presented a more sophisticated approach to represent temporal knowledge which is based on the development and integration of a special purpose temporal constraint solver.

439

References

[All93] J. F. Allen. Maintaining knowledge about temporal intervals. *Communications of the ACM*, 16(11), November 1993.

[BM93] Michael Böhlen and Robert Marti. Handling temporal knowledge in a deductive database system. In *Datenbanksysteme in Büro, Technik und Wissenschaft*, 1993.

[BM94] Michael Böhlen and Robert Marti. On the completeness of temporal database query languages. In *Proc. 1st Int. Conf. on Temporal Logic*, July 1994.

[Böh94] Michael Böhlen. *Managing Temporal Knowledge in Deductive Databases*. PhD thesis, ETH Zurich No. 10802, 1994.

[Bur92] Jan Burse. ProQuel: Using Prolog to implement a deductive database system. Technical Report TR 177, Departement Informatik ETH Zürich Switzerland, 1992.

[CGT90] Stefano Ceri, Georg Gottlob, and Letizia Tanca. *Logic Programming and Databases*. Surveys in Computer Science. Springer Verlag, 1990.

[GM93] Roman Gross and Robert Marti. Intensional answers in generalized deductive databases. In *Proc. Workshop on Deductive Databases, 10th Int. Conf. on Logic Programming*, Budapest, June 1993.

[GM94a] Roman Gross and Robert Marti. Compile-time constraint solving in a constraint database system. In *Workshop Constraints and Databases, Int. Logic Programming Symposium*, Ithaca, November 1994.

[GM94b] Roman Gross and Robert Marti. Handling constraints and generating intensional answers in a deductive database system. *Journal of Computers and Artificial Intelligence*, 13(2-3):233–256, 1994.

[JCE⁺94] C. S. Jensen, J. Clifford, R. Elmasri, S. K. Gadia, P. Hayes, and S. Jajodia (eds). A glossary of temporal database concepts. *SIGMOD Record*, 23(1), March 1994.

[JL87] Joxan Jaffar and Jean-Louis Lassez. Constraint logic programming. In *Proc. of the 14th ACM Symposium on Principles of Programming Languages*, pages 111–119, January 1987.

[JM94] Joxan Jaffar and Michael J. Maher. Constraint logic programming: A survey. *Journal of Logic Programming*, 19/20:503–582, 1994.

[KKR90] Paris C. Kanellakis, Gabriel M. Kuper, and Peter Z. Revesz. Constraint query languages. In *Proc. 9th ACM Symp. on Principles of Database Systems (PODS)*, pages 299–313, Nashville, 1990.

[MWW89] R. Marti, C. Wieland, and B. Wüthrich. Adding inferencing to a relational database management system. In *Datenbanksysteme in Büro, Technik und Wissenschaft*. T. Härder, 1989.

[Ram88] Raghu Ramakrishnan. Magic Templates: A spellbinding approach to logic programs. In *Proc. Int. Conf. on Logic Programming*, pages 140–159, 1988.

[RSSS93] Raghu Ramakrishnan, Divesh Srivastava, S. Sudarshan, and P. Seshadri. Implementation of the CORAL deductive database system. In *Proc. ACM Conf. on Management of Data (SIGMOD)*, 1993.

[SS94] Peter J. Stuckey and S. Sudarshan. Compiling query constraints. In *Proc. ACM Symp. on Principles of Database Systems (PODS)*, 1994.

[TCG⁺93] Adbullah Uz Tansel, James Clifford, Shashi K. Gadia, Sushil Hajodia, Arie Segev, and Richard Snodgras. *Temporal Databases: Theory, Design and Implementation*. Benjamin/Cummings Publishing Company, Inc., 1993.

[TCR94] David Toman, Jan Chomicki, and David S. Rogers. Datalog with integer periodicity constraints. In *Proc. Int. Logic Programming Symposium*, November 1994.

[VRK⁺91] J. Vaghani, K. Ramamohanarao, D. Kemp, Z. Somogyi, and Peter Stuckey. Design overview of the Aditi deductive database system. In *Proc. 7th Int. Conf. on Data Engineering*, pages 240–247, 1991.

Ein Werkzeug zur Gewinnung semantischer Constraints aus natürlichsprachlichen Eingaben und Beispieldaten *

Meike Albrecht[1,2], Edith Buchholz[2], Antje Düsterhöft[2], Bernhard Thalheim[1]

[1] Technische Universität Cottbus, Fachbereich Informatik
e-mail: thalheim@informatik.tu-cottbus.de
[2] Universität Rostock, Fachbereich Informatik
e-mail: {meike/buch/duest}@informatik.uni-rostock.de

Zusammenfassung Die vollständige und richtige Angabe der Semantik ist insbesondere für größere Anwendungen eine der schwierigsten Aufgaben im Datenbankentwurf. Im Rahmen des Projektes Rapid Application Database Development (RADD [3]) wurden Erfahrungen bei der informalen Modellierung von Strukturen einer Datenbank gesammelt. In dem hier vorgestellten Werkzeug wird die Semantik durch eine Analyse natürlichsprachlicher Beschreibungen, die Auswertung von Beispieldaten und Nachfragen in Form einer Beispieldiskussion gewonnen. Aus natürlichsprachlicher Information können Kandidaten geltender Constraints abgeleitet werden. Durch Beispiele kann die intendierte Bedeutung der ermittelten Constraints geklärt und gemeinsam mit dem Entwerfer validiert werden. Der Dialog läßt sich in einfacher und auch für ungeübte Entwerfer verständlicher Form bis zur vollständigen Erfassung der Semantik fortführen. Dieser Zugang kann ebenfalls für die Modellierung von Funktionalität und Verhalten einer Datenbankanwendung erweitert werden.

1   Einleitung

Bereits mit dem Entwurf eines Informationssystems, insbesondere einer Datenbank, werden wesentliche Entscheidungen für die effektive Nutzung des Systems getroffen. Ein schlechter Entwurf kann die Ursache für Probleme wie Inkonsistenz, Instabilität, Ineffektivität oder auch fehlende Robustheit eines Systems sein. Die Qualität eines Entwurfsproduktes hängt sehr stark von der Eingangsinformation, der Professionalität des Entwerfers und der Qualität der Unterstützung ab. Auch wenn zum Datenbankentwurf höhere Modelle wie das Entity-Relationship Modell oder objektorientierte Modelle verwendet werden, ist eine Unterstützung des Entwerfers notwendig.

---

* Die Arbeiten am Projekt werden z.T. über die DFG unter dem Kennzeichen Th465/2 unterstützt.

[3] Ehemals RAD abgekürzt, da dieser Name bereits für ein lizensiertes Softwarewerkzeug im europäischen und amerikanischen Raum vergeben ist, erfolgte die Änderung.

Obwohl die Bedeutung des Entwurfs allgemein anerkannt ist, stehen weniger umfangreich als das sonst der Fall ist, Leitfäden und Tools zur Unterstützung des Entwurfs zur Verfügung. Das veranlaßt einen Entwerfer sehr oft zu einem intuitiven, informalen Entwurf in einem Inspirationsstil. Deshalb ist die Entwicklung von Tools nach wie vor von Bedeutung. Solche Tools müssen den gesamten Entwurfsprozeß in seiner vollen Komplexität als einen Prozeß unterstützen und sich an den Entwerfer anpassen können. Kein Entwurfssystem kann einen hochwertigen Entwurf garantieren, aber ein solches System kann es erleichtern, einen guten Entwurf zu finden.

In Zusammenarbeit mit Arbeitgruppen der Universitäten Münster und Dresden wird eine integrierte Toolbox zur Unterstützung des gesamten Entwurfsprozesses entwickelt, die auf der Grundlage eines erweiterten Entity-Relationship Modells [BOT90] nicht nur einem oder mehreren Entwerfern die Darstellung von Struktur, Semantik, Funktionalität und Verhalten einer Datenbankanwendung erlaubt, sondern auch über Transformations-, Modifikations-, Nutzerberatungs- und -anpassungstools verfügt (Vorstellung des Gesamtprojektes in [TAA94]).

Im Rahmen dieser Arbeit werden Methoden zur Semantikakquisition vorgestellt, die

- das linguistische Wissen für den Datenbankentwurf und die Erfassung der semantischen Zusammenhänge verwenden,
- zeigen, inwieweit eine Suche nach semantischen Constraints mit Heuristiken und eine informale Validierung der Constraints möglich ist,
- diese Zugänge in das RADD-Projekt integrieren und entsprechende Tools implementieren.

Dabei werden zunächst allgemeine Probleme, die bei der Semantikakquisition auftreten, erläutert. Anschließend wird ein Lösungsansatz zur informalen Semantikakquisition gezeigt.

2 Probleme bei der Semantikakquisition

Semantische Constraints werden verwendet, um die Bedeutung der Strukturen einer Datenbank darzustellen. Anhand dieser werden korrekte Datenbankzustände von inkorrekten unterschieden. Semantische Constraints sind notwendig, um richtige Umstrukturierungen vornehmen zu können. Falsche oder unvollständige Mengen von Constraints können also direkte Auswirkungen auf die Richtigkeit der Datenbanken haben.

Die formale Angabe semantischer Constraints ist eine der schwierigsten Aufgaben im Datenbankentwurf. In dem hier vorgestellten Zugang beschränken wir uns auf die im Datenbankentwurf am häufigsten verwendeten Constraints (Schlüssel, funktionale Abhängigkeiten, Inklusions- und Exklusionsabhängigkeiten, Kardinalitäten). Die Schwierigkeit der Erfragung dieser Constraints ist auf folgende Probleme zurückführbar:

- Der traditionelle Zugang zur Erfassung der Semantik basiert auf einer *abstrakten mathematischen Darstellung von Integritätsbedingungen*. Sogar bei kleinen Schemata ist der Abstraktionsgrad dabei so hoch, daß selbst erfahrene Datenbankentwerfer überfordert werden, wie einige Tests mit Nutzergruppen verschiedener Systeme ergaben.

- Fast alle Entwurfsmethoden erwarten vom Entwerfer eine *vollständige Angabe der Semantik*. Normalisierungsalgorithmen liefern z.B. nur dann eine korrekte Normalform, wenn die Menge der funktionalen (und mehrwertigen) Abhängigkeiten vollständig angegeben wurde.

  Oft werden aber einige semantische Constraints vergessen, obwohl oder auch weil sie offensichtlich sind, oder semantische Constraints sind zu *kompliziert*, besonders, wenn sie über mehreren Attributen definiert sind, und werden deshalb entweder gar nicht gesehen oder falsch angegeben.

Wünschenswert wäre also eine *Unterstützung bei der Semantikakquisition*, bei der dem Entwerfer semantische Constraints vorgeschlagen werden. Dabei treten weitere Probleme auf:

- Insbesondere bei komplizierten semantischen Constraints, die über mehreren Attributen definiert sind, ist es schwer zu entscheiden, ob diese gelten oder nicht.
- Nicht alle Constraints können in einfacher und unmißverständlicher Form graphisch dargestellt werden.
- Es müssen potentiell exponentiell viele mögliche semantische Constraints untersucht werden, um die vollständige Menge semantischer Constraints zu finden.

Als Lösung dieser Probleme bieten sich folgende Ansätze an:
1. Es ist möglich, semantische Constraints *informal* zu erfragen.
2. Eine *starke Einschränkung des Suchraumes* kann durch einen intelligenten Zugang, der Heuristiken zur Beschleunigung der Suche verwendet, erreicht werden.
3. Günstig ist es, bereits beim Entwurf der Strukturen Informationen über die *Semantik* zu erfassen. Die Semantikakquisition und die Untersuchung des Verhaltens ist dann kein nachfolgender Prozeß, sondern Teil des Entwurfes.
Ein Ansatz, der diese Möglichkeiten nutzt, soll hier gezeigt werden.

3 Ein Lösungsansatz

Der Entwurf einer Datenbank kann über die Analyse natürlichsprachlicher Eingaben erstellt werden. Aus natürlichsprachlichen Sätzen, die ein Anwendungsgebiet beschreiben, lassen sich Informationen über die Struktur der Datenbank und Kandidaten für die Semantik ableiten *(Abschnitt 5)*. Aussagen in natürlicher Sprache sind oft mehrdeutig und unexakt. Daher stellen die abgeleiteten Entwürfe und die Semantikinformationen vages Wissen dar. Die Validierung des Strukturentwurfes wird in *Abschnitt 6* gezeigt. Es ist ein Tool erforderlich, das die abgeleiteten Kandidaten für semantische Constraints untersucht *(Abschnitt 7)*. Da die Beschreibungen in natürlicher Sprache meist unvollständig sind, ist es erforderlich, weitere Kandidaten für semantische Constraints durch Heuristiken zu ermitteln. Die Kandidaten für semantische Constraints werden gewichtet, um zuerst die Kandidaten zu validieren, die am plausibelsten erscheinen. Im Dialog mit dem Entwerfer kann dann anhand von Beispielen eine Validierung der Kandidaten erfolgen. Das folgende Bild zeigt die Kombination dieser Methoden.

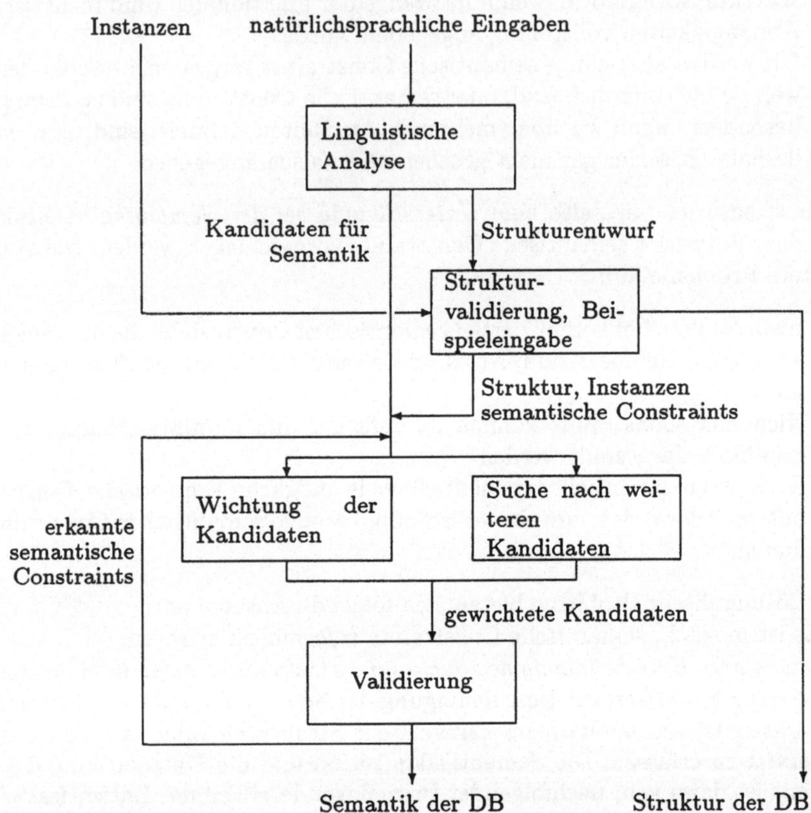

Dieser Ansatz ist auch für ungeübte Nutzer verwendbar. Erstens ist die Erfassung von Informationen mittels natürlicher Sprache eine informale Möglichkeit, Wissen vom Entwerfer zu erfragen. Zweitens erfolgt die Validierung der Ergebnisse ausschließlich über generierte Beispiele. Diese Beispiele illustrieren die semantischen Constraints gleichfalls in einfacher und verständlicher Weise.

4   Einordnung und Abgrenzung gegenüber anderen Arbeiten

Ausgehend von [Che83] existieren zur Abbildung auf Entity-Relationsship- Modelle aus natürlichsprachlichen Äußerungen eine Reihe von Veröffentlichungen (z.B. [FPR85] oder [TjB93]). Im Projekt ANNAPURA ([Eic84]) wird natürliche Sprache genutzt, um im Dialog Anforderungsspezifikationen in Form eines

Modells zu erarbeiten. Ansätze zur Erfassung von Semantik und Verhalten der Datenbank aus natürlicher Sprache finden sich in [CGS83]. [Ort93] untersucht die in Arbeitssituationen verwendete (Fach)Sprache mit dem Ziel, eine normierte Unternehmensfachsprache zu entwickeln, um sie für das Software-Engeneering zu nutzen. Die Idee unserer Arbeit liegt in der Entwicklung eines komplexen Tools, in dem mittels Dialog Wissen über die Struktur, als auch über die Semantik und das Verhalten einer zu entwickelnden Datenbank aus natürlicher Fach- und Alltagssprache akquiriert wird.

Informale Semantikakquisition wird in der Literatur nur wenig behandelt. Bekannt sind Methoden zur Ableitung von Schlüsseln und funktionalen Abhängigkeiten aus Daten [CaS93], [MaR92]. Oft wird dabei eine Closed-World-Assumption vorausgesetzt oder es erfolgt eine einfache Bestätigung der abgeleiteten Constraints (pseudonatürlichsprachliche Erfragung in [BGM85] und Armstrongrelationen u.a. in [MaR92]). Aus der Literatur sind einfache Heuristiken zur Schlüsselsuche [StG88] und Fremdschlüsselsuche [CBS94] bekannt. Der hier vorgestellte Ansatz erweitert diese und stellt Heuristiken zur Suche nach weiteren Constraints vor. Außerdem werden Methoden der effizienten Erfragung der Constraints genutzt, nicht geltende Constraints werden hier ebenfalls ausgewertet. Zur Validierung der Constraints wird eine Erfragung anhand von Beispielen, die jeweils ein semantisches Constraint repräsentieren, verwendet.

5 Linguistischer Zugang

5.1 Motivation und Ziele des linguistischen Zugangs

Das Ziel der natürlichsprachlichen Komponente ist es, dem Entwerfer die Möglichkeit zu bieten, sein informales Wissen in natürlicher Sprache darzustellen. Grundvoraussetzung für die adäquate Modellierung eines Problems bezüglich des Datenbankentwurfs ist dessen Formulierung. Eine für die meisten Nutzer übliche Darstellungsweise ist die Muttersprache - im Gegensatz zu formalen Modellen wie z. B. Diagramme. Wir gehen davon aus, daß ein in natürlicher Sprache formuliertes Problem mehr Informationen zu dessen Struktur und insbesondere zu dessen Semantik und Verhalten liefert.

Im Datenbankentwurf wird zuerst die Strukturierung einer Anwendung im Groben festgelegt. Zugleich wird eine eingeschränkte Fachsprache gewählt, in der Worte nicht mehr über alle möglichen Interpretationsmöglichkeiten verfügen. Mit dieser Fachsprache sind auftretende Ambiguitäten oft eindeutig auflösbar. Gerade die deutsche Sprache verfügt aufgrund ihrer variablen Satzstruktur über noch umfangreichere Darstellungsmittel in dieser Beziehung als die englische Sprache.

Die Computerlinguistik hat in den letzten Jahren eine ganze Reihe von beachtlichen Beiträgen zur automatischen Verarbeitung und Bearbeitung der natürlichen Sprache erbracht (hinsichtlich der Semantik z.B. [Pin93]). Diese Resultate waren nicht bekannt, als die meisten Datenbankentwurfstools der zweiten Generation entwickelt wurden. Um dieses 'know-how' in Entwurfstools der dritten

Generation einsetzen zu können, ist jedoch eine weitere tiefgründige linguistische Analyse und eine Einschränkung auf Teilsprachbereiche notwendig.

Es hat sich aber auch gezeigt, daß ein 'general-purpose-system' für komplexere Anwendungen nicht realisierbar erscheint. Komplexere Anwendungen zeichnen sich sowohl durch eine semantische Vielfalt als auch durch eine stärkere Benutzung formalisierbarer Teile aus. Der Datenbankentwurf ist ein Beispiel einer solchen komplexen Anwendung. Er führt zum einen auf eine formalisierte Beschreibung, setzt aber zum anderen eine Sprache voraus, die bereits eine gewisse Standardform besitzt. Dadurch ist der Datenbankentwurf sehr gut geeignet, die bereits zum Teil vollständig ausgearbeiteten Verfahren der Computerlinguistik zu verwenden und zum anderen zu zeigen, wie durch ein natürlichsprachliches Interface der Entwurf effektiver gestaltet werden kann.

5.2 Prinzipielle Analyse natürlichsprachlicher Eingaben

Das natürlichsprachliche Interface (NLI) ist als ein dialogartiges, mit den anderen RADD-Komponenten interaktiv zusammenwirkendes Teilsystem konzipiert. Es besteht aus Dialog-, Syntax-, Semantik- und Pragmatik-Tool. Eine ausführlichere Darstellung der einzelnen Komponenten findet sich in [BuD94a] bzw. [BuD94b]. Aufgabe des *Dialog-Tools* ist es, einen moderierten Entwerfer-Dialog zu führen. Der Entwerfer hat die Möglichkeit, seine Anwendung in deutschen Sätzen zu beschreiben. Das NLI wertet die Eingaben aus und stellt Nachfragen zur Vervollständigung der linguistischen und pragmatischen Analyse-Ergebnisse.

Über das *Syntax-Tool* wird die syntaktische Analyse der Eingabe des Entwerfers durchgeführt. Dazu wird ein spezieller Parser, ein ID/LP-Parser (Immediate Dependence Linear Precedence), eingesetzt. Gleichzeitig wird eine eingeschränkte, repräsentative Menge deutscher Grammatikregeln genutzt. Die Basis der Syntax-Analyse bildet das Lexikon deutscher Wörter und Wendungen, das größtenteils anwendungsunabhängig ist.

Das *Semantik-Tool* weist der Entwerfereingabe in zwei Stufen eine Wort- und eine Satzsemantik zu. Grundlage der Satzsemantik ist das linguistische Rollenkonzept. Das Rollenkonzept beschreibt die Zuordnung von bestimmten Elementen im Satz zu definierten Funktionsrollen.

In der *Pragmatik* werden die Ergebnisse der Syntax- und der Semantikanalyse genutzt, um die Eingabe ausgerichtet auf den Zweck zu interpretieren und in den aktuellen Entwurf einzuordnen. Die Interpretation erfolgt mit einer attributierten Grammatik. Das Interpretationsergebnis umfaßt einen Skelettentwurf und eine Aufstellung über mögliche semantischen Constraints sowie Informationen zum Verhalten. Schnittstellen-Routinen bilden die Ergebnisse auf die Data-Dictionary-Struktur ab.

5.3 Extraktion von Semantik — Linguistische und Pragmatische Basis

Transformationsprozeß. Die Erfassung von Datenbank-Semantik aus natürlichsprachlichen Eingaben erfolgt während des Interpretationsprozesses, also in der Pragmatik. Es werden Funktionen innerhalb der eingesetzten attributierten Grammatik genutzt, um die Semantik des Satzes bzw. der Wörter auf die Datenbank-Semantik (z.B. Erkennen von Schlüsseln, Kardinalitäten) abzubilden. Dazu werden semantische Feinheiten, die der Entwerfer meist unbewußt nutzt, ausgewertet. Erkenntnisse der Computerlinguistik unterstützen diesen Transformationprozeß ([Pin93]).

Computerlinguistische Prinzipien. Für die Semantikerfassung können wir eine Reihe von linguistischen/ computerlinguistischen Methoden nutzen, die Regeln für die Bedeutungszuordnungen zu natürlichsprachlichen Äußerungen beschreiben.

Prinzip der Kompositionalität. [GaM89, 280] beschreiben das Fregesche Prinzip als: 'The meaning of the whole sentence is a function of the meaning of the parts.' Die Bedeutung eines Satzes setzt sich somit zusammen aus der Bedeutung der Satzteile. Die Bedeutung dieser wird dann durch die Bedeutung der Subphrasen beschrieben und so weiter; letztlich gilt es, die Bedeutung der Wörter zu untersuchen. Grundlage für die Satzsemantik bildet also eine im Lexikon definierte Wortsemantik.

Betrachten wir dieses Prinzip für unsere Anwendung, den Datenbankentwurf, so müssen wir klären, welche Satzphrasen eine wichtige Rolle bei der Semantikakquisition spielen und welche Wörter die Basis der Phrasen bilden (vgl. auch [Pin86]).

Bedeutung als Referenz. Wenn wir das Prinzip der Kompositionalität annehmen, dann gilt es auch, die Frage zu erläutern, wie Bedeutungsbeziehungen zwischen Phrasen/Wörtern realisiert werden. Dazu ist eine gewisse Klassifizierung von Wortarten vorzunehmen, um differenziert Beziehungsrelationen aufstellen zu können. Diese Relationen müssen im Lexikon definiert werden. (Zum Beispiel könnte das Verb 'essen' zur Klasse der Tätigkeitsverben gehören, die mit der Substantivklasse Nahrungsmittel korrelliert.) Diese Klassifizierungen und Relationen sind nur zum Teil anwendungsunabhängig gestaltbar. Spezielle Informationen zur Domaine sind für alle Anwendungen notwendig. In diesem Sinne wird die Bedeutungsbeschreibung auch als 'feature instantiation' beschrieben.

Pragmatischer Ansatz. Gewisse Teile der Fachsprachen sowie Teile der Umgangssprache allgemein zeichnen sich durch bestimmte über die Anwendungsgebiete hinausgehende pragmatische Eigenschaften aus. Diese auf Beobachtungen basierenden Eigenschaften betreffen insbesondere gewisse Lesarten von Wörtern/Sätzen die dem Nutzer plausibler oder 'auf den ersten Blick logischer' erscheinen. Zum Beispiel wird mit dem Wort 'mehrere' meistens eine Menge von Elementen, die größer als zwei ist, beschrieben; selten ist eine Menge mit zwei Elementen gemeint.

Die Erfassung von semantischen Informationen hinsichtlich der zu entwerfenden Datenbank stützt sich auf eine Reihe solcher heuristischen, linguistisch motivierten Annahmen, die in die Wissensbasis integriert sind. Der folgende Abschnitt beschreibt einige dieser Annahmen.

5.4 Ausgewählte Beispiele der Semantikerfassung

Schlüsselkandidaten. Annahmen für das Erkennen von Schlüsselkandidaten sind:

1. das zuerst genannte Attribut eines Entities wird als Schlüsselkandidat aufgestellt
2. Attribute, die Nummerncharakter haben, sind Schlüsselkandidaten
3. künstlich eingeführte, im Lexikon ausgezeichnete, identifizierende Substantive sind Schlüsselkandidaten.

Die erfaßten Schlüsselkandidaten werden in der Form keycand(Entity-Relationship,Schlüsselattribut) dargestellt.

Die erste Annahme beruht auf der Beobachtung, daß der Nutzer das ihm wichtigste Attribut zuerst nennt.

> Beipiel: 'Ein Gewässer hat einen Namen und einen Standort.'
> Schlüssel: keycand(gewässer,name)

Annahme 2 entspricht der Tatsache, daß das genannte Attribut eine Numerierung widerspiegelt. Nummerncharakter besitzen z.B. die Substantive Hausnummer, Kartennummer, Datum, Zeit oder auch Substantive, in denen diese Wörter als Teilwörter auftreten. In der Wissensbasis können Substantive, die Nummerncharakter in einem Anwendungsbereich besitzen, explizit definiert werden (z.B. ISBN).

> Beispiel: 'Eine Messung ist gekennzeichnet durch ein Datum, eine Uhrzeit und eine Konzentration.'
> Schlüssel: keycand(messung,datum)
> keycand(messung,uhrzeit)

Der dritten Annahme liegt eine Charakterisierung von bestimmten Substantiven zugrunde, die diese als identifizierend einstuft. Zu dieser gehören z.B. Wörter wie Kennzeichnung, Bezeichnung, Benennung, Identifikator.

> Beispiel: 'Eine Ionenkonzentration hat eine Bezeichnung und einen Typ.'
> Schlüssel: keycand(ionenkonzentration,bezeichnung)

Bei der Erfassung von Wörtern, die Schlüsselannahmen reflektieren, werden Synonym- und Häufigkeitswörterbücher genutzt.

Kardinalitäten. Bei der Akquisition von Kardinalitäten aus natürlichsprachlichen Eingaben liefern uns linguistische Untersuchungen zum Auftreten von bestimmten Determinantien (z.B. ein, der, jeder, mehrere) die Grundlage für die pragmatische Umsetzung. Der Entwerfer beschreibt (bewußt oder unbewußt) mittels dieser Wörter seine Anwendung insofern scharf, daß er mögliche Kardinalitäten definiert und ihm dabei eine bestimmte Lesart plausibler erscheint als eine andere. Diese Reihenfolge wird durch die in den Fakten enthaltene Numerierung beschrieben. Die folgenden Beispiele illustrieren die Sichtweise auf bestimmte Determinantien.

Die erfaßten Kardinalitäten werden in der Form cardcand(Nr,Relationship-Name,Entity-Name,MinKard,MaxKard) dargestellt.

Zum Beispiel kann das Wort 'ein' immer nur bedeuten:
- mindestens ein (1:n) oder
- genau ein (1:1).

Alle anderen Möglichkeiten der Verwendung von 'ein' werden ausgeschlossen. Benutzt der Entwerfer explizit in seiner Beschreibung dieses Wort, so nehmen wir an, daß er eher eine 1:1 Kardinalität darstellen möchte.

Beispiel: 'Ein Gewässer weist eine Ionenkonzentration auf.'

Kardinalitäten: cardcand(1,aufweisen,gewässer,1,1)
cardcand(2,aufweisen,gewässer,1,n)
cardcand(1,aufweisen,ionenkonzentration,1,1)
cardcand(2,aufweisen,ionenkonzentration,1,n)

Der Nullartikel (Auftretens keines Artikels) wird meistens in Verbindung mit Pluralia gebraucht. Diese suggerieren das wiederholte Vorkommen der Objekte oder Aktanten (Ausführende). Wir gehen davon aus, daß der Entwerfer bei Verwendung des Nullartikels keine Konkretisierung Objekte/Aktanten beschreiben will, sondern daß ihm eine 1:n Kardinalität plausibler erscheint.

Beispiel: 'Gewässer werden durch Faunen besiedelt.'

Kardinalitäten: cardcand(1,besiedeln,gewässer,1,n)
cardcand(2,besiedeln,gewässer,1,1)
cardcand(1,besiedeln,fauna,1,n)
cardcand(2,besiedeln,fauna,1,1)

Das Wort 'mehrere' im Gegensatz zu 'ein' referenziert immer eine 1:n Beziehung. Die Betrachtung von 'genau ein' ist unwahrscheinlich.

Beispiel: 'Für ein Gewässer werden mehrere Eintrittspunkte definiert.'

Kardinalitäten: cardcand(1,definieren,gewässer,1,1)
cardcand(2,definieren,gewässer,1,n)
cardcand(1,definieren,eintrittspunkt,1,n)

Bei der Aufnahme von Determinantien in die Wissensbasis müssen diese hinsichtlich ihrer Kardinalitäten-Mächtigkeit untersucht und gekennzeichnet werden. (Für das Deutsche sind die Determinantien eine überschaubare, endliche Menge von Wörtern.) Die Angaben zur Kardinalitäten-Mächtigkeit beschreiben innere zwingende und mögliche Eigenschaften der Determinantien und sind somit anwendungsunabhängig.

In- und Exklusionsabhängigkeiten. In- bzw. Exklusionsabhängigkeiten werden durch die natürlichsprachliche Unterstützung in Aufzählungen von Entities vermutet, zu denen ein Oberbegriff existiert. Aufzählungen treten auf, wenn Substantive mittels Konnektoren verbunden sind; z.B. und, oder, sowohl als auch. Die erkannten In- und Exklusionsabhängigkeiten werden in der Form inklcand(Entity/ Relationship, enthaltenes Entity/ Relationship), exklcand(Liste der Entities/ Relationship) dargestellt.

Beispiel: 'Seen, Flüsse und Teiche sind Gewässer.'

Exklusionsabhängigkeit: exklcand([see,fluss,teich])

Inklusionsabhängigkeit: inklcand(gewässer,see)
inklcand(gewässer,fluss)
inklcand(gewässer,teich)

Synonyme Für die weitere Bestimmung der In- und Exklusionsabhängigkeiten durch Beispiele werden in der linguistischen Unterstützung für alle auftretenden Identifikatoren (Entity-Namen, Relationship-Namen, Attributnamen) aus dem Lexikon entsprechende Synonyme gesucht. Treten diese Synonyme auch im Skelettentwurf auf, so werden sie in Form eines Faktes synonym(identifikator,listeder-synonyme) bereitgestellt.

5.5   Ein Beispieldialog

Der folgende Beispieldialog illustriert den prinzipiellen Dialogverlauf. Im Dialog äußert der Entwerfer sogenannte Inhaltsaussagen wie z.B. 'Für ein Gewässer werden mehrere Eintrittspunkte definiert.' auf sogenannte Inhaltsabforderungen, die sich im Beispieldialog hinter der Aufforderung 'Gibt es weitere Details?' verbergen. Das System stellt linguistisch und pragmatisch orientierte Nachfragen. Eine linguistische Nachfrage wäre z.B. 'Auf welche Art und Weise wird die Aktion - definieren - durchgeführt?' Die Nachfrage vom System 'Wodurch ist - Eintrittspunkt - gekennzeichnet?' ist eine pragmatische Nachfrage, die darauf zielt, den Entwurf zu vervollständigen.

Betrachten wir die prinzipielle Erfassung von Wissen durch natürlichsprachliche Eingaben im Dialog, so liegt es nahe, dem Entwerfer pragmatische Nachfragen zu stellen, die die *exakte* Definition der Kardinalitäten betreffen. Da sich jedoch durch diese Nachfragen der Dialog sehr langatmig gestaltet und der Entwerfer nach unseren Erfahrungen meist auch nicht in der Lage ist, diese Fragen richtig zu beantworten, werden nur Kandidaten für Kardinalitäten aufgestellt. Diese können dann mittels Beispieldaten (siehe Abschnitt 7) konkretisiert werden.

```
>: ...
- Ein Gewässer weist Ionen auf.
>: Wodurch ist - Gewässer - gekennzeichnet?
- Ein Gewässer hat einen Namen und einen Standort.
>: Wodurch ist - Ion - gekennzeichnet?
- Durch den Typ, die Art und eine Bezeichnung.
>: Gibt es weitere Details?
- Seen, Flüsse und Teiche sind Gewässer.
>: Muß man - See - außer mit
- Name -
- Standort -
noch weiter kennzeichnen? Wenn ja, wie?
- Ein See hat eine Größe und eine Tiefe.
>: Muß man - Fluß - außer mit
- Name -
- Standort -
noch weiter kennzeichnen? Wenn ja, wie?
- Ein Fluß hat eine Länge.
...
```

>: Gibt es weitere Details?
- Für ein Gewässer werden mehrere Eintrittspunkte definiert.
>: Auf welche Art und Weise wird die Aktion - definieren - durchgeführt?
- Mit einer Datenblattnummer.
>: Wodurch ist - Eintrittspunkt - gekennzeichnet?
- Ort, Tiefe, Fließvektor.
>: Gibt es weitere Details?
- An jedem Eintrittspunkt werden Ionen gemessen.
>: Auf welche Art und Weise wird die Aktion - messen - durchgeführt?
- Es wird eine Konzentration an einem bestimmten Tag und in einer bestimmten Tiefe gemessen.
>: Gibt es weitere Details?
- Gewässer werden durch Faunen besiedelt.
...

Folgender erster Strukturentwurf wurde aus diesem Beispieldialog abgeleitet:

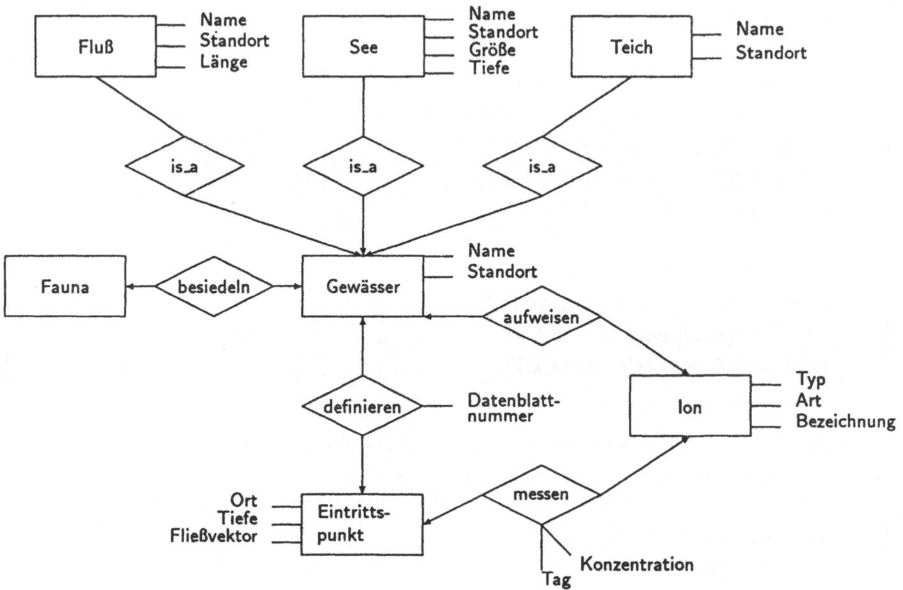

Aus dem Dialog wurden folgende Schlüsselkandidaten abgeleitet:

```
keycand(gewässer,name).
keycand(ion,bezeichnung).
keycand(see,name).
keycand(fluß,name).
keycand(teich,name).
keycand(see,größe).
keycand(see,tiefe).
keycand(fluß,länge).
keycand(definieren,datenblattnummer).
keycand(eintrittspunkt,tiefe).
keycand(messen,tag).
keycand(messen,tiefe).
```

Folgende Kandidaten für Kardinalitäten wurden aus dem Dialog erstellt:

```
cardcand(1,aufweisen,gewässer,1,1).
cardcand(2,aufweisen,gewässer,1,n).
cardcand(1,aufweisen,ion,1,n).
cardcand(2,aufweisen,ion,1,1).
cardcand(1,definieren,gewässer,1,1).
cardcand(2,definieren,gewässer,1,n).
cardcand(1,definieren,eintrittspunkt,1,n).
cardcand(1,messen,eintrittspunkt,1,1).
cardcand(2,messen,eintrittspunkt,1,n).
cardcand(1,messen,ion,1,n).
cardcand(2,messen,ion,1,1).
cardcand(1,besiedeln,gewässer,1,n).
cardcand(2,besiedeln,gewässer,1,1).
cardcand(1,besiedeln,fauna,1,n).
cardcand(2,besiedeln,fauna,1,1).
```

Aus dem Dialog wurden folgende In- und Exklusionsabhängigkeiten erstellt sowie folgende Synonyme aus dem Lexikon extrahiert:

```
exklcand([see,fluß,teich]).
inklcand(gewässer,see).
inklcand(gewässer,fluß).
inklcand(gewässer,teich).
synonym(name,[bezeichnung]).
synonym(standort,[ort]).
```

Nach der Analyse der natürlichsprachlichen Eingaben hat man auf diese Weise einen ersten Datenbankentwurf sowie Kandidaten für semantische Constraints erhalten.

6   Strukturvalidierung und Beispieldateneingabe

Die erhaltenen Datenbankentwürfe müssen bestätigt oder korrigiert werden.
Dazu ist eine *graphische Darstellung* der entworfenen Strukturen in Entity-
Relationship Diagrammen, wie sie im vorigen Abschnitt gezeigt wurde, günstig.
Die graphische Darstellung erfolgt in einem Editor (vorgestellt in [TAA94]), hier
kann der abgeleitete Entwurf vom Entwerfer verändert werden. Der graphische
Editor ist nicht nur ein Zeichentool, er enthält Erklärungs- und Nutzerführungs-
komponenten, die die Bestätigung oder Änderung der Entwürfe erleichtern.
Die entstandenen Entwürfe müssen gegebenenfalls noch um *Attributtypen und -
längen vervollständigt* werden. Dieses sind technische Details, es ist deshalb nicht
sinnvoll, sie bereits im natürlichsprachlichen Entwurf vollständig zu erfragen.
Weiterhin ist es günstig, frühzeitig *Beispieldaten* zu der entworfenen Datenbank
eingeben zu lassen. Hierbei werden zunächst zu den Entities in der Datenbank
Beispieldaten erfragt.

...

See:

Name	Standort	Größe	Tiefe
Pel	14_10'_15" /47_50'_05"	10.2	28
Rie	14_10'_15" /47_50'_05"	5.3	30
Saa	14_10'_35" /47_48'_85"	15.9	25
Wald	14_10'_32" /47_49'_25"	4.8	34

...

Ion:

Typ	Bezeichnung
Kation	Fe^{3+}
Kation	Mn^{2+}
Anion	Cl^-
Anion	$SO_4{}^{2-}$

...

Zum Einlesen von Werten für Relationships müssen Schlüssel der zugehörigen
Entities bekannt sein. Diese können mit den im nächsten Kapitel beschriebenen
Methoden bestimmt werden. Erst dann können Daten für Relationships erfragt
werden, da dazu Fremdschlüssel in die Relation aufgenommen werden müssen,
um die Zusammenhänge zu den betreffenden Entities herstellen zu können. Beispiel:

...

messen:

Eintrittspunkt.Ort	Ion.Bezeichnung	Tag	Konzentration
92/295m	Fe^{3+}	15.8.94	0.20
138/530m	Mn^{2+}	15.8.94	0.30
20/128m	Fe^{3+}	20.8.94	0.06

...

Durch die frühzeitige Verwendung von Beispieldaten im Entwurf können vom
Entwerfer Unvollständigkeiten und Fehler in der Datenbank gefunden werden.

Weiterhin können die eingegebenen Beispiele verwendet werden, um zu überprüfen, ob die Kandidaten für semantische Constraints wirklich gelten können und wie plausibel sie sind. Diese Überprüfung wird im nächsten Abschnitt gezeigt.

7 Semantikakquisition und informelle Semantikvalidierung

Nach Ergänzen der strukturellen Daten und Beispieleingabe hat man also einen ersten Strukturentwurf, der vom Entwerfer bestätigt wurde, sowie korrekte Beispieldaten. Weiterhin kennt man Kandidaten für semantische Constraints. In diesem Abschnitt wird gezeigt, wie weitere Kandidaten bestimmt werden können, die Plausibilität aller ermittelten Kandidaten ermittelt werden kann und eine informale Validierung erfolgen kann.
Die Validierung der Semantik ist ein iterativer Prozeß, aus bekannten semantischen Constraints lassen sich mit Hilfe von Heuristiken weitere Kandidaten ableiten. Deshalb werden die anschließend beschriebenen Teile mehrfach durchlaufen.

7.1 Ermittlung weiterer Kandidaten für semantische Constraints

Die aus der natürlichsprachlichen Eingabe abgeleiteten Kandidaten können unvollständig sein. Deshalb wird auch unabhängig von diesen nach weiteren Kandidaten für semantische Constraints gesucht. Dazu werden Heuristiken verwendet. Es gibt in der Struktur, den bereits bekannten semantischen Constraints und den Beispieldaten vage Hinweise, die verwendet werden können, um Kandidaten für semantische Constraints zu bestimmen und gleichzeitig zu ermitteln, wie plausibel diese Kandidaten sind.
Es werden mehrere Heuristiken angewendet (ausführlich vorgestellt in [Alb94b]), eine Auswahl dieser soll hier aufgezählt und kurz erläutert werden.

Heuristiken zur Schlüsselsuche. In der Struktur, den Beispieldaten und der bereits bekannten Semantik können Hinweise auf Schlüssel vorhanden sein. Einige davon werden hier aufgezählt.

- Kandidaten für Schlüssel können aus Attributnamen (bestimmten Teilstrings in den Namen wie -name-, -nummer-, -#-, -id-) vermutet werden.
- Oft existieren in Relationen künstliche Schlüssel, die als sehr große Integerwerte vereinbart sind. Ist eines der Attribute so definiert, so kann es Schlüssel sein.
- Laufende Nummern in den Beispieldaten sind ebenfalls ein starker Hinweis darauf, daß dieses Attribut Schlüssel ist.
- Tritt in der Relation eine Attributmenge auf, die in einer anderen Relation bereits als Schlüssel bestimmt wurde, so kann die Schlüsseleigenschaft auch in dieser Relation gelten.

Attribute, bei denen eine dieser Eigenschaften erfüllt ist, können Schlüssel sein. Schlüssel können auch aus mehreren Attributen zusammengesetzt sein. Am plausibelsten sind dabei die Kandidaten, bei denen die meisten Heuristiken auf eine Schlüsseleigenschaft hinweisen. Die Kandidaten sind jedoch vage, deshalb müssen sie validiert werden.

Heuristiken zur Suche nach Inklusions- und Exklusionsabhängigkeiten. Um Kandidaten für Inklusions- und Exklusionsabhängigkeiten zu suchen, muß zuerst nach Attributen gesucht werden, die die gleiche Bedeutung haben. Diese werden im folgenden *Analoga* genannt. Nur über solchen Attributen sind Inklusions- und Exklusionsabhängigkeiten sinnvoll definiert.

Nicht immer sind Attribute mit dem gleichen Attributnamen Analoga. Es kann Bezeichnungen geben (z.B. Nummer, Name, Preis), die mehrfach innerhalb einer Datenbank verwendet werden und dabei unterschiedliche Bedeutung haben. Deshalb wird die Suche nach Analoga nicht nur auf Attributnamen aufgebaut:

- Die notwendige Bedingung zur Suche nach Analoga ist, daß Attribute in den Typen übereinstimmen müssen und mit ähnlichen oder gleichen Längen definiert sein müssen.
- Gleiche oder synonyme Attributnamen sind ein Hinweis auf Analoga. (Aus dem Wörterbuch der natürlichsprachlichen Analyse kann ermittelt werden, welche Substantive synonym verwendet wurden.)
- Ebenfalls deuten Entity-/Relationshipnamen, die synonym verwendet werden können oder gleiche Teilstring in diesen Namen darauf hin, daß sich zwischen diesen Entities bzw. Relationships Analoga befinden.
- Kommen in den Beispieleinträgen gleiche Werte vor, so ist das ebenfalls ein Hinweis auf Analoga.
- Werden zwischen zwei Knoten bereits Attribute mit gleicher Bedeutung gefunden, so können hier auch weitere Analoga auftreten.
- Besteht zwischen mehreren Attributen die gleiche intrarelationale Semantik (Schlüssel der Relation oder funktionale Abhängigkeiten zwischen diesen Attributen), so ist das ein zusätzlicher Hinweis auf Analoga.

Hat man Analoga gefunden, so werden in Auswertung der Beispieleinträge Kandidaten für Inklusions- und Exklusionsabhängigkeit über diesen ermittelt.
Treten in den Beispieleinträgen dieser Analoga *keine gemeinsamen Werte* auf, so wird eine *Exklusionsabhängigkeit* vermutet. Treten *gemeinsame Einträge* auf, so wird angenommen, daß eine *Inklusionsabhängigkeit* gilt.
Ist die Validierung dieser Constraints nicht erfolgreich, so muß versucht werden, die nicht geltenden Constraints zu präzisieren. Wurde z.B. herausgefunden, daß eine Exklusionsabhängigkeit nicht gilt, so muß man untersuchen, ob hier eine Inklusionsabhängigkeit auftritt.

Heuristiken zur Suche nach weiteren Constraints. Auch zur Suche nach funktionalen Abhängigkeiten und Kardinalitäten gibt es verschiedene Heuristiken. Diese werten vorwiegend die Beispieldaten, sowie die bereits validierten semantischen Constraints aus.

7.2 Überprüfung, ob ermittelte Kandidaten möglich sind

Es wurde gezeigt, daß sowohl über die natürlichsprachliche Analyse als auch über Heuristiken Kandidaten für semantische Constraints ermittelt werden. Man verfügt über weitere Informationen zur Datenbank, die Beispieleinträge und die bereits validierte Semantik.

Einige ermittelte Kandidaten für semantische Constraints können bereits *in den Beispieldaten nicht erfüllt* sein. Z.B. können vermutete Schlüssel bereits im Beispiel nicht gelten, da dort bei den Attributen des vermuteten Schlüssels in mehreren Tupeln gleiche Werte auftreten. Auch funktionale Abhängigkeiten, Exklusionsabhängigkeiten oder Kardinalitäten können bereits im Beispiel nicht erfüllt sein.

Folgende semantische Constraints der natürlichsprachlichen Analyse sind bereit durch die in Abschnitt 6 gezeigten Beispieldaten widerlegt:

```
keycand(see,tiefe)
keycand(messen,tag)
cardcand(1,messen,eintrittspunkt,1,1)
cardcand(2,messen,ion,1,1)
```

In diesen Fällen sind die ermittelten Kandidaten falsch und werden nicht weiter untersucht.

Es ist auch möglich, daß Kandidaten für semantische Constraints bereits *aus anderen semantischen Constraints ableitbar* sind, diese müssen dann ebenfalls nicht weiter untersucht werden, da diese Information redundant ist. Z.B. ist eine vermutete funktionale Abhängigkeit redundant, wenn die linke Seite der Abhängigkeit als Schlüssel der Relation ermittelt wurde.

Kandidaten für Constraints können auch im *Widerspruch* zu bereits ermittelten *semantischen Constraints* stehen. In diesem Fall weiß man, daß diese Kandidaten nicht gelten können, es wurden also falsche Kandidaten abgeleitet.

Es müssen nur solche Kandidaten weiter untersucht werden, die nicht im Widerspruch zum Beispiel oder zu den bereits validierten semantischen Constraints stehen und aus den semantischen Constraints auch noch nicht ableitbar sind.

7.3 Wichtung der Kandidaten für semantische Constraints

Die *Reihenfolge der Validierung* unbekannter semantischer Constraints ist von großer Bedeutung, da die *Akzeptanz* durch den Entwerfer wesentlich davon abhängt, wie sinnvoll ihm die einzelnen Dialogschritte erscheinen. Außerdem können aus semantischen Constraints weitere Constraints abgeleitet werden. Man möchte deshalb frühzeitig in der Validierung die geltenden Constraints finden, da sich so die *Anzahl der Dialogschritte minimieren* läßt. Die Reihenfolge der Erfragung wird damit insbesondere bei der effizienten Validierung der Constraints in großen Relationen und großen Datenbanken relevant.

Die ermittelten Kandidaten werden deshalb vor der Validierung gewichtet, d.h. es wird abgeschätzt, wie plausibel diese Kandidaten sind.

Zur Wichtung der Kandidaten werden die in Abschnitt 7.1 beschriebenen Heuristiken angewendet und gegeneinander gewichtet. Eine einfache Näherungsformel wird zur Abschätzung eingesetzt. Für das Beispiel Schlüssel:

Plausibilität (A ist Schlüsselattribut) $:= w_1 r_1(A) + w_2 r_2(A) + w_3 r_3(A) + w_4 r_4(A)$

$$r_i \text{ - Ergebnis der Heuristikregel } i \in [0..1]$$
$$w_i \text{ sind die Gewichte zwischen } 0..100 \text{ und}$$
$$w_1 + w_2 + w_3 + w_4 = 100$$

Die einzelnen Gewichte werden zu Beginn der Semantikakquisition festgesetzt, sie werden im Verlauf der Suche nach semantischen Constraints geändert. Heuristiken, die erfolgreich waren, werden dann stärker gewichtet als Regeln, die keine richtigen Hinweise lieferten. Damit wird eine *Anpassung der Heuristiken an das Anwendungsgebiet und den Entwerfer* möglich.

Mit dieser Abschätzung der Plausibilität wird eine Reihenfolge der Validierung festgelegt. Eine Methode zur Validierung wird im nächsten Abschnitt beschrieben.

7.4 Informale Validierung

Da der vorgestellte Zugang ein Hilfsmittel für ungeübte Datenbankentwerfer sein soll, muß auch die Validierung der ermittelten Kandidaten für semantische Constraints einfach und informal sein. Es wird deshalb ein *beispielorientierter Zugang* gewählt, die Erfragung der Kandidaten für semantische Constraints erfolgt anhand eines generierten Beispiels. Dieser Zugang ist für Schlüssel, funktionale Abhängigkeiten, Inklusions- und Exklusionsabhängigkeiten und Kardinalitäten möglich. Zwei Beispiele werden dafür gezeigt.

Für die ermittelte Exklusionsabhängigkeit zwischen See und Fluß müssen zuerst Analoga zwischen den Entities ermittelt werden, um die Exklusionsabhängigkeit zu konkretisieren. Diese werden hier leicht gefunden, da beide Entities den gleichen Schlüssel (Name) haben. Die Erfragung dieses Constraints sieht dann so aus:

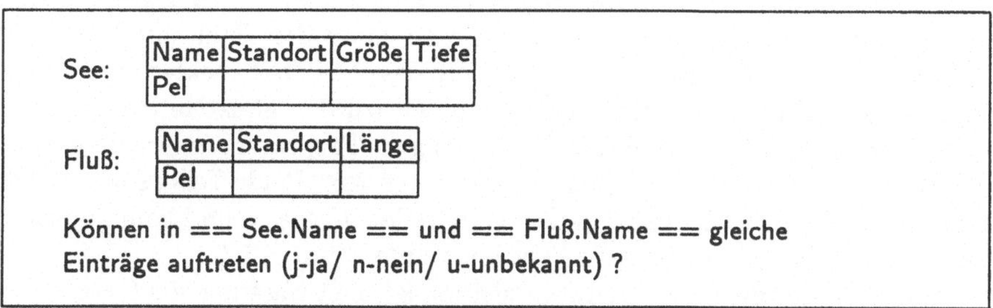

Aus der Antwort des Entwerfers lassen sich folgende Schlußfolgerungen ableiten:

ja   → exklcand(see,fluß) gilt nicht
nein → exklcand(see,fluß) gilt

Die Validierung anhand einer Beispieldiskussion soll auch für Kardinalitäten gezeigt werden:

<table>
<tr><td rowspan="4">aufweisen:</td><td>Gewässer.Name</td><td>Ion.Bezeichnung</td></tr>
<tr><td>Pel</td><td>Fe^{3+}</td></tr>
<tr><td>Pel</td><td>Mn^{2+}</td></tr>
<tr><td>Pel</td><td>$SO_4{}^{2-}$</td></tr>
</table>

Können dem gleichen Wert in == Gewässer.Name == verschiedene
Werte für == Ion.Bezeichnung == zugeordnet sein
(j-ja/ n-nein/ u-unbekannt) ?

In diesem Fall läßt sich aus der Antwort des Entwerfers ableiten:

ja   → cardcand(1,aufweisen,gewässer,1,1) ist falsch

nein → cardcand(1,aufweisen,gewässer,1,1) ist richtig

Die Validierung der Semantik anhand von Beispielen ist für alle hier betrachteten Constraints analog möglich. Aus den Antworten des Nutzers können dabei immer formale semantische Constraints abgeleitet werden.

Man hat also im Ergebnis der Validierung Informationen über semantische Constraints, die gelten und semantische Constraints, die nicht erfüllt sind. Constraints, über die noch keine Aussage bekannt oder ableitbar ist, sind unbekannt. Durch diese "Negativinformationen" setzt man *keine Closed-World-Assumption* voraus. Man kann dadurch bestimmen, wann alle semantischen Constraints einer Relation oder Datenbank bekannt sind.

Bei der vollständigen Akquisition der Semantik müssen alle unbekannten Constraints erfragt werden. Begonnen wird dabei mit den plausibelsten Kandidaten.

8   Zusammenfassung/Ausblick

In dieser Arbeit wurde eine unkonventionelle Methode vorgestellt, mit der Struktur und Semantik einer Datenbank über die Analyse natürlichsprachlicher Eingaben erkannt und validiert werden können. Diese Zugang ist informal und ermöglicht damit auch ungeübten Benutzern den Entwurf einer Datenbank.

Die natürlichsprachliche Entwurfskomponente sowie das Tool zur Akquisition von Semantik aus Beispielen wurde innerhalb des RADD-Projektes prototypisch implementiert. Für die einzelnen Komponenten wurden günstige Programmiersprachen gewählt, z.B. wird für das NLI Prolog als Programmiersprache genutzt, die Semantikvalidierung ist in Modula2 implementiert. Beide Teile, sowie alle anderen Tools im RADD-Projekt, laufen als parallele Prozesse und kommunizieren über ein Data Dictionary. Das Projekt läuft unter SunOS 5.3.

In analoger Weise wie die Semantikakquisition ist die Erfassung von Operationen und Verhaltensinformationen über der Datenbank möglich. Dazu wird für die natürlichsprachliche Analyse ein Modell benötigt, welches Aufschluß über den Zusammenhang von Prozessen gibt. Dieses wird in die Wissensbasis integriert. Alle konkret auftretenden Prozesse werden in dieses Modell eingeordnet. Für

einen bestimmten Prozeß sind dann, nach einer Klassifizierung, Aussagen über
notwendige Pre- und Postprozesse möglich. Das Problem bei der Erstellung eines
solchen Modells besteht darin, daß es möglichst allgemein gestaltet wird.
Die Ableitung semantischer Constraints aus Daten, die Heuristiken zur Ermittlung von Kandidaten für semantische Constraints und die informale Validierung
können in analoger Weise im Reverse-Engineering angewendet werden. Mit diesen Methoden können die in bestehenden Datenbanken geltenden semantischen
Constraints ermittelt werden. Diese Constraints sind Voraussetzung zur Übertragung bestehender Datenbanken in andere Datenmodelle.

9 Danksagung

Wir möchten uns an dieser Stelle bei Andreas Heuer für die Hinweise zu früheren
Versionen dieses Artikels bedanken.

References

[Alb93] M. Albrecht, Akquisition von Datenbankabhängigkeiten unter Verwendung
von Beispielen, GI-Workshop, Grundlagen von Informationssystemen Graal-
Müritz, 1993, Universität Rostock, Informatik-Berichte 3/93, S. 5-9

[Alb94a] M. Albrecht, Ansätze zur Akquisition von Inklusions- und Exklusionsabhängigkeiten in Datenbanken, GI-Workshop, Tutzing, 1994, Informatik-
Berichte, Universität Hannover, S.162-169

[Alb94b] M. Albrecht, Semantikakquisition im Reverse-Engineering, Technische Universität Cottbus, Reihe Informatik I-4/1994

[BCN92] C. Batini, S. Ceri, S. B. Navathe, Conceptual Database Design, The Benja-
min/ Cummings Publishing Company, Inc., 1992

[BGM85] M. Bouzeghoub, G. Gardarin, E. Metais, An Expert System Approach, Proceedings Very Large Databases, 1985, pp. 82-94

[Buc93] B. G. Buchanan, Readings in knowledge acquisition and learning, San Mateo:
Morgan Kaufmann Publishers, 1993

[BuD94a] E. Buchholz, A. Düsterhöft: The linguistic backbone of a natural language interface for database design. Forthcoming. In: Literary and Linguistic
Computing, Oxford University Press

[BuD94b] E. Buchholz, A. Düsterhöft: Using natural language for database design. In:
Proceedings Deutsche Jahrestagung für Künstliche Intelligenz 1994 - Work-
shop 'Reasoning about Structured Objects: Knowledge Representation meets
Databases'. 18-23. September 1994

[BOT90] P. Bachmann, W. Oberschelp, B. Thalheim, G. Vossen, The Design of RAD:
Towards to an Interactive Toolbox for Database Design, RWTH Aachen, FG
Informatik, Aachener Informatikberichte 90-28

[CaS93] M. Castellonos, F. Saltor, Extraction of Data Dependencies, Universitat Po-
litecnica de Catalunya, Barcelona, Spain, Report LSI-93-2-R

[Che83] P.P. Chen: English Sentence Structure and Entity Relationship Diagrams.
In: Information Science 29(2),1983,S.127-149

[CBS94] R. H. L. Chiang, T. M. Barron, V. C. Storey, Reverse engineering of relational
databases: Extraction of an EER model from a relational database, Data &
Knowledge Engineering 12 (1994), 107-142

[CGS83]   M. Colombetti, G. Guida, M. Somalvico: NLDA: A Natural Language Reasoning System for the Analysis of Data Base Requirements. In: Ceri, S. (ed.): Methodology and Tools for Data Base Design. North-Holland, 1983

[Eic84]   Ch. F. Eick: From Natural Language Requirements to Good Data Base Definitions - A Data Base Design Methodology. In: Proc. of the International Conference on Data Engineering, pp.324-331, Los Angeles, USA, 24.-27.4.1984

[FaV94]   C. Fahrner, G. Vossen, A Survey of Database Design Transformations Based on the Entity-Relationship Model Universtität Münster, Angewandte Mathematik und Informatik, Bericht Nr. 14/94-I

[FPR85]   B. Flores, C. Proix, C. Rolland: An Intelligent Tool for Information Design. Proc. of the Fourth Scandinavian Research Seminar of Information Modeling and Data Base Management. Ellivuori, Finnland, 1985

[GaM89]   G. Gazdar, C. Mellish: Natural language processing in PROLOG: an introduction to computational linguistics. Addison-Wesley Wokingham, England,1989

[MaR92]   H. Mannila, K.-J. Räihä, The Design of Relational Databases, Addison Wesley, 1992

[Ort93]   E. Ortner: KASPER - Konstanzer Sprachkritik-Programm für das Software-Engineering. Universität Konstanz, Informationswissenschaft, Bericht 36-93, September 1993

[Pin86]   M. Pinkal: Definite noun phrases and the semantics of discourse. COLING-86, S.368-373

[Pin93]   M. Pinkal: Semantikformalismen für die Sprachverarbeitung. Universität des Saarlandes, CLAUS-Report Nr.26, Januar 1993

[StG88]   V. C. Storey, R. C. Goldstein, Methodology for Creating User Views in Database Design, ACM Transactions on Database Systems, Sept. 1988, pp 305-338

[TAA94]   B. Thalheim, M. Albrecht, E. Buchholz, A. Düsterhöft, K.-D. Schewe, Die Intelligente Tool Box zum Datenbankentwurf RAD, GI-Tagung, Kassel, 1994, Datenbankrundbrief, Ausgabe 13, Mai, S. 28-30

[Tha93]   B. Thalheim, Fundamentals of Entity-Relationship Modelling, Annals of Mathematics and Artificial Intelligence, J. C. Baltzer AG, Vol. 7 (1993), No 1-4, S. 197-256

[TjB93]   A M. Tjoa, L. Berger: Transformation of Requirements Specifications Expressed in Natural Language into an EER Model. Proceeding of the 12thInternational Conference on ER-Approach, Airlington, Texas USA,Dec. 15-17th, 1993